TEACHING WORLD HISTORY

Sources and Studies in World History

Kevin Reilly, Series Editor

TEACHING WORLD HISTORY

A Resource Book

Heidi Roupp
EDITOR

M.E. Sharpe
Armonk, New York
London, England

Library of Congress Cataloging-in-Publication Data

Teaching world history : a resource book /
Heidi Roupp, editor.
p. cm.
Sources and studies in world history
Includes bibliographical references and index
ISBN 1-56324-419-5. — ISBN 1-56324-420-9 (pbk.)
1. History—Study and teaching—United States.
I. Roupp, Heidi.
D16.3.T38   1996
907′.1—dc20
96–23391
CIP

Printed in the United States of America

The paper used in this publication meets the minimum requirements of the
American National Standard for Information Sciences—
Permanence of Paper for Printed Library Materials,
ANSI Z 39.48-1984.

∞

BM (c)   10   9   8   7   6   5   4   3   2   1
BM (p)   10   9   8   7   6   5   4   3   2   1

In loving memory of my mentor, John Hazard,
and my colleague Darlene E. Fisher

Contents

List of Contributors

Paul Vauthier Adams Shippensburg University, Shippensburg, Pennsylvania

Carol A. Adamson The International School of Stockholm, Stockholm, Sweden

JoAnn Alberghini Lakeview Junior High School, Santa Maria, California

Bob Andrian Loomis Chaffee School, Windsor, Connecticut

Trudi Arnold Fairfax Public Schools, Fairfax, Virginia

Robert B. Bain Beachwood High School and John Carroll University, Cleveland Heights, Ohio

Jerry H. Bentley University of Hawaii, Honolulu, Hawaii

Daniel Berman Fox Lane High School, Bedford, New York

Richard W. Bulliet Columbia University, New York, New York

Mary O. Burton Clarke Central High School, Athens, Georgia

George Camp Lamar High School, Houston, Texas

A.J. Carlson Austin College, Sherman, Texas

Pat Carney Standley Lake High School, Westminster, Colorado

Timothy C. Connell Laurel School, Shaker Heights, Ohio

Sammy Crawford Soldotna High School, Kenai, Alaska

Robert Cummings United States Air Force Academy, Colorado Springs, Colorado

Philip D. Curtin The Johns Hopkins University, Baltimore, Maryland

Felicia C. Eppley Lamar High School, Houston, Texas

Darlene E. Fisher New Trier Township High School, Winnetka, Illinois

Nancy Fogelson Cincinnati Country Day School, Cincinnati, Ohio

Michele Forman Middlebury Union High School, Middlebury, Vermont

Sandra Garcia Watkinson School, Hartford, Connecticut

Dwight Gibb Lakeside School, Seattle, Washington

Corinne Lathrop Gilb Wayne State University, Professor Emeritus, Detroit, Michigan

Helen Grady Springside School, Philadelphia, Pennsylvania

David Harbison Cate School, Carpenteria, California

Charles Hart Carl Sandberg High School, Holland Park, Illinois

Marilynn Hitchens Wheatridge High School, Jefferson County, Colorado

Bernard C. Hollister Illinois Mathematics and Science Academy, Aurora, Illinois

Michele Hubley Pope John XXIII Regional High School, Sparta, New Jersey

Sarah S. Hughes Shippensburg University, Shippensburg, Pennsylvania

Judy Lightfoot Lakeside School, Seattle, Washington

Bullitt Lowry University of North Texas, Denton, Texas

Lawrence W. McBride Illinois State University, Normal, Illinois

Carrie H. McIver San Diego County Office of Education, San Diego, California

Marianna McJimsey Colorado College, Colorado Springs, Colorado

William H. McNeill University of Chicago, Professor Emeritus, Chicago, Illinois

John A. Mears Southern Methodist University, Dallas, Texas

Bill Mendelsohn The School District of Clayton, Clayton, Missouri

Linda Miller Fairfax Public Schools, Fairfax, Virginia

Gil Morrison Fairfax Public Schools, Fairfax, Virginia

Patricia O'Neill Central Oregon Community College, Bend, Oregon

Dale M. Owens L.B. Landry Magnet School, New Orleans, Louisiana

Ellen Pike Lancaster Country Day School, Lancaster, Pennsylvania

Susan Pojer Maria Regina High School, Yonkers, New York

Mary A. Price Libertyville High School, Libertyville, Illinois

Dennis Reinhartz University of Texas at Arlington, Arlington, Texas

Judy Reinhartz University of Texas at Arlington, Arlington, Texas

Robert Rittner Hastings High School, Spring Valley, New York

Sue Robertson Mills E. Godwin High School, Richmond, Virginia

Mary Rossabi The Fieldston School, New York, New York

Laurie Schmitt Friends' Central School, Wynnewood, Pennsylvania

Lynda Shaffer Tufts University, Medford, Massachusetts

Leften S. Stavrianos Northwestern University, Professor Emeritus, Evanston, Illinois

Peter von Sivers University of Utah, Salt Lake City, Utah

Connie Wood Rufus King High School, Milwaukee, Wisconsin

Foreword

This book meets a deeply felt need of teachers of world history, on both the school and the college levels. While educational theorists, school administrators, and college faculty across the country have recognized the importance of teaching world history, and urged their faculties to teach it, most historians were, and are, encouraged to specialize. Only recently have graduate schools offered courses in comparative or global history, and the number who attempt to train new world historians is still very small.

This is, in fact, the first book on the teaching of world history. It brings together some of the best advice available, from both leading scholars and daily practitioners. *Teaching World History* is a compendium of conceptual overviews, essays on relevant topics, successful lessons, teaching strategies, and fruitful ideas. Among the contributors are the "founding fathers" of contemporary world history education: William H. McNeill, L.S. Stavrianos, and Philip Curtin, and dozens of scholars and teachers who have found their own ways to bring world history to the classroom.

Heidi Roupp is the ideal editor for such a volume. An enthusiastic teacher of world history at Aspen High School, participant in the founding of the World History Association in 1982, organizer of regional WHA meetings at Aspen, she is also current vice president and president-elect of the association. As this volume demonstrates, Heidi Roupp has the range of intellect, interests, and contacts as well as the energy and patience to cajole many other busy historians into contributing to this volume and to gather and edit their work.

Like the World History Association, which from its origin included teachers and scholars—from schools, colleges, and universities—this is not a guide from on high for the workers in the trenches. While there may be few trenches in Aspen, Heidi Roupp is well aware, as I became at meetings she organized, that when it comes to teaching strategies, the exemplary models come from teachers in the schools more often than from college professors. Thus, this volume is offered to those at all levels of world history teaching in the hope and expectation that we can learn a good deal from each other.

Kevin Reilly
Series Editor

Introduction

Today's current events, like the changing patterns of a kaleidoscope, shift bits of the past into new configurations of the present as new interrelated patterns continue to form and disappear from view. World historians seek to understand larger global patterns by using tools of comparison and analysis. They are both scientists and artists: scientific in their research, artistic in their ability to synthesize patterns of change and interpret their findings to a wider audience. Their questions have encouraged new research. Because the questions are different, the answers require a different investigation of the past.

Technology has changed the kaleidoscopic pattern. The global market, Internet, movies, and television have linked together vigorous, cosmopolitan societies with international interests. Yet among today's students, confronted by rapid global change, the desire remains to understand how one's own values and the values of others have been shaped by previous cultural traditions. To understand their own place in time, students seek to understand how they fit within the larger context of human history. Not only do students need to know who they are and the story of their own nation's history; they also must know how their story fits into a global pattern.

World history is a rapidly developing subfield of history with new course offerings in schools and universities across the country, yet few who are teaching the subject have actually taken a world history course. To be useful, world history must be more than the story of selected societies or even geographic regions through time. Just as U.S. history is not the history of fifty individual states but a national history of the American experience, world history is not just the study of nation-states or separate civilizations but a global history of human experience. Teachers and professors are faced with the challenge of constructing a coherent course narrative for world history. Faced with the need for a narrative and the amorphous nature of the subject, founding members of the World History Association pioneered the development of an organization of teachers and professors to serve as a forum for world history. Since its inception in 1982, the WHA has fostered research and discussion among professionals representing all levels of instruction. This book is the product of that work. This collection also reflects the ideas of Ross Dunn and world history teachers who participated in the Woodrow Wilson National Fellowship Foundation–DeWitt Wallace Reader's Digest program at Princeton from 1991 to 1993. The course descriptions, essays, and lessons reflect the changing nature of world history and offer a wide range of useful ideas for teaching a world history course.

I have been extremely fortunate as a teacher to be guided by many friends and colleagues. Leften Stavrianos and William McNeill have unselfishly continued to answer questions both big and small and provided new ideas to direct my study of world history. I am especially indebted to Marilynn Hitchens, Kevin Reilly, Lynda Shaffer, Ray Lorantas, Morris Rossabi, Anne Barstow, John Mears, Judith Zinsser, Arnie Schrier, and Carl Reddell as well as many other friends in the Rocky Mountains and across the country who have tirelessly guided my efforts to learn and teach world history. I would also like to thank Nancy Arnold, Dale Koepp, and Carolyn Wilson of the Woodrow Wilson National Fellowship Foundation, whose efforts addressed the need for scholarly exchange among teachers. Michael Weber's advice and expertise were invaluable. Typing of this manuscript was made possible through funding by Ken and Harle Montgomery. As in other facets of my life, my mother's caring demand for excellence and my husband's sustaining love and support have made this book possible.

TEACHING WORLD HISTORY

Part I

Approaches

During the past decade world history courses have been organized by instructors and authors of textbooks using three general approaches: the comparative study of civilizations, the study of human societies using themes or topics, and the chronological survey. The choice of approach is determined by the expertise of faculty, the resources available, and the characteristics of students. World history does, however, offer an ideal opportunity for interdisciplinary, cooperative teaching units using art, literature, or computer programs to enrich the student experience.

In this book are found examples of courses of study, curricula, and texts that are useful maps of the world history landscape. William McNeill offers a rationale for world history and identifies landmarks in the human story. Leften S. Stavrianos emphasizes the importance of teaching world history from a global perspective rather than the history of Western civilization supplemented with non-Western topics. Marilynn Hitchens examines the approaches used by several textbooks to organize their surveys of world history and the organizing chronology of the National World History Standards; she concludes with the recently published *SAT II World History* course outline. Bob Andrian describes a one-year required world history course written by the World History Planning Group at the Loomis Chaffee School in Windsor, Connecticut. Loomis Chaffee uses a topical approach to devise a world history, designed to engage actively ninth- and tenth-grade students in the story of human experience. Robert Bain explains a seven-step process for teaching world history by the comparative method. For graduate courses, Philip Curtin advocates using comparative themes, studying published works on aspects of comparative world history, or researching a comparative topic in an experimental exercise.

Another approach to a world history course is using a repeating theme. Bernard Hollister and Lawrence McBride challenge students to define civilization through careful consideration of the relationship of historical processes and social systems in various societies. Connie Wood uses the "isms" that shape modern history as a "Wheel of Fortune" to order the study of modern history. Dwight Gibb breaks with the tradition of these approaches by beginning with the student rather than the subject matter. As his students fashion their own identities, he helps them relate their experiences to a global perspective through lessons that emphasize critical thinking skills.

How do world history courses fit into larger curriculum designs? Traditionally, children are first introduced to history through family stories beginning with "When I was your age. . . ." The family stories are supplemented in elementary school with lessons about the child's neighborhood and town. Children often compare their families and neighborhoods with those in other parts of the world as class projects. Younger children listen to folk tales from long ago and far away and learn about the holidays others celebrate and the foods children in other countries enjoy. Older students are initiated into the discipline of history, the process of questioning, analysis, and research, through an increasingly academic course of study. The purpose is to develop critical thinking and historical perspectives, knowledge useful to future citizens of a republic.

As communications around the globe continue to expand, new curricula reflect the need for more knowledge about the world. Current trends indicate that U.S. and world history will supply the story line for new social studies programs. Clayton, Missouri, has designed a curriculum with a global perspective under the leadership of Bill Mendelsohn, the social studies curriculum coordinator. The new plan begins in elementary school with a comparative study of societies. Each year elementary children are introduced to a new geographical region and people around the world whose societies share similar characteristics of place. A three-year middle school program acquaints students with American history in grades five through seven. Grades eight through ten include a three-year sequence of world history that considers American history as part of the story from 1400 to the present. Elective and advanced placement courses are offered to students in their junior and senior years. Several world history units written by Clayton teachers demonstrate how world history and American history are integrated into the world history sequence. The goals and courses of the California Framework for Social Studies in the next chapter offer an interesting comparison to the Clayton model. "The History–Social Science Framework for California Public Schools, Kindergarten through Grade Twelve" represented a major change in the curricula design and courses of study for California schools when it was published by the California State Department of Education in 1988. Charlotte A. Crabtree and Daine Ravitch were the principal writers.

The final articles provide a sampling of world history at colleges and universities. Patricia O'Neill teaches a world history survey. She uses a chronological approach but supplements the text and lectures with study guides on topical subjects. An example of her study guides, entitled "Sacred Writing of the World's Religions," is included with her course of study and paper topics. These guides direct the study of entry-level students who may find the accumulation of unfamiliar names and places overwhelming. Jerry Bentley's "Seminar in World History" offers the reader an interesting comparative approach to world history. Bentley's syllabus also represents an excellent reading list for individuals wishing to extend their knowledge of world history. Peter von Sivers has organized his survey course using McNeill's *History of the Human Community* as the general text and three other texts dealing with specific topics. His course description and requirements indicate the fundamentals first- and second-year students master. At the University of Utah globally oriented courses begin with a survey course, "World History Since 1500 C.E." Descriptions of other world history courses at the University of Utah indicate the range of course offerings students may take after they have completed the survey.

1
World History

William H. McNeill

What can a teacher do with the buzzing, blooming confusion that is world history? The problem is twofold. On the one hand, the subject is infinite. On the other hand, considerable attention must be paid to the heritage of Western civilization that shaped American institutions and made the country what it is. Mere confusion will inevitably result from an indiscriminate effort to deal with everything we know about the past; and if too little emphasis is placed on the world-transforming character of Western civilization throughout the past five hundred years, then our heritage from that truly remarkable epoch of world history will be inexcusably undervalued. As yet, there are no generally agreed upon models; historians have only recently begun to try to frame a coherent vision of the history of the world.

Yet the imperatives pointing toward a world history are obvious. In the first place, our country has become part of an intensely interactive world system that no longer revolves solely around events in Europe, as was (or at least seemed to be) the case as recently as the 1930s. To deal effectively with Asians, Africans, Latin Americans, and Europeans, we need to know how the historical past has shaped their diverse outlooks upon the world. In the second place, migrants from Asia, Africa, and Latin America have filled our classrooms with students whose ethnic and cultural background is now "Western." They need a past they can share with Americans of European descent; and equally, Americans of European descent need a past they can share with all their fellow citizens, including the indigenous Indian population that got here before anyone else. World history fits these needs, and only world history can hope to do so.

How then should the history of human adventure on earth be presented in our classrooms? We need a clear and distinct idea about what matters most. Teachers might rely on a few simple rules of thumb:

1. Human power and wealth have increased through time because people strive for them. People are perpetually on the lookout for new skills or ideas that will increase their wealth and power. Borrowing interesting new capabilities from strangers may upset existing relationships; it may arouse in some the desire to maintain local practices undefiled, and it may hurt some people while it benefits others. Still, the changeability of human history results from the modification of established ways of thinking and acting provoked most often by contact with strangers.

2. People are often unaware of the consequences and implications of particular actions or choices, so that human purposes are a very imperfect guide to what actually occurs. Side effects regularly distort purposes. Multiple causes are everywhere, and so are cross purposes. The open-endedness of human experience needs continual emphasis to counteract the tendency to treat whatever did happen as somehow foreordained.

3. Students should try to make moral judgments about the past, but only after they have thought about the norms and expectations that prevailed among those being judged. Students need to know that human beings make sense of their lives by striving to conform to the norms of behavior that group membership imposes on them.

These rules of thumb about how to approach human history still do not answer the practical question of how to distribute classroom time among the infinite possibilities that world history offers. Two overarching goals should guide decision making.

First, students need to realize that they share the earth with people whose beliefs and actions are different from their own and arise from divergent cultural heritages. The way to make this clear is to define as fully and richly as possible the distinctive national traditions of the United States, and then to sample other cultural traditions, choosing for closer study those cultures of importance for global affairs in our time. Schools must therefore teach both the national history of the United States and the history of the rest of the world, paying special attention to the principal civilizations of Eurasia (including that of western Europe) because they shaped the worldviews of the majority of human beings today. Africa,

McNeill, William H., "World History," in *Charting a Course: Social Studies for the 21st Century,* Report of the Curriculum Task Force of the National Commission on Social Studies in the Schools. Washington, D.C.: NCSS, 1989. © National Council for the Social Studies. Reprinted by permission.

Latin America, North America, as well as Eurasia, came to share in the European heritage owing to the same processes of expansion that operated within Eurasia itself.

Second, students need to know that the various cultures and different civilizations that divide humanity are all part of a larger process of historical development whereby successful ideas and skills, wherever initiated, spread from people to people and culture to culture. Elaboration and diffusion of skills are as old as the emergence of humanity, whose distinctive trait is learning how to do things from others. Finds of obsidian and other scarce minerals in places remote from their origin show that Paleolithic hunters communicated across long distances. In subsequent ages, trading and raiding, missionary enterprise and mere wandering linked communities. This means that the One World of our time is not new. The speed of communication and rapidity of reaction have increased enormously, but the process of innovation and diffusion of skills is age old.

Indeed that is what defines the pattern of world history as distinct from the pattern of more local histories, including the history of separate civilizations. Accordingly, world history ought to be more organized around major breakthroughs in communication that, step by step, intensified interactions within ever larger regions of the earth until instant global communications became the pervasive reality of our own time. By focusing on the pattern of interaction, and showing how borrowed skills and ideas always had to be adapted to fit local geographical and cultural environments, a simple and commonsensical pattern for world history emerges within which detailed study of any chosen time and place will fit smoothly.

The course of study should begin with a sampling of the culture of preliterate societies. Hunters and gatherers and autonomous villages of food producers prevailed in the distant past. A few such societies survived into modern times, allowing anthropologists to study them with insight and sympathy. That insight can and should be communicated to students just because their lives are set in an utterly different sort of social environment. But this can only be preliminary. The major focus of attention must be upon the major civilization of Eurasia.

Studying European, Chinese, Indian, and Middle Eastern civilizations with sufficient sympathy to be able to present their ideas and institutions, so to speak, "from the inside" is a formidable task. But art and literature—the "classics" of each civilization—are available, and even small excerpts from such classics can convey something of the spirit and distinctive flavor of the civilization in question. Looking at the reproductions of great works of art and reading translations from the world's great literature invites students to react as individuals to the treasures of the human past. That experience ought to be part of every course in world history.

But random sampling of the world classics will only create confusion. Teachers can simplify without unduly distorting the reality of the four principal Eurasian cultural traditions by showing how each was built around a master institution, with a ruling idea to match. For ancient Greece, the territorial state was the ruling institution and the matching idea was natural law, applicable both to humans within the polis and to inanimate nature. For China, the extended family and the notion of decorum played a similar organizing role for the behavior of human beings and of the cosmos. For India, the ruling institution was caste and the organizing idea was transcendentalism, that is, the reality of the spiritual realm above and beyond the illusory world of sense. And for the Middle East, bureaucratic monarchy and monotheism played the same organizing roles.

Obviously, these four separate institutional-and-idea systems mingled through subsequent time. Thus, with the rise of the Roman Empire and spread of Christianity, European civilization blended the Middle Eastern and part of the Indian with its Greek heritage. Similarly, China, Japan, and the adjacent East Asian peoples borrowed a great deal of the Indian heritage when Buddhism spread to that part of the world. Middle Easterners combined the Greek heritage with their own after Alexander's conquests and borrowed Indian transcendentalism a few centuries later. India, likewise, toyed with Middle Eastern ideas of bureaucratic monarchy as early as the third century B.C.E., and explored the full complexity of both Middle Eastern and European civilizations after 1000, when first Moslem and then European conquerors intruded upon Hindu society as a new ruling caste.

Since each of the major Eurasian civilizations took form long ago—before 400 B.C.E. in Western Eurasia and before 100 B.C.E. in East Asia—a course in world history must devote considerable emphasis to this classical, formative stage. But once a grasp of the enduring character of each civilization has been achieved, emphasis ought to shift to the processes of interaction across civilizational boundaries and the subsequent blending of what had begun as separate traditions.

Main landmarks of that process may be listed as follows:

1. The rise of cities, writing, and occupational specialization, centered initially in the Middle East. The impact of Middle Eastern skills and ideas extended all the way across Eurasia by 1500 B.C.E., when the Shang dynasty brought chariots and such characteristic ideas as the seven-day week to the valley of the Yellow River.

2. The opening of regular caravan connections between China and Rome, and between the Middle East and India about 100 B.C.E. At about the same time, Mediterranean sailors discovered the monsoons of the Indian Ocean and

began to participate in a much older seaborne commercial network uniting the Indian Ocean with the South China Sea. The so-called Silk Road was the most famous overland route, but the caravan world extended north and south of the Silk Road proper, and in common with the navigation of the southern seas, created a slender Eurasian world market for luxury goods that could bear the cost of long-distance transport.

3. The development and spread of the so-called higher religions of Judaism, Buddhism, Christianity, and Islam between 500 B.C.E. and 630 C.E. These faiths provided a moral universe that countered the injustices and impersonality of urban bureaucratic and hierarchical society by inviting their followers to create communities of believers wherever they found themselves. This stabilized human relations within the expanding Eurasian civilizations, and, through conscious and deliberate missionary activity, attracted neighboring peoples into the widening and ever intensifying circles of interacting civilizations.

4. The large-scale domestication of camels after about 300 C.E. Caravans could now cross hot deserts, with the effect of bringing Arabia and West Africa into the interacting circles of civilizations. The Moslem Middle East became the principal center of the resulting system of trade and transport, and Moslem skills spread in every direction. In particular, Moslem merchants taught the rules of bazaar trading to the nomad world of the Eurasian steppe and also to the Chinese.

5. Cheap and dependable water transport resulting from technical advances in shipbuilding and, equally important, from the extensive canalization of rivers, especially in China. The horizon point of this development came about 1000 C.E. when long-distance trade ceased to be confined to luxuries and began to alter everyday life for ordinary people because goods of common consumption could now bear the cost of transport across hundreds and even thousands of miles. In many ways, this represents the dawn of the modern age, as much as or more than the familiar date of 1500. China was the principal center of the resulting intensification of exchanges, and, like the Moslems before them, the Chinese swiftly developed skills superior to the rest of the world.

6. The establishment of the political unity throughout much of Eurasia by the Mongols in the thirteenth century. This was the principal medium for the diffusion of Chinese skills westward, for as the career of Marco Polo illustrates, the Mongol peace allowed literally thousands of people to move back and forth between China and the rest of the Eurasian world. Chinese skills therefore spread westward—notably gunpowder, printing, and the compass, three key technological elements in Europe's subsequent assumption of world leadership.

7. The familiar opening of the oceans by the Europeans just before and after 1500. European merchants established trading posts on the coasts and islands of the Indian Ocean and played an increasingly active part in the trade and politics of the southern seas and East and West Africa thereafter. In addition, the Americas entered abruptly into the circle of Eurasian interactions, exposing the Amerindians to repeated disease disasters and allowing Europeans to establish thriving colonies in the New World. (From this point onward, the history of the United States becomes part of world history and ought to be treated as such. Some separate treatment of United States history is needed, but world history ought not to omit our national past. Instead, world history courses should put the national past in perspective.)

8. The tapping of mechanical power for industrial production and then for transport and communication, beginning in a dramatic way, about 1750. From this time onward, the threefold structure suggested in our ideal curriculum becomes a practicable guide for directing attention toward the most important traits of the modern age: (a) the democratic revolution in government; (b) the industrial revolution in economics; and (c) the demographic upsurge.

In studying this increasingly far ranging and intensive interaction, the way each step prepared the way for the next is worth emphasizing. But as always, history is not a simple success story. Costs must be counted as well as gains. The loss of autonomy for local peoples and cultures that resulted from the arrival of powerful strangers in their midst was always the price of admission to the interacting circle of sophisticated skills and exchanges. Exposure to new and lethal infectious diseases was another cost of the civilizing process. Each expansion of the range of communications put new populations at risk, and the resulting die-off from the sudden onset of smallpox and other diseases regularly weakened local peoples and sometimes crippled or even destroyed them. The case of the American Indians is the most dramatic example, but Australians, Polynesians, and peoples of the Siberian forests suffered parallel disease disasters in modern times; and catastrophic disease encounters in earlier ages—the Black Death and the Antonine plagues—are also worth attention.

World history built along these lines can prepare students to live in the interactive world of the twenty-first century more serenely and wisely than would otherwise be possible for them. It would also give appropriate weight and attention to the primacy of Western civilization in the last five hundred years.

Study of world history with the help of simple ideas like these can be an intellectually uplifting experience; it is also an essential preparation for citizenship. World history is therefore very much worth doing, and doing well. It belongs with the national history of our country at the core of K–12 social studies.

2

A Global Perspective in the Organization of World History

Leften S. Stavrianos

First and foremost, the world history course should deal with world history. This observation may seem perversely trite. Actually, it is wildly Utopian. The fact is that the great majority of the so-called world history courses now taught are Western civilization courses, with or without an Afro-Asian fig leaf. And naturally so, since virtually all introductory history courses on university campuses also are concerned essentially with Western civilization, regardless of the titles they may bear. At both levels the basic organization, aside from afterthought additions, is traditional and familiar: the ancient Near East, classical Greece and Rome, northwestern Europe, and the United States. The result is "world history" courses that ignore the histories of about three-quarters of the people of the world.

Since World War II this West-oriented coverage has become so patently inadequate that new materials have been added, usually in response to current newspaper headlines. Numerous Asian countries won their independence during the first postwar decade; accordingly, they were squeezed in at the tail-end of courses. For the same reason, African countries attracted attention during the next decade, and presumably we can look forward to a Latin American cycle in the near future.

This patchwork tinkering is intellectually indefensible and pedagogically disastrous. It is indefensible because the end product is neither fish nor fowl, neither Western civilization nor world history. Japan is mentioned in order to set the stage for Admiral Perry, India in order to introduce Robert Clive, and Africa for David Livingstone and Cecil Rhodes. This sort of thing may be correctly defined as "Europe and its world relationships." But no matter how much the "world relationships" are stressed, such a course is not world history, in the same manner that a "History of France and its European relationships," even in the periods of Louis XIV or the French Revolution, is not European history.

The patchwork tinkering is also pedagogically disastrous because it has bloated courses to the bursting point. Consider what we have done to our textbooks during the past half-century. First, we added chapters on economic and social and cultural developments for the sake of broader coverage. Then we added more chapters on the interwar years and on World War II and on postwar developments in order to bring the textbooks up to date. And now we are adding still more chapters on Africa, the Middle East, India, and China in an effort to attain global perspective. It is scarcely surprising that both courses and textbooks have become virtually unmanageable. . . .

This past record points to the following conclusions: that the world history and Western civilization courses are inherently and fundamentally different; that they cannot and should not be combined or integrated in any fashion; that each teacher must make the basic policy decision as to whether to offer Western civilization or world history; that if the choice is Western civilization, the teacher will be able to continue substantially with what is now being taught; that if the choice is world history, the teacher will need to start afresh with a basically new global perspective.

What does this new perspective mean and what does it involve? It means the perspective of an observer perched on the moon rather than ensconced in London or Paris or Washington. It means that for every period of history we are interested in events and movements of global rather than regional or national significance. More specifically, it means the realization that in the classical period Han China was the equal of the Roman Empire in every respect; that in the medieval period the Mongols were infinitely more significant than Magna Carta; that in early modern times Russia's expansion overland and western Europe's expansion overseas were likewise more noteworthy than the Reformation or the Wars of Religion; and that today the globally significant developments have to do not with Cold War blocs and crises but rather with the passing of Western hegemony and the emergence of new global concerns such as the ecological.

With these general propositions by way of rationale, the

Stavrianos, Leften S., "A Global Perspective in the Organization of World History," in *New Perspective in World History,* Bulletin 64. Washington, D.C.: NCSS, 1964. © National Council for the Social Studies. Reprinted by permission.

following three recommendations are submitted as guidelines for organizing a world history course.

1. The course should include an overview of the entire history of humanity from a consistent global viewpoint. This is essential in order to make clear the dynamics of world history and its regional interrelationships. Compartmentalized study of a given region loses much of its value if it is not preceded by an understanding of the relationship of that region with others and with world history as a whole. . . .

2. When the structure of the whole has been grasped, then the study of its parts (or of regions) becomes meaningful and comprehensible. A detailed study of several regions is an instructive form of "post-holing." It makes possible an examination in depth of the histories and cultures of various peoples. The precise number will vary with the time available and the background and ability of the students. In any case there is no need to rush breathlessly and superficially from one region to another in order to cover them all. A study of one Communist country, for example, will suffice if the distinctive Communist features of that society are made clear, so that the students will understand the meaning and nature of communism in theory and in practice. Likewise, a study of one underdeveloped country will suffice if the students have recognized and comprehended the "profile" of an underdeveloped society—for example, its low productivity and per capita income, its high birth rate and death rate, and its poorly developed education facilities and technological skills.

3. Every effort should be made to relate the past to the present, so that world history might have maximum relevance and interest for the student. With this in mind, I and my collaborators published in 1966 the world history text *The Global History of Man,* in which the "region" chapters are organized on the flashback principle.[1] First, we describe and analyze existing conditions, and then we trace their historical evolution through the ages. The response of students to this device is one of relief to discover that history need not be the pointless "one damn thing after another" variety, to use Toynbee's phrase. Furthermore, the flashback technique meets the basic problem of selection that plagues every teacher who uses the "region" approach. It has often been argued that since it is difficult enough to deal with Western civilization alone in one year, how can one possibly cover also the civilizations of India and China and the Middle East and Africa and all the rest? The answer, of course, is that it is impossible to do this in any meaningful way if by "cover" is meant a frantic dash through the millennia of the histories of all these regions. The flashback technique helps to cope with this very real problem by confining attention to those events and forces and personalities in the past that help to explain the present. Purists who are wont to deprecate what they term "present-mindedness" might consider the following observation by the distinguished British historian C.V. Wedgwood: "The greater number of historians failed entirely to understand what was expected of them. They . . . turned deliberately from the present to the past. They began to consider with misguided conscientiousness their duty to the dead. This was nonsense, for no one has a duty to the dead except in relation to the living."[2]

The above comments are presented as *one* approach to the teaching of world history—an approach that has been widely tested both before and after publication, and with gratifying results. Undoubtedly, other methods will evolve, now that the needs and potentialities of the world history course are being recognized. We live today in a period that is at least as creative and exciting as that of Periclean Athens or Renaissance Italy or Elizabethan England. It is also a period when humans stand poised at a fateful crossroads, with one path leading to security and well-being for all, and the other to devastation and misery for all. World history can be, and should be, the most exciting and meaningful course in the curriculum. I do not mean to minimize the difficulties in teaching world history, but neither should we exaggerate them. We might bear in mind the sage observation of a teacher at a recent conference: "When you teach well, it always seems as if seventy-five percent of the students are above the median."

Notes

1. *The Global History of Man* that Stavrianos refers to was published by Allyn & Bacon, Inc., in 1966 and is now out of print. Stavrianos has recently published two new world histories based on the approach presented in this article. They are *Lifelines from Our Past: A New World History* (Armonk, NY: M.E. Sharpe, 1992) and *A Global History: From Prehistory to the Present* (Englewood Cliffs, NJ: Prentice Hall, 1995).

2. C.V. Wedgwood, *Velvet Studies* (London: Cape, 1946), p. 157.

3

World History as a Course of Study

Rationale, Goals, and Formulations

Marilynn Hitchens

Perhaps the waning of national history and the rise of world history is not so new. Lord Acton wrote in 1896 in *The Cambridge Modern History*, "Universal history moves in a succession to which the nations are subsidiary. Their story will be told, not for its own sake, but in reference and subordination to a higher series, according to the time and degree in which they contribute to the common fortunes of mankind." Nor is the propensity for a world historical view such a novelty to other civilizations. The Chinese, for instance, have always tended to tell their story as if it were a universal one with them at the center, while the Western world has tended to see its history as a universal story of progress applicable to the rest of the world. So what is new in world history, and why are we trying to tell a new story?

From whatever vantage point, extended ethnocentrism or some higher view of things, we find ourselves in times that have awakened in us a new consciousness regarding the world's shared struggles and achievements. In the West, some have seen this new course as the "third stage in citizenship." The first course was the American history course that was developed in the second half of the nineteenth century. It was designed to be a vehicle for molding a nation of immigrants into a nation of Americans. The second was the Western civilization course that was invented when America was preoccupied with two world wars. It gave America and Europe a common identity. The third stage has emerged in the post–world war period when America has global commitments and markets and is a nation of immigrants whose primary origin is outside Europe. Others see the emergence of world history less in terms of politics and civics and more in terms of an emerging world culture that is directly related to new communications technologies.

Whatever the reason, historians are trying to write a new story and we are trying to tell it in the classrooms. We think it is the key to understanding our common past, to a shared civic and cultural identity in our present, and to progressive passage into the future. We are so bold, or vain as the case might be, as to think that the world's stability and future creativity rest on a new narrative.

Goals

The cognitive goals of a world history course can be discussed in terms of conceptual goals, content goals, and discipline goals. Framing all of these goals, however, are certain inclusionary and exclusionary historical principles peculiar to world history.

The inclusionary principles have to do with the gathering of evidence. As Thucydides pointed out so long ago, the validity of history in some measure rests on the breadth and factuality of the evidentiary base. In world history this means that confining the evidence to written histories of great civilizations is no longer sufficient to tell the whole story. Nontraditional types of history like oral history, myth, and unwritten histories must be given a wide exposure in a world history course as must other affiliated disciplines like anthropology, archaeology, and sociology.

The exclusionary principles have to do with the selectivity of material. What are the principles on which selectivity of material from this wide evidentiary base rests? The concepts and content selected must reflect streams of activity that are of importance to the whole global human community over time. Therefore, regionalism, "presentism," and elitism of all sorts, from class to culture, should be avoided. The course, for example, cannot confine itself to a study of great civilizations, the period from 1500, or the twentieth century. Much that has occurred of importance in the common history of humanity has occurred at its fringes before modern times. In attempting to reorient one's thinking along those lines, it is helpful to picture a spinning globe and a vertical timeline, and then ask if the material that is about to be included can stand the test of wide impact over space, time, and class.

Conceptual Goals

The conceptual goals for a world history course might include the following:

1. The first conceptual goal of world history is to expand historical thinking geographically and chronologically. This

does not mean that every culture, event, and place must be given space in the story. Nor does it mean that it should be guided by the Western history model whose narrative is based on ideas of Western "progress," or on models of grand civilization like China and India. Rather, it means that the narrative should be based on human change over time, that is, on events, people, times, and places that have had a significant impact on the history of the world, on large groups of people and large areas, and that have proven important to human beings generally over time. A successful world history course will stretch a student's chronological and spatial world to the point that he can sense life's infinite patterns and durability, his proper place in the universe, and the extraordinary achievements of the past upon which his present rests.

2. The world history course should be rooted in chronology and not take an exclusively thematic approach. The reason is that too often the latter starts with present concerns like ecology, ethnicity, democratization, and technology and reads them back through time. While themes should play a central role in course conceptualization, they cannot take priority over chronology, the key to ordering patterns of causation. However, this does not condone an empty timeline approach, which obscures the nature of change and continuity in world history. Rather, it remains true to the basic framework of history, which is chronology. Within a chronological approach, there are a variety of ways to order world history. The teacher should feel free to choose one over the other, as long as students are somehow apprised along the way that there are alternatives.

3. The world history course should address the issue of change and continuity by including certain developments bounded by time but of unusual significance in all cultural regions, such as the development of agricultural society or the industrial revolution. This is in contrast to themes that cut across time, such as political systems and class structure.

4. The world history course should emphasize history as a lived experience. It is all too easy to focus on questions of why certain cultures "failed," or did not follow a Western pattern of development. The decisions of people in the past must be situated in the context of the values, traditions, environments, and institutions that distinguished them.

5. The world history course should address not only the internal dynamics of cultural regions, but also interrelationships between or across cultural areas. Cultures and civilizations are rarely self-contained, and the richest are those that have been the products of fertile exchanges and cross-cultural encounters. Comparative history and supracultural history should play a major role in a world history course.

Content Goals

1. World history should acquaint students with the major changes in lifestyle in the past. These changes include standing upright; peopling the earth; the nature of hunter-gatherer societies; the agricultural and pastoral revolutions; the development of ethical patterns of social interaction; and the commercial, industrial, and technological revolutions. The course must investigate why these changes and revolutions occurred, the ecological and cultural context in which they occurred, and the results of such change. These are the major shared stories of world history.

2. A world history course should include study of points of differentiation among peoples. This can be done by examining major world civilizations and cultures and examining their intellectual and cultural underpinnings. The course, therefore, should include study of Japanese, Chinese, Southeast Asian, Indian, Persian, Judaic, Greek, Roman, West African, European, and American civilizations.

3. A world history course should include study of the major forces of exchange and spread of cultures like trade complexes, religious conversion movements, migrations, wars, environmental changes, and technological advancements.

Discipline Goals

1. The first discipline goal is that students should be encouraged to read widely and from many different viewpoints and sources. The course should be geared to teaching students how to read historically. This includes recognizing the analytical components of culture like politics, economics, and social and cultural strands; recognizing cause and effect; identifying viewpoint and context; becoming visually sensitive; identifying theme and factual supporting evidence; and examining spatial and chronological factors.

2. The second disciplinary goal is that students should develop the ability to write an analytical historical essay. The course should help students to learn how to examine historical problems and write about them. Students should be able to make a generalization, back it up with historical facts, and come to conclusions that derive from the facts presented. This will show students that history is not a single truth but an understanding based on evidence.

3. The third discipline goal is that students learn how to write a narrative essay or research paper. In this instance, students should try to become historians, picking a historical topic, gathering large amounts and varied types of evidence, weighing the evidence, properly citing the evidence, and then delivering a compelling narrative that includes a beginning and an end, rising tension, geographical and chronological context, ethical components, lyrical style, and exciting

verbiage. This kind of activity also lends itself to other mediums like videos, diaries, newspaper articles, and reenactments.

By studying world history, students will recognize that history draws on other humanities and social studies disciplines. They will understand that history is not linear or a story of progress, but a complex process of change and continuity characterized by contingency. One hopes they will develop understanding and respect, not remorse or guilt, for the varieties of human experience and recognize the validity of multiple perspectives. They will recognize the historical roles of both human agency and factors beyond human control. They will become literate and functional in a world context. They will gain a sense of perspective and proportion about their own lives.

When asked why he collected rare Chinese art of the Shang dynasty, Dr. Arthur Sackler, who gave his collection to the Smithsonian, once answered, "So as not to be so lonely." I hope this course will allow students to be less imprisoned by the confines of time and space and to live at a broader, deeper, and richer level. World history is about a bigger world and new frontiers, concomitant with the world we live in—a world of expanding space frontiers, a world of interconnection between the remotest village and the biggest metropolis, and the infinite unseen worlds of science and math.

Course Formulations

A world history course should strive not to become a course in great civilizations, a study of various regions of the world, or a global issues course. What it should be is the study of human change and continuity over time. Within that broad mandate there have emerged various formulations and a gradual consensus. The conceptualization and periodization of a survey world history course has been a major preoccupation of the world history movement since its inception in the early 1980s.

The wrestling that has taken place in working out a new course has inspired new scholarship, which in itself has helped these new formulations along. Research into broader topics like the Atlantic Exchange and "Southernization" has promoted a more elegant and refined course formulation. Still, course formulation is very much in flux, and the course chosen will to some extent depend on resources available, curricular and content mandates, and the interests of training the staff.

Following are a few of the most important course formulations prevalent in professional circles today. Representative tables of contents and outlines are shown at the end of this chapter.

1. The Western civilization course with add-ons. This is probably the most common type of course formulation today, mostly because it is led by the textbook companies, which are following a gradual market shift from Western civilization to world history. It is a legitimate formulation in the sense that it responds to a teaching corps that was trained in Western civilization not world history, to available resources, and to an entrenched curriculum that is slow to change.

The course typically takes the Western civilization progression from ancient to classical to medieval to modern civilization and includes other areas of the world along the way.

A typical formulation from Wallbank et al., *History and Life,* illustrates this formulation (see its table of contents on p. 13).

2. The horizontal history formulation. This type of world history concentrates on matters of links, exchanges, and movements of peoples. Two illustrations of this type are from George Brooks, *The Aspen World History Handbook* (see p. 13), and Ross Dunn, *A World History—Links Across Time and Place* (see p. 14).

This formulation pushes the world history story beyond the framework of civilization and progress. Its emphasis on geography and movement elevates the merchants to high rank and forces a look at hitherto hidden stories like the great Polynesian exploration and the settlement of the Pacific (encompassing an area three times that of the Atlantic exchanges). The weaknesses are its unfamiliarity to most teachers and its tendency to become a geographical rather than a chronological time line, which lists and describes rather than narrates.

3. *The National Standards for History* formulation (see p. 16). From the work of historians and teachers over a period of two to three years has come a world history formulation that is a cross between the Western civilization with add-ons approach and the horizontal history approach. Eras 1, 2, 3, and 7 are reminiscent of the former, and 4, 5, and 6 of the latter. It has tried to include the latest scholarship and to acquaint students with both the great classical traditions of human history and the important movements and exchanges.

4. The assessment-based formulation. Because of increased public pressure for increased accountability and measurable outcomes, historians and teachers have begun to formulate world history courses on the basis of testing procedures and well-defined content outcomes. Two types of tests have produced two types of course conceptualizations. Writing tests that tend to ask students to write analytical or narrative essays based on historical documents and factual material has tended to produce more discipline-driven than content-driven courses. The content tends to be varied, flex-

ible, and less restricted. The course might introduce students to large concepts, such as the agricultural revolution, and then ask them to write analytically or narratively using any number of examples, such as China, India, Southwest Asia, or the Americas. The students would have to know how to collect, select, and interpret evidence and then write coherently on the subject. Since the test usually offers a number of choices, students are free to select a topic in which they are well versed. The other type of test, a multiple-choice test, tends to make a course more content- than discipline-driven, though multiple-choice tests are beginning to incorporate historical thinking skills by asking students to interpret works of art, graphs, charts, and historical methodology. Such a course has been worked out for the new Scholastic Aptitude Test, or SAT II. It is a course designed to cover the major areas, events, changes, themes, cultures, and processes that constitute content literacy in world history.

Conclusion

The world history course of today and tomorrow is a course aimed at both civic education and personal enlightenment. Its focus is human change over time, not civilizations, nation-states, geographical areas, or global issues. It should embrace large themes that are given substance with concrete chronological and geographical examples. (A course outline illustrating these considerations can be found on pages 17–19.) It should concentrate on enhancement of student literacy. It should be approached with the idea that, like our own society, it is in constant flux, not made up of mutable truths. While humbling, it should not be intimidating. Rather, it should be approached as an exploration for which, on a daily basis, teachers and students will find surprising and fascinating connections and meanings.

Table of Contents of *History and Life,* Wallbank et al.
(New York: Scott Foresman, 1987)

Unit 1: Civilization Begins
1. Early Humans
2. The First Civilizations

Unit 2: Classical Civilizations
3. The Golden Age of India
4. The Great Age of China
5. The Golden Age of Greece
6. The Roman Empire

Unit 3: The World of Christendom and Islam
7. The Rise of Christendom
8. Western Christendom in the Middle Ages
9. Byzantine Civilization and the Formation of Russia
10. The Rise of Islam and the Muslim Empire

11. Islamic Civilization

Unit 4: The Worlds of Africa and the Americas
12. The Lands and Peoples of Africa
13. African Civilizations South of the Sahara
14. Early Cultures in the Americas

Unit 5: The World of Asia
15. India under Muslim Rule
16. China from the Songs through the Manchus
17. The Emergence of Japan

Unit 6: The Rise of the West
18. The Development of Nations
19. The European Renaissance
20. The Reformation and National Power
21. The Age of Exploration
22. The Formation of Latin America

Unit 7: Revolutionary Changes in the West
23. Science and the Age of Reason
24. The Age of Democratic Revolutions
25. The Growth of Liberalism, Nationalism, and Democracy
26. The Industrial Revolution
27. Social Protest and Mass Society

Unit 8: The World in Upheaval
28. The Building of Empires
29. World War I
30. The Rise of Communism in Russia
31. The Growth of Nationalism and Dictatorship
32. World Depression and World War II

Unit 9: The Contemporary World
33. The Aftermath of World War II
34. The Forging of Nations in Asia and Africa
35. Instability in the Middle East and Latin America
36. A New Pattern of World Relationships

Table of Contents of *The Aspen World History Handbook,*
edited by George E. Brooks, Dik A. Daso,
Marilynn Hitchens, and Heidi Roupp
(Denver: Aspen World History Institute, 1994)

Teaching a Non-Centric World History Course
1. Introduction to the Course
2. The Contemporary—and Future—World
3. Paleolithic Times to the Neolithic "Evolution"
4. The "Secondary" Neolithic: Tigris-Euphrates, Nile, Indus, and Yellow River Valleys
5. Eurasia to c. 500 B.C., Indo-European Migrations
6. Mediterranean Trade Diasporas: Phoenicians, Greeks, and Romans
7. Eurasian Social and Cultural Interchanges
8. The Closing of the Ecumene from China to the

———

Table of Contents of *A World History—Links Across Time and Place,* Ross Dunn (New York: McDougal, Littell, 1988)

———

The National History Standards, National Standards for History in the Schools (Los Angeles, CA: National Standards for History in the Schools, 1996)

Standards Integrating Historical Thinking and Understandings in World History for Grades Five through Twelve Overview of World History

Era 1: The Beginnings of Human Society
  Standard 1: The biological and cultural processes that gave rise to the earliest human communities
  Standard 2: The processes that led to the emergence of agricultural societies around the world

Era 2: Early Civilizations and the Rise of Pastoral Peoples (4000–1000 B.C.E.)

Standard 1: The major characteristics of civilization and how civilizations emerged in Mesopotamia, Egypt, and the Indus valley.
Standard 2: Agrarian societies spread and new states emerge in the third and second millennia B.C.E.
Standard 3: The political, social, and cultural consequences of population movements and militarization in Eurasia in the second millennium B.C.E.

Era 3: Classical Traditions, World Faiths, and Extensive Empires (1000–600 B.C.E.)
  Standard 1: Empire-building, trade, and migrations contribute to increasingly complex relations among peoples of the Mediterranean basin, Africa, and Central Asia, 1000–6000 B.C.E.
  Standard 2: The rise of Aegean civilization and the interrelations that developed between Hellenism and the cultural traditions of Southwest Asia and Egypt, 600–200 B.C.E.
  Standard 3: The rise of large-scale empires in the Mediterranean basin, China, and India, 600–300 B.C.E.
  Standard 4: The rise of early agrarian civilizations in Mesoamerica

Era 4: Expanding Zones of Exchange and Encounter, 300–1000 C.E.
  Standard 1: Imperial crises and their aftermath, 300–700 C.E.
  Standard 2: Causes and consequences of the rise of Islamic civilization between the seventh and tenth centuries
  Standard 3: Major developments in East Asia in the era of the Tang dynasty, 600–900 C.E.
  Standard 4: The search for political and social order in Europe, 500–1000 C.E.
  Standard 5: The spread of agrarian populations and rise of states in Africa south of the Sahara
  Standard 6: The rise of centers of civilization in Mesoamerica and Andean South America in the first millennium C.E.

Era 5: Intensified Hemispheric Interactions, 1000–1500 C.E.
  Standard 1: The maturing of an interregional system of communication, trade, and cultural exchange in an era of Chinese economic power and Islamic expansion
  Standard 2: The Rise of European society and culture 1000–1300 C.E.
  Standard 3: The rise of the Mongol empire and its importance for Afro-Eurasian peoples, 1200–1350
  Standard 4: The growth of states, towns, and trade in Sub-Saharan Africa between the 11th and 15th centuries

Standard 5: Patterns of crisis and recovery in
Afro-Eurasia, 1300–1450
Standard 6: The expansion of states and civilizations in
the Americas, 1000–1500

Era 6: Global Expansion and Encounter, 1450–1770
Standard 1: How the trans-oceanic interlinking of all
major regions of the world in the 1450–1600
period led to important global transformations
Standard 2: How European society experienced
political, economic, and cultural transformations in
the age of global intercommunication, 1450–1750
Standard 3: How large territorial empires dominated
much of Eurasia between the 16th and 18th centuries
Standard 4: Economic, political, and cultural
interrelations among peoples of Africa, Europe,
and the Americas, 1500–1750
Standard 5: How Asian societies responded to the
challenges of expanding European power and
forces of the world economy

Era 7: The Age of Revolutions, 1750–1914
Standard 1: The causes and consequences of political
revolutions in the late 18th and early 19th centuries
Standard 2: The causes and consequences of the
agricultural and industrial revolutions, 1700–1850
Standard 3: The transformation of Eurasian societies in
an era of global trade and rising European power,
1750–1850
Standard 4: Patterns of nationalism, state-building, and
social reform in Europe and North America,
1830–1914
Standard 5: Patterns of global change in the era of
Western military and economic domination,
1850–1914

Era 8: The Twentieth Century
Standard 1: The causes and global consequences of
World War I
Standard 2: The search for peace and stability in the
years between the wars
Standard 3: The causes and global consequences of
World War II
Standard 4: How new international power relations
took shape following World War II
Standard 5: Promises and paradoxes of the second half
of the 20th century

Table of Contents of *How to Prepare for SAT II:
World History*, Marilynn Hitchens and Heidi Roupp
(Hauppauge, NY:
Barron's Educational Series, 1996)

National Liberation in China, Southeast Asia,
    Africa, and Latin America

Modernization

    Patterns of Development—The Capitalist and
        Socialist Models

    The Ecological Results—The Green
        Revolution, Pollution, and Resource
        Depletion

    Science and Technology

    The Triumph of Liberalism

Society and Culture

    Race, Ethnicity, and Gender

    Mass Media, Culture, Education, and
        Metropolis

    Art, Protest, and Counterculture

    Population and Migration

Cross-Regional Developments

Legacies

4

World History

Not Why? but What? and How?

Bob Andrian

World history at Loomis Chaffee: Year One, Day One, September 14, 1993: A group of students holds up and presents its world map drawn from memory on poster board with magic marker. We are not sure how many world maps they remember from the summer, but that does not matter. Other groups with their masterpieces wait patiently, listening and looking at the map presently on display. Furrowed brows seem to abound as this particular group strives to explain why North America, and specifically the United States, appears so large (and so central), easily dwarfing Africa and Asia combined. Another group arises and proceeds to show a map with South America somewhat oversized and the nation of Colombia (again rather centrally located) casting a giant shadow over Brazil and Argentina. A third group's map would assuredly satisfy the natives of Greenland (and post-humously, mapmaker Mercator), and a fourth's would make the Micronesian sailor cringe as land masses appear to cover six-sevenths of the entire poster board, even though there is a fair amount of *terra incognita*. (Perhaps Columbus was familiar with such a map?)

A general discussion ensues. "It makes sense to put your country at the center of the map," someone explains, and many agree. (Thoughts of national perspective and the notion of ethnocentrism come to the teacher's mind but remain unstated for the time being.) "What about the size of the land masses and the bodies of water?" the teacher asks. "Well, you need someone reliable to get an accurate map," comes the reply. "But it depends on where the guy who drew the map lives," interjects another. "Wouldn't all maps be accurate if they each had a specific function and tried to convey a certain perspective?" the teacher wondered. "Then how can we get a world map that everyone will want to use?" someone asked. "Well, you just can't do that with a flat map." "Yeah, what we need is a globe." (General agreement among the crowd.) The teacher tosses out a plastic globe. (Murmurs and giggles are heard.) The student lucky enough to catch it now has to describe the location of her right index finger on the globe. (It's on Egypt.) "It's below the Mediterranean Sea; it's bordered by another sea on the right; it's in Africa, and it's in the Mideast," offers the student. "From the Egyptian

perspective, what's the Mideast?" the teacher queries. Saved by the bell, the class prepares to depart. "Write a short reflection on the function and power of maps," the teacher insists. (Lots of consternation, furrowed brows again.) "This is confusing," frets one boy. The teacher smiles. End of Day One.

The eminent world historian William McNeill once observed, "Try to teach world history, and you will find that it can be done."[1] The first attempt at such an enterprise in synthesis took place in 1821 at the Boston English High School, where students first learned that civilization had essentially followed in the footsteps of Christianity. Later in the century the theme of progress was substituted for Providence, and the "history of the civilized world [became] the history of the Aryan, Semitic, and Hematic races."[2] The course focused on political history, wars, kings, queens, popes, emperors, dates, names, the Mediterranean basin, western Europe, the New World, and briefly, Asia and Africa. As well as being a conceptual flop, it was boring.[3]

In the twentieth century, especially after World War I, world history, a required tenth-grade course (the other requirement, of course, was U.S. history), masqueraded as "European" history. Then when a "larger" world opened up to us in the 1960s and 1970s, thanks to the computer and communications technology and the Space Age, world history adopted a more global perspective. Unfortunately, while successful at discrediting the old Eurocentrism, the new courses fell short in creating new parameters and conceptualizations. In trying to answer the question, "What is world history?" scholars, rather than searching for key principles of selection in the midst of too much material, retreated to the safety of specialization. The results then led to world history courses masquerading as area studies.

The 1980s brought a turn inward and away from internationalism. With this historical perspective in mind, and with several conferences and institutes under their belts, the members of the Loomis Chaffee World History Planning Group (Bert Thurber, Cindy Bertozzi, Jeff Ross, Mara Lytle, Dave Beare, Greg Hunter, and Al Beebe) began to meet in 1992 to create a one-year required course for freshmen and sophomores called "World History." The challenge was obvious: to determine how most effectively and efficiently to unite the whole human past, to identify the "elegant" ideas that would undergird this unity, and to do so without denying a fundamental premise, especially prominent in this century, that separate peoples need separate histories to balance the notion that we are all world citizens. Thus, the group formulated a set of "commitments" around which the course curriculum would be structured. First and foremost among these commitments is the examination of themes of cultural diffusion, migration, and encounter, for cultural interaction represents the driving force of world history. Studies of cultural encounter at key junctures in world history allow students to place their own Western civilization comparatively within a larger and longer history of an ecumenical global community. What happens when people—and all of the culture they carry as baggage: plants, animals, diseases, ideas, values, dreams—bump into each other makes for fascinating study and allows kids to better understand their own historical and cultural identities.

In the first half of the year this theme of cultural interaction is introduced by examining cultural diffusion through trade, religion (and religious art and music), conflict, disease, and travel. A main goal is to begin to get students to wonder how and why much of the world had become so interconnected by the end of the Mongol Empire (c. 1350). In part, especially concerning the role of trade in diffusing material and nonmaterial aspects of culture, they also learn that the North and the West must wait a long time before catching up with a richer and more prosperous South and East.[4] The list of ideas and products is rather impressive from these southern and eastern regions of the globe: Indian cotton and mathematics (our numerals including the number zero may have been delivered by the Arabs, but they are in fact from India), Molucca Island spices (cloves, nutmeg, cinnamon, pepper, etc.), Chinese silk, porcelain, gunpowder, and, of course, the compass, Arab traders (and Muslim pilgrims and travelers) across the Sahara into and throughout the Middle East and into Spain, Mongol conquests of Muslim areas opening up trade routes between Mediterranean Europe and the Pacific (Marco Polo, the appearance of printing, the compass, gunpowder in Italy), and a Turkish-Mongolian-Persian Muslim cultural mix expanding into eastern Europe (Constantinople), Central Asia, Northwestern India, Southeast Asia, and East and West Africa—and all of this activity *before* Columbus.

In addition to commercial activity, along the Silk Route from India to China migrated one of the world's great universal religions, Buddhism (which in a different form also moved with Hinduism to Southeast Asia). By looking at some of the sculpture and cave paintings in the caves along the Silk Route, students are able to discern the influence of Greek, Roman, Persian, and Chinese artistic sensibilities upon Buddhist images. Hence, we begin to see religion as a prominent vehicle for the diffusion of culture in world history.

Students in different groups investigate simultaneously the spread of Buddhism into China and Southeast Asia, Christianity throughout the Roman Empire, and the expansion of the vast Islamic Empire from Spain to West Africa to India to Southeast Asia. Jerusalem becomes a focal point for a comparative study of Judaism, Christianity, and Islam (a study later revived by looking at Arab-Islamic Spain in Granada and Cordoba). In thinking about the ongoing, contemporary prospects for peace in the Mideast, students wonder why three religious traditions that have much in common could end up in such hostile situations. These concerns are highlighted by Islam's encounter with both Western and Eastern Christians and Jews, but specifically those Christians sent to recapture the Holy City during the Crusades.

Of course, empire-builders, religious figures, and other world travelers could also carry disease with them, as the Mongols ably demonstrated with the bubonic plague. Students observe that the "Black Death" (which like AIDS quickly became a pandemic) spread along the same routes that traders and religious pilgrims and missionaries (Hindu, Buddhist, Christian, Muslim) and members of the Jewish diaspora traveled. A knight returning home from Jerusalem after surviving the conflict between the Crusaders and the Muslims might well have been infected with the pestilence.

After a lengthy consideration of how and why much of the world became so interconnected by the dawn of the fifteenth century, students begin to examine factors within Europe that would affect the course of European exploration and expansion and future cultural encounters. Included among these factors are the European Renaissance, the Protestant and Catholic Reformations, the emergence of rival nation-states on the Continent, and the pivotal role England played. No one should underestimate the significance of the exploits of Portugal's Prince Henry or of "Spain's" Columbus (or of China's Zheng Ho, for that matter). But Columbus's dreams for his "Enterprise of the Indies" essentially disappeared when the Spanish "discovered" a distinct *lack* of gold on Hispaniola and took their wrath out on the indigenous peoples. Then, out of the ocean blue, Cortes came to the rescue. The encounter between the Spanish and the Aztecs represents but one of a number of case studies of cultural encounter resulting from Portuguese and Spanish exploration (the pope having graciously split the entire world in half between the two countries in 1494) and, later, following the Reformation, Dutch and English and French competition for the "New" World. Other case studies examine the interaction between the southern New England Indians (Algonkians), particularly the Connecticut River Pequots, and the English Puritans; the Canadian Indians (Hurons and Iroquois) and the French Jesuits; and the Japanese of the late sixteenth and early seventeenth centuries (pre- and early Tokugawa Japan) and the Portuguese.[5]

Like much of the work in the course, these case studies are collaborative in nature. Each group works with a number of different sources, many original, that represent different viewpoints, styles, and narrative accounts. Each group of students offers a presentation to the class, complete with maps, outlines, reflections, perhaps costumes, a video, computer-enhanced graphics, etc. Where feasible, two classes combine to share presentations. This approach allows for more case studies to occur. In addition, for example, to the four encounters noted above, students investigate interaction in the Incan Empire, West Africa, the Chesapeake Bay region, and what is now Indonesia.

The case study approach to cultural encounter continues with an investigation of three specific regions of the Atlantic Ocean trading complex focusing on the slave trade. After a consideration of the origins of the slave trade and its impact on African populations, students analyze the interaction between African slaves and their descendants and owners of sugar plantations in Haiti and Brazil and rice plantations in South Carolina. Another investigation is being planned that would compare the impact of African–native interaction in the Caribbean (Black Caribs) with that in Florida (Black Seminoles).

At times a form of cultural interaction might be "manufactured" or staged by a teacher for purposes of comparative study and an ongoing insistence on providing a more global context in which students can think historically. One might consider, for example, the rise of European humanism during the Renaissance in conjunction with the neo-Confucian movement in China and the neo-Persian Renaissance. In another case, rather than look solely at Europe's intellectual and scientific revolutions, students might participate in a grand convention of some of the world's great thinkers. Alongside revolutionaries like Galileo and Copernicus and Newton might appear an African educator from Sangore University in Timbuktu, the great Arab doctor ar-Razi (long since dead, of course, but that's precisely the point), and the Chinese inventor of the compass, *all* of whom have contributed to the *evolution* of scientific and intellectual advancement. As reason challenged the primacy of faith in Europe, it is worth remembering the influence the great Arab-Muslim thinker Ibn Rushd had on the great Christian theologian St. Thomas Aquinas. Science and religion could indeed work harmoniously, Galileo's recantation to Pope Urban notwithstanding. To be sure, the rise and triumph of the West indeed occurred in the eighteenth century with the advent of the industrial revolution and the rise of economic and political nationalism and subsequently imperialism and colonialism. These developments foreshadowed the emergence of a twentieth-century richer North and a poorer South (the reverse of some 1,500 prior years of world history), a subject that receives treatment in the modern period.

Later in the year, students examine the encounter between imperial nations and those regions they occupy in the nineteenth and twentieth centuries through further case studies. These studies include the British in West and East Africa and India, the French in Southeast Asia, the Americans in Hawaii, the Europeans and the Japanese in China, the British and French in the Mideast, and the Dutch in South Africa. Colonialism, however, and particularly colonialism in the context of the world at war in the first half century, paves the way for anticolonial movements for national independence in the non-Western world. Students then begin to brainstorm about the problems newly independent nations face and come to recognize that many of these difficulties are products of colonial legacies. This approach leads students into a lengthy consideration of the theme of development and ultimately the realization that all countries and regions of the world find themselves in a continuous state of development. In other words, we are all *developing* peoples and cultures attempting to improve the quality of our lives. Moreover, students learn the need to see the concept of development as more than simply an economic process and one that will assure that while we work to meet the needs of the present, we will not compromise the lives of those who live after us. Hence our concern for environmental and ecological issues and the importance of social justice.

A second "commitment" in the world history survey course involves cultivating both geographic and cultural perspective in students' minds. To be sure, this goal will be attainable only if students are given a framework in which to study the concepts of geography and culture. Talking about geography using terms like *location, place, movement, region,* and *human-environment interaction* (borrowed from the National Geographic Society) and defining what culture is in both material and nonmaterial terms begin to provide such a framework. Attempts at encouraging this kind of thinking start on Day One as described at the beginning of the article. In wrestling, as they did that first day, with the notion of the function and power of maps, students come to realize that every flat map is subjective in that it cannot help but distort the sizes and shapes of the earth's features. In the end, that such maps are bedeviled by an inherent contradiction—namely, "a claim to represent objectively a world they can only subjectively present, a claim made to win acceptance for a view of the world whose utility lies precisely in its partiality"[6]—reflects the political and cultural ramifications of geographic perspective. Our own cultural conditioning, which breeds a healthy dose of ethnocentrism, can sometimes lead us to believe that *our* way is *the* way. Unhealthy ethnocentrism or chauvinism or exceptionalism is quickly reflected in the cultural stereotyping and cultural lumping of other peoples, a practice that contradicts the reality that humankind throughout world history has devised *different* solutions to common problems (survival, order, growth, etc.). Thus early in the world history course, students are confronted with the significance of cultural perspective.

Yet another component in the study of geographical, and by implication, cultural perspective is the notion of "Big Geography."[7] Is it conceivable, for example, rather than viewing the arbitrary designation of the continents of Africa, Asia, and Europe as three distinct land masses, to see them as one solid land mass called Afrasia.[8] Afrasia contains a great arid zone that includes the west end of the Sahara, the Arabian desert (which the Red Sea breaks), and then China and the Gobi Desert. In this concept, one might envision the Mediterranean Sea as a big lake and the Red Sea as a small one. And, by viewing Europe, Africa, and Asia on a geographic continuum, the "Age of Exploration," for example, can be seen in its proper world-historical context. Thus, "Portugal and Spain do not magically initiate exploration and trade, but act within an already existent, often dynamic system of world exploration and trade and communication (begun long ago)."[9] Similarly, Big Geography affects our labeling of oceans. Why not picture the Indian and Pacific oceans as one enormous body of water, which would help to explain how the peoples of the Southern and Eastern hemispheres assisted in connecting the world for so long before Prince Henry and Columbus. Such a view gives students the added advantage of recognizing the perspective and predominance of *water*, while the usual perspective of land (many maps in Columbus's day had land covering six-sevenths of the earth's surface) takes a back seat.

One means by which to further the discussion of cultural perspective is to have students consider the origins of the universe and humankind. By providing students with various creation myths from around the world, teachers begin to get them to think about the function and power of myths as they impact a people's cultural and historical identity. The course attempts to reinforce this relationship along the way. Introducing students to creation myth early in the course offers additional advantages. Many of these myths illustrate a "Mother Earth–Father Sky" paradigm, which will be useful in discussing gender relations, issues of power, etc., and which invariably prompts a few students to wonder how and why the paradigm has changed in many cultures over time. The stories of peoples' origins can also give students different conceptions of time and even space, affording the teacher an opportunity to return to compare and contrast these cultural conceptions as the course evolves. How very different, for example, is American time "by appointment"—remem-

ber that Loomis Chaffee planbook—from Islamic time in which the day is measured by calls to prayer, each day a repeating cycle, or Hindu time, a never-ending cycle of creation and destruction. And myths, because they raise and answer several questions related to the concept of religion (the relationship of human beings to the Creator, the means to form order from chaos, the question of life after death, etc.), can begin to help students formulate a working definition of religion that can be applied to their comparative study of major civilizations during the course. Part of this study may include a small unit on comparative religious art in world history around the year 1500. Finally, when the teacher combines the archaeological and anthropological dimensions with the religious and philosophical to help explore the beginnings of our world, students become aware of the complexity of the study of world history and its interdisciplinary nature. Is that example of prehistoric African rock art a product of artistic imagination, religious expression, or the historical record—isn't it really *all of these*?[10]

While the world history course is not committed to a "civilization's" approach of study, it does devote time, in the midst of exploring the interactive global community, to a comparative study of the classical features of the world's major civilizations during periods of great empires. The existence of empires greatly facilitated cross-cultural contact. Greece (Golden Age of Pericles and Empire of Alexander the Great), Rome (Roman Empire), India (Mauryan and Gupta empires), China (Han and Tang dynasties), West Africa (Ghana and Malia and Songhai empires), and Meso-America (Mayan Empire) are among those studied. The course makes an even more challenging commitment, namely, to address the relationship between settled and unsettled peoples, the "core" and the "periphery." Of course, this means confronting important terminology, loaded words like *civilized* and *barbarian, advanced* and *primitive*. While cultural anthropologists have identified several criteria which constitute a "civilization," based around the concept of urbanism, are we prepared to state that early African and Amerindian societies, just because of the absence of a written historical tradition (and thus technically considered to be "prehistoric"), were not civilized? What may seem civilized to one culture can be primitive to the next. How the settled peoples of the twentieth century encounter the unsettled peoples, and how the latter find ways to survive, represent some of the final questions that students investigate in the course.

In conjunction with these major commitments noted above, the Planning Group thought that there should be a number of major coordinated events during the year at which many all world history students (all 130 of them) could be present. In the fall of 1993, the renowned Nicaraguan poet and liberation theologian Father Ernesto Cardenal read dramatically from his latest anthology, with Loomis Chaffee Spanish students reading translations. In the spring of 1994, as part of a unit on the global impact of World Wars I and II, and, in particular, Holocaust studies, all students went to see the epic film *Schindler's List*. During the winter of 1995, students attended a special Old World–New World Burrito Lunch, illustrating the impact of the Columbian exchange. Students could enjoy the gastronomical experience while trying to remember the place of origin of various food and drink.

In an interdisciplinary extravaganza in the winter of 1995–96, students, teachers, and faculty members representing other teaching disciplines participated in an early eleventh-century Banquet at the Alhambra Palace in Granada, Spain, complete with Arabic food, music from the world of Islam, games, Islamic art decoration. The banquet afforded the opportunity for students and teachers to assume various roles, among others, for Ibn Rushd to converse with Thomas Aquinas about the compatibility of faith and reason.[11] After being entertained by an acting troupe that performed a theatrical version of an Arab folk tale, the guests were rudely interrupted (and transported in time) by an unannounced visit by Ferdinand and Isabella and then guards of the Spanish Inquisition. The Christian reconquest of Andalusia in the sixteenth century ended the intellectual exchange among Jews, Christians, and Muslims, as the Jews and Muslims among the banquet guests soon discovered. While Ferdinand and Isabella proceeded to burn books and manuscripts seized from the dinner guests, their guards herded all the Jews and Muslims (those who did not convert on the spot) into the Parton Room, thereby expelling them from their homes and businesses in Spain.

Several students reflected in their journals about how effective the entire banquet experience had been, particularly in terms of being able to meet so many different and very bright people from different cultures. Many noted that what happened at the end was incredibly shocking and provided an important contrast with the atmosphere of the dinner. Some wondered how those forced to leave could cope with what occurred to their families. A few took the time to examine the forces of faith and reason and the purpose of religion.

Recently a World History Film Festival has been instituted. Several students attended the showing of *The Mission*, having already watched *The Black Robe* as part of the course curriculum. Other feature films include the Cuban film *The Last Supper* and the epic *Gandhi*. Concerning current affairs in the world, each student must keep a collection of *New York Times* articles, which they write about in terms of what they have been studying in the course. Finally, a trip to Ellis Island may occur in future years.

Representing medieval personalities, Alison Thurber '98 and Titania Barrett '98 are served mint tea, eggplant, and kufta by Bob Andrian as might have been the custom in eleventh-century Arab-Muslim Spain. Photo by Wayne Dombroski.

Needless to say, World History at Loomis Chaffee has signified an ambitious undertaking. The Planning Group already has thought of ways to revise and tinker with the curriculum of the survey course in order to weave together a more coherent and compelling narrative. Student and faculty concerns about the pace of the course will mean more editing after all is said and done, but the major course "commitments" seem both desirable and reasonable. And as we end our third year, staff and students alike have worked hard and had fun. In the final analysis, students may not remember a great deal of *what* has been learned in a school year. Summers have a marvelous way of facilitating forgetfulness. On the other hand, if we have taught the students to become better thinkers, to wonder about "how we know what we know," if we have piqued their intellectual curiosity, broadened their sense of perspective, inspired and excited them about the study of world history and history itself, then they will be on the road to lifelong learning as citizens of the world, a process that summer will also eventually facilitate. As Brian Hershcopf '97 concluded in his course evaluation: "I had fun in class this year, and I really felt challenged. This was the first history class in which I had to think, and I really enjoyed that!"

Fall-Term Topical Syllabus

This syllabus is organized by topics in the order in which we will study them this term. Your notebook should be organized by topic, as we have discussed already. Remember that you will submit your notebook when you take the exam at the end of the term.

Topic 1: An introduction to geographic and cultural perspective

Different perspectives of world maps . . . the five geographic themes: *location, place, human-environment interaction, movement, region* . . . different map projections with different biases . . . the notion of "Big Geography," for example, the "continent" of *Afrasia,* one continent versus three (Europe, Africa, Asia) . . . the power of maps . . . defining culture: material versus nonmaterial culture . . . differing cultural perspectives . . . the problem of ethnocentrism . . . different conceptions of time . . .

Topic 2: Wondering how the world/humankind began as a means to understanding the richness and complexity of the study of world history, in trying to answer the question: "How do we know what we know?"

Thinking about the role and power of myth in comparing various creation myths from different cultures . . . the significance of religion in creating order out of chaos, in establishing meaning in people's lives . . . archaeological and anthropological origins of humans . . . break-up of land masses (and land bridges), rock art and cave paintings . . .

Topic 3: Transition from hunting-and-gathering societies to village life

Examining the agricultural revolution (domestication of plants and animals) through the eyes of women and men . . . understanding the transition from matrilineal and matriarchal societies in settled villages to patrilineal and patriarchal societies in cities . . .

Topic 4: Defining civilization as a subset of culture, using Egypt and Mesopotamia as case studies

Designing your own city . . . exploring the terms *civilized* and *primitive* . . . the relationship between the "urban" life and the "hinterland," the "wilds" of pastoral or nomadic life (*Epic of Gilgamesh—Gilgamesh* and *Enkidu*) . . . comparing Sumerian, Babylonian, Hebrew, and Egyptian societies (moral and legal codes; life after death; *human-environment interaction,* especially with the Tigris-Euphrates and the Nile rivers; *movement,* e.g., travels of the Hebrews) . . .

Topic 5: A comparative cultural study of "classical" civilizations

What is meant by *classical?* . . . key features, legacies, heroes, role players, the importance of geography; in short, the investigation of each civilization using the definition of material and nonmaterial culture as guideline . . . the ideal and the real Greece (Athens primarily) during the "Golden Age" of Pericles . . . Rome during the height of the empire, the Pax Romana of Augustus (first century C.E.) . . . the sacred essence of Indian civilization, Benares and the Ganges . . .

China, the center of the universe, group harmony, Confucius and codes of conduct (first and second century C.E.) . . . West Africa, Ghana, c. 500–700 C.E. . . . the Mayans and an isolated but sophisticated civilization . . .

Topic 6: Beginning to explore the notion of the interacting global community through trade brought about by expanding empires and adventuresome sailors

Alexander the Great's empire and the spread of Hellenism . . . the *cosmopolitan* city of Constantinople in 550 (or Baghdad in 750) . . . the importance of *movement* and, in particular, the emergence (starting in 300 B.C.E.) of the process called *Southernization,* the evolution of an Indo-Pacific Ocean trading network . . . Malay sailors . . . Indian sailors and the *Indianization* of Southeast Asia . . . Chinese sailors and traders . . . reviewing technological catalyst towards interacting global community (iron) . . .

Topic 7: Cultural diffusion through religion and religious art along similar trade routes

Case study of the rise and spread of Buddhism from India to China along Silk Route . . . Buddhist cave painting revealing several cultural influences (Greco-Roman, Indian, Chinese) . . . appeal of *Bodhisattva* to the Chinese . . . possibilities of salvation . . .

Topic 8: Continued cultural diffusion through religion and trade: pilgrims, crusaders, missionaries, and conflict

Learning about the shared "holiness" of Jerusalem among Jews, Christians, and Muslims . . . comparing the values of tenets of Christianity as espoused by Jesus and later Paul (the conversion of Paul from Saul), Moses and the Ten Commandments, Muhammad and the Qu'ran . . . pilgrimages to Makkah *(hajj),* Jerusalem, Benares (Hindus bathing in the Ganges), along the Silk Road from Chang'an (present day Xian) westward . . . the split (1054) between Western (Roman Catholic) Christians and Eastern (Orthodox) Christians and "Holy Wars," the Crusades (Pope Urban's attempt to regain Jerusalem and reunite the Christian world and the Muslim response (Saladin) . . . the spread of Islam and with it *Southernization* . . .

Note that for each topic there are several relevant maps to be found in the text. You will also see different maps shown on transparencies in class that pertain to the above topics.

Fall-Term Exam Questions

Below are nine questions for which you should prepare responses. Three will be selected at exam time.

1. We have thought a great deal about the "power of maps" and the idea of geographic perspective this term. What is meant by the "power of maps"? How can you apply this notion to what we have been studying? (Be specific in

your applications.) How would a map of *Afrasia* or the *Indo-Pacific Ocean* alter our geographic perspective in the study of world history?

2. "How do we know what we know" about the origins and evolution of early humankind from creation to hunting and gathering to village to city life?

3. What is myth? Discuss the relationship between myth and culture in world history from creation to the Black Death (c. 1300 C.E.). Be sure to cite specific examples.

4. You, as a cultural anthropologist, have just discovered a "new" civilization. In order to find out more about it, who would you talk to and what kinds of questions would you ask? What would you want to see?

5. Discuss the roles of men and women in agricultural (village) societies. Then compare their roles and status in *one* of the following pairs of "classical" civilizations: China and India *or* Maya and West Africa *or* Greece and Rome.

6. In what ways were the Buddhist cave paintings powerful illustrations of cultural diffusion?

7. Hammurabi, Moses, Jesus, Muhammad, Osiris, Buddha, Confucius, Asoka, Hindu warrior (Arjuna): Choose any *three* of these world history personalities and construct a discussion about *either* religion *or* society's rules of behavior, customs, and traditions.

8. Describe Jerusalem around 1200 C.E.

9. What is meant by *Southernization*? What groups contributed to this process (300 B.C.E.–1200 C.E.) and what did they contribute?

Winter-Term Topical Syllabus

Topic 1: The interactive global community, 1000–1500

World travelers . . . Mongol conquests and their impact . . . Turkish-Mongolian cultural mix and the spread of Islam, "Southernizing the Mediterranean" . . . case studies of major regions (and in some cases how one region has influenced another) . . . India–Southeast Asia, China–Japan . . . continued cultural diffusion through the spread of disease (the Black Death of bubonic plague) . . . origins and evolution of the plague, perceptions of the disease, responses to it in Europe and the Mideast, its impact on population data, societies, economies, etc., how and why it spread so fast . . . comparisons with the AIDS epidemic . . .

Topic 2: The state of cartography in the world during the Middle Ages

Examining the state of cartography during all of this cultural diffusion (how did people know where to go?) . . . the loss of Greek science to Christian dogma . . . the brilliance of Chinese and Arab cartography and the spread of Southernization . . .

Topic 3: Exploring the roots of European exploration and expansion in a global context

European humanism and tension between individualism and communalism (*The Return of Martin Guerre*) . . . Renaissance and Reformation and Counter-Reformation . . . European humanism and Chinese humanism . . . motivations to explore (Portuguese, Spanish) or not to explore anymore (Chinese) . . . the Columbian exchange (people, plants, animals, disease) and initial perceptions of cultural encounter . . . Old World–New World gastronomical gathering . . .

Topic 4: Discovery, invasion, encounter—the world 1500–1650

Four case studies: Devising questions to investigate cultural encounter . . . examining Pequots and the English, French Jesuits and the Canadians (Hurons), Aztecs and the Spanish, Portuguese and the Japanese . . .

Topic 5: African slavery and the Atlantic slave trade in world history

Three case studies: Framing questions about the slave trade . . . examining slavery and cultural diffusion and interaction (and forms of resistance, rebellion, and revolution) in Haiti, Brazil, and South Carolina and the Georgia Sea Islands . . .

Topic 6: The significance of the Columbian exchange "Pulling Things Together."

Winter-Term Essay: "The Significance of the Columbian Exchange"

For a long time in this century students who thought they were learning about world history actually were learning only about the history of the West and how it affected the rest of the "unknown" or "uncivilized" world. Textbooks managed to persuasively convey the false notion that exploration and expansion and thus the unification of the globe had been magically initiated by Portuguese and Spanish and later Dutch (and other) intrepid sailors and heroic sea captains who sailed for proud rulers—who bore the sword and the cross—in their homelands (or, in the case of Columbus's "Enterprise of the Indies," whoever would finally buy into his proposal). In this light, the voyages of Christopher Columbus and the subsequent Columbian encounter could be represented (and were) as simply, the "discovery" of America. Fortunately, the intellectual curiosity and honesty of students like you have come to the rescue in recent years.

You are well aware by now that European exploration and expansion in general and the Columbian encounter and exchange in particular occurred within the context of an already existing vibrant and dynamic interactive global community, which had seen cultural diffusion through trade, religion, war and conquest, and disease for two thousand years. (You remember that Afrasian continent, don't you, and what about the Indo-Pacific Ocean???) The process of "Southernization" had made its way to the shores of the Mediterranean, and the Mongol conquests provided even greater opportunities for world travelers and traders and proselytizers. More directly, the advent and spread of a kind of Turkish-Mongolian Islam, which had overtaken present-day Turkey and then Constantinople in 1453, helped to intensify Spanish and Portuguese efforts to strengthen Christianity and weaken Islam. Thus, the Spaniards were able to retake Spain from the Moors (expelling the Jews in the process as well), and the Portuguese successfully evaded the Muslims of North Africa by sailing down the West African coast to the source of that region's gold. In doing so, the Portuguese sailors learned a great deal about the wind patterns and ocean currents west of Africa, knowledge that would be valuable to the success of Columbus's voyages. Placing the Columbian exchange in this "global" context should enhance rather than diminish its significance as something far more substantial than the "discovery" of America, or, more accurately, than Columbus himself (after all, someone else would have done what he did soon enough).

Your task is to continue to illustrate the limitless bounds of your intellectual curiosity and imagination and powers of interpretation (not to mention writing skills) by thinking *DEEPLY* about the significance of the Columbian exchange. How and why has it been so important, given your work over the last several weeks? How would you assess it from various cultural perspectives? What carefully reasoned moral judgments would you make?

Your essay should be about 3–4 pages.

Spring-Term Topical Syllabus

Topic 1: Cultural evolution and revolution in the early modern and modern world

The enlightenment and ideas, forces, tensions at work in government and the economy leading to nationalism and cultural imperialism: 1600–1914 . . .

Topic 2: European cultural imperialism in Africa, East Asia, India, and the Mideast during the nineteenth and twentieth centuries

An evaluation based on a few case studies . . .

Topic 3: The world in crisis in the first half of the twentieth century

World War I and its impact: from nation-state to ideological conflict . . . totalitarianism vs. democracy . . . Russian revolution and communism and the rise of Hitler and Nazism . . . World War II and its aftermath . . .

Topic 4: Anticolonial movements for national independence in the world

Africa, India, the Mideast, East and Southeast Asia . . .

Topic 5: Toward an understanding of human development and cultural identity in the contemporary world

Examining models of development . . . cultural conflict in Northern Ireland, the Balkans, South Africa, Latin America, and the Mideast . . .

Topic 6: Americans as World Citizens
Trips to Ellis Island and prepare for exam . . .

Final Exam Project: Cultural Identity and Development

As we have discovered in our study since we began to brainstorm about the problems newly independent nations would face after breaking away from colonial powers, *all* countries and regions of the world find themselves in a continuous state of development. In other words, we are all "developing" peoples and cultures, attempting to improve the quality of our lives. Moreover, we have learned that we need to see the concept of development as more than simply an economic process (it includes the political, social, cultural, etc., evolution) and one that will assure that while we work to meet the needs of the present, we will also not compromise the lives of those who live after us. Hence our concern for environmental and ecological issues and the importance of social justice leads us to an awareness of the idea of *sustainable development.*

Until 1989, countries and regions around the globe faced the challenges of "developing" in the midst of significant changes (many of which you read about in *A Global Village* and watched on a recent video about the world after World War II) and in the context of the Cold War and ideological conflict between the U.S. and the USSR. Since 1990, however, with the fall of Soviet and Eastern European communism, the world political landscape has changed. Apocalyptic events—witness the election of Nelson Mandela in South Africa—and significant world conferences concerning the environment, trade, population, growth, disease, women, and human rights have taken place. New "maps" have been and will continue to be drawn. And, in the words of one political scientist, ideological conflict has been replaced by "cultural identity" conflict.

In this larger, global context of change, peoples and cultures the world over must continue to wrestle with their identities and with various challenges in order to "sustain their development" for generations to come. How they resolve these problems and difficulties will say much about "who they are" as cultures and in what directions their lives will be headed. Your task, working in pairs, will be to work with a specific country or region and to respond to the following three questions:

1. What are the problems or difficulties facing your country or region? (Note: Remember the scope of the concept of development.)
2. Given your understanding of the ideas behind *sustainable development,* what solutions for the future would you propose to the leadership of your country?

3. As curator of the _____ Cultural Museum, take a visitor on a tour of your major exhibits (all five of them), and explain why you have selected these particular exhibits.

    Here are the countries/regions:

    Americas: Haiti and Brazil

    Europe and the Mideast: Bosnia and Israel/Palestine

    Africa: South Africa and West Africa

    Asia: India and Vietnam

Expectations: In your exam period, you will submit your written report (typed), which should include all pertinent maps, charts, etc. You will be asked to present a 5–10-minute synopsis of your findings to the class.

Some Thoughts about Your Research:

You will be researching your country or region using sources since 1990. At first, you should consult your text to review any historical background necessary as well as any contemporary material that might be included. You should also make use of the MacGlobe software (and/or the "MAPS" software available at the library), which includes country/regional maps, charts, country reports, flags, anthems, and a wealth of data related to "development" issues. Then you will use the library resources, which will constitute the bulk of your research. These sources include various books and publications that will be available at the reserve desk (titles to be given later) and newspaper and periodical sources derived through computer use. These latter sources include the *New York Times* (a useful place to begin), Wilson Line (which can access recent periodical titles and article abstracts), and EBSCO (which can provide the full text of pertinent articles in a number of important periodicals, a list of which will be provided to you). At the beginning of work on this unit, your class will go to the library and, with the expert help of one of the library staff, you will be introduced to our computer resources and how to use them. During the last week of classes, you will report to the library each day for work there. You may, after checking in, go to the computer center as well. For some groups, additional work beyond class time at the library may be needed.

Good Luck!!!

Notes

1. William H. McNeill, "The World History Survey Course," as quoted in Gilbert Allardyce, "Toward World History: American Historians and the Coming of the World History Course," in *Journal of World History* 1, no. 1 (Honolulu, 1990):26.

2. William Swinton, *Outlines of World History,* as quoted in Allardyce, p. 45.

3. Ibid., p. 47.

4. The historian Lynda Shaffer has labeled the process by which the Southern and Eastern hemispheres helped to insure the economic development of first the Mediterranean and then the rest of Europe, "Southernization." Thus, an interactive global community was much in place *prior* to the Mongol conquests. From 1500 on, of course, Southernization gave way to Westernization, which, in turn, one might argue, yielded to the "Americanization" of the twentieth century. See Shaffer's recently published article "Southernization," in the *World History Journal,* May–June 1994.

5. The author gratefully acknowledges the work of colleague Mark Williams in creating the "Pequot War" case study as part of several units on Connecticut history. He also teaches a course entitled "The World After Columbus, 1500–1700," which offers an in-depth study of cultural interaction as a result of the Columbian exchange.

6. Dennis Wood, "The Power of Maps," *Scientific American,* May 1993, p. 93.

7. The concept of "Big Geography" originated with the *Pacesetter* World History Task Force established by ETS and the College Board.

8. The notion of "Afrasia" came from curriculum development at the 1991 DeWitt Wallace World History Institute at Princeton University.

9. "Power of Perspective: Map Projections" is a curriculum unit developed at the 1991 DeWitt Wallace World History Institute.

10. Heidi Roupp, Aspen High School World History Curriculum, 1993.

11. "A Medieval Banquet in the Alhambra Palace" comes from the curriculum unit of the same name designed by Audrey Shabbas and published by AWAIR, Arab World and Islamic Resources and School Services in Berkeley, California.

5

Building an Essential World History Tool

Teaching Comparative History

Robert B. Bain

"To compare" is a key verb in the history teacher's vocabulary. Comparison may be the most widely used demonstration of higher-level thinking in history courses. Teachers consciously use comparison to make connections, to demonstrate history's value, and to challenge students to analyze events, eras, and people. And even without the verb, comparison hides in teachers' analogies and metaphors. "Any treatment of society or literary tradition," historian Peter Stearns holds, "invites implicit comparisons by encouraging some sense of distinctiveness."[1]

However, implicit comparisons are often poor comparisons. Using little or no comparative methodology, people allow surface similarity or difference to pass for analysis or evidence. Teachers often assume students can compare because everyone makes comparisons so often. Yet frequency of activity does not guarantee the quality.

For example, I recently heard a nationally respected superintendent and leader in educational reform compare special education to the Holocaust. "Special educators are like Nazis. They label children like the Nazis burned numbers into Jewish arms." As a history teacher, I was shocked, immediately struck by the way a superficial, weak link between situations passed for insight. I was also taken by the power of the analogy—the way it silenced the audience, channeled ideas, and narrowed the realm of dissent. Beware the dangers of incomplete comparison, bad analogies, and shoddy history! They are the shadows that cloud minds.

In *Historians' Fallacies,* David Hackett Fisher refers to the misuse of comparison as the fallacy of appositive proof, a "complex form of empirical error, which consists in an attempt to establish the existence of a quality in A by contract with a quality in B—and B is *misrepresented or misunderstood.*" This misuse is an "invidious mistake." Though the real attention is on event A, Fisher explains, the "erroneous B is bootlegged" into the discussion of evidence.[2]

How often are history teachers and students guilty of such error? How often do they "bootleg" comparisons into classes? How often do teachers shape the understanding by the type of comparison they allow in their classrooms?

The problem inheres in implied, quick, assumed, or vague comparisons. "The remedy for comparative error," Fisher urges, "is not less comparative history but more of it, more that is explicit and more that is empirical."[3]

This chapter makes a case for teaching comparative history, making it both *explicit* and *systematic.* Why is comparative history valuable for world history students? What are the processes, the habits of mind, that constitute comparative history? This chapter speaks of the educational treasure stored in comparative study. It suggests an overt way to teach the steps in comparison, to reinforce and critique the comparative methods students use. For students and teachers, clarity in the comparative method yields deeper understanding of world history.

The Value of Comparative History

All the recent calls for improving history in schools make comparative history an element of reform. For example, the Bradley Commission labeled comparison as one of history's unique and most valuable perspectives.[4] World historian Philip Curtin sees comparative history as revitalizing the survey course. Though writing about graduate study, Curtin tells us that "[a] slightly deeper superficial knowledge of world history is not likely to produce much gain in real understanding. The key to understanding is not in the survey, but in the way the parts are linked together, that is, comparative history."[5]

We should take a minute to consider the value of comparative history, if only to justify the time and effort it takes to teach the comparative method. Why is comparison considered so valuable for history students?

Comparison locates the distinctive. For students, history is too often one damn thing after another. What makes one historical event significant? What makes one more important than another? Comparative history highlights the distinctive. This allows students to assess what is unique in a situation, event, idea, or person's life. Through comparison, the distinguishing features step from the background. Locating the distinctive and significant is one of the great values in comparative history.

Comparison locates the common. The reverse is also true—comparative history allows students to ask whether or not an event was truly distinctive. How common was a movement, trend, or system? In world history, such comparison allows the constructing of broader world patterns. It encourages students to develop concepts that apply beyond a single locale, nation, or even region. Locating the common is crucial in understanding whether specific attributes of a situation are generalizable to others.

Therefore, comparisons identify the common while attending to the particular. This is the heart that pumps life into world-scale history.

Comparison locates hidden elements in a situation. In the short story "Silver Blade," Sherlock Holmes cracks the case by pointing to the key clue—the dog that did not bark. Holmes uncovered the missing evidence—the nonevidence—by comparing what happened with what should have happened if a stranger had appeared. Such comparison, though fanciful, demonstrates the value of holding two situations side by side. Studying a situation in isolation typically encourages historians and students to attend to the most obvious and dramatic elements in the situation. Focusing exclusively on one situation often blinds us to nuance, obscuring subtler characteristics. Applying what is obvious in one situation to another or asking questions raised in one place of another can reveal hidden attributes.

Comparative history stimulates students to use higher-level thinking skills. Directly, formally teaching the processes of comparative history should improve thinking skills. Eventually the formal steps of method become habits of thought. Comparative thinking, of course, transcends the historical realm. Most thinking employs implied comparison, analogy, and metaphor. Improving students' comparative facility will sharpen their analytical saw.

Thinking the Comparative Method

No matter how old students are, we must formally introduce or reintroduce the concept of and steps in making informed comparisons. We must not assume students understand how to "compare and contrast." This is analogous to athletic coaches who begin an initial training session by reviewing or reteaching fundamentals. Baseball's spring training always begins with the basic stances, positions, and movements. Obviously, the time spent in stressing fundamentals depends upon the players, but no coach assumes automatic carryover from the previous season. Neither should history

teachers. If it is important enough to build upon, we should review the fundamentals.

In *Dimensions of Learning,* a wonderful book on developing student thinking, the authors suggest four fundamental steps in the comparative process:

1. Select the items you want to compare.
2. Select the characteristics of the items on which you want to base your comparison.
3. Explain how the items are similar and different with respect to the characteristics you selected.
4. Summarize what you have learned.[6]

While these clear, concise steps are a solid foundation, they are too general for effective comparative history. History has unique elements—time and culture—that teachers must include in the comparative process. Further, historians must carefully consider the cases and categories they select for comparison. These factors are elements in teaching the comparative process in history. Therefore, general steps for comparison must be elaborated to reflect the special characteristics of doing comparative history.

The key steps in teaching the comparative process in history are:

1. Introducing comparison and comparative history.
2. Forming a problem and selecting historical cases.
3. Choosing the elements of comparison.
4. Collecting information and analyzing each case.
5. Making an initial comparison.
6. Summarizing the results.
7. Reconsidering each case.
8. Final comparison and conclusions.

Introducing Comparison and Comparative History

Teachers should always introduce or reintroduce the *concept* of comparison and comparative history. From the outset, students must understand that comparison is a particular type of thinking, with its own strengths and weaknesses. The comparative process itself becomes an object of study.[7]

Teachers can vividly begin the study of comparative history by investigating ways people typically make comparisons. One way is to locate examples from advertisements, commercials, or politics. Or student-generated examples might introduce the concept, a technique I often use. Comparison colors much of my students' conversations. In fact, they compare colorfully, contrasting one school to another, one year to another, one class to another, one teacher to another, one film to another, or one musician to another. Often, their comparisons are historical, comparing items in the past or cases across time. "High school is much harder than middle school." "I can't believe I once liked that song . . . it stinks!" "Nothing ever changes here at school. One year is just like another."

Together, teachers and students analyze the examples to discuss when and why people make comparisons, and to establish the value and power of comparative thinking. The discussion typically centers on what people gain or lose by a comparative method. Students should be able to explain how comparing cases produces different insights from studying cases in isolation. Teachers also could take this opportunity to discuss the problems in quick, loose, or implied comparison.

Another way to introduce the idea of comparison is to have students collect their own examples. Students might maintain a "Comparison Log," keeping a record of examples they've heard or read. Together, teacher and students reflect on how the examples shaped a conversation, argument, or thought. Did the comparison further understanding? Did it make a judgment, holding one case as better or worse than the other? Was it exaggerated? Careful? Fair? Did the comparison clarify or confuse? When is comparison most useful? Does everything need methodological comparison?

While time consuming, such discussion helps students connect new meaning to the verb "compare." Most significantly, the introduction elevates comparison to an object of study and a skill that merits mastery.

Forming a Problem and Selecting Historical Cases

Students should begin their comparison with a clear understanding of their comparative problem or question. They also must identify the type of comparison they will be working with.

There are three general types of historical comparisons: (1) comparing a case across time, (2) comparing across culture or region, and (3) a combination of the two. Each presents unique advantages and dangers.

Comparison across time. One comparative problem uses cases drawn from the same region or culture but at different *times* in history. For example, we might compare how people in the west farmed in different eras, developed a relationship with nature, fought each other, or reared children. The historian consciously selects time as the key variable. Cross-temporal comparison enables us to assess the changes within a society, culture, or region over a specific time.

Charles Rosenberg, for example, used this type of comparison effectively in *The Cholera Years*.[8] Rosenberg contrasted how the United States responded to cholera during three different epidemics. His data pointed to new institutions, attitudes, and methods of fighting disease. Placing the

three temporal cases side by side dramatically demonstrated the changes.

Cross-cultural comparison. The second type compares the same item across cultures or regions within the same era. This allows historians to investigate the cultural commonalities and variations of a phenomenon. For example, one could have compared reactions to cholera epidemics within the same time frame in England, China, Australia, and America.

Peter Stearns, for example, used this type of comparison in *The Industrial Revolution in World History*.[9] He took the same item, industrial growth, and compared it in England, France, Russia, Japan, and throughout the world. This demonstrated important cultural similarities and differences. It expanded our understanding of global industrialism. Too often people indiscriminately apply concepts developed or formulated in one culture to another. Further, people often reify concepts developed in one culture, making them universal without testing them. Cross-cultural comparison reduces these problems.

Comparing across time and across culture. This type of comparison is obviously more involved, and teachers should most likely hold these problems for more advanced students. However, the methodology suggested here applies equally to all the categories.

It is crucial to formulate a problem or question—a problem whose solution lies in comparison. What changes? What remains constant? What is distinctive? Does the concept apply equally well everywhere? This problem is the real hook for doing the comparison. Students do *authentic* comparative history when they work to answer the question or resolve the problem.

I begin teaching this process immediately. The agricultural revolution presents a marvelous opportunity to teach the steps in this process. This teacher-guided comparison fully demonstrates the method. The question we study is either the cross-cultural "What is the difference between Paleolithic and Neolithic cultures?" or the cross-temporal "What effect did farming have on people?"

Choosing the Elements of Comparison

After forming the comparative problem, students need to identify the elements of the cases that will guide data collections, and eventually the comparison itself. To answer the larger comparative questions or solve the comparative problem, what must we know about each case? What information will we need about each case to compare?

This important step structures and limits the process—an important yet also potentially dangerous procedure. Without clear categories, the comparative task overwhelms students. They may collect information in a random or an unbalanced

Table 5.1

Agricultural Revolution Comparison

Categories	Paleolithic	Neolithic
Maintaining order?		
Producing and distributing goods/services?		
Raising young?		
Transmitting traditions, skills, and knowledge?		
Common beliefs?		
Systems of communication?		

way. Further, when they try to compare cases, they often find that they do not have sufficient information on comparable items. Comparison then turns into parallel descriptions. So, determining the elements for comparison provides important direction for students.

However, predetermining analytical categories also funnels the data collection and the analysis along a prescribed path. This may restrict student thinking to the most familiar, well-traveled roads. As students decide which elements they will want to compare to resolve their problem or answer their questions, teachers must remind them to leave room for new questions or categories. To ensure such reconsideration, step 7 below, "Reconsidering Each Case," formally revises the categories for comparison.

At this point, teachers might want to set up charts to help students keep their thinking straight. Comparative history lends itself well to concept mapping, charts, and other visuals. One suggestion is to place the comparative cases (either temporal or cultural) in the columns of a chart and put the items of comparison in the rows.

In the agricultural revolution comparison, the students work out five or six elements they will use to analyze and then compare Paleolithic or Neolithic people. Sometimes, I introduce six elements of social life as the categories for comparison: how people maintain order, produce and distribute goods and services, raise young children, transmit their traditions and knowledge and skills; the common beliefs that bind them; and their systems for communication.

A chart then for this lesson could look like Table 5.1.

Collecting Information and Analyzing Each Case

Students now collect data on each cultural or temporal case. They analyze the cases separately, working to acquire information and to understand the specific case. If they create charts, they work to complete the charts, one column (case) at a time.

Students might want to skip the individual data collection stage and move immediately to comparing the cases. Teachers should prevent this, especially with younger students.

Initially, these steps should remain separated, as mixing cases too quickly has risks. Comparing before understanding the specifics of the cases often leads students to ignore key elements in one case or apply standards from one case to the other.

In the agricultural revolution lesson, students might work in cooperative groups. Each group would provide information on a case (Paleolithic or Neolithic society). Within the group, students would assume responsibility for gathering information about each category or element of analysis.

Making an Initial Comparison

After students analyze each case, they consider the similarities and differences between the cases. What do these cases have in common? What is different? What is present in one case that is not present in the other? What is missing? If a person from one case traveled to another, what would be most surprising? Least surprising? What if a traveler went in the other direction?

Here students would contrast the way that Paleolithic and Neolithic people kept order, produced and distributed goods and services, raised their young, transmitted traditions, developed common beliefs, and developed systems for communication.

Summarizing the Results

It is important for students to record what they learned from their comparisons. What did they discover? What is similar or different in the cases? This is a wonderful opportunity for students to write in a journal, "publish" a draft of a paper, write a letter explaining the difference from one case to another, or participate in a discussion with other students.

Reconsidering Each Case

Too often, comparison stops with the initial comparison. In history, we must return to each case informed by the ideas and information from the initial comparison. Ask students to reconsider each case now that they have seen the other case.

Ask them to reconsider each case from the perspective of the other. What did they miss the first time? Did the initial questions or categories too narrowly define the study? What elements might we compare that we had not considered initially?

One of the dangers of a generic comparative method is that it presupposes we know from the outset what the effective categories of comparison are. One of the strengths of the comparative method in history is that it questions that assumption. Historians recognize that comparative categories are both time and culture bound. Therefore, they understand that new insights, questions, and categories arise after initial comparison. They review the cases, guided by the new insights, asking new questions, and analyzing with the new categories.

Students should use their initial comparison to add items for analysis. They return to individual cases to gather more information, and they restructure their categories and questions for a deeper comparison.

For example, the initial comparison of Paleolithic and Neolithic societies typically raises questions about changed gender relationships, or relationship to nature, or issues of distribution of goods. Students do not raise these questions initially. The new questions grow from the comparative soil. We then place our new items on the chart, and students return to their investigations of the specific cases to gather information on gender, ecology, or social structure of the Paleolithic and Neolithic societies.

Final Comparison and Conclusions

Students now compare the cases again, reconsidering each category and the new categories or questions. They work to answer their initial question, to resolve their initial problem. As a final step, they analyze the method itself.

This process is initially laborious. The steps are a bit exaggerated, though they do become less rigid with practice. Students can use the method to develop comparative essays or to criticize the comparisons and analogies of others. Most important, the comparative method allows students to make sophisticated connections, to test and retest ideas across times and/or cultures, to deepen and extend their understanding of world history.

Notes

1. Peter N. Stearns, *Meaning over Memory: Recasting the Teaching of Culture and History* (Chapel Hill: University of North Carolina Press, 1993), p. 159.
2. David Hackett Fisher, *Historians' Fallacies: Toward a Logic of Historical Thought* (New York: Harper Colophon Books, 1970), pp. 56–58 (emphasis added).
3. Ibid., p. 58.
4. Paul Gagnon and the Bradley Commission on History, eds., *Historical Literacy* (Boston: Houghton Mifflin Company, 1989).
5. Philip Curtin, "Graduate Teaching in World History," *Journal of World History* 2 (Spring, 1991):82.
6. Robert Marazano et al., *Dimensions of Learning: Teachers Manual* (Alexandria, VA: Association for Supervision and Curriculum Development, 1992), pp. 89–96.
7. Marazano et al. make a similar case for introducing the concept of comparison at the beginning. See *Dimensions of Learning*.
8. Charles Rosenberg, *The Cholera Years: The United States in 1832, 1849 and 1866* (Chicago: University of Chicago Press, 1964).
9. Peter N. Stearns, *The Industrial Revolution in World History* (Boulder: Westview Press, 1993).

Bibliography

Curtin, Philip. "Graduate Teaching in World History," *Journal of World History* 2 (Spring, 1991):81–89.

Fisher, David Hackett. *Historians' Fallacies: Toward a Logic of Historical Thought.* New York: Harper Colophon Books, 1970.

Gagnon, Paul, and the Bradley Commission on History, eds. *Historical Literacy.* Boston: Houghton Mifflin Company, 1989.

Marazano, Robert, Debra Pickering, Daisy Arredondo, Guy Blackburn, Ronald Brandt, and Cerylle Moffett. *Dimensions of Learning: Teacher's Manual.* Alexandria, VA: Association for Supervision and Curriculum Development, 1992.

Rosenberg, Charles. *Cholera Years: The United States in 1832, 1849 and 1866.* Chicago: University of Chicago Press, 1964.

Stearns, Peter N. *Meaning over Memory: Recasting the Teaching of Culture and History.* Chapel Hill: University of North Carolina Press, 1993.

Stearns, Peter N. *The Industrial Revolution in World History.* Boulder: Westview Press, 1993.

6

Graduate Training in World History

Philip D. Curtin

The problems of graduate training in world history are not very different from the problems of graduate training in any other field of knowledge—or from the problems of education at all levels. The crucial fact is that available knowledge is increasing at a faster rate than ever before in history, and it promises to go on increasing at a similar rate for the foreseeable future.

One reaction is to build bigger libraries with new technology for information retrieval. This is all very well, but access to information is not necessarily knowledge, much less wisdom. The recipients have to know what to do with the information: how to assimilate it to what they already know and fit it into their understanding of the world and their place in it. Libraries can be larger, but human beings have to struggle with the same limitations they have always had. Consequently, while available information grows, areas of professional specialization shrink to keep them within the bounds of human capacity. The problem of any graduate education is to combine the demands of increasing specialization with enough breadth to keep that specialized knowledge in perspective. This is true of every kind of graduate education across the whole range of arts and sciences.

For world history, as for other fields of knowledge, one theoretical possibility would be to set up graduate training for generalists, or people whose specialty would be to know a little bit about everything. No such option now exists, nor should it. Everyone who now teaches world history at the university level began with some narrower field of specialization in the history of some particular time and place, and that is the correct point of departure. Our ability to understand the nature and validity of broad generalizations depends on our knowledge of the underpinnings at scattered points. Otherwise, it would be hard to imagine what lies beneath the surface. The conventional wisdom is correct: that the best understanding comes from an appropriate combination of depth with a broad span of knowledge.

How to translate this general proposition into a particular program of training? Let us begin with the assumption that graduate students in the twenty-first century will still be

asked to show knowledge of a certain limited number of areas of history that will still be called "fields." We can assume for convenience that these students of the future will have to demonstrate proficiency in four to six fields, taking four as a convenient example.

Should one of these be a field in world history? I think not. By that time, students who have already come through primary and secondary schools and universities will already have been exposed to a variety of courses in world history—more in the twenty-first century than today. They should have adequate superficial knowledge. A slightly deeper superficial knowledge of world history is not likely to produce much gain in real understanding. The key to understanding is not in the survey, but in the way the parts are linked together, that is, comparative history.

Comparative history is a difficult concept because it has so many different meanings to different people. The kind of comparative history I have in mind crosses the boundaries of the major culture areas to pick out similarities or differences and to make comparisons in the perspective of world history. In the twenty-first century, many (perhaps most) academic historians will teach world history, but the *specialists* in world history will not be "worldists" or "globalists"; they will be "comparatists."

How might a graduate field in comparative history be organized? One component would certainly be a course in comparative world history: a course where lectures, discussions, and readings actually make comparisons that reach across the major barriers of culture, time, and space. Many models already exist. Kevin Reilly's collection of reading lists in world and comparative history, published by Markus Wiener in 1991,[1] illustrates the possibilities with twenty-two different undergraduate courses that would qualify as some kind of comparative world history.

My course, called "The World and the West," is concerned with the impact of the West on the rest of the world since about 1000 C.E. The basic approach is somewhat anthropological. The central theme is the way in which human ways of life have changed through interaction between peoples of varying cultures. The method is to consider a number of case studies as a basis for generalization. The

Originally published as "Graduate Teaching in World History," *Journal of World History* 2 (1991): 81–89. Reprinted with permission.

course tries to draw on data on all the major culture areas, but changing human culture remains at the center of the picture.

I have already raided my lectures for that course to publish two books, one on cross-cultural trade and one on plantations.[2] Other themes are concerned with the comparative movement of European frontiers overseas; the reception of Western culture in places as various as Uganda, Turkey, and Japan; and the revolt against European colonialism, viewed comparatively with examples from Ghana and Indonesia. Other people's courses in comparative modernization have some of these same elements, but any such course will be most effective when instructors deal with themes that especially interest them. Variety is therefore desirable.

Comparative courses are put together in different ways. Some instructors pick a particular geographical focus. Another possibility is to consider intercommunication between culture areas across Eurasia from Japan to Europe. Still another centers on a body of water and the people who live on its shores. The Indian Ocean is one such body of water. The Atlantic after Columbus is another.

Still another approach is to choose parts of the world that have had a common experience defined in some other way. The comparative history of the tropical world is one possibility, sometimes discussed as the history of the third world. Another possibility is a topical subject, like women's history, treated on a global basis. Still another is intentionally to choose comparisons between societies that are distinctly different—like a course on the history of the family in England and China taught at the University of Pennsylvania or one on peasant societies in France and China at Columbia.

The important point is not so much the choice of things to compare, but the way the comparisons and contrasts can be used to deepen our understanding of the way human societies change through time. Many of these comparative courses are designed for undergraduates. The University of Manitoba has a whole range from a freshman survey to graduate courses—all offered as part of a history concentration in modern world history.[3] At both graduate and undergraduate levels, the goal is the same, and such courses are an appropriate part of graduate training in world history.

A second kind of comparative training already present in American universities involves a seminar or proseminar where the students read and discuss published works in cross-cultural comparative history. This approach is used, among other places, at the University of Hawaii and at Johns Hopkins University.[4] The choice of texts is even wider than in the variety of courses in comparative world history. At the broader end of the spectrum are works that take a theme through some part of world history: McNeill's *The Rise of the West,*[5] Von Laue's *The World Revolution of Westernization: The Twentieth Century in Global Perspective,*[6] Eric Wolf's *Europe and the People without History,*[7] Immanuel

Wallerstein's *Modern World-System,*[8] and Janet L. Abu-Lughod's *Before European Hegemony.*[9]

In another category are the worldwide histories of changing technologies. Here we have Daniel Headrick's two books on technology transfer from Europe, books that are already widely used in world history courses.[10] And, of course, McNeill comes in again with *The Pursuit of Power,*[11] along with Geoffrey Parker's more recent entry, *The Military Revolution.*[12]

Cross-cultural environmental history is still another category of comparative history, with McNeill represented this time by *Plagues and Peoples.*[13] Other examples are Alfred Crosby's *Columbian Exchange* and *Ecological Imperialism,*[14] and my own *Death by Migration.*[15]

The Vietnam War and other recent disturbances served as impetus for a spate of books on the comparative histories of revolutions, mostly taking in revolutions of the past two centuries, if not merely those of the recent past. Here the earlier tradition of comparative revolutionary studies in the manner of Crane Brinton[16] became cross-cultural and often worldwide, with political scientists, anthropologists, and sociologists (such as Barrington Moore, Theda Skocpol, and Eric Wolf)[17] entering alongside the professional historians.

The list of possible topics could be extended to take in comparative millenarian and nativist movements with authors like Michael Adas and Peter Worsley.[18] Comparative frontier studies go back to Owen Lattimore on the *Inner Asian Frontiers of China*[19] and come down to Howard Lamar and Leonard Thompson in *The Frontier in History.*[20] Comparative urban histories range from Robert Adams's *Evolution of Urban Society,*[21] which compares ancient Mesopotamia and ancient Middle America, to Gilbert Rozman's studies on urban networks in Russia, China, and Japan.[22] Taken together, the discussion of these works can carry the student toward an understanding of what comparative history can and cannot do to broaden our understanding of world history as a whole.

A third approach to teaching comparative history involves another kind of seminar, which might be called a research seminar but in a special sense of that term. Most comparative history has to rest on secondary authorities rather than basic research with source material. It is nevertheless possible and desirable to try to arrive at generalizations, even when the sources have not been explored in detail. The model I have in mind originated as the seminar in comparative tropical history at the University of Wisconsin, beginning in the early 1960s. Over a semester, a group of students worked on a single problem in comparative history. The topic had to be chosen with some care. It had to be divisible into fifteen or twenty cases for comparison, so that each student could present one or two cases for discussion during the course of the semester, and information on each case had to be available in the secondary literature. As the semester progressed, student discussions helped to refine the questions being asked of each new case. Some cases had to be rejected as inappropriate, while others did not work well for lack of sufficient evidence. If all went well, the seminar would arrive at a general statement based on the comparisons. That statement might not be the last word about the problem at hand, but it could usually tell something about the patterns, uniformities, or lack of patterns illustrated by the topic chosen.

Several different kinds of topics are appropriate for this kind of exercise. One I used was the comparative study of trade diasporas, with each student doing two papers of about ten pages, each reporting on a particular trade diaspora. Many possible topics owed their quality of comparability to the wide spread of colonial regimes to different culture areas beyond Europe. One successful topic, for example, was the comparative study of the relationships between changes in land tenure introduced by colonial regimes and the accompanying changes in social structure. The *zamindari* settlement in Bengal toward the end of the eighteenth century is a famous example, but others can be found on almost all continents.

Another kind of example is culture change among the European colonists who moved overseas or, more interesting still, culture change that took place among Europeans who settled beyond the frontier line of European control. These trans-frontiersmen could be found in the eighteenth and nineteenth centuries in places as various as the Canadian prairie provinces, the Karoo in South Africa, or among pastoralists like the gauchos of Argentina and the *llaneros* of Venezuela. Comparative forms of resistance to European rule or to the spread of European culture is another source of workable comparative topics, from comparative primary resistance to the different forms of local nationalism or group identity that appeared as colonialism faded.

Whatever the topic, the point of the exercise is not to discover truth or to produce a publishable set of papers as a conclusion to the seminar. Some comparative seminar topics can lead to publishable books: a comparative seminar on trade diasporas in 1973 became a pilot project for a book on cross-cultural trade that appeared in 1984.[23] But that is not the object. The object is to work through the problems that make comparative history one of the more frustrating and difficult forms of historical writing. Learning by doing is a significant step beyond merely reading and criticizing the comparative works that have already appeared.

To return to the Ph.D. field in comparative history: One would hope that in the twenty-first century, a program can be prepared using some combination of these existing techniques for teaching comparative history, and that more experience with the subject and with world history generally will lead to still better ways. Doctoral programs offering a field in some form of comparative world history already exist at Hawaii, Manitoba, Minnesota, and Johns Hopkins, and probably at several other universities. The further experience of these programs is bound to lead to innovations and improvements. Nevertheless, variants of the three approaches I just outlined may still be around. These are, in summary, courses incorporating comparative themes in a broad world history; second, the study of published works on aspects of comparative world history; and finally, experimental exercises in a joint effort to make comparisons the source of historical generalizations.

But the comparative field should be only one field among several in the training of historians. Historians need depth as well as span. This means, among other things, that they need detailed knowledge of some particular segment of time and space, and this includes knowledge of the techniques necessary to investigate in that field. These techniques may include languages, diplomatics, statistics, training in gathering and interpretation of oral data, or cross-disciplinary training that can reach into fields as diverse as economics, linguistics, medicine, archaeology, and biology. This proposed graduate program for the next century assumes that about half a student's predissertation time will be devoted to his or her major geographical area, or two of the four fields.

The fourth field should deal with another segment of time and space, and one from another culture area. Each student should be required to prepare a field from *at least two* of the major culture areas of the world: the West (including both Europe and North America), East Asia, Africa, Latin America, South Asia, and Southeast Asia. That would provide world historians with a reasonable beginning toward the kind of broader knowledge they will need to master later in their careers.

So far, I have recommended in the guise of predicting, and recommending is easy. Getting recommendations accepted is a more serious problem. I must therefore hesitate before predicting that *any* of these recommendations will ever become common practice. On the other hand, world history as a fundamental course in the history curriculum seems to have an assured future, not necessarily as a replacement for the common Western civilization survey, but at least as a second kind of survey. In spite of increasing specialization, enough historians seem willing to move out of their narrow specialties to staff such courses. This in itself may change attitudes, as it has at places like the University of Hawaii or the Air Force Academy, where a survey of world civilizations is required of all.

On the other hand, the explicit programs in comparative world history that once flourished at Wisconsin and Santa Cruz have since been canceled. But closing these formal programs had some trade-offs—several of the people who had been involved in them went on doing the same kind of teaching in new settings. The variety of new comparative world history courses—without a formal program—is far more important. The full range is not well publicized; even Kevin Reilly's extensive collection of syllabi is not complete, simply because many historians who teach cross-cultural courses do not think of themselves as world history specialists, only as people with an interest in a subject like comparative urban history or the comparative industrialization of Japan and the West.

These trends suggest that a broader conception of historical study is making more progress against the dominant graduate training of the 1990s, still overwhelmingly designed to turn out specialists on narrow areas in time and space. Unless that pattern is changed, overspecialization will continue to be the easy way intellectually and the easy way to professional advancement. Time will tell.

Notes

1. Kevin Reilly, ed., *World History: Selected Reading Lists and Course Outlines from American Colleges and Universities* (New York: Markus Wiener, 1991).

2. P.D. Curtin, *Cross-Cultural Trade in World History* (New York: Cambridge University Press, 1984); *The Rise and Fall of the Plantation Complex* (New York: Cambridge University Press, 1990).

3. T.E. Vadney, "World History as an Advanced Academic Field," *Journal of World History* 1 (1990):209–24.

4. Craig Lockard, "World History Graduate Program: University of Hawaii," *World History Bulletin* 5, no. 2 (1988):2–11.

5. William H. McNeill, *The Rise of the West* (Chicago: University of Chicago Press, 1963).

6. Theodore H. Von Laue, *The World Revolution of Westernization: The Twentieth Century in Global Perspective* (New York: Oxford University Press, 1987).

7. Eric Wolf, *Europe and the People without History* (Berkeley: University of California Press, 1982).

8. Immanuel Wallerstein, *The Modern World-System,* 3 vols. to date (New York: Academic Press, 1974–).

9. Janet L. Abu-Lughod, *Before European Hegemony: The World System, A.D. 1250–1350* (New York: Oxford University Press, 1989).

10. Daniel R. Headrick, *The Tools of Empire: Technology and European Imperialism in the Nineteenth Century* (New York: Oxford University Press, 1981); *The Tentacles of Progress: Technology Transfer in the Age of Imperialism, 1850–1940* (New York: Oxford University Press, 1988).

11. William H. McNeill, *The Pursuit of Power* (Chicago: University of Chicago Press, 1982).

12. Geoffrey Parker, *The Military Revolution* (Cambridge: Cambridge University Press, 1988).

13. William H. McNeill, *Plagues and Peoples* (Garden City, NY: Doubleday, 1976).

14. Alfred W. Crosby, *The Columbian Exchange: Biological and Cultural Consequences of 1492* (Westport, CN: Greenwood Press, 1972); *Ecological Imperialism: The Biological Expansion of Europe, 900–1900* (Cambridge: Cambridge University Press, 1986).

15. P.D. Curtin, *Death by Migration: Europe's Encounter with the Tropical World in the Nineteenth Century* (New York: Cambridge University Press, 1989).

16. Crane Brinton, *The Anatomy of Revolution,* 2nd ed. (New York: Prentice Hall, 1972).

17. Barrington Moore, Jr., *Social Origins of Dictatorship and Democracy: Lord and Peasant in the Making of the Modern World* (Boston: Beacon Press, 1966); Theda Skocpol, *States and Social Revolutions: A Comparative Analysis of France, Russia, and China* (Cambridge: Cambridge University Press, 1979); Eric Wolf, *Peasant Wars of the Twentieth Century* (Englewood Cliffs, NJ: Prentice Hall, 1969).

18. Michael Adas, *Prophets of Rebellion: Millenarian Protest Movements against the European Colonial Order* (New York: Cambridge University Press, 1987); Peter Worsley, *The Trumpet Shall Sound: A Study of Cargo Cults in Melanesia,* 2nd ed. (New York: Shocken, 1974).

19. Owen Lattimore, *Inner Asian Frontiers of China,* 2nd ed. (New York: American Geographical Society, 1951).

20. Howard Lamar and Leonard Thompson, eds., *The Frontier in History: North America and Southern Africa Compared* (New Haven: Yale University Press, 1981).

21. Robert Adams, *Evolution of Urban Society* (Chicago: Chicago University Press, 1965).

22. Gilbert Rozman, *Urban Networks in Russia, 1750–1800 and Premodern Periodization* (Princeton: Princeton University Press, 1976; *Urban Networks in Ch'ing China and Tokugawa Japan* (Princeton: Princeton University Press, 1973).

23. Curtin, *Cross-Cultural Trade.*

7

Introducing Students to Civilization

Lawrence W. McBride and Bernard C. Hollister

The term *civilization* is the fundamental construct of the world history course. Typically, the high school course surveys the so-called great civilizations in chronological order, moving serially from one region of the world to the next. As students proceed around the world and through tens of thousands of years in 180 school days, they span the earliest bands of gatherers and hunters to the multicultural civilizations that have existed from ancient times to the present day. Along the way, students may be asked to list—or in the more challenging classes, to analyze—the important contributions to humanity made by the particular civilization that is passing in review. They may also be asked to compare and contrast the characteristics of two or more civilizations: the Babylonian and the Egyptian, or the Greek and the Roman, or the sub-Saharan Meroe and the Mesoamerican Aztec.

It all sounds so straightforward, but teachers know that this agenda is not easy to complete. Coverage, however, is only part of the problem. We believe a more fundamental problem is that the concept of civilization is presented without much thought; and without a basic understanding of the factors that constitute a civilization, students cannot fully understand the development of the human community over time.

This chapter describes a unit of study, "To C or not 2C?" that is designed to introduce students to the concept of civilization during the first three or four weeks of the world history course. During this introductory unit, the students' principal task is to determine the relationships that exist among the historical processes and social systems that, when taken together, might define a civilization. Students create mathematical models that represent the product of their thinking. Specifically, the students are asked to solve the mathematical equation: Civilization = x, in which x represents the various factors that combine to shape a civilization.

In addition to helping students think about the term *civilization,* we had several other goals in mind when we developed this unit. The first goal was to create a new point of departure for the world history course. We wanted to convey to the students at the beginning of the school year our belief that the discipline of history is more than just a vacuous list of names, dates, and events. Instead, we wanted students to understand that history is a method of thinking that involves formulating a hypothesis, asking questions, gathering evidence, reviewing informed opinion, and reaching conclusions that help to answer the initial questions and pose new ones. We also wanted to devise an activity that would present to the students an immediate challenge—an adventure in thinking—at the beginning of the course, one that would involve their intuitive powers of analysis and their higher-order thinking skills, rather than watching them merely begin to catalog facts for Friday quizzes and the monthly exam. And, finally, we wanted to engage students in metacognitive activities in which they would reflect on their own ways of knowing, learning, and thinking.

Getting Started

"To C or Not 2C?" begins at the beginning, a few million years ago, before the story of the human community began to take shape with the appearance of the human species on the planet and the human diaspora around the earth. Too often, this long period of history is either ignored or compressed into one or two days' teaching. The academic calendar compels teachers to press forward to the early civilizations of what is now known as the Middle East. This urge to cover content is often misguided. Students are deprived of the opportunity of encountering the work of physical scientists and anthropologists who have much information that students can use to develop their understanding of the early cultural groups and that they can apply during their study of past and contemporary civilizations. The unit opens with a week-long overview of the geologic ages of the earth and the so-called ages of human history. The time spent on the geologic ages is important because of the role that minerals, plants, and animals have played in shaping the ongoing development of human history. Students should have some idea of the origins and relationships among all of them. Students should also compare the time span of the geologic ages with the ages of human history. Chronologies of key events in geologic and human history, time lines, and periodization charts are the three most efficient means of presenting the overview.

In the second week of the unit, the students explore the question, What is a human society? Here, students encounter the formation of the first cultural groups during the period between the Paleolithic and Neolithic ages. This period of early world history is included for three reasons. First, by focusing on the history of early human beings, the students are challenged to abandon present-mindedness when they discuss family structure, religious and political elites, and social role, among other issues. Second, the long view of human history provides them with the opportunity to consider the pattern of change and continuity in human history over a long period of time. Third, students should have knowledge about the transition from life in nomadic bands of gatherers and hunters to life in settled agricultural communities, and later, in urban societies—two of the pivotal events in human history. Activities that highlight this part of the unit are brainstorming sessions in which students develop possible answers to the following questions: How might such factors as the physical environment, technology, religious beliefs, and social organization change during the transformation from one mode of living to another? What might happen when people in a society come into contact with strangers—either "barbarians" or others more "civil"—from regions beyond their frontier? The students' thinking is facilitated by discussing the approaches of historical sociologists and cultural anthropologists.

Building on the information about the earliest human experiences and the processes that affected the transition from life in nomadic bands of gatherers and hunters to settled agricultural societies, students are now ready to consider the term *civilization*. We begin to build the centerpiece of the unit by discussing its culminating activity: the creation of an algebraic equation that will show the relationship among all the factors the students believe shape a civilization. The in-class procedures and the resources the students can use to develop their equation are explained. They learn that the class sessions will involve two instructional techniques: inductive thinking, which will help them create knowledge about civilization; and a review of several scholars' ideas about civilization, which students can apply deductively as they develop their mathematical models. Students are given the option of working cooperatively in a small group or completing the assignment as an individual. Most choose the former. All students, however, are required to make entries in their own journal, called a "Thinking Log," in which each class member can sort out his or her ideas as their equation takes shape. (These logs are described in more detail below in the section on evaluation.) Students are also required to write a brief essay in which they present their rationale—a synthesis—for the arrangement of the factors and terms in the equation. As individuals or as members of a team, students must prepare and deliver an oral presentation about their models. The oral presentations take place in one of the school's hallways, where the equations are displayed on

large sheets of paper, 3 × 5 feet. (In the Chicago area where this project was developed, the students use butcher paper for the posters.) The students are told that their equations will attract considerable interest from passersby; therefore, clarity of design, the use of color, and other drafting techniques should be brought to bear on the final presentation.

The time constraint for completing this phase of the project is at least ten class hours; an additional week is used to complete the equation and the essay and to prepare the oral presentation. Students learn they will be assessed in several ways: by their ability to respond to questions in class; by an examination of their individual and, if appropriate, their team's work in progress; by an evaluation of their portfolios—the Thinking Log, the final essay, and the equation; and by observation of their performance during the oral presentation and their subsequent interaction with an audience of their peers.

Solving the Equation

The students begin with brainstorming sessions in which they exercise the free play of their imaginations and draw on their life experience to generate ideas about civilization. Next, they use their textbooks (McKay, Hill, and Buckler, *A History of World Societies,* 2nd edition, 1987; and Wallbank and Taylor et al., *Civilization Past and Present,* 1987) to read about the history of early Mesopotamian civilization. In this exercise, the students make an inventory of the factors the authors use to define that civilization. As this work progresses, we employ the familiar "Persia" model—it is timely in this context—to help students think about civilization. The six parts of this mnenomic device stand for:

P (political system)
E (economic system)
R (religious system)
S (social structure)
I (intellectual developments)
A (artistic achievements)

Students begin to create equations using this generic mnemonic. The particular historical processes and social systems that might constitute a civilization become the equation's mathematical terms or factors. Each process or system is given symbolic representation for use in the equation. The initial effort based on the Persia mnemonic usually consists of a long string of terms connected by plus signs:

$$C = P + E + R + S + I + A$$

But our aim is much higher, and, in any case, the mnemonic is inadequate. For example, students draw on the first week's work and quickly point out that Persia ignores important geographic and environmental factors. It also fails to provide room for the nuances that shape each of these factors. To fill this gap and to provide more factors to consider for the equation, the students look further in their textbooks to gather information about other civilizations. Utilized this way, the textbook becomes more than a reader; it becomes a resource.

Meanwhile, the students' early models are continued, deductively, as the knowledge and perspectives of historians, sociologists, and anthropologists are provided on handouts and through assigned or optional readings. For example, the students review quotes and short readings about class structure, the theory of leisure, power elites, and more. One book that we have found useful for its blending of the social sciences and history is J.M. Blaut's *The Colonizer's Model of the World: Geographical Diffusionism and Eurocentric History* (1993). Michael Adas's edited volume, *Islamic and European Expansion: The Forging of a Global Order* (1993), provides some historians' views on gender and ethnicity. Other material is available in textbooks that are used in introductory sociology and anthropology courses at the high school and college levels.

We also provide students with quotes and short passages that highlight historians' thinking on the construct of civilization. Teachers can easily locate the received wisdom about world history from historians over the years in the prefaces and opening chapters of old high school world history textbooks. Poking around in an older school's attic or storeroom or using the local interlibrary loan system, teachers can turn up such classic works as Philip Van Ness Meyers, *General History for Colleges and High Schools* (1908); H.G. Wells, *The Outline of History* (1920); James Harvey Robinson et al., *Our World Today and Yesterday: A History of Modern Civilization* (1934); and William Habberton and Lawrence Roth, *Man's Achievements Through the Ages* (1958). The authors of the texts—many others could be mentioned—listed the factors that they believed constituted civilization, and they proffered notions about both the hierarchical ranking of civilizations and the course of human progress as one civilization came to influence the development of another. Most of these old texts are emphatically Eurocentric.

Research in other secondary sources can provide students with information that may have been too complex to find its way into the typical textbooks. Students may wish to consider Jacob Burckhardt's triad of the state, religion, and culture; Oswald Spengler's assertion that every civilization is a unique experience; Georg Hegel's ideas about political and economic power in the development of stages of civilization; Arnold Toynbee's idea about the transfer of cultural traits by mutation and diffusion; Fernand Braudel's insis-

tence on the *longue durée;* and McNeill's ideas about the interplay between urbanized central places and the nomadic or agricultural peoples on the frontier. (We have included at the end of this chapter a list of additional sources that teachers can consult to find great quotes and passages for discussion by students.)

As the students weigh the information from the historians and social scientists, they record their thoughts in the Thinking Log, which quickly becomes the crucible for the entire project. Through the process of writing, their equations become more complex. They fuse two or more factors; they reconfigure the relationships between and among factors; and they deconstruct factors into component parts. Students have a great deal of fun with this part of the assignment. To help clarify their thinking, some students draw flow charts or webbed "concept maps"; some use bar graphs; other use ratios; other use geometric diagrams.

The students must decide, for example, if the factor T (technology) is strong enough to stand on its own, or if it should appear in the equation in a more detailed manner, as: I (innovation) + D (demand) ÷ E (energy supply) + M (materials) + L (labor supply). What about the role of religion? Or should the equation also include ethics and values? Do some factors, perhaps war—especially if a civilization can be crushed—always have a negative effect on civilization? What if the army is powerful and generally wins? How should these variables appear in the final equation? Are some factors so influential that they must have components? What is the relative importance of communication to a civilization? Must a civilization have a written language? Can there be combinations of methods of communication? If so, how can that variety be shown in the equation? What about the chance of natural disasters or the failure to prepare for disasters that might happen? How, then, the students wonder, can our group use some irrational numbers in the equation? Should our equation reflect a modern, urban civilization, or an ancient, lost civilization, or an idealized, imaginary civilization?

Whatever solutions the students find, each factor and term in the equation must have a rationale in the final essay, and, if asked about it during the oral presentation, the students must be able to explain their decisions. Slowly, the equations assume their final shape.

Examples 1 and 2 illustrate how some students developed various component parts of their equation. Excerpts in Example 1, taken from one individual's Thinking Log, show his team at work on the factor of technology in civilization. Once the team began to think about technology, the members realized that there was more to it than met the eye. Logic dictated to the team that resources and the people who had ideas about what to do with them had to be reckoned with in tandem.

Example 1

$$T = \ln(Cm \times R)$$

In this equation, technology (T) is equated to innovation (In) times the quantity of the creative minority (Cm) times the resources (R). These are the factors that we consider important to the definition of technology as it relates to civilization. Without the creative minority to utilize the resources, there would not be any type of advancing technology; all knowledge and innovation would remain stagnant.

The student then goes on in this section of the log to consider the importance of resources and geographic and environmental features. Each has its own equation and written rationale.

$$R = A(a + f + v + an + m)$$

Resources, as defined above, are the relationship between geographic area (A) and its secondary factors. These secondary factors are: air (a), food (f), vegetation (v), animals (an), and minerals (m). As the area of civilization increases, the amount of resources also increases.

This group of students then concluded their thoughts on the problem of technology by tackling the factor of people with ideas: their "creative minority."

$$P = Cm^1 + Um$$

This equation denotes the impact of the creative minority (Cm) and the unwashed masses (Um): Population. The hierarchical creative minority is raised to the "innovation power," and then added to the unwashed masses, showing the huge importance of a permanent creative minority to a thriving civilization. This also shows how the creative minority grows exponentially as the innovation increases.

Example 2 presents the Thinking Log of another student as she described the work of her group. For these students, no food supply = no civilization.

Example 2

Pretty much *the* most important factors of civilization were domesticated plants and animals. The way we see it, unless humans can control their food sources, they cannot have surpluses for an extended period of time. As higher yield per farmer comes about, fewer people are needed to work the fields, which leads to the rise of artisans and more time to develop tools and metallurgy, which in turn leads again to an increase in crops. More time [could be devoted to tools], more miscellaneous items such as clothes and jewelry [could be produced], which gives rise to trade. Trade, then, stimulates contact, shared knowledge, development of language, other languages. As a people sees that others have greater resources, war comes about and metallurgy receives a second boost.

Example 3 demonstrates how another student's group advanced its thinking. The entries in her Thinking Log, #19, #21, and #22, point out the level of analysis attempted by

these young learners as they worked through the various factors that they determined constituted a civilization. The first entry here shows the group coming to a consensus on the factors. The next two entries detail this group's thinking about the relationships among the factors.

Example 3

Entry #19: When we set to work to build our equation of civilization, we first decided to attempt to define what civilization actually means. We defined it as "a group based on self-expression of art, agriculture, religion, and technology."

Entry #21: After we decided what we were going to put in our equation of civilization, we decided to chart the factors in civilization: P = population; M = masses; CM = creative minority; PE = power elite; UW = ultimate weapon; A = area; T = technology; E = energy; CH = change; EM = extraneous measures (like natural disasters, other civilizations, time. In other words, things that the civilization cannot control).

Entry #22: Next, we decided to write down some simple statements about the [relationships among] factors in the equation:

- When CM is in control of the M, then CM raises T, which leads to positive or negative CH.
- When CM is more powerful than PE, then T increases.
- When PE is more powerful than CM, then T and CH remain stable.
- T and E are balanced off each other. When T increases, the need for E increases, so E will increase. If E doesn't increase along with T, then T will decrease.
- CM causes change.
- PE wants no change.
- CM creates change.
- PE brings change to M.

So, CM was placed over PE because, generally, the CM are directly affected by the PE.

Then, a ratio was set up with E over T because of their direct balance. This ratio was placed over PE as well.
  Another ratio, P over A, was set up. This represents population density. The greater the population density, the greater a detriment it is to the civilization, so it was placed on the bottom.
  UW was placed on the bottom because of its obvious negative effects on civilization (e.g., the atomic bomb.) This entire ratio is multiplied by CH because change affects the other factors greatly. For the same reasons, the entire formula is multiplied to the EM-power because EM affects change even more.

After the students are satisfied with their exploration of the parts of the various factors that would make up the final equation, they move on to solve the equation. The student group in example 4 used the textbook chapters on Mesopotamia as the basis of their inventory of factors and their final equation. Most of the factors this group identified have two or more component parts, which other student groups might have placed in different orders and arrangements.

Example 4

Factors of Civilization

1. Time = T
2. Change = Ch
3. Population = P
4. Technology = Ty
5. Creative Minority = CM
6. Agriculture = A
7. External Forces = Ext
8. Energy = E

Explanation of Factors

1. *Time*—time to develop the other factors of civilizations.
2. *Change*—result of other factors over time (e.g., revolution, deterioration, elimination).
3. *Population*—increase/decrease of number of people in a population.
4. *Technology*—level of sophistication of tools (e.g., knife vs. power saw).
5. *Creative Minority*—that part of the population that contributes most new ideas to the civilization.
6. *Agriculture*—crops grown and amount of surplus/deficit.
7. *External Forces*—natural disasters, human-made disasters (e.g., macroparasites, ultimate weapon).
8. *Energy*—per capita energy required by the civilization.

Factors Excluded

1. *Area*—civilizations adapt to limitations of land space and overcome them.
2. *Masses*—fits within population, does not have substantial effect by itself to alter civilization.
3. *Language*—inherent to the most basic of societies; human beings cannot progress to civilization without language; therefore language is a given factor:

$$C = (Ext*T) - 1\{[Ch(A*(P = CM))]\ (E^{Ty})\}$$

Example 5 provides an example of a student's summary ideas as recorded in her Thinking Log, in which she concludes that some civilizations have a better chance of survival than others.

Example 5

$$C = C \times E \times P \times Tech \times Area \times Communication$$

This equation is meant to have numerical values assigned to it that will produce a number that represents the "viability" of the civilization. (Note: I believe that this will work for hunter-gatherer societies just as well.) I shall explain.

C =   change: Change is a necessary part of civilization; it allows people to adopt to different situations and challenges and helps them grow in technology as well as in "enlightened" human values.

E =   energy: Energy is the basis of everything in a civilization, from the necessities of life to the growth of technology. Without energy there is no civilization. (This factor is in units of kilocalories.)

P =   population: The greater the population of a civilization, the greater the likelihood of survival, especially if it has a wide genetic base.

Tech =   technology: It says it all. Technology is what has brought us to control our world; without it we would be intelligent animals. For humans at least, technology is a necessity, whatever its form, from simple stone tools to the space shuttle.

Area: What civilization can survive without a place to stand? With a lever and a place to stand we can move the earth, but without it we are nothing.

Communication: Civilization is communication. I don't just mean vocal; a civilization could be based on a manual language, but the people must interact or else there is no civilization, by definition.

(Note: If any of those variables drop to zero, the civilization will not survive.)

Example 6 presents another group's final equation as well as one of the group's conclusions about the problem of defining the construct of civilization.

Example 6

$$C = TPH^2\ \frac{\left[\dfrac{Ed \times Tech \times Ag \times E \times Ec}{M \times Geo \times Cm}\right]}{Ch^2}$$

C   = civilization
T   = time
P   = population
H   = human ethics
Cm   = creative minority
Ed   = education
Tech = technology
Ag   = agriculture
E   = energy
Ec   = economy
M   = Masses
Geo = geography
Ch   = change

After explaining the component parts and the rationale for each part of this complicated equation, one student (who persisted in confusing "society" with "civilization") began to wonder about the cultural bias entering into the final determination of the equation, particularly if the definitions were used to rank order one civilization over others.

Because each society is biased to the characteristics of one's own society as good, this assignment is virtually impossible. I believe each civilization was at its best sometime during existence. The only people who can decide a society is changing for the worse (or the better) are the people who live in that society. The values of a society change as time goes by. For example in the 80s the American society seemed very obsessed with success and material objects. In the 90s there is a movement toward environmental awareness and traditional family values. If a society changes that much in only a decade, how can they judge other civilizations? I don't think we can. I think each civilization should just be accepted as it is and not judged as to its greatness.

A Word about Evaluation

The Thinking Logs are evaluated following a rubric adapted for our purposes from a method originally used in New York State to score essay examinations. The students are given three-ring binders—the logs—on the first day of classes. They also receive a two-page handout that explains the log's purpose. The key element in the handout is the information that the students are to demonstrate through their entries that they are active learners. Not all entries are expected to be formal. For grading, a sliding scale, A to F (the New York model has a 1–6 scale), is employed. An A log will have a continuous narrative of thoughtful entries, be carefully written, and be particularly meticulous when formal writing is required. It will show attention to detail, including polished grammar and neatness in illustrations. B and C logs will be of lesser quality in each of these categories. If students fail to keep a log or turn in sloppy work that shows little or no effort to come to grips with the assigned material, they risk a grade of D or F. The final essay is graded by standard scoring procedures that are familiar to all teachers. The log and the essay carry the heaviest amount of the assessment load for this project. It should be added that the Thinking Log continues to be an integral part of the world history course in subsequent units of study.

The oral presentations that describe the algebraic symbolism take about ten minutes per team or individual. Each team member must participate on this occasion and explain part of the thinking that went into the creation of the equation. During the question-and-answer part of the presentation, particular students often get to shine, either as questioners or as answerers. We are alert for the opportunity to reward students for that on-the-spot activity. We have not awarded a specific number of points for either the presentations or the artistic quality of the posters. In the case of the former, the students tend to stick very close to the summaries in their Thinking Log; but in the latter case, an artistic presentation of the equation certainly can work its magic in the overall assessment of the project. Finally, the closer an equation comes to representing a meaningful mathematical model, the more we like it.

Implications for Students and Teachers

Approximately seventy-five equations have been developed since 1991 when this unit first took shape. The students realize that no two models are going to be exactly alike, although one model may turn out to be similar to others. The important point is that students learn not to accept a particular construct as the definitive one. The students also learn, however, that paradigms do exist, and that they shift over time. This insight into historical interpretation will be rein-forced later on in the course when the students encounter other civilizations. It will also be reinforced in other course contexts when the students transfer their knowledge and insight to consider such constructs as feudalism, colonialism, Marxism, and almost any other "ism" that depends for its definition on either the analysis of only a few historical examples or a dogmatic interpretation. With this understanding in mind, the students realize the value of undertaking a close analysis of a historical problem—trying to define a civilization is one of them—as well as the limitations of reductionist thinking.

There are other important outcomes as well. The students begin to build the mental apparatus—the habits of the mind—that they will need to analyze change and continuity in the human experience across space and time; to consider individuals or groups of people who made a contribution to a given society; to make comparisons of major developments in history; and to understand and appreciate the common bonds that make us one people on the planet.

This unit—"To C or Not 2C?"—also has a number of additional implications. Some of its benefits in basic skill development will come as no surprise to teachers. Students learn when they practice writing and speaking skills and when they participate in cooperative learning activities. The latter is an especially useful teaching technique when it is employed at the beginning of the school year to develop interpersonal communication abilities, which can then be used all year long. In addition, students find new uses for their textbooks, and they learn that they must go to outside sources for supplemental information. The unit also has the benefit of demonstrating to students the inter-connectedness of knowledge. Using the discipline of history as a point of departure, the unit adopts an inter-disciplinary approach to the social sciences, humanities, geology, mathematics, and logic. Finally, because much of the unit depends on inductive thinking, in which students create and then modify their knowledge of civilization, the unit places students at the center of their learning. They have the power to learn about and solve a historical problem on their own terms.

Suggested Readings for Teachers

Alder, Douglas D., and William F. Lye. "Dare We Teach World History? Dare We Not?" *The History Teacher* 20, no. 3 (1987):328–32.

Christian, David. "The Case for Big History." *Journal of World History* 2, no. 2 (1991):223–38.

Engle, Shirley H., ed. *New Perspectives in World History*. Washington, DC: National Council for the Social Studies, 1964.

Hollister, Bernard. "Using Social Studies Learning Logs to Assess Student Learning." *The Councilor* 53 (October 1993):39–47.

McNeill, William H. "The Rise of the West after Twenty-Five Years." *Journal of World History* 4, no. 3 (1990): 1–21.

Mears, John A. "Conceptual Strategies for Survey Courses." *World History Bulletin* 4, no. 3 (1987):8–14.

Reilly, Kevin, et al. "What Is an Attainable Global Perspective for Undergraduates in History?" *The History Teacher* 18, no. 4 (1985):501–36.

Simme, Brian, and Thomas Berry. *The Universe Story*. San Francisco: Harper Publishers, 1992.

Stavrianos, L.S. *Lifelines from Our Past: A New History*. New York: Pantheon Books, 1989.

Welter, Mark. "World History: Some Suggestions for Organization and Application." *World History Bulletin* 4, no. 3 (1987):18–22.

Wenke, Robert J. *Patterns in Prehistory*. New York: Oxford University Press, 1984.

White, H. Loring. "A Technological Model of Global History." *The History Teacher* 20, no. 4 (1987):495–517.

8

Wheel of Fortune

An Alternative Approach to the Second Semester

Connie Wood

Despite the wisdom of the old saw, I maintain desperation, not necessity, is the mother of invention. After years of dreading teaching second-semester world history, I tried something radically different. Most curricula for world history include the seventeenth through the twentieth centuries in the second semester. This is almost as impossible a task as the first semester, which often includes prehistory up to the seventeenth century. However, in the minds of many world history students, the first semester, with its cavemen, Egyptians, Greeks, Romans, Early Chinese and Indians, medieval knights in shining armor, and Renaissance figures, is much more interesting. The second semester offers an endless and often deadly boring succession of events that seem unrelated but that the teacher says are important. Students often walk away from world history understanding little about the relationship between the rise of national states, industrialism, and the political "isms" of the seventeenth through the twentieth centuries, or the relationship of those concepts to revolutions and imperialism in the nineteenth and twentieth centuries. How then does the world history teacher aid the fledging history student in understanding the major agents that influence the second semester of world history?

Throw out the standard chronological approach and introduce a conceptual approach aimed at establishing patterns that allow prediction of events and enhance the ability of students to understand the agents that have led to the current situations, as well as anticipate future activity in the sphere of world history. To accomplish this task requires an organizing structure that helps the student see the patterns that emerge from history. The Wheel of Fortune is such a tool. The wheel contains seven major conceptual factors influencing history in the seventeenth through the twentieth centuries: industrialism, nationalism, Marxism, republicanism, fascism, imperialism, and revolution. By manipulating the wheel and analyzing the results, recognizable patterns emerge, which enables students to predict or at least speculate on future events.

Example: The scope and sequence of history viewed via the Wheel of Fortune incorporates many of the same histor-ical events taught in the standard world history curricula, but these events are combined in a set of units focused around the agents of change and the variety of combinations leading to the final results. (See "Curriculum Scope and Sequence" on p. 46.) The combination of conceptual factors that result in recognizable patterns rather than the concept of chronological order is the premier mover of the study of events.

This is how the Wheel of Fortune works. The seven conceptual factors are marked on three separate circles and are assembled and fastened in the center on a "bull's eye" wheel. (See Figure 8.1 and "Constructing the Wheel" on p. 47.) As students study the second-semester material, they use the wheel to manipulate ideas by combining the concepts and examining the results in a variety of cultures and across a number of chronological eras. Since the movement of most nations in the time frame of the seventeenth through the twentieth centuries has been to become more industrialized, the core of the wheel is industrialism. This motivating economic factor combined with the several political factors has repeatedly resulted in one of two patterns: imperialism or revolution. Thus, imperialism becomes the result of nationalism and industrialism in one era. For example, the imperialism of the nineteenth century results from the aggressive rivalry of European nations in Africa and Asia to acquire raw materials and markets in an age of rising global competition. In another era imperialism is the result of nationalism, fascism, and industrialism, as in the twentieth-century Japanese desire to assert hegemony in the Pacific Rim in the years prior to the Second World War.

It is important that the combinations be studied in areas other than the traditional Western setting that is often the major focus of second-semester world history. The republican revolutions of the Western Hemisphere in the nineteenth century provide as valid a look at republicanism and nationalism and revolution as do the nationalistic revolutions of European nations. An excellent vehicle to study nationalism, Marxism, and revolution is provided by Cuban history, for example.

Using the Wheel of Fortune requires a different attitude

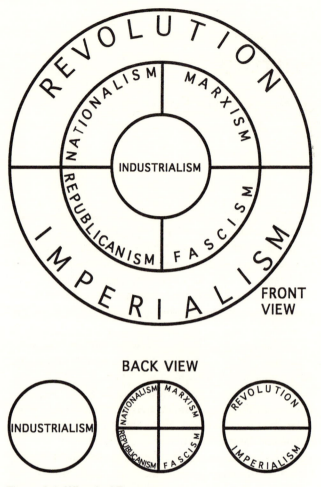

Figure 8.1 **Wheel of Fortune**

in this plan. However, with judicious selection the teacher can structure a set of mutual experiences supplemented with a variety of individual experiences that would be shared with the entire class in the patterns-perception segment of each unit. As an example, in the nationalism and revolution unit some students could be assigned liberal nationalism in the nineteenth century and integral nationalism in the twentieth century. Students would then be responsible to share what they have learned with others who have had other experiences. To be certain that each student has a variety of cultural experiences, the individual work could be rotated so that all students have experiences in the various geographical areas and time frames. As a facilitator of the learning, the teacher must always be aware of the need to relate the various concepts to each other before moving on to the next major unit.

Evaluation of the students' mastery may be achieved by giving them a set of materials that identify the essentials of an actual historical case. The students assess the information and predict the results. They will need to understand that the successful project of results will rest on their ability to extract the basic elements of a particular situation. The actual event could then be revealed and students could evaluate their individual performance. Another method of evaluation may be to use the past as preface to facilitate the discussion of a "now" event. The students could be asked to identify the basic elements and to examine events to see if, in fact, they correspond to patterns already observed, and then to predict possible future activities.

In some ways, the Wheel of Fortune shows that history does repeat itself in the patterns it establishes. The study of history in this way does other things as well. It requires critical thought and analysis of the events of history and not just a rote memorization of chronological material. It helps students see that the motivations of nations in various areas of the world are often reflections of past patterns. And as William Shakespeare observed, "What is past is prologue." Obviously, the method should not be construed as totally deterministic but as simply a method to aid younger scholars by giving them a framework with which to examine the events of history and to draw some conclusions. The Wheel of Fortune is a far better way to deal with second-semester world history than slogging through endless chronological material in the hope that some semblance of order will be perceived by the student—a risky expectation at best.

Curriculum Scope and Sequence

Industrialism

A. Definition of concept
B. In the Western Hemisphere in the seventeenth, eighteenth, and nineteenth centuries

on the part of both the teacher and the student. Beginning the semester with the construction of an actual wheel should be a signal that something different is happening. Students can often be convinced that after acquiring the concepts of the wheel they will be equipped to solve the "mysteries" of the second semester and to predict future events. Teachers, on the other hand, should be forewarned that the concepts are not easy and patience is needed to bring students to the essential understandings this conceptual framework requires.

The Wheel of Fortune serves as a visual reminder of the concepts throughout the entire semester. Introduction of each new unit is accompanied by spinning the wheel and reviewing the basics of the concepts that come up on the wheel. Finally, uppermost in the mind of the teacher should be the idea that understanding these concepts will give the student a framework that may be utilized to evaluate events of history and to project eventual results on the basis of the patterns learned.

Suffice it to say that extensive and thorough coverage of all the topics in the scope and sequence would be very difficult. Individual and group cooperative learning experiences are essential to cover the immense amount of material

C. In Japan in the nineteenth century

D. In the Pacific Rim (or other LDCs) in the twentieth century

E. Patterns perceived

Note: After this point industrialism may be assumed to be occurring and a motivating factor even though it is not incorporated in the headings.

Republicanism and Revolution

A. Definition of concept

B. Republicanism and revolution in western Europe in the eighteenth and nineteenth centuries, especially the French Revolution

C. Republicanism and revolution in the Western Hemisphere in the eighteenth and nineteenth centuries, including the United States, Latin America, and Canada

D. Patterns perceived

Nationalism and Revolution

A. Definition of concept—liberal/integral (*Note:* Liberal nationalism generally is thought to be a common feeling of community in response to domination by what is perceived as a foreign power. Integral nationalism is the voluntary or imposed "unification" of groups identifying with a sense of commonality among themselves [i.e., geographic, ethnic]).

B. Liberal nationalism in the nineteenth century in Europe (Revolution 1830–1848)

C. Liberal nationalism in the twentieth century in Mexico, India, and the African states

D. Integral nationalism in the nineteenth century in Europe (Italian and German unification)

E. Integral nationalism in twentieth-century Yugoslavia, CIS, and Rwanda

F. Patterns perceived

Nationalism, Marxism, and Revolution

A. Definition of concept of Marxism

B. Russian Revolution

C. Chinese revolution

D. Cuban revolution

E. Nicaraguan revolution

F. Patterns perceived

Nationalism and Imperialism

A. Definition of concept

B. Imperialism by western European nations in Africa and Asia in the nineteenth century

C. Imperialism leading to World War I

E. Imperialism by Japan in Asia in the twentieth century

F. Patterns perceived

Nationalism, Fascism, and Imperialism

A. Concepts defined

B. Concepts applied to Germany, Italy, and Japan and leading to World War II

C. Patterns perceived

Nationalism, Republicanism, Marxism, and Imperialism

A. Concept of Cold War

B. The Cold War in the Western Hemisphere including Cuba, Nicaragua, Chile, Granada

C. The Cold War in Asia including Korea and Vietnam

D. The Cold War in Africa including Angola and the Congo

E. The Cold War in the Middle East including Israel, Iran, and Iraq

F. Patterns perceived

Constructing the Wheel

1. Each student receives a sheet with the three circles drawn on it. The students cut out the circles and, on the front side, label them as shown in Figure 8.1.

2. On the back of each circle a definition of the concepts is recorded as follows:

   Smallest Circle

   Industrialism: Social and economic organization marked by large-scale manufacturing and urbanization.

   Middle Circle

   Nationalism: The belief that one's distinctive culture and interests are more important than all other interests.

   Marxism: An economic and political doctrine advocated by Karl Marx in which a classless society owns all property and means of production.

   Fascism: A political doctrine characterized by a single-party state and aggressive nationalism.

   Republicanism: A political doctrine characterized by a system of government in which the citizens choose the leaders.

   Largest Circle

   Revolution: The overthrow of a government with another taking its place.

   Imperialism: Domination by one country of the political, economic, or cultural life of another country.

Note: In the case of the interior circles, if the placement of the definitions is planned in advance, the definitions can be read by simply bending the paper circle.

3. The circles are attached with a brass fastener, which allows them to be turned.

Use of the Wheel

A large classroom-sized wheel (approximately 36 inches in diameter) should be constructed to constantly remind students of the theme of the semester. Before engaging in the specific units of study like Republicanism and Revolution, the teacher should be certain that the major concepts are minimally understood. A deeper understanding will emerge as the concepts are further developed and utilized. For each of the major units the students "spin" the wheel to create the combination required for that unit of instruction and review the concepts used. Review is the next activity after spinning the wheel. Both the classroom wheel and the student's wheel should be repositioned. The individual student's wheel has explanations on the back that can be used to aid in the review of the concepts. All students will have the same definition from which to work and discuss the concepts.

Interior Dimensions of World History

A Process Approach

Dwight Gibb

Theory

Exterior Dimensions

In world history the question of content receives the most frequent attention, and it arrives framed in nearly identical terms each time. Writers express the desire to extend the subject matter but immediately lament that they do not know "what they can leave out." This formulation is not only a negative one—what to omit, rather than what to include—but it assumes that what we presently teach is important, even though we recognize that our lenses have been honed by the stones of dominant cultures.

Next in order of frequency come calls for an "organizing framework"—for one idea that may make world history "intelligible, and hence teachable." Yet grand schemes that attempt to integrate human behavior have too often generated only controversy and counterschemes.

An array of other external features follows. In discussions participants often blur the line between "world history" and a "world history course" and focus on the latter. A course is usually assumed to be a *survey* course. Conversations turn to *textbooks,* perceived as fundaments of courses, and thence to lists of what a student *ought to know.* An example from the College Board specifies that students should understand:

> The basic features of major societies and cultures in the contemporary world: their geography, major economic and social structures, political systems, and religions.
> The historical developments underlying present connections and similarities among the world's peoples, and the major differences dividing them.
> The chronology and significance of major events and movements in world history (for example the Renaissance, the industrial revolution, and the spread of Islam).
> The international context of contemporary diplomacy and economics.[1]

Portions of this chapter originally appeared as "Europe and the World Since 1500" and "The U.S. and the World" by Dwight Gibb, in *The Creation of an Interrelated World, 1550–1750.* The DeWitt Wallace–Reader's Digest Fund 1992 Curriculum Model. Princeton, NJ, 1992.

Most responses to such onerous imperatives have been either to use an area-studies method or to pattern information according to concepts. Both approaches involve pitfalls. In the area-studies model there is an overemphasis on memorization, and in the conceptual one, excessive abstraction, leading to such phenomena as textbooks with two-page descriptions of the French Revolution.

Interior Dimensions

It seems to this writer that what is essential to world history is to be revealed not in the surface aspects of the subject matter described above but in the values expressed and implied by the writers. These ideas shine through so brightly that it is surprising that they have yet to be articulated as the basis for a pedagogy:

- The writers decry the reductionism of modern scholarship, and they affirm that history in a postmodern era must be more than a process of detached analysis. They seek connections between parts that have been denied a broader context.
- They affirm diversity but, more than that, a certain passion—a rejection of the "cognitive imperialism" implicit in so many curricula, and a call for justice on a scale not yet exhibited by the academic community at large.
- They emphasize critical thinking, and they imply that there resides within it the capacity for a higher conception of human dignity.
- They suggest that by studying more broadly, we may become more human.
- They perceive the study of world history as a journey without a map, and they affirm that it is best to travel so, without a preconceived destination.

We suggest that this may be the tie that binds world historians. The shared values constitute an *approach.* If what we share is an approach, that is what we should teach. We do not need to teach all of the world in one year, but merely to assist students to think globally. A redirected focus on the thought processes of students may be a paradigm shift, or it may constitute the organizing idea sought by some writers.

At the least it may liberate us from impossibly extended survey courses.

If our aim is to teach a mode of thought, it follows that for the purposes of design we should concentrate first not on content but on the mental processes of our learners. Of course, the idea that processes are as important as content is not new. Teachers agree on it routinely—but often only parenthetically, after which their conversations revert quickly to content. Content is familiar, much of graduate training is defined by it. It is also well served by language, because it is concrete, whereas processes, which involve the inner dimensions of thought and creativity, may be only imperfectly articulated in words.

Nonetheless, if we recognize that it is no longer possible to achieve our aims by "covering the important material," we will need to discuss processes intentionally. We must ask: What do we mean by global thinking? Which processes are conducive to learning it? And how should we teach them? It is not that we are abandoning content so much as adding more explicit language to the learning processes toward which the content will be addressed. The need for explicit description may be illustrated by Kevin Reilly's collection of college syllabi, which are replete with fascinating possibilities for instruction.[2] The limitations for the reader are that many syllabi represent the fruition of a professor's academic career, and that the descriptions of each course are predominantly in terms of content. A careful perusal reveals that many instructors do orient their material toward the ways students learn, but the techniques are only implied or mentioned briefly in introductions. The world history novitiate, who lacks training in the new areas, and who must infer the methods involved, finds the prospect of starting out intimidating. The purpose of this chapter is to render the underlying structure of one person's work visible, so that a reader may try it out, or use it as a reference for his or her own system. Since in my case, it has taken two decades of experimentation to achieve a process-based approach, and another five years to put it into words, my fondest aspiration is that I may save some lucky soul a quarter century of trial and error!

I would like to suggest that a focus on processes is both natural and radical: natural, because all teachers know that what they have to offer is something deeper than the content, most of which the students will forget over time; radical, because this orientation goes to the very foundations of educational practice. We all know that education should be for the welfare of students and not for the convenience of teachers, but in the press of the hour, the day, the term, we are prone to slip into the areas of content with which we are most familiar. A commitment to learning, such as may make an entire course or a curriculum work for students, requires a plan, an architecture, that will bring into actuality the processes that we say we believe in. It means that we must shape the content to the plan and must refer to the plan periodically. It will also involve asking the students at times how the plan is working for them. A student-centered format, since it operates close to the students' interests, is rewarding to teach, but it does involve reflection on a different plane, experimentation, and the transference of some forms of power from teacher to student.

In arguing this, it is essential to acknowledge that it is difficult for some instructors to set content aside, even temporarily for the purposes of design. They may be thinkers who incline naturally to information. They may enjoy memorization and pride themselves on retention. They may have entered the profession because they were stimulated by their first survey courses. They may be less interested in the art of communicating than in presenting data artistically. These preferences are real, and they may reside at the center of the instructor's personal style. Nevertheless, we would urge attention to process in spite of this discomfort. In our age of burgeoning information, when we find ourselves at the point of designing a course or a curriculum, a divide appears before us. The path of content leads to excessive concern for coverage, to crowded educational formats, and to competition with other programs, which may in turn be overextended. The path of process enables a less encumbered design. It facilitates winnowing and integration, and it can suggest ways of working with other programs in a synergetic fashion. We believe that the instructor who is willing to delay thinking about content until he or she has achieved an architecture of processes will emerge with a structure to which the content can be attached, will be able to enjoy teaching at a relaxed and reflective pace, and, ultimately, will be able to teach the content more effectively.

In the method suggested in Table 9.1 we "plan backwards" by setting goals in the right column. In the middle column we place learning processes that conduce toward the goals. In the left column we break these processes into smaller, more teachable units termed themes. The themes will constitute the architecture of a course. We select the content, displayed in appendix I, only after the themes have been established. An advantage of this method is that in many cases one may start with whatever content one is familiar with, leaving to the future, opportunities to add new areas as our spectrum of competence broadens.

From the students' vantage the course will appear to consist of the content, and, indeed, on a daily basis most of the instructor's attention will be directed to it. But the fundamental organization of the course will derive from the themes, and the instructor will return to them recursively. The purposive reintroduction of themes will have a cumulative effect, as individual students catch on to the processes at different times.

Table 9.1

**Themes, Processes, and Goals for a
Tenth-Grade Course**

Themes	Processes	Goals
Reading Patterning Abstraction Analysis	Historicity	Transmission of culture
Culture Multiple perspectives Responsibility	Openness Altruism	Multicultural understanding
Justice Prejudice Migrations Violence Peace Wealth	Synthesis Systemic thinking	Globalism Ecology Humanity

Objectivity
Bias
Paradigms
Acceptance of
  uncertainty
Sources of motivation
Choice
	Inquiry
	Thinking at a
	  level of
	  complexity
		Social responsibility
		Citizenship

Practice

Which teaching methods may match and amplify the ideas implicit in a process-based format? There is no set formula, but the following elements may assist the reader in assembling a bag of pedagogical tricks.[3]

Inquiry

All of the writers surveyed emphasize critical thinking, but they do not specify why. We believe that the particular force of critical thinking lies in the fact that, in the act of thinking for oneself, one experiences power in relation to information. Our guide is Paolo Freire.[4]

Freire taught literacy to Brazilian peasants in the 1960s with the conviction that education could be a source of liberation. He distinguished between libertarian education and what he called "banking" education. In banking education, the teacher chooses the content and then makes deposits in students' minds in the form of lectures and reading, deposits that the teacher withdraws periodically in the form of examinations. Banking education, he noted, is used by all oppressive governments as a means of control.

Freire relied on a student-based and thematic method. Teams of instructors would visit a village, ask the peasants about their lives, and, from the information gleaned, choose themes that made up a schematic description of their lives. Freire called this collection the "minimum thematic uni-

verse" of the peasants. Subsequently, the team presented the peasants with information connected to the themes—always in the form of problems to solve. With practice in problem solving, the peasants learned to see their world with new eyes and to envision exerting power in it. Freire's work was so invigorating that the Brazilian government saw fit to imprison him briefly and expel him from the country.

Although our students are not oppressed in the ways that peasants are, the complexities of a technical society and the perception that change derives from forces beyond their control renders education through inquiry liberating for them as well. Presented with orchestrated problems to consider, they achieve power in reference to complex information, and they are able to glimpse the possibility of acting on their convictions. For examples of thematic organization, see appendix II.

Learning Theory and Diversity

We live at a transition when a veritable science of learning is emerging. Just as we may use inquiry techniques as a source of engagement with the world, so we may use the varied ways students learn as a *praxis* for diversity. The classroom is part of the world of our students, and relationships within it provide experiential opportunities.

In practice a reading assignment and a day's discussion may suffice as an introduction to learning styles.[5] Students are relieved to discover that their varied styles are not flaws. Awareness of their strengths opens up greater choice in tackling academic tasks, and it enables the teacher to assist the class when specific types of material are difficult for some students. Given affirmation of individual talents, students bring enthusiasm to their projects, and the quality of the work that arrives at the instructor's desk is greatly improved. Most important, a mutual understanding of how different people learn creates a more sympathetic relationship among students. This experience of compassion in reference to learning can then be extended to ethnic, religious, and gender differences within the institution, and then outward to a consideration of other cultures. The assignment illustrated in appendix III provides choices grouped according to learning differences.

Broader and more fundamental than learning styles is information about multiple intelligences. Given the theoretical base achieved in the past decade, practitioners are devising methods of tailoring assignments to enable the application of several intelligences at one time or in appropriate sequences.[6]

All this has many implications. While survey courses with lectures and textbooks may suit some learners, those students constitute only part of any classroom population. A course that is assessed only by mid-terms, specified papers, and a final exam would probably not tap the talent of the majority of the students. This is not to say that instructors should abandon these forms, but it suggests inclusion of other techniques—division of classes into small groups, oral reports, exhibits, journals, portfolios, exams without time limits, the Believing Exercise described below, and assignments that allow broad choice. Jerold Starr describes a method for teaching, entirely without lectures or discussion, by using extended and sequenced role-playing exercises.[7] For examples of role-playing formats, see Appendix IV.

Methodological Belief

Teachers have long understood that to ask students to view information from more than one perspective is a valuable way to teach altruism. Peter Elbow has extended this idea in a now classic essay by developing a technique for systematic belief as well as for systematic criticism. He has fashioned this into a procedure called the Believing Exercise.[8] The idea is that there is an overemphasis on criticism in education. Although we say that we believe in open-mindedness, in fact, halls of learning so emphasize critical faculties that we do not give an equal hearing to ideas that we disagree with. In the very act of listening we are accustomed to formulating a response, which means that we do not attend completely to the other person's argument. In the believing exercise, a group suspends criticism and devotes all attention to trying to understand a point of view. After a presentation, the moderator limits questions to those that will help students to understand the presenter. The exercise can be used with readings, films, and speakers. Sets of opposed statements may accompany each other for several sessions in a row or be interspersed over longer periods.[9]

Visiting speakers provide the most exciting opportunities for the Believing Exercise format. We invite speakers on separate days to preclude a debate atmosphere. We inform the speakers ahead of time about our guidelines and assure them that they will not have to defend their ideas. Possible combinations of speakers are myriad and can be juxtaposed for mild or severe impact—for example: a former medical missionary to El Salvador and a media personality who argues that American policy fosters democracy in Latin America, or a member of a group that espouses segregation and a Holocaust survivor. As students question speakers with the intent to learn how they think, they become engaged personally, and they experience compassion, even in reference to ideas that they find repugnant.

The Believing Exercise is especially challenging for people with strong opinions. In a classroom the task of moving students away from recitals of ideas uncritically absorbed to a reformulated personal value system is a slow process. One of the way-stations to this is reaching a new level of open-mindedness. The Believing Exercise is especially effective in this regard. Participants initially experience a sort of terror that, if they listen to so many perspectives, they may "lose their values." With time and experience they discover that they are able to become more flexible. They realize that accepting uncertainty is essential to taking a subject to a level of complexity, and they find that the conclusions they settle on are not only more meaningfully based but also more accessible to revision if new information should warrant a change.

In administering the Believing Exercise, it is important to set guidelines beforehand and to make clear that the discussions after the presentations are not free-form. Some specific questions: What is the thesis of this presentation? What sort of documentation does the presenter utilize? What are some believable elements of this argument? What are some of the values and assumptions on which this argument is based? Questions that withhold criticism tease the participants for later reflection and discussion at the same time that they induce the discipline of paying attention. The believing process is also a method of conflict resolution. By listening, by asking the speaker to explain, one encourages reflection on the part of the speaker. Students who practice the Believing Exercise treat each other's ideas with increased respect, and class dynamics change for the better.

Systemic Thinking

Systems analysis holds a useful position in fields as diverse as computer programming, ecology, and psychotherapy, and it can be applied in history as well. One may teach the habit of viewing information in terms of wholes as one proceeds, and this becomes an avenue to understanding information that does not make sense in other ways.

In our work we start with small systems and progress toward larger ones. We begin with glimpses into discrete social systems, by viewing taboos and lifestyles of traditional cultures. We study the plantation system as an economic form that, though relatively simple, had powerful effects. Eighteenth-century France affords a more complex social system. Viewing genocide as a system in our study of the Holocaust involves more sophisticated thinking. We conclude with a research project on tropical commodities as they affect people in northern and southern countries, and a unit on environmental issues. By this time, we are viewing the entire world as a system. By expanding our scope from smaller to larger systems, we render each one manageable yet also achieve a cumulative effect.

As students learn to think systemically, they discover that systems are interconnected—that plantation economies link with industrial ones, that ecological realities have to do with systems of exploitation and racism. Students come to realize that all parts inhere in larger wholes, and they begin to look for underlying systems when they meet specific data. Their thinking thus moves naturally toward an inquiry into the hows and whys of history.

Students report that they remember information learned within a systemic context better than that acquired in more isolated formats. Another advantage of systemic study is that, once acquired as a skill, it is readily transferable. This fits with Howard Gardner's definition of education at a level of understanding—learning in such a way that one is able to apply acquired information in a new situation.[10] Some months after completing a U.S. history course centered on systems, one student related that she was able to understand the complexities of the civil rights movement in the 1990s as a result of our study of the reforms of the 1960s. A few months later she reported that she had been in Moscow during the coup of 1991 and had been able to understand what was happening "because she had a balanced view of the world." Now she is preparing for a major in international studies and working with a group to reduce racism in colleges, and she connects these things with having learned to see information in terms of wholes. Another student, now attending Spelman College, reports that, even though she questioned whether her attendance at a predominantly white school had been beneficial, she recognized that the systemic treatment of genocide in tenth grade and of American racism in eleventh was an important element in assisting her to fashion her identity as an African American woman.

Conclusion

We must remember, when we discuss processes, that our focus is on the minds of the students and not on those of instructors. It is an occupational hazard of teachers, as they increase in age, in familiarity with content, and in the capacity to associate broadly, that these strengths may draw them away from the world of the students. It is the essence of process-based instruction that teachers enable students to consider ideas personally and in their broadest significance at the same time. This conforms with Piaget's idea that education at all levels is a matter of learning about oneself and one's world.

Appendix I: Syllabus for Tenth-Grade Course

The World

Content	Themes	Notes
Cultural values	Culture Systemic thinking	A tour of difference cultures introduces students to the relativism of cultural norms.
	Liberty	What is the role of the individual in a society?
The world in 1400	Globalism	Students are introduced to the possibility that one might be able to comprehend the entire world.

The West and the World

Content	Themes	Notes
1492: The expulsion of Jews and Moors from Spain	Perspectives	Note role of Jews in Andalusia, Morocco, and later in Antwerp and the New World.
	Antisemitism	Anticipate later work with antisemitism.
Exchanges of flora, fauna, and diseases	Interdependence	These exchanges represent an explosion from the Eurasian continent outward to peripheries—the Western Hemisphere, Australia, and Oceania—and illustrate dramatically the effects of European expansion.
The plantation system and slavery	Systems	The opportunity to view economic development as a system enables learning in a holistic manner. The content includes introductions to the terminology of both mercantilism and capitalism.
	Interdependence	The transition from Mediterranean to Atlantic trade is replete with connections to European and African history.
	Migrations	The migrations of Europeans and Africans to the New World presage migrations during the industrial period.

Religious Change and State Formation

Content	Themes	Notes
Religious pluralism under the Ottoman Empire	Openness	Used as backdrop for European religious conflicts.
Reformations in German states, France, and England	Liberty	Religious ferment seen as an extension of "modern" thinking in the Renaissance, and as a preface to the development of ideas about political liberty.
Stuart England	Liberty	Religious and political struggles combined.
Absolutism in France	Systems	Introduction to the French social system.
Prussia, Russia, and Austria		Introduced briefly for future reference.

Intellectual Change

Content	Themes	Notes
Social contract theories	Abstraction Liberty	Develop skill with abstract ideas. Sources of political authority.
Locke Rousseau	Authority above the law?	Anticipates issues of French Revolution, Holocaust.
French philosophers	Liberty Choice	Practice in reading varied writing styles.

Political Change

Content	Themes	Notes
French Revolution	Abstraction	Connect abstract ideas about politics to concrete events of the revolution.
	Uncertainty Choice Complexity	Students are assigned roles as individuals in France. With each advance of the revolution they must choose whether they support or oppose it.
Revolution in Haiti	Interdependence	Reconnect with Latin America. Compare landholdings, class relations, stages of revolution with those in France.

Economic Change

Content	Themes	Notes
Agricultural and industrial revolutions	Systems	Compare agricultural, plantation, and industrial systems.
The social question	Liberty	Liberty, extended to the economic realm, becomes a more complicated idea.
"New Imperialism"	Racism	Why were "natural rights," so arduously achieved in Europe, not extended to other continents?
	Interdependence	Anticipate North-South relations in final unit to tropical commodities.

Parliamentary Systems

Content	Themes	Notes
English Reform Bill	Abstraction	Concepts of representation and ministerial responsibility take the idea of liberty to a more sophisticated level.
German politics under Bismarck	Liberty	Failure of representation under Bismarck.

International Relations

Content	Themes	Notes
Origins of World War I World War I	Perspectives	View crises from multiple perspectives.
Versailles Treaty	Uncertainty	Special emphasis on import for Germany, in anticipation of the next unit.

Genocide

Content	Themes	Notes
Introduction		After the introductory work of the fall and the relatively standard topics of the winter, this in-depth treatment of a demanding subject offers students a chance to think deeply about themselves and their roles in society.
Decision making	Motivation	Individual and peer group. Emphasis on social roles and ways they influence decision making.
Antisemitism	Prejudice	Survey of antisemitism since Roman times, with emphasis on eastern European aspects.
Weimar	Liberty	Students observe effects of breakdown of processes of representation. Connections made with the era of Bismarck.
	Abstraction	Emphasis on constitutional thinking.
	Uncertainty	Neither the failure of Weimar nor the rise of Nazism was inevitable.
Nazism	Choice	Examples of individuals who allowed the government to think for them and of those who resisted.
	Prejudice	Used as an instrument of policy.
Fascist aggression		Connection with Versailles.
Second World War		
Holocaust	Liberty	Choices available to various parties.
Nuremberg Tribunal	Complexity Choices	Was justice achieved?

Ecology

Content	Themes	Notes
Tropical commodities in North-South economic relations	Interdependence	Research topic: Examine one commodity in a tropical country: How is the commodity produced and marketed, and how does its role in the economic systems of this country affect the way people live? What level of production of these commodities would be beneficial for the year 2014?
	Wealth	What constitutes wealth for both southern and northern societies?
Ecology	Liberty	In the unit on the Holocaust, students have learned the costs of inaction in the face of "incremental evil," i.e., small steps toward a destructive end. Does the same idea apply in regard to the environment today?
	Choices	Investigation of opportunities for the future.

Appendix II: Thematic Organization

To apply Freire's methods to a contemporary school—for example, the minimum thematic universe of tenth-grade students in my school, private, suburban, and college-oriented—could be described as follows: the students are very physical, because their bodies are changing; they are at a transition point mentally, their brains developing rapidly in the capacity for abstraction; and they are sensitive to their relationships with peers. It is possible to choose topics keyed to these themes: in reference to physicality, lots of concrete and personalized data early on; for abstraction, an increasing emphasis on conceptual development as the year progresses; and for peer relations, the use of relationships of individual and group as an analogy for that of citizen and society. Appendix I shows a scheme for such a course. Its globalism resides partly in its content, which includes some parts of the world, and also in its orientation to the "universe" of the students.

The idea of attaching content to themes may be illustrated in the decision to devote a major segment to the Holocaust. Study of this subject provides an opportunity to examine why so many German citizens allowed themselves to close their eyes to moral issues. Tenth graders, who must decide on a daily basis whether to act on their own ideals or to conform to the direction of the peer group, find this subject gripping. In addition, an in-depth study of prejudice in a society removed from ours provides a graduated introduction to the subject of racism, which they will meet close-up in the following year's U.S. history course. In sum, the Holocaust, though it could be termed Eurocentric, is well suited to the "world" of the students, and it provides a foundation for learning about diversity and justice on a global scale.

Appendix III: An Assignment Keyed to Learning Styles[11]

What follows is a list of different learning styles, each accompanied by a selection of research projects on that learning style. Select and prepare one project, using assigned reading and research sources. You may choose any project—your selection does not have to be listed with one of your learning styles.

1. I am well organized. I like structure and precise instructions. I enjoy facts and details, and I prefer tangible things and hands-on projects.
   - Create a display of Atlantic trade in the sixteenth and seventeenth centuries, showing ship design, routes, winds, and cargo. Include written information to explain the display to the viewer.
   - Draw maps of Africa for the period 1500–1700 showing climatic features, political structures, economic activities, and relations with Muslims and Europeans.
   - Research the role of the pig, the cow, or the horse in the New World.
2. I am an information person. I like ideas, facts, and theories. I work best with clear structures, and I like to analyze things.
   - How did European forms of governance and administration apply and change when transferred to the New World?
   - Describe the evolution of European merchant ships, including important features of time-weight-distance considerations.
   - Describe world bullion flow, 1400–1700, and discuss its implications.
3. I am a people person. I try for personal understanding of what I learn. I care about values and feelings, and I like to look at things from different points of view. I also enjoy an artistic approach.
   - Describe slavery in Africa from the perspective of African political leaders and from the vantage of the people running the Atlantic slave trade. What were the political, economic, and cultural forces at work in each case?
   - Write a short story based on an intercultural encounter.
   - Draw a huge mind-map, in color, of the plantation system.
   - It is 1530, and Amerindians are dying in droves in Tenochtitlan. Describe the event from the perspectives of the Amerindians, of the Spanish, and of an Islamic observer who is traveling through.
4. I am experimental and independent. I like to take risks when I learn. The process of working with an idea is more interesting to me than the final product.
   - Write a hypothetical history of the Caribbean, describing an arrangement that could have met European needs while providing better conditions for agricultural laborers.
   - Design your own questions and have them approved by the instructor.

Appendix IV: Role-Playing Formats

Role-playing is a powerful method that can be applied to diverse topics. In the course described in Appendix I we have used role perspectives for the study of the French Revolution. When we begin study of eighteenth-century French society, we distribute to each student a role card that provides a name and a brief description of a hypothetical delegate to the meeting of the Estates General. Our three "estates" meet in groups to discuss individual differences and shared objectives and to read sample *cahiers* for their estates.

As we survey the events of 1789, students imagine their presence at Versailles and discuss the events from the perspective of their roles. They vote individually on whether they support the illegal action of the Third Estate in declaring itself the National Assembly. We then separate them into "revolutionaries" and "counterrevolutionaries." Within each group there are subdivisions, by estate, social class, or interest, as the ideas demand. From there we proceed, for two weeks, through the increasingly radical choices made during the years 1789–1795, allowing students to change sides as their ideas develop but requiring that they explain to the class why they change each time. Students write daily in their notebooks about how they interpret the development of the revolution and why they make choices as they do.

Role-playing can include re-enactment: In our unit on the Holocaust, when we come to the Nuremberg trials, we have students devise their own arguments and their own disposi-

tion of the case, by dividing the class into three groups: Allied prosecutors, German defense attorneys, and tribunal judges. They report in their journals that they struggle mightily with the responsibilities of their roles, and that they gain new insights.

The advantages of role-playing include: an emotional engagement with the topic; the need to discriminate between multiple responsibilities, e.g., to one's constituents, to one's nation, and to one's conscience; a struggle with the question of how to interpret one's role; the experience of making choices in unclear situations; and a developing awareness of the value of viewing information at a level of complexity. Students read more carefully while role-playing, and they write with greater investment. Role-playing is one of the best ways for them to view information from varied perspectives. A final benefit is that students who are more advanced in "interpersonal intelligence" are the superstars of role-playing, and they assume active roles in classes that analytic thinkers might otherwise dominate.

Notes

1. Douglas D. Alder and William F. Lye, "Dare We Teach World History? Dare We Not?" *The History Teacher* 20 (1987): 328.

2. Kevin Reilly, ed., *World History* (New York: Markus Wiener, 1991), is a collection of syllabi, rich in suggestions. See also George Brooks, "An Undergraduate World History Curriculum for the Twenty-first Century," *Journal of World History* 2 (1991): 65–79.

3. My lens for these suggestions is that of Educators for Social Responsibility, an organization founded at the same time as the World History Association, which has focused on engaged citizenship at local and global levels. The pedagogical techniques that they have developed appear ideally suited to the intellectual thrust of world history. For insights into the work of a number of instructors who use these techniques, see: Sheldon Berman and Phyllis LaFarge, eds., *Promising Practices in Teaching for Social Responsibility* (Albany: SUNY Press, 1993).

4. Paolo Freire, *Pedagogy of the Oppressed* (New York: Seabury Press, 1970).

5. Kathleen Butler, *It's All in Your Mind: A Student's Guide to Learning Style* (Columbia, CT: The Learner's Dimension, 1988), is a manual for students that is also very helpful for instructors. It includes a self-examination that is sufficient to introduce a class to the basic ideas.

6. Howard Gardner, *Frames of Mind: The Theory of Multiple Intelligences* (New York: Basic Books, 1983), is the standard statement. For applications in classes see: Bruce Campbell, Linda Campbell, and Dee Dickinson, *Teaching and Learning through Multiple Intelligences* (Stanwood, WA: New Horizons for Learning, 1992).

7. Jerold Starr, *Lessons of the Vietnam War: Teacher's Manual* (Pittsburgh: Center for Social Studies Education, 1988).

8. Peter Elbow, "The Doubting Game and the Believing Game—An Analysis of the Intellectual Enterprise," in *Writing Without Teachers* (New York: Oxford University Press, 1973), pp. 149–91.

9. For descriptions of how three teachers have used the Believing Exercise, see Berman and LaFarge, *Promising Practices in Teaching*, pp. 152–57, 169–71.

10. *The Unschooled Mind: How Children Think and How Schools Should Teach* (New York, Basic Books, 1991). Gardner maintains that most education does not take place at a level of understanding. He explains why and suggests methods for education at a deeper level.

11. Kathleen Butler, *Learning and Teaching Style in Theory and Practice* (Columbia, CT: Learner's Dimension, 1984), is the inspiration for this format. This manual is replete with effective ways of teaching to the various ways that students learn.

10

The Social Studies Curriculum, K–12

Bill Mendelsohn

Course Description

The Curriculum Review Committee of the School District of Clayton, Missouri, during the 1991–1992 school year studied all of the major reports on scope and sequence (National Commission on the Social Studies in the Schools, Bradley Commission, National Council for the Social Studies, California Framework) and examined the course sequence of many school districts both locally and nationally. We have developed a sequence that is conservative in certain respects yet bold in conception. It reflects the thinking and spirit of the most recent critiques of the social studies in this country. At the same time, it offers some exciting and unique approaches to our discipline, especially at the elementary level.

The following factors were in the forefront of our thoughts as we designed this sequence. The School District of Clayton's social studies course sequence:

- reflects our philosophy and belief statements for social studies.
- flows logically, in terms of subject matter, from grade to grade. In addition, the six content strands spiral through the sequence.
- offers substance and depth at the elementary level.
- is developmentally appropriate as our students progress from grade to grade.
- is multicultural in nature.
- strikes a balance between national and international content.
- ensures that our students will study the present as well as the past.
- provides opportunities for teachers to blend social studies content with content from other disciplines.

The Six Learning Strands

Six learning strands form the core of the K–12 social studies curriculum: history, geography, economics, civics, culture, and contemporary applications.

Kindergarten

All six strands—history, geography, economics, civics, culture, and contemporary applications—will be introduced during this year, but special emphasis will be placed on the geography and culture strands. "Celebrations: Living Together in Families and Communities" will be the central theme for the course. Students will explore four holiday festivals, one for each season of the year, beginning with harvest festivals in the fall. The remaining three holidays that will be studied are celebrated by people in other countries. Since the science curriculum units explore the seasons of the year, our units will provide opportunities for blending the two disciplines.

Grades One through Four

Geography and culture will continue to be the focuses for students. Each year, students will study peoples around the world who live in the same geographical region. For example, students in first grade will study peoples who live in desert regions. Second graders will study people who live in forest regions. Third graders will study peoples who live in plains and grasslands. Fourth graders will study peoples who live near rivers. By the end of fourth grade, students will have studied people and cultures, past and present, from all over the world. They will learn how humans interact with a variety of environments. They will be able to make comparisons and learn about the similarities and differences among cultures.

Each unit will include a historical component, which will grow in significance from grade to grade. Students will also learn basic economic and civics concepts when they learn how the societies they study organize themselves and provide for their basic needs. The committee intends that these units be interdisciplinary in nature. For example, tying in with language arts, students will read stories, myths, biographies, and legends related to the people and places they are studying. Regions for each grade level were carefully chosen to enable teachers to blend content with the science curriculum. For example, second graders study soil and rainforests in science. One of the units will involve studying the people who live in the Amazon rainforest. The opportunities for making connections, both within the social studies and between social studies and other disciplines, are rich.

Grades Five through Seven

Traditionally, social studies takes some interesting twists and turns in grades five through eight. By fifth grade, most students are considered ready to explore history in a chronological fashion. Across this nation, students take American history in fifth grade and study this topic from the era of Columbus through westward expansion during the antebellum era. The sixth-grade year shifts to a world cultures course. The next two years students pick up American history once more. Only instead of beginning where the fifth grade left off, the students begin with Columbus again. There is simply no logic to this approach.

Our students will explore American history in a three-year sequence that will flow from grade to grade, avoiding needless breaks and repetition. The fifth-grade classes will study American history from the era of Columbus to the War of 1812. Students will study the founding of our nation and the creation of our constitution. Sixth graders will begin with westward expansion and continue through the nineteenth century to 1914. Their year will culminate with a unit on immigration. The seventh grade will explore American history from World War I to the present. The seventh-grade year is especially noteworthy because it ensures that our students will really study events in recent history and even spend a little time pondering the future. The committee also plans to weave St. Louis history into these three years so that our students begin to make the connections between this region and our nation. We plan to work with the Clayton Historical Society and the Missouri Historical Society to accomplish this goal. Local history, if energetically pursued, can begin to break down the barriers between school and the larger world.

Grades Eight through Ten

By the time our students reach eighth grade, we hope that they will have a solid foundation in all six strand areas in addition to American history. They will be ready to explore world history. Therefore, in grade eight, our students will study world civilizations to about 1400. The great civilizations from all corners of the globe will form the heart of this course. The units will follow chronological order, but the approach will also have thematic and comparative elements. In grades nine and ten, students will study world history *and* U.S. history. Ninth graders will explore the world's history between 1400 and 1800. Tenth graders will continue the story to the present day. Their second semester will be entirely devoted to the twentieth century.

The advantages of combining the study of American and world history are several. First, the most recent scholarship in world history is approaching the subject from a more global, as opposed to regional, perspective. Scholars are beginning to research and explicate the interrelatedness of world history. Cultures and civilizations rarely have developed in total isolation from each other, yet that is how traditional history classes have always approached the subject. Historians are now realizing that one cannot truly understand such basic concepts as cause and effect, change and continuity, and cultural diffusion in world affairs without studying how various cultures and empires developed in relationship to one another. This idea applies to the study of American history. One cannot fully understand such essential elements of American history as our revolution, basic political beliefs and institutions, slavery, expansion westward, or economic development without studying them in the larger context of global development. Second, this approach encourages students to make connections when they examine world affairs. They will develop habits of mind that will enable them to better comprehend the constantly changing and ever more complex world we live in.

It is for these two reasons that the National Commission for the Social Studies in the Schools made its recommendations. Two members of the Curriculum Review Committee and the high school department chair visited Aspen High School, where this approach has been offered since 1984. We were impressed with their program, finding it enriching and substantial. The students were engaged in learning activities that required them to make connections between historical developments in a variety of geographical regions. They used many resources in addition to their textbooks to learn about the past. The teachers worked closely with the librarian to develop research activities that challenged and stimulated the students.

Grades Eleven and Twelve: Electives

By the end of grade ten, our students will have completed a three-year world and American history sequence and will have fulfilled Missouri's U.S. history requirement. With a solid foundation in history, they will then have the opportunity to explore the social studies in greater depth through an expanded electives program. During their junior or senior year, all students will be required to take American government, a semester-length course that fulfills a state requirement. Currently, Clayton students take this course during their sophomore year. The proposed changes result in our students studying our nation's political system nearer to the time when they become eligible to vote. To fulfill Clayton's graduation requirements, students will need to complete one more semester of social studies. They will be able to select the course to meet this requirement.

Elective Program: High School
(1995–1996 School Year)

Social Sciences	Area Studies	Integrated Studies
American Government*	AP American History	Classical Civilization
Behavioral Psychology	AP European History	American Studies
Economics	East Asian Studies	The Civil War and Frontier in American History
International Politics: 1945–Present	Latin American Studies	
Political Philosophy	Current Issues in American Society	
Psychology II	African Studies	

   *American Government is a required course.

Course Sequence for Social Studies

Kindergarten

*Celebration: Living Together in Families
and Communities*

1. United States: Harvest Festivals—Thanksgiving and Kwanzaa
2. China: Chinese New Year
3. Japan: Festivals of the Boys and the Girls
4. Mexico: Cinco de Mayo

First Grade

Challenge: Cultures of the Desert

1. Introduction to Deserts
2. United States: Navajos Then and Now
3. Australia: Aborigines of the Outback
4. India: People of the Thar Desert

Second Grade

Interdependence: Cultures of the Forest

1. Introduction to Forests
2. United States: Totem Tribes of the Pacific Northwest
3. Brazil: Amazonian Tribes of the Rainforest
4. Germany: Tales from the Black Forest
5. Japan: Past and Present

Third Grade

*Conflicts and Cooperation: Cultures
of the Grasslands*

1. Introduction to Grasslands
2. United States: Life on the Great Plains
3. Argentina: Life on the Pampas
4. Kenya: Life on the Savannah

Fourth Grade

Civilization: Cultures of River Systems

1. Introduction to Rivers
2. Ancient Egypt and the Nile River
3. China and the Yangtze River
4. England and the Thames River
5. St. Louis and the Mississippi River

Fifth Grade

American History to 1812

1. Africa, Europe, and America
2. Establishing Colonies in America
3. From British Colonies to the United States of America
4. The New Nation

Sixth Grade

American History from 1812 to 1914

1. Expansion
2. Pre–Civil War
3. Civil War and Reconstruction
4. Vanishing Frontier
5. Rise of Industry
6. Immigration

Seventh Grade

American History from 1914 to the Present

1. The Nation Transformed
2. World Power
3. Boom or Bust
4. World Leadership
5. Times of Turmoil
6. Toward a New Century

Eighth Grade

World Civilizations to 1400

1. Understanding History
2. Ancient River Civilizations
3. Rise of Classical Civilizations
4. Asian Civilizations
5. Forces of Change
6. Europe in the Middle Ages
7. Early African Civilizations

Ninth Grade

World and American History: 1400–1815

1. Kingdoms and Empires
2. Exploration and the Clash of Cultures
3. Comparative Government: Kings, Constitutions, and Colonies
4. Comparative Social Structures: Early Modern World
5. Atlantic and Indian Ocean Communities of the 1600s
6. Global Conflict and Conquest
7. Transformation and Tradition: The World of the Eighteenth Century
8. Revolution and the New Political Order

Tenth Grade

World and American History: 1815–Present

1. Responses to Democratic Revolutions
2. Industrial Revolution
3. Nationalism
4. Imperialism and the World
5. Life in Industrial Society
6. World War I and the Russian Revolution
7. The World Between the Wars
8. Totalitarianism and the Crisis of Democracy
9. The Contemporary World

Unit Overviews

What follows are three unit overviews, one from the ninth-grade curriculum and two from the tenth-grade curriculum. They should give one an idea of the underlying structure of the high school courses.

Unit Title: Democratic Revolutions (Grade 9)

This unit will be a comparative study in revolutions. We will use the American, French, and Latin American revolutions of the late eighteenth and nineteenth centuries to see what effects the Enlightenment ideas had upon the real lives of people. Students will spend some time studying the immediate causes and the paths of each revolution, drawing their own conclusions about how similar and dissimilar they were.

Topics/Content by Strand

History

- American colonialism
- Latin American colonialism
- French and Indian War
- Independence movement in America
- American Revolution
- Breakdown of old order in France
- National Assembly of 1789
- French Revolution
- Republican France
- Reign of Terror
- Thermidorian reaction
- Latin American revolutions

Geography

- Values of land and natural resources
- America's Proclamation of 1763
- Military strategy and the land

Economics

- Mercantilism
- Taxes
- Class and power
- The three estates
- Slavery and forced labor in Latin America

Civics

- Liberty and equality
- Citizenship
- American Revolution or war for independence?

Culture

- Importance of mass literacy, printing press, speeches

Contemporary Applications

- Compare to recent revolutions in eastern Europe

Connections with Other Disciplines

Coordinate with Spanish and French foreign language teachers to compare independence ceremonies of France, United States, and Latin American countries.

Essential Questions

- What caused this era of revolution?
- What were the ideas and objectives of the men and women who rose up violently to undo the established system?
- What were the gains and losses for privileged groups and for ordinary people in a generation of war and upheaval?

Assessment

- Mock trial of King Louis XVI (interact simulation). Students write about and role play various historical figures from the era.
- Students write a Declaration of Independence for colonies of Spain and/or Great Britain.
- Students write comparison/contrast essay about American, French, and Latin American revolutions.
- Primary-source evaluations
- Objective and subjective unit test

Core Outcomes

History

- Demonstrate an understanding of the role of leadership in history.
- Demonstrate an understanding and appreciation of the effect of irrational and accidental events in history.
- Appreciate history as an interesting and relevant subject.

Geography

- Give examples of movement from place to place of people, materials, and ideas.

Economics

- Appreciate the role of economics in political decisions.

Civics

- Identify and analyze the various ways leadership develops and manifests itself.
- Identify and interpret the role of law and its relationship to social and political systems.

Culture

- Demonstrate understanding that all societies have ideals and standards of behavior.

Contemporary Applications

- Identify, describe, and appreciate the responsibilities of citizenship in their community, their nation, and the world.

Suggested Texts

- Jantzen, Kreisler, and Neal, *World History* (Lexington, MA: D.C. Heath, 1988).
- McKay, Hill, and Bucker, *A History of World Societies* (Boston: Houghton Mifflin, 1992).
- Jordan, Greenblatt, and Bowes, *The Americans* (Evanston, IL: McDougal-Littel, 1988).
- Bailey and Kennedy, *The American Pageant* (Lexington, MA: D.C. Heath, 1991).

Teacher Background Material

- R.R. Palmer, *The Age of Democratic Revolutions* (Princeton, NJ: Princeton University, 1959).

Teacher Resource Material

- Crane Brinton, *The Anatomy of Revolution* (New York: Random House, 1972).
- Krasnow and Levy, *A Guidebook for Teaching United States History*

Unit Title: Responses to Democratic Revolutions (Grade 10)

The students will be taking their knowledge from the previous comparative unit on democratic revolutions and following through to see if the revolutions accomplished what they set out to do. Once again, the United States, France, and Latin America will be the basis for this study. The students will also look at the different models used to resume peaceful lives after the revolutions, with an emphasis on the U.S. Constitution and the Bill of Rights.

Topics/Content by Strand

History

- U.S. Confederation period
- Why the U.S. Constitution and the Bill of Rights?
- Federalists and Antifederalists
- Napoleon's rule of France
- The Bourbon restoration
- Latin American neocolonialism and military dictatorships

Geography

- Congress of Vienna model
- Federalist model
- Military dictatorship

Culture

- Civic mythology of revolutionary heroes
- Art as political ideology

Contemporary Applications

• Third world revolutions today

Essential Questions

• Why did the democratic revolutions have such varied results?
• How did these revolutions prepare the way for the industrial revolution?

Core Outcomes

History

• Interpret and respond to artifacts, documents, photographs, art, cartoons, and other sources used by historians to understand the past and present.
• Demonstrate knowledge of chronology and major cultures, people, and events in history.
• Demonstrate an understanding and cite examples of cause-and-effect relationships and multiple causation in history.

Geography

• Locate places using relative terms.
• Locate places using reference systems.

Economics

• Describe and analyze how specific economic systems make judgments about value, allocation, and distribution of resources.

Civics

• Identify, describe, analyze, and compare political systems, especially with respect to government organization, allocation of power, constitutions, roles of people, rights and responsibilities, and legal systems.
• Demonstrate understanding of how governing bodies make decisions and how people participate in those decisions.

Culture

• Analyze the ability to personalize history, i.e., to take information from the social studies role models and frameworks that can result in self-understanding.

Unit Title: Imperialism and the World (Grade 10)

This unit will allow students to look at the expansion of the major Western nations around the turn of the century and at the effects of this imperialism on both parties, the conqueror and the conquered. Students will be able to gain an understanding of the many different cultures and peoples of the world and how some of the values and attitudes that are still prevalent today developed.

Topics/Content by Strand

History

• Industrial revolution and nationalism causing/allowing imperialism
• Africa in the nineteenth century
• India in the nineteenth century
• The Middle East in the nineteenth century
• Japan in the nineteenth century
• China in the nineteenth century
• Latin America in the nineteenth century
• The American West

Geography

• Trade routes and coaling stations
• Suez and Panama canals

Economics

• Supply and demand
• Raw materials and finished products
• Workers and owners, race and class

Civics

• Imperial rule
• Self-determination and home rule
• Rebellion

Culture

• Comparative cultures of the late nineteenth century

Contemporary Applications

• Anti-Western sentiment
• Racism today

Essential Questions

• How and why did the many-sided, epoch-making expansion occur in the nineteenth century?
• What were some of its consequences for the West and for the rest of the world?
• How did the political, social, and economic goals of imperialism impact race and class around the world?

Core Outcomes

History

• Analyze and cite examples of cultural diffusion through history.
• Analyze and cite examples of the effect of geography on history and on the development of cities.

- Identify, describe, and analyze the causes and consequences of conflict and cooperation among nations, peoples, and cultures.
- Make judgments about the past after considering the norms and expectations prevailing in the culture at the time.

Geography

- Identify reasons for the location of places.
- Describe the human and/or cultural characteristics of a place.
- Describe how geographic factors have influenced historical events.

Economics

- Demonstrate the use of economic concepts in everyday choices.
- Appreciate the role of economics in political decisions.

Civics

- Analyze and interpret the reciprocal relationship between an individual and a group, an individual and an institution, and an individual and a political system.

Culture

- Identify characteristics of a culture.
- Describe how culture is transmitted in various societies.
- Identify, describe, and value the multicultural and multiethnic dimensions of our society, including the contributions made by the various groups that constitute our society.

Contemporary Applications

- Identify, describe, and analyze current issues.
- Apply knowledge from the social studies to help enrich lifelong personal experiences, resulting in a deeper appreciation of travel, art, dance, music, and literature.

11

History–Social Science Framework

California Public Schools

The distinguishing characteristics of the California history–social science framework are as follows:

1. This framework is centered in the chronological study of history.
2. This framework proposes both an integrated and correlated approach to the teaching of history–social science.
3. This framework emphasizes the importance of history as a story well told.
4. This framework emphasizes the importance of enriching the study of world history with the use of literature, both literature of the period and literature about the period.
5. This framework introduces a new curricular approach for the early grades (kindergarten through grade three).
6. This framework emphasizes the importance of studying major historical events and periods in depth as opposed to superficial skimming of enormous amounts of material.
7. This framework proposes a sequential curriculum, one in which knowledge and understanding are built up in a carefully planned and systematic fashion from kindergarten through grade twelve.
8. This framework incorporates a multicultural perspective through the history–social science curriculum.
9. This framework increases the place of world history in the curriculum to three years (at grades six, seven, and ten), organized chronologically.
10. This framework emphasizes the importance of the application of ethical understanding and civic virtue to public affairs.
11. This framework encourages the development of civic and democratic values and an integral element of good citizenship.
12. This framework supports the frequent study and discussion of the fundamental principles embodied in the United States Constitution and the Bill of Rights.

13. This framework encourages teachers to present controversial issues honestly and accurately within their historical or contemporary context.
14. This framework acknowledges the importance of religion in human history.
15. This framework proposes that critical thinking skills be included at every grade level.
16. This framework supports a variety of content-appropriate teaching methods that engage students actively in the learning process.
17. This framework provides opportunities for students' participation in school and community service programs and activities.

Course Descriptions

Kindergarten—Learning and Working Now and Long Ago
Grade One—A Child's Place in Time and Space
Grade Two—People Who Make a Difference
Grade Three—Continuity and Change
Grade Four—California: A Changing State
Grade Five—United States History and Geography: Making a New Nation
Grade Six—World History and Geography: Ancient Civilizations
Grade Seven—World History and Geography: Medieval and Early Modern Times
Grade Eight—United States History and Geography: Growth and Conflict
Grade Nine—Elective Courses in History–Social Science
Grade Ten—World History and Geography: The Modern World
Grade Eleven—United States History and Geography: Continuity and Change in the Twentieth Century
Grade Twelve—Principles of American Democracy (one semester) and Economics (one semester)

United States and World History Courses

The curriculum departs from current practice by significantly increasing the time allocated to chronological his-

This material is quoted from pages 3–6, 23, and 25 of the *History–Social Science Framework for California Public Schools, Kindergarten through Grade Twelve,* which was published by the California State Department of Education in 1988.

tory. The three courses in United States history (grades five, eight, and eleven) and the three courses in world history (grades six, seven, and ten) have the following characteristics:

1. Beginning with grade six, each course in this series contributes to students' learning of historical chronology. The course in grade six emphasizes the ancient world to 500 C.E. The grade-seven course continues world history through medieval and early modern times, 500–1789 C.E. The grade-eight course establishes the new American nation in the context of the European Enlightenment, with which the grade-seven course just concluded, and emphasizes the years 1783–1914. The grade-ten course emphasizes the modern world, 1789 to the present day. The grade-eleven course emphasizes United States history in the twentieth century. This interplay between world and United States history helps students recognize the global context in which their nation's history developed and allows teachers to illustrate events that were developing concurrently throughout the world.

2. Each course gives major emphasis to a selected historical period that students will study in depth.

3. Beginning with grade seven, each course provides for a review of learning from earlier grades.

4. Each course provides opportunities to link the past with the present.

12

World History

A Community College Course Syllabus

Patricia O'Neill

Information Sheet for Students

History 104–105–106 is designed to be a year-long survey course of world history. The nature of a world history survey course is such that we can study only major historical events in a global context. This is not an attempt to present human history as a whole but rather to identify major civilizations, illustrate the parallel processes and contacts that define the principal time periods of world history, and compare and assess these civilizations within an increasingly interdependent context.

The course is structured in three distinct parts. The *fall term* is essentially focused on the ancient time period and the development of the "classical" civilizations such as China, India, and Rome. The *winter term* has as its time period what we in the West think of as the Middle Ages, when the classical civilizations move out of their geographical centers into an ever widening world system. The *spring term* deals with world history in the past 550 years, in what is thought of as the "modern" period, and the new global patterns of interaction between societies.

Each of these terms of history can be taken separately; that is, it is not necessary to take the fall term in order to enroll in, or understand, the other two terms of history. However, I expect that the student would acquire the necessary background information and terminology to successfully complete the course work.

The textbook used in the class is widely acclaimed as a well-balanced and readable textbook. It is written by Stearns, Adas, and Schwartz, who are all major scholars in their field, and is entitled *World Civilizations: The Global Experience*. In addition, I have assigned supplementary readings from a book edited by Stearns entitled *Documents in World History*. This gives students exposure to primary source material from each time period and many of the societies we are covering. I will also distribute handouts of relevant material throughout the year.

The course is structured so that each week we will cover approximately one to two chapters of the textbook. Although this does not seem like a heavy reading load, we will deal with an enormous variety of places, dates, and people, which will require careful reading. I try to have my lectures complement the information in the textbook, highlighting the main points of each chapter and offering some broad themes that might help you analyze the information more effectively.

Slides, overheads, and computer-assisted displays are used to provide a visual complement to the lectures. These include the important names, places, dates, and themes for quick reference and an aid to notetaking. As many audiovisual aids as time permits will be used as supplements to our reading.

In each term of world history, there will be a paper assignment. For the fall and winter terms, the paper should be five pages in length, with an additional section for the bibliography. Research papers should include citations—as a separate section at the end (endnotes), at the bottom of the page (footnotes), or, using a system such as that of the Modern Language Association, after each sentence (author, date, page). The paper will count for 25 points out of a total of 125 points of the final grade.

There will be three examinations, equally weighted, and not cumulative. The first one will be given after approximately 30 percent of the course has been completed; the second after approximately 60 percent of the course; and the last during finals. There will be no makeup exams unless prior arrangements have been made. The first exam will be 80 percent multiple choice and 20 percent short essay questions. The second exam will be 80 percent short essay and 20 percent multiple choice questions. The final exam will be 50 percent multiple choice, 50 percent short essay.

Grade Computation		Final Grade Equivalency
Average of three exams	100 Points	113–125 = A
Paper grade	25	100–112 = B
Total maximum	125	88–99 = C
		75–87 = D
		Below 74 = F

67

Course Syllabus, Fall Term

Required Reading: Stearns, Adas, Schwartz, *World Civilizations;* Stearns, *Documents in World History,* volume 1

Note to teachers: These syllabi are based on a Monday–Wednesday–Friday class schedule.

Class 1: General Information
Class 2: Paleolithic Age
Class 3: Neolithic Age
Reading: *World Civilizations,* Chapter 1

Class 4: Mesopotamia
Class 5: Egypt
Class 6: Early Mediterranean Area
Reading: *World Civilizations,* Chapter 2
Documents: Mesopotamian Values, Babylonian Law, Ancient Egypt, Judaism

Class 7: Beginnings of Indus Valley
Class 8: Beginnings of China
Class 9: Pastoral Nomadism
Reading: *World Civilizations,* Chapters 3 and 4

Class 10: Imperial Unity—Qin China
Class 11: China's Classical Age—Han Dynasty
Class 12: First Exam
Reading: *World Civilizations,* Chapter 5
Documents: Key Chinese Values, Legalism, Chinese Politics in Practice, Women in Classical China

Class 13: Greece as a Classical Civilization
Class 14: Persia
Class 15: India—Brahman Dominance
Reading: *World Civilizations,* Chapters 6 and 7 (first half)
Documents: Greek Political Tradition, Greek Science, Caste and Duty in India

Class 16: The Rise of Buddhism
Class 17: India's Golden Age
Class 18: The Roman Republic
Reading: *World Civilizations,* Chapter 7 (second half) and 8
Documents: Four Noble Truths of Buddhism, State and Society in India, Gender Relations in India

Class 19: The Roman Empire
Class 20: The Birth of Christianity
Class 21: Mesoamerican Civilizations
Reading: *World Civilizations,* Chapters 8 and 9
Documents: Grandeur of Roman Empire

Class 22: Spread of Civilization in Africa
Class 23: Spread of Chinese Civilization to Japan
Reading: *World Civilizations,* Chapter 10
Documents: Uncommon Woman in China, Rise of Samurai in Japan

Class 24: Second Exam
Class 25: Decline and Fall of India and China
Class 26: Decline and Fall of Rome
Reading: *World Civilizations,* Chapter 11
Documents: Marco Polo in China, India Society in Seventh Century

Class 27: The Birth of Islam
Class 28: The Arab Islamic Empire
Reading: *World Civilizations,* Chapter 12
Documents: The Koran and the Family, The Islamic Religion, Religious and Political Organization in Islamic Middle East

Class 29: Coming of Islam to Asia
Class 30: African Civilization
Class 31: The Spread of Islam
Reading: *World Civilizations,* Chapters 13 and 14
Documents: Islamic Culture, Islam Comes to India

Paper Topics

During the fall term of world history, students are required to write a five-page research paper on one of the following selected topics. There are thirteen topics to choose from, and they cover a broad range of issues as well as geographical areas.

1. One of the major components of the classical civilizations was the development of a writing system. Take two of these writing systems—for instance, cuneiform and Chinese ideographs—and compare them. What was their origin? What was the initial reason for developing a writing system? How do they differ? What was the relationship of the writing system to religion in each society? Who controlled the writing system and for what purpose? What were the long-term consequences of the writing system on the society?

2. Compare and contrast sedentary society with nomadic society. What differences were there between two types of societies in such areas as social stratification, gender equality, political organization, technological development, population density, and occupational specialization?

3. The classical civilizations of the ancient world were largely grouped into those in an imperial system and those in a city-state system. Compare and contrast the two forms

of society in terms of their political, social, and economic structures.

4. Compare and contrast the Harappan civilization in the Indus River valley with that of ancient China. Look at their agricultural systems, religious practices, political organization, response to outsiders, and long-term development.

5. How does Greek civilization compare with the Han Chinese civilization? Think about their political, social, and economic systems, their philosophical and religious beliefs, and the underlying values of each society.

6. Compare *two* of the following religions: Hinduism, Buddhism, Christianity. How did each view the afterlife? What was the role of monasticism in each? What was the place of the individual in each religion? What sort of structural organization did each have? Who championed the religion in each society and for what purpose?

7. Compare the political, social, and religious organization of Gupta India with that of Han China or the Roman Empire.

8. Compare one of the American civilizations with one of the Eurasian civilizations prior to the intrusion of the West into the Americas. What were the differences in areas such as political organization, social stratification, economic specialization, monumental architecture, writing, and the use of physical resources?

9. How were the Celtic, Germanic, and Slavic cultures of northern Europe similar? Discuss the type of economic and social organization, the degree of urbanization, the development of writing, and religious practices.

10. Compare one of the developing societies of Africa, northern Europe, Japan, or Polynesia with one of the classical cultures of the core civilizations. Look at the social, political, and economic organization, the religious practices, and the development of urbanization, writing, and technology.

11. How did Islam address the fundamental problems of Arabic society?

12. Compare the initial spread of Islam throughout the Mediterranean and the Middle East with the Islamic incursions into India and Southeast Asia.

13. What were the "common elements" in African societies prior to the intrusion of the West?

Fall Term Study Guide: Sacred Writing of the World's Religions

Since all of the world's major religious traditions have produced written documents, it is possible and legitimate to ask: What are the equivalents of the Christian Bible in those different traditions? What and where are the historic copies of their scriptures?

Answers to these questions, however, quickly indicate not only the expected diversity of documents, but also very different significances that have been ascribed to the documents. The written word does not always have the same function in the lives of Buddhists, Hindus, Muslims, and others as it does in the lives of Christians—even acknowledging that there is a variety among Christians themselves. Verbal literacy has been variously valued in different times and places, and the unique authority that Christians, particularly Protestants, ascribe to a book, is placed in individuals, certain ritual behavior, or mystical experiences in other religions.

The Muslim situation is the closest to that of Jews and Christians, and for good reason: the religion of Islam sees itself as the fulfillment of the two older traditions, which, like Islam, are rooted in the faith of Abraham. This fulfillment focuses explicitly on scripture, the Koran (Qur'an, meaning "recitation"). In Muslim understanding, this scripture was revealed piecemeal to the Prophet Muhammad. The words are understood as the flawless word of God himself, not as Muhammad's personal utterances.

The Koran stands as the corrective to the faulty scriptures of other "People of the Book": the one God (Allah) had previously spoken through a series of prophets to Jews and Christians, but his message was distorted in the course of writing it down. The Koran serves to amend these previous partial misunderstandings and to provide comprehensive guidance for human conduct, both individual and social.

Islam is in many ways the most "scriptural" of the world's religions, not just in the comprehensive significance it ascribes to the Koran, but in the rapidity with which a definitive version was assembled. Oral transmission remained crucial, however, because of the incomplete system of writing Arabic, and it was nearly three hundred years before a text with vowel pronunciation was produced. From that point on, there has been a standard version of the Koran. However, the oral recitation of the Koran is equally emphasized because there are still so many functionally illiterate Muslims who carry the entire "text" verbatim within their hearts.

The Hindu situation could not be more different. The symbolic center of the tradition is in the Rig Veda, a collection of 1,028 Sanskrit hymns, composed for religious use over three thousand years ago. They are among the earliest compositions in any Indo-European language. Yet Indian culture has consistently affirmed that the power of these (and most other) words lies in their oral and aural (hearing) quality, and so has resisted reducing them to writing. The Rig Veda was not, in fact, publicly accessible until its first published edition appeared in the mid-1800s. That work, significantly, was accomplished by an Oxford professor and is of virtually no religious consequence for Hindus themselves. The Rig Veda's significance is symbolic, a cultural and religious reference point, not literal or applicable to daily life.

In modern times, partly in response to imported Western ideas about "religions" having "scripture," efforts have been made to present the Bhagavad Gita, which is Krishna's instruction on knowledge, morality, and devotion, as the "Bible" of Hinduism. This text has become, after the Christian Bible, the second most translated book in world history. The Gita has doubtless been widely prized over the course of the past two thousand years, but it has never commanded the exclusive attention of Hindus as a whole.

As it is with gods in Hinduism, so it is with scriptures. There are a very great number, and which one is the "right" one really depends on region, time of year, family tradition, caste, language, century, and so on. Certain texts may attain a near biblical status in particular contexts, but the core of Hindu religion lies, not in its texts, but in its stories about gods and goddesses. It is these stories that lie in Hindu hearts and that get told and retold, interpreted and amended and re-interpreted over and over and over again.

Buddhists lie somewhere in between Muslims and Hindus in their attitudes toward holy writing. Like Muslims, they have an idea of a standard text, but like the Hindus, they have an open-ended and expansive attitude toward what may appropriately be considered standard. The decisive measure is what is consistent with "the word of Buddha," but this does not mean absolute loyalty to the historic founder, Siddhartha. Rather, it means teaching that accord with the experience of enlightenment, as taught by the historical Buddha and as lived by later followers.

This dynamic quality gives the Buddhist writing great diversity. The holy writing of Theravada Buddhism (South and Southeast Asia) was composed and written down by the first century C.E., but it was not widely published until the nineteenth century. It consists of thirty-one texts of varying antiquity, divided into three groups (Tripitaka): rules for monastic practice, sayings of the Buddha, and scholastic analysis. The rise of Mahayana Buddhism, and its spread to East Asia, produced a Chinese holy writing, whose first block printing was completed in 983. It includes some 1,076 items and is approximately seventy times the length of the Christian Bible. However, sectarian and individual practice has tended to emphasize one particular text, and such scriptures as the Lotus Sutra have been enormously popular.

Tibetan Buddhism also has a massive body of holy writing, consisting of over thirty volumes, dating from the fourteenth century, much of it based on translations of Indian sources now lost. Here too, the daily life of both monks and normal people focuses on a few selected texts for meditational, ritual, and philosophical elaboration.

To inquire into "Bibles" elsewhere in the world thus reveals a stunning variety of content, of attitudes toward texts, and of ideas about what it means to be religious. This discovery should caution us against a simplistic cross-cultural comparison of scriptures. At the same time, it should invite us to think more deeply about the distinctive features of the Bible, and of Judeo-Christian attitudes toward it, while pondering other traditions, and other expressions, of religious faith.

Course Syllabus, Winter Term

Required Reading: Stearns, Adas, Schwartz, *World Civilizations: The Global Experience;* Stearns, *Documents in World History,* volumes 1, 2

Class 1: Civilization in Eastern Europe
Class 2: Civilization in Western Europe
Reading: Stearns, Chapters 15 and 16
Documents: Russia Converts to . . . , Feudal Monarchy: Magna, Medieval Intellectual

Class 3: Postclassical Mesoamerica
Class 4: Aztec Society
Class 5: Incan Society
Reading: Stearns, Chapter 17
Documents: Tribute under the Aztecs

Class 6: Reunification of China: Tang and Song
Class 7: Spread of Chinese Civilization
Class 8: Japan and Korea
Reading: Stearns, Chapters 18 and 19
Documents: Poetry and Society in Tang, Uncommon Woman in Song

Class 9: First exam
Class 10: The Mongol Challenge
Class 11: Marco Polo's Travels
Reading: Stearns, Chapter 20
Documents: Noble and Magnificent City

Class 12: The Rise of the West
Class 13: The Expansion of the West
Class 14: The Gunpowder Empires
Reading: Stearns, Chapters 21 and 22
Documents: New Tension in Western . . . , Scientific Revolution in . . .

Class 15: The West and the World
Class 16: Colonial Expansion
Class 17: The Rise of Russia
Reading: Stearns, Chapters 23 and 24
Documents: Peter the Great Reforms

Class 18: Second exam
Class 19: Early Latin America
Class 20: Spanish and Portuguese Conquests
Reading: Stearns, Chapter 25
Documents: Economy and Society in . . .

Class 21: The Ottoman Empire
Class 22: The Mogul Empire
Reading: Stearns, Chapter 26
Documents: Suleiman the Lawgiver, Akbar's India

Class 23: The African Slave Trade; papers due
Class 24: The African Diaspora
Class 25: Impact of Slavery on Africa

Class 26: The Asian Trading World
Class 27: Ming China
Class 28: Japanese Civilization
Reading: Stearns, Chapter 28
Documents: Matteo Ricci on Ming China, The Rise of the
    Samurai
Final exam

Paper Topic

The winter term of world history covers the time period from
what we call the Middle Ages through the Age of Exploration in western European historical terms. It is a time period
full of people and events, many of which are especially
interesting to students.

Instead of a research paper, I would like you to write a
creative paper. The paper should be written from the "voice"
of a person or a thing from this time period. For instance, you
might want to be a knight going out on Crusade or an African
slave or a sailor on a Chinese ship during the Ming voyages
of discovery. There are really endless possibilities. By using
this focus, it will allow you to put yourself back in that time
period and have a better sense of what it was like to live in
the twelfth or the fifteenth century.

Course Syllabus, Spring Term

Required Reading: Stearns, Adas, Schwartz, *World Civilizations: The Global Experience;* Stearns, *Documents in World
History,* volume 2

Class 1: General Information
Class 2: The French Revolution
Class 3: The Industrial Revolution
Reading: Stearns, Chapter 29
Documents: New Tensions in Western Political Tradition;
    Absolutism and Parliament; Work and Workers in the
    Industrial Revolution

Class 4: Industrialization and Imperialism
Class 5: Latin American Revolutions in the Twentieth Century
Class 6: Latin American Economies
Reading: Stearns, Chapters 30 and 31
Documents: Political Styles in Latin America: Colonial Bu-
    reaucracy and National Liberation; Baroque Culture in
    Latin America; The Decades of Imperialism in Africa;
    The Interaction between Western and African Cultures;
    "Tradition Falls Apart"

Class 7: Islamic Civilizations in Crisis
Class 8: Russian Reforms and Protests
Class 9: Japanese Modernization; research proposals due
Reading: Stearns, Chapters 32 and 33
Documents: Russian Peasants: Serfdom and Emancipation;
    Japan and the West in the Nineteenth Century; The Views
    of a Japanese Educator; Islam and the West in the Nine-
    teenth Century; The Views of a Muslim Intellectual

Class 10: First exam
Class 11: World War I
Class 12: The Great Depression
Reading: Stearns, Chapter 34
Documents: The Twentieth-Century Western State

Class 13: World War II
Class 14: The Russian Revolution
Class 15: The Soviet Union
Reading: Stearns, Chapters 35 and 36
Documents: The Feminist Revolt; Lenin and the Russian
    Revolution; Stalin and the Soviet Union during the 1930s;
    Progress and Terror; To Combine Motherhood with Ac-
    tive Participation in Labor; Family and Gender in the
    Contemporary Soviet Union

Class 16: Japan in the Twentieth Century
Class 17: East Asia in the Postwar Era
Class 18: Pacific Rim Mini-Dragons; paper outline due
Reading: Stearns, Chapter 37
Documents: Gender and Age in Contemporary Japan

Class 19: The Mexican Revolution
Class 20: Latin American Revolutions
Class 21: Second exam
Reading: Stearns, Chapter 38
Documents: Twentieth-Century Latin American Politics;
    Searching for the Soul of the Latin American Experience;
    Underemployment, the Social Crisis of Latin America in
    the Twentieth Century

Class 22: Africa in the Era of Independence
Class 23: Asia in the Era of Independence

Class 24: The Third World Experience
Reading: Stearns, Chapters 39 and 40
Documents: The Emergence of Arab Nationalism: Two
    Views from the 1930s; Middle Eastern Dreams in Con-
    flict: Two Views; The Resurgence of Islam in the Con-
    temporary Middle East; African Nationalism; Changes in
    African Society

Class 25: The Struggle for China
Class 26: Mao's China and Beyond
Class 27: Revolution in Vietnam; papers due
Reading: Stearns, Chapter 41

Class 28: Trends in World Societies
Class 29: Regions, Civilizations, and World Forces
Reading: Stearns, Chapter 42
Final exam

Paper Topics

In the spring term of world history, students are required to
research and write a paper on a contemporary topic. The
body of the paper should be seven or eight typed (if possible)
pages.

Students also are required to turn in a one-page topic
statement/research proposal that clearly explains what the
paper topic will be. A few weeks after handing in the topic
statement, students will turn in an actual outline of the paper
that shows in much more detail what the structure of the
paper will be.

Topic Possibilities

1. One of the major areas of global unrest today is the
former Yugoslavia. Examine the conflict's historical origins
and relate them to the present-day situation in that region. As
a conclusion, in what way will this situation be resolved—
"peace by piece" (one region at a time) or a unilateral
settlement with United Nations troops stationed there?

2. Mexico is faced with a home-grown rebellion by
Mayan Indian guerrillas in the southern state of Chiapas.
This rebellion shattered the image of Mexico as a politically
stable nation. What are the issues surrounding this rebellion,
and what do you think will be the likely outcome of this
rebellion?

3. The United Nations was established in 1945 as an
organization that would be able to resolve international
conflicts without resorting to military force. The United
Nations has always been dependent on voluntary contributions of money and troops, and it is forbidden from interfer-
ing with the internal affairs of any nation. Assess the United
Nations in terms of its mission. How successful has it been

in resolving international conflicts? What do you think the
future of the United Nations will be?

4. An increasingly difficult global problem is that of
refugees. Choose one group of refugees—Palestinians,
e.g.—and examine their predicament. What were the circumstances in which this group became refugees? What
efforts have been made to resolve their plight? What obstacles are there to successfully restoring them to their homeland?

5. Choose one *global* ecological issue, such as acid
rain or nuclear proliferation, and research what has been
done to solve this problem at an international level. What
are some of the issues that complicate the process of
international agreement? The description of the problem
should be only the introductory paragraph for this paper.
The paper is oriented toward international policy solutions
to the problem.

6. In South Africa, apartheid and white-dominated government seem to be things of the past. Two possible ideas for
a paper on South Africa: (1) choose one aspect of society
(education, employment, etc.) and analyze the obstacles to
full integration of black Africans into that part of society and
also what efforts the government is making to successfully
realize this goal; (2) examine the divisions within the black
majority of South Africa and what the future conflicts might
be in this area.

7. The international trading system has been based on
GATT (General Agreement on Tariffs and Trade) since
1948. Some analysts suggest that a structure less favorable
to Western nations might be more beneficial for the less
advantaged nations in our global community. Examine the
history of GATT and its international trade system and the
proposals for alternate trade systems.

8. The ancient Western world was centered upon the
Mediterranean Sea. The early modern world was controlled
by those countries fronting the Atlantic Ocean. Some people
feel that this postmodern world will be dominated by those
nations that face the Pacific Ocean. Examine this theory and
present an argument that supports or refutes this idea. A good
starting point for this topic is a book by Simon Winchester
entitled *Pacific Rising*. It is readily available at most local
libraries.

9. One of the pressing problems of the twenty-first century is the existence of "lesser developed countries." At
present there are forty-two such countries, inhabited by four
hundred million people (about 10 percent of the world's
population, according to United Nations 1993 statistics).
These are nations such as Niger, Mozambique, Samoa,
Yemen, and Burma. Choose one of these countries and
examine how it became a lesser developed country, or compare two of them. In either case, your conclusion should
include what the future holds for such countries.

10. Asia is a collection of dynamic regional groupings in which regional entities are beginning to pool their resources of capital, labor, and raw materials. Choose one of these regional groupings: Greater China (China, Taiwan, Hong Kong), Greater Indochina (Thailand, Laos, Cambodia), or Greater Malaysia (Singapore, Malaysia, Indonesia) and research how this regional entity has structured itself. What are the obstacles to its competing in the global economy? What are the advantages this regional grouping has in comparison with other regional groupings?

11. We are familiar with the genocide practiced by Adolf Hitler and the Nazis. Choose a contemporary example of genocide. Why is genocide being practiced against this particular group? What international efforts are being made to stop this situation?

12. The 1980s were years of staggering economic decline for black Africa. This area of the world is now on the brink of economic disintegration as well as political and social decay. To spur development, many of these nations adopted state-controlled, one-party socialist systems, which were then turned into instruments of oppression and exploitation. Choose one of these nations and examine the problems confronting that society today. How can such a society transform itself into a successful, "modern" society?

13. The decades of conflict in Central America have changed the civil societies in that region. Choose one Central American nation and examine its postrevolution situation. What strategies are being used for economic recovery? How will politics be conducted from now on? What will happen to the revolutionary elite?

14. Central Asia is a vast geographical area inhabited by diverse groups of people. One of the largest groups of people is that group descended from Turkish nomadic ancestry. Many of those Turkish people were under Soviet domination for fifty years and have recently experienced independence again. Two possible ideas for a research topic: (1) Choose one of these nations, such as Turkmenistan, and examine its contemporary situation. Examine its attempts to become a modern independent nation state. Discuss what obstacles it must overcome to achieve such a goal (ethnic conflict, lack of economic foundation, etc.). (2) This area of the world has seen the emergence of what is called "Pan-Turkism," in which the common cultural and linguistic elements will be used to mold the Central Asians into a powerful global entity, and one in which fundamentalist Islam will replace communism as the underlying justification of their society.

13

Seminar in World History

Jerry H. Bentley

World history is a fast-emerging and exciting subfield of the broader discipline of history. The purpose of this reading seminar is to provide an introduction to the most important literature, themes, theories, concepts, and methods of world history as a field of research and scholarship. The works listed in this syllabus all deal with world history in one sense or another: they explicitly compare experiences across the boundary lines of societies and cultural regions, they analyze processes of cross-cultural interaction, or they examine large-scale patterns that influence historical development on a transregional or global scale. Some works represent efforts at macrohistory in that they deal with the whole world or large parts of it. Most, however, examine the workings of large-scale processes in local or regional contexts. Many bring the results of basic research to bear on global themes.

Each member of the seminar will read one book for each of the weekly themes, or at least ten books during the course of the semester, and will prepare incisive analyses, with copies for all other members. In addition, each member of the seminar will provide an introduction to the literature and will help facilitate discussions for one of the weekly themes. Course grades will be based on class discussion and book analyses.

Themes and Readings

Week 1: Conceptions of World History

H.G. Wells, *The Outline of History*
Oswald Spengler, *The Decline of the West*
Arnold Toynbee, *A Study of History*
William H. McNeill, *The Rise of the West*
Marshall G.S. Hodgson, *Rethinking World History*
Bruce Mazlish and Ralph Buultjens, eds., *Conceptualizing Global History*
Patricia A. Crone, *Pre-Industrial Societies*
Stephen K. Sanderson, *Social Transformations*
P.A. Sorokin, *Social and Cultural Dynamics*

Paul Costello, *World Historians and Their Goals*
Jerry H. Bentley, *Shapes of World History in Twentieth-Century Scholarship*

Week 2: Modernization Analysis

W.W. Rostow, *The Stages of Economic Growth*
————, *How It All Began*
Cyril E. Black, *The Dynamics of Modernization*
Cyril E. Black et al., *The Modernization of Japan and Russia*
————, ed., *Comparative Modernization*
Reinhard Bendix, *Nation-Building and Citizenship*
————, *Kings or Peoples*
S.N. Eisenstadt, ed., *The Protestant Ethic and Modernization*
Barrington Moore, *Social Origins of Dictatorship and Democracy*
Wilbert E. Moore, *World Modernization*
Daniel Chirot, *Social Change in the Modern Era*
E.L. Jones, *Growth Recurring*
————, *The European Miracle*, 2d ed.
E.L. Jones, Lionel Frost, and Colin White, *Coming Full Circle*
Peter N. Stearns, *The Industrial Revolution in World History*

Week 3: Dependency and World-System Analysis

Immanuel Wallerstein, *The Modern World-System*, 3 vols. to date
————, *Geopolitics and Geoculture*
Andre Gunder Frank, *World Accumulation*
————, *Dependent Accumulation and Underdevelopment*
Andre Gunder Frank and B. Gills, *The World System: Five Hundred Years or Five Thousand?*
Eric Williams, *Capitalism and Slavery*
Walter Rodney, *How Europe Underdeveloped Africa*
J.M. Blaut, *The Colonizer's Model of the World*
Eric Wolf, *Europe and the People without History*
Janet L. Abu-Lughod, *Before European Hegemony*

L.S. Stavrianos, *Global Rift*
Fernand Braudel, *The Perspective of the World*
Daniel Chirot, *Social Change in the Twentieth Century*
Frances Moulder, *Japan, China, and the Modern World Economy*
Alvin So and Stephen Chiu, *East Asia and the World-Economy*

Week 4: Cross-Cultural Trade: Premodern

Philip D. Curtin, *Cross-Cultural Trade in World History*
C.G.F. Simkin, *The Traditional Trade of Asia*
S. Ratnagar, *Encounters: The Westerly Trade of the Harappa Civilization*
Michael Rowlands et al., eds., *Centre and Periphery in the Ancient World*
Ying-shih Yu, *Trade and Expansion in Han China*
J. Innes Miller, *The Spice Trade of the Roman Empire*
Vimala Begley and Richard Daniel de Puma, eds., *Rome and India*
Liu Xinru, *Ancient India and Ancient China*
Richard Hodges, ed., *Mohammed, Charlemagne and the Origins of Europe*
K.N. Chaudhuri, *Asia before Europe*
————, *Trade and Civilisation in the Indian Ocean*
S.D. Goitein, *A Mediterranean Society*, 6 vols.
Olivia Remie Constable, *Trade and Traders in Muslim Spain*
Janet L. Abu-Lughod, *Before European Hegemony*
E.W. Bovill, *The Golden Trade of the Moors*
Kenneth Hall, *Maritime Trade and State Development in Early Southeast Asia*

Week 5: Cross-Cultural Trade: Early Modern

Philip D. Curtin, *Cross-Cultural Trade in World History*
James D. Tracy, ed., *The Rise of Merchant Empires*
————, ed., *The Political Economy of Merchant Empires*
K.N. Chaudhuri, *Trading World of Asia and the English East India Company*
Niels Steensgaard, *The Asian Trade Revolution of the Seventeenth Century*
L. Blusse and F.S. Gaastra, eds., *Companies and Trade*
R. Ptak and D. Rothermund, eds., *Emporia, Commodities, and Entrepreneurs*
Holden Fuber, *Rival Empires of Trade in the Orient*
D. Lombard and J. Augin, eds., *Marchands et hommes d'affaires asiatiques*
A. Das Gupta and M.N. Pearson, eds., *India and the Indian Ocean*
Michael Pearson, *Before Colonialism*
————, *The Portuguese in India*
Sanjay Subrahmanyan, *The Portuguese Empire in Asia*
M.A.P. Meilink-Roelofsz, *Asian Trade and European Influence*

Om Prakesh, *The Dutch East India Company and the Economy of Bengal*
John E. Wills, *Embassies and Illusions*
Rhoads Murphey, *The Outsiders*
Nicholas Thomas, *Entangled Objects*

Week 6: Migrations and Diasporas

J.P. Mallory, *In Search of the Indo-Europeans*
Irving Rouse, *Migrations in Prehistory*
Philip D. Curtin, *The Atlantic Slave Trade*
————, *The Rise and Fall of the Plantation Complex*
John K. Thornton, *Africa and Africans in the Making of the Atlantic World*
Mechal Sobel, *The World They Made Together*
Patrick A. Manning, *Slavery and African Life*
J. Inikori, ed., *The Atlantic Slave Trade*
Barbara Solow, ed., *Slavery and the Rise of the Atlantic System*
Allison Blakely, *Blacks in the Dutch World*
Paul Gilroy, *The Black Atlantic*
Martin L. Kilson and Robert I. Rotberg, eds., *The African Diaspora*
Hugh Tinker, *A New System of Slavery*
Paul Northrup, *Indentured Labor in the Age of Imperialism*
Lynn Pan, *Sons of the Yellow Emperor*
Gabriel Sheffer, ed., *Modern Diasporas in International Politics*

Week 7: The Age of European Imperialism

Daniel R. Headrick, *The Tentacles of Progress*
————, *The Tools of Empire*
Carlo Cipolla, *Guns, Sails, and Empires*
D.K. Fieldhouse, *The Colonial Empires*
————, *Economics and Empire*
V.G. Kiernan, *From Conquest to Collapse*
————, *Imperialism and Its Contradictions*
R. Robinson and J. Gallagher, *Africa and the Victorians*
S. Gallagher, *Decline, Revival, and Fall of the British Empire*
Sidney Mintz, *Sweetness and Power*
Michael Adas, *Prophets of the Rebellion*
————, *Machines as Measure of Men*
Margaret Strobel, *European Women and the Second British Empire*
N. Chaudhuri and M. Strobel, eds., *Western Women and Imperialism*

Week 8: Post-Colonial Perspectives

Edward W. Said, *Orientalism*
————, *Culture and Imperialism*

James Clifford, *The Predicament of Culture*
James Clifford and G. Marcus, eds., *Writing Culture*
Bernard McGrane, *Beyond Anthropology*
Nicholas Thomas, *Colonialism's Culture*
Paul Gilroy, *The Black Atlantic*
———, *There Ain't No Black in the Union Jack*
Mary Louise Pratt, *Imperial Eyes*
Vicente L. Rafael, *Contracting Colonialism*
Timothy Mitchell, *Colonising Egypt*
Bernard Smith, *European Vision and the South Pacific*
———, *Imagining the Pacific*
Henry Louis Gates, Jr., ed., *"Race," Writing, and Difference*
Benedict Anderson, *Imagined Communities,* 2d ed.
Partha Chatterjee, *Nationalist Thought and the Colonial World*
———, *The Nation and Its Fragments*
Homi Bhabha, *Location of Culture*
———, ed., *Nation and Narration*
History Workshop Journal, no. 36 (autumn 1993)

Week 9: Biological and Ecological Exchanges

Andrew Watson, *Agricultural Innovation in the Early Islamic World*
Alfred W. Crosby, *Ecological Imperialism*
———, *The Columbian Exchange*
William Cronon, *Changes in the Land*
Timothy H. Silver, *A New Face on the Countryside*
Donald Worster, *Rivers of Empire*
———, ed., *The Ends of the Earth*
William H. McNeill, *Plagues and Peoples*
———, *The Global Condition*
Richard H. Grove, *Green Imperialism*
William M. Denevan, ed., *The Native Population of the Americas in 1492*
Philip D. Curtin, *Death by Migration*
Clive Ponting, *A Green History of the World*

Week 10: Cross-Cultural Encounters

Mary W. Helms, *Ulysses' Sail*
Jerry H. Bentley, *Old World Encounters*
Jean W. Sedlar, *India and the Greek World*
Edward H. Schafer, *The Golden Peaches of Samarkand*
———, *The Vermilion Bird*
Clifford Geertz, *Islam Observed*
Stuart B. Schwartz, ed., *Implicit Understandings*
Peter Hulme, *Colonial Encounters*
Sabine MacCormack, *Religion in the Andes*
James Axtell, *The European and the Indian*
———, *The Invasion Within*
———, *After Columbus*

———, *Beyond 1492*
Jacques Lafaye, *Quetzalcoatl and Guadalupe*
Louis M. Burkhart, *The Slippery Earth*
John Leddy Phelan, *The Hispanization of the Philippines*
Jean and John Comaroff, *Of Revelation and Revolution*
Greg Dening, *Islands and Beaches*
Arnold Pacey, *Technology in World Civilization*
Richard W. Bulliet, *The Camel and the Wheel*
Lynn White, Jr., *Medieval Technology and Social Change*

Week 11: Frontiers

William H. McNeill, *The Great Frontier*
———, *Polyethnicity and National Unity in World History*
Owen Lattimore, *Inner Asian Frontiers of China*
Thomas J. Barfield, *The Perilous Frontier*
Barry Cunliffe, *Greeks, Romans and Barbarians*
Richard Price, *First-Time*
———, *Alabi's World*
Richard White, *The Middle Ground*
Frances Karttunen, *Between Worlds*
David J. Weber, *The Spanish Frontier in North America*
Patricia Nelson Limerick, *The Legacy of Conquest*
Patricia Nelson Limerick et al., eds., *Trails: Toward a New Western History*
Nancy M. Farriss, *Maya Society under Colonial Rule*
Inga Clendinnen, *Ambivalent Conquests*

Week 12: Spread of Religions and Ideologies

Arthur Darby Nock, *Conversion*
Jerry H. Bentley, *Old World Encounters*
Johannes Geffcken, *The Last Days of Greco-Roman Paganism*
Ramsay MacMullen, *Christianizing the Roman Empire*
S.N.C. Lieu, *Manichaeism in the Later Roman Empire and Medieval China*
Jacques Gernet, *Les aspects economiques de bouddhisme*
Liu Xinru, *Ancient India and Ancient China*
Arthur W. Wright, *Buddhism in Chinese History*
E. Zurcher, *The Buddhist Conquest of China*
Richard W. Bulliet, *Conversion to Islam in the Medieval Period*
Daniel C. Dennett, *Conversion and the Poll Tax in Early Islam*
S.M. Ikram, *Muslim Civilization in India*
J. Spencer Trimingham, *The Influence of Islam upon Africa*
Nehemiah Levtzion, ed., *Conversion to Islam*
Michael Gervers and Ramzi Jibran Bichazi, eds., *Conversion and Continuity*
Speros Vyronis, *The Decline of Medieval Hellenism in Asia Minor*
Robert W. Hefner, ed., *Conversion to Christianity*

University of Utah Course Offerings and the Introductory Survey Course Syllabus

World History, 1500–Present

Peter von Sivers

Course Description

Today it is possible for humans to orbit the earth and view it in its totality from deep space. Yet on earth, in many respects, we don't seem to think of the world as being one. Or if we do, then only with ourselves at the center. After all, is the United States not the most powerful and technologically advanced country in the world? Aren't even the Russians now imitating the very system that has made us prominent—capitalism? On the one hand, many of us regard people on other continents as almost being from different planets, while on the other hand, we allow them the chance of one day becoming like us if they will only embrace rationality and develop themselves in the right direction.

One of the primary purposes of this course is to wake us all up from our complacent Western-centrism, which causes us to have no more than a dim awareness of the vast world around us. This course is designed to show us that Western civilization is merely one among many civilizations and that its apparent technological superiority does not condemn the others to lesser significance. Quite the contrary, Latin Americans, Middle Easterners, Indians, Chinese, and Africans are all currently in a phase in which they emphasize their own cultural heritage more or less aggressively against what they consider Western cultural hegemony. Understandably, we don't like anti-Americanism, but the best way of meeting it is by making an effort to understand other cultures and civilizations with the same interest and sympathy we devote to understanding our own roots. In the long run, our survival will depend on this effort.

Course Requirements

1. Students will take two exams, a midterm and a final. The relative weight of the exams is 40 and 60 percent, respectively.

2. One general text is assigned to this course. William H. McNeill, *A History of the Human Community,* 4th ed. (Englewood Cliffs, NJ: Prentice Hall, 1993). In addition, three texts deal with specific topics representing the civilizations of China, Europe, and the Middle East: Jonathan Spence, *The Death of Woman Wang* (Harmondsworth, Middlesex: Viking, 1978); Friedrich Engels, *The Condition of the Working Class in England,* translated by W.O. Henderson and W.H. Chaloner (Stanford, CA: Stanford University Press, 1968); and Naguib Mahfouz, *The Beggar,* translated by Kristin Walker Henry and Nariman Khales Naili al-Warraki (New York: Anchor Books, 1986). The class is structured around the textbook; the other books will be drawn into the class discussions at the appropriate times, as indicated in the class schedule below.

Course Schedule and Reading Assignments

Note: All readings are to be completed on the weekend prior to the week for which they are listed.

Week 1: Introduction—European Explorations, c. 1500
Reading: McNeill, Introduction and Chapter 15

Week 2: European Origins of Modernity, 1500–1650
Reading: McNeill, Chapter 16

Week 3: European Expansion and World Reaction, 1500–1700
Reading: McNeill, Chapter 17

Week 4: Chinese Civilization in the Seventeenth Century
Reading: Spence, *Woman Wang*

Week 5: Absolutist and Imperial Regimes in the World, 1700–1800
Reading: McNeill, Chapters 18 and 19

Week 6: The Democratic and Industrial Revolutions, 1800–1850
Reading: McNeill, Chapter 20

Week 7: Engels's View of the English Industrial Revolution
Reading: Engels, *Working Class,* ix–149

Week 8: European Nationalism and the Colonization of the World, 1850–1914

Reading: McNeill, Chapters 21 and 22

Week 9: A Century of Ideologies and War, 1914–1989

Reading: McNeill, pp. 608–61

Week 10: Modernity in Thought and Culture, Twentieth Century

Reading: McNeill, pp. 662–85, Mahfouz, *The Beggar*

Week 11: Conclusion—Multiculturalism in the World

Reading: McNeill, pp. 686–87

World History Course Offerings, University of Utah

World History since 1500 C.E.

This course focuses on broad themes that explain the evolution of global society from the age of European and Islamic expansion to the present. Themes include nation-states and empires, religion, imperialism, nationalism, global conflict, ideology, among others. These themes are considered on a chronological basis. The course is aimed at first- and second-year students.

Themes in World History

This course approaches world history from a purely thematic perspective. Each week students and faculty examine a specific theme. Topics range from global migration and global cities to borderless corporations/trading companies and cultural encounters. Students will generally read a book every week, participate in class discussions, and complete several papers.

World Health

This is a world history course that focuses on health conditions and problems in various cultures and in various historical contexts. The impact of epidemics, the role of medicine in imperialism and colonialism, the work of medical missionaries, and international health agencies such as the Rockefeller Foundation are included in the content of this course.

Warfare in the Middle East and the West since 1450 C.E.

This course approaches the study of warfare from a comparative and global context. We will examine the changing nature of warfare and the shifting imbalance between the Middle East and the West. In the sixteenth and seventeenth centuries, for example, the Ottoman Empire held sway as a leading military power whose reach extended from the western Mediterranean to the Indian Ocean. By the nineteenth century, European states had achieved a similar position. In the mid-twentieth century, the United States had become a truly global superpower challenged only by the USSR. States and societies in the Middle East, once dominant in regional affairs, often acted as surrogates for the United States and the USSR.

America in Global Perspective

This course seeks to place the United States in the broader, global perspective. Key issues will be approached from regional, global, and/or comparative position. For example, slavery will be placed in an Atlantic context and will encompass West Africa, Brazil, the Caribbean, and the American South. The rise of the corporation will be considered from a comparative perspective that will include the United States, Great Britain, and Germany. In all cases, the United States will be linked to other societies and regions.

Europe in the Americas: Colonization in Cross-Cultural Perspective

This course focuses on the questions of cross-cultural influence in the colonization of the Americas. We begin with the assumption that it is necessary to understand imperial types in the context of indigenous American societies and resources and that variations among European colonies reflect the diversity of their populations and environments. Topics include the geography of indigenous America, sugar, slaves, the proliferation of the plantation complex, African-American communities and identities, missions, presidios, resistance and rebellions, and colonial and postcolonial worlds.

Part II

Articles

Since few who are now organizing courses in world history received training in the field, individuals teaching world history find it essential to read widely and become familiar with current world history scholarship. Histories by Alfred Crosby, Philip Curtin, Marshall Hodgson, William McNeill, and Leften Stavrianos equip new world historians with a solid grounding in the field. Publications of the World History Association; *The Journal of World History,* which serves as a forum for scholarly research in world history; and the *World History Bulletin,* which includes materials related to teaching, provide teachers and professors with current developments in a rapidly expanding field.

The following essays offer valuable insights for teaching world history. The ideas proposed by the authors of these essays are best used to complement and enhance student learning rather than to heap more subject matter on a full plate. John Mears proposes a world history course that integrates prehistory, 99 percent of human experience, and recorded history into a single, coherent vision of the human story. He divides world history into three radical transmutations: the emergence of Cro-Magnons, the development of complex societies, and the twentieth-century watershed. Sarah Hughes finds that a study of gender relationships identifies "critical differences in the family foundations of societies—varying from how marriages were contracted and ancestry calculated to how property was transferred and classes formed." Mary Rossabi identifies the procession, a recurrent theme in the art of many societies, as a visual source for analysis and comparative study. Dick Bulliet highlights themes and topics that emphasize interconnections between societies and historical developments shared or similarly experienced by several world regions. These themes and topics offer a structure and coherency for seemingly unrelated textbook materials. Lynda Shaffer argues that in the premodern period the impact of developments that originated in South Asia was a catalyst for global change and laid the groundwork for European Westernization. Paul Vauthier Adams examines the role of the frontier not just in terms of the United States but also as a repeating theme worldwide, spanning three thousand years of history. A.J. Carlson frames the story of the Reformation in its global context to illustrate how better understanding a regional event, its causes and consequences, is possible within a global context. Literature, like art, enriches the study of history. Judy Lightfoot proposes a new paradigm for literature, with American literature as the core. Through a comparative study of voices from world literature, students develop a better understanding of their own literary traditions.

15

Integrating Prehistory into the Study of Humanity's Common Past

John A. Mears

The ultimate purpose of the study of world history, most of us would probably agree, is to provide comprehensive perspectives on the human historical experience. Such perspectives obviously must be long as well as large, capable of highlighting powerful continuities along with the decisive turning points, while emphasizing both the diversity and the common denominators of humanity's past. From these assumptions it surely follows that one way world historians must expand their field of vision is through the integration of what we have learned to call prehistory with our customary consideration of events since the advent of ancient Sumer. The task is daunting, for if we want to take more than a cursory look at the origins of humankind, then we must be prepared to venture into the foreboding—and forbidden—domain of the anthropologist, whose assumptions, methods, and source materials are sometimes unfamiliar to us, and whose slender bodies of evidence often preclude the possibility of firm conclusions and seldom yield the narrative detail historians regard as essential to their tasks. Whatever our hesitations, we might overcome them by reminding ourselves of the compelling reasons for mounting a serious dialogue between the two disciplines, particularly with the problem of interpreting prehistory in mind. For more than 99 percent of the time our hominid ancestors lived on this earth, they functioned within hunting-gathering contexts. Much of what makes us human evolved in our pre-agricultural past. Moreover, the principal components of the other major human adaptations defined and systematically studied by anthropologists—pastoralism, the agricultural village, and the city—had emerged by the end of the Neolithic period. As a consequence of their efforts to understand the patterns of prehistory, anthropologists have also been compelled to wrestle with a variety of important theoretical issues. As world historians, we can profit from their thinking about how cultures relate to their total environments and why they change over time.

Our attempts to connect what anthropologists understand about the patterns of prehistory with the large structures of world history over the last five thousand years must contend with three radical transmutations in the human condition: the advent of anatomically modern humans, the origins of complex societies (civilizations), and the global integration of human societies. All three coincided with periods of remarkable technological innovations that substantially altered the way people related to the natural environment, and that supported exponential population growth by increasing the carrying capacity of the earth. They all marked breaks with existing cultural patterns and introduced deep changes in the organization of societies that affected virtually every aspect of human existence. By dramatically expanding exploitable resources, most especially the energy extracted from nature, these great watersheds spawned true economic revolutions, the first based on refined tool making, the second on the advent of agriculture, and the third on the spread of industrialism. In all of them, certain historical processes reached some kind of culmination while others were beginning to germinate. Viewed in these terms, the three great milestones in the human adaptation to life on our planet can serve as pivotal points in an analytical framework with sufficient explanatory power to integrate the grand outlines of humanity's total past into a single interpretation. What follows is a brief elucidation of the proposed framework.

The earliest of the great transmutations centered on the abrupt emergence of contemporary humans (40,000–35,000 B.C.E.) as the earth's sole surviving hominids. In widely separated places at slightly different times, anatomically modern people replaced Neanderthals and other archaic *Homo sapiens,* probably through a gradual accumulation of numerous small, imperceptible evolutionary modifications. Collectively known as Cro-Magnons, after the earliest known European specimens of our kind, *Homo sapiens sapiens* may have appeared initially in Africa, but seem to have existed in the Near East and Southeast Asia somewhat before Neanderthals became extinct in Europe. Wherever they emerged in the Eastern Hemisphere, they possessed the physical attributes required for articulating elaborate speech patterns that permitted the full maturation of language. Associated with the perceptual-cognitive complexities of modern speech, there must have been enlarged mental abilities, the ultimate source of the many rapid cultural advances made by early *Homo sapiens sapiens.* After three million years of comparatively modest improvements in tool-making techniques, a sudden technological shift took place with the advent of Cro-Magnons, a shift that yielded many conceptually innovative, special-purpose tools, including a cutter used to make other implements and more efficient, durable items combining stone with bone, antler, and wood. The spread thrower, the bow and arrow, and ingenious fishing devices were among Cro-Magnon's seminal inventions. Expanded tool kits, together with an enhanced mastery of fire, permitted intensified exploitation of the natural environment, which in turn sustained higher population levels and enabled some human groups to move toward sedentary lifestyles. Along with settled living came striking intellectual and spiritual achievements. Cro-Magnons demonstrated impressive artistic creativity reflecting a level of abstract symbolizing unique to contemporary humans. Their cave paintings and sculptures revealed an astonishing aesthetic sense as well as a concern for the mysteries of birth, death, and other aspects of existence that mark the origins of religious belief. So quickly did the various manifestations of Cro-Magnon potential appear and so far beyond Neanderthal practices did they take our kind that John Pfeiffer has justifiably referred to them together as "the creative explosion."[1]

Examined in terms of what had preceded the first great transmutation, alterations in the human condition we now link with the triumph of *Homo sapiens sapiens* can be understood as the fulfillment of trends that had shaped the course of hominid evolution over a period of four million to six million years. We can trace hunting-gathering patterns and tool-making to *Australopithecus africanus* and find clear evidence for the nuclear family with *Homo habilis,* the earliest true hominid, at least two million years ago. Right-handedness, the controlled use of fire, and perhaps the rudiments of language came with *Homo erectus,* who ranged far beyond Africa into Europe and Asia, and with whom cultural evolution began to outpace biological evolution more than one million years ago. Similarly, it was Neanderthals among the varieties of archaic *Homo sapiens* who expanded into the northern forests and Arctic tundra of Eurasia, and who embraced the complete spectrum of human behavior by extending their conscious activities into the realms of art and magic more than fifty thousand years ago.

Careful consideration of prehistory's overarching themes should heighten our appreciation of the first great transmutation as a true dividing line in the human experience. No later than thirty thousand years ago, technological innovation and cultural adaptation virtually replaced physical evolution. The first significant alterations between human beings and their natural environment occurred with the extinction of several large mammal species. At the same time, continuities running through the first great transmutation do

seem readily apparent. Hunting and gathering remained the universal means of subsistence until almost twelve thousand years ago. With the ultimate success of the hunting-gathering adaptation, many distinctly human attributes, such as the division of labor between the sexes, cooperation and sharing, artistic expression, and the bonding of the males and females, that stem directly from it received enduring definition. However, despite the obvious continuities, the first great transmutation did push humankind onto hitherto untraveled paths leading toward the development of complex societies typically based on sedentary food production and the city.

In some respects, we understand the second transmutation in human history better than the other two. In the case of the emergence of the first modern humans, we can apply a long perspective but lack sufficient data to cover all the gaps in our knowledge. In the case of the watershed over which humankind is currently passing, we possess immense quantities of data but stand so close to events taking place around us that we struggle to establish sufficient perspective to grasp the meaning of what we encounter day by day. When we turn to the origins of complex societies, we enjoy not only adequate perspective but, thanks to the rich scholarship of the last forty years, also rapidly growing bodies of evidence. We know that the shift to sedentary food production happened gradually. By twenty thousand years ago, some hunting-gathering societies were paving the way by drawing a broad spectrum of foods from diverse environments and learning to make microlith tools, enabling them to exploit new food sources and construct pottery and bins to store surpluses. By nine thousand years ago, expanding populations of sedentary hunter-gatherers, boasting artisan specialists, were tied to permanent villages of several hundred people located in the Near East and had already begun to domesticate plants and animals. By seven thousand years ago, widely separated societies in the Fertile Crescent, southeastern Europe, northern China, Southeast Asia, Mesoamerica, and possibly Andean South America had started to make the transition to sedentary food production, most likely under pressures of population growth that accompanied the other vital preadaptations. Settled agriculture came after human beings had occupied nearly every habitable region of the planet. A logical extension of what highly evolved hunting-gathering societies had achieved, it allowed humans to dominate nature far more intensely than ever before, making us a truly abundant species for the first time in our history.

Like the introduction of agriculture, the subsequent emergence of cities hastened the unfolding of historical development in civilizational centers whose enlarged geographical scope and intensified patterns of interaction amplified the range of human choices and sustained such unprecedented institutions as monarchies and cults of the gods, that thrived in the river valleys of the ancient Near East. In contrast with the nomadic and more egalitarian societies still prevalent at the time of the first great transmutation, urban-based societies performed highly diverse functions within hierarchical—and patriarchal—structures of wealth, status, and power, which had already started to coalesce in the increasingly sedentary gathering-and-hunting societies of the Mesolithic and Neolithic periods (c. 12,000–c. 3500 B.C.E. The upshot was the breakthrough to the levels of societal complexity we call civilization in Mesopotamia, Egypt, and the Indus River valley.

Nothing more dramatically marks this second great transmutation as another dividing line in world history than the fundamental alterations it brought to the context of human existence. For countless millennia, gathering-and-hunting peoples functioned in harmony with their environments. Life for them was typically nomadic, leisurely, and egalitarian. From the outset, the second great transmutation decisively modified those dispositions. Civilizations have always subsisted on agriculture. Food-producing peasants usually constituted as much as 90 percent of the population. Living in small village communities and maintaining themselves barely above subsistence levels, they labored under the authority of tiny ruling elites often concentrated in towns and cities. Hierarchy, specialization, and inequality were among the distinguishing attributes of urban-centered societies. The essential character of human communities in this context was no longer imposed by nature, or by genetic potential, but by systems of coercion and legitimation alien even to a competing adaptation like pastoral nomadism.

Just as the larger consequences of the first great transmutation pointed toward the second, so the enduring implications of the second pointed toward the third. Integrated analytically with the patterns of prehistory, the last five thousand years can be understood as a distinct unit in the history of humankind despite the uninterrupted sequences of events that we can find running back through the Neolithic Age to our Paleolithic ancestors. Bracketed by two momentous watersheds in the context of human existence, this entire period was characterized by the emergence of complex societies and their spread throughout the globe, so that pastoral nomads along with gathering-and-hunting peoples were ultimately overwhelmed by the tremendous power generated in civilizational centers. The second great transmutation had broken through the developmental ceilings that limited the accomplishments of hunters and gatherers by providing human beings with the capacity to enlarge their resource base in relationship to population levels. At the same time, it had shattered the relative equilibrium of the hunting-gathering context, making the last five thousand years a period of chronic instability and conflict. Until the onset of modern industrialism, traditional societies could not sustain a developmental takeoff of any kind. Only in recent centuries has

humankind begun to transcend the restrictions on its creative potential dictated by the second great transmutation.

As the consequences of worldwide economic and cultural integration have become increasingly difficult to ignore at the close of the twentieth century, leaders in all walks of life and from virtually every nation have been using the word *globalization* to describe the complicated and often contradictory realities with which they must deal. Typically they are referring to phenomena that once operated regionally but that now embrace the entire world or at least are very broad and far-reaching in scope. The concept seems to encapsulate the dominant forces of change in our times. It embraces the extraordinary processes of interaction that are rapidly drawing together hitherto separate peoples and autonomous regions as never before in human experience. With globalization has come technological breakthroughs that are automating many of our commonplace activities, urban growth that is turning historic cities into sprawling metropolitan areas, and industrial development that is raising productivity while reducing farm populations to dwindling minorities. While the trends associated with globalization have a long history behind them, they are in a fundamental sense contemporary, World War II probably being the earliest moment when events induced by human actions exercised an impact on nearly every society almost simultaneously. In the past fifty years we truly have been living in a global age shaped by universal patterns of integration that have conditioned the most significant changes and defined the key problems of the period.

The worldwide integration of diverse regions has been stimulated in particular by international business enterprise and accelerated by revolutionary modes of mechanical transport and communication, beginning in the mid-nineteenth century with the railroad, telegraph, and ocean-going steamship. As networks of power and influence have tightened, interactions between distant places have become more intense and competitive. Many of the consequences—the formation of international elites, for example, or the emergence of cultural forms with worldwide appeal—have been long anticipated; others, such as the sharp juxtaposition of affluence and poverty, have come as a surprise even to the experts. While some of the implications appear to be fundamentally promising, such as the liberation of women, many are deeply disturbing: the threat of drastic environmental deterioration, the rising tide of ethnic-religious violence accompanying the mixing of peoples and societies, and the various ways in which processes of globalization have challenged the capacity of the nation-state to organize and control its own affairs. Ironically, rapid global integration has led repeatedly to the assertion of autonomy and struggles to define stronger local identities. Global interdependence, far from creating a bland sameness, has generated fragmentation and the resurgence of differences between human groups. Humankind seems to be moving toward a highly decentralized world in which the experiences of every region have become relevant because all now participate more or less in the universal processes of globalization.[2]

Like the first and second transmutations, the third did not take off suddenly. On the contrary, it could only commence when the possibilities inherent in complex societies had been thoroughly exploited. During the era of the two twentieth-century world wars, forces that had been operative since at least the emergence of sedentary hunter-gatherers during the Upper Paleolithic were working their way toward completion at the same time that unanticipated novelties were already carrying some segments of humankind across another threshold. We can anticipate that this third transmutation will ultimately settle into a global system bearing the historic imprint of diverse regional cultures rather than a bland, all-encompassing uniformity. Humankind will surely remain connected to the heritage of the civilization epoch as well as the gathering-and-hunting adaption even as its history deviates from previous realities. In short, the overall dynamics of our global age will resemble those of the two critical junctures that preceded it so long ago.

What has been sketched in this essay is a bare outline of dominant themes that world historians might employ to integrate prehistory and recorded history into a single coherent vision of humankind in the making. Such a vision, derived from serious conversations between our own and other disciplines, most especially anthropology, is more than feasible. It has become indispensable. With such a vision, we can construct a flexible schema that will allow us to consider the contemporary era from the longest possible perspective. We might then be better positioned to pursue the ultimate aims of world history, which above all should give us an approach to the past that bears directly on our abiding concerns about the present.

Notes

1. See J.E. Pfeiffer, *The Creative Explosion: on Inquiry into the Origins of Our Religion* (New York: Harper and Row, 1982).
2. These reflections on the global integration of contemporary societies have been influenced by my recent reading of Michael Geyer and Charles Bright, "World History in a Global Age," *The American Historical Review* 100, no. 4 (October 1995):1034–60.

16

Gender at the Base of World History

Sarah S. Hughes

Gender is one fundamental organizing principle of human societies. As such, it should be integral to world history survey courses—as basic as economic systems, growth of cities and states, trade, conquest, and religion. Students need to learn about the changing and various distinctions of gender that have divided the lives of women and men from prehistory to the modern period. Pervasive assumptions that women have always kept house and cared for children should yield to knowledge about women's productive labor in gathering and growing crops, in weaving textiles in homes and factories, in marketing, and in providing essential social services. Considering gender reveals critical differences in the family foundations of societies—varying from how marriages were contracted and ancestry calculated to how property was transferred and classes formed. That women had no public role in classical Athens is relevant to democratic theory and to understanding why American women's demand for voting rights was ridiculed before 1920. Whether considering religion, literacy, health, art, slavery, war, or trade, gender usually mattered, and to teach world history accurately, we need to explore this and explain how it mattered.

Judith Zinsser, in *History and Feminism: A Glass Half Full,* points out that it has been nearly twenty years since women historians called for systematic analysis of gender relationships as a "fundamental category of historical thought."[1] Except among pioneers like Steve Gosch, this has not happened in university world history courses.[2] Instead, a few women may be added, usually to discussions of Western societies—added to what is not human history, but men's history. If you doubt this, recollect discussions of the modern democratic state; what meaning does "democracy" have if half of adults are disfranchised? Do your students learn about women's access to basic civil and political rights in the twentieth century? Do they know that women voted in Thailand and Turkey before they did in France?[3] There is, I believe, more leadership at the secondary-school level, exhibited in state mandates that women be included in history courses and in curriculum transformation efforts such as

Philadelphia's Women in World History Project, which is creating units parallel to the district's model world history syllabus. A weakness of this approach is already apparent; it is hard to "add and stir" women into an impersonal batter. Comparative history needs rethinking to incorporate significant patterns of masculine and feminine behavior.[4]

My title, "Gender at the Base of World History," is, then, more reflective of intention than of what I actually accomplish now working within the traditional paradigm. I teach three sections of world history each semester in a department where forty sections are scheduled; I use standard textbooks and conform to departmental guidelines of chronology, extent of reading, writing assignments, and exams. So what I propose is a pragmatic approach to incorporating gender within the framework of world history as it is now conceived. Five years ago this was difficult, but the proliferation of new resources—both theoretical and empirical—makes doing it easier each year.

I think about gender in planning courses—considering how it might fit with each topic and about where the ordinary texts or organizations omit critical gendered historical developments. Squeezing more explanatory factors into a world history syllabus is hard, and I can devote few classes only to gender. So, it is critical to establish early that discerning the social meanings of *male* and *female* is one major historical theme. This is stated in my course description and reinforced in syllabus topics.

In selecting required readings, gender is a primary focus of at least one book. It might be explicit, as in Sarah Pomeroy's *Goddesses, Whores, Wives and Slaves: Women in Classical Antiquity,* or embedded in a text like Jonathan Spence's *The Death of Woman Wang.* I find that students who have learned to look at history in gendered ways find evidence of its patterns even in books chosen to illustrate other historical factors—such as the Chinese Judge Dee mysteries. In designing written assignments based on readings, I've learned to leave open the selection of themes so that students may analyze gender or avoid it. It is particularly important in a required general education course to avoid making male or female students believe that feminism—a feared and hated word among Shippensburg freshmen—is

Originally published in *History Teacher* 27, no. 4 (August 1994). Reprinted with permission.

being forced on them. Even when I assigned Gerda Lerner's *Creation of Patriarchy,* suggested themes for papers included some gender-neutral topics.

In the classroom, I mention gender regularly in lectures and discussions. World history has a tendency to omit actual people—even most famous men—in favor of broad, impersonal, but implicitly masculine, forces. I try to remind students that we are talking about women and men, whose collective behavior is consequential. Seeing gender can become habitual. Teach them to look at television news shots as vignettes of people, not unlike themselves, and to see gender patterns when the street demonstrators and soldiers are overwhelmingly male and when the refugees are only women and children, as the United Nations estimates 70–80 percent today are. What we have seen in Somalia and Bosnia makes it easier to understand how warfare in the ancient Near East and North Africa so often led to enslavement of women. Often it takes very little class time to indicate the gender-specificity of war, slavery, education, migration, or citizenship in the state. Thorough analysis of masculinity and femininity is never possible in a survey, and generalized types are more necessary than I like, but there is usually time to be accurate in using the words *human, male,* and *female,* as well as gendered pronouns.

Because students believe grades are important, gender must also be incorporated in testing. Questions of fact and analysis appear regularly in my multiple-choice items and essays. I distribute study questions prior to essay exams and intersperse gender topics among more traditional ones. Here are samples from several semesters for the period 1300 to 1500 C.E.:

1. Were the ideals for women's behavior developed in classical Islamic societies practiced by the women of fourteenth-century Cairo?[5] Explain your answers with appropriate examples.
2. If, in a previous life, you were a young, unmarried person born into a family of ordinary wealth about 1400, would you choose to have been born in (a) western Europe, (b) Southeast Asia, or (c) Peruvian Inca society? Explain your choice of gender and geography as you compare and contrast daily life in these places.[6]
3. Describe the character and lifestyle of a typical Italian Renaissance man. Where was he born? How was he educated? What were his values or beliefs? How did he spend his time?

These topics draw upon social or intellectual history; economic and political history are also important to the project of gendering world history.

Few issues are as critical as the division of labor, beginning with prehistoric gathering-and-hunting societies. Stu-

dent misconceptions are so deeply entrenched that I spend one class on the importance of women's gathering to the sustenance of their families, on their participation in some hunting activities, on patterns of shared childcare, and on the relative equality anthropologists find in later similar societies. *Gender and Anthropology,* published by the American Anthropological Association, has useful essays and suggestions for class projects that range from primates to modern gathering-hunting peoples.[7] The transition from foraging to agricultural societies may be included in this unit or developed later. What is important is to stress that both women and men participated in producing vegetative and animal food. Human societies depend on productive labor by most adults but usually divide it into male and female tasks. A book that is comparative and useful in its categorization of gendering in agriculture is Ester Boserup's *Woman's Role in Economic Development.*[8] As we encounter new regions and new crops, women's farming responsibilities can be quickly introduced. As trade develops, who owns and has the rights to market various agricultural products needs to be established when possible.

Early in the first semester we also discuss food processing and cooking. Students tend to equate women's domestic work with what they know, with the spacious houses they know—that are full of appliances, furniture, linens, and clothes. Before 1800, most women and men lived in small, sparsely furnished spaces, had few clothes, and spent far more time producing rudimentary products for survival. I also introduce early in the course the variability of gender assignment of other tasks of hand manufacture—spinning, weaving, potting, leather work, building construction—but the tendency for blacksmithing and metalwork to be done by men. Slides are useful—particularly those that show African men sitting at a loom or women building a house. My intention is to shake the students' received notions of "natural" gender patterns and to make them question relationships of work and power between the sexes in any historical society.

In world history classes, I avoid several unanswerable issues of the prehistorical era. One is the role of goddesses. Another is the origin of patriarchy. I find Gerda Lerner's exploration of patriarchy's historical beginnings too narrow because of its Western bias. Furthermore, historical evidence suggests to me not a single pattern of male oppression of women but much more complex negotiations of power. Rather than trying to explain why or how men subjugated women, I demonstrate how patriarchy was associated with the major ancient civilizations of Mesopotamia, Persia, Greece, China, India, and Rome. We discuss how the benefits of civilized life most often arose beside domination of women, class inequalities, and slavery. Discussion of the explicit inequality of women and men embedded in law, marriage, philosophy, religion, and government is shocking to many of my students. Athens and China are important examples both because one need add only a little to the facts in textbooks and because the philosophies of Plato, Aristotle, and Confucius influenced conceptions of male and female for millennia in broad regions. In Athens, where the conception of manhood is central to the society, the intertwining of gender, age, sexuality, and power offers an opportunity to introduce homosexuality. Sarah Pomeroy's *Goddesses, Whores, Wives and Slaves* discusses gender in both Greece and Rome. Within the Mediterranean, Egyptian women had relatively high status, with more choices in marriage, work, and law than their Asian or European neighbors. Yet they were as likely to be slaves. Hatshepsut and Cleopatra had little in common with their serving women. Establishing the privileges of free women in dynastic Egypt sets a stage for showing significant Egyptian influence on women's rising status in the Hellenistic Mediterranean and East Africa.[9]

Sometime in the first semester student consternation and depression mounts over women's seeming perpetual and universal low status. This may appear among male students who are overwhelmed with guilt. There is a concomitant tendency to leap to the false conclusion that everything was terrible until the American Revolution liberated women. So it is important to deal with societies besides Egypt in which women had high status. I rely on a unit on Southeast Asia, based largely on readings from Anthony Reid's *Southeast Asia in the Age of Commerce*. Here women were thought to be more competent than men in business, were more often literate, and expected sexual satisfaction from men. The beauty of this picture for female students is marred by a preference for blackened teeth, tattooed bodies, and androgynous dressing, while male students may be horrified by descriptions of genital surgery to enhance men's appeal to women. Discussion of gender in Southeast Asia serves a further purpose in illustrating the selectivity of Indian and Chinese influences. If one only looks at the Buddhist temples of Pagan, Borobudor, or Angkor Wat, India's influence can seem overwhelming; persistence of diametrically different ideals of masculinity and femininity suggests more complex cultural interaction. Lorraine Gesick first showed me that in medieval Thailand local women merchants enabled foreign men to maintain long-distance trade. Once observed, this practice can be found on continents beyond Southeast Asia. One day, I believe gender will transform our understanding not only of trade, but of the spread of religion and culture. Think about the meaning to be deconstructed from a textbook phrase such as "Muslim traders spread Islam as they married local women." This implies that agency or power was male, while closer scrutiny may reveal how tenuous his position as a foreigner was.

My final example concerns gender and colonialism. I find the Peruvian case useful, for Irene Silverblatt, in *Moon, Sun, and Witches,* briefly explicates how the Incas used gender to solidify their conquests of adjacent peoples and then how the Spanish imposition of European gender ideology both enhanced their control of Andean peoples and oppressed women especially. Andean women's resistance to loss of status earned them prosecution as witches in the seventeenth century. The role of gender in European conquest of the Americas can also be explored in examples drawn from Canadian Hurons or the New Mexican pueblos.[10] Kathleen M. Brown suggests considering "the relationship between gender and colonialism" as "cultural encounters . . . occurring along gender frontiers. . . ." Such gender frontiers were not distinct from economic, linguistic, political, or religious confrontations but pervaded these aspects of culture, with each society defining its gender categories as "natural." Brown concludes that "the struggle of competing groups for the power that comes with controlling definitions of 'the natural' makes gender frontiers a useful concept for understanding colonial encounters."[11] Exploring these issues might extend into the nineteenth and twentieth centuries, for Africanists have developed a significant body of work connecting European exploitation of gender with the slave trade, colonization, capitalism, and apartheid.[12] Perhaps only the literature on women and the welfare state compares to it in significance for world history.

I have scarcely touched on the modern period, because it is easier to incorporate gender as sources become more plentiful and women move from the household into the public arena. A final recommendation is perhaps the most important. The indispensable source everyone needs is a volume of short interpretative essay and bibliographies, published by the Organization of American Historians, entitled *Restoring Women to History: Teaching Packets for Integrating Women's History into Courses on Africa, Asia, Latin America, the Caribbean and the Middle East.*[13]

Notes

1. Judith P. Zinsser, *History and Feminism: A Glass Half Full* (New York: Twayne Publishers, 1993), citing Joan Kelly's essay "The Social Relations of the Sexes," p. 40.

2. Stephen S. Gosch, "Using Documents to Integrate the History of Women into World History Courses," *World History Bulletin* 5, no. 1 (Fall/Winter 1987–1988).

3. *The World's Women, 1970–1990: Trends and Statistics* (New York: United Nations, 1991); table 3 lists the year women gained the right to vote in all countries, with Thailand in 1932, Turkey in 1934, and France in 1944. The volume contains extensive data on work, households, education, and health.

4. For a beginning, see Cheryl Johnson-Odim and Margaret Strobel, "Conceptualizing the History of Women in Africa, Asia, Latin America and the Caribbean, and the Middle East," *Journal of Women's History* 1, no. 1 (Spring 1989).

5. Huda Lutfi, "Manners and Customs of Fourteenth Century

Cairene Women: Female Anarchy Versus Male Shar'i Order in Muslim Prescriptive Treatises," in Nikki R. Keddie and Beth Baron, eds., *Women in Middle Eastern History* (New Haven: Yale University Press, 1991), a reserve library reading, was the basis for this essay. This reading is more successful in revealing the complexity of women in Islamic cultures than others I have tried.

6. Reserve library readings from Anthony Reid, *Southeast Asia in the Age of Commerce, 1450–1680,* volume 1: *The Lands Below the Winds* (New Haven: Yale University, 1988), and Irene Silverblatt, *Moon, Sun, and Witches: Gender Ideologies and Class in Inca and Colonial Peru* (Princeton: Princeton University Press, 1987), were the basis of this question, along with John P. McKay, B. Hill, and J. Buckler, *A History of World Societies,* vol. 1, 3d ed. (Boston: Houghton Mifflin Company, 1992).

7. Sandra Morgan, ed., *Gender and Anthropology: Critical Reviews for Research and Teaching* (Washington: American Anthropological Society, 1989). Kevin Reilly, ed., *Readings in World Civilizations,* volume 1: *The Great Traditions,* 2d ed. (New York: St. Martin's Press, 1992) has a useful section.

8. Ester Boserup, *Women's Role in Economic Development* (New York: St. Martin's Press, 1970).

9. See Gay Robins, *Women in Ancient Egypt* (Cambridge: Harvard University Press, 1993), and Sarah B. Pomeroy, *Women in Hellenistic Egypt from Alexander to Cleopatra* (New York: Schocken Books, 1984).

10. Karen Anderson, *Chain Her by One Foot: The Subjugation of Women in Seventeenth-Century New France* (London: Routledge, 1991); Ramon A. Gutierrez, *When Jesus Came, the Corn Mothers Went Away: Marriage, Sexuality, and Power in New Mexico, 1500–1846* (Stanford, CA: Stanford University Press, 1991).

11. Kathleen M. Brown, "Brave New Worlds: Women's and Gender History," *The William and Mary Quarterly,* 3d series, 1, no. 2 (April 1993):318–19. This is a fine guide to gender literature of the European/African/American frontiers of 1500–1800.

12. Cherryl Walker, ed., *Women and Gender in Southern Africa to 1945* (London: James Currey, 1990); Elizabeth Schmidt, *Peasants, Traders, and Wives: Shona Women in the History of Zimbabwe, 1870–1939* (Portsmouth, NH: Heinemann, 1992); Claire Robertson and Iris Berger, eds., *Women and Class in Africa* (New York: Holmes and Meier, 1986); and Sharon Stichter and Jane Parpart, eds., *Patriarchy and Class: African Women in the Home and Workforce* (Boulder, CO: Westview, 1988).

13. Edited by Cheryl Johnson-Odim and Margaret Strobel in 1988, the volume is available in paperback from the OAH for $20.00.

17

The Procession Portrayed

Using Art History in the Global Curriculum

Mary Rossabi

Similar themes and subjects appear in the art of most civilizations. Representation of the family, the mother and child, animals, and music making are found on objects around the world and have been the subjects of scholarly interest. The recurrent theme of the procession, however, has received little attention from historians and art historians, even though, over time, it can be found in the arts of Africa, Asia, Europe, and the Americas. The procession portrays rituals and ceremonies, celebrates civil and religious authority, and illustrates social activities. It, therefore, reflects a civilization's social structure and its political and religious power in depictions of marriages, funerals, births, coronations, religious activities, pageants, military parades and maneuvers, tribute bearing, and triumphal entries:

> From the Panathenes or funeral marches of antiquity to the demonstrations of the labor unions, political parties, and "groupuscles" of May 1968 in Paris, from the Corpus Christi procession of the High Renaissance to the Red Square parades during the anniversary celebration of the October Revolution, we can see that order is an essential means for getting across the "message" be that message religious, civic, political, philosophical, or social. Often the intended message becomes complex due to the participants' reciprocal relationships and relative positions within the parade.[1]

The procession throughout art history can become a focal point in any history curriculum; in a global history course, this major theme can unite many diverse cultures. A procession of religious or civil figures, gods, acolytes, worshipers, and warriors can also be read as a sign signifying attitudes toward power, spiritual belief, women, children, and outsiders of any sort. In studying the position of the participants in the procession, their posture, their dress, the contiguity of the figures, and their gaze or eye contact, the viewer learns about social relationships between those signified and their signifiers, between artists, patrons, and those portrayed, and between the viewer and the processional work itself:

> More generally, parade, cortege, and procession create through their narrative aspect a system of values from which any parade, cortege, procession, or demonstration derives its legitimacy. The process of legitimization or actualization may, in turn, serve to formalize relationships between participants, such as the political relationship between a sovereign and a city.[2]

Since most of the works of art were or are exhibited either on temples or in churches, in town squares, in the residences of patrons, and finally in museums, they have been seen by different audiences, and their reception must, if possible, be considered if their impact is to be analyzed.

The setting of the procession also offers valuable glimpses of the period's architecture and urban and rural landscapes, while the medium and placement or location of the actual procession lead the observer to further conclusions about the place of ritual and authority in a particular society. The art historical genre of history painting, therefore, includes many processions.

A study of the procession rewards the viewer with insights into the prosperity and politics of a particular society, and specific questions about the political, social, and economic functions of that society can be addressed. Is the procession generally optimistic in depicting a positive event? Other than funerals (and, as we shall see, not even all funerals), do processions ever reflect the misery and sadness connected to the disasters of war, famine, disease, or political and economic unrest? Is the pictorial procession, as commissioned by a person in authority, a type of visual control in which those portrayed are horizontally organized to complement (or counteract?) the vertical or hierarchical control the rulers or institutions impose on their societies? If so, when does the visual control weaken? Are there fewer depictions of processions in more democratic or unstructured societies? Does the human eye respond to a line of figures positively? Does the procession need beginning and ending points so that this line is "aesthetically" resolved? These questions can help focus analyses and discussions of the artworks themselves, and at the same time can serve to connect the art to the social and political history surrounding it. The works included in this chapter are accessible and well known, found in basic art history texts, history books, major museums, and soon on CD-ROM. A study of why they have become art historical "icons" or classics serves to uncover some of the stereotypes and values different societies uphold.

An introductory art history course usually begins with a study of the Lascaux frescoes and concludes with the art of the late twentieth century. Most courses concentrate on Western art as it develops out of the art of the Middle East (Mesopotamia and Egypt) and ancient Greece, although there are often units devoted to the art of Africa and the Far East. In the texts generally followed in an introductory course, whether A. Janson's *History of Art,* H. Gardner's *Art Through the Ages,* or F. Hartt's *Art, a History,* reproductions of processions occur throughout, the earliest being the parade of animals in the "Great Hall" at Lascaux. This glorious array of beasts leaves no doubt in the viewer's mind of the priorities of this ancient cave civilization, although it is difficult to categorize this procession. One of the earliest processions after these frescoes is the Sumerian Standard of Ur, a triumphal entry, eliciting praise for the victorious king who subdued the enemy captives he parades behind his chariot. The best-known processions from antiquity, however, are the Parthenon Friezes, the Ara Pacis, and the circular reliefs on Trajan's Column. The first work depicts a religious ceremony in which tribute bearers offer gifts to Athena. The other two reliefs record military victories. The Ara Pacis celebrates the Roman emperor Augustus's victory over Spain, and the reliefs on Trajan's Column describe the subjugation of the Dacians. This procession through Western art history moves into the early Christian era with the Ravenna Mosaics of Theodora and Justinian and their retinues and the Bayeux Tapestry with its depiction of the Norman invasion of England.

During both the classical and the early Christian periods, the instructor can introduce the student to the contemporaneous stone relief processions in the arts of China, India, and Indonesia. Chou and Han dynasty military and royal processions can be compared to Trajan's spiraling soldiers; Gandharan stair risers, with their classical figures in procession, can be studied against the Ara Pacis; and an Ajanta procession of dwarfs and Borobodur reliefs of Prince Sudhara and his women can be contrasted with the Ravenna Mosaics. There are time discrepancies in some of these comparisons, but by studying the same theme and artistic form in very different cultures, students can ask the questions and follow the approaches suggested earlier in this chapter as a starting point for further exploration. (Just as the Western references can be found in the reproductions from the standard texts already mentioned, most of the oriental references are located in S. Lee's *History of Far Eastern Art,* J. Spence's *Search for Modern China,* and J. Fairbank, E. Reischaur, and A. Craig's *East Asia: Tradition and Transformation.*)

In the West, the medieval religious figures have a rigid military air about them, in great part because of their frontal style, lack of perspective, and contrapposto, but also, perhaps, because the early Church relied upon militancy for its survival. In the high Middle Ages, many twelfth-century reliefs, like those on churches along the French pilgrimage route to Santiago de Compostella in Spain, lose some of the stiffness of earlier hierarchical processions. The rows of figures from the reliefs at Autun, Vezelay, and Conques are sent to heaven or are thrust into the jaws of hell. At Angkor Wat in Cambodia, a twelfth-century relief of heaven and hell includes "an ecstatic procession of the saved"[3] and offers a rich comparison with the aforementioned French works. Thirteenth-century animal processions from Mysore in India can also be contrasted.

From the thirteenth and fourteenth centuries, Duccio's *Christ Entering Jerusalem*, Martini's *The Road to Calvary*, and Giotto's *Pieta*, all egg tempera on wood, depict groups of figures in a procession where Christ is the focal point. Toward Giotto's dead Christ the mourners approach and stop; Duccio's Christ enters Jerusalem triumphantly on a donkey, leading his disciples; and Martini's Savior bears his cross to Golgotha surrounded by his devoted followers. Lorenzetti's fresco *Good and Bad Government in the Country* uses civil processions of courtiers and urban officials from early Renaissance Siena to expose the uses and abuses of political power.

Aztec relief on a pyramid outside Mexico City offers a chronological point of comparison with these late medieval–early Renaissance paintings, but because of the very different media, one could also contrast these flat stone sculptures with the medieval French reliefs:

> The processional type reappears in Aztec sculpture of the fifteenth century, on friezes and slabs in the National Museum, notably the Tizoc stone. The procession of individuals converging from left to right upon an image of the god, or upon a symbol of blood sacrifice, is a recurrent theme. The costumes, attributes, and physical types differ enough in these processions to justify their identification as historical figures, perhaps a convocation of tribal leaders allied under the unifying cult of the Morning Star deity.[4]

The processional theme is found less frequently in the "icons" of Renaissance Italy than in the frescoes and manuscripts used to adorn the palaces of the Italian princes. Perhaps art historians and other connoisseurs preferred to focus on and thus popularize works that illustrated the assumption of individual power and the ascendancy of the princely city-states after the Middle Ages. Perhaps more portraits or intimate religious scenes were selected by Renaissance patrons to reflect or magnify their own importance, making the procession as a theme in Renaissance art less familiar than in the periods already described.

In the Vatican apartments, Raphael's popular fresco *The*

School of Athens" does, however, offer an intriguing hint of a procession, with Plato and Aristotle the only participants. The use of perspective frontality, physical bulk, and dimensional space separates this work from its medieval predecessors. However, northern European painters of the same period use the processional form in many of their works. The Van Eyck brothers' *Adoration of the Lamb* from the Ghent Altarpiece depicts four processions of religious figures converging on the lamb of God; Bosch's *Garden of Delights* presents a bizarre circular procession of nude men and women mounted on wild beasts; and Peter Brueghel the Elder's *The Blind Leading the Blind* captures a procession of the sixteenth-century beggars while illustrating verse 15:14 from the Book of Matthew.

From the fifteenth through the eighteenth centuries, the West African kingdom of Benin produced splendid bronze plaques to decorate the royal palaces of the oba, or king. Most of these sculptures exalted the monarch and his rule by depicting him and/or his officials in authoritative stances. "These plaques also served as historical documents, recording people and events."[5] In some of these bronze reliefs, halted processions of warriors, dressed for battle with their swords and shields, face forward. Surrounding them are animals representing the oba. Other plaques show lines of musicians who also serve the ruler of Benin. One might ask in studying these West African processions if other African societies with a less formal royal structure and a less well-developed and powerful court life also employed the processional form in their art.

These processional plaques were fashioned to hang on the walls of the monarch's dwelling in the same way that processional frescoes and other pictures were created for the palaces of the elite of Renaissance Italy. Earlier, when contrasting the stone reliefs of fifteenth-century Mexico with late medieval Italian paintings, we could see that the diversity of media, although a hindrance to a precise comparison, informs the student where these very different works were placed. He or she can then make hypotheses about the architecture, the climate, the economy, patronage, and living styles in these disparate societies.

Like the Benin bronzes, seventeenth-century European processions glorify royal power. Rubens's series celebrating the queen of France, Maria de Medici, includes a painting of her debarkation procession in the Marseilles harbor as she alights from a mighty galleon above cavorting sea nymphs. Rubens's painterly style is in sharp contrast to the stark linear bronzes of the Benin royalty.

Seventeenth- and eighteenth-century European processions also portray the middle class, which prospered from trade with Africa, Asia, and Latin America and commissioned its own memorials. In Holland, the Dutch burgher class made its triumphal entry in Rembrandt's *Night Watch*.

The Chinese reaction to Europe's scramble for trade is recorded in a late eighteenth-century Chinese tapestry in which a procession of Chinese porters, in the employ of British lord Macartney's embassy, carry scientific and technological instruments in the hope of "gaining diplomatic and commercial concessions from the Qing. . . . But Qianlong's responses in an edict to King George III was 'we never valued ingenious articles, nor do we have the slightest need of your country's manufactures.'"[6]

The rise of the merchant class in early Romanov Russia, and its reaction to the reforms of Peter the Great, is reflected in several satirical woodcuts by anonymous Old Believer artists, whose sect resisted the changes Peter introduced. In one print, Peter is caricatured as a dead cat, sometimes with his mustachios clipped in the modern fashion so antipathetic to the Old Believers, pulled to his funeral by a procession of mice, each one representing a different trade or geographical area of Russia. This lubok, or woodblock print, has become a classic to Russian and foreign viewers who know of it in a variety of reproductions.

By the nineteenth century, processions were a striking feature of several French masterpieces that recorded social and political protest and change. Delacroix's *Liberty Leading the People* of 1830 celebrated the victory of Lady Liberty, who led a rather disorderly band of followers through the burning boulevards of Paris, over the slain bodies of their countrymen. The loosely organized procession reflects this diffuse group of rebels, which moves toward the viewer but makes no eye contact, limiting thereby the emotional impact and casting this work as a history painting rather than a call to arms. A contrasting Japanese print, also from the 1830s, shows two parallel processions of territorial lords (or daimyos) as their "entourages pass the gates of a daimyo mansion on the way to the Shogun's castle on New Year's day."[7] The style is more conventional, with the figures moving from right to left in an orderly file, not toward the picture surface as in Delacroix's work. A comparison of these two processions would encourage students to do research into early nineteenth-century Japanese and French social and political history, as well as studying the conventional characteristics and signifiers of the procession.

Courbet's enormous canvas of 1840–1850, *The Burial at Ornans*, portrays a procession of French peasant mourners gathered at a graveside. The painting was considered outrageous because Courbet did not portray the grand personages usually found in history paintings but depicted instead the country folk found in popular prints like *Les Images D'Epinal*. Some fifty years after *Liberty Leading the People*, Seurat painted a stratum of French society different from that of either Delacroix or Courbet in his *Sunday Afternoon on the Island of La Grande Jatte*. Here the middle class, in all its finery, enjoys its leisure while strolling in a disjointed, discontinuous parade. Robert Hughes, in *The Shock of the New,* states:

> Seurat wanted to paint the processional aspect of modern life—something formal, rigorous, and impressive. . . . "I want to show moderns moving about on friezes, stripped of their essentials, to place them in paintings arranged in harmonies of colours, in harmonies of line, line and color fitted to each other. . . ." And so, in "La Grande Jatte," the vision of pleasure takes on the gravity of history painting.[8]

There is no formal procession in this painting, only fragments, but the image of a procession of elegant Parisians ambling along the Seine could be imprinted in the viewer's mind's eye. However, the viewer might also "read" the painting as a record of disconnectedness and alienation as Linda Nochlin suggests in her essay "Seurat's La Grande Jatte: An Anti-Utopian Allegory."[9] The unity of purpose expressed in Delacroix's dramatic processional confrontation, Courbet's funeral cortege, and the grand parades of the daimyos, is gone. Each person remains isolated; even the mother and child do not touch or hold hands. The disintegration of the processional form coincides with the growing significance and power of the individual and the weakening of that individual's affiliation with a larger institution or group, be it religion and the Church, a civic organization, or a political hierarchy. The processions discussed earlier in this chapter are all the reflection of some larger entity, while Seurat's fragmented procession mirrors the separation from the group and the isolation of the individual.

Reflections of social change in early twentieth-century West Africa are also found in the processions of the Yoruba, a neighboring tribe of the Benin people. Entry doors for the palace at Ikere, completed by the court artists in 1916, depict "a full court ceremonial of 1897 . . . [in which] the Oba received the British Captain Ambrose, travelling Commissioner for the province. Seated in his litter, the European is depicted as smaller than the Yoruba king. Each has his own retinue. . . . The Oba's entourage included a cluster of wives with children on their backs."[10] The members of the captain's procession move toward the king as if about to pay tribute. While the figures in the Western procession appear glum, the followers of the oba smile, displaying their superiority before these Europeans who invaded their territory and made it part of the British colony of Lagos in 1861.

Even before the Ikere palace doors were fashioned, African imagery had exerted a strong influence on European art, as can be seen in Picasso's *Les Demoiselles d'Avignon* of 1907. African masks and their planar construction were instrumental in the development of cubism and the shattering of Renaissance perspective, which had defined European painting for nearly five hundred years. This weakening and,

for many twentieth-century artists, demise of one-point perspective coincided with the disintegration of the procession as it was seen in many "classics" of art history.

The procession in some European paintings began to move toward abstraction. Marcel Duchamp's *Nude Descending a Staircase* of 1912 can be read as a time-motion study of one figure or, in spite of the title, as a procession of abstract figures exploding on the canvas. Form is all, and there is no recognizable narrative. What seems merely a representation of shapes in a line, however, can, by its very nonobjectivity, permit the viewer to react to this painting unhindered by more traditional subject matter and convention.

Through this emancipation, artists like El Lissitsky in revolutionary Russia used processions of squares, triangles, and circles in his *Beat the Whites with the Red Wedge* to signify a new socialist order. At the same time as the Russian avant-garde artists were using neutral and value-free geometric forms to celebrate the triumphal entry of socialism into Russia, the socialist realists were proclaiming the proletarian state in their victorious processions of flag-bearers, workers, and soldiers. Denikin's portrayal of a procession of troops in *Defense of Petrograd* (1927) is certainly more accessible and moving than the paintings of El Lissitsky. Throughout the Communist world, processions of peasants, workers, and soldiers celebrate the victory of their personal fulfillment through the triumph of the collective state. This theme is illustrated in an anonymous Chinese painting entitled *Follow Closely Chairman Mao's Great Strategic Plan, 1968*, in which Mao, in the bottom left corner of the painting, holds up his left hand in front of a winding procession of distant figures.[11] In Mexico City, Diego Rivera's murals in the National Palace, 1929–1935, depict the "past, present and future of mankind . . . as a dialectical march from the glories of the primitive past . . . into the sunlit upland of Marxian communism."[12] The murals are filled with processions of Aztecs, conquistadors, and workers, and the whole series can be seen as the procession of Mexican history, culminating in the triumph of communism. Narrative prevails; there is no abstraction here.

By the mid-twentieth century, however, the procession had ceased to provide the inspiration for most artists who created the "icons" of art history. Picasso's *Guernica* of 1937, considered by Robert Hughes as the last great history painting, is, with its parade of agonized victims, also the last great procession. After *Guernica*, Hughes states, artists no longer believed they could influence their viewers:

> The idea that an artist, by making painting or sculpture, could insert images into the stream of public speech and thus change political discourse has gone, probably for good. . . . Mass media took away the political speech of art.[13]

The processional form in relief and in painting became, therefore, irrelevant, replaced by the never-ending procession of television images. In the global curriculum, however, the processional form throughout history and across cultures remains useful in studying the art and civilizations of Africa, Asia, Europe, and the Americas.

Notes

1. L. Marin, "Notes on a Semiotic Approach to Parade, Cortege, and Procession" in A. Falassi, ed., *Time Out of Time: Essays on the Festival* (Albuquerque: University of New Mexico, 1987), p. 226.

2. Ibid., p. 225.

3. S. Lee, *A History of Far Eastern Art* (New York: Abrams, n.d.), pp. 168–70.

4. G. Kubler, *The Art and Architecture of Ancient America* (New York: Penguin, 1984), pp. 87–88.

5. W. Forman, B. Forman, and P. Dark, *Benin Art* (London: P. Hamlyn, 1960), p. 11.

6. J. Spence, *The Search for Modern China* (New York: W.W. Norton, 1990), following p. 132.

7. J. Fairbank, E. Reischauer, and A. Craig, *East Asia: Tradition and Transformation* (Boston: Houghton Mifflin, 1973), p. 404.

8. R. Hughes, *The Shock of the New* (New York: Knopf, 1991), p. 116.

9. L. Nochlin, *The Politics of Vision* (New York: Harper and Row, 1991).

10. L. Silver, *Art in History* (New York: Abbeville Press, 1993).

11. E.J. Laing, *The Winking Owl* (Berkeley: University of California Press, 1988), plate (anonymous, "Mao Zedong's Thought Illumines the Theatre," poster, 1968).

12. B.D. Wolfe, *The Fabulous Life of Diego Rivera* (New York: Stein and Day, 1963), p. 266.

13. Hughes, *The Shock of the New,* p. 11.

18

Themes, Conjunctures, and Comparisons

Richard W. Bulliet

No single scheme for teaching world history is unquestionably the best, and it is not my intention to put forward an inflexible model. Instead, my aim is to suggest some of the main themes that characterize global history in each of the major periods and then to highlight a few important topics, some of them possibly unfamiliar, that can help illuminate those themes. Obviously, teachers can adopt or adapt the structure and use the topics selectively in whatever way best suits their classroom needs and the organization of the textbook they are using.

My choice of themes and topics aims at emphasizing global interconnections and highlighting historical experiences shared, or similarly experienced, by several world regions. It is also meant to complement rather than overlap textbook coverage and therefore puts less stress on European history, recent history, and superstructure than current textbooks commonly do. At the same time, since, like everyone, I have gaps in my own historical education, examples drawn from the histories of sub-Saharan Africa, pre-Columbian America, and Latin America are less numerous and fully developed than they should be.

You and your colleagues or students might wish to work up themes and topics of your own to fill in these and other gaps. Highlighting specific themes and topics is a good way to fine-tune the structure of a course to the needs and student profile of a particular classroom.

Each topic is labeled either a Conjuncture or a Comparison. Conjunctures are points in time and place when circumstance leads different parts of the world to become connected or to change their relationship in significant ways. Comparisons are instructive contrasts between situations that are unconnected in time or in place. Conjunctures, therefore, are actual episodes in world history seen as a global phenomenon, while Comparisons use situations from different parts of the world to illuminate each other.

Encourage students to think of history in these terms, too. Memorization of facts is desirable, but few students can realistically be expected to remember most facts, particularly

about the non-Western world, for long after the examination. Even fewer will be able to bring the facts they do remember to bear in discussion. However, if students think in terms of specific instances when parts of the world somehow came together and of specific comparisons of different parts of the world, they may retain a sense of global interconnection and of the value of knowing about other peoples even after the facts have dimmed in their memories.

The Early Ancient Period

Whether your course begins with the appearance of farming, pottery, and animal domestication during the Neolithic period or with the development of the first civilizations five thousand years later, there are certain themes that warrant attention in the Early Ancient period:

Scale

Human populations were small and dispersed in ancient times, especially in comparison with your students' own experience of the world. Let them talk about what it means to call a place with five thousand inhabitants a city. Communications were slow, too; twenty miles a day is a good rule of thumb for caravans. Talk about how long it took for a messenger or an army to get from one extremity of some state or empire to another. The larger the polity, the more precarious its control in distant parts. If a provincial official was strong and independent enough to control an army and defend against rebellions and invasions, what kept him loyal to the central ruler? The average size of states tends to grow throughout the early ancient period from city-states and tribal states to kingdoms, to empires, though most empires of this period were fragile and short-lived.

Subsistence

The great preponderance of all people lived on the product of their own labor. Money came into use in Anatolia (modern Turkey) in the seventh century B.C.E., but most people used barter and remained outside the orbit of monetary exchange for centuries. Domesticated plants and animals had their own

This paper was commissioned by The College Board. © 1991 by The College Board.

characteristics that governed the calendars of farmers and herders. Digging sticks and hoes, such as those used in sub-Saharan Africa or pre-Columbian America, did not require animal labor; plows normally did. Some very hot regions, such as Egypt and Mesopotamia, grew crops during the winter; temperate European countries grew crops during the summer. Very few people anywhere in the world participated in high culture.

Gods

Students who have grown up with no exposure to polytheism tend to look down on polytheistic systems. But polytheistic systems varied greatly and were both emotionally and spiritually rich. The cults of Mesopotamia centered on rituals performed by specialists in elaborately organized and staffed temples. The common people were little involved, although there was great interest in divining the future either from the livers of slaughtered animals or from the heavens. This indicates a belief in the idea of a pattern to existence that carried over consistently from the realm of the stars, to the hidden parts of animals, to the minutiae of daily life.

Unlike Mesopotamians, the Egyptians, and later the Aztecs, had a cheerful view of death and elaborate death rituals that touched many strata of society. Egyptian archaeological remains of this period are overwhelmingly funerary in character.

The Indian priests who compiled and recited the hymns of the Rig Veda always performed their rituals outdoors without using temples. Hence, there is little archaeological evidence for early Indian religion. The ancient Europeans shared many of the same gods because the Vedic Indians and the Europeans share a prehistoric cultural origin in western Central Asia or eastern Turkey. The Vedic sky god Dyaus was the same as the Greek god Zeus, though neither the Indians nor the Greeks realized it. Both gods were the fathers of other gods, so the Roman form of the name became Ju the Father. Since "father" in Latin is *pater,* this yielded the name Jupiter.

Texts and archaeological discoveries document differences between religious cultures, but for the most part they do not convey much about the spiritual lives of common people. Modern anthropological data on the spiritual richness of sacred dances, legends, and symbols can sometimes be used to get a fuller picture.

Civilization

Different texts define civilization in different ways, all of which have to be used cautiously. Writing is a useful criterion, but the Incas did not have it. Where the Mycenaean Greeks used writing to keep financial records, and apparently for little else, the Incans kept similar records very accurately using knotted strings called *quipus.* Writing, as such, was less important than what writing was used for.

Cities are hallmarks of civilization in China, Mesopotamia, the pre-Vedic Indus Valley, and Mesoamerica, but cities were apparently not so important in ancient Egypt and Turkmenistan, which are often seen as early civilized areas. Archaeologists now believe that huge stone and earth monuments in southern and western Europe—Stonehenge is the best known—were made by local people without any accompanying urban development.

It should also be remembered that comparatively insignificant palaces and temples survived for millennia when built out of stone and baked brick while much grander structures perished when built out of wood. Perishable construction materials are the reason ancient urban sites are scarce in India and Southeast Asia.

A more reliable mark of civilization is the division of labor, but there is a question as to what degree of division constitutes civilization. Accumulation of agricultural surpluses by taxation, trade, or force makes it possible for a small percentage of a population, often in cities, to devote their lives to high cultural activities. Traders, warriors, tax collectors, priests, and scribes all used specialized skills and represent a division of tasks in society. This division evolved from a presumed original situation in which all families in a community engaged in roughly the same tasks, mostly involving food production.

Later, some people became specialized herders of animals, and others concentrated on farming. The herders produced animal skins, and at some point they began to trade their skins to people who specialized in making leather, fur, or hair products. These people used dyes and tanning materials collected by themselves or by specialists. Still further division led to tanners providing leather for other specialists, such as shoemakers and saddlers. Responding to growing diversity in demand, the shoemakers then subdivided into sandal makers, booters, makers of fancy shoes, makers of work shoes, etc.

In every field of endeavor early history reveals evidence of increasing division of labor in association with what we consider civilization.

Conjunctures

Diffusionism and Prehistoric Trade

The common idea of long-distance trade does not always apply in the ancient world. Marketplaces where goods from distant lands are openly bartered or sold were probably less common than situations in which powerful figures, such as rulers or temple priests, arranged for goods to be imported without a market to determine prices or to balance supply and demand. Consequently, it is hard to determine how long-distance trade originated. Nevertheless, it certainly existed before civilization.

Pieces of obsidian, a volcanic glass that was particularly good for chipping into sharp blades, have been discovered at a number of archaeological sites and traced by chemical analysis to a specific island in the Mediterranean Sea. Similarly, a soft, dark blue, precious stone called lapis lazuli, which even now is most abundant in the northeastern panhandle of Afghanistan, was used prehistorically for jewelry and decoration fifteen hundred miles away in Mesopotamia. These are two examples of valuable materials that were carried long distances before the development of states or empires.

How did people in Afghanistan discover that Mesopotamians prized their stones? Did someone carry a backpack full of them all the way to the Tigris River by chance? Or was there a chain of intermediate exchange points? Archaeology cannot answer these questions clearly, but probably goods that traveled far passed through many hands and were part of a complex network of exchange that began before most hallmarks of civilization became evident.

Communication and exchange between human groups is natural and continuous and does not depend upon cities, or civilization, or even merchants. One of the most important scholarly debates of the prehistoric and early ancient periods concerns diffusionism. Diffusionism is the belief that similar or identical things, styles, and ideas are more likely to originate in one place and spread from there than to originate in two unconnected places. In its extreme form diffusionism borders on racism, as in the case of the theory that Egyptian civilization was started by a conquering race of superior people who were not African.

In the case of Mediterranean obsidian and Afghan lapis lazuli, it can be proven that specific items were carried enormous distances in prehistoric and early historic times. In other cases of supposed diffusion, such as that of Stonehenge, where it was theorized that visitors from the "civilized" eastern Mediterranean brought with them the idea of massive stone buildings, archaeologists have disproved the connection. So some things do diffuse, and others develop independently. There is no single right theory. Increasingly, however, scholars are testing each case of apparent diffusion as scientifically as possible and preferring the idea of continual contact and exchange through networks and intermediaries to ideas about conquering races or trader adventurers.

The Conquests of Alexander the Great

Alexander of Macedon accomplished the first great coming together of Europe, Asia, and Africa. His career, short though it was, is a pivotal event in ancient history. Textbooks that

deal with ancient history at all give the basic information about Alexander's conquests, which extended from Egypt to Pakistan. They do not always point out, however, how enduring Alexander's image was in the lands he affected.

Alexandria of Egypt was one of the cities Alexander founded. After his death it became the greatest city of the age. Being situated well west of the mouth of the Nile, Alexandria did not become the capital of Egypt so much as the capital of an eastern Mediterranean world unified by Alexander. Alexandretta on the coast of Syria was also founded by Alexander, and the generals who divided his empire after him followed his example by founding other cities, including Antioch, the principal ancient city of northern Syria, founded by Antiochus.

The archaeological site of Ay Khanum in northern Afghanistan, a region that was conquered by Alexander and became a separate kingdom after his death, has all the characteristics of a Greek city. Moreover, Greek art from northern Afghanistan heavily influenced the early development of Buddhist sculpture in northern Pakistan.

The heritage of Alexander survived more generally in poems and legends about him written down over a thousand years later in Persian and Arabic. Iskandar remains a popular man's name in several Middle Eastern languages down to the present day, just as Alexander does in English. The Alexander legend spread as far as Indonesia, where it was believed that the first mythical king was the brother of the king of China, on the one hand, and Alexander the Great, on the other. In that legend Alexander is called the king of Rome, however, which shows how jumbled historical memories can be.

A few rare individuals—Alexander, Julius Caesar, Genghis Khan, Napoleon—leave profound personal impacts on history more because of their deeds than their ideas. It is important to know what they actually did; but it is equally important to realize that legends and stories about them, even wildly inaccurate ones, influence people's lives for generations and even centuries after their deaths.

Comparisons

The Origins of Writing: China and Mesopotamia

It is important to realize that writing did not originate in just one way or for just one purpose. The earliest writings in Mesopotamia and in Mycenaean Greek reflect a need to keep track of things. They are mostly composed of storage records, delivery records, and so forth. Only after the technique was developed did it become a means of recording ideas, laws, and historical information.

In the Mesopotamian case, it appears that originally tiny

baked clay tokens in different shapes were used as counters. If a clay triangle represented one storage jar of wheat, for example, the door of a storeroom might be sealed with a ball of clay with a number of triangles packed inside it equal to the number of jars in the room. The practice of pressing the shape of the token onto the outside of the clay ball to show what was sealed on the inside may have been the origin of writing on clay. Certainly, some of the earliest signs for things have the same shapes as the tokens found by archaeologists. Later, other signs were invented.

Sounds came to be represented as well as things, and there was a shift to making marks by pressing the triangular point of a stylus into the clay instead of scratching lines. These changes marked the invention of cuneiform, or wedge-shaped, writing, which was used for a number of languages in and around Mesopotamia from the beginning of civilization until after Alexander's conquests.

By contrast, in China, as in Egypt, the earliest known writing had little to do with record keeping. Tortoise shells and animal bones bearing early forms of some of the Chinese characters still in use today date to before 1000 B.C.E. The characters are accompanied by carved indentations in the shell or bone, burn marks in the indentations, and cracks spreading outward from the indentations. The purpose of the "oracle bones" was to divine the future. A hot poker was placed in a carved indentation, and the character of the crack produced by the heat foretold the future. The writing then made a record of the act of divination.

Ritual divining was an important duty of the earliest Chinese kings and a source of their authority. This impression of writing being used as an accompaniment of ritual, rather than for financial records, is reinforced by the appearance of other early Chinese characters cast in bronze on ritually important vessels and bells.

The lesson this comparison teaches is that the actual technique of conveying language by written signs has little to do with what the language is used for. The haphazard preservation of early writing also distorts our understanding of its purposes. For example, the Chinese may have written storage inventories on perishable bark that has entirely disappeared, leaving only the oracle bones and bronzes.

Eventually, of course, all societies adopted writing for the same array of purposes. Originally, however, writing seems to have played very different roles in different societies. While the Sumerians in Mesopotamia used cuneiform for record keeping and the Chinese used character writing for divining, the ancient Indians believed the sacred hymns of the Rig Veda should be passed from generation to generation by memory alone. They thus created a sophisticated, and unquestionably civilized, literature many centuries before belatedly adopting a writing system and committing the Rig Veda to writing.

Irrigation and Society

Karl Wittfogel wrote an influential book called *Oriental Despotism* in which he argued that the need to coerce people into working together to build and maintain irrigation systems was an important factor in the origin of civilization. This "hydraulic theory" of history is no longer popular because it was too exaggerated, but Wittfogel rightly demonstrated an important connection between irrigation and social organization. However, there are several different types of connection.

In ancient Egypt the Nile River rose gently at the end of each summer and inundated the valley on either side. Just as today, it was virtually the only fresh water source in Egypt, but today the Aswan High Dam contains the flood and keeps the river level steady all year round. The Nile valley was originally swampy until the climate achieved its present state of extreme dryness around 2500 B.C.E. Gradually, farmers moved from side valleys and the desert fringe into the flood area. They had to cooperate in building temporary dikes to hold the water on the land so it could soak in, but there was no need to organize a unified irrigation system for the country as a whole.

Egypt became a unified kingdom early in its history, but the Nile's influence on the process had more to do with it being the country's main transportation route and providing a common environment and life experience for the people living near it—and few people lived anywhere else in Egypt—than with its irrigation system.

Mesopotamia, on the other hand, contained two rivers, the Tigris and the Euphrates, that flooded tumultuously every spring. The floods were dangerous and destructive. Farming was done not during the torrid summer but during the cooler winter, so irrigating the crops meant lifting or channeling water from the rivers during their low stage rather than trying to utilize the floods. This meant building partial dams to raise water levels, digging long canals, and keeping the dams and canals in good repair. Mesopotamia seems, therefore, to provide a good example of what Wittfogel proposed. Yet as in Egypt, civilization began in Mesopotamia when the land was much wetter than it later became, and the people in the earliest city-states used small-scale irrigation rather than lengthy canals.

A third example comes from Iran, where even today thousands of villages get their water by *qanat*. A qanat is like an artificial spring. It is an underground canal that leads ground water from a hillside to the lands below. Canals may be as long as fifteen kilometers. Specialists are hired to calculate the underground slope and supervise the digging. The process requires a great deal of labor and money, and any village that depends on a qanat has a common need to keep it in good repair. But each qanat is separate and does not necessitate cooperation between villages.

Irrigation, therefore, can lead to or accompany social organization on a large scale or a small scale. It is not the sole explanation of the rise of civilization, however. Nor is it the only basis for social organization. Mayan civilization in the Yucatan, for example, utilized farming techniques that required cooperative building of elevated fields; and elaborate terracing of hillsides, which requires planning and cooperation, is an ancient practice in Lebanon.

The Late Ancient Period

The Greco-Roman world from Spain to Syria and the rise of the Han dynasty in northern China represent the poles of historical documentation and interest in this period. The Silk Road across Iran and Central Asia connected these regions, but contact remained fairly slight, just as Roman forays across the Sahara were insufficient to bring sub-Saharan Africa into the ken of Roman civilization. Themes worth mentioning that might not be highlighted in your textbook are:

Africa

The general outline of Western civilization that has been followed for generations has Greece as the first major focus but recognizes some sort of earlier role for Egypt. Egypt provided a model of civilized life that the Greeks appreciated and borrowed from, but it was a model that owed nothing to the ethnic groups inhabiting Europe. That the Egyptians were Africans is too often ignored.

In the same way, North Africa is too often considered simply the southern shore of the Mediterranean Sea. The Sahara desert is similar to the Mediterranean in being both a barrier and a connector. In both cases, it was usually safer and easier to go around the edges than to go directly across. Consequently, the Nile valley was an important link to sub-Saharan Africa. A less important link existed between Morocco and sub-Saharan Africa in the west. Crossing the Sahara in the center was seldom done.

The question of the skin color of the Africans who created and sustained Egyptian civilization remains under debate, though Africans who would be considered "black" in present-day American terms certainly played a role. It should be recognized that the Egyptians remained Africans even while being ruled by the Greek Ptolemies and by the Romans.

India

Strikingly little is known about the history of India in ancient times. The reason is that there are very few written sources. Yet the religious and philosophical literature of ancient India is sophisticated and abundant. This phenomenon can be used to discuss whether an interest in recording history is a natural inclination of civilized people. If recording history is simply a cultural choice that some literate, civilized peoples make and other don't, as the Indian example seems to show, then students can usefully discuss why people decide to record their history at all. History should be seen not as something natural or automatic but as an idea. Different peoples developed different ideas about what was important and worth recording, and some of them simply didn't think historical facts were worth the effort.

City-States

The term *city-state* covers many types of political organization. The ancient city-states of Mesopotamia coalesced around kings and gods considered as the guardians of the city. The Greek *polis,* on the other hand, conveyed a stronger conception of citizenship than of urbanism. Sparta, for example, did not have a heavily urbanized center, but it had a fierce sense of citizenship. The Greeks believed citizenship meant participating in the affairs of the polis, sometimes as voters and sometimes as fighters. People who lived far away from the polis, in overseas colonies, for example, could not really function as citizens. Therefore, they made their colony into a new polis.

Rome began as a small farming town. When it passed from being a monarchy to being a republic, notions of participatory citizenship were added to older ideas of local tribes, kings, and gods. But the Romans gradually dispensed with the idea that citizens had to be local residents. They pioneered new concepts of citizenship that culminated, under the Roman Empire, in the idea of everyone being a citizen of Rome.

The Christian idea of all Christians sharing a kind of citizenship in the "City of God" takes off from this Roman conception of geographically dispersed citizenship. In both cases, citizens were bound to one another by shared beliefs and laws rather than by proximity or ethnic identity.

Conjunctures

Hellenism

In the centuries following Alexander the Great's conquests, Hellenism became an international culture. Throughout the Mediterranean basin and as far eastward as northern Afghanistan and Pakistan, educated, urbanized people came to esteem the art, philosophy, literature, and drama of the Greeks, or Hellenes. Greek was the lingua franca of this culture, but Hellenism influenced people who wrote in other languages as well. Roman art and Latin literature, for example, drew heavily upon Greek models and ideals.

Many different peoples adopting a single language for high culture alongside their own languages and cultures is not uncommon historically. The Chinese culture of northern China gradually spread in medieval times to become the dominant high culture of all China, not to mention Japan and Korea. The international Latin culture of medieval Europe has left traces down to today. The Sanskrit culture of India, originally restricted to certain northern areas, became dominant throughout the peninsula and influential in Indonesia and Southeast Asia. Today, English is increasingly becoming the vehicle of Western culture throughout the world.

International cultures have institutional frameworks. The Roman Catholic church and the late medieval universities fostered Latin culture in Europe, for example. Hellenism was supported by the *gymnasium,* a kind of secondary school found in every Hellenistic city. Gymnasia were uncommon before Alexander, but they became the means of sustaining Greek ideals and language in the farflung *poleis* he and his successors established, as well as instruments for teaching these things to non-Greek citizens.

Alexandria became the center of Hellenistic culture. Established in Egypt by Alexander himself, it was nevertheless more Mediterranean than Egyptian, partly because it was not on the Nile River. People from many lands around the Mediterranean came to the melting pot of Alexandria and contributed their talents to a culture that made important advances in science and learning. The Alexandrian pattern of cosmopolitan learning was repeated in Pergamon in Turkey and on the Aegean island of Cos.

Later, the Byzantine cities of Constantinople and Antioch and the Sassanid city of Jundishapur continued this pattern, which culminated in the medieval Muslim learning centers of Baghdad, Cairo, and Nishapur. The impact of Hellenism thus extended centuries beyond the actual domination of Greek and Macedonian rulers.

The Silk Road

The earliest historically known inhabitants of Central Asia spoke Indo-European languages related to those of India, Iran, and Europe. They herded cattle and engaged in agriculture. Yet they also wandered, some of them settling as far to the east as northwest China. They used oxen for plowing and drawing carts, and in the fourth millennium B.C.E. they adapted two-humped, or Bactrian, camels to these purposes.

At roughly the same period, they began to use domesticated horses. The Indo-European warrior class became enamored of the chariot, a fast, light war vehicle. By the sixth century B.C.E. or so, the Central Asians began to switch from fighting from chariots to fighting on horseback, though they continued to use wheeled vehicles for other purposes. Riding horses instead of using them to draw vehicles gave the Central Asians greater mobility and freedom from settled arts and crafts. Horse-based pastoralism as a way of life spread and was adopted by Eastern peoples speaking Turko-Mongolian languages. These peoples in turn spread westward and mixed with the Indo-Europeans.

The spread of pastoral nomadism and the increased mobility of the Central Asians prepared the way for the Silk Road. The Parthians, who gradually supplanted Alexander the Great's successors in Iran, were pastoral tribesmen from northeast Iran and also, apparently, the earliest Western people to trade regularly with China. Camels, many of them hybrids bred by crossing one-humped (dromedaries) and two-humped animals, carried loads of precious goods from Mesopotamia, across northern Iran, northeastward into Central Asia, across the desert basin of the Tarim River, and down onto the North China Plain. A reverse traffic brought Chinese goods westward.

Pottery figurines of loaded camels are found in contemporary Chinese graves and occasionally at Mesopotamian sites. Many products of Chinese origin, such as citrus fruits and silk, became known in the West this way; and vice versa. Central Asian cities along the Silk Road flourished, and the trade made Central Asia a focal point of Eurasian cultural exchange for almost two millennia.

Comparisons

Buddhism-Taoism-Epicureanism

While there are many differences between religious traditions, certain human inclinations reappear again and again. One of these is mysticism, a feeling of spiritually uniting with something higher and greater than oneself. Another is renunciation of the world either to escape its pains and sorrows or to lead an effortless, natural life. Buddhism, Daoism (Taoism by older transliteration), and Epicureanism all share the tendency to renounce worldly attachments. This does not mean, however, that they are directly connected.

Buddha preached that life is suffering and that the suffering is caused by attachment to things of this world. By renouncing worldly attachments one can hope to minimize suffering until, after many rebirths, one achieves final release through a snuffing out of existence. Daoism, one of the main currents of early Chinese thought, taught that living apart and refusing to be involved in worldly affairs was the way to inner peace and a truly natural life. Epicurus, a Greek philosopher who lived in the third century B.C.E., advocated a withdrawn life of intellectual pleasures enjoyed among friends as an alternative to active involvement with politics and family.

These three schools of thought differ substantially in detail. In the branch of Buddhism characteristic of Southeast

Asia worldly renunciation manifests itself in mendicant monks; Daoist renunciation has come in time to be epitomized by wise and saintly hermits; and the aloof intellectuality of Epicureanism has become popularly, though incorrectly, associated with pleasure seeking. But the three represent parallel ways of reacting to the world.

Comparing religious systems in terms of the promises or hopes they set forth for believers, rather than in terms of specific doctrines, can help students understand common features of human societies. Other topics might include salvation as understood by early Christians and by Egyptian Isis worshipers, sacrifice as understood by the Vedic religion and Aztec religion, and religious law as understood by Judaism and by Islam.

Barbarians

The word *barbarian* conjures up more for us than the original Greek notion of someone whose unintelligible non-Greek language sounds like "bar-bar-bar." It stands for violence, destruction, inhumanity, and uncivilized behavior in general. The peoples whom historians have labeled barbarians, however, were only occasionally guilty of these faults and perhaps no more guilty than their "civilized" foes.

The Germanic tribes on the Roman frontier lived by farming, and the Hsiung-nu on the northern border of China were horse nomads. Both were barbarians in the eyes of the empires they encroached upon, but they were also peoples with sophisticated social systems and codes of behavior. Sometimes political circumstances made raiding so profitable, or conditions of life in their homelands became so precarious, that groups like these (and civilized states, as well!) gave themselves over entirely to warfare. This may have been the case with the Vikings, for example, who apparently suffered from a growing population and a worsening climate in Scandinavia. But most "barbarians" lived peaceable lives most of the time.

Settled states referred to external enemies (and even friends) who did not share their culture as barbarians to emphasize the differences between them. Yet populations continually intermixed in frontier regions, and imperial military forces frequently recruited barbarians into their ranks. When empires fall in the course of conflict with such peoples, as did the western Roman Empire and the Han dynasty, it is superficial to concentrate solely on the barbarian attacks.

Borders between empires and barbarians were social and economic as well as military, and barbarians often played a constructive as much as a destructive role in troubled times. Classical Chinese writings make a distinction between "raw" and "cooked' barbarians. The former, from the Chinese point of view, were inferior because of their lack of familiarity with Chinese culture. They didn't wear silk or drink tea. The latter were accustomed or drawn to silk, tea, and other goods. For this reason they were also targets for Chinese expansion.

This distinction illustrates that there is a gradual continuum between peoples beyond imperial frontiers whose cultures are comparatively autonomous and other peoples whose cultures are heavily influenced by the imperial culture. From the point of view of raw barbarians, cooked barbarians might seem to have abandoned the age-old traditions the raw barbarians remain devoted to. Using the word *barbarian* as Roman or Chinese officials would have used it is therefore highly misleading, since it is a term that by its very nature signifies a prejudicial point of view.

All societies, unfortunately, sometimes think in terms of "us" and "them." This can be recognized historically without accepting the rigidity of definition and the prejudicial implications of the terms used by historical actors. In this sense, a discussion of how barbarians were and are thought of, and by whom, can lead into discussion of stereotyping and prejudicial language in contemporary American society.

The Early Medieval Period

This is an epoch of unprecedented discovery and cultural exchange in Asia, Africa, and eastern Europe, combined with equally remarkable isolation and introversion in western Europe. Buddhism spread from India to China and Southeast Asia. Islam began in the seventh century and spread from Spain to Pakistan. Viking warriors and traders traveled down the rivers of Russia to trade with Iran and serve in the Byzantine army. Turkic tribes increasingly intermingled with Indo-European peoples in Central Asia. The trans-Saharan caravan trade in gold, salt, and slaves forged new connections between North Africa and sub-Saharan Africa. And after centuries of rule in China by small post-Han states, the expansive Tang dynasty created a bigger and stronger empire in the seventh century.

Discovery and cultural exchange were accompanied by scientific, technological, intellectual, and artistic advances of many different sorts. Knowledge of papermaking, printing, and gunpowder spread from China; new concepts in mathematics and physics developed in the Middle East; and philosophy in India culminated in the thought of Shankara (ninth century), the paramount figure in the still pervasive Vedanta religious outlook.

Western Europe's isolation from all of this was due partly to economic decline following the collapse of Roman rule, and partly to hostility and defensiveness vis-à-vis Eastern Christianity and Islam, the two cultures that cut western Europe off from contact with Asia and Africa. Europe's development of a distinctive culture and social system during this period set the stage for its resuming contact with the outside world in the Late Medieval period, when it belatedly adopted many of the Asian scientific and intellectual advances. It can be compared to Japan's isolation from outside influences throughout the Early Modern period, which facilitated a cultural distinctiveness that is an important fact in the world today. Students can debate the cultural benefits and liabilities of isolation and interconnection.

Conjunctures

Conversion to Islam

Like the conquests of Alexander the Great, this is an obvious focus for discussion of world interconnections. The problem is what to concentrate on. There is no way to tell what shares faith in Islam, desire for booty, and military and political leadership had in the extraordinary success of the Arab armies that between 632, when Muhammad died, and 711 created an empire, called the caliphate, from the Pyrenees to the Indus River.

Conversion of the conquered peoples to Islam was a slow process taking three to four centuries. Though Muslims were ruling, they seem not to have planned for or expected wide-scale conversion. Some scholars have argued that people converted out of fear or to escape taxation, which was heavier for non-Muslims; but these explanations are not well supported by evidence. Probably some people converted to improve their social standing or for financial gain, others because they were convinced of the truth of the new faith, and others simply because their friends and relatives had done so. Regardless of people's reasons for converting to it, the Islamic religion, embodying reverence for the Arabic language of the Koran, slowly became the faith of the majority of the population.

The caliphate went from having a thin layer of Muslim Arabs dominating a vast, non-Muslim population to having a common, religiously oriented culture in which almost everyone participated irrespective of native language and previous culture. Some countries, such as Egypt, Syria, and Iraq, adopted the Arabic language and became Arab; others, such as Iran, did not. But the medieval Muslims gave little importance to the differences between Egyptians and Iranians.

Within the Islamic world, movement from city to city and land to land was far easier and more commonplace than in Europe. Muslims traveled far beyond the borders of the caliphate, as well, though seldom into unfriendly western Europe. Travelers became informal emissaries of the Islamic faith and seem to have been the main agents in bringing Islam to many new peoples in sub-Saharan Africa, Central Asia, India, and China from the tenth century onward. The conversion of Indonesia and other parts of Southeast Asia occurred several centuries later under similar influences.

The Crusades

The history of the armed pilgrimages to the Holy Land that came to be known as the Crusades normally concentrates on the four principalities established there by the first crusaders. In terms of meaningful cultural contact and lasting effect, however, less well-known manifestations of the same impulse were more important.

The *Reconquista* in Spain, the early phases of which provided a model for the Crusades, was accompanied by a determined effort to get to know the Muslim enemy's culture. Books translated from Arabic into Latin in Spain brought Europe a new awareness of ancient Greek culture, which the Muslims had preserved and added to. In the Late Medieval period, the expulsion of the Jews (1492) caused the highly learned culture of Spanish Judaism to spread to Holland, North Africa, Greece, Turkey, and Palestine. The more gradual expulsion of the remaining Muslims introduced another new and highly cultured element into North African society. The Norman conquest of Muslim Sicily similarly fostered European learning about the Islamic world, and the Fourth Crusade's sack of Constantinople and subsequent establishment of Latin principalities in Greece and Turkey provided yet a third avenue for Greek and Arabic learning to reach Europe.

The crusading idea remained in vogue for several centuries. Hostility to Islam spurred Portuguese and Spanish attacks on the Muslim kingdoms of North Africa, and hence the voyages of exploration were launched in an effort to bypass those kingdoms and find the source of their riches by sailing down the African coast. European exploration in general might have been less bent on conquest and spreading Christianity if the explorers hadn't had generations of indoctrination in the spirit of crusading behind them.

Comparing the European era of discovery with the earlier era of discovery when Islam, Christianity, and Buddhism traversed the trade routes of Asia and Africa and brought widely separated peoples into cultural contact, we see that what is most striking is the openness of societies in the earlier period and their willingness to engage in cultural give and take without insisting on or fearing domination. The Europeans were decidedly more domineering and insistent on their cultural superiority. This can be seen, in part, as a long-run effect of the Crusades.

Comparisons

Missionaries and Pilgrims

Many religious cultures revere similar types of people: priests who perform rituals, ascetics, mystics, and religious scholars. The religions may differ widely in rituals and in defining asceticism, mysticism, and scholarship, but these activities commonly require a devotion to high and self-denying ideals that impresses less devoted believers favorably. Two less universal religious types, missionaries and pilgrims, played important roles as cultural intermediaries in the Early Medieval period.

Missionaries are better known in Christianity than in other religions. Accounts of their semilegendary exploits, mainly in unconverted regions of northern and eastern Europe, left a tradition in Christianity that later revived as Christians encountered the rest of the world during and after the voyages of discovery. Islam and Buddhism, which spread as widely as Christianity, put much less emphasis on missionaries. Hinduism, Zoroastrianism, and Judaism, which saw themselves exclusively as the religions of the Indians, the Iranians, and the Israelites, put little emphasis on missionaries.

Pilgrims were more common than missionaries and were important agents of communication between far distant regions. European Christian pilgrims flocked to Rome, Constantinople, the Holy Land, and Santiago de Compostella in northwest Spain. Thousands of Muslims traveled to Mecca for the annual pilgrimage Islam requires the faithful to make, if they are able, at least once in a lifetime. Muslims, like Christians and others, also visited hundreds of smaller holy places closer to home. Hindus traveled to Varanasi (Benares) to bathe in the Ganges River and made pilgrimages to other river shrines as well. And there were many popular Buddhist pilgrimage sites in India, Sri Lanka, Burma, China, and Japan.

Buddhism gives the greatest historical prominence to pilgrims. The men who traveled from China across Central Asia or around Southeast Asia to visit early Buddhist sites in India earned special historical recognition because of the sacred texts they brought back with them for translation. This phenomenon is similarly important, though less celebrated, in other religions. Islamic reform movements in eighteenth-century China and Indonesia, for example, owed much to the lessons learned and writings brought back by pilgrims to Mecca.

Seafaring

After the opening of the Suez Canal in 1869, it became commonplace to think of the Red Sea as the link between the Mediterranean Sea and the Indian Ocean. But prior to then, the unfavorable winds of the Red Sea had made it more often a barrier to communication. It was so effective a barrier, in fact, that the ship-building technology and sail designs of the ancient and medieval Mediterranean were entirely different from those of the Indian Ocean. European shipwrights nailed a skeleton of ribs to the plank sides of their boats, while dhow builders in the Persian Gulf bored holes in the planks and tied them together with palm-fiber ropes. The Mediterranean

craft used square sails that made it difficult to maneuver against the wind, while the Indian Ocean dhows used more maneuverable triangular sails.

Since maneuverability and speed were important in war, galleys dominated Mediterranean naval engagements. But the large numbers of oarsmen who rowed the galleys required large quantities of food and water. This severely limited the length of time galleys could stay at sea. Naval battles, usually fought close to shore, stressed rowing at top speed to ram and board enemy ships. Cannon were used only when ramming was about to occur, not from long distances.

Though the Vikings used galleys in the stormy North Sea and Atlantic Ocean, ships with higher sides were safer there; and longer voyages could be made by carrying fewer sailors and relying more on the wind. The ships used by Spanish and Portuguese explorers evolved from these considerations. Fewer sailors led to greater reliance on cannon fired from a distance. European ships and naval tactics, developed for the Atlantic Ocean, quickly became dominant in the Indian Ocean after the Europeans reached Asian waters at the end of the fifteenth century, but galleys remained popular in Mediterranean navies for several centuries.

The Late Medieval Period

This is probably the most crucial period to get across to students. They know that the West is the dominant force in today's world, but down to the Late Medieval period they have studied a world that has been only partially and sporadically interconnected. In the Late Medieval period, Europe discovers the rest of the world and simultaneously experiences an intellectual rebirth prompted by the rediscovery of ancient Greek culture. The burgeoning economies of several highly competitive European states capitalize on the discoveries made by the explorers. Exotic goods reach Europe from many lands, and the seeds of later colonial exploitation are sown.

Charting Europe's rise to dominance in this period risks losing sight of the rest of the world. It also raises questions about the periodization. Europe expanded out of its early medieval isolation and provinciality and gained phenomenal momentum, which then carried it into the rest of the world, and into the modern period. By contrast, the other world cultures seemed to subside into comparative isolation or continued to operate within restricted geographical orbits. If dynamism were to be selected as the sole hallmark of the era, therefore, Europe would appear to outclass the world, and the designation of this as a distinctive era would be Eurocentric.

But on the other hand, it was during this period that many cultures attained a culminating expression that later came to be regarded as classical, particularly in Western eyes. That Andean civilization culminated in the Incas and indigenous

Mexican civilization in the Aztecs is obvious since no indigenous empires survived the Spanish onslaught. But what was demonstrably true in those cases, namely, that European political and economic impingement distorted patterns of development in other parts of the world, was true elsewhere to a significant, though lesser, degree.

The Late Medieval period, therefore, may best be thought of as a period of culmination—sometimes, as in Ming China, triumphant culmination—prior to Europe's expansion, and of the revving of the engine of that expansion. Later political and cultural achievements of the Early Modern period may, in some cases, have been more impressive, as in Mogul India; but their attainment was inevitably conditioned, and even distorted, by the presence of a dynamic, expansive Europe.

While fragmented Europe was laying the groundwork for economically based world domination, the colossal, though short-lived achievement of the Mongols in uniting China and the Middle East in a trans-Asian empire dissolved into a number of fragmented Asian states. Though several of these states were very large, the cosmopolitan intermixing that had marked the Mongol period, particularly in bringing Chinese arts and technology, notably printing and gunpowder, westward, slowly gave way to isolation.

China and Japan both became inward looking at the end of the medieval period. So did India under the Delhi sultans and later Mogul emperors. The Ottomans were expansive in Europe and took over most of the Arab world, but the Safavid Empire in Iran stood as a Shi'ite Muslim barrier blocking any possible connection between the Ottomans, the Muslims of South and Southeast Asia, and the Mongol successor states in Central Asia—all peopled predominately by Sunnis.

Why was Asia so amendable to cultural interchange in medieval times and thereafter so inward looking? No one has definitively answered this question, but students can discuss the possible paralyzing impact of European dynamism and expansion, the collapse of Central Asia as a crossroads of civilization in the post-Mongol period, and, as in the Chinese case, the possibility of satisfaction with the level of culture and civilization that had finally been achieved.

From a chronological point of view, this is also a reasonable time to discuss pre-Columbian America and sub-Saharan Africa. Archaeological data about pre-Columbian America reach back into much earlier periods, but the transition from life before the Spaniards to life in the colonial period makes for a vivid lesson. It is important to stress the devastating population decline in the Americas caused by diseases brought by the Europeans. It makes the transition from the wealth and glory of the Incas and Aztecs to the subordination and exploitation of colonial domination more understandable. It also lays the groundwork for later discussion of multi-ethnic society, e.g., African, Indian, and European, in Latin America.

As for Africa, it is important to lay a firm foundation by describing the early historical kingdoms and cultures, such as Zimbabwe in the south and Ghana in the north, before getting into the issue of Muslim and European contacts and slavery. Though few details are known about these kingdoms, they bridge the historical and geographical gap between ancient Egypt and Ethiopia and make it clear that Africa has its own history and identity and was not simply a stage for foreigners to play upon.

Conjunctures

The Mongols

From looking at the Mongols purely as destroyers, many historians have turned to seeing them as politically creative and culturally open-minded. The destruction wrought by the mixed Turkic and Mongol armies of Genghis Khan and his grandsons Hulagu (in the Middle East) and Kublai (in China) struck horror into the hearts of their enemies and was vividly detailed by historians working for the Mongols themselves. The terror they evoked among conquered populations by publicizing the destruction of cities and slaughter of populations undoubtedly helped them to rule their enormous empire with little internal opposition. Messengers carrying the arrow that marked them as emissaries of the Great Khans could travel safely from China to Syria, and Christian missionaries and traders could travel from Europe to China.

The Mongol rulers were religiously tolerant. Members of ruling families frequently belonged to different religions. They also recognized talent among their subjects and called upon their services regardless of ethnic or religious identity. It is unimaginable that a medieval European king would have taken a non-Christian Chinese or Mongol into his service the way Kublai Khan in China did Marco Polo.

The Mongols favored trade and tried to restore economic vitality to the lands they devastated. In the Middle East, much of the destruction blamed on the Mongols had taken place earlier in the course of wars between the petty kingdoms that arose with the breakup of the Islamic caliphate. The Mongols were more attracted to Chinese culture than to Islamic or Christian culture. Among the Chinese cultural traits that reached the West during Mongol times were painting styles that helped transform Persian miniature painting from crude book illustration into a magnificent art form. A more ominous import was gunpowder.

It can be instructive to compare the conquering Arabs, who destroyed relatively little and implanted a new language and religion, with the conquering Mongols, who destroyed and then rebuilt, practiced tolerance, and left little permanent trace. The fact that early Russian history takes place in the shadow of various Mongol successor states should not be interpreted solely as a negative influence. In some of the ways mentioned, the Mongols were more enlightened and creative than the late Byzantines, who also influenced early Russia.

Crossing the Sahara

Rock paintings and inscriptions in the mountainous regions of the central Sahara, where there is sufficient water to sustain a sparse population, show a succession of styles. Different styles are associated with different animals. The earliest paintings show giraffes, elephants, and other big game that could not survive in the Sahara today. These presumably date from before 2500 B.C.E. Then come beautiful depictions of cattle-herding peoples. Many of these pictures bring to mind the cattle herders who today live farther south in the grasslands bordering the desert. Since these pictures must also date from a time when the Sahara was somewhat more moist, the antiquity of African cattle-herding cultures seems apparent. Some of the motifs in the pictures indicate a likely cultural connection with the Nile valley.

Horse people succeeded the cattle people, and many rock paintings depict chariots. Since archaeologists have never found any chariot remains and the climate and terrain make it difficult to see how they could ever have been common, some scholars see the chariot pictures as a visual motif deriving from cultural contact with the Mediterranean world or from population migration from the north.

Camels, originally native to Arabia, began to appear gradually late in the horse period, perhaps around 200 B.C.E. The camel saddle designs indicate a derivation of animals and equipment from the Nile Valley, not from across the Sahara, where camels were unknown until several centuries later and where a different technology was used.

Until the eighth century C.E., therefore, communication and trade across the Sahara seems to have been rare. The sub-Saharan cultures developed separately, with external influences coming from the Nile Valley and from Indian Ocean seafarers who reached the African coast from faraway Indonesia and implanted their language on the island of Madagascar.

By the tenth century, however, Saharan trade with North Africa had become a major enterprise. Gold from the Niger River region was the mainstay of Islamic coinage in the Mediterranean lands. The organization of caravans brought merchants from northern oases, Saharan camel nomads, and sub-Saharan peoples into a complex and productive relationship. Important caravan cities, such as Timbuktu, developed in the south, and Islam became an important religious influence and source of political organization. Most Africans living north of the forest zone of Central Africa are Muslim today because of the connections with Mediterranean Islamic culture forged at that time. Enormous trucks now traverse the Sahara in the place of camel caravans, and strong political connections between the north and south sides of the desert continue.

Comparisons

Bureaucratic States: The Ottoman Empire and Ming China

Empires have always experienced common problems of controlling outlying areas, defending frontiers, and collecting revenues. In ancient times most empires were really collections of separate peoples with different customs, religions, political traditions, and methods of fighting. Paramount kings often ruled through alliances with the many minor kings and chiefs within their realm. In the war between Alexander the Great and the Iranian king Darius III, for example, both armies were divided into ethnic groups that followed their own customs.

The Roman Empire evolved a new concept with the idea of universal Roman citizenship. The Islamic caliphate and Byzantine Empire combined that concept with religion, saying that dominion belonged to all of the members of the dominant faith irrespective of ethnic background. Local customs and loyalties persisted, of course, but they became less important politically.

The Early Medieval period ended with political fragmentation and disruption rife in most of Europe, Asia, and the historically known parts of Africa. The Late Medieval period, by contrast, witnessed the development of increasingly effective centralized kingdoms in Europe, namely, the Holy Roman Empire, France, and England, and the establishment of several large centralized states elsewhere: the Ottoman Empire in Turkey, the Balkans, and the Middle East; the Safavid Empire in Iran; the Mogul Empire in India; and the Ming dynasty in China. All of these states were faced with problems stemming from the acceleration of trade and economic life in the preceding period and the spreading use of firearms. Firearms undermined the position of medieval warrior elites by making it possible for a minimally trained soldier to kill a knight.

The Ottoman and Ming states responded to these problems in different ways, building on earlier practices in their respective regions. The Ottomans created a professional, and technically enslaved, soldiery by taking boys from Christian communities under their control, educating them and converting them to Islam in training barracks, and assigning them to the janissary corps, a special infantry force equipped with firearms.

The most talented recruits were trained in the palace school in Istanbul and assigned jobs in the sultan's palace service. From there they might be promoted to become military commanders and even grand viziers. This system provided the state with an elite centralized army, the best in Europe, complemented by rural-based Muslim cavalrymen; a well-educated and loyal group of top commanders and administrators; and an ethos that elevated the prestige of "being an Ottoman" and speaking the refined Turkish of the court. Though the empire was multi-ethnic and multireligious, its core ruling class surmounted such divisions and developed a centralized system. By the seventeenth century, however, internal cleavages and economic difficulties were combining with pressure from external enemies to break the system down.

The Ming dynasty, in contrast with the bellicose Ottomans, held military service in low regard. A civilian ruling elite was recruited through a nationwide examination system begun under the preceding Song dynasty. Aspirants spent years studying the Confucian classics in hopes of passing the examination. Those who were successful usually came from well-to-do families that could afford good tutors and did not need their sons for other purposes. Once part of the imperial educated elite, Ming officials, or mandarins, were rotated frequently from province to province to prevent their developing strong local attachments. The highest-ranking mandarins controlled the examination system from the capital and formed a core of powerful advisers who coached the emperor in his decisions.

The ideal of merit-based civilian government with a national interest and outlook fostered by a systematic rotation of officials seems like a sound basis for stable and prolonged rule. But monarchies are vulnerable internally to the indolence or incompetence of rulers and to the formation of court factions, and autocratic regimes dominated by socially isolated elite groups frequently lose touch with the common citizenry and fail to appreciate their discontent. (These are problems of all bureaucratic empires down to and including the former Soviet Union.) Like the Ottomans, the Ming could not sustain the effectiveness and unity of their system indefinitely. Internal rebellion, factional infighting at court, and finally Manchu invasion from the north brought the dynasty to an end at the beginning of the seventeenth century.

The Ottoman and Ming empires, and other centralizing kingdoms that might be brought into comparison with them, such as the Moguls in India and the Holy Roman Empire under Charles V in Europe, exhibited creative but ultimately inflexible solutions to the problems of the era. Complex economies, large territories, and diverse populations could not easily be welded into an empire on the previously adequate basis of ethnic or personal loyalty. Imperial success or failure in the Late Medieval period was largely determined by each regime's effectiveness in forging new governing techniques from earlier traditions. By this measure, the Ottoman and Ming empires were notably successful.

Japan was one of the few regions to escape the new trend by isolating itself and totally abolishing the use of firearms. Ethnic homogeneity, limited territory, government built on personal loyalty of a feudal character, and universal devotion to the person and cult of a symbolic, nonruling emperor highlight the differences between Japan and the Ottoman and Ming empires.

The Early Modern Period

The work of Immanuel Wallerstein and other historians sharing his views has become increasingly influential in discussions of the Early Modern period. Wallerstein maintains that during that period a "world system" matured in which Europe was the economic world center, and other regions, including outlying parts of Europe itself, were on the periphery. The European center directly or indirectly exerted economic and political control over the periphery and subordinated the economies of the peripheral regions to European consumption needs. Independent cultural and social traditions slowly withered as the impact of the European economy deepened, and new social and political structures developed to cater to European needs. This resulted, by the end of the period, in enforced underdevelopment and intellectual stagnation in the periphery while Europe luxuriated in increasing wealth, intellectual dynamism, and political power.

The Wallerstein approach describes Europe's sudden rise to world domination from a perspective in which the Enlightenment and the industrial revolution are seen not just as episodes in European history, but as manifestations of a European world system that simultaneously stifled intellectual and economic dynamism in the periphery. This approach has the advantage of making the "underdevelopment" of the non-Western world in the early twentieth century easier to understand, but many historians feel that it overstresses economic factors and concentrates unduly on European history and on the European aspects of non-European history.

After World War II many thinkers, particularly in the United States, thought that the world was destined to become more and more uniform as "modernization" guided the world's peoples toward Western-style democracy, industry, and secularism. According to this vision of the future, non-Western cultures and traditions would gradually cease to be important. Today, however, it is recognized that despite the Western origin of our increasingly worldwide industrial society, other parts of the world are bringing their own distinct traditions and historical viewpoints into that society as they become part of it.

Consequently, it is important in teaching the Early Modern period to balance the story of European efflorescence and domination with stories of how other cultures developed and survived. Possible focuses are: (1) the survival of African traditions in the Americas and the Caribbean during colonial times, to be followed up later by a discussion of their integration into the culture of the Americas in modern times; (2) the efforts at internal reform and resistance to European pressure made by eighteenth-century Muslim groups in Arabia (the Wahhabis) and sub-Saharan Africa (the Fulani jihads), to be followed up later by discussion of the Iranian revolution and today's worldwide reassertion of Muslim identity.

Conjunctures

The Impact of American Gold and Silver

Many different substances have served as money, from shells in Africa and Southeast Asia, to beads in North America, to bits of metal in most historic societies, to pieces of paper today. To be effective tokens of exchange, money must be controlled in quantity and value. If the amount of money grows faster than the supply of goods people want to buy, inflation results. If too little money is in circulation, people have a hard time transacting business.

Until modern times, however, governments did not keep track of how much money was in circulation. Since coins last much longer than paper money, there was always a possibility of too much money flooding the market. On the other hand, if the metal used for coins became scarce, there might be too little money in circulation. The advantage of using gold and silver for coinage, other than the fact that they look pretty and don't rust away, was that they were comparatively rare. Metal for new coins came from melting down old coins, foreign coins, jewelry, and ornaments and from newly mined gold and silver. Since the amount of new gold and silver mined each year was small and fairly steady, the gold- and silver-based coinage systems—the Chinese used copper—were fairly stable, with the rate of exchange between the two metals changing only slowly over the centuries.

When the Spaniards conquered the Incas and Aztecs in the sixteenth century, they took possession of enormous quantities of gold and silver. This fluke of fate provided a powerful stimulus for further European exploring. Indeed, one wonders whether the Chinese of the late medieval Ming dynasty would have sent out more exploring expeditions than they did if one of their captains had brought back an equivalent shipload of gold. The initial shipments from the New World were followed by many more, as silver mines in Mexico and South America were exploited using forced Indian labor.

This "cheap" silver unbalanced the monetary systems of Europe. Inflation brought on a collapse of the Spanish economy at the end of the sixteenth century, and inflationary forces caused severe problems as far east as the Ottoman Empire and beyond. A price revolution set in as prices rose

to meet the increased volume of coinage in circulation. People living on fixed amounts of money, from certain feudal dues, for example, suffered. People investing in growing commercial enterprises prospered. In short, the historical accident that the Spanish explorers happened upon the richest parts of the New World, instead of the forests of Maine or the Amazon jungles, played an important role in transforming the European and world economies in the Early Modern period.

Joint Stock Companies and Asian Trade

Since ancient times long-distance trade has been organized in many ways. Sometimes rulers have controlled it. Sometimes traders have been left to their own devices. In medieval times merchant partnerships became common in both Europe and the Islamic world. Partners would share risks and profits, sometimes with one partner contributing the money to buy the trade goods and the other contributing his time and labor by doing the actual traveling.

Transport and communications being slow and prices fluctuating irregularly, a trader always ran the risk that the buying or selling prices in the city he was heading for would change before he got there. Therefore, the better informed a trader was about market conditions, the better his chance of making a good profit. Knowledge was power, and it was jealously guarded. Many traders preferred to deal only with family or with members of their religious or ethnic group. Venetian, Florentine, Jewish, Armenian, and Hindu traders all tended to stick together.

The appearance of the joint stock company at the beginning of the seventeenth century set off a major change in the world's way of doing business. The Dutch East India Company and the English East India Company were the pioneers. Many partners bought shares in the company, which hired personnel to man its ships and trading posts and defend its interests. More money meant more ships and men and a greater ability to dominate markets.

As time went on, it became clear that the best way to dominate a market was to control production of a product and set its price for all traders. Sugar plantations were established in Europe's West Indian colonies, and the competition destroyed the earlier sugar industry of Egypt and the Mediterranean islands. Coffee, since its initial development in the fourteenth century as the main export of Yemen, was transplanted to Dutch plantations in Java and Spanish plantations in Colombia. The market for Yemeni coffee collapsed.

As joint stock companies and plantation economies increasingly dominated world trade, traditional trading networks withered away. Non-European merchants turned to small-scale or local trading, or found a way to serve the Europeans. One permanent casualty was the Silk Road.

Camel caravans made up of many individual traders could not compete with the European seaborne trading empires. As a result, Central Asia, which had played an important role in world history since the time of Alexander the Great, became an economic and political backwater.

Comparisons

Sufism, Protestantism, and Zen Buddhism

The Islamic world from Indonesia to West Africa saw a proliferation of Sufi brotherhoods from the fourteenth century onward. At the core of each brotherhood were meditative practices and rituals that were supposed to lead the devotees to higher and higher levels of spiritual awareness culminating in a feeling of union with God. Many brotherhoods had chapters in different cities, with each chapter headed by a saintly master. Besides the devotees who were sworn to obey the master, there were many sympathizers who respected the Sufis and revered the masters without following the prescribed practices. In many Muslim cities virtually every male belonged to or associated with at least one brotherhood.

During this same period of time Protestantism arose and spread in Europe. The Protestants divided into sects following the teachings of different leaders. Just as the Sufis wanted to get away from the dry, legalistic teaching of the established Muslim scholars, the Protestants wanted to escape the hierarchy and control of the Roman Catholic church. Both movements stressed a closer, more personal experience of God. Protestantism was a significant force helping spur the emergence of northern Europe as an adventurous and economically aggressive region.

A similar movement away from dry rules and doctrines toward individual religious experience had occurred earlier with the development in Japan of Zen Buddhism (called Chan in China). Personal meditation was the hallmark of Zen teaching. The strong personal discipline required of Zen devotees made it the favorite doctrine of Japan's dominant military class, but it also inspired austerely beautiful achievements in art in both Japan and China.

Movement away from strong divides between religious officials and common believers and toward more personalized religious experience seems characteristic of Late Medieval and Early Modern religion. Meditation and mysticism are frequently stressed. Why at this time so many people in different parts of the world decided they wanted a richer and more personal spiritual experience than the traditional priests and religious legal systems could supply is unclear. It could be related, however, to slowly growing levels of literacy and education, which broke down the monopoly on higher learning that religious specialists had previously so often held.

Slavery Old and New

Slavery is the only common word in English for a less than free condition of life. This is unfortunate, because the world has known many forms of limited freedom, but for Americans the word *slavery* always calls up images of oppressed black farm laborers. When students read of Turkish *mamluks* in Egypt being highly trained soldiers and dominating Egyptian society, calling them slave-soldiers, as is commonly done, seems out of place. What kind of slave owner would train his slaves in military arts and then give them weapons? In the context of the history of the Americas, fear of slave rebellion was common and slaves were not trained to fight. So what does the word *slave* mean in this context?

If by purchase, capture in war, or voluntary contract one person becomes the property of another, we call that acquired person a slave. This concentration on the circumstances in which freedom was lost obscures significant differences, however. Some slaves could look forward to being freed, especially in Islamic lands, where giving slaves their freedom was a pious act. But others knew that their descendants would be slaves in perpetuity, as was the case with most black slaves in the Americas. Some slaves were valued for their education, as were many Greek slaves in Roman times. Others were deliberately kept illiterate and ignorant. Some slaves were put into elite military units and rose to exercise great political power over ordinary citizens, as did the mamluks of Egypt and the Ottoman janissaries. Others were utterly deprived of any political role, as were slaves in ancient Greece and in the United States.

The massive and gruesome exportation of Africans to the New World and to the Islamic world should be seen as a distinctive and particularly heinous form of slavery. In the New World it should also be seen as an outgrowth of the plantation system, which demanded cheap labor, and therefore a characteristic feature of the Early Modern period. Black slaves in the Islamic world were less numerous and generally fared somewhat better, since there was no plantation system to consume their labor. Students can be prompted to discuss whether freed slaves who remained bound by poverty and lack of skills to their old jobs or masters can properly be called free. This phenomenon is of common occurrence in the history of slavery.

The Modern Period

As we near the end of the twentieth century, it becomes increasingly clear that the nineteenth and twentieth centuries fit very well together as a historical period. The twenty-first century, on the other hand, is extremely difficult to visualize as a simple projection of what we see in the world around us today. Imperialism climaxed in the nineteenth century with the scramble for Africa, and it collapsed in the late twentieth century with worldwide decolonization. Socialism began as a radical vision in the nineteenth century, climaxed with the rise of the Soviet Union to potential world domination, and collapsed in the last decade of the twentieth century. Nationalism was invented in the nineteenth century, achieved repeated success in providing the foundations for new states, and began to become dysfunctional in the late twentieth century as ethnic groups pressed for autonomy in some countries, and migration diminished ethnic homogeneity in others.

Throughout the rise and fall of "isms," however, some trends remained fairly constant and fundamentally changed the character of the world. World population vastly increased. Pressure on resources, with attendant degradation of the environment and loss of wild places, increased. War and civil violence became increasingly destructive. Public health and biomedical discoveries lengthened lifespans, controlled serious diseases, and improved health. Literacy and education became more widespread. Transportation and communication became faster and more available.

In each of these areas, the Early Modern period from 1600 to 1800 saw only modest change. The nineteenth century was the take-off period of rapid change, and the twentieth century marked the climax of world transformation. Where the late nineteenth century saw a world dominated by a confident Europe that had little inkling of the disasters—war, revolution, loss of empire—awaiting it, most people today see more problems than bright spots when they look toward the coming century.

As for the non-Western world, scarcely a generation has passed since the achievement of independence from imperialistic domination. Today's high school students live in a world in which the problems and demands of the poorer non-Western nations and the economic dynamism of the richer non-Western nations reduce the role of Europe and North America in world affairs to proportions more in keeping with their size and resources. If the creation of a world system with Europe at its core is viewed as the main defining characteristic of global history in the Early Modern and Modern periods, it seems certain that a new world system is in the offing.

Although even professional twentieth-century historians have a difficult time doing it, it is desirable to rise above the minutiae of world wars, revolutions, and presidencies and talk to students about how the history of the late twentieth century is the prologue to their own lives. People who lived through the Great Depression, or World War II, or the Cold War, or the Vietnamese War sometimes feel that younger people don't understand the "lessons" of history that they themselves learned the hard way. But in teaching students how we got to where we are today, it is important to remember that their future will be different from our past. We should teach them about the recent past not didactically or moralistically, but with an eye toward what the students may see as coming next.

Conjunctures

An Era of Migration

Small shiploads of adventurers and emigrants and migrating bands of farmers and herders have made history from earliest times by pioneering new territory or encroaching on other people's land. Improved transportation and population growth in the Modern period, however, made possible a tremendous increase in human migration. Immigration history in the nineteenth century is well known to most American students, since the United States was a prime beneficiary. Students are less aware, however, of population movements since World War II.

World War II caused much more human displacement than World War I, most notably by accelerating the migration of European Jews to Palestine (after 1948 Israel). Postwar decolonization and political upheaval in some of the new Asian and African states brought large numbers of immigrants to Europe: colonists returning from Algeria to France, Indians fleeing to Great Britain from persecution in East Africa, Latin Americans escaping dictatorial rule to Spain and North America, and so forth. Some countries with growing populations pushed into sparsely settled areas, most notably the Chinese in Tibet and Central Asia, and the Brazilians in the Amazon basin. Other countries—Vietnam, Lebanon, Afghanistan, and Iran, for example—suffered wars or revolutions that forced thousands into exile. *Refugee* is one of the key words of the late twentieth century.

Economic necessity was probably a greater spur to movement than anything else, however. Mexicans and Latin Americans were attracted by greater opportunities in North America. Arabs and Turks flocked to Europe for jobs. And Pakistanis and other Asian Muslims found employment in the newly rich oil states of the Arabian Peninsula. In the extreme case of the contemporary United Arab Emirates, 80 percent of the population is foreign born. In all of these cases, the welcome such economic immigrants received was tempered by fears that they might stay permanently and seek citizenship.

One of the hallmarks of world politics in the Modern period has been nationalism, the belief that people who share a common language and territory deserve political recognition and independence. Before the nineteenth century, shared religious beliefs or being subjects of a common monarch were generally thought of as adequate bases for political identity. Nationalism sprang up partly as a substitute for religious identity and partly because the scientific study of languages made people aware of the shared traits of different dialects. For example, nationalistic Italians in the nineteenth century built a unified kingdom and supported it with an ideology in which the separate dialects of Naples, Venice, and Sicily were recognized as mere variants of a single, shared Italian language. In the twentieth century the Arabs tried the same thing by calling, unsuccessfully, for a unified Arab nation even though the colloquial Arabic of Morocco is almost unintelligible to the man on the street in Iraq.

Today, worldwide population movements are breaking down the assumptions of linguistic and territorial homogeneity that underlies nationalism. The idea of a multilingual united Europe is a postnationalist phenomenon, but even advocates of European unity are sometimes dismayed by the growing proportion of immigrant Muslims in their midst. Some Americans are similarly apprehensive of the large numbers of new immigrants in the United States. What is important to convey to students is that the massive population movements of the Modern period have fundamentally changed the world and are continuing to change it, but that there is nothing inherently good or bad about the phenomenon as a whole.

The Changing Face of War

The Modern period began with the Napoleonic Wars, which haunted Europe for the rest of the nineteenth century. It is culminating in the waning of the threat of nuclear annihilation. Between these two points, the growth of the importance and destructiveness of war has been a hallmark of the period. The desire to defend themselves against European intrusion stimulated the Chinese and the Ottomans to begin modernizing their armies and societies in the early nineteenth century, and a desire to compete with the Europeans in territorial expansion caused Japan to create a powerful army in the early twentieth century. Meanwhile, armament makers invented the machine gun, dynamite, poison gas, aerial bombardment, and much more.

Economists have tried with limited success to calculate the benefits of military research and technological development. Many of the outstanding scientific achievements of the Modern period have been made in response to military needs. Atomic power and space exploration are obvious examples. Yet who is to say that devoting those same scientific resources to civilian needs would not have produced equivalent achievements? Japan's rapid rise to a dominating position in electronics owed little or nothing to the Japanese defense budget.

Regardless of whether one can discover economic benefits in war and preparation for war, modern warfare has caused unbelievable suffering and loss in almost every part of the world. Never before has the power to kill and destroy been so great or so indiscriminately applied. Nor has there ever been a historical equivalent to the fear of global annihilation that the current generations have lived with.

Until recently, it was generally accepted that European armaments and politics were the governing considerations in most modern wars. In the nineteenth century colonial wars between rival European powers, or between Europeans and non-Europeans, were fought all over the world. In the last few decades, wars between Pakistan and India, Israel and the Arab states, and Ethiopia and Somalia were fought with weapons produced by the United States and the Soviet Union and ended when supplies ran short.

The war between Iran and Iraq was the first major conflict since World War II over which the Western powers and the Soviet Union had only limited control. Partly this is because many countries now manufacture and export modern arms, and partly it is because the rivalry between Arab nationalism and Islamic revolution has almost nothing to do with Western politics. As a possible harbinger of things to come, the Iran-Iraq war is another indicator that the era of European, or American-European, world domination is coming to an end.

Conclusion

The foregoing presentation on themes, conjectures, and comparisons in world history was written as a chapter of an unpublished longer work on teaching world history at the precollege level. After writing it, I became one of six authors of a college-level world history textbook, *The Earth and Its Peoples.* This experience reinforced my conviction that even the best-conceived textbook confronts teachers with a lot of trees and only a sketchy map of the forest.

A century ago, the idea of progress, variously defined, served as a beacon guiding historians through the undergrowth. Following this beacon proved psychologically rewarding for European and American historians because Europe and America seemed to be the motherland and logical culmination of historical progress. Today, few historians would confidently predict a long continuation of Euro-American world supremacy. But then again, few historians, looking back on the work of their predecessors, see the light of progress as a beacon. It more often looks like a paralyzing beam in the dark preventing a doomed animal from looking elsewhere.

Today's students will live their lives in the twenty-first century, which seems destined to evolve very differently from its two predecessors. Lessons on how their forebears emerged for a while on the top of the heap of world events are of less use to them than lessons on the ebb and flow of power and achievement in world history and the necessity of seeing the world whole in order to come to an understanding of their own place in it.

19

Southernization

Lynda Shaffer

The term *southernization* is a new one. It is used here to refer to a multifaceted process that began in southern Asia and spread from there to various other places around the globe. The process included so many interrelated strands of development that it is impossible to do more here than sketch out the general outlines of a few of them. Among the most important that will be omitted from this discussion are the metallurgical, the medical, and the literary. Those included are the development of mathematics; the production and marketing of subtropical or tropical spices; the pioneering of new trade routes; the cultivation, processing, and marketing of southern crops such as sugar and cotton; and the development of various related technologies.

The term *southernization* is meant to be analogous to *westernization*. Westernization refers to certain developments that first occurred in western Europe. Those developments changed Europe and eventually spread to other places and changed them as well. In the same way, southernization changed southern Asia and later spread to other areas, which then underwent a process of change.

Southernization was well under way in southern Asia by the fifth century C.E., during the reign of India's Gupta kings (320–535 C.E.). It was by that time already spreading to China. In the eighth century various elements characteristic of southernization began spreading through the lands of the Muslim caliphates. Both in China and in the lands of the caliphate, the process led to dramatic changes, and by the year 1200 it was beginning to have an impact on the Christian Mediterranean. One could argue that within the Northern Hemisphere, by this time the process of southernization had created an Eastern Hemisphere characterized by a rich south and a north that was poor in comparison. And one might even go so far as to suggest that in Europe and its colonies, the process of southernization laid the foundation for westernization.

The Indian Beginning

Southernization was the result of developments that took place in many parts of southern Asia, both on the Indian

subcontinent and in Southeast Asia. By the time of the Gupta kings, several of its constituent parts already had a long history in India. Perhaps the oldest strand in the process was the cultivation of cotton and the production of cotton textiles for export. Cotton was first domesticated in the Indus River valley some time between 2300 and 1760 B.C.E.,[1] and by the second millennium B.C.E. the Indians had begun to develop sophisticated dyeing techniques.[2] During these early millennia Indus River valley merchants are known to have lived in Mesopotamia, where they sold cotton textiles.[3]

In the first century C.E. Egypt became an important overseas market for Indian cottons. By the next century there was a strong demand for these textiles both in the Mediterranean and in East Africa,[4] and by the fifth century they were being traded in Southeast Asia.[5] The Indian textile trade continued to grow throughout the next millennium. Even after the arrival of European ships in Asian ports at the turn of the sixteenth century, it continued unscathed. According to one textile expert, "India virtually clothed the world" by the mid-eighteenth century.[6] The subcontinent's position was not undermined until Britain's industrial revolution, when steam engines began to power the production of cotton textiles.

Another strand in the process of southernization, the search for new sources of bullion, can be traced in India to the end of the Mauryan Empire (321–185 B.C.E.). During Mauryan rule Siberia had been India's main source of gold, but nomadic disturbances in Central Asia disrupted the traffic between Siberia and India at about the time that the Mauryans fell. Indian sailors then began to travel to the Malay Peninsula and the islands of Indonesia in search of an alternative source,[7] which they most likely "discovered" with the help of local peoples who knew the sites. (This is generally the case with bullion discoveries, including those made by Arabs and Europeans.) What the Indians (and others later on) did do was introduce this gold to international trade routes.

The Indians' search for gold may also have led them to the shores of Africa. Although its interpretation is controversial, some archaeological evidence suggests the existence of Indian influence on parts of East Africa as early as 300 C.E. There is also one report that gold was being sought in East

From *Journal of World History* 5 (1994):1–21. Reprinted with permission.

Africa by Ethiopian merchants, who were among India's most important trading partners. The sixth-century Byzantine geographer Cosmas Indicopleustes described Ethiopian merchants who went to some location inland from the East African coast to obtain gold. "Every other year they would sail far to the south, then march inland, and in return for various made-up articles they would come back laden with ingots of gold."[8] The fact that the expeditions left every other year suggests that it took two years to get to their destination and return. If so, their destination, even at this early date, may have been Zimbabwe. The wind patterns are such that sailors who ride the monsoon south as far as Kilwa can catch the return monsoon to the Red Sea area within the same year. But if they go beyond Kilwa to the Zambezi River, from which they might go inland to Zimbabwe, they cannot return until the following year.

Indian voyages on the Indian Ocean were part of a more general development, more or less contemporary with the Mauryan Empire, in which sailors of various nationalities began to knit together the shores of the "Southern Ocean," a Chinese term referring to all the waters from the South China Sea to the eastern coast of Africa. During this period there is no doubt that the most intrepid sailors were the Malays, peoples who lived in what is now Malaysia, Indonesia, the southeastern coast of Vietnam, and the Philippines.[9]

Sometime before 300 B.C.E. Malay sailors began to ride the monsoons, the seasonal winds that blow off the continent of Asia in the colder months and onto its shores in the warmer months. Chinese records indicate that by the third century B.C.E. *Kunlun* sailors, the Chinese term for the Malay seamen, were sailing north to the southern coasts of China. They may also have been sailing east to India, through the straits now called Malacca and Sunda. If so, they may have been the first to establish contact between India and Southeast Asia.

Malay sailors had reached the eastern coast of Africa at least by the first century B.C.E., if not earlier. Their presence in East African waters is testified to by the peoples of Madagascar, who still speak a Malayo-Polynesian language. Some evidence also suggests that Malay sailors had settled in the Red Sea area. Indeed, it appears that they were the first to develop a long-distance trade in a southern spice. In the last centuries B.C.E., if not earlier, Malay sailors were delivering cinnamon from South China seaports to East Africa and the Red Sea.[10]

By about 400 C.E. Malay sailors could be found two-thirds of the way around the world, from Easter Island to East Africa. They rode the monsoons without a compass, out of sight of land, and often at latitudes below the equator where the northern pole star cannot be seen. They navigated by the wind and the stars, by cloud formations, the color of the water, and swell and wave patterns on the ocean's surface. They could discern the presence of an island some thirty miles from its shores by noting the behavior of birds, the animal and plant life in the water, and the swell and wave patterns. Given their manner of sailing, their most likely route to Africa and the Red Sea would have been by way of the island clusters, the Maldives, the Chagos, the Seychelles, and the Comoros.[11]

Malay ships used balanced lug sails, which were square in shape and mounted so that they could pivot. This made it possible for sailors to tack against the wind, that is, to sail into the wind by going diagonally against it, first one way and then the other. Because of the way the sails were mounted, they appeared somewhat triangular in shape, and thus the Malays' balance lug sail may well be the prototype of the triangular lateen, which can also be used to tack against the wind. The latter was invented by the Polynesians to the Malays' east and by the Arabs to their west,[12] both of whom had ample opportunity to see the Malays' ships in action.

It appears that the pepper trade developed after the cinnamon trade. In the first century C.E. southern India began supplying the Mediterranean with large quantities of pepper. Thereafter, Indian merchants could be found living on the island of Socotra, near the mouth of the Red Sea, and Greek-speaking sailors, including the anonymous author of the *Periplus of the Erythraean Sea,* could be found sailing in the Red Sea and riding the monsoons from there to India.

Indian traders and shippers and Malay sailors were also responsible for opening up an all-sea route to China. The traders' desire for silk drew them out into dangerous waters in search of a more direct way to its source. By the second century C.E. Indian merchants could make the trip by sea, but the route was slow, and it took at least two years to make a round trip. Merchants leaving from India's eastern coast rounded the shores of the Bay of Bengal. When they came to the Isthmus of Kra, the narrowest part of the Malay Peninsula, the ships were unloaded, and the goods were portaged across to the Gulf of Thailand. The cargo was then reloaded on ships that rounded the gulf until they reached Funan, a kingdom on what is now the Kampuchea-Vietnam border. There they had to wait for the winds to shift, before embarking upon a ship that rode the monsoon to China.[13]

Sometime before 400 C.E. travelers began to use a new all-sea route to China, a route that went around the Malay Peninsula and thus avoided the Isthmus of Kra portage. The ships left from Sri Lanka and sailed before the monsoon, far from any coasts, through either the Strait of Malacca or the Strait of Sunda into the Java Sea. After waiting in the Java Sea port for the winds to shift, they rode the monsoon to southern China.[14] The most likely developers of this route were Malay sailors, since the new stopover ports were located within their territories.

Not until the latter part of the fourth century, at about the same time as the new all-sea route began to direct commercial traffic through the Java Sea, did the fine spices—cloves, nutmeg, and mace—begin to assume importance on international markets. These rare and expensive spices came from the Moluccas, several island groups about a thousand miles east of Java. Cloves were produced on about five minuscule islands off the western coast of Halmahera; nutmeg and mace came from only a few of the Banda Islands, some ten islands with a total area of seventeen square miles, located in the middle of the Banda Sea. Until 1621 these Moluccan islands were the only places in the world able to produce cloves, nutmeg, and mace in commercial quantities.[15] The Moluccan producers themselves brought their spices to the international markets of the Java Sea ports and created the market for them.[16]

It was also during the time of the Gupta kings, around 350 C.E., that the Indians discovered how to crystallize sugar.[17] There is considerable disagreement about where sugar was first domesticated. Some believe that the plant was native to New Guinea and domesticated there, and others argue that it was domesticated by Southeast Asian peoples living in what is now southern China.[18] In any case, sugar cultivation spread to the Indian subcontinent. Sugar did not become an important item of trade, however, until the Indians discovered how to turn sugarcane juice into granulated crystals that could be easily stored and transported. This was a momentous development, and it may have been encouraged by Indian sailing, for sugar and clarified butter (ghee) were among the dietary mainstays of Indian sailors.[19]

The Indians also laid the foundation for modern mathematics during the time of the Guptas. Western numerals, which the Europeans called Arabic since they acquired them from the Arabs, actually come from India. (The Arabs call them Hindi numbers.) The most significant feature of the Indian system was the invention of the zero as a number concept. The oldest extant treatise that uses the zero in the modern way is a mathematical appendix attached to Aryabhata's text on astronomy, which is dated 499 C.E.[20]

The Indian zero made the place-value system of writing numbers superior to all others. Without it, the use of this system, base ten or otherwise, was fraught with difficulties and did not seem any better than alternative systems. With the zero the Indians were able to perform calculations rapidly and accurately, to perform much more complicated calculations, and to discern mathematical relationships more aptly. These numerals and the mathematics that the Indians developed with them are now universal—just one indication of the global significance of southernization.

As a result of these developments India acquired a reputation as a place of marvels, a reputation that was maintained for many centuries after the Gupta dynasty fell. As late as the ninth century 'Amr ibn Bahr al Jahiz (c. 776–868), one of the most influential writers of Arabic, had the following to say about India:

As regards the Indians, they are among the leaders in astronomy, mathematics—in particular, they have Indian numerals—and medicine; they alone possess the secrets of the latter, and use them to practice some remarkable forms of treatment. They have the art of carving statues and painted figures. They possess the game of chess, which is the noblest of games and requires more judgment and intelligence than any other. They make Kedah swords, and excel in their use. They have splendid music. . . . They possess a script capable of expressing the sounds of all languages, as well as many numerals. They have a great deal of poetry, many long treatises, and a deep understanding of philosophy and letters; the book *Kalila wa-Dimna* originated with them. They are intelligent and courageous. . . . Their sound judgment and sensible habits led them to invent pins, cork, toothpicks, the drape of clothes and the dyeing of hair. They are handsome, attractive and forbearing, their women are proverbial, and their country produces the matchless Indian aloes which are supplied to kings. They were the originators of the science of *fikr,* by which a poison can be counteracted after it has been used, and of astronomical reckoning, subsequently adopted by the rest of the world. When Adam descended from Paradise, it was to their land that he made his way.[21]

The Southernization of China

These southern Asian developments began to have a significant impact on China after 350 C.E. The Han dynasty had fallen in 221 C.E., and for more than 350 years thereafter China was ruled by an ever-changing collection of regional kingdoms. During these centuries Buddhism became increasingly important in China, Buddhist monasteries spread throughout the disunited realm, and cultural exchange between India and China grew accordingly.[22] By 581, when the Sui dynasty reunited the empire, processes associated with southernization had already had a major impact on China. The influence of southernization continued during the Tang (618–906) and Song (960–1279) dynasties. One might even go so far as to suggest that the process of southernization underlay the revolutionary social, political, economic, and technological developments of the Tang and Song.

The Chinese reformed their mathematics, incorporating the advantages of the Indian system, even though they did not adopt the Indian numerals at that time.[23] They then went on to develop an advanced mathematics, which was flourishing by the time of the Song dynasty.[24] Cotton and indigo became well established, giving rise to the blue-black peasant garb that is still omnipresent in China. Also in the Song period the Chinese first developed cotton canvas, which they used to make a more efficient sail for ocean-going ships.[25]

Although sugar had long been grown in some parts of southern China, it did not become an important crop in this region until the process of southernization was well under way. The process also introduced new varieties of rice. The most important of these was what the Chinese called Champa rice, since it came to China from Champa, a Malay kingdom located on what is now the southeastern coast of Vietnam.

Champa rice was a drought-resistant, early ripening variety that made it possible to extend cultivation up well-watered hillsides, thereby doubling the area of rice cultivation in China.[26] The eleventh-century Buddhist monk Shu Weny-ing left an account explaining how the Champa rice had arrived in China:

> Emperor Cheng-tsung [Zhengzong (998–1022)], being deeply concerned with agriculture, came to know that the Champa rice was drought-resistant and that the green lentils of India were famous for their heavy yield and large seeds. Special envoys, bringing precious things, were dispatched [to these states], with a view to securing these varieties. . . . When the first harvests were reaped in the autumn, [the emperor] called his intimate ministers to taste them and composed poems for Champa rice and Indian green lentils.[27]

In southern China the further development of rice produc-tion brought significant changes in the landscape. Before the introduction of Champa rice, rice cultivation had been con-fined to lowlands, deltas, basins, and river valleys. Once Champa rice was introduced and rice cultivation spread up the hillsides, the Chinese began systematic terracing and made use of sophisticated techniques of water control on mountain slopes. Between the mid-eighth and the early twelfth centuries the population of southern China tripled, and the total Chinese population doubled. According to Song dynasty household registration figures for 1102 and 1110—figures that Song dynasty specialists have shown to be reli-able—there were one hundred million people in China by the first decade of the twelfth century.[28]

Before the process of southernization, northern China had always been predominant, intellectually, socially, and polit-ically. The imperial center of gravity was clearly in the north, and the southern part of China was perceived as a frontier area. But southernization changed this situation dramati-cally. By 600, southern China was well on its way to becom-ing the most prosperous and most commercial part of the empire.[29] The most telling evidence for this is the construc-tion of the Grand Canal, which was completed around 610, during the Sui dynasty. Even though the rulers of the Sui had managed to put the pieces of the empire back together in 581 and rule the whole of China again from a single northern capital, they were dependent on the new southern crops. Thus it is no coincidence that this dynasty felt the need to build a canal that could deliver southern rice to northern cities.[30]

The Tang dynasty, when Buddhist influence in China was especially strong, saw two exceedingly important technolog-ical innovations—the invention of printing and gunpowder. These developments may also be linked to southernization. Printing seems to have developed within the walls of Bud-dhist monasteries between 700 and 750, and subtropical Sichuan was one of the earliest centers of the art.[31] The

invention of gunpowder in China by Daoist alchemists in the ninth century may also be related to the linkages between India and China created by Buddhism. In 644 an Indian monk identified soils in China that contained saltpeter and demon-strated the purple flame that results from its ignition.[32] As early as 919 C.E. gunpowder was used as an igniter in a flame thrower, and the tenth century also saw the use of flaming arrows, rockets, and bombs thrown by catapults.[33] The ear-liest evidence of a cannon or bombard (1127) has been found in Sichuan, quite near the Tibetan border, across the Hima-layas from India.[34]

By the time of the Song the Chinese also had perfected the "south-pointing needle," otherwise known as the com-pass. Various prototypes of the compass had existed in China from the third century B.C.E., but the new version developed during the Song was particularly well suited for navigation. Soon Chinese mariners were using the south-pointing needle on the oceans, publishing "needle charts" for the benefit of sea captains and following "needle routes" on the Southern Ocean.[35]

Once the Chinese had the compass, they, like Columbus, set out to find a direct route to the spice markets of Java and ultimately to the Spice Islands in the Moluccas. Unlike Columbus, they found them. They did not bump into an obstacle, now known as the Western Hemisphere, on their way, since it was not located between China and the Spice Islands. If it had been so situated, the Chinese would have found it some 500 years before Columbus.

Cities on China's southern coasts became centers of over-seas commerce. Silk remained an important export, and by the Tang dynasty it had been joined by a true porcelain, which was developed in China sometime before 400 C.E. China and its East Asian neighbors had a monopoly on the manufacture of true porcelain until the early eighteenth century. Many attempts were made to imitate it, and some of the resulting imitations were economically and stylistically important. China's southern ports were also exporting to Southeast Asia large quantities of ordinary consumer goods, including iron hardware, such as needles, scissors, and cook-ing pots. Although iron manufacturing was concentrated in the north, the large quantity of goods produced was a direct result of the size of the market in southern China and over-seas. Until the British industrial revolution of the eighteenth century, no other place ever equaled the iron production of Song China.[36]

The Muslim Caliphates

In the seventh century C.E. Arab cavalries, recently con-verted to the new religion of Islam, conquered eastern and southern Mediterranean shores that had been Byzantine (and Christian), as well as the Sassanian Empire (Zoroastrian) in what is now Iraq and Iran. In the eighth century they went on to conquer Spain and Turko-Iranian areas of Central Asia, as well as northwestern India. Once established on the Indian frontier, they became acquainted with many of the elements of southernization.

The Arabs were responsible for the spread of many important crops, developed or improved in India, to the Middle East, North Africa, and Islamic Spain. Among the most important were sugar, cotton, and citrus fruits.[37] Although sugarcane and cotton cultivation may have spread to Iraq and Ethiopia before the Arab conquests,[38] only after the establishment of the caliphates did these southern crops have a major impact throughout the Middle East and North Africa.

The Arabs were the first to import large numbers of enslaved Africans in order to produce sugar. Fields in the vicinity of Basra, at the northern end of the Persian Gulf, were the most important sugar-producing areas within the caliphates, but before this land could be used, it had to be desalinated. To accomplish this task, the Arabs imported East African (Zanj) slaves. This African community remained in the area, where they worked as agricultural laborers. The famous writer al Jahiz, whose essay on India was quoted earlier, was a descendant of Zanj slaves. In 869, one year after his death, the Zanj slaves in Iraq rebelled. It took the caliphate fifteen years of hard fighting to defeat them, and thereafter Muslim owners rarely used slaves for purposes that would require their concentration in large numbers.[39]

The Arabs were responsible for moving sugarcane cultivation and sugar manufacturing westward from southern Iraq into other relatively arid lands. Growers had to adapt the plant to new conditions, and they had to develop more efficient irrigation technologies. By 1000 or so sugarcane had become an important crop in the Yemen; in Arabian oases; in irrigated areas of Syria, Lebanon, Palestine, Egypt, and the Mahgrib; in Spain; and on Mediterranean islands controlled by Muslims. By the tenth century cotton also had become a major crop in the lands of the caliphate, from Iran and Central Asia to Spain and the Mediterranean islands. Cotton industries sprang up wherever the plant was cultivated, producing for both local and distant markets.[40]

The introduction of Indian crops, such as sugar and cotton, led to a much more intensive agriculture in the Middle East and some parts of the Mediterranean. Before the arrival of these crops, farmers had planted in the fall to take advantage of autumn rains and harvested in the spring. In the heat of the summer their fields usually lay fallow. But the new southern crops preferred the heat of the summer, and thus farmers began to use their fields throughout the year. They also began to use a system of multiple cropping, a practice that seems to have come from India. This led to an increased interest in soil fertility, and to manuals that advised farmers about adding such things as animal dung and vegetable and mineral materials to the soil to maintain its productivity.[41]

Under Arab auspices, Indian mathematics followed the same routes as the crops.[42] Al-Kharazmi (c. 780–847) introduced Indian mathematics to the Arabic-reading world in his *Treatise on Calculation with the Hindu Numerals,* written around 825. Mathematicians within the caliphates then could draw upon the Indian tradition, as well as the Greek and Persian. On this foundation Muslim scientists of many nationalities, including al-Battani (d. 929), who came from the northern reaches of the Mesopotamian plain, and the Persian Umar Khayyam (d. 1123), made remarkable advances in both algebra and trigonometry.[43]

The Arab conquests also led to an increase in long-distance commerce and the "discovery" of new sources of bullion. Soon after the Abbasid caliphate established its capital at Baghdad, the caliph al-Mansur (r. 745–775) reportedly remarked, "This is the Tigris; there is no obstacle between us and China; everything on the sea can come to us."[44] By this time Arab ships were plying the maritime routes from the Persian Gulf to China, and they soon outnumbered all others using these routes. By the ninth century they had acquired the compass (in China, most likely), and they may well have been the first to use it for marine navigation, since the Chinese do not seem to have used it for this purpose until after the tenth century.

After their conquest of Central Asia the Arabs discovered a silver mine near Tashkent and a veritable mountain of silver in present-day Afghanistan, a find quite comparable to Potosí in South America. The Arabs mined and coined so much silver that by 850 its value, relative to gold, had fallen from 10:1 to 17:1.[45] By 940 the ratio had recovered to 12:1, in large part because the Arabs had access to larger quantities of gold. After the conquest of North Africa, they had discovered that gold came across the Sahara, and they then became intent on going to Ghana, its source.

Thus it was that the Arabs "pioneered" or improved an existing long-distance route across the Sahara, an ocean of sand rather than water. Routes across this desert had always existed, and trade and other contacts between West Africa and the Mediterranean date back at least to the Phoenician period. Still, the numbers of people and animals crossing this great ocean of sand were limited until the eighth century, when Arabs, desiring to go directly to the source of the gold, prompted an expansion of trade across the Sahara. Also during the eighth century Abdul al-Rahman, an Arab ruler of Morocco, sponsored the construction of wells on the trans-Saharan route from Sijilmasa to Wadidara to facilitate this traffic. This Arab discovery of West African gold eventually doubled the amount of gold in international circulation.[46] East Africa, too, became a source of gold for the Arabs. By the tenth century Kilwa had become an important source of Zimbabwean gold.[47]

Developments after 1200: The Mongolian Conquest and the Southernization of the European Mediterranean

By 1200 the process of southernization had created a prosperous south from China to the Muslim Mediterranean. Although mathematics, the pioneering of new ocean routes, and discoveries of bullion are not inextricably connected to locations within forty degrees of the equator, several crucial elements in the process of southernization were closely linked to latitude. Cotton generally does not grow above the fortieth parallel. Sugar, cinnamon, and pepper are tropical or subtropical crops, and the fine spices will grow only on particular tropical islands. Thus for many centuries the more southern parts of Asia and the Muslim Mediterranean enjoyed the profits that these developments brought, while locations that were too far north to grow these southern crops were unable to participate in such lucrative agricultural enterprises.

The process of southernization reached its zenith after 1200, in large part because of the tumultuous events of the thirteenth century. During that century in both hemispheres there were major transformations in the distribution of power, wealth, and prestige. In the Western Hemisphere several great powers went down. Cahokia (near East St. Louis, Illinois), which for three centuries had been the largest and most influential of the Mississippian mound-building centers, declined after 1200, and in Mexico Toltec power collapsed. In the Mediterranean the prestige of the Byzantine Empire was destroyed when Venetians seized its capital in 1204. From 1212 to 1270 the Christians conquered southern Spain, except for Granada. In West Africa, Ghana fell to Sosso, and so did Mali, one of Ghana's allies. But by about 1230 Mali, in the process of seeking its own revenge, had created an empire even larger than Ghana's. At the same time, Zimbabwe was also becoming a major power in southern Africa.

The grandest conquerors of the thirteenth century were the Central Asians. Turkish invaders established the Delhi sultanate in India. Mongolian cavalries devastated Baghdad, the seat of the Abbasid caliphate since the eighth century, and they captured Kiev, further weakening Byzantium. By the end of the century they had captured China, Korea, and parts of mainland Southeast Asia as well.

Because the Mongols were pagans at the time of their conquests, the western Europeans cheered them on as they laid waste to one after another Muslim center of power in the Middle East. The Mongols were stopped only when they encountered the Mamluks of Egypt at Damascus. In East Asia and Southeast Asia only the Japanese and the Javanese were able to defeat them. The victors in Java went on to found Majapahit, whose power and prestige then spread through maritime Southeast Asia.

Both hemispheres were reorganized profoundly during this turmoil. Many places that had flourished were toppled, and power gravitated to new locales. In the Eastern Hemisphere the Central Asian conquerors had done great damage to traditional southern centers just about everywhere, except in Africa, southern China, southern India, and maritime Southeast Asia. At the same time the Mongols' control of overland routes between Europe and Asia in the thirteenth and early fourteenth centuries fostered unprecedented contacts between Europeans and peoples from those areas that had long been southernized. Marco Polo's long sojourn in Yuan dynasty China is just one example of such interaction.

Under the Mongols overland trade routes in Asia shifted north and converged on the Black Sea. After the Genoese helped the Byzantines to retake Constantinople from the Venetians in 1261, the Genoese were granted special privileges of trade in the Black Sea. Italy then became directly linked to the Mongolian routes. Genoese traders were among the first and were certainly the most numerous to open up trade with the Mongolian states in southern Russia and Iran. In the words of one Western historian, in their Black Sea colonies they "admitted to citizenship" people of many nationalities, including those of "strange background and questionable belief," and they "wound up christening children of the best ancestry with such uncanny names as Saladin, Hethum, or Hulugu."[48]

Such contacts contributed to the southernization of the Christian Mediterranean during this period of Mongolian hegemony. Although European conquerors sometimes had taken over sugar and cotton lands in the Middle East during the Crusades, not until some time after 1200 did the European-held Mediterranean islands become important exporters. Also after 1200 Indian mathematics began to have a significant impact in Europe. Before that time a few western European scholars had become acquainted with Indian numerals in Spain, where the works of al-Kharazmi, al-Battani, and other mathematicians had been translated into Latin. Nevertheless, Indian numerals and mathematics did not become important in western Europe until the thirteenth century, after the book *Liber abaci* (1202), written by Leonardo Fibonacci of Pisa (c. 1170–1250), introduced them to the commercial centers of Italy. Leonardo had grown up in North Africa (in what is now Bejala, Algeria), where his father, consul over the Pisan merchants in that port, had sent him to study calculation with an Arab master.[49]

In the seventeenth century, when Francis Bacon observed the "force and virtue and consequences of discoveries," he singled out three technologies in particular that "have changed the whole face and state of things throughout the world."[50] These were all Chinese inventions—the compass, printing, and gunpowder. All three were first acquired by Europeans during this time of hemispheric reorganization.

It was most likely the Arabs who introduced the compass to Mediterranean waters, either at the end of the twelfth or in the thirteenth century. Block printing, gunpowder, and cannon appeared first in Italy in the fourteenth century, apparently after making a single great leap from Mongolian-held regions of East Asia to Italy. How this great leap was accomplished is not known, but the most likely scenario is one suggested by Lynn White, Jr., in an article concerning how various other southern (rather than eastern) Asian technologies reached western Europe at about this time. He thought it most likely that they were introduced by "Tatar" slaves, Lama Buddhists from the frontiers of China whom the Genoese purchased in Black Sea marts and delivered to Italy. By 1450, when this trade reached its peak, there were thousands of these Asian slaves in every major Italian city.[51]

Yet another consequence of the increased traffic and communication on the more northern trade routes traversing the Eurasian steppe was the transmission of the bubonic plague from China to the Black Sea. The plague had broken out first in China in 1331, and apparently rats and lice infected with the disease rode westward in the saddlebags of Mongolian post messengers, horsemen who were capable of traveling one hundred miles per day. By 1346 it had reached a Black Sea port, whence it made its way to the Middle East and Europe.[52]

During the latter part of the fourteenth century the unity of the Mongolian Empire began to disintegrate, and new regional powers began to emerge in its wake. Throughout much of Asia the chief beneficiaries of imperial disintegration were Turkic or Turko-Mongolian powers of the Muslim faith. The importance of Islam in Africa was also growing at this time, and the peoples of Southeast Asia, from the Malay Peninsula to the southern Philippines, were converting to the faith.

Indeed, the world's most obvious dynamic in the centuries before Columbus was the expansion of the Islamic faith. Under Turkish auspices Islam was even spreading into eastern Europe, a development marked by the Ottoman conquest of Constantinople in 1453. This traumatic event lent a special urgency to Iberian expansion. The Iberians came to see themselves as the chosen defenders of Christendom. Ever since the twelfth century, while Christian Byzantium had been losing Anatolia and parts of southeastern Europe to Islam, they had been retaking the Iberian Peninsula for Christendom.

One way to weaken the Ottomans and Islam was to go around the North African Muslims and find a new oceanic route to the source of West African gold. Before the Portuguese efforts, sailing routes had never developed off the western shore of Africa, since the winds there blow in the same direction all year long, from north to south. (Earlier European sailors could have gone to West Africa, but they would not have been able to return home.)

The Portuguese success would have been impossible without the Chinese compass, Arabic tables indicating the declination of the noonday sun at various latitudes, and the lateen sail, which was also an Arab innovation. The Portuguese caravels were of mixed, or multiple, ancestry, with a traditional Atlantic hull and a rigging that combined the traditional Atlantic square sail with the lateen sail of Southern Ocean provenance. With the lateen sail the Portuguese could tack against the wind for the trip homeward.

The new route to West Africa led to Portugal's rounding of Africa and direct participation in Southern Ocean trade. While making the voyages to West Africa, European sailors learned the wind patterns and ocean currents west of Africa, knowledge that made the Columbian voyages possible. The Portuguese moved the sugarcane plant from Sicily to Madeira, in the Atlantic, and they found new sources of gold, first in West Africa and then in East Africa. Given that there was little demand in Southern Ocean ports for European trade goods, they would not have been able to sustain their Asian trade without this African gold.

The Rise of Europe's North

The rise of the North, or more precisely, the rise of Europe's northwest, began with the appropriation of those elements of southernization that were not confined by geography. In the wake of their southern European neighbors, Europeans of the northwest became partially southernized, but they could not engage in all aspects of the process because of their distance from the equator. Full southernization and the wealth that we now associate with northwestern Europe came about only after their outright seizure of tropical and subtropical territories and their rounding of Africa and participation in Southern Ocean trade.

In the West Indies and along the coast of South America, the Dutch, the French, and the English acquired lands where for the first time they were able to become producers of sugar and cotton, though with African labor on Native American land. In West Africa the Dutch seized the Portuguese fort at Elmina, Portugal's most important source of gold. And in the East Indies, the Dutch seized Portuguese trading posts in the Moluccas and in 1621 conquered the Banda Islands, thereby gaining a stranglehold on the fine spices. Without such southern possessions the more northern Europeans had been unable to participate fully in the southernization process, since their homelands are too far north to grow either cotton or sugar, much less cinnamon, pepper, or the fine spices.

Even though the significance of indigenous developments in the rise of northwestern Europe should not be minimized, it should be emphasized that many of the most important causes of the rise of the West are not to be found within the bounds of Europe. Rather, they are the result of the transformation of western Europe's relationships with other regions of the Eastern Hemisphere. Europe began its rise only after the thirteenth-century reorganization of the Eastern Hemisphere facilitated its southernization, and Europe's northwest did not rise until it too was reaping the profits of southernization. Thus the rise of the North Atlantic powers should not be oversimplified so that it appears to be an isolated and solely European phenomenon, with roots that spread no farther afield than Greece. Rather, it should be portrayed as one part of a hemisphere-wide process, in which a northwestern Europe ran to catch up with a more developed south—a race not completed until the eighteenth century.

Conclusion

The patterns of southernization become apparent when one considers "the long duration," more or less from the fourth century to the eighteenth. It began as a southern Asia phenomenon and spread through the warmer latitudes of the Eastern Hemisphere north of the equator. Both in China and in the Middle East it stimulated new developments and acquired new elements, and its potential continued to unfold. After 1200 the radical transformations throughout the Eastern Hemisphere brought about by the Mongolians and many others created conditions that led to the spread of southernization to Europe and Europe's colonies in the Western Hemisphere. Ultimately, it transformed East Asia, the Middle East, Africa, the Mediterranean, northwestern Europe, and portions of the Western Hemisphere, more or less in that order.

Southernization was not overtaken by westernization until the industrial revolution of the eighteenth century. At that time the nations of northwestern Europe were catapulted into a position of global dominance, an event marked by the British takeover of Bengal and other parts of India. By the nineteenth century, using the new "tools of empire" provided by the industrial revolution, the northern powers for the first time were capable of imposing their will and their way on the rest of the world.[53]

Both the ocean crossing that knit together two hemispheres and the industrial revolution were indeed unprecedented. But their roots are inseparable from the process of southernization. Only after the northwestern Europeans had added to their own repertoire every one of the elements of southernization did the world become divided into a powerful, prestigious, and rich north and an impoverished south perceived to be in need of development.

Notes

1. Andrew Watson, *Agricultural Innovation in the Early Islamic World: The Diffusion of Crops and Farming Techniques, 700–1100* (Cambridge: Cambridge University Press, 1983), p. 32.

2. Mattiebelle Gittinger, *Master Dyers to the World: Technique and Trade in Early Indian Dyed Cotton Textiles* (Washington, DC: Textile Museum, 1982), p. 19. For a discussion of the significance of cotton textiles in Indonesia, see Gittinger, *Splendid Symbols: Textiles and Traditions in Indonesia* (Washington, DC: Textile Museum, 1979).

3. Moti Chandra, *Trade and Trade Routes of Ancient India* (New Delhi: Abhinav Publications, 1977), p. 35.

4. Ibid., p. 126.

5. Gittinger, *Splendid Symbols,* pp. 13, 19.

6. Ibid, p. 15.

7. Paul Wheatley, *The Golden Khersonese: Studies in the Historical Geography of the Malay Peninsula Before A.D. 1500* (Westport, CT: Greenwood Press, 1973), p. 188.

8. D.W. Phillipson, "The Beginnings of the Iron Age in Southern Africa," in *UNESCO General History of Africa,* vol. 2: *Ancient Civilizations of Africa,* ed. G. Mokhtar (Berkeley: University of California Press, 1981), pp. 679–80, 688–90. In the same volume, see also M. Posnansky, "The Societies of Africa South of the Sahara in the Early Iron Age," p. 726. Phillipson indicates that there is evidence of exchange between Zimbabwe and the coast in this early period, and Posnansky refers to the work of R.F.H. Summers, who believes that early prospecting and mining techniques in East Africa reveal Indian influence. The description of Ethiopian merchants seeking gold in East Africa is from Steven Runciman, *Byzantine Style and Civilization* (Middlesex, England: Penguin Books, 1975), p. 132. Information about the monsoon is from A.M.H. Sheriff, "The East Africa Coast and Its Role in Maritime Trade," in *Ancient Civilizations of Africa,* ed. Mokhtar, pp. 556–57.

9. Anthony Reid, *Southeast Asia in the Age of Commerce, 1450–1680,* 2 vols. (New Haven, CT: Yale University Press, 1988–93) 1:4.

10. Keith Taylor, "Madagascar in the Ancient Malayo-Polynesian Myths," in *Explorations in Early Southeast Asian History: The Origins of Southeast Asian Statecraft,* ed. Kenneth Hall and John Whitmore (Ann Arbor: University of Michigan, Center for South and Southeast Asian Studies, 1976), p. 39. An excellent source on the early spice trade is James Innes Miller, *The Spice Trade of the Roman Empire, 29 B.C. to A.D. 649* (Oxford: Clarendon Press, 1969).

11. Taylor, "Madagascar," pp. 30–31, 52.

12. George Hourani, *Arab Seafaring in the Indian Ocean in Ancient and Medieval Times* (Princeton, NJ: Princeton University Press, 1951), p. 102.

13. Kenneth Hall, *Maritime Trade and State Formation in Southeast Asia* (Honolulu: University of Hawaii Press, 1985), p. 20.

14. Ibid., p. 72.

15. Henry N. Ridley, *Spices* (London: Macmillan, 1912), p. 105.

16. Hall, *Maritime Trade and State Formation,* p. 21.

17. Joseph E. Schwartzberg, *A Historical Atlas of South Asia* (Chicago: University of Chicago Press, 1978). The date 350 C.E. appears in "A Chronology of South Asia," a pocket insert in the atlas.

18. For a discussion on its domestication in southern China by the ancestors of the Southeast Asians, see Peter Bellwood, "Southeast Asia before History," in Nicholas Tarling, ed., *Cambridge History of Southeast Asia* (Cambridge: Cambridge University Press, 1992), 1:90–91. Also see Sidney W. Mintz, *Sweetness and Power: The Place of Sugar in Modern History* (New York: Viking, 1985), p. 19. Mintz agrees with those who argue that sugar was domesticated in New Guinea. He also suggests that crystallized sugar may have been produced in India as early as 400–350 B.C.E.

19. Chandra, *Trade and Trade Routes of Ancient India,* p. 61.

20. Georges Ifrah, *From One to Zero: A Universal History of*

Numbers, trans. Lowell Blair (New York: Viking, 1985), pp. 382, 434. This is an excellent book that explains many mysteries and contradictions in the literature. Even those who are not mathematically inclined will enjoy it.

21. 'Amr ibn Bahr al Jahiz, *The Life and Works of Jahiz,* trans. from Arabic by Charles Pellat, trans. from French by D.W. Hauter (Berkeley: University of California Press, 1969), pp. 197–98.

22. See Liu Xinru, *Ancient India and Ancient China: Trade and Religious Exchanges, A.D. 1–600* (Delhi: Oxford University Press, 1988).

23. Ifrah, *From One to Zero,* p. 461.

24. Joseph Needham, *Science and Civilisation in China,* 6 vols. to date, vol. 3: *Mathematics and the Sciences of the Heavens and Earth* (Cambridge: Cambridge University Press: 1959), pp. 40–50.

25. Lo Jung-pang, "The Emergence of China as a Sea Power during the Late Sung and Early Yüan Dynasties," *Far Eastern Economic Review* 14 (1955):500.

26. Ho Ping-ti, "Early-Ripening Rice in Chinese History," *Economic History Review* 9 (1956):201.

27. Ibid., p. 207.

28. Ibid., pp. 211–12.

29. Ibid., pp. 205–6.

30. Ibid., p. 206.

31. Thomas Francis Carter, *The Invention of Printing in China and Its Spread Westward* (New York: Columbia University Press, 1955), pp. 68, 38–40.

32. For a reference to the Indian monk, see Arnold Paley, *Technology in World Civilization: A Thousand Year History* (Cambridge, MA: MIT Press, 1991), p. 16.

Other information on gunpowder included here comes from Joseph Needham, "Science and China's Influence on the World," in Raymond Dawson, ed., *The Legacy of China* (Oxford: Oxford University Press, 1964), p. 246. This article is an excellent brief account of Chinese science and technology and their global significance. James R. Partington's *A History of Greek Fire and Gunpowder* (Cambridge: W. Heffer, 1960) is still useful.

33. Lo, "The Emergence of China as a Seapower," pp. 500–501.

34. Lu Gwei-Djen, Joseph Needham, and Phan Che-Hsing, "The Oldest Representation of a Bombard," in Joseph Needham, *Science and Civilisation in China,* vol. 5, part 7: *Military Technology: The Gunpowder Epoch* (Cambridge: Cambridge University Press, 1986), appendix A, pp. 580–81. (I am indebted to Robin Yates for this information.)

35. Lo, "The Emergence of China as a Seapower," p. 500. Other useful articles by Lo include: "Maritime Commerce and Its Relation to the Song Navy," *Journal of the Economic and Social History of the Orient* 12 (1969):57–101; and "The Termination of the Early Ming Naval Expeditions," in *Papers in Honor of Professor Woodbridge Bingham: A Festschrift for His Seventy-fifth Birthday,* ed. James B. Parsons (San Francisco: Chinese Materials Center, 1976), pp. 127–41.

36. Robert Hartwell, "A Revolution in the Chinese Iron and Coal Industries during the Northern Sung, 960–1126 A.D.," *Journal of Asian Studies* 21 (1962):155; and Hartwell, "Markets, Technol-

ogy, and the Structure of Enterprise in the Development of the Eleventh-Century Chinese Iron and Steel Industry," *Journal of Economic History* 26 (1966):54. See also Hartwell, "A Cycle of Economic Change in Imperial China: Coal and Iron in Northeast China, 750–1350," *Journal of the Social and Economic History of the Orient* 10 (1967):102–59. For an excellent overview of the transformations in Tang and Song China, see Mark Elvin, *The Patterns of the Chinese Past* (Stanford: Stanford University Press, 1973).

37. Watson, *Agricultural Innovation in the Early Islamic World,* pp. 78–80.

38. Sheriff, "The East African Coast," p. 566.

39. William D. Phillips, *Slavery from Roman Times to the Early Transatlantic Trade* (Minneapolis: University of Minnesota Press, 1985), p. 76.

40. Watson, *Agricultural Innovation in the Early Islamic World,* pp. 29, 39–41.

41. Ibid., pp. 123–25.

42. Ifrah, *From One to Zero,* p. 465.

43. R.M. Savory, *Introduction to Islamic Civilization* (Cambridge: Cambridge University Press, 1976), pp. 116–17.

44. C.G.F. Simkins, *The Traditional Trade of Asia* (Oxford: Oxford University Press, 1968), p. 81.

45. Sture Bolin, "Mohammed, Charlemagne, and Ruric," *Scandinavian Economic History Review* 1 (1953):16. In the past, Sture's interpretation of the Carolingians has been disputed. The article has, however, stood the test of time. For example, see the assessment of it in Richard Hodges and David Whitehouse, *Mohammed, Charlemagne and the Origins of Europe* (Ithaca: Cornell University Press, 1983). The information about Scandinavia's relationship with the caliphates is especially valuable.

46. Anthony Hopkins, *An Economic History of West Africa* (New York: Columbia University Press, 1973), p. 82.

47. F.T. Masao and H.W. Mutoro, "The East African Coast and the Comoro Islands, in *UNESCO General History of Africa,* vol. 3: *Africa from the Seventh to the Eleventh Century,* ed. M. El Fasi (Berkeley: University of California Press, 1988), pp. 611–15.

48. Robert S. Lopez, "Market Expansion: The Case of Genoa," *Journal of Economic History* 24 (1964):447–49. See also Lopez, "Back to Gold, 1252," in *Economic History Review* 9 (1956):219–40. The latter includes a discussion of the relationship between western European coinage and the trans-Saharan gold trade.

49. Ifrah, *From One to Zero,* pp. 465, 481. See also Joseph and Frances Gies, *Leonardo of Pisa and the New Mathematics of the Middle Ages* (New York: Crowell, 1969).

50. Bacon is cited in Needham, "Science and China's Influence on the World," p. 242.

51. Lynn White, Jr., "Tibet, India, and Malay as Sources of Western Medieval Technology," *American Historical Review* 65 (1960):515–26. This is an important, if little known, article.

52. William H. McNeill, *Plagues and Peoples* (Garden City, NY: Anchor Press, 1976), pp. 133, 145.

53. The term comes from Daniel Headrick's excellent book *The Tools of Empire: Technology and European Imperialism in the Nineteenth Century* (New York: Oxford University Press, 1981).

20

The United States in World History

An Economic and Demographic Scheme

Paul Vauthier Adams

On the domed ceiling of the municipal library in Carcassonne is a painting that I noticed for the first time in the summer of 1969. It struck me not only for its beauty but also for what it instantly told me about the history of Mediterranean France, and now much later about the history of the world. In the foreground crouches a primitive man clad in animal skins; concealed behind bushes at the top of a forested cliff, he stares in astonishment at what appears to be a Mycenaean ship moored just offshore. On the beach below a few men dressed in Mycenaean warriors' costume are at work loading cargo—barrels, newly killed game—evidently having stopped in this cove to take on provisions. The artist evidently knew the prehistory of the region, for early Greek and Phoenician voyagers have left ample archaeological evidence of their presence in these waters of western Languedoc and Roussillon, where the Corbieres and Pyrenees mountains run down to the sea. In the Mycenaean age the western Mediterranean was a frontier into which civilization advanced gradually over the next five centuries. By the beginning of the seventh century civilization had reached the Atlantic coast of North America. Now the advancing Europeans carried different weapons, dressed differently, and spoke different languages. Yet they still arrived at the frontier by ship; first the Mediterranean, then the Atlantic became accessible waterways carrying civilized humanity to new and abundant resources.

The advance of civilization across a global frontier is the overwhelming phenomenon of the last three millennia, possibly five millennia if we include the advance of agricultural cultures and urban societies hard on their heels since c. 3000 B.C.E. Of course, the significance of the frontier is by no means a new concept to American history, but its significance is understood in the last decade of the twentieth century perhaps better than and differently from the way it was understood in Frederick Jackson Turner's heyday. A frontier was not unique to American society, nor did it

necessarily produce freedom, but it was enormously important. The frontier envisaged here is more on the order of that described by Walter Prescott Webb in *The Great Frontier* (1951). For Webb the European discoveries and exploration of the sixteenth century opened a vast frontier across North and South America, Australia, New Zealand, and Oceania, and it opened with dramatic suddenness. However, Webb's frontier was clearly not the first, nor did it necessarily begin in the sixteenth century, nor, except from the perspectives of European farmers and artisans who moved into its empty spaces, swept of indigenous inhabitants by diseases, trappers, miners, and soldiers, was it a joyful, liberating process. These points can be demonstrated by comparing a set of events on two widely separated frontiers. The first is taken from the American West, the Cheyenne Sand Creek Massacre of 1864:

> By 1859 the [Cheyenne and Arapaho] Indians were compressed into a small circle of territory which straddled a main line of white emigration. In 1861 the Indians were persuaded by government officials to sell that land to the United States and move to a gameless, arid section of the southeastern Colorado Territory. The Indians claimed that they had been cheated and had misunderstood the treaty; in 1864 some tribes in Colorado were goaded into a war and killed many settlers. The Cheyenne, who were then at peace under Chief Black Kettle, gave up their arms and camped where they were promised protection by federal troops against the Colorado militia. Those promises were not kept. A contingent of Colorado militia under the command of Colonel J.M. Chivington, a Methodist pastor in civil life, fell upon the unsuspecting camp, refused to acknowledge a white flag of surrender, and slaughtered and mutilated perhaps as many as 450 men, women, and children. The soldiers scalped the dead and dying, then cut out the genitals of the women and stuck them on poles or wore them in their hats. Chivington later remarked that the children had to be killed because "nits make lice. . . ."

The following account is from the testimony of John S. Smith, an Indian agent well known to the Cheyenne and present during the raid, before the Joint Committee on the Conduct of the War: "Massacre of the Cheyenne Indians," 38th Congress, 2nd Session, III (1865):

> "By the time I got up with the battery to the place where these Indians were surrounded there had been some considerable firing. Four or five soldiers had been killed, some with arrows and some with bullets. The soldiers continued firing on these Indians, who numbered about one hundred, until they had almost

This paper was originally presented at the American Historical Association, 103d Annual Meeting, December 27–30, 1988, Cincinnati, Ohio.

completely destroyed them. I think I saw altogether some seventy dead bodies lying there; the greater portion women and children. There may have been thirty warriors, old and young; the rest were women and small children of different ages and sizes."

Question: "Were the women and children slaughtered indiscriminately, or only so far as they were with warriors?"

Answer: "Indiscriminately."

Question: "Were there any acts of barbarity perpetrated there that came under your own observation?"

Answer: "Yes, sir; I saw the bodies of those lying there cut all to pieces, worse mutilated than any I ever saw before; the women cut all to pieces."

Question: "How cut?"

Answer: "With knives; scalped; their brains knocked out; children two or three months old; all ages lying there, from sucking infants up to warriors. . . . They were terribly mutilated, lying there in the water and sand; most of them in the bed of the creek, dead and dying, making many struggles. They were so badly mutilated and covered with sand and water that it was very hard for me to tell one from another." (Richard Hofstadter and Michael Wallace, eds., *American Violence, A Documentary History* [New York: Knopf, 1963], pp. 274–77)

On an entirely different frontier, in India in about the eighth century B.C.E. Indian peasantry and their Aryan lords moved gradually from the upper Indus valley eastward into the forests of the northern Ganges. In the *Mahabharata* the process is described as follows:

The lord [Agni] took on his fiery form and began to burn the forest. Surrounding it on all sides with his Seven Flames, the Fire angrily burned the Khandava, as though to exhibit the end of the Eon. . . . Standing on their chariots at both ends of the forest, the two tiger-like men Krishna and Arjuna started a vast massacre of the creatures on every side. Indeed, whenever the heroes saw live creatures escaping, such as lived in the Khandava, they cased them down. They saw no hole to escape, because of the vigorous speed of the chariots—both the grand chariots and their warriors seemed to be strung together. As the Khandava was burning, the creatures in their thousands leaped up in all directions, screeching their terrifying screams. Many were burning in one spot, others were scorched—they were shattered mindlessly, their eyes abursting. Some embraced their sons, others their father and mothers, unable to abandon them, and thus went to their perdition. Still others jumped up by the thousands, faces distorted, and darting hither and thither fell into the Fire. . . . When they jumped out, the Partha cut them to pieces with his arrows and, laughing, threw them back into the blazing Fire. Their bodies covered with arrows and screeching fiercely, they leaped upward nimbly and fell back into the Fire. The noise of the forest animals, as they were hit by the arrows and left to burn, was like the ocean's when it was being churned. (J.A.B. van Buitenen, trans., *The Mahabharata, I: The Book of the Beginning* [Chicago: University of Chicago Press, 1973], pp. 216–17)

So much more evocative is the epic poem than testimony before a committee. The massacres they both describe nevertheless confirm what is well known but too often neglected in adulatory narrative national histories: frontiers advanced at great human cost. Everywhere the process has involved the elimination, enslavement, or acculturation of the indigenes, whether by microbes, most spectacularly in the cases of peoples beyond Eurasia and Africa, or by warfare and conquest. Trade, to be sure, advanced civilization by exchanges of technology and learning—philosophy, religion, and knowledge of the material world. But colonization advanced with great violence, indeed the term is a euphemism really for massacring the inhabitants and transforming the ecological systems of the not-yet agricultural and civilized domains of the world.

Far apart in space and time, the frontiers of the American West and the Ganges are but two examples. The two most important for global history are the frontiers of Chinese and Mediterranean Greco-Roman civilizations. Their comparison yields some intriguing notions. First, both conquered and annexed vast expanses of land at about the same time, conquering small neighboring states and peoples in the fourth and third centuries B.C.E. (Ch'in in China, early Republic in Rome), and then massive territorial expansion in the second and first centuries B.C.E. as they overran pastoral and agricultural people (Han in China, latter Republic and early Empire in Rome). Both empires experienced severe political, military, and financial crises in the third century C.E.; both assimilated barbarian immigrants from the North, whose assimilation was preceded by partial acculturation. Then their histories diverge sharply. By 589 the Chinese Empire was reunited and thereafter remained intact except for brief intervals from 907 to 959 and from 1127 to 1275 when Mongols ruled the north; their subsequent conquest of the southern Sung (1276–1367) restored unity until the twentieth century. Dynasties came and went, but the empire held. By contrast the division of the Roman Empire and the political disintegration of its western half in the fifth century was never fully reversed. In their very different political experiences lies one of the keys to understanding world history, but that is not the subject at hand.

Their frontiers are, and these too were quite different. The southern Chinese frontier became a second core area (the Huang-he valley and North China Plain being the first), situated between the Yangtze and Hsi river valleys and across South China to Annam. There were, of course, massive assaults north and westward against the Hsuing-nu (Hunnic peoples) of Mongolia and into Szechuan and Manchuria in the second century B.C.E., and far into Central Asia in the first century. But South China became the principal area where Chinese civilization and the empire became firmly established. By contrast Mediterranean civilization gave rise to its second core area in the northwest, on the Great North European Plain. Their economic growths were roughly contemporaneous, i.e., from the ninth through the

Table 20.1

World Population Sizes, 1000–1975 C.E. (Total Population by World Areas, in millions)

Continents	1000	1700	1800	1900	1975
Europe	36	120	180	390	635
Asia (includes Near East)	185	415	625	970	2,300
Africa	33	61	70	110	385
Americas	9	13	24	145	545
Oceania (includes Australia)	1.5	2.25	2.5	6.75	23
Totals	264.5	611.25	901.5	1,621.75	3,888

Table 20.2

Percentage or Proportions of Total World Population

	1000	1700	1800	1900	1975
Europe	13.6	19.6	19.7	24.0	16.3
Asia	69.6	67.6	69.3	59.8	59.2
Africa	12.4	10.0	7.8	6.8	9.9
Americas	3.4	2.1	2.7	8.9	14.0
Oceania	0.6	0.4	0.3	0.4	0.6

Table 20.3

Changes in Proportions since 1000 C.E., Setting All Equal to 100 in That Year

	1000	1700	1800	1900	1975
Europe	100	333	500	1,083	1,764
Asia	100	224	338	524	1,243
Africa	100	185	212	333	1,167
Americas	100	144	267	1,611	6,056
Oceania	100	150	167	450	1,533
World	100	231	341	613	1,470

Source: Colin McEvedy and Richard Jones, *Atlas of World Population History* (New York: Penguin Books 1978).

thirteenth centuries, but their geographies and ecologies, and consequently their technologies, were profoundly different. To borrow William McNeill's terminology, Chinese civilization moved up a sharp disease gradient; its peoples had to become seasoned or immune to the disease environment of the South. European civilization moved down a disease gradient into a cooler, healthier, and temperate environment. In their new settings each experienced the massive medieval economic revolution. In China its distinctive features were wet-rice cultivation, year-round multicropping, hydrological systems—the dam, sluice-gate, noria (peripheral pot-wheel), and treadle water-pump—its cash-producing cottage industry was silk. In northwestern Europe its features were the heavy wheeled plow, the axe, harnesses, and livestock: cattle (especially oxen), horses, and sheep. Its cottage industry was woolens.

This digression into the history of Rome and early medieval Europe and China from the Han through Mongol eras helps to identify the factors that set off European global expansion. Europe's medieval economic revolution was land and labor extensive; China's was land and labor intensive. Perhaps because of its massive territorial expansion after c. 1000 Europe's new core area experienced dramatic population growth c. 1000–1700 at rates more rapid than Asia or even China considered alone. (See, Tables 20.1, 20.2, 20.3.) Indeed, the overarching reality of global history after c. 1000 has been Europe's massive territorial expansion across wide frontiers, while other centers of world civilization remained, essentially, at home. Why this should be so is the great riddle of world history, and, to me at least, provides the essential conceptual schema for the organization of its mass of information. This is the *problematique* that helps one to cope with the historian's fundamental question: What is important? And it provides the setting for American history.

The establishment of European outposts of civilization in the Americas represents the continuation of a process that began in northwestern Europe in the ninth century, in what

Marc Bloch termed the Age of the Assarters. The forests fell and lands came under the heavy wheeled plow, populations grew, manors multiplied, trade increased, fairs became towns, merchant fleets increased, urbanization advanced, social structures became more stratified, and a complex literate and artistic Christian culture emerged. By the latter half of the eleventh century, west European civilization, including the Italian states, was sending out its first expansionist probes: the Reconquista in Spain, the Crusades in the Levant, and, begun earlier, Viking colonization of Iceland and Greenland, and the *Drang nach Osten* across the Elbe River. The extreme thrusts northwestward by the Vikings and the Frankish adventure in Jerusalem were overextensions into inhospitable climatic and epidemiological environments, but Spain, eastern Europe, much of the Mediterranean sea, and Iceland held fast and became integral parts of what now was becoming the European world system. The Atlantic Ocean was not at all a barrier; instead, it was itself a frontier that yielded fish, furs (seals), and oil (seals and whales). By the beginning of the fourteenth century, European sailors were braving the Atlantic already with the intention of circling Africa. As Alfred Crosby describes the efforts of the Vivaldi brothers, who set out in 1291: "The Vivaldi venture was the beginning of the most important new development for the human and many other species since the Neolithic Revolution" (*Ecological Imperialism,* p. 71). By 1439 the king of Portugal granted lands to colonists in the Azores. By the end of the fifteenth century, Spanish and Portuguese had wholly conquered and colonized the Madeiras and Canaries, bringing with them first weapons and disease, then plants and animals. In another brilliant sentence Crosby sums it up: "These three archipelagoes of the eastern Atlantic were the laboratories, the pilot programs, for the new European imperialism, and the lessons learned there would crucially influence world history for centuries to come" (p. 100). One of the most distinctive systems of New World colonization was invented in these Fortunate Isles: enslavement of Africans on plantations to produce durable, portable cash crops: first sugar, then tobacco and cotton.

Transplantation of this system, complete with its portmanteau biota—diseases, animals, plants, slaves, masters, and subordinate free men—to the Caribbean and American mainland was but another, albeit large, step, not the beginning but rather the culmination of a process begun five centuries earlier with an agricultural revolution on the North European Plain. I sometimes ask my students to reconsider their understanding of American and world history by asking them to explain the following statement: "Columbus did not discover America. Rather American historians and their European city-cousins invented Columbus." The response should be, of course, both historical and historiographical.

Now to take a different tack on the date 1500 as a landmark in world history: It was really not until about 1600 that west Europeans had developed the navigational or military technology sufficient to exploit the resources of the vast domain that yawned open before them. Moreover, not until the demographic explosion of c. 1750–1850 had accumulated population reserves could Europeans export themselves in great numbers. In the Americas the processes were roughly as follows:

The frontiers were emptied of indigenous peoples by diseases that ran far ahead of advancing Europeans, clearing the way, as it were. Then came the rest: plants, animals, and peoples, the latter well armed and not at all reluctant to eliminate what remaining indigenes their microbes had spared. As they became colonized, the new lands yielded vast quantities of agricultural products, primarily because of very favorable land-to-labor ratios: much land, and locally the best of it, per unit of labor input, resulting in high real wages and the formation of surplus in the forms of material goods, savings, and investments. Part of the surplus, of course, supported population growth. All across the frontiers, well documented in the United States and Canada, a high fertility zone followed closely behind. For several decades the increase in population contributed to still greater per capita output, the point of diminishing return to labor not coming until after a substantial lag in time, in the United States probably not until the end of the 1920s. Meanwhile, still in agriculture, investment in improved technology increased per capita output. These took the forms of improved crops, rotation systems, livestock breeds, buildings, and farm tools and machinery, this last very important in labor-scarce America. Improvements in transportation permitted regional specialization by facilitating the flow of agricultural products and the growing range of consumer goods and agricultural supplies upon which commercial agriculture increasingly came to depend. Agricultural surplus also sustained growth of the nonagricultural sectors: the entire range of manufactures, first artisanal, then industrial and commerce. Commercialization and marketization represented the achievement of economic maturity.

It would not be appropriate to continue into a discussion of political power and its institutional forms, but one must observe that slavery and other forms of servitude in the new worlds of the Americas and Australia were due to labor scarcity, as serfdom had been in northwestern and eastern Europe in its colonial phase. Freedom was a possible but not a necessary outcome of the opening frontier.

The medieval economic revolution in eastern Asia and western Europe had involved similar processes, but they had been much slower, almost sluggish by comparison. What was unique and spectacular about the Americas was the vastness of its land and resources and the amazing rapidity of its conquest, exploitation, and civilization. From their beginnings to the fruition of their respective medieval economic revolutions, the Chinese Empire and northwestern Europe passed through about a thousand years. In the New World it was all accomplished in less than four hundred years, 1500 to 1900, and in North America the dramatic economic and demographic growth came in the latter two centuries.

Tables 20.1, 20.2, and 20.3 present estimates of world populations by world areas or continents from 1000 to 1975. These are rough orders of magnitude; some of these estimates are more reliable than others, but given their broad temporal and global scale, they are accurate enough to suggest some general notions. First, it is clear that Europe, Asia, and Africa contained over 95 percent of the world's population before 1700, Eurasia having about 88 percent, and Asia alone clearly dominating with nearly 70 percent of the total. No surprise. If we look more closely, some surprising features do emerge. From 1000 to 1700 the area of most dynamic growth was Europe, not Asia; Europe's population tripled, Asia's doubled. China, considered apart, did no better despite its economic revolution. So Europe, Black Death and all, led the world's population explosion. As proportions to the world's total, all other areas diminished. By 1800 this phenomenon was more pronounced: Europe's population increased 5 times, Asia by 3.4, Africa by 2, the Americas—now receiving immigrants—by 2.7. Then from 1800 to 1900 a remarkable shift occurred: Europe's increase was now 10.8 times, while the Americas increased enormously, by 16 times, both easily outstripping growth rates in the rest of the world. The familiar explosion of population in Asia and Africa, the teeming billions of Indians and Chinese featured in the public media are a phenomenon of the twentieth century alone. European populations, by contrast, exploded into the world, overrunning three entire continents. The world population explosion until very, very recent times has been preeminently an American and European phenomenon.

It is in this context, then, that America, north and south, finds its place in world history. The reasons for this massive surge of population—leaving aside the exact demographic mechanisms—are familiar enough. Everyone knows that Western civilization in the eighteenth and nineteenth centuries experienced the industrial revolution, urbanization, and a population explosion. Yet the erroneous notion persists in textbooks and lecture halls that something called the industrial revolution was first of all industrial; that it began in England, then spread, by emulation, to Europe and North America; and that population growth—modest by Asian standards—accompanied all this, just how is not clear. I hope to underscore here several crucial, obvious, but nevertheless regularly overlooked features of the "world revolution of westernization" considered from an economic and demographic perspective.

1. It began in the medieval economic revolution, whose epicenter was in the North European Plain.
2. Its driving force was increased agricultural output produced by massive and incremental input of land and improved agricultural technology. These sustained population growth rates led the world.
3. This emergent European economic system was expansionist in nature by the mid-eleventh or twelfth century, and by the sixteenth century was extending its range eastward beyond the Urals into Central Asia and beginning to exploit the Americas.

Much of our history is placed on a Procrustean bed of inherited forms. William McNeill's "inherited shape of European history" also intrudes into global history. The periodization and conceptual terms we have inherited from late eighteenth- and nineteenth-century European nationalists and Eurocentric historiography are obstacles that block our understanding of history as the story of the entire human condition. They must be removed or radically redesigned if we are to advance understanding of the human condition. Among them are: the English industrial revolution, the Renaissance, the Middle Ages, the Dark Ages, and of course the dates 476, 1500, 1750, or their variants.

One great inherited shape, the dominant one perhaps, is history conceived and constructed in national units; even world cultural areas, e.g., the world of Islam, the Confucian world, the Christian world, echo nationalist assumptions. The place of the United States in the history of the world is in a sense a *question mal posé*. Rather, one should consider the place of the Americas in a process of global diffusion of modern agriculture, industry, and the concomitant population explosion.

From this perspective the overwhelming phenomenon of our age, for the human species, is that the frontier has closed, slammed shut. For millennia technologically advanced civilization expanded across widening frontiers, carelessly, unconsciously transforming the environment in ultimately destructive ways. Then suddenly, within little more than our lifetimes, the frontier filled up and the resources—air, water, land—are in distress. Learning how to cope with scarce resources after millennia of wastefulness is the true challenge to the human race; the most formidable challenge now is an inward frontier—ourselves. For historians who study humanity as a whole, our mission is to develop a new paradigm; global history requires a Kuhnian revolution. The rise of the new social history, now considered in global and comparative terms, promises a new paradigm and a new synthesis in the interests of humanity. Am I wrong in imagining that one is in the formative stages?

Selected Bibliography

Boserup, Ester. *The Conditions of Agricultural Growth.* Chicago: Aldine, 1965.

————. *Population and Technological Change: A Study of Long-Term Trends.* Chicago: University of Chicago Press, 1983.

Cronon, William. *Changes in the Land: Indians, Colonists and the Ecology of New England.* New York: Hill and Wang, 1983.

Crosby, Alfred W. *The Columbian Exchange.* Westport, CT: Greenwood, 1972.

————. *Ecological Imperialism: The Biological Expansion of Europe.* New York: Cambridge University Press, 1986.

Curtin, Philip D. *Cross-Cultural Trade in World History.* New York: Cambridge University Press, 1984.

Elvin, Mark. *The Pattern of the Chinese Past: A Social and Economic Interpretation.* Stanford, CA: Stanford University Press, 1973.

Gernet, Jacques. *A History of Chinese Civilization.* New York: Cambridge University Press, 1982.

Jones, Eric L. *The European Miracle: Environments, Economies and Geopolitics in the History of Europe and Asia.* New York: Cambridge University Press, 1981.

McNeill, William H. *Plagues and Peoples.* Garden City, NY: Anchor Press, 1976.

————. *The Shape of European History.* New York: Oxford University Press, 1974.

Pirenne, Henri. *Mohammed and Charlemagne.* New York: Barnes and Noble, 1939.

Reinhard, Marcel, André Armengaud, and Jacques Dupaquier. *Histoire générale de la population mondiale.* Paris: Montchrestien, 1968.

Slicher van Bath, B.H. *The Agrarian History of Western Europe.* London: St. Martin's Press, 1963.

Von Laue, Theodore. *The World Revolution of Westernization: The Twentieth Century in Global Perspective.* New York: Oxford University Press, 1987.

Webb, Walter Prescott. *The Great Frontier.* Austin: University of Texas Press, 1964.

White, Lynn. *Medieval Technology and Social Change.* New York: Oxford University Press, 1962.

————. *The Transformation of the Roman World: Gibbon's Problem after Two Centuries.* Berkeley: University of California Press, 1966.

21

Teaching the Reformation as World History

A.J. Carlson

Most of us—when we consider the sixteenth-century Reformation—immediately think of Martin Luther in October 1517 nailing up his Ninety-five Theses against indulgences on the door of the Castle Church in Wittenburg. By his act, this obscure Augustinian professor, quite rightly, has been regarded as the catalyst of a protest movement that shook the Western world. No matter that what probably was posted represented a mere handwritten "list" of theses, and it wasn't until February of 1518 when his *Sermon on Indulgences and Grace* was printed that Dr. Luther produced the "first best seller of the Reformation."[1] Yet we may still pinpoint October 31, 1517, as *the* critical point of departure for the creation of Protestant Europe.

And there is nothing wrong with this approach: Students like to understand history by studying real people as opposed to statistical tables, and they appreciate specific dates—so long as there aren't too many of them. What the teacher of a world history course faces, however, is a myriad of dates and a surfeit of faces. In the case of the sixteenth-century Reformation, one will never have either the space or the time in which to detail the causes and effects of what is now seen as both a Catholic and a Protestant re-formation in this period.

What then is the world history teacher to do? One possibility is to find what William H. McNeill calls "connections" or points of disjunction in which we might build toward what is now being called by Samuel Huntington and others "the Clash of Civilizations."[2] If we can agree that the sixteenth century does comprise a period of disjunction with "medieval Europe" (whatever that means) and that Europe in that century also experienced connections with the rest of the world, it may be possible to help our students grasp some of the essential background to understand our own crazy world.

Much discussion has taken place recently in the light of the quincentennary of Columbus's discoveries as to how much Europe knew or didn't know about the world at large in the early sixteenth century. But Martin Luther in 1530 wrote a preface for a reprint of a book on the religion and customs of the Turks. He concluded with the hope "that our Gospel, now shining forth with a light so great, will, before Judgment Day, make an attack also on the abominable prophet Mohammed. May our Lord Jesus Christ do this soon."[3] Luther's urgency represents a pastoral response to the fact that in September 1529, the Ottoman Turks, under perhaps the finest field general of the sixteenth century, Suleyman, laid siege to the walls of Vienna itself. For the first time since the early medieval period, Europe was threatened by a Muslim invasion force that would become a factor in Europe for the next five hundred years. To be sure, the Serbs today still lament the Battle of Kossovo (1389) as the start of their struggle against the might of Islam; but it was the failure of the Christian West to expel the Turks from the Danube basin, after a stubborn defense of Vienna in 1529, and again in 1532, when the emperor's brother, Ferdinand, refused to organize a "crusade" against the Ottomans, that led Luther to comment: "A smart Turk makes a better ruler than a dumb Christian."[4]

For our history today, Suleyman's withdrawal into Hungary and Bosnia led to multiracial cultures in the Balkans, which did survive in relative harmony until the latter twentieth century. Recent research suggests that the *Timar* or field system of Ottoman landholding, which used to be seen as "feudal," was in fact under Suleyman ruthlessly controlled by the Ottoman center, granting lands to Christians and Muslims alike who supported this command structure.[5] Thus no "blood" aristocracy arose to challenge the power of the sultans, who were content to allow separate ethnic groups to live in relative harmony. After his failure to push beyond Vienna in 1532, Suleyman turned his attention eastward to Baghdad, where he proceeded to restore Sunni Islamic rites, though he allowed the Shi'ite Muslims to dominate Iran, as they have done to the present.

In an even more interesting stretch of historical "maybes," the proximity of the Ottoman army during the 1530s probably accounts for the failure of the Emperor Charles V to be able to deal decisively with the emerging alliance of Protestant princes, the Schmalkaldic League (1529), until it was too late for anything beyond the compromise of the 1547 Interim Settlement. So one might argue, as Lewis Spitz does, that the Turkish threat forced Charles V to curry favor with the Lutheran princes and caused his brother Ferdinand to recognize Suleyman as "father and suzerain," giving up Habsburg claims to Hungary and paying an annual tribute of thirty thousand ducats to the sultan.[6] Or, put more boldly, it was the pressure of the Ottoman Turks on the Habsburgs from 1529 to 1550 that permitted Lutheranism to become sufficiently entrenched in north Germany, so that the Habsburg emperor, "His Most Catholic Majesty," was forced to acquiesce to Lutheranism's survival in the Peace of Augsburg in September 1555. Spitz would insist that this overstates the case,[7] but in the ambit of the "Clash of Civilizations" thesis, today's students should recognize that by the mid-sixteenth century the Christian world of Charles V did dominate the Mediterranean and the West, whereas the vast Ottoman Empire would remain physically intact and used by the Venetians, the French, and later by the Russians as a counterweight in power politics until nearly the end of the nineteenth century.

In spite of the "Clash" thesis, examples of continued connections remain. For one, the son of a Genoese nobleman and a Turkish woman, one "Scipione," who was captured by Muslim seamen, grew up in Constantinople to become a distinguished admiral and vizier, but maintained a lively correspondence with family and friends in his native Genoa;[8] or, earlier, the brother of the sultan, Prince Jem, who was at the Renaissance papal court in Rome from 1489 to 1495, attracted attention through a love affair with a French baron's daughter, and showed up in Castiglione's *Book of the Courtier* "as a counter to cinquecento gaiety."[9] Castiglione wrote that when queried about jousting as he saw it in late fifteenth-century Italy, Prince Jem commented that "it seemed to him too much if done in play and too little if done in earnest."[10]

Such anecdotal evidence softens, perhaps, the impact of the "conflict" of civilizations thesis that Professor Huntington is currently delivering, and while one may accept much of what he says as bearing on potential for conflict in the future, both the Christian West and Islam (two of Huntington's "civilizations") ultimately are based on a sense of moral order, which does bring us back to the sixteenth-century Reformation. Here students need to be reminded that there was both a "Catholic" reformation and a Protestant reform, which took different directions.

Catholic scholars are quick to recognize that the origins of successful Catholic reform occurred before Luther's break with Rome. Cardinal Ximenes (Jiménez de Cesneros, 1436–1517), Queen Isabella's confessor, sought to reform the Spanish church during the first years of the sixteenth century, after the terrors of Torquemada had led to the expulsion of the Jews from Spain in 1492. Ximenes did continue the excesses of the Holy Office—it was, after all, a bloody and intolerant age—but he also condemned indulgences issued for the rebuilding of St. Peter's. And from his own resources he founded the University of Alcalá, the glory of which was the trilingual Complutensian Polyglot Bible in six volumes, printed between 1514 and 1517, with the Latin Vulgate text printed between the Hebrew and Septuagint Greek (the preface says, as Christ was crucified between two thieves), with Chaldee and Hebrew notes across the bottom and in the margin of the text.

Students should understand that Erasmus's New Testament, also printed in 1517, and this Iberian polyglot Bible, along with Luther's New Testament in 1522, in many ways changed the whole course of religious debate, to examine what Father George Tavard calls *Holy Writ or Holy Church,* to which Luther would have responded, *Sola Fide* and *Sola Scriptura.*

For Catholics, stung by the onslaughts of Protestant reformers, the response came, as always, with reform of old orders, such as the Capuchins and Luther's own Augustinians, or with the creation of new orders, such as the Theatines founded by Giovanni Pietro Carafa (later Pope Paul IV), who sought to create "an army of zealous priests," and the Ursulines under St. Angelo Merici, who became the teachers to girls as the Jesuits would be to boys. It is hard to overstate the impact on the sixteenth century of this latter group, the Society of Jesus, whose founder, Inigo Lopez Recalde, was born in 1491 in Basque country at the castle of Loyola. His life as a soldier, conversion in 1521, and subsequent study in Spain and at the University of Paris (at the same time as Calvin in the early 1530s), as well as the influence of his disciplined meditation—*Spiritual Exercises*—are all well known. What should be emphasized to students in a world history course is the missionary zeal of these young members of "the Company of Jesus" after 1540, who wanted to raise chickens in Rome to feed the marginalized, and by the death of their founder in 1556 had sent more than a thousand Jesuits worldwide: from Francis Xavier to Goa in 1542 and later to Japan; to Antonio Possevino to Poland and Russia, the first Westerner to describe Muscovy Russia firsthand; and, finally, to Matteo Ricci from 1582 to 1610, dressed in Chinese silks and reading Chinese classics, who would serve the Ming dynasty as what Anthony Grafton calls "the first Christian Mandarin." Collectively, Grafton describes these first Jesuits as "spiritual entrepreneurs who wanted to break open new markets" for the faith.[11]

It was this renewed energy that galvanized the medieval Church into the Counter-Reformation at the long awaited Council of Trent during the middle years of the century, 1547 to 1563, to create what we recognize today as the Roman Catholic church. Here the Trentine emphasis was upon a reformed clergy and a diocesan structure that sought to use both the educational humanist reforms of Alcalá (mixed with Thomist theology) and the priestly zeal of the new orders to counter the emerging power of Protestantism.

Dealing with reforms in the existing medieval Church first certainly allows us to see Luther's own hope and expectation. As late as the creation of the Augsburg Confession in 1539, and even at the conference at Ratisbon in 1541, Martin

Luther hoped for some type of restoration within the medieval church. Indeed, for beginning students the key words are *restoration, revolution,* and *reformation.*[12]

Luther's total effort was concentrated on restoring what he perceived to be the commitment of the early Church to an emphasis on *individual* salvation. His Pauline-inspired doctrine of justification by faith, i.e., *sola fide,* emphasized the almost mystical commitment to the individual who receives the word, i.e., *sola scriptura.* He wrote in his pamphlet *On Christian Liberty* (1520):[13]

> Just as the heated iron glares like fire because of the union of fire with it, so the Word imparts its qualities to the soul.

This son of a German miner may well have had the image of molten metal before his mind as he pondered the effect of scripture on the new faithful. Yet to his German neighbors Luther also insisted (as did St. Augustine):

> A man does not live for himself alone in this mortal body to work for it alone, but he lives also for all men as well; rather, he lives only for others and not for himself.

It is this kind of commitment that makes the German Lutheran a strong servant with an urgency to become a member of this new moral community based on a *restored* biblical faith.

Such language, however, did propel some of Luther's listeners and readers to seize upon the creation of new communities with a radically different vision of society. Those German peasants in 1524–1525 who heard the words *Christian freedom* proclaimed a social liberty that the conservative Martin Luther never intended. Those so-called spiritualists, who carried individual faith to the level of complete authority were indeed *revolutionaries* and attacked their landlords led by preachers such as Thomas Münzer, of whom Luther said: "I wouldn't believe Münzer if he swallowed the Holy Ghost feathers and all!" Even more radical for the future were the Zürich Christians who read Luther and heard the sermons of Huldreich Zwingli and believed individuals should be rebaptized as adults with the true spirit, the so-called Anabaptists (Calvin grimly called them Catabaptists). But the efforts of the Zürich Anabaptists, such as Conrad Grebel and Georg Blaurock, to form new communities of believers in gathered churches quite apart from society laid down the beginnings in Western religious thought of the autonomous lay churches that would form one source for later emerging representative democracy in both Europe and the United States.

The third term, *reformation,* fits best with the work of John Calvin in Geneva: trained in law, with a humanist commitment to mind and body that allowed him to emphasize both the omnipotence of God and the moral depravity of humankind. To a larger degree than Luther, Calvin saw the Church as an agent of discipline composed of both the clergy and the laity, who must reform a sinful world. His *Ecclesiastical Ordinances* of 1541 altered Church polity into a balance of clergy and laymen that remains the model in the Reformed churches to the present. However, Calvin's last few paragraphs of the 1559 edition of *The Institutes of the Christian Religion* carry this concept of reformation, for the first time, directly into the political arena. Whether intentionally or not (and Calvin was hardly revolutionary himself), in these latter sections it becomes the duty of the Christian magistrate to reform ungodly kings into their true role as "ministers of God," as he wrote the French king in his preface to the first edition of his *Institutes.* And while Calvin attempts to forestall individuals acting out any implied theory of Tyrannicide, his language in Chapter XXXI of Book IV leaves little doubt of the responsibility of elected magistrates "to oppose the violence or cruelty of kings." The ultimate impact of such language would be political revolutions in Holland, France, England, and ultimately, the United States.

One further example of reformation comes out of the sixteenth century—that of the political magistrates, i.e., the monarch themselves. In England, which is perhaps the cleanest example of "magisterial reformation," from Henry VIII to Elizabeth I, Europe saw the results of the state-reformed church. Catholic in liturgical form and doctrine under King Henry and loosely Protestant under his younger daughter Elizabeth, England survived the latter sixteenth century without religious civil war (delayed, of course, only until the clumsiness of the Stuart kings caused war in the mid-seventeenth century). For students who would smile at the reasons for his break with Rome (all those six wives), Henry VIII's desire to reform Church orders and to grant permission for an English Bible was grounded in a deep sense of responsibility. His second daughter, Elizabeth, pushed one step further, to emphasize the responsibility of the state for the Church and for society, which led, in part, to the Elizabeth Poor Laws and grudging acknowledgment of the rights to free speech in Parliament and pulpit wrested from the queen by her "loyal" Puritan subjects.

All of these movements during the sixteenth-century Reformation—reform of the medieval Church by Roman Catholicism, different models of ecclesiastical reforms by Protestants, as well as state commitment to reform for laity and clergy—were a large part of the transformation of our own heritage. Teachers should emphasize this fact for students to realize a sense of individual moral responsibility.

Notes

1. Heiko A. Oberman, *Luther: Man Between God and the Devil* (New Haven: Yale University Press, 1989), p. 192.

2. S.P. Huntington, "The Clash of Civilizations," *Foreign Affairs* (summer 1993):22–49; cf. W.H. McNeill, "The Rise of the West after Twenty-five Years," *Journal of World History* (spring 1990):1–22.

3. *What Luther Says: An Anthology,* E.M. Plass, ed. (St. Louis: Concordia Press, 1959), 2:958.

4. Lewis W. Spitz, *The Protestant Reformation, 1517–1559* (New York: Harper and Row, 1985), p. 330.

5. Cemel Kafadar, "The Ottomans and Europe," *Handbook of European History, 1400–1600, Late Middle Ages, Renaissance and Reformation,* T.A. Brady, Jr., Heiko A. Oberman, and James D. Tracy, eds. (Leiden: E.J. Brill, 1994), 1:588–628.

6. Spitz, *Protestant Reformation,* p. 331.

7. Ibid., p. 317.

8. Kafadar, 1:620.

9. Ibid., p. 607.

10. B. Castiglione, *The Book of the Courtier,* C.S. Singleton, tr. (New York: Doubleday, 1959), Bk. II, par. 66.

11. Anthony Grafton, "The Soul's Entrepreneurs," *New York Review of Books* (March 3, 1994):33–37.

12. E. Harris Harbison, *The Age of the Reformation* (Ithaca: Cornell, 1956), *passim.*

13. Martin Luther, *Christian Liberty,* W.A. Lambert, tr. (Philadelphia: Fortress, 1957), pp. 12, 27.

Bibliography

Luther and the Reformation

Bainton, Roland H. *Here I Stand: A Life of Martin Luther.* Nashville: Abington, 1950.

Oberman, Heiko A. *Luther: Man Between God and the Devil.* New Haven: Yale University Press, 1989.

Spitz, Lewis W., *The Protestant Reformation, 1517–1559.* New York: Harper and Row, 1985.

The Ottoman Turks and Europe

Itzkowitz, Norman. *Ottoman Empire and Islamic Tradition.* New York: Knopf, 1972.

Lewis, Bernard. *Istanbul and the Civilization of the Ottoman.* Norman: University of Oklahoma Press, 1963.

The Catholic Reformation

Daniel-Rops, Henri. *The Catholic Reformation.* 2 vols. J. Warrington, tr. New York: Doubleday, 1962.

Dickens, A.G. *The CounterReformation.* History of European Civilization series. New York: Harcourt Brace, 1969.

Grafton, Anthony. "The Soul's Entrepreneurs." *New York Review of Books,* March 3, 1994, 33–37.

O'Malley, John. *The First Jesuits.* Cambridge, MA: Harvard University Press, 1994.

The Protestant Reformation

Bainton, Roland H., *The Reformation of the Sixteenth Century.* Boston: Beacon Press, 1952.

———. *Women of the Reformation.* Minneapolis: Augsburg Press, Vol. I, *Germany and Italy* (1971); Vol. 2, *France and England* (1973); Vol. 3, *From Spain to Scandinavia* (1977).

Grimm, Harold J. *The Reformation Era, 1500–1650.* 2nd edition. New York: Macmillan, 1973.

Harbison, E. Harris. *The Age of the Reformation.* Ithaca, NY: Cornell University Press, 1956.

22

An American-Centered Paradigm for a Global Literary Curriculum

Judy Lightfoot

A Multicultural American Literary Curriculum . . .

When revising the content of my English courses over the past twelve years, I've tried to follow a principle that may sound both grandiose and banally obvious: I try to choose course content on the basis of what all my students, regardless of race, ethnic origin, or sex, might need as American citizens of the world of the twenty-first century. What they most need, I think, is help in conceiving of themselves and others as belonging to two enormous cultural families—an American one and a global one. These are sprawling and contentious families to be sure, with rivalries and alliances reaching back centuries and speaking too many dialects and languages for any one person to master. But the diverse members of these families are alike in having ideas about how to live and how to talk about living, and the diversity of these ideas provides a desirable and necessary multiplicity of positions for our students to occupy, ponder, act on, and grow from. So I try to make literary study a way of introducing students to a wide variety of American and international perspectives and modes of representation. Doing so with reasonable coherence has been quite a challenge.

I start by counting myself less an advocate of multiculturalism in ways it is often defined than the opponent of *mono*culturalisms so narrowly conceived that they prevent full and rich identification with voices of male and female authors of all races. For example, I think every African-American man needs to grow up having had the opportunity to feel that *The Autobiography of Benjamin Franklin* is part of his birthright and a potential source of inspiration, and that he can take sides in Hawthorne's argument against Franklinian opportunism or in Melville's quarrel with Emerson's transcendentalism even though he is not a white reader. Similarly, every Euro-American woman, me, for example, should be able to make Henry David Thoreau her artistic exemplar or question Maxine Hong Kingston's response to being caught between cultures.

But it is difficult to remember that it is the emotional, imaginative, intellectual, and spiritual interest of *everyone* to study various literatures when so many public arguments for multiculturalism are based on a simplistic notion of fairness—that the exclusion of works by nonwhite and female authors deprives nonwhite and women students of equal opportunity with white and male students to be reflected or otherwise affirmed in the literature they study. Fairness as a curricular goal invites a mindless reliance on quotas, generates backlash, and without adequate conceptual frameworks tends to promote either tokenism or separatism.

One problem with tokenism is that it tends to create racist and sexist stereotypes instead of countering them, as when a few nonmainstream works are sprinkled into a study of mainstream literature and are consequently received as factual reports on the lives of eccentric others. An African-American student enrolled in such a course at my school privately expressed the feeling of several classmates to me: "You just know the white students are thinking crazy things about black people. Listen to what they say in class about *Native Son*. We catch ourselves wanting to explain, 'Our life isn't like that,' then have to laugh at ourselves for feeling defensive. But the books are a problem." A book by a woman is a problem, too, when so poorly contextualized that its style and subject make it an uncomfortable course anomaly. Last year, in two different sections of the survey of American authors at my school, the first day on Cather's *A Lost Lady* began with almost identical challenges from (as it happened) thoughtful boys. They said they realized that "in those days" women writers lacked the opportunities men had, "but why should we read second-rate books because of this?" Neither teacher was satisfied with the discussion that followed.

Some schools that resist tokenism do so by instituting separate courses for the literature of different social groups—African-American Literature and Women's Studies, for example. And some separatist reformers go so far as to claim that special homogeneous courses are the only way to make nonmainstream readings feel less dissonant or exotic and to inspire a ready, full reception, even from students whose origins might be thought to ease their identification with the literature. Others say all white students should be required to take at least one special ethnic studies course. Yet "separate but equal" policies within schools create problems similar to ones they used to create between schools, and ethnic studies requirements generate their own kinds of backlash. In many instances, then, attempts at creating separate programs that fairly represent different groups have fostered social misunderstanding and polarization while weakening curricular coherence.

So I start with the assumption that all my students have deep personal and social needs for participating in dialogues among different literary voices, and that no student should be deprived of strains of the nation's and the world's literatures because some educator wants to place a traditionalist or a compensatory emphasis on writers with particular backgrounds. Nor should these literatures be divided into Mirrors for the Self and Windows on alien Others. This notion is false because literature everywhere provides, not unmediated encounters with persons or life, but imagined representations of them in verbal form. It is divisive, too, in that it asks us to read literature as members of subgroups possessing mutually exclusive identities and interests instead of as a people sharing not only specific cultures and subcultures but also a whole planet.

. . . At the Center of a Global Literary Curriculum

Even with a clearer goal in mind, though, it was hard for me to revise the content of my courses because an Anglo-European primacy in my department's conceptions of English continued unchanged. At my school, almost half the literature presented is British in origin, and almost a fifth consists of European or ancient classics. Thus about two-thirds of the program has always been devoted to Anglo-European writings (most of them pre-twentieth century), while only a third is left for American works and only a negligible fraction for addressing literature from other countries. An unquestioned Anglo-European predominance in a reading curriculum implicitly defined as a collection of revered artifacts makes it difficult to include more voices in the literary conversation even when compelling reasons exist for doing so.

However, a critique of Anglo-European domination in English programs is facilitated if a teacher's central goal is to help students develop an understanding of their own culture. One can concede, for example, that it may have made sense a hundred years ago to place the literature of England at the center of the U.S. language arts curriculum because British literature, considered the cultural matrix of America, was also considered to be more important than anything that might grow out of it. But augmented by a century more of American writing, by discoveries of forgotten or previously unpublished manuscripts, and by transcripts of native oral traditions, American literary culture has come to be highly

regarded in its own right—so highly regarded, in fact, that it is *the* culture whose popular versions are most widely exported throughout the world today. Surely our students should have a deeper, broader acquaintance with American literary works and ways than what many foreign nations ask their students to acquire. In short, it seems simply mistaken now to teach as if our nation were more the stepchild of a distant tradition than our own cultural motherland—however much contempt our familiarity with it may breed.

Thus I have come to assume that the center of the American school literary curriculum ought to be American literature, and rather than devote only a minor third of the program to the subject, I see it as requiring at least half the available time. Such a move might on the surface seem revolutionary only to independent schools like mine, and not to the many schools in which American literature already happens to dominate the reading lists. But even in places where most of the works now taught are written by U.S. authors, the liberating and shaping implications of making American literature the *chosen* curricular focus of English have gone largely unrecognized. To me, this choice implies a logical center for a global literary curriculum.

For if my goal is to acquaint students with their home tradition, can they fully know what it is, or what any tradition is, if they do not see theirs as one among others? In order to realize the multiple qualities of their own extended cultural family, they need to compare it with ones around the world. So besides a nonmonocultural American literacy of the kind discussed above, my students need to develop a second kind: a knowledge of foreign literatures whose contrasts with literature of their own nation will improve their understanding of it and will encourage a habit central to literacy, that of questioning their interpretations.

In light of these purposes, Anglo-European literature becomes just one part (though still an important part) of available worldwide cultural resources. That is, students from kindergarten onward do need to read literature that contributed to their home literary tradition—stories from the Bible and classical myth, Sophocles, Shakespeare, the British romantics, Tolstoy, and Kafka. But is unreasonable today for British literature automatically to preside over the American reading program as the compulsory examination of Anglo-Saxon and English cultural monuments from the Dark Ages onward. It makes more sense to choose British writings from among a number of international traditions (not all of them Western) that speak to each other and the American tradition in ways important for high school students to know. As a basic image from which to derive a literary curriculum, then, I have stopped picturing a finite hierarchy of collections of essential artifacts: at the top the Western Literature Collection (Ancient, then European, then British, then American) and at the bottom a shelf called Other, which some reformers are trying to enlarge. Instead, I imagine something like a world map (or clock face) with American literature at the center and the literatures of the world surrounding it, from European literature at about NNE (or 1:00) to African literature at SE (4:00) or thereabouts, Latin American literature farther south (6:00), and on around the global circle to the literatures of India, Japan, and China (see appendix, p. 133.

Coping Strategies for Teachers Lacking Expertise in Noncanonical Literature

Professional anxiety due to lack of acquaintance with literature called multicultural is a significant and very understandable reason that educators across the nation have been slow to alter their programs. Indeed, like most English teachers my age, I was not well educated in noncanonical American literature, and like most high school teachers in the United States, I hardly encountered foreign literatures beyond those considered roots of the Western tradition. In my ignorance, and in the absence of a coherent institutional direction for curricular reform, the way I address unfamiliar books and traditions is by teaching them to make them familiar, mainly by counting on my students to instruct themselves and each other—and me in the process.

Not surprisingly, my students have taught me that appropriate contexts are more useful than apologia when introducing literature with striking differences into the mainstream. For example, I describe elsewhere how years ago, before published commentary about Zora Neale Hurston's *Their Eyes Were Watching God* became as plentiful as it is now, the novel was readily integrated into a tenth-grade course of mainstream literature by students making oral presentations of library research on the Harlem Renaissance and Hurston's life prior to reading it.[1] Having given each other a meaningful context for the book, they avoided stereotyped notions while coming to appreciate new literary styles, characters, and subjects. They learned more than just the text, and they enjoyed helping me gain a gradual acquaintance with an area of literature and literary history that significantly enlarges an appreciation of the arts and concerns of the American 1920s. For similar contextualizing purposes I asked the same class to draft a collaborative introduction and footnotes for Kingston's *The Woman Warrior* after we read the book. To do so, we looked in ancient Chinese legends and customs, modern Chinese history, the lives of Asian immigrants in the United States from the mid-nineteenth century on, and background material on Kingston's life and art. The Chinese-American student who asked whether a Chinatown Renaissance had ever occurred in the United States found much to tell the class about why there had not been one, while other students conducted retellings of ancient Chinese myths

of heroic women, speculated about why these stories thrived in a culture so oppressive to females, and compared them with the few tales of Western heroines they already knew, along with the more numerous Native American stories they were able to find.

My first experiment in teaching the literature of a non-Western nation to deepen an understanding of American culture was also designed so that my students and I could teach ourselves cultural contexts for the literature as the weeks unfolded. In this senior course in twentieth-century Japanese writing, we started with and periodically returned to the question, What is American about American writing?—at times recalling material and ideas from their survey of American authors the preceding year. Together we set as a principal goal the framing of adequate responses to a comparable question about Japan, while acknowledging the provisional nature of any conclusions we might eventually draw. After reading several essays on Zen, two articles about traditional forms such as *tanka* and *haiku,* and a few passages from Reischauer's latest book on Japanese culture and character, we studied the novels *Botchan* and *Black Rain* and an anthology of short fiction in which a few writers such as Shiga Naoya, Yasunari Kawabata, and Kobo Abe are each represented by several stories. Throughout the term, students gave presentations on aspects of Japanese and Japanese-American history and culture they researched in the library. By term's end, my students and I had become more sophisticated about problems of interpretation, especially across cultures, and we better understood how we and our American culture are influenced by particular definitions of self and group, by a heritage of philosophical dualism, by aesthetics of restraint and extravagance, and by Western conceptions of literary character, plot, and subject. In course evaluations the most frequent (and, for me, most gratifying) response from students was this: "I think I'm beginning to understand Western culture."

I have had similar good luck with other experiences of integrating into my courses literature called multicultural that is new to me, but in no case could I have framed the outcomes summarized above as explicit goals before teaching the new material. I had to learn along with students the value of what we did by doing it, and I always felt surprised when things turned out so well. But my experience does help me feel more eager to teach unfamiliar American and foreign literatures without years of prior reeducation, and it suggests that other teachers can do the same by planning student-centered work on relevant cultural contexts to complement the readings—an approach that also, fortunately, helps keep studies of nonmainstream and foreign literature from becoming a historical Disneyland tour through the planet's exotica.

My experience has generated other guidelines for future experiments. First, I keep in mind that my purpose in affirming American literature as the curricular center and dislodging Anglo-European literature from conscious or unconscious primacy is not "political" in a narrow sense—i.e., is not to facilitate a form of quid pro quo between historically ignored and so-called hegemonic authors. Nor is it to pretend that all literature from everywhere in the world is comparable in subject or equally important to teach my students. My purpose is to outline a curricular paradigm that will bring more of the world's literary voices into my range of available options, will assist the creation of coherence among the voices I decide to teach, and will give me ways of learning enough about them while a new course unfolds to enable me to choose the most appropriate ones for students in the future.

So far, the paradigm of ongoing conversations within American literature and between American and foreign literatures has worked well for me. I will try to sketch here the sort of conversation I mean:

What does this book (A) say about who we are? If there is a "we," is there a "they"? What constitutes "life" in this book? What are some of the ways people live it? How, according to the book, should people live? Can we describe the voice, imagery, point of view, and structural features that represent these various matters? What is missing from the overall picture? Why do you suppose all this is so?

If the other books we have read (B, C, D, etc.) could talk, how might they (separately, together) respond to A's claims and thoughts as we interpret them? Where would these books agree with A? Disagree? Go off on their own tangents? Would the voices or structures of their responses resemble or differ from the styles of A? What is missing here? Why do you suppose all this is the case?

. . . and so on. Of course, the conversation that a class might invent between book A and other books would consist of interwoven exchanges, not a pair of uninterrupted monologues, and each of the questions is really a generalized rubric for many related and subtle questions about visions, voices, and traditions that would take days or months to explore.

Given the purpose of evoking coherent conversations among works and traditions of literature around the world in order to help my students understand their own culture, then, I more readily remember that the way to select readings is not to start by asking, Which are the best?—a question that begs the retort, "Best for what?" The wonderful books in the world already number more than could possibly be taught, so beyond apparent or reputed creative genius, the more useful question is this: To what extent are these works likely to spark interesting, instructive dialogues with each other and with American literature?

To illustrate: When choosing examples of British literature to include in a reading program, I acknowledge that Shakespeare, the romantic poets, the nineteenth-century novelists, and the moderns produced splendidly complex, teachable cultural monuments. However, what makes them good choices from the whole range of British literature for an American-centered high school program is not their monumental value but their value in helping my students better understand their home literary culture. So I continue to teach Shakespeare because of his concern with themes and rhetorics that mark important transitions between Western medieval and modern conceptions of the world; the conflict between obedience and self-assertion in his plays and his celebration of high to low styles of spoken English are excellent reference points for discussion of analogous concerns in American writing. In a similar vein, British novels and romantic poetry offer clarifying counterpoints to an American romanticism that continues to dominate our cultural life, and British modernism has figured in our aesthetic arguments for nearly a century. Thus, though I would not want to teach all the British literature currently presented in my school's English program, I would want to teach some of it—for reasons different from (and, I think, better than) those that prevailed when I was a student.

Designing the non–Anglo-American segment of a literary program is more difficult because the goal of teaching students how to read their own culture well through interpreting another across barriers of difference does not in itself compel a particular choice among Asian, Latin American, African, or Middle Eastern literary traditions. Again one must ask, Which ones have the greatest potential to generate rich conversations with American literature? And when the scholarship required to make a convincing case for one or another is lacking, the following reminder can mitigate anxiety about choosing erroneously: A culture-based exploration of American literature provides key recurring concepts that can be used to open pathways into literatures around the world: e.g., freedom, society, individual rights, wealth, revolution, nature, art, spirit, originality, romanticism, modernity, tradition. For Americans each of these terms possesses, if not always a commonly accepted cultural definition, at least a common cultural history of evolving and conflicting definitions. Students who have had sustained experience in using and reflecting on such concepts while discussing American literature can be shown how to sift foreign texts for evidence of these concepts at work in one way or another. In doing so, they see that other cultures define some of these concepts differently, ignore many of them entirely, and occupy themselves with ideas of their own that may not readily leap to an American reader's mind when contemplating literary art—for example, the aesthetic of extreme verbal austerity in Japanese traditions, or their tendency to represent freedom in spiritual rather than political terms. As a consequence of having chosen an American-centered focus for literary study, then, I am provided with a language that virtually guarantees relevant, illuminating conversations between American literature and any foreign one. After having engaged students in several different studies of foreign literature, it is possible to begin deciding the comparative appropriateness of each for future curriculum choices.

A National Humanities Curriculum for U.S. Schools?

It is probable that only plans that take kindergarten through secondary reading programs into account could adequately address the goal of teaching American students their literary tradition within an international context. So, having articulated here some thoughts about curriculum revision that have proven more useful in my work than the current ways in which multiculturalism is being defined and promoted in schools, I find it hard to resist imagining changes on a grander scale than just my classroom.

Perhaps a concentrically imagined American-international focus in K–12 curricula across the nation would enhance a sense of cultural unity instead of contributing to what now seems a cacophony of cross-purpose, sometimes internecine instruction. People persuaded (as I am) by some of E.D. Hirsch's arguments in favor of creating a common core for American schools' humanities curricula may see that a sensible selection of readings in American and international literatures might more readily be made within such a concentric framework than amid the confusion of existing programs and the presently debased state of public discourse about multiculturalism. A single detailed curriculum would have limited application and value for schools across as large and diverse a country as ours, but different communities can produce locally tailored versions of a nationwide program if they have a frame of reference suggesting at least broad goals in common. And it is exciting to me to think in terms of a frame of reference that could inaugurate a third era of English in America.

That is, if the first era of literary studies in American English departments were termed:

The Era of British Literature (c. 1890–1950)—a reading program focused on major periods and works of British literature from Anglo-Saxon times to the present, with judicious selections from American literature (e.g., Hawthorne, Emerson, Bryant, Irving),

the second era of American literary studies might be called:

The Era of British and American Literature (c. 1950–2000)—a reading program consisting of major periods and works of British and American literature.

Now is the time to work toward establishing:

The Era of American and World Literatures (2000–?)—a reading program divided equally between literature of the United States drawn from native and immigrant strains, and foreign works from Western and non-Western literatures, written by men and women.

Be that as it may, looking back over two decades of my teaching, I see that construing the English reading curriculum as an array of indispensable artifacts gave my students limited notions of literature and its value while making even self-motivated changes in my own courses awkward and sometimes impossible. My difficulties only increased when I supposed that multicultural reform meant replacing white male traditions with formerly excluded ones, or dividing my students into Selves and Others for whom equitable numbers of Mirrors and Windows need to be found. I've found that it is more conducive to needed reform as well as more accurate about literature, traditions, readers, and the world today to think of the literary curriculum as a continuing conversation among multiple voices of American and foreign literatures.

Note

1. Judith Lightfoot, "Studying the Harlem Renaissance and *Their Eyes Were Watching God*," in *Vital Signs 1: Bringing Together Reading and Writing,* ed. James L. Collins (Portsmouth, NH: Heinemann-Boynton/Cook, 1990), pp. 70–83.

Appendix

Picturing U.S. literature at the center of our English reading programs, surrounded by a range of literatures from elsewhere in the world, we would have less need to think in terms of a hierarchy of traditions resembling this:

THE LITERATURE OF THE WEST*
Ancient Literature
British Literature
European Literature
American Literature
Other

*Mostly white authors, with few nonwhite and female authors mixed in.

The mental map from which a U.S.-centered literary curriculum was drawn would look more like this:

LITERATURES OF THE UNITED STATES AND THE WORLD

However, just as a Mercator map shapes the continents differently from other global projections, this sketch of a map has its distortions. I do not offer it as a full list of worldwide sources for readings—in which case the bagginess of the category "Eastern Europe" would be unhelpful, and the absence of specific references to Egypt or Iraq might suggest ignorance or bias. Similarly, unwarranted detail seems to be supplied by the list of individual Asian nations when it is compared with the undifferentiated abstractness of "Western Europe." This sketch is only an outline of a visual image meant to open a wider, more complex perspective on the literary world than the simple ladder-image most of us inherited.

Part III

Strategies and Lessons

Introduction

Since the whole history of the world is possible subject matter for world history, selecting world history lessons quickly becomes a daunting task. The cardinal rule for success is Keep It Simple. Arnie Schrier, professor at the University of Cincinnati and author of the textbook *History and Life,* occasionally can be enticed to retell the story of his first teaching adventure, which illustrates this cardinal rule:

In 1949 I was a student teacher in a tenth-grade social studies class at Evanston Township High School in Evanston, Illinois. After observing the class for several weeks, I was asked by the teacher if I would be willing to take over the class the following week and base my lesson on Chapter 25 in the textbook. I agreed, though I didn't have the text with me and didn't know what Chapter 25 covered. When I got back to my room and checked the text, I nearly panicked. Chapter 25 was entitled "Democracy, Communism, and Socialism," and I was to cover it all in one class session!

Stress can sometimes be the mother of inventiveness. I decided that what I needed to do, given the short time I had for the lesson, was to focus on some key concepts and have the students provide examples from the recent past or from their contemporary world to illustrate those concepts. It was a way to get the students quickly involved and for them to gain some basic understanding of important ideas.

When I came to class on the day of my lesson, I made two columns on the blackboard. One I headed "Political Systems" and the other "Economic Systems." Then I asked students to give me the names of two fundamental political systems and two fundamental economic systems. On the political side they suggested democracy and dictatorship; on the economic side, capitalism and socialism. Each time a term was suggested, we briefly discussed its essential features.

The next step was to point out that every country had its own combination of political and economic systems. Referring to the columns on the board, I told the students that we would make different combinations and then try to think of countries that best represented those combinations. When I said "democracy" and "capitalism," the immediate response was the United States. When I asked about "democracy" and "socialism," the response was not so immediate, but eventually we decided on Sweden.

Combining "dictatorship" and "capitalism" caused some confusion because many of the students thought "capitalism" was synonymous with "democracy." Once the confusion was cleared up, we were able to point to Nazi Germany and Fascist Spain as examples of the dictatorship-capitalist combination.

Finally, in asking about "dictatorship" and "socialism," virtually all students named the Soviet Union.

We concluded the lesson within the class period. Of course, there was no time to dwell on the many complex varieties in these combinations. But at the very least, I hoped, we had been able to sort out some key ideas.

While the goals and general course outlines are interesting reading the first day of class, the lesson is the message. Good textbooks are accompanied with an instructor's manual bulging with ideas for teaching the political and cultural achievements of one civilization at a time. But world history extends beyond the study of each civilization. The goal of world history is to help students acquire a working knowledge of the world with its many interrelated parts. World history lessons that reflect new research and extend beyond the traditional, mental boundaries of civilizations or modern countries are not as readily available. The following lessons, which include comparative, cross-cultural, and global approaches, enable students to develop a broader vision. Comparative studies allow students to gain important perspectives, not only about the aspects of the societies compared but also about their own time and culture. Lessons with the theme of cross-cultural exchange offer students insights into the process of cultural diffusion—how societies change as they adopt, reject, or adapt to foreign ideas. Lessons that teach a global theme trace the impact of a process on various societies around the world. Global lessons provide students with the opportunity to identify common, shared characteristics in the human story and characteristics that are unique to a particular society.

Develop rubrics to evaluate the usefulness of the lesson. The following questions provide a possible starting point for developing lesson evaluations.

1. Is the lesson consistent with the goals and framework of the course?
2. Is this lesson a realistic challenge for students in terms of their abilities?
3. Are the materials for teaching the lesson adequate?
4. Are the lesson goals consistent with the plans for evaluation?
5. What historical thinking skills are included in the lesson?
6. Does the content of this lesson extend the historical knowledge of students?

7. Does this lesson engage students as active learners?
8. How successfully did students demonstrate their mastery of skills and content?

Perhaps a few housekeeping suggestions are in order. At the beginning of the year consider the general abilities and range of individual differences in the incoming class. Good lessons engage the student as a participant. Less academically gifted students profit from shorter units, more opportunities to practice critical thinking skills, concrete examples of historical concepts, and biographical and autobiographical accounts of real people. Compare the world history course with other courses being taught to eliminate unnecessary redundancies and overlapping content. Organizing world history teaching files so that clippings, handouts, copies of tests, lesson plans, primary sources, and technology materials are accessible is rather like designing an index for the Internet, but don't give up. Use the computer to keep an inventory of articles, ideas, and materials categorized according to the course of study. Keep revising and personalizing your system. A filing system passes muster when students have the right material at the right time in class. Accurate notes concerning class progress, new ideas for research and development, and considered revisions are invaluable the following year. This section begins with strategies, technologies, and teaching ideas that may be applied throughout the year and are followed with lessons organized chronologically, as they might appear in a world history survey course.

23

Mixing It Up in the Classroom

JoAnn Alberghini

Varied approaches to subject matter keep students engaged and learning. JoAnn Alberghini has developed a variety of generic activities to combine with specific subject matter. Every activity is written separately on a brightly colored index card. With each lesson JoAnn selects new activities from her repertoire that serve as intriguing springboards into the subject matter.

Hot Seat

This is a group activity that allows students to assume the persona of a character in history or literature. The student (in character) answers questions from others in the group, requiring that the student live in the shoes of the selected character. Divide the class into groups of three to five students. Each student selects a different character to become. In turn, students are given two minutes to respond "in character" to questions posed by other members of the group. To facilitate implementation, brainstorm possible questions in groups. Questions might focus on why a character did something or how she or he felt about something that happened. For responding to questions, put students in expert character groups to share ideas about characters. Lead-in activities might include using puppets, character masks, or living murals.

Duologue

This is a spontaneous conversation between two students who assume the persona of characters in history or literature; it encourages them to develop an in-depth understanding of the thoughts and actions of two characters. A scene is chosen from history or from a story in which a conversation could have taken place between two characters but did not. Students begin talking and develop a conversation as it might have taken place.

Historical Fiction Book Projects

Here are several suggested book-project assignments for students:

• Construct a History Notebook on the people and events in your book. Your notebook might include mini-reports on such topics as: customs, clothing styles, folklore, food preparation, occupations, leisure activities, speech patterns, and the major problems facing the people who lived in the time and place that your book covers. Include an illustrated cover, a title page, a table of contents, an index, and a bibliography.

• Assume you are a character in the book you are reading. Construct and write a Historical Journal describing your thoughts and actions during a critical time in the book. Include as many details as possible describing what life was like during the time you were alive (and writing your journal).

• Create a Relief Map of a specific location in your book. Identify the important buildings, roads, landmarks, and geographic features on your map. Color your map and include a scale of miles and a map key to help identify the features.

• Write an Archaeologist's Log describing the locations in your book by listing both "cultural artifacts" (customs, language, old sayings, superstitions, folk medicine, beliefs) and "physical artifacts" (any physical object created and used by human beings). For each artifact you find, give a detailed description of what it is, where you found it, and what it tells you about the people in the story.

• Design and create an Illustrated Timeline showing, through pictures and words, the major events in the story that had a significant effect upon the main character(s).

• Write a "What If" History as if you could have been there to have changed events. Choose an episode from your book and rewrite "history" the way you would want it to turn out.

• Choose a scene or incident from the book and rewrite it in a Funny History satire, poking fun at what is going on. Be as creative as you can. Use as many details from the book as you can.

A History Recipe

Students list "ingredients" for an event in history such as an invasion or a revolution, all written as measured quantities as in a recipe. They should describe how the ingredients should be mixed and prepared in a way similar to a cooking process.

Storyboards

This is a graphic depiction of the major events in a historical episode or story. Students are asked to illustrate (in sequence) *exactly* eight major events of that episode. Students share their storyboards, since no two will be alike. This activity may be done individually or in groups.

Venn Diagram

This is an organization device for charting similarities and differences. The Venn Diagram consists of two overlapping circles. The part that overlaps is for the similarities; the rest of each circle is for the differences. This part should be labeled. Words or phrases or even illustrations may be used. Groups, partners, or individuals can make these diagrams.

Found Poem

This is a collection of luminous words or phrases quoted from a piece of literature or primary source material and then written in poetry form. It enables individuals, groups, or the entire class to return to a reading to focus on those vivid words or phrases used by the author. For example:

> The cool winds of the night
> Blew across the desert.
> It was time to move on.
> They had escaped the cruel
> Rays of the desert sun by
> Resting that day at a small
> Oasis one night's journey from Cairo.

Freehand Map

Instead of handing out a copy of a map, have students sketch the map freehand. Or they can graph a map: prepare a 4×4 graph on the map you plan to draw. Have students fold an $8\frac{1}{2} \times 11$ piece of paper into sixteen squares, and then, using the graph squares as a guide, enlarge the map.

Tableau

This is a strategy that allows students to visualize and interpret text in a dramatic pose. Working in groups, they select and create a frozen scene from literature, the text, or a primary source. A leader will tap a person in the scene who will, while the others remain frozen, speak "in character." The character stops when tapped again. Each character gets an opportunity to speak. Only one character speaks at a time. A member of the group can be selected to control the scene. This strategy draws students into the text and allows interpretation beyond the text.

Silent Dialogue

This is a silent written assignment between two students who assume the persona of characters in literature or history. One paper is passed back and forth between the two students as they "talk" to each other, writing down their "conversation" in script form.

The "Write" Picture

This activity exposes students to creative writing-across-the-curriculum and helps them identify personally and emotionally with historical figures and events. Choose an interesting and thought-provoking historical painting, drawing, or photograph related to what you are studying. Either have a slide of the picture to project to the class or duplicate it on paper for each student to refer to. Instruct the students to study the chosen picture with their eyes. Ask them to write all the things they *see* in the picture. Have them label this as "sight." Give the students two or three minutes. Next, have them choose one person in the picture that they will become for the next twenty or thirty minutes. Now direct them to list or jot down all the things they might *hear* as if they were the person they chose in the picture. (Give them two to three minutes.) Repeat with *smell, touch, taste,* and finally how they *emotionally feel* as the person they have become. Give them two to three minutes to write on each of these senses. At this point, instruct the students to write a diary entry or a letter to a friend as the person they chose, writing in the first person. Instruct them to hit all the senses when writing on this particular subject, using their paper and picture as a guide. Finally, ask for volunteers to read their diary or letter selections while viewing the picture. The teacher may also want to share his or her writing.

Biopoem

This is a good activity for those students who have difficulty expressing themselves in long writings. It involves a great deal of thinking and a minimal amount of writing, yet the completed poem is very revealing about the person. Encourage students to use phrases or short sentences in lines 4–9 rather than single words, unless they are $100 words!

Line 1: **First name**
Line 2: **Four words of description**
Line 3: **Relative of** (one person, thing, or idea)
Line 4: **Lover of** (three things or ideas)
Line 5: **Who feels** (three things or ideas)
Line 6: **Who needs** (three things or ideas)
Line 7: **Who fears** (three things or ideas)
Line 8: **Who gives** (three things or ideas)
Line 9: **Who would like to see** (three things or ideas)
Line 10: **Resident of** (one real or fictional place)
Line 11: **Last name**

For example:

> Michelangelo
> Outgoing, ambitious, confident, stubborn.
> Relative of pain and happiness.
> Lover of Tessina de Medici—in a special way; those who love him; sculpture, not painting.
> Who feels art should have inspiration; people should be free to make their own choices; he is alone.
> Who needs work to survive; people to know a sculptor is someone who releases a statue already placed inside the marble by God; supporting patrons.
> Who fears losing his talent; he won't complete all his work in time; the High Renaissance will come to an end.
> Who gives 110 percent in each artwork he does; his opinion on important matters but only a glance to men who criticize him and his art.
> Who would like to see the foolishness of war end; the world wait for when he is ready for what matters; people understand his art.
> Resident of the patrons who support him.
> Buonarroti
>
> (Mike Anderson, seventh grader)

Epitaph

The students create an imaginary tombstone for a famous person, including the name, date of birth, and date of death if the person is dead. Have them try to capture the essence of what made this person significant. What were her or his main contributions to society? What would she or he want to be remembered for? How did she or he influence the thoughts and actions of others? This must be *concise*. Use all $100 words! Include some type of decorative work and display the result on a bulletin board titled "History Hall of Fame."

Literary/Historical Report Card

At the end of a study introduce this activity to ascertain the merits of characters. In cooperative groups determine ten or so criteria for assigning grades A through F. Evaluate the characters on these criteria and assign grades. Have groups compare their grades.

Infocube

Fold a piece of heavy construction paper into a three-dimensional cube. On five of the six sides draw a picture to illustrate one aspect of a theme. Save one side for the title: Stone Age Tools, Renaissance Artists, or some such. Fold and glue together.

Text Rendering

After reading a piece of literature or primary source material, students choose a favorite sentence or two that they find interesting because of content or description. After everyone has chosen one or two, the class begins to read *in no special order* without being called on by the teacher. Selections may be from any part of the reading. It becomes an interesting way to recall a piece of literature or primary source.

R.A.F.T. Writings

This is an approach to writing that has the students writing in character for various audiences. R = role, A = audience, F = form, T = tense. The teacher sets up a situation, for example: You are a Muslim *[role]* who is explaining the religion of Islam to a Christian friend *[audience]*. Write a dialogue *[form]* of your conversation. Be sure to write in the *present tense*.

It immerses the writer in a specific scene. It also allows students to write for an audience other than the teacher.

Acrostic

After studying a person or event in history, take the name of that person or event and write it vertically on a piece of paper for the class. Ask students to think about the most important aspects of this person or event and write them across the name. Students should try to use the letter of the name within the sentence and connect the words at the end of the line to ideas in the next line. See the following example using the name "Renaissance person."

> A **R**enaissance person is
> int**E**rested in many
> thi**N**gs;
> such a person is **A**lways looking for new
> **I**deas.
> S/he i**S** an inventor, a creator,
> **S**eeking
> **A**lways a better way,
> **N**ever satisfied with
> medio**C**rity.
> S/h**E** is not limited in the
> sco**P**e of his/her
> int**E**rests;
> a**R**t and
> mu**S**ic help to
> create a well-r**O**unded
> i**N**dividual.

Video Reaction Paper

While they view a video or film, have the students complete the following statements:

Appreciation: I liked
Confusion: I don't understand
Connections: This reminded me of
Observations: I noticed that
Speculation: It seemed to me that
Question:

Zip-Around

This is a good review activity. Write a question at the bottom of a 3 × 5 card and the answer at the top of another 3 × 5 card. Write another question at the bottom of the second card and the answer at the top of a new card. After you have all the questions written, write the answer to the last question at the top of the *first* card. Pass out the cards. Have a student read his or her question. The person with the answer stands up and reads the answer. The same person then reads his or her question and sits down when it is answered. Hints: Make enough cards for each student and have no repeat answers.

Wall Newspaper

This is a one-page newspaper for which students create the articles and advertisements, which are then pasted to a large piece of poster board or construction paper (24 × 36). Include articles from all parts of a newspaper that might have been written in the period being studied. Classified ads, advertisements, and "Dear Abby" columns are particularly fun for students to create "in the period." This works well with cooperative groups.

Historical Dinner

Ask students to imagine they have invited J.D. Rockefeller, Andrew Carnegie, Jane Addams, Lewis Hine, Upton Sinclair, a child mine worker, or a meat factory worker from the turn of the century to dinner at their home and to write a two-page dialogue that they might have with their guest during dinner. They should be creative but historically accurate. Some possible subjects to give the students: What is your guest wearing, and how does she or he enter your home? What do you serve your guest? Describe his or her manners at the table. Your guest might bring you a gift; what is it? Pick historical topics to discuss at dinner to better understand your guest. Your guest might make some comments about your home and some things in it; what are they? Give your guest a gift you believe might be useful in his or her time period and explain how to use it. What event might end your dinner together? You might also bring a guest to lunch instead of dinner. How might your meal together change history?

Historical Fictional Character

Students are asked to create a character, complete with personal documents, who might have lived in a given time and place, based on research about the period and location. The purposes are to gain experience doing research; to examine everyday life of the historical past; and to learn about the types of documents historians frequently work with.

Student assignment: Choose any century and setting of world history that interests you. Imagine you are a person who lived in that setting during that period. You may be of any race, sex, nationality, political group, social class, or occupation you wish. You must have lived a minimum of twenty-five years but no more than seventy-five. You are to create a set of documents for this person that might have been collected or created during her or his lifetime. These may include any of the following that you feel are appropriate: a diary or journal, a newspaper article about your character, a will, a birth (or death) certificate, awards, land deeds, marriage (or other) license, report cards, etc. You must also include a two-page autobiography of your character's life. All information must accurately reflect the time period: descriptions of people, food, dress, customs, transportation, economics, tools, religion, sports and leisure activities, etc., must be as authentic as possible. If your character took part in a significant historical event, the event must be accurately described.

When your project is complete, it must be arranged in the following order:

1. Cover—illustrated and attractive; include character's name and your name.
2. Table of contents—list of documents with page numbers.
3. Two-page autobiography of character's life.
4. Documents—minimum of three, maximum of five.
5. Bibliography—minimum of three references used for factual information.
6. Statement of Learning—explain what you learned while doing this project.

Timeline It!

Timelines help students develop a sense of proportion and perspective for events of the past. Below is a list of possible ways to do timelines with students. Try linking some of these lists with other activities.

Choose a Subject
For example, "The History of . . ."

• Individuals
• Your house
• Transportation
• Famous people

- Games, recreation, toys, sports
- Founding of places
- Events
- Architecture
- Inventors
- Wildlife (animals, plants, etc.)

Timelines May Include

- Dates and labels
- Dates and pictures (drawings/photos)
- Dates and short, written descriptions
- Different shapes or themes for labels (leaves, cars, etc.)

Make a Creative Format

- Clothesline and clothespin timelines
- Quilt style (pictures, captions, dates in squares)
- Accordion style (folded paper timelines)
- Hanging timelines (illustrate both sides, hang pictures with dates from wire or coathanger)
- Time capsule timelines (use shoebox, label with year, put inside objects, pictures, and writings from that period)
- Railroad track timelines (dates and events are on the tracks or on railroad cars)
- Creek or river timelines (the flow of local history)
- Victorian house timelines (windows with dates that open and tell a story)
- Tall tree with sequence of historical events on the branches

Key Words for Encouraging Higher-Level Thinking

Bloom's Taxonomy
Begin your instructions with these words:

To Assess Knowledge

Know	Recall	Cite
Define	Name	Enumerate
Memorize	Relate	Tell
Repeat	Collect	Recount
Record	Label	
List	Specify	

To Assess Application

Exhibit	Employ	Illustrate
Solve	Use	Operate
Interview	Demonstrate	Calculate
Simulate	Dramatize	Show
Apply	Practice	Experiment

To Assess Synthesis

Compose	Arrange	Incorporate
Plan	Assemble	Generalize
Propose	Construct	Originate
Produce	Create	Predict
Invent	Set Up	Contrive
Develop	Prepare	Concoct
Design	Imagine	Systematize
Formulate	Hypothesize	

To Assess Comprehension

Restate	Explain	Retell
Summarize	Express	Review
Discuss	Identify	Translate
Describe	Locate	
Recognize	Report	

To Assess Analysis

Interpret	Discover	Survey
Analyze	Inquire	Dissect
Differentiate	Detect	Inventory
Compare	Inspect	Question
Contrast	Classify	Test
Scrutinize	Arrange	Distinguish
Categorize	Group	Diagram
Probe	Organize	
Investigate	Examine	

To Assess Evaluation

Judge	Revise	Infer
Decide	Conclude	Deduce
Appraise	Select	Score
Evaluate	Criticize	Predict
Rate	Assess	Choose
Compare	Measure	Recommend
Value	Estimate	Determine

Historical Event Pyramid

This activity is designed to encourage students to focus on a historical event, identify the participants, place them in the proper environment, and sequence the actions.

1. Person or event
2. Two words describing person or event
3. Three words describing setting
4. Four words stating problem
5. Five words describing first incident
6. Six words describing second incident

7. Seven words describing third incident
8. Eight words describing solution

Lesson Potpourri for Students

- Create or analyze a map.
- Write an editorial or a letter to the editor.
- Write an obituary for a famous person.
- Cartoon balloons—fill in with an appropriate conversation.
- Write a fictional story or a legend.
- Draw a cartoon strip as a timeline.
- Write a caption under a given picture(s) or political cartoon.
- Draw before-and-after pictures to show cause and effect.
- Write a historical poem or lyrics to a popular or common tune.
- Create a bumper sticker or political button.

- Create a propaganda poster for a political belief.
- Write a speech for a character in history.
- Prioritize facts and justify why #1 is first, etc.
- Place political cartoons or pictures of presidents in chronological order.
- Identify the meaning or the author of given quotes.
- Create or analyze a political cartoon.
- Place data in a graph or diagram.
- Imagine yourself as a shoe or boot and ask, *Where have I gone?* or *What have I seen?*
- Substitute a coin, wagon, suitcase, or carpetbag for the shoe or boot above.
- Draw a trunk. Create documents that might have been in the trunk: letters, maps, personal documents, or maybe even personal belongings. Other students can try to discover what kind of a person owned the trunk and where it has been.

Miscellaneous Ideas

a letter	advertisement	art gallery
bulletin board	choral reading	clay sculpture
collage	collection	comic strip
costumes	demonstration	detailed illustration
diary	diorama	display
edibles	fact file	family tree
game	illustrated story	interview
journal	labeled diagram	learning center
map with legend	mobile	mural
museum exhibit	newspaper story	oral report
pamphlet	picture story for young children	poetry
pop-up book	project cube *(InfoCube)*	puppet (show)
rebus story	role-play	slogan
song	story pyramid	transparency
travel brochure		

24

Forging Links in Time and Space with Computers and HyperCard

Nancy Fogelson

Nancy Folgelson integrates the computer as another tool for combining good research, critical thinking, and writing. She introduces students to computers through HyperCard stacks. Her units can just as easily be used on a Web site or as visual, oral, and written presentations in classrooms without computers.

Introduction: Why Computers and World History

Using computer technology as a tool for teaching world history encourages and fosters student involvement in exploring themes essential to a world history course. By developing their own programs, students learn to define, investigate, and draw conclusions about the threads that are the fabric of a global approach to history: trade, societies, government, and transfer of culture. Freed from paragraph and outline restrictions, students can incorporate new details expressed in visual or audio images without disrupting the flow of ideas. Using HyperCard (or any of the hypertext and multimedia programs) as a tool to create links between subjects as well as to integrate a multimedia approach to history, students have the freedom to explore a subject in depth in a pattern that more closely resembles a web than a formal outline. This web approach encourages using information as evidence of a concept rather than as an end in itself. Because a central aspect of world history is integration rather than exceptionalism, connections are clearer using a web than using an outline.

Grouping students to prepare programs is an important part of using computers as a teaching tool. This group format requires students to interact, teaching each other about what they have found through individual research, negotiating over use of material, and evaluating the pertinence of both material and arrangement. Evaluation of a program should be based on a combination of information and links established, demonstrating understanding of interrelationships. Careful assembly of data should be given high priority, although it can be difficult to refrain from grading a program on the basis of its graphics. Expertise with the computer should not be confused with expertise in history. Therefore, programs should be evaluated not by comparing programs within a class but on the value of the information and linkages prepared by each group. Designing computer programs for world history is an excellent model for implementing student-centered cooperative learning with a framework that provides supportive teacher monitoring.

Although the most exciting programs use the full graphic and multimedia capability of computers and require an expertise usually developed in conjunction with computer departments, programs can be constructed with a minimum of computer experience. These may be less visually exciting but can be academically outstanding and intellectually as rigorous as more sophisticated programs. Ideally, partners should be arranged so that each team is a composite of different skills and interests such as computer experience, interest in art and architecture, and curiosity about culture. The best way to integrate project development into a world history course is to set aside a regular class period for work on the program. Because a successful program requires extensive research into as broad a set of materials as a school has access to, the ideal location for work is in or near the Learning Resource Center. By allotting one period a week and requiring students to work on the program as part of their ongoing homework assignments, the program develops not as an outside project but as an integral part of the thematic approach taken in world history.

The following material describes program projects that can be used, or modified for use, in high school classes. Each project can be as complex as students wish. Basic directions are given, followed by instructions for expanding the program to fit different levels of ability and levels of computer skills. Basic projects can be completed in four weeks; more sophisticated projects can take a whole semester. Projects are organized to correspond with basic themes as they unfold during the year.

Three basic programs and variations are described in detail. Each can be modified or expanded to suit the talents of the students and can be focused on a specific time period or subject. The examples range from broad topics to very narrow and short subjects. Each project has been developed for either grade nine or ten. If world history is offered as a grade twelve course, similar projects can be used but should be expanded to take into account the level of achievement expected of high school seniors. Remember that the function of the teacher is to encourage students to use what they have learned as a basis for acquiring additional information and experimenting with organizing that information around central ideas. The projects reflect the students' development of critical thinking skills. The computers are only the tools; the students are the artisans.

The Computer and HyperCard

The basic characteristics of a computer that a history teacher will use are the capacity to store, retrieve, and organize information. Remember that as a tool for understanding world history a computer is only as useful as the quality and quantity of information put into its memory and as efficient as its ability to retrieve and organize that information. Programs are like precooked dinners that just have to be heated in the microwave. Copied onto the computer, they contain information and make the computer work. All you have to do is push the buttons. You can learn how these programs work if you wish, but it is not necessary. You can start using computers with more curiosity than expertise.

Pointing an arrow (using a mouse) at a command and seeing what happens is the first step to using the computer, and this should be done with a sense of curiosity minus any fear that the computer will break or that the project will be ruined. The primary program for using computers with world history is HyperCard, which allows the student to connect screens of information by using "buttons" or "arrows," a process that connects ideas from a primary screen to multiple screens. For use with HyperCard, the screens (the whole project) is called a stack. Throughout this chapter the terms *card* and *stack* will be used. Sometimes *project* will be substituted for *stack* because as students become more adept at using HyperCard, they can actually create more than one stack for a project. This is the heart of using the computer: the ability to connect ideas, text, and images. Making the connections, or buttons to link one card with another, requires three or four basic steps that are clearly detailed when the HyperCard program is opened. Predrawn images can be inserted, or students can create their own. Images can be inserted (called scanning) when students are ready for more complex projects. HyperCard comes with maps, but other map programs can be used. The manuals cited at the end of this chapter are most important. They contain simple visual directions that cannot be summarized in a few paragraphs. The most important thing to remember is to experiment and to understand that students are probably more adept and eager to experiment with the computer than the teacher. Learn from the students!

The most important role you have as a teacher is to show students you enjoy experimenting and then allow them to use the mouse and the HyperCard program *to experiment and explore on their own*. Create some stacks *made up of three or four cards* before starting students on a serious project. Remember, students still need the teacher for guidance in selecting content and organizing ideas. Projects should be simple to begin with and should involve discussion about goals and expectations before beginning. Computers can stimulate students to link ideas and discover connections.

First Semester: Sixteenth-Century Western Expansion to Nineteenth-Century Revolutions

Basic Topic: Exploration and the Transfer of Culture

European Exploration of the Western Hemisphere 1500–1650

Goals
1. To understand the drive of European monarchies to acquire wealth and power by exploring the Western Hemisphere, India, and the Pacific Ocean basin.
2. To appreciate the advances in science and technology as they were applied to exploration during the Renaissance period.
3. To demonstrate what transfer of culture meant during the Renaissance and the consequences of exploration, trade, and migration for the twentieth century.

This project can be completed in four weeks using one class period per week plus free time. The best projects, developed with extensive use of historical atlases, music, monographs, and specialized encyclopedias, can take from one quarter to one semester. If the purpose is to introduce students to research and to give them an opportunity to become familiar with the computer, it is best to keep the project short. For students with an interest and some expertise in using the computer, it is important to expand each segment and provide sufficient time to develop each aspect of the program.

Project Description
Create a stack that demonstrates your understanding of the long- and short-term consequences of exploration. Maps are integral to the success of this project.

1. Choose a major explorer whose expeditions took place between 1500 and 1650.
2. Provide enough background information to build a clear portrait of the man.
3. Include a description of the crew.
4. Explain who sponsored voyages and why.

5. Re-create the route taken and include information on the kinds of ships used, navigation instruments, and cargoes.

6. Provide a description of land explored, including geo-physical features, climate, flora and fauna, and the culture of the indigenous people.

7. Conclude the project with a description of the area today, including language, impact of history on the geography of the area, and aspects of culture that reflect the past as well as the present. This is an excellent opportunity to include Spanish and French as part of learning history. Re-creations of diaries can be included as well as lyrics from songs that represent integration of Spanish and/or French culture with the indigenous culture. Text to accompany the conclusion should be an essay that explains what is meant by the phrase "historic transfer of culture."

Note: Students should be encouraged to use their own pictures as faces of the crew. This can be done by digitalizing photos or using scanned photos and then modifying the picture to reflect the period. If this option is chosen, students continue with this tactic in each project for the course, again emphasizing physical similarities and differences over time and reflecting conditions peculiar to a particular place or period, especially during periods of epidemics such as small pox. Film clips from videos and scanned pictures can be inserted, providing more authentic images.

Nature, Nutrients, and Nurturing

Goals

1. To develop an understanding of the impact of history on geography.

2. To explore the relationship between social systems and land use.

3. To appreciate the importance of food and its preparation in the development of family traditions and folklore.

Project Development

1. Each group will choose one of the following and trace its origins and spread globally, beginning with the Columbian period and moving through the seventeenth, nineteenth, and twentieth centuries:
   - rice
   - sugar
   - potatoes
   - cattle

2. Explain the impact of the item on the land, its use as a basic food, and the modification of its use with industrialization.

3. Include recipes and directions for preparation and serving, using both to discuss or describe lifestyle, family organization, and festivals.

4. Conclude with a description of gender roles and the roles of children and the elderly in society.

Note: This can be fairly straightforward or it can serve as a vehicle to explore the connections between settlement and land use, trade, government, and changes in the population. Two books that can serve as excellent reference guides and could inspire students to engage in research are *Seeds of Change* by Henry Hobhouse and *Why We Eat What We Eat* by Raymond Sokolov. Students interested in new applications of biological research could branch this out to include genetic experiments with grains, vegetable, and cattle. A study of nutritional diseases could also be part of this project. The more complicated it becomes, the more time must be set aside. Working in a group enables students to prepare an expanded project because each member can take the responsibility for a particular thread. The larger the group, the more interesting the project, but keep the group size within the bounds of successful organization. A group of more than four students could easily break down.

Basic Topic: Generational History, Revolution and Nationalism

The French Revolution, Napoleonic Wars, and the Revolutions of 1848

A similar program can be constructed for the period 1900–1945: World Wars I and II.

Goals

1. To understand the causes and short- and long-term consequences of the eighteenth-century revolutionary period.

2. To promote an appreciation for the spread of ideas.

3. To explore the connections between political and social positions taken by individuals and their economic status, age, and personal history.

4. To understand that history is made both at the top and from the bottom.

This project can be completed in five weeks, using one class period per week plus free time. Allowing a full quarter, or even longer, will produce the best projects because students will have the time to gather more information about a broader set of subjects. One important skill incorporated in this project is learning that historical evidence is more than written documents.

Project Description

Buyers of a 250-year-old house in France (exact location to be determined by students) discover diaries, letters, drawings, clothing, personal and household objects, and other artifacts hidden in a secluded corner of the attic. Out of this cache, they put together a history of the family and of the period.

1. Each team constructs a French family consisting of husband, wife, and children between ten and sixteen. The

project begins in 1783 (the end of the American Revolution) and ends in 1848.

2. Students decide the status or class of the family and prepare a scenario so that the family becomes real: ages, personalities, how they lived and earned a living—basically as much information and substance as they can gather. This portrait is contained in letters, diaries, and (by scanning copies of paintings or inserting footage from art CDs) family pictures.

3. This family responds to the political and social conditions of the following time periods, keeping in mind the changing ages, death, and new generations that will appear. This approach combines the "great men" and "from the bottom up" theories of history by incorporating significant events with how people at the time were involved in those events.
   - 1783
   - 1787–1789
   - 1792–1800
   - 1800–1812
   - 1815
   - 1830–1836
   - 1848

   For short projects of two or three weeks, use only 1787–1789 and the Napoleonic Wars.

4. In each time period, members of this family will be involved with the social, political, and economic history of the time, either as aristocrats, peasants, merchants, artists, or urban laborers. They will take part in the Napoleonic Wars in some capacity and may remain in France, move to another country, or migrate between countries, but they must move back to France by 1848. In 1848, they will have a position on the revolutions depending on their politics, position in society.

5. The project should end with a final entry by this fictitious (but historically accurate) family on the quality of life in 1848 and with a new diary entry added by the family now occupying the house about quality of life in the present.

Note: The family will be more authentic if students can use their own faces, modified to fit the time periods and conditions, such as small pox. Excerpts from films, videos, and music CDs will add to the impact of this project. Using *Les Miserables*—the book, the play, or the film (or any combination)—will add to the excitement of the project. Having some of the family move to different countries will add to the authenticity of the history of migration, especially if moves come at the time of the Napoleonic Wars and just after the revolutions of 1848. Letters from these expatriates (or emigrants) with details of their life in a new country again will add to the understanding of a constantly changing population.

Second Semester

Basic Topic: Museum of Culture

Museums of World Civilization in the Twentieth Century

Goals

1. To connect culture, society, and civilization.
2. To understand the development of culture on the basis of indigenous factors as well as contact and interaction with outside forces.
3. To appreciate different social characteristics and to understand the connection with universal values such as dignity, justice, and community.

This should be a semester-long project because it requires extensive research in as broad a set of materials as are available. The project should include art, law, literature, music, crafts, family life, religion, and festivals. The real danger is that students will try to do more than is possible in one semester. Working with the music, art, and computer departments will be a big help because the ability to use a multimedia approach is what will bring this project to life. There are numerous CD-ROMs with encyclopedic information and images that can be incorporated into this project as well as clips from films and National Geographic videos. Once more, students should try to place themselves in this project by inserting their own ethnic history and their own image, illustrating the complex web of ancestry we all share. Programs such as Morph would be perfect if the computer capability of the students allows them to use it.

Project Description

Create a museum with a room or area for each category of culture (art; religion, including rituals of marriage, birth, and death; festivals; music; crafts; and family). In each room include samples from three different ethnic groups or geographic locations. Wherever possible, samples of language should be included. The same group or location may be represented in more than one room.

1. The museum exterior should be the product of the students' creativity and may include ideas gathered from materials such as *Architecture Digest*.
2. Rooms or areas should be arranged to illustrate the connections between the various aspects of culture.
3. Samples displayed should include information on why the sample was chosen: why it is important to the people it represents and why it is important to the viewers.
4. Each room or area should be built or arranged to reflect the three cultures or geographic areas chosen. The completed museum should contain samples from a variety of cultures. Encourage students to create their own mix of cultures.
5. Sample combinations that emphasize similarities:
   - tropical Africa, Amazon basin, Haiti

- Canadian Innuit, Siberians, North American Native American nations from the Great Plains
- Mexico, Spain, Maya
- Korea, China, Vietnam
6. Sample combinations that emphasize differences:
   - Kenya, Nicaragua, Rumania
   - Iran, Philippines, Sri Lanka
   - Christianity, Judaism, Islam, Buddhism
   - Egypt, Argentina, Japan

Museum of Ancient and Medieval History

Goals
1. To understand the contributions of ancient and medieval societies to concepts of law, government, science and technology, literature, art, and architecture.
2. To explore the relationships among Egypt, Greece, Rome, and medieval Europe.
3. To appreciate the universality of the history of civilizations.

Project Description
Create a museum that contains examples of the most important aspect of each civilization. The exterior should reflect the twenty-first century, and each room or area should reflect the appropriate ancient or medieval civilization. The collection can be composed of art, artifacts, and examples of philosophy, law, and government. Each item should be accompanied by an explanation of why it was important in its time, why it deserves to be preserved in a museum, and why it is important in the present and to the future.

1. Use a variety of materials, including historical atlases, art books, and CD-ROMs.
2. Each civilization should include a map locating the principal cities, geophysical features, and ethnic, religious, and linguistic groups.
3. Rooms or areas should be arranged to indicate the relationship between them and the order of importance. Students should be encouraged to devise their own arrangement, justifying or explaining the arrangement in a concluding essay.

This project could be completed in one quarter but ideally should be worked on for a semester. It encourages sharing of information and perceptions and requires cooperation in research and arrangement of material and forming conclusions.

Conclusion

I remember the year I taught second grade, and a little boy looked up and hollered out, "I can read! I can *read!*" Of course, he had been reading, at least decoding, before that, but the recognition of what reading meant had just become clear to him. The joy and excitement he expressed reflected an internal understanding of what being able to read really meant. The words were ideas and the ideas were his. The computer is a tool that encourages that same internal understanding of history. It provides the setting for creative use of materials. The linking capacity of HyperCard makes research a treasure hunt because students can easily integrate new material and insights without disrupting the flow of the subject under study. Initial steps in using HyperCard are fairly easy to learn. Each of the projects described can be produced with a minimum of steps by creating fields and buttons and scanning in art work and maps. Simple illustrations can be created using a HyperCard capability called Art Bits and using the variety of drawing tools. Practice using scripting or ways to tell parts of the stack what to do to achieve more elaborate visual effects. After the first encounter, students and teachers who approach learning with a sense of adventure can create exciting projects by experimenting—pushing buttons. The student creates; the buttons do all the work.

The following sources are excellent guides to using HyperCard and the newer resources such as laser disks, CD-ROMs, and data bases:

Franklin, Carl, and Susan K. Kinnell. *Hypertext/Hypermedia in Schools: A Resources Book.* Santa Barbara, CA: ABC-CLIO, 1990.

Hofmeister, Joseph, and Joyce Rudowski. *Learning with HyperCard* and *Flying Solo.* Southwestern Publishing Co., 5101 Madison Rd., Cincinnati, OH 45227–1490. (800) 543–7972; fax (800) 453–7882.

Parisi, Lynn S., and Virginia L. Jones. *Directory of Online Databases and CD-ROM Resources for High Schools.* Santa Barbara: ABC-CLIO, CA 1988. This directory contains an excellent bibliography on sources for using computers, especially HyperCard.

25

Investigating History

Charles Hart

Charles Hart begins and ends his world history classes with a focus on research. He challenges his students to begin a lifelong search to find evidence to test their ideas. To give students a notion of how the present is shaped by the past, he challenges them to find the sources of traditional twentieth-century rivalries, to debate turning points in history, or to find historical examples that illustrate axioms about human behavior.

When history teachers are asked what it was as students that excited them most about their discipline, a common answer is "the investigation": searching through the academic haystack for that tiny needle of information. This search not only can prepare the individual for a lifelong learning process but also can be transferred to other topics. Along with the excitement of the hunt comes the methodology, the content, the detail, and the concepts. The lesson plans that follow are offered as a sampling of what students can do when they become detectives. One hopes they will enter the course as detectives and leave it as prospectors.

Axioms in History

What follows is a list of historical "truisms" as documented by my students. The list is the result of a take-home exam question. At the beginning of the semester, the students are presented with the assignment, which is simply to identify an axiom that explains human behavior throughout history. They have eighteen weeks to work on it. It is turned in as part of the final exam. The evaluation is based upon originality (is it a worn cliché, or are other students using it?), level of sophistication (is it so obvious and simplistic it does not warrant investigation?), use of historical examples (are the examples used to justify it from different time periods as well as different regions of the globe?), and whether the answer is written in an acceptable essay format.

I like this assignment because it lends relevance to what we do daily in class, it strikes at the essence of history, and I am constantly surprised at what the students come up with. The students like this assignment because they appreciate this kind of challenge, and it puts them in the driver's seat. The list below is what my second-semester freshman class came up with last year.

"An unjust peace is the mother of war."
"Love is the cause of all war."
"Power tends to corrupt, and absolute power corrupts absolutely."
"Power sometimes makes rulers turn bad."
"Politics is every person's opportunity to look stupid."
"Freedom is slavery."
"No guts, no glory."
"If you can't beat them, join them."
"What goes around comes around."
"No good deed goes unpunished."
"Knowledge is power."
"With great power, there comes even greater responsibility."
"People live off a feast or famine mentality."
"It is easier to make war than peace."
"The greater the good, the harder the blow."
"I am woman, hear my roar."
"Every society needs something to worship."
"Power is often lost when searching for more."
"Courage is contagious."
"You have not converted individuals because you have silenced them."
"A person is finished only when he quits."
"The work of the individual is the spark that moves humanity forward."
"Never mistake kindness for weakness."
"Nothing fails like success."
"Those who live by the sword die by the sword."
"Little decisions are made with the mind; big ones are made with the heart."
"The impossible is always possible."
"All successful conquerors died an undignified death."
"Actions speak louder than words."
"Hatred can be an acid that does more damage to the vessel in which it is stored than to the object on which it is poured."
"The teacher can open the door, but the pupil must walk through him/herself."
"The lessons of history are rarely learned by the actors."
"Love is blind."
"Nice guys finish last."
"For every action there is an equal and opposite reaction."

"A country must first regress before it can progress."
"A sword may end a war, but a plume can start one."
"Perfection lies in the eye of the beholder."
"You're damned if you do and damned if you don't."
"One always wants the apples from his neighbor's tree."
"Those who win the war write the history."
"For every revolution there is a counterrevolution."
"Might makes right."

Debate on Important Events in History

Students generally like debates. I have paired up events that seem to lend themselves to debate under the theme "Important Events in History." Sometimes students want to make up their own topics; that is fine, but make sure there is enough "meat" to carry the selected topic. Emphasize historical examples, or the students will fall back on emotional redundancies. I allow the class to vote on the winning side and give that team the opportunity to proceed to an extra credit round.

Instructions for Students

Select a topic below that intrigues you. Each person will be placed in a group of three who have selected the same topic, and each group believes their event to be a pivotal turning point in history. You will be debating your stance against the other side. You are to convince the remainder of the class (who determines which side wins and advances for extra credit points) by proving your point and rebutting the opposing side's point.

Each student will be graded individually. I will be looking for ability to present an argument in a clear and logical manner, appearance of preparation, use of specific historical examples, ability to rebut the opposing side, and ability to defend your own arguments.

Topics

Agricultural revolution vs. the industrial revolution
The birth of Christ vs. the Battle of Milvian Bridge
Control of steam vs. the invention of the computer
Irrigation vs. the domestication of animals
The Black Death vs. the cure for malaria
Bloody Sunday vs. the Battle of Tsushima
Journey of Marco Polo vs. the invention of the internal combustion engine
Assassination of Archduke Franz Ferdinand vs. the Japanese attack on Pearl Harbor
The life of Confucius vs. the life of Plato
The Battle of Marathon vs. the Napoleonic Wars
The Glorious Revolution vs. the French Revolution
WWI vs. WWII
The jet engine vs. atomic energy
The birth control pill vs. the credit card
Publication of the *Principia Mathematica* vs. publication of *The Origin of the Species*
The exploration of Cortes vs. the exploration of Columbus

The Origin of Traditional Rivalries

This is the assignment I have used in the past to introduce the second semester. I enjoy giving students assignments in which they have choices; it seems to help them buy into the work.

Instructions for Students

This is to be either a written or an oral report. If your report is written, it must be a minimum of five pages in length and must include a bibliography. A written report must contain information on what the current situation is, how it evolved, and what you believe must happen in order for the issue to be resolved. If your report is to be oral, an outline must be given to the teacher at the time of the presentation. You must present your report along with another student; each of you will take a side and argue your case to the class. Remember, facts and examples speak louder than emotions and expletives. The combined oral presentation should not be longer than fifteen minutes. Pertinent visual aides are always welcome. I always appreciate an opportunity for the entire class to learn.

Topics

Britain vs. France	Iraqi vs. Kurd
England vs. Ireland	Ibos vs. Hausa Yoruba
Christian vs. Jew	Ethiopian vs. Somalian
Israeli vs. Palestinian	Tamil vs. Singhalese
Black vs. white (outside the United States)	Basque vs. Spaniard
pastoralist vs. farmer	French Canadian vs. English Canadian
Muslim vs. Hindu	Athens vs. Sparta
Protestant vs. Catholic	Tibet vs. China
Chinese vs. Japanese	French vs. Tahitian
Chinese vs. Southeast Asian	Korean vs. Japanese
Chinese vs. Mongol	Ainu vs. Japanese
terrorist vs. established government	Turk vs. Armenian
Sunni vs. Shi'ite	French vs. Spaniard
Croatian vs. Serb	Orthodox vs. Catholic
Greek vs. Turk	English vs. Afrikaner
	English vs. Hindu

26

Geography and History

Dennis Reinhartz and Judy Reinhartz

Dennis Reinhartz and Judy Reinhartz explore the common ground linking history and geography. They have included practical lessons that assist students with an understanding of that relationship. The strength of these lessons is that they can be adapted in a variety of ways as geography-history lessons and used throughout the year.

Contemporary Geography

What Is Geography?

Before we can consider the importance of geography's contribution to general education or the actual teaching of geography, a working definition must be established. Over its long development, and as an academic discipline, geography has never remained static. It has taken on many meanings and given rise to as many misconceptions. Today these misconceptions still exercise a major influence over popular attitudes about geography and its importance, or lack thereof, to the well-rounded person.

To many people, geography conjures up memories from their own school years of rote learning of massive numbers of facts about different places and their inhabitants. Essentially, the various "tests" and "polls" that have been administered to students and young adults in the past decade have reflected their degree of mastery of this almost encyclopedic knowledge. In addition, the poor test results have been interpreted as revealing an appalling lack of understanding on the part of students about the world around them. Yet, many of these exercises are unreliable in determining the true state of "useful geographic knowledge" possessed by students upon completion of their schooling.[1] This contention in turn has spawned a growing controversy among educators, community leaders, and parents not only over the value of geography, but also, more specifically, over what "kind" of geography is important to general education.

Part of the basis for this controversy is rooted in the second popular conception about geography—it is related to

Excerpted from *Geography and the Curriculum* by Dennis Reinhartz and Judy Reinhartz. © 1990. Washington, DC: National Education Association. Reprinted by permission of the NEA Professional Library.

discovery and travel. Over the centuries a large body of literature has chronicled real and fictitious expeditions, journeys, and adventures, such as those of Marco Polo and Lewis and Clark as well as those of Gulliver and Captain Kirk. A third view associates geography with maps, their creation, interpretation, and use. While all these perceptions reflect the evolution of geography as a disciplined body of thought, and to some extent are valid and encompassed in a modern definition of geography, there is much more.

The first significant contributions to the development of geography were made by ancient Greek and Roman scholars such as Herodotus (c. 485–425 B.C.E.) and Strabo (65 B.C.E.–20 C.E.), who wrote topographical accounts of places in their world, describing and explaining geographical phenomena and placing events in geographical perspective. The term *geography* was first used by the scholars at the great museum and library at Alexandria in the fourth century B.C.E. Ptolemy (90–168), working in Alexandria, considered the importance of maps and offered instructions on how to draw them in his multivolume *Geographia*. During the Middle Ages and the Renaissance the ancient tradition was carried forward by major Muslim geographer-travelers such as al-Muqaddasi (945–988), al-Idrisi (1099–1180), and Ibn Khaldun (1332–1406), among others, ushering in the great age of Western discovery. The Enlightenment brought structure and order to the field. But only in the nineteenth century did it become an institutionalized academic discipline, with the founding of professional geographic organizations such as the British Royal Geographical Society in 1830, which was influenced by the development of modern science.

Contemporary geography emerges from this diverse historical process of maturation as the systematic study of the "interaction of people and environments."[2] "Geographical training should develop the ability to 'see geographically,' to observe and interpret a natural or cultural landscape in the field and/or through the study of maps, aerial photographs, and other visual representations."[3] Consequently, the *region* as delineated by some human and/or physical uniformity is the basic unit of study, and the multidisciplinary nature of geographical analysis makes geography a bridge between the arts and the sciences.[4] "Thus geographic education requires knowing *where* things are located, but more importantly requires a system for inquiring *why* they are there and where they should be."[5]

In addition, geography is a mode of scientific inquiry through which we gain an understanding of *how* and *why* the world can support its people now and in the future. We live in a time of instant communication, with film footage on television from India, Germany, Israel, etc. A global perspective is essential as our world continues to get smaller in time and space. It no longer takes weeks or months for news to travel across the oceans. As events unfold, they are televised via satellites. It is this multidisciplinary nature that greatly facilitates the integration of geography into the school curriculum for the teaching of "useful geographic information." Geography can be the framework for studying and learning about the world.[6]

The Importance of Geography to General Education

Geography, then, is the systematic study of the interaction of people and environments as revealed in the character of specific locations or regions. And it is in its "distinctive focus upon the *study of place*" and spatial relationships that its role in general education lies. For example, in a general education setting geography poses several unique questions:

- Where is this place? (Location—the latitude and longitude give its global address)
- What is this place like, and how does it differ from or resemble other places? (Place—the study of historical and cultural features)
- How is this place connected with other places? (Interaction—how people respond and change the physical environment)
- How and why is this place changing? (Movement—focus on systems of transportation and communication that connect people with the environment)
- What would it feel like to be in this place? (Affect—response to the environment)

Obviously, geographic learning in this context requires more than the rote memorization of such facts as capitals, commodities, and demographics: it requires that students be taught to apply this learning.[7] What is more important—knowing how to use an atlas (i.e., acquiring skills to gain knowledge) or committing to memory the fact that Ndjamena is the capital of Chad?

The Importance of Maps

As we have indicated, maps are an intimate part of geography and geographic education. But what is a map? And why is an understanding of maps considered so crucial to getting along in the future?

Simply stated, a map is the "drawn representation of geographical space."[8] Maps make up a powerful, widely used, complex, and little understood system of communication that is as old as the spoken word. Humanity achieved "graphicacy" well before it achieved literacy. Early humans learned to draw before they learned to write and probably to draw maps before they learned to write.[9] Maps graphically convey spatial images and relationships and are the point at which art and science meet. Because maps are interdisciplinary, they can be the sources of much data and should be evaluated and taught accordingly.

Cartography, the making of maps, evolved independently among many peoples in many parts of the earth; the earliest recognizable maps date back to about 15,000 B.C.E. The teaching of map skills and maps as learning devices has been important since the later Renaissance. By the year 1000 the Chinese were printing maps with ink on paper and using them with early examples of magnetic compasses. Modern science and technology produce maps, charts, globes, and atlases of ever greater accuracy and scope, leading to mass dissemination of cartographic aids and their increased accessibility. Today, we continue to map not only our own shrinking planet, but the expanding universe as well.[10] Maps are artifacts that communicate across the ages to the present.

> Maps are significant landmarks of historical development and achievement, summarizing the scientific, technological, and intellectual strengths of an era and recording the political, economic, and social values of the times in which they were created. Since the beginning of history they have been intimately involved in human development. They have helped people define who they are, where they are, and how they move about. Maps delineate physical, political, economic, and social features and depict the effect the environment has on us as well as our impact on the environment. . . . Maps also can be viewed as art, part of the wider human aesthetic experience. . . .[11]

Consequently, old maps, or good facsimiles thereof, can be invaluable to teachers of history and social studies.

And as the preceding quotation intimates, the aesthetics of maps should not be overlooked in the teaching-learning process. Art historian Rudolf Arnheim has observed that maps are "a dynamic expression of color and shape" and they provide a "luxurious enrichment" of geographical and historical data. Stressing graphic communication, Arnheim also has pointed out that the aesthetic appeal of maps is like that of paintings by encouraging the viewer to ask, "Who are you and what are you like?"[12]

Graphicacy

The use of maps emphasizes visual education and sharpens visual perception, thereby stimulating the development of the student's graphicacy,[13] or communication by nonverbal, nonliterary, and non-numerical means. Graphicacy is the embodiment of the old adage that a picture can be worth more than a thousand words. As Thomas Jefferson, himself a cartographer, once pointed out, "A map can give a better idea of a region than any description in writing."[14]

Like articulacy, literacy, and numeracy, graphicacy is essential for full productive participation in modern society, where people are confronted daily by maps, graphs, charts, and diagrams in such dispensable and inescapable forms as road maps and signs, news, weather, and business reports, education television, and advertising. Graphicacy also is basic to computer literacy.[15]

The following activity uses two of the four most common and often ignored maps in everyday life: road maps, weather maps, news maps, and advertising logos. How many people are familiar with them? How many take them and most maps for granted?

What Is a Map?

This activity introduces students at all grade levels to the complexities of maps—all that maps can tell us and how they tell us. At the same time, it is an experience in problem solving, viewing the map as an artifact—what a map tells us about its creators and their environment. Since maps are nonliterary documents, it also is an exercise in "graphicacy," the interpretation of data presented in graphic form.

The only resources necessary are copies of a standard state road map for students. Teachers can obtain these maps free from state highway departments. The rules are simple. Students are told that they are the leaders of an extraterrestrial "greenie" expedition that has landed on a small water planet that has a high radiation count and is orbiting a moderately sized, unimpressive yellow star. On the planet, they have found the widely scattered ruins of a long-lost civilization of which no survivors remain. All that the members of the expedition must know about this civilization and its creators will be derived from the ruins and other artifacts.

Road maps are the major form of evidence discovered thus far for the leaders to consider. Using this source, the class members who function as greenie department heads have been asked to determine what they can learn about the beings who once dominated the earth. The teacher tells students that they must play the roles of greenie scientists and technicians and that all their earthly knowledge of road maps must be forgotten. For example, once the maps are distributed, the students' first tendency would be to open them, thus showing that they are still earth people. A greenie scientist, on the other hand, would examine the folded map *in situ* first. The teacher's role, then, is to enforce this prohibition against previous earthly knowledge and to guide

the analytical interchange by pointing out what kind of knowledge the greenies do possess—the state of their science and technology. Obviously, since they have journeyed far across space and time to reach the earth, the state of their science and technology is high.

The teacher continues by asking questions and giving directions as needed. For example, the sequence of questions and directions might be as follows:

- What do you notice first about the artifact? (multiple copies)
- What else do you notice about it? (portable)
- And? (folded)
- Open the artifact.
- In opening it, what becomes apparent about the physiology of the being who employed it? (structural similarity)
- What else? (polychromatic vision)
- What do you notice now about the artifact? (color)
- What else do you notice about it? (line and form)
- What else? (organization)
- What types of symbols and conventions are used? (colors, letters, and numbers)
- How do you know? (scales, inset charts, directions)
- What is the artifact? (a map)
- What was it used for? (navigation on roads)
- How do you know? (use of lines explained in key)
- What does the map's function tell us about its creators? (highly mobile)
- What do the material and manufacture tell us about the map's creators? (high scientific development and state of technology)
- What level of scientific and technological development is revealed by the map? (high)
- How do you know? (use of mathematics, printing, design, etc.)
- What level of aesthetic sensibility is revealed by the map? (high)
- How do you know? (use of color, line, shape, form in design)

The teacher then tells the greenie scientists-students to take the knowledge derived from the map and construct a written sketch of its creators and their civilization. They should use only information derived from and related to the map. Students will reconvene at an appointed time with their individual sketches to formulate a combined final report.

Finally, greenie scientists-students are given a related artifact—a weather map copied from a local newspaper—and told to analyze it in writing using the same rules they used for the road map.

Geography and History

Of all the subjects in the school curriculum, geography is probably most closely related to history. Geography is a major causative factor in historical development. History has even been defined by geographic determinists as nothing more than "geography over time." Classically, whereas history has posed the related questions When? and Why? geography has posed the related questions Where? and Why? Moreover, according to Backler, geography and history also converge as they relate to five historical concepts: (1) understanding time and chronology, (2) analyzing cause-and-effect relationships, (3) examining continuity and change, (4) recognizing and participating in a common memory, and (5) developing historical empathy.[16] And the disciplines actually do come together in a legitimate subfield of both—historical geography.

Historical geography is the geography of the past or geography carried back to the past. It brings together the basic questions of both disciplines in its stress on "regional effect," the environmental impact of the region on its historical development. So, for example, it is impossible to relate accurately to students the development of one of the first civilizations, such as Bronze Age Egypt, without referring to the regional effect—the impact of the Nile River coupled with the climate—on ancient Egypt. Similarly, the history of the North American Great Plains in the nineteenth century cannot be understood without reference to the topography and aridity of the region.

Maps, too, form a connective tissue between geography and history. They are important both to geographers and to historians, albeit sometimes for different yet not wholly unrelated reasons. In their teaching and their research, geographers and historians nevertheless often are map users and makers.

The following activities demonstrate connective tissue between history and geography.

The World of the Medieval Monastery

A world civilization class is directed to read the appropriate sections in textbooks, dealing with monastic life in western Europe during the Middle Ages. Students also read all or part of Umberto Eco's mystery novel *The Name of the Rose,* which is set in a medieval monastery. (If it is more practical, the teacher can provide students with a summary of the novel and have the students read only appropriate passages; a student or group of students can report on this novel for the rest of the class; or students can view a videotape of the movie made from the novel. Teachers of younger students should preview and select scenes or excerpts carefully to omit sexually explicit material.) By reading and using this novel, students are asked to draw on the research tools of reading, interpreting, and creative imagining.

The teacher asks students to assume the role of adolescents in the Middle Ages living with their families in a community at the center of which is a great monastery. They must describe in their own words what their lives are like, their values, and the day-to-day activities of themselves and their families in making a living. They must also voice their knowledge of and attitudes toward the world outside their community. What is their world view? How do they interact with the medieval environment?

Using the descriptive passages in the novel, the teacher asks students to draw maps of the monastery and the library labyrinth that is at its center. The students then use their maps to explain the daily routines common in a medieval monastery. They can check the accuracy of their maps and visions with those supplied by the author in the novel.

The Geography of a Novel

When students read a novel, a play, or a poem in an English class, geographic themes can be emphasized. For example, Davenport used James Michener's *Caravans* to help his students learn about the geography, the people, and the culture of this remote region of the world (south-central Asia—specifically Afghanistan).[17] Students are introduced to "the geographic elements" and facts about Afghanistan while reading Michener's novel. To some, it is like reading the *National Geographic* without pictures.

In addition to reading the novel for its storyline and characters, *Caravans* can be read for its geographic content by emphasizing the following:

- Landscape—physical as well as human, including climate, vegetation, drainage, topography, cities, villages, and farms.
- Human ecology—the human relationship to the land and its influence on the quality of life.
- Economics—the way people make a living, the communication and transportation systems, and the products produced.
- Regionalism—the reflection of the area uniformity as defined by the physical and/or human cultural characteristics.[18]

To better understand such physical elements as the climate of Afghanistan, comparisons can be made between south-central Asia and the American Southwest—Texas, for example. Climate determines where and how people live, types of transportation routes, the way people spend leisure time, and decisions regarding land use.[19] In the novel *Caravans,* the human element is exemplified by the nomads and their seasonal migration routes as related to the climate and the availability of pastureland for their flocks. When Davenport followed the seasonal migration patterns on the basis of the information in the text, he found an apparent contradiction in the annual route of nomadic Kocki.[20] The use of films, too, can be helpful, "to provide pictorial reinforcement of images created by [the] prose."[21] Salter and Lloyd advocate using literary settings and characters to encourage greater sensitivity to geographical space.[22] The authors' treatment of the landscape and personal space helps to link the reader with the physical and cultural geography of the location.

In this activity the teacher uses a literary work as a tool to integrate the study of world history and contemporary literature with geographic content. Students engage in an in-depth examination of Afghanistan, the description of the people, their country, and their way of life. Using the storyline in *Caravans,* for example, and maps, students have an opportunity to learn about people who are thousands of miles away. Geographic knowledge about a different culture and way of life helps students understand who they are, and by studying about where Afghans live, they learn how they live and how geography influences their lives.

Once students locate the described places on a map of south-central Asia, the information in the novel comes alive and they can plot the migration routes that the nomads took to feed their families and animals. They become familiar with the names of the mountain ranges, major cities, ideal places to graze animals, daily tasks of family members, and foods served during the course of a day.

To extend the technique of geographic inquiry, along with developing writing skills, students pretend they are newspaper reporters and plan a trip to Afghanistan. Michener's Afghanistan is very different from the country today. All reporters should be prepared to face a country ravaged by war and should have information about the following:

1. The major economic centers and their historical significance. (students develop a report)
2. The inoculations they will need in order to travel.
3. The clothes they will need. (students generate a list)
4. The transportation routes they will take once they are in the country. (students prepare an itinerary for internal travel)

In addition, the reporters should prepare sets of questions to ask the men, women, and children they will meet to write the story, "Now That the War Is Over."

Notes

1. A. Robinson, R. Sale, and J. Morison, *Elements of Cartography,* 4th ed. (New York: John Wiley and Sons, 1978), p. 1.
2. R. Daugherty, *Geography in the National Curriculum* (London: Geographical Association, 1989), p. 6.
3. A. Holt-Jensen, *Geography: History and Concepts—A Student's Guide,* 2d ed., trans. Brian Fullerton (Totowa, NJ: Barnes and Noble Books, 1988), p. 2.
4. Daugherty, *Geography in the National Curriculum.*
5. *Guidelines for Geographic Education,* prepared by Joint Committee on Geographic Education (Washington, DC: Association of American Geographers, 1984), p. 2.

6. *Five Themes of Geography,* booklet (Washington, DC: National Geographic Society, 1988).
7. S. Midgely, "Teachers Oppose Learning by Rote," *Independent* (London), March 29, 1989, p. 3.
8. Robinson, Sale, and Morrison, *Elements of Cartography,* p. 1.
9. D. Reinhartz, "Teaching History with Maps: A Graphic Dimension," in *Walter Prescott Webb and the Teaching of History,* ed. D. Reinhartz and S.E. Maizlish (College Station: Texas A&M University Press, 1985), p. 79.
10. J. Reinhartz and D. Reinhartz, *Teach-Practice-Apply: The TPA Instruction Model, 7–12* (Washington, DC: National Education Association, 1988).
11. D. Reinhartz, "Teaching History with Maps," p. 82.
12. R. Arnheim, "The Perception of Maps," *American Cartographer* 3 (1976):5–6.
13. E.T. Parker and M.P. Conzen, "Using Maps as Evidence: Lessons in American Social and Economic History," ERIC Document Reproduction Service, ED 125 395, 1975.
14. Reinhartz, "Teaching History with Maps," p. 86. See also in Walter Prescott, *Webb and the Teaching of History,* 1985.
15. Ibid.
16. Alan Backler, "Teaching Geography in American History," ERIC Document Reproduction Service, ED 299 222, 1988.
17. D.P. Davenport, "Caravans and Classrooms: The Novel as a Teaching Aid," *Journal of Geography* 80, no. 7 (December 1981):259–63.
18. Ibid.
19. *Guidelines for Geographic Education,* Joint Committee on Geographic Education.
20. Davenport, "Caravans and Classrooms."
21. Ibid., p. 263.
22. C.L. Salter and W.J. Lloyd, "Landscape in Literature," ERIC Document Reproduction Service, ED 157 067, 1977.

Bibliography

Austin, C.M. "Geography and Interdisciplinary, Future-Oriented Education," 1980. ERIC Document Reproduction Service, ED 199 167.

Balchin, W.C.V., and A.M. Coleman. "Graphicacy Should Be the Fourth Ace in the Pack." *Times Education Supplement* (London), November 5, 1965.

Connections. Washington, DC: National Geographic Society, 1989. Videotape.

Coones, P., and C.V. Stoddard. "A Hundred Years of Geography at Oxford and Cambridge." *Geographic Journal* 155 (March 1989):13–32.

Forsyth, A.S., Jr. "How We Learn Place Location: Bringing Theory and Practice Together." *Social Education* (November/December 1986):500–503.

Fuller, M.J., et al. "Using State and Local Studies to Teach Geographical Concepts." *Journal of Geography* 81, no. 6 (November/December 1982):242–45.

Geography: Making Sense of Where We Are. Washington, DC: National Geographic Society, 1988.

Grosvenor, G.M. "The Case for Geography Education." *Educational Leadership* 47, no. 3 (November 1989):29–32.

———. "Geographic Education and Global Understanding." *NASSP Curriculum Report* (September 1986):2.

———. "Integration of Geography Instruction Urged for Every Subject." *Education USA* 32 (February 1990):24.

Muir, S.P., and H.N. Cheek. "A Developmental Mapping Program Integrating Geography and Mathematics," 1983. ERIC Document Reproduction Service, ED 238 796.

Natoli, S.J., and C.F. Gritzer. "Modern Geography." In *Strengthening Geography in the Social Studies*. Bulletin no. 81. Washington, DC: National Council for the Social Studies, 1988.

O'Neil, J. "Global Education: Controversy Remains, But Support Growing." *ASCD Curriculum Update*. Washington, DC: ASCD, January 1989.

Sunal, D.S., and B.G. Warask. "Mapping with Young Children," 1984. ERIC Document Reproduction Service, ED 248 163.

Teaching Geography: A Model for Action. Washington, DC: National Geographic Society, 1988.

Wise, J.H. "The Value and Use of Music in Geographic Education," 1979. ERIC Document Reproduction Service, ED 186 337.

World Wildlife Fund. *Rain Forest Rap*. Videotape. 6.5 min. World Wildlife Fund, 1250 24th St., N.W., Washington, DC 20036.

General Resources

Articles

Allenman-Brooks, J., A.A. Clegg, and A.P. Sebolt. "Making the Past Come Alive." *Social Studies* 68 (January–February 1977):6.

Olmstead, C.W. "Knowing and Being Who We Are." *Journal of Geography* 86, no. 1 (January–February 1987):3–4.

Pannivitt, B., ed. "Locating Geography on the Curriculum Map," 1986. ERIC Document Reproduction Service, ED 281 786.

Parry, J.H. "Old Maps Are Slippery Witnesses." *Harvard Magazine* 32 (April 1976).

Reinhartz, D. "The Remapping of Civilization: An Artifactual Approach to Teaching World History." *Proceedings of the Sixth International Conference on Improving University Teaching*. Lausanne, Switzerland (College Park, University of Maryland), July 1980, pp. 911–12.

Roberts, M. "Using Videocassettes." *Teaching Geography* 12, no. 3 (1987):114–17.

Sack, D. "The Popularity of Grade-School Geography: A Texas Case Study." Unpublished manuscript, University of Utah, 1987.

Walsh, S.J. "Geographic Information Systems: An Instructional Tool for Earth Science Educators." *Journal of Geography* 87, no. 1 (January–February 1988):17–25.

Watson, W.J. *Mental Images and Geographical Reality in the Settlement of North America*. Nottingham, U.K.: University of Nottingham, Cust Foundation Lecture, 1967.

Whitmore, P.M. "Mapping a Course." *Science and Children* 25, no. 4 (January 1988):15–17.

Wolf, A. "100 Jahre Putzger—100 Jahre Geschichtsbild in Deutschland (1877–1977)" (100 Years of Putzger—100 Years of Historical Maps in Germany [1877–1977]), *Geschichte in Wissenschaft und Unterricht* 29 (1978):702–18.

Zuckerman, D.W., and R.E. Horn. "The Guide to Simulations/Games for Education and Training," June 1973. ERIC Document Reproduction Service, ED 072 667.

Books

Adventures in Your National Parks (3–8). National Geographic Society, no. 00707. $9.50.

Bargrow, L., and R.A. Skelton. *History of Cartography*. Cambridge, MA: Harvard University Press, 1964.

Boardman, D. *Graphicacy and Geography Teaching*. London: Croom Helm, 1983.

Brown, L.A. *The Story of Maps*. New York: Dover Publications, 1977.

Geo-whiz, Why on Earth (3–8). National Geographic Society, no. 00662. $9.50.

Harley, B.W., and D. Woodward. *History of Cartography*, Vol. 1. Chicago: University of Chicago Press, 1987.

Living on Earth (high school). 1988. National Geographic Society, no. 00736. $31.95.

Malthus, T.R. *Essay on the Principle of Population*. New York: W.W. Norton, 1976.

Martin, J.C., and R.S. Martin. *Maps of Texas and the Southwest, 1513–1900*. Albuquerque: University of New Mexico Press, 1984.

Montesquieu, B.C. *Spirit of Laws* New York: Free Press, 1969.

Peden, W., ed. *Thomas Jefferson, Notes on the State of Virginia*. Chapel Hill: University of North Carolina Press, 1955, p. 5.

Schwartz, S., and R.E. Ehrenberg. *The Mapping of America*. New York: Harry N. Abrams, 1980.

Southworth, M., and S. Southworth. *Maps: A Visual Survey and Design Guide*. Boston: Little, Brown, 1982.

Turner, F.J. *The Frontier in American History*. Tucson: University of Arizona Press, 1985.

Webb, W.P. *The Great Frontier*. Austin, TX: University of Texas Press, 1964.

Webb, W.P. *The Great Plains*. New York: Grosset and Dunlap, 1931.

Wilford, J.N. *The Mapmakers*. New York: Alfred A. Knopf, 1981.

Buenos Días King Tut, Mazal Tov Confucius (I've Got the Whole World in My Notebook)

An Investigation into the Relationship between Early Civilizations and Their Environments

George Camp and Felicia C. Eppley

Through a rigorous program of research, discussion, and writing, students in the classes of George Camp and Felicia Eppley create products, evaluate their work through peer review, and investigate the relationship among geography, climate, and early civilization. A dazzling array of products and their scoring rubrics make this lesson an excellent model for other lessons.

Most world history courses study the four early river civilizations of Afro-Asia—Egypt, Mesopotamia, China, and India. Although these are perhaps among the earliest civilizations, they are not the only civilizations in the world that developed from isolated agrarian cultures. In the Western Hemisphere, for example, the Mayan and Inca civilizations were among the earliest. Interestingly enough, they did not arise along major rivers. Why not?

In order to explore this divergence while still keeping the scope of the unit manageable, we will explore the Mayan civilization along with the Chinese, Egyptian, and Sumerian. This will also lend a more global perspective to our inquiry.

In the course of this unit, students will be asked to examine the four civilizations and to filter their data through the lens of geographic-climatic determinism. The Big Question: How do geography and climate affect various aspects of civilizations? Each student will be asked to exhibit mastery of the material by producing a product (puppet show, children's book, poem/rap, etc.), which will be part of a student exhibition. Students will also participate in a Socratic Seminar, in which they will discuss the effects of geography on civilization in general.

Objectives

1. To explore the art of inquiry.
2. To develop basic skills: research, map interpretation, social interaction, decision making, critical thinking, presentation, vocabulary, metacognition.
3. To develop a global perspective.
4. To think critically about the reasons civilizations, cultures, and people differ from one other.
5. To study the nature of civilization in general, early civilizations in particular.
6. To explore the relationship between civilization and geography and climate toward a level of awareness of our own world.
7. To become aware of one's learning style and the process of learning.

Program

1. In class: Students will explore the basic features of civilization in general and the basic features of Egyptian, Mesopotamian, Chinese, and Mayan civilizations in particular.
2. In class: Students will become part of a Civilization Team and will be assigned responsibility for researching one aspect/department of that civilization. For example, if the civilization is Chinese, the department might be Politics.
3. In class/outside of class: Students will learn basic information about all four civilizations (through discussion, activities, homework). There will be a test on this information.
4. Outside of class: (a) Students will collect data on the details of the way in which China was governed—the ruler, the laws, punishments, defense, conflicts with other nations, collapse of ruling elites, etc.; and (b) having collected the data, students will then ask, How have these aspects of Chinese government been molded by Chinese geography and climate?
5. In class: About halfway through the project, each student will submit an outline or sketch of his product. He will

exchange outlines/sketches with a member of his Civilization Team. Each student will read his partner's paper and write constructive suggestions for ways in which the project could be improved. These suggestions will be considered, responded to (explaining how the project was altered in keeping with the suggestions or why it wasn't) in writing. This document will be submitted as part of the "process" folder along with the project.

6. Outside of class: Student will produce a product (children's history, diorama, poem, puppet show, radio/TV newscast) exhibiting mastery of the relationship between Chinese government and the geography and climate of China.

7. In class: Each student will bring a rough draft, sketch, model of his or her project and submit it to Peer Review. This means that the student will discuss the project with a member of the Civilization Team. The team member will evaluate the project and make suggestions (in writing) for alterations. The student-creator will respond to these suggestions (in writing) and either make the alterations suggested or explain why the alterations have not been made.

8. In class: Students' projects will constitute an in-class Student Exhibition. Each student will be asked to examine four or five projects and produce a Reaction Paper for each.

9. In class: As a Civilization Team, students will exchange information about the various aspects of the civilization and produce a poster displaying the relationship between geography and climate and the nature of their civilization.

10. In class: Students will then reorganize themselves according to "departments"—Politics, Science/Engineering, etc.—and share findings across civilizations. Each group will write a Consensus Paper explaining to what extent, in their opinion, the influence of geography and climate is similar and to what extent it is different in reference to their department.

11. In class: The culminating activity will be a Socratic Seminar, in which students address the Big Question of geographic-climatic determinism.

Evaluation

Daily Grade. Quizzes, peer review process, participation. _____/300

Test. One for this unit. _____/100

Project Process. The following items will be included in a folder to be submitted with your product.

- Cornell notes: a form with key words/questions/topics/ideas, page #s, source #s, effective abbreviation system on the left; make notes—no sentences—on the right

(draw a line down a sheet of paper, with one-third of the paper to the left of the line, two-thirds to the right). _____/20

- Sources: minimum of three with only one encyclopedia, depth of data (except for Mayan civilization—ask). _____/40

- Quality control documents: required rough plan/sketch/outline for all elements of unit with clear evidence of peer review and revision on each. _____/40

Project Product. See rubrics (grading parameters) for each type on following pages. _____/100

Poster. Group; see directions for Poster Project (item 9 earlier on this page. _____/100

Reaction Paper. Four individual papers at 25 points each. _____/100

Seminar. The Big Question. _____/100

Consensus Paper. Group. _____/100

Metacognition Survey. _____/100

Projects and Rubrics

Children's Book with Illustrations

Description

Create book for children that explains the relationship between your "department" (Politics, Science/Engineering, etc.) and geography and climate. This book could be a fable, a Richard Scarry–type book, an ABC book, etc. Go to the children's section of the public library for inspiration.

Rubric

1. Does product address the Big Question (How have geography and climate influenced your department of this civilization?) 0–20

2. Does it present at least three aspects of your department—e.g., "Lifestyle": sports, clothes, food? 0–20

3. Is information presented coherently, with perceptive interpretations and transitions? 0–10

4. Is the material presented creatively, with adequate illustrations where applicable? 0–10

5. Does product reflect one or more higher-order intellectual processes (association, classification, comparison, contrast, differentiation, distinction, organization, relation, explanation, formulation, interpretation, summarization)? 0–20

6. Is it presented neatly? 0–5

Total 0–100

Radio/TV Script

Description

Create a script for radio or TV that explains the relationship between your department and geography and climate. This script could be for a newscast, a soap opera, a game show, a children's show, MTV, etc. It could also be performed on tape. Regardless of whether it is performed, videotaped, or audiotaped, a script must be submitted for a grade. Performance will, of course, enhance the grade.

Rubric

Same as rubric for children's book, p. 157.

Diorama/Display

Description

Create a three-dimensional display exhibiting aspects of your research. For example, if your department were science and engineering, you might build a model of a Mayan community showing men crawling toward underground cenotes for water, while on the surface others build temples of local stone, etc. Explanation (250 words minimum) may be in the form of an accompanying paper or labels.

Rubric

Same as rubric for children's book, p. 157.

Poem or Rap

Description

Create a poem or rap that conveys the information you have gleaned from your research. A poem could rhyme or be blank verse. The poem or rap could tell a story or simply convey information.

Rubric

Same as rubric for children's book, p. 157.

Puppet Show

Description

Create a puppet show that conveys the information you have gleaned from your research. It could enact a fable or tell a real-life story. It should involve costumes, dialogue, etc.

Whether or not the puppet show is performed, it requires the submission of a script in order to get a grade. Performance will, of course, enhance the grade.

Rubric

Same as rubric for children's book, p. 157.

Role-Play/Script

Description

Create a character who will convey the information you have gleaned from your research. The script must let the reader know at least ten specific things about the character (name, age, family, situation, finances, occupation, etc.). It must include "point of view." Even if you perform your role-play, you must also submit a script. Performance will, of course, enhance the grade.

Rubric

Same as rubric for children's book, p. 157.

Edibles

Description

Create dishes that are representative of your civilization, that reflect what you have learned through your research. A written explanation of 250 words or more should accompany the dishes to explain their significance and to address the Big Question.

Rubric

1. Does product address the Big Question?   0–20
2. Does it cover at least three aspects of your department? 0–20
3. Is material presented coherently?   0–10
4. Does product reflect one or more higher-order intellectual processes?   0–20
5. Are the dishes historically relevant?   0–15
6. Is the preparation attractive and creative?   0–15

   Total 0–100

Journal or Diary

Description

Entries must cover at least one year in the life of their author. A preface must give at least ten details about the author (e.g., name, occupation, age, family situation, finances, etc.). Each entry must include action, location or setting, and the author's "point of view" or feelings about the data. Minimum 1,000 words overall.

Rubric

1. Does product address the Big Question?   0–20
2. Does it cover at least three aspects of your department? 0–20
3. Is material presented coherently?   0–20
4. Does it reflect one or more higher-order intellectual processes?   0–20
5. Are the requirements in the "Description" adequately met?   0–15
6. Is it presented neatly?   0–5

Total 0–100

Essay

Description

The essay must have a thesis, e.g., the nature of Mayan agriculture was significantly determined by the geography and climate of the Yucatan Peninsula. Or, you could take the opposite position. In any event, you must marshal evidence to support your position. It should be about four handwritten pages, 1,000 words minimum.

Rubric

1. Does product address the Big Question?   0–20
2. Does it cover at least three aspects of your department? 0–20
3. Is material presented coherently with perceptive interpretations and transitions?   0–20
4. Does it reflect one or more higher-order intellectual processes?   0–20
5. Is there a thesis statement, and is it supported adequately? 0–15
6. Is the product presented neatly?   0–5

Total 0–100

Reaction Paper

Name:
Period:
Project Title:
Project Author:

1. In what way does this project deal with the Big Question?
2. What did you learn from this project that you didn't know before?
3. Indicate what you liked most about this project.
4. Suggest one way in which this project could be improved.

28

Historical Themes through Ancient Literature

Bullitt Lowry

Bullitt Lowry has developed a book review that enables students to identify historical themes in the literature of ancient and classical societies and analyze these themes in terms of the society. Students enjoy the work and can acquire interesting insights into the lives of ancient and classical peoples. While this particular assignment applies to early periods, the same review is just as applicable to later periods of history.

When our history department first moved from Western civilization to world civilization, I, like everyone else who has faced such a sea change, was frightened to death. Fortunately for the first semester's offering, "World History to 1500," I was familiar with Kevin Reilly's excellent textbook *The West and the World,* which organizes the otherwise overwhelming material through themes, and that gave me a point from which to start. (For the second semester—in our case, "World History Since 1500"—I use other materials.) Since I was using Reilly's themes, I thought it might be sensible to reinforce them through other written requirements, and therefore I developed a book review that requires students to explore historical themes in other writings.

That became the assignment, "Historical Themes through Ancient Literature." Below, I reproduce the handouts I give to the students. The reader will note that the literature to which the students are limited is heavily Greek and Roman. The same assignment would work equally well if the list included, or were limited to, the literature of ancient China or India. I have not offered this course for several years, and the next time I teach it, I plan to add material from ancient Asia. I could also add specific writings from other European traditions, like *Beowulf.*

Book List

Please take one of the works listed below (or any other work for which I have given *prior* approval), read it, and in six pages (typed, *maximum*), describe the contents and show how they apply to, or illustrate, one of the themes of this course. You will get a separate handout discussing those themes and giving you more details on what you need to include in your paper.

Inanna, Queen of Heaven and Earth
The Epic of Gilgamesh
The Story of Sinuhe, the Egyptian
Aeschylus, *Agamemnon*
Aeschylus, *Prometheus Bound*
Sophocles, *Electra*
Aristophanes, *The Frogs*
Aristophanes, *Lysistrata*
Aristophanes, *The Clouds*
Thucydides, *Peloponnesian War*
Juvenal, *Satires*
Caesar, *Conquest of Gaul*
Tacitus, *Annals*
Lucan, *Pharsalia*
Xenophon, *Anabasis*
Plautus, *Menaechmi*
Terence, *The Woman of* [sometimes *Maid of* or *Girl from*) *Andros*
Terence, *The Eunuch*
Seneca, *Medea*
Petronius, *Satirae* [*Satyricon*]
Ovid, *The Art of Love*

The reader will note that this list is directed, to some degree, toward the interests of the average student, with sex and violence being overrepresented. Many of the plots reappear in the works of Shakespeare, Molière, and others, so students often make a voyage of literary discovery. Some obvious works I omit. At one time, I included the *Iliad,* the *Odyssey,* and the *Aeneid,* but I got poor results from them. They are so long that students are tempted, perhaps, to skip over parts they should not skip. Also, those works are so complex that the student is hard pressed to pick a single theme and follow through.

When I get to the themes of the course, I confess that I have modified Reilly's definitions. He should not be excoriated for what I have done with the themes he presents in *The West and the World.*

Directions for Preparing the Paper

The assignment asks you to examine a work of ancient literature and to point out how the work illustrates one of the themes developed in this course. Any of the works listed might illustrate all of the themes, but because of the page limit set (six pages, typed and double-spaced), it would be hard for you to develop more than one course theme adequately.

You will need to make the assumption that the work you are reading is representative of a given society. Whether the author is reporting what he or she thinks is true, exhorting the reader to a particular course of action, or satirizing what he or she thinks is absurd, treat the work as representative of the author's society.

I recommend the following procedure. Read the work you choose carefully. Intermittently, as you read, refresh your mind on the possible themes. When you have finished that first reading, pick the course theme you wish to explore. Then go back through the work, this time taking notes on matters that illustrate what you want to say.

The Course Themes

Masculine and Feminine Roles

Societies have differing views on the appropriate roles of men and women, their work, duties, responsibilities, rewards, relationship to authority, and general behavior. What roles does the work you are reading describe? What social mechanisms support those roles? Which character traits are considered masculine and which feminine?

Sex and Love

Sex is a biological function. How and why does a particular society regulate it? What rituals do they bind it in? Love is an emotion that is not expressed in some societies. If it is expressed in the society you are discussing, how does the work you have read explain or describe it? How is love related to sex, if, in the work you are examining, it is? Are there courtship rituals? How does the society punish people who defy its teachings?

Cities and Civilizations

How and why do cities grow? What role does a city play in the society you are exploring? What attitudes toward cities does the work reveal? How are different types of cities treated?

War and Peace

Whether or not aggression is part of human nature—and it may not be—no society can allow its members to express aggression without limits. What limits on violence are shown in the work you are examining? How does the society regu-

late violence? How does the work depict war? Are some types of society more prone to violence and war than others? Is peace considered to be a normal condition that war disturbs, or is the opposite suggested? Are martial qualities—strength, bravery, and so on—considered to be particularly virtuous, or are peacemakers especially blessed?

Individual and Society

The relationship between an individual and society shows as many different patterns as there are societies (and possibly individuals). Nevertheless, any society will demand that an individual follow a general pattern. Does the individual exist to be a part of society, a faceless piece of an operating system, or does the society exist so that the individual may flourish? Some sort of compromise on this point is necessary, but it will lean to one side or the other. How does a society train an individual to play an assigned role? How does it punish an individual who refuses to play the assigned role? What goals does society set for the individual? How does it reward an individual who meets those goals? How does an individual act to change society, if the thought ever crosses the individual's mind?

Politics and Religion (Morality)

None of the themes mentioned thus far is clearly separate from the others. Masculine and feminine roles involve sex and love. War and peace necessarily are interwoven with individual and society. "Politics and Religion (Morality)," too, contains elements of all the other themes, because this theme involves the interaction between decision making and belief systems. Does a society act in some relation to the belief system of its members? Do actions of society cause changes in belief systems, or do changes in belief systems cause changes in society's decision making? To ask those questions is to answer them. A person examining this theme would be less concerned with proving that a relationship existed than with showing how the process worked in the particular society under discussion.

Organization of the Paper

After reading the work, thinking, rereading, and making notes, the student might organize the paper in this way:

Title of Paper. The title is: Blank (the course theme) in Blankety-blank (title of the work you are examining).

Bibliographic Heading. (That is, information on the book you are discussing.) Author (period) title (underlined, period) translator (period). (That should look like Translated by Sam Smith.) Series (if any, semicolon) place of publication (colon) publisher (comma) date (period). Put this information just beneath the title of your paper.

Introduction. In three or four sentences, give some information about the author: birth and death dates, if known; major facts or myths about the author's life, etc. Then in a few sentences summarize what the work covers. This whole introduction should take no more than one and one-half pages.

The Course Theme. Briefly state the nature of the theme you are examining. Show how that theme works in the material you have read. Give specific examples, but summarize. Do not quote excessively. Take care to do more than produce a scrapbook on a theme.

Conclusions. Save at least one page for your *own* conclusions and personal reflections on the theme and the material.

I have found this assignment a useful one. The students like it, too, perhaps because it gives them some room for self-expression, and approved self-expression is often difficult to find in lower-division classes. The average class grade on this paper is generally high, which suggest that the students work hard at doing this assignment well.

29

Thousands of Years Ago the World Was Connected by a Caterpillar . . .

Michele Forman

An excellent way to structure a lesson that crosses cultures and lays the groundwork for analysis of cultural diffusion is to begin with a study of trade. Michele Forman has constructed just such a unit.

I use this lesson very early in the year. Our tenth-grade curriculum begins with units on India and China (approximately 600 B.C.E.–600 C.E. Just before this activity, we spend time discussing and exploring some of the problems of constructing history. We look at history as a human construct and, as such, not an absolute. We grapple with ways of organizing the past so that it makes sense. We examine how some textbooks categorize history, and we brainstorm some alternative schemata. I ask them to consider how we can best study phenomena that take place over a large area and over a long period of time. This activity can take a long time (a week), and I let it lead us into a study of Chinese civilizations in a global context. I use it this way because it helps set a "messy" framework. That is, it helps kids see that history can't be neatly categorized by civilization or time period. And it makes a fun introduction to our study of China, naturally linking it to much of the rest of the world. I also like being able to refer to it later in the year as an example of how connected and messy history is.

Objectives

Students will:

- Define the concept of luxury goods and recognize their importance in world trade.
- Construct questions that form the basis of their history inquiry.
- Explain the extent of the silk trade over time and distance and analyze its role in connecting peoples.
- Discuss how trade led to the exchange of ideas.
- Interpret and use information from a variety of sources.
- Evaluate the importance of places along the Silk Road and of events connected to the silk trade.
- Apply information from their research to the construction

of maps, charts, and timelines.
- Report their findings in a written essay containing a thesis and supporting evidence.

Introduction

I explain to students that we'll be researching and learning about how "things" connected people. We brainstorm a list of things (stuff) that we value today (bikes, cars, CDs, etc.), and we talk about what makes these valuable, i.e., why we want them. We talk about the difference between "necessities" (I don't usually consider any of the things on our list to be necessities; they do, of course—how can one live without CDs?) and "luxuries." We agree upon some items today that are considered luxuries or things that are nice to have.

I ask them to think about what things might have been considered luxuries a hundred years ago, a thousand years ago, two thousand years ago. I ask if they can think of anything that has been a luxury for people throughout a large area of the world over thousands of years. After some discussion, I mention that silk has played such a role. I ask how silk is made, where it comes from, etc., and explain that throughout much of history over much of the world, many people have felt about silk the way that we (they) feel about bikes, cars, CDs, etc. We talk about how our luxury goods connect us to other people around the world today. Who made your CD? Who grew the beans for my cup of coffee? etc.

Research

We generate some questions about silk. I ask them, if they want to understand how this "thing" affected the world, what questions would they have to answer? I keep pushing them to be more specific until we have a decent set of historical questions for our research. I have everyone write these in his or her research journal. Typical questions include: Why was silk valued, what qualities about it were prized? What was traded for silk? How far did silk travel? Who bought the silk? How much was traded? Why didn't other peoples manufacture silk? I explain that these questions will define our study and the evaluation for this unit. (They like the idea that they've just created their own evaluation instrument.)

Working in groups, different students choose different questions for research. I support them but give them a lot of freedom with their work. Some of the activities I assign to help guide their research (with some classes I'm much more directive than with others) include:

1. Create a map. You may choose to illustrate your map. Label at least twenty (twenty-five, thirty) important points on the Silk Road(s) and be prepared to explain why each was important. Attach dates to your map and, of course, include a legend.
2. Create an annotated, illustrated timeline of the silk trade.
3. Create a silk trader's journal. Be sure to include plenty of historical specifics. Include sketches. Be sure to describe your experiences and observations from a historically correct perspective (point of view).
4. You are a silk trader. Create a logo and advertisement for your product. The advertisement may be a poster, a brochure, a jingle, a skit, or a video. Define the audience for your ad and explain how you are targeting that audience.
5. Write an essay on the following: "Thousands of years ago, the world was connected by a caterpillar." (I've used this as the summative evaluation for the unit sometimes.)

Projects are shared and presented, of course. I like *big,* colorful displays, so they usually fill a wall with their maps, timelines (using a computer Timeliner program, they've made timelines that wrap around the room—high up on the walls), posters, etc.

Teacher Notes

I use just these for review in helping me guide students in their research.

The Silk Trade

Silk is a symbol of ancient Chinese civilization, and the silk trade provides a vehicle for studying China's connections with the rest of the world over time. Silk has been produced in China for four thousand to five thousand years. Some of the early evidence of its importance appears in writings on bones and tortoise shells from the Shang dynasty (sixteenth to eleventh century B.C.E.) and tells of silk and silkworms.

Silk was ideally suited for long-distance trade. As a prized luxury good, its price was high, but its weight and volume per yard are very low. In India it's said that a fine silk sari, six yards long, can be held in one closed hand. Silk readily absorbs brilliant dye colors, drapes gracefully, and is very comfortable to wear. It lasts for a long period of time without decay; indeed an Egyptian mummy from 1000 B.C.E. has been discovered with strands of silk still identifiable in her hair.

The Silk Road, a sprawling, extended trade network, linked China with many cultural centers of the ancient world. For many, China became identified with silk; in the Old Testament Book of Isaiah, the Chinese are referred to as *Sinim,* or silk men, and the Greeks called China *Seres,* or the nation of silk. Silk cultivation was so important that in some dynasties peasants were required to plant mulberry trees and pay their taxes in silk.

Evidence of an important and extensive silk trade extends back to a number of early civilizations in different parts of the world. A silk saddle cover made in 770–475 B.C.E. was found in an ancient tomb in southern Siberia, and silk has been found in seventh-century B.C.E. graves in Germany.

Trade networks extended from China to points in the Persian Empire in the sixth and fifth centuries B.C.E., and to Greece in the fourth century B.C.E. After the fifth century B.C.E., Alexandria became a silk textile center. The silk trade introduced many Westerners to China and encouraged them to learn about Chinese culture. Ptolemy, the Greek geographer and mathematician, wrote about the silk trade.

In the fourth century B.C.E. Sichuan merchants traveled to Assam and then to parts of India. The Maurya regime in India traded goods for silk during 320–185 B.C.E.

Ancient Romans prized silk highly; emperors, for example, wore togas of Chinese silk. Queen Cleopatra wore silk. The Romans thought silk grew on trees, and in Julius Caesar's time, silk was worth its weight in gold. Chinese silk trade with the Roman Empire peaked in 280–289 C.E.

The Silk Road's land terminus was Constantinople/Istanbul, where it met the sea portion of its trade route.

China traded silk with Malaysia in the first century B.C.E.

In the fifteenth century, Malacca was an important trade center.

Favorite Sources

Institute of the History of Natural Sciences, Chinese Academy of Sciences. *Ancient China's Technology and Science.* Beijing, China: Foreign Languages Press, 1986. This source contains an excellent discussion of sericulture, including its history and the technology and methods of its production. It has wonderful primary-source selections, including illustrations of silkworm decorations on bronze objects of the Shang dynasty and drawings of women picking mulberry leaves from the Warring States period. 632 pp.

Muqi, Che. *The Silk Road, Past and Present.* Beijing, China: Foreign Languages Press, 1989. The author of this work recently journeyed along the Silk Road. His account weaves the history of the Silk Road with descriptions of current places and people he meets. The book is rich in the history of the Silk Road and contains excellent maps and good photos. 319 pp.

Wilford, John Noble. "Even Earlier Trade on Fabled Silk Road." *New York Times,* March 10, 1993. This brief article describes the recent discovery of strands of silk in the hair of an Egyptian mummy from about 1000 B.C.E. It discusses the teamwork of scientists, archaeologists, and historians in reconstructing the story of the silk trade.

The article, which includes a map of the Silk Road, is an excellent source for students.

Yan, Xing, ed. *From Venice to Osaka: UNESCO Retraces the Maritime Silk Route*. Beijing, China: China Pictorial Publishing House, 1992. This beautiful book recounts the UNESCO project, retracing the maritime Silk Route. It contains some good discussions of the history of the silk trade and many spectacular photos. It provides a superb pictorial demonstration of the diversity of lands, civilizations, and peoples connected by the Silk Road.

30

Comparison of Confucius and Christ as Important Influences on Their Cultures

David Harbison

David Harbison establishes the foundation for comparative study with a lesson on Confucius and Christ. He continues comparative work by assigning a series of short essays on a particular world religion or philosophy over a four-week period. Students have ample time to discuss and revise their short essays, which become the basis of their final paper.

The two- or three-day activity outlined below is designed to introduce students to the ideas of two influential people, Confucius and Christ. The activity enables students to compare what are very dissimilar world views and to investigate the influences of each on the development of their respective societies.

Having spent part of a class asking my (mostly) Western students to identify what they think are the most important sources of the Western tradition (usually they will come up with Judeo-Christian sources and name the Old and New Testaments as well as the Grateful Dead and more recent sources), I point out that all cultures have sources of this magnitude and introduce Confucius as the most influential source for the Chinese tradition. I then assign my students the following readings for homework:

- The Beatitudes from Matthew 5:1–18, the Lord's Prayer from Matthew 6:1–34, the Golden Rule from Matthew 7:1–29 (King James Version).
- Various Confucian analects. (There are many sources for these. One very good and easy-to-find source is the standard work *Sources of the Chinese Tradition.*)

Read through the New Testament sources above and then select appropriate analects.

I also provide my students with the following guide questions to help them identify the most important ideas in the readings:

1. Judging by what Christ says, what do you think is his purpose?
2. Judging by what Confucius says, what do you think is his purpose?

3. How would Christ and Confucius describe a good life?
4. In what specific ways are the goals of Christ and Confucius different?

Depending on your circumstances, you as teacher can proceed from here in any number of ways. Perhaps you will ask your students to write paragraph answers to some or all of these questions. Perhaps you will lead a group discussion based on these questions. Do what you think will work best for you. Some (but not all) of the ideas that you hope to elicit from your students include:

- Christ is divine; Confucius is not.
- Christ hopes to ensure "life after death" by showing the individual how to live; Confucius has no interest in "life after death" but seeks to create a better collective society by encouraging self-sacrifice in the interest of collective society.
- Christ commands obedience and outlines consequences for noncompliance; Confucius encourages virtue and a good personal example within strict guidelines.
- Christ suggests equality; Confucius values inequality.

From here I trust you see many other discussions to have that compare the West and the East. For example, compare Western concepts of law and Chinese systems.

World Religion and Philosophy Project

The project outlined below is designed as an ambitious, student-centered, cross-cultural research project for strong ninth or tenth graders who have access to a reasonably well-stocked library. Computers, while tremendously valuable for this project for reasons that will reveal themselves to you as read through it, are not essential to the design of the project. Note that the series of short papers is what distinguishes this project. This approach reduces the intimidation of researching and writing about such a big and usually unfamiliar topic. In fact, my students always find producing the final longer paper more secretarial than daunting because the process has acquainted them so thoroughly with their topic. My list of topics, my list of questions, and the time frame can be modified to match your interests and circumstances. Finally, a follow-up discussion and/or writing assignment that explores common ground among the topics presented by students in groups or as individuals is also effective.

Assignment

1. To produce a five-page report detailing what you think are the essential characteristics or aspects of the religion or philosophy you have selected or been assigned. This report will be word-processed and double-spaced and will include a formal bibliography. Our research topics include Islam, Hinduism, Buddhism, Catholicism, Protestantism, Judaism, and Confucianism.

2. To present orally to the class the information that you think is most important and most interesting about your topic. Oral presentations will be in pairs where more than one person in a given class is presenting the same topic. Feel free to include visual aids, handouts, etc.

Process

To help focus your thinking and research, I have written a series of questions that you will answer formally in writing as we proceed through the project. Each answer will be *at least one page* in length and include a bibliography where appropriate (see attached style sheet). You may answer most of the questions in any order, but you must answer all of them in accordance with the schedule below. As you answer them, be certain to save them in a single text file. Also, be certain to identify by letter which questions you are answering with any hard copy you produce. Keep a back-up file! The questions are:

1. Do you understand the process you will undertake to complete this project? What will be the most challenging aspect of the project for you? Do you consider yourself an organized person? Do you tend to procrastinate? If yes, what can you do about it?
2. List a handful of people associated with your topic. Write a short biographical sketch of two of the people on your list who have influenced your topic the most. What were those contributions?
3. Write a historical sketch of your topic. Where did it originate? Under what conditions? How and why did it spread? What were some of the major historical turning points? Include a timeline of major events and turning points.

4. How many believers are there today? Where are they? What current issues are relevant to the members of this religion/philosophy today? What are the important sects today?
5. Describe the religious life of a believer.
6. What are the roles of men and women in this religion/philosophy? Do they differ? Have they changed over time?
7. Is there a specific birth-life-death cycle? If yes, describe it. If not, what happens when a believer dies?
8. How tolerant or intolerant of other faiths is this religion/philosophy? Today? Historically? Give examples.
9. Does this religion/philosophy have an ethical system or worldview to which members are expected to subscribe? In short, does it tell you what to believe and how to act?
10. What are the sacred texts of this religion/philosophy? Provide some important examples.
11. Describe in detail an important ceremony associated with this religion/philosophy.
12. What is something you find especially interesting about this religion/philosophy?
13. Interview someone who practices this religion/philosophy. What did you learn?
14. What topic headings or terms other than "Hinduism" or "Religion" did you trace to find information about your topic? Describe something you have learned about the research process.

Below find the schedule you will follow for turning in your various answers:

Class 1—Introduction to project. Visit the librarian. Do research in library.
Class 2—Question 1 due.
Class 3—Two sources in list form due.
Class 4—Research.

Week 2

Class 1—Research in library.
Class 2—Question 2 due.
Class 3—Any question due; research.
Class 4—Research.

Week 3

Class 1—Any two questions due.
Class 2—Research; any two questions due.
Class 3—Research.
Class 4—Any one question due.

Week 4

    Class 1—Research; any one question due.
    Class 2—Research; any one question due.
    Class 3—Research; any two questions due.
    Class 4—Any two questions due.

Week 5

    Class 1—Oral presentations.
    Class 2—Oral presentations.
    Class 3—Oral presentations (if necessary).
    Class 4—Final papers due.

31

The Great Mandala

The Circle of Life

Mary A. Price

Mary Price uses the mandala or circle, a symbol present in the art of many cultures, as a repeating visual theme in her world history course. She uses it to identify religious traditions and discuss the religious ideas in many societies. In this lesson she gives examples of student work and provides instructions for teaching this material.

A mandala is a circular design arranged in layers radiating from the center. The word comes from Hindu Sanskrit, the classical language of India, and means circle or center. The Hindus used mandala designs for meditation. The mandala also appears in many cultures other than those of the Eastern world. Mandalas can be found in the rose windows of medieval cathedrals of Europe. The Aztecs of Mexico created a magnificent stone mandala for their calendar. At its center was a mask of the sun god. Surrounding the mask were symbols depicting an earthquake that the Aztecs thought would end the world. Around that was a band with the signs for the days of the Aztec year. The Navaho of the American Southwest have a healing ritual in which multicolored sands are used to create circular patterns. The patient is placed in the center of the mandala design and is encircled by a ring of prayers.

The Swiss psychiatrist C.G. Jung (1875–1961) made psychological studies of the mandala and used it in treating patients. Jung and his patient would draw a mandala, starting

Section of an Aztec Calendar Stone

the design at the center and continuing outward. Taking turns, the patient drew, then doctor, then patient, until they felt the mandala was complete.

The steps demonstrated below show one way of creating a mandala design. Look at these steps before you begin your own.

Step 1　　Step 2

Step 3　　Step 4

Begin with a center design. Add details within. Add more designs, symmetrically filling in open spaces. Finally, add shading to highlight special areas.

Exercise Set

1. What are some examples of mandala design that you've seen or know about?
2. What company designs or logos are also mandalas?
3. Find a quiet moment and create your own mandala. Color it.

Islamic art uses designs of repeating geometric patterns. *The Mathematics of Islamic Art,* Rosanne Wasserman, ed., is a packet of slides, information, and directions for creating Islamic designs. This may be purchased from the Metropolitan Museum of Art.

169

**Frances Wong
Geometry student**

**Scott Shanks
Geometry student**

Design by the author

**Donna Chang
Geometry student**

32

Europe and India

Corinne Lathrop Gilb

Corinne Lathrop Gilb is a true pathfinder. She has developed a lesson that provides the subject matter essential for developing an understanding of the rarely taught connection of trade and cultural diffusion between India and Europe. The information in this lesson may be used as one lesson or divided into mini-lessons and used as focal points in a world history survey.

The purpose of this lesson is to understand the common heritage of India and Europe, such as the Indo-European language; how the cultures of each influenced the other, such as India's contribution of a number system to Europe; how the two regions were economically interrelated; and how trade spread culture both ways. Note that both had relations with East Asia.

Background

1. The Indo-Europeans, who were in India by 1500 B.C.E. or earlier, may have originated in Europe's far north. They eventually spread throughout most of India, parts of the Middle East, and into some eastern parts of Europe. They influenced many European languages as well as Sanskrit in India.

Greeks began to have contact with India in the sixth century B.C.E. and invaded India in 327 B.C.E. There were later Indo-Greek kingdoms in northwest India. The two cultures influenced one another and traded.

Show a table of Indo-European languages. Explain that so-called Arabic numerals came from India.

2. India was divided among many rulers throughout most of its history. Among them were the Kuṣāṇas, who came from northwest China. Their empire in North India (c. 78 B.C.E. to 248 or 300 C.E.) existed at roughly the same time as the Roman Empire. There had been international trade between India and the Middle East for a long time. Trade flourished between India and the Romans at the time of the Kuṣāṇas. Roman caravans began in Antioch or Palmyra or Petra and went east to Merv, from which some caravans went south into India; or caravans went to the Red Sea or sometimes the Persian Gulf, and then the goods went by sea to major Indian ports. Indian goods were exported by the same routes in reverse. The Kuṣāṇas helped trade and regulated it.

Early Roman trade with India was not direct but was carried on by Greek, Syrian, Jewish, Armenian, and other merchants, all of whom were under Roman rule. Often the ships belonged to the Colas, who ruled in South India. Roman ships came directly to India during the first century C.E. The ships became very large. The Romans bought much more from Indians than they sold to India. India traded with the Far East to get goods the Romans wanted. They also traded with East Africa.

Show maps of Eurasia from the first century B.C.E. to the end of the fourth century C.E. Show pictures of ships of that time. Discuss the meaning of balance of payments.

3. After 100 B.C.E., people from the Roman Empire began to settle in the major southern Indian seaports or along parts of the land route to India. In 69–79 C.E., when the Roman Empire had shortages of gold and silver because it sent so much away to pay for Indian goods, the Roman emperor Vespasian forbade the export of precious metals out of the Roman Empire. Indian merchants began to trade more with East Bengal and Southeast Asia. Roman trade with India declined after the third century C.E.

Show where East Bengal and Southeast Asia are on the map in relation to India.

Discuss Hindu and Buddhist beliefs and how these spread eastward when Indians traded more with the East.

4. Both the Roman and Kuṣāṇa empires declined in the third and fourth centuries. Both were being invaded by foreign tribes and both were splitting up internally. In both, cities began to decline. The western Roman Empire went into a lengthy period of breaking up when the emperor Constantine moved the capital from Rome to Constantinople. After the Kuṣāṇas came a period of political chaos in India.

Show Constantinople and the Byzantine Empire on maps.

Discuss how economic prosperity and trade depend on political stability.

5. In India feudalism appeared, the area was divided among various regimes, and trade declined until the tenth century. During this period China was usually prosperous, and Chinese private merchants had entered the Indian Ocean trade by the tenth century.

Define feudalism; show China on maps.

6. After the Islamic Empire spread over the Middle East

and later North Africa from the seventh century onward, trade in the Mediterranean was badly disrupted by warfare. There was little trade between the Muslim Middle East and Europe for 250 years. From 845 and especially after 906, European trade with China was also disrupted. During the same period, Muslim industry grew, gold flowed into the Muslim Empire from Africa, Muslim trade grew, and Muslim merchant colonies appeared in India.

Discuss the basic tenets of Islam. Show maps of the spread of Islam.

7. Indians played an increasingly important role in the Indian Ocean trade. Early in the fourteenth century, Marco Polo brought news of the Spice Islands to Europe. Spices were carried to the West by sea by Indian and Arab merchants.

Discuss the role of spices as preservatives.

8. Muslim Turks ruled parts of northern India in the thirteenth and fourteenth centuries. Muslims began to take over India's seagoing trade. In 1483 the Muslim Mogul Empire began to take over parts of India. It was willing to let foreign merchants come in. Indian Ocean trade prospered in the fourteenth and fifteenth centuries.

Show maps of Muslim India.

9. Christians gradually pushed Muslims out of Spain and Portugal. The Muslim center of Granada in Spain was defeated in 1492. Now the Christians were in complete control in Spain and Portugal, and yet Muslim Turks took over Constantinople in 1453 and Baghdad in 1534. When France and England ended their Hundred Years' War in 1453, both needed rebuilding. With Muslims still blocking land routes to India, western Europe needed new trade routes. This was the situation when the Portuguese sailed along the African coast and Columbus sailed across the Atlantic, looking for new routes to India.

Discuss ways India was important to Europe and why it remained important for a long time.

Show maps of sea trade.

Individual Project

On an outline map of the world centered on Eurasia c. 1500 B.C.E., color areas where Indo-Europeans lived and make broad arrows showing the paths over which they moved into Europe, the Middle East, and India.

On another outline map of Eurasia, use different-colored pencils to draw land routes and sea routes between Europe and India c. 50 C.E. (For a map of the Silk Road, see page 10

of Judy Bonavta, *The Silk Road,* London: The Guidebook Co., 1988.) Put dots on the map for Damascus, Antioch, Constantinople, Merv, Kashgar, Anxi, Lanzhou, Xian. Also dots for Tyre, Palmyra, and Petra. Draw lines from Merv to Kabul, Taxila, and from there to Banares in the Ganges Valley and to Tamralipiti in Bengal.

Use a different-colored pencil for sea routes from ports on India's east coast (Karikal, Madras, Masulipatam, Pondicherry-Arikmedu, Camara, and Sopatma) and India's west coast (Barbaricum, Barygaza [Broach], Muziris-Nelcynda, and Bocare) to along the offshore edges of the northern Indian Ocean, and from there to the head of the Persian Gulf, to Adulis in East Africa, and up the Red Sea. Put a dot on the map for Alexandria in Egypt.

Team Project

Divide the class into small groups to design a Monopoly-type board game that requires the players to use the information and locations in the lessons. Use additional library sources to enhance the game, or students may design a word search using words from a chart on Indo-European languages.

Suggested Reading

McEvedy, Colin. *The Penguin Atlas of Ancient History.* Baltimore: Penguin, latest edition. Has a chart showing the relations of Indo-Europeans to others. Covers the area from western Europe to Persia from 8500 B.C.E. to 362, with maps and discussion of towns and trade.

Robinson, Francis, ed. *The Cambridge Encyclopedia of India, Pakistan, Bangladesh, Sri Lanka, Nepal, Bhutan, and the Maldives.* Cambridge: Cambridge University Press, 1989. Has maps, pictures, tables of states and rulers, and bibliography.

Bibliography

Abu-Lughod, Janet L. *Before European Hegemony: The World System C.E. 1250–1350.* New York: Oxford University Press, 1989.

Ballard, George. *Rulers of the Indian Ocean.* Delhi: Neeraj Publishing, 1984.

Chaudhuri, K.N. *Trade and Civilization with the Indian Ocean.* Cambridge: Cambridge University Press, 1985.

Miller, J. Innes. *The Spice Trade of the Roman Empire.* Oxford: Clarendon Press, 1969.

33

The Nature of Civilization

A Final Exam

Laurie Schmitt

Laurie Schmitt begins her course with the final examination. She begins teaching using the ideas of Islamic historian Ibn Khaldoun to structure a final essay. She includes in this chapter an example of a sophomore essay by one of her students. This assignment may be used as a template with ideas of twentieth-century world historians providing the structure of the final exam second semester.

When the students walk into ancient civilizations class on the first day of school, I hand them their final exam. Their first assignment, to be repeated at the end of the year, is to write an essay based on the following description of the observations of Ibn Khaldoun, the fourteenth-century Islamic historian, about the nature of civilization:

> Ibn Khaldoun was concerned with the *nature* of civilization, its rise and decline. He considered that settled cooperative human life was the goal of civilization, the attainment of a certain level of luxury; that it went in cycles of growth and decay, like all forms of life. He thought that overconsumption in society was an inevitable cause of decline, but that under certain favorable conditions of geography and climate and the character and customs of the people, culture could acquire a rootedness that he called the "habit of civilization."

This assignment, inspired by the *Legacy* video series by Michael Wood, provides the backbone for the year's study of ancient cultures. Showing relevant episodes of *Legacy* in class during the course of study of various subject areas such as Mesopotamia, Mesoamerica, and Egypt, helps the students to reflect on the application of Ibn Khaldoun's ideas. At the end of each unit, we return to reflect on their relevance for the civilization we have just studied.

Each student does a substantial amount of independent research for this course, so that each has a different perspective to bring to his or her analysis. As an example, the first major research project is to examine archaeological data for the development of early cultural complexity. The students are assigned primary civilizations from various parts of the globe, with the goal of contributing specific information to decide, as a class, if there is a common pattern that can be used as a model to predict the evolution of civilization. Their individual input, as well as the corporate results of the project, forms a basis for comparison as we progress through the year.

For the final exam, I encourage students to compose an outline that encompasses all of their primary areas of study and research. They are allowed to write for two hours. The exam itself is open-book, since I am far less interested in memorization than I am in how the student processes information. The exam is graded according to how well the student has incorporated each of the subject areas into his or her overall analysis of Ibn Khaldoun's observations. A part of their evaluation is based on the long-term development of their thought by comparing their essay from the beginning of the year with the final exam.

The following essay, by tenth-grader Clio Mallin, was an especially successful summary of her year of study in this course. She included elements from all of our major areas of investigation to consider Ibn Khaldoun's ideas, bringing evidence from work we did as a class as well as from her own research into early civilization in Southwest Asia.

Final Exam—Ancient Civilizations

Ibn Khaldoun provides a reasonable argument concerning the nature of civilization. However, he does not mention that unequal distribution of power in any complex society (which accompanied the changeover from a pastoral to an agrarian economy) makes social injustice a powerful fact of every civilization.

Whether we look at modern Western civilization or such ancient civilizations as the Mesopotamian, Egyptian or Greek, we are always looking at man's patterns of power distribution accompanying cultural complexity. Different variables will affect the way that cultures meet the needs of the individual and of the society and attain levels of cooperation. One would wish that the noblest ideals of humankind and high civilization could always be met, but civilizations have engendered their share of violence, greed and destruction based on power distribution. Nevertheless, the desirable goal of social cooperation does, in spite of all else, drive mankind towards the "habits of civilization." This paper will look at the various civilizations to see how Ibn Khaldoun's assessment applies.

Civilization does not just automatically "occur." It takes time for development of community and progression to happen. There seems to be a process that takes place and certain elements that are necessary for cultural complexity and "civilization." From the hunter/gatherer stage, where survival is the main focus, we move into a stage where people become more settled and start living in communities. These groups of people have usually centered themselves around a river or some other water source. Agriculture allows man to settle in one place and to build cooperative communities, and to know that the plants and animals that they domesticate will be right there when they are hungry, as a constant food supply. Also not having to work all the time and spend all his time gathering food, man is now able to develop art and culture, so that specialization comes forth. Man is far more able to control his environment. Agriculture presumes other inventions: weaving, metalworking, the wheel, the plow and even writing. It is when man learns how to control the water sources available to him that he has the ability to make genuine progress. Generally, there were two types of agriculture that developed: one was rainfall and the other, riverbased. A rainfall-based agricultural society can have small multi-centered villages that are semi-nomadic. However, those who were using the technique of riverbased agricultures (which implies a certain amount of fertile soil around the riverbed) will most likely have been organized and used irrigation to water their fields and crops. With control of the water source, they have a kind of stability that can be relied on, whereas those depending on the rain have a much less predictable and reliable source. So the riverbased people would probably see a population increase, occupational specialization, class structures, writing, differentiation of burials, monumental architecture, warfare, fortifications, weaponry, and eventually an empire may emerge to engulf the small rainfall-based groups. So, with favorable conditions and climate and geography (good soil, temperate climate, water source, natural boundaries, etc.), there is a good chance that early civilizations and complex societies will develop. . . .

The Late Bronze Age was a time of mixing and trading. Empires were fluctuating, and changes in diplomacy were taking place. Different power configurations and different kinds of trade were most likely based on the search for bronze. However, dominant powers declined at the end of this period, as palaces were burned in Crete and mainland Greece, the Trojan War perhaps being a part of this unrest. War, migrations and depopulation led to the destruction of the Hittite empire. The Egyptians were forced back to their own borders because of the Sea Peoples, and their empire, too, was lost. These events usher in the Iron Age, a time when dominant empires were in decline, allowing smaller groups to emerge and make their mark. The Phoenicians and the Hebrews were two such groups.

On the subject of ancient religions and Ibn Khaldoun's ideas, religion extends the unit of human cooperation beyond the immediate family, and for the ancient Hebrews, who had been patriarchal and nomadic, the monotheism of Moses bound the people closely even when all around them, religion was polytheistic. The force of the Ten Commandments and the belief in one god was powerful, but might not have led to social cohesion had the Hebrews been politically stronger in the ancient world. Since they could not master the Canaanites or the Philistines, and were in constant danger of being attacked, clinging to their religious beliefs and to their movable, omniscient God gave the Hebrews a sense of togetherness and inner strength. Later, after the destruction of their temples and the fall of Jerusalem, this cohesion persisted. If Ibn Khaldoun is right and overabundance leads to decay, then in the modern world when Jewish life is threatened, it grows strong, whereas when it has the luxury of flourishing openly, Jewish life tends to decline.

For the Greeks, religion contained the notion of fate, a hierarchy of Olympian gods, and rituals. But Greek social cohesion and high civilization came from their ability to humanize their gods and confidently express a realistic acceptance and appreciation of the limits of human life. Not gods, but man, with his creativity and vitality, was seen as the center of the universe. At its peak in the fifth century B.C.E., Hellenism permitted an astonishing psychological health and freedom from repression in its citizens. Greek beliefs made the enjoyment of a natural existence possible and promoted man's confidence in his ability to guide his life by using reason. It is said that as individualism became dominant, it was more important than the welfare of the social whole (as Ibn Khaldoun might have said, individualism "overconsumed") and Greek civilization began its decline. Greek culture and civilization flourished during its Golden Age, when Athens reached its height of power and prosperity. This was a time of great artistic and literary accomplishment and huge monumental structures (the Parthenon on the Acropolis) were built to show this wealth and power. The Peloponnesian War (beginning in 431 B.C.E.) ended the Golden Age of Athens. The war was ruinous and lasted for over twenty years, totally weakening Athens. The war was not necessary, but it was perhaps inevitable. It all comes down to power and control, two major determinants of process and progress among groups of people. The "real" cause of war was the tremendous growth of power in Athens and the alarm that this caused Sparta. Once the desire for power comes in, the concern centers around who has the power, who has the most, and who can get it from whom. So, in a way, war was inevitable between Athens and Sparta. The human desire and want and need for control and power are usually the underlying cause of events. . . .

Clio traces the development of early civilizations of Southwest Asia and, applying the material she learned during the semester, she concludes with the following paragraphs:

In all our work this year with ancient civilizations, it is clear that man is a glorious creature—imaginative, creative, and sometimes even wise—in building civilizations and aiming for improvement in the conditions of human life. But human greed and rivalry for the control of resources (including human resources), property and people can lead to tragic imbalances of power within individual civilizations and between civilizations.

In the fourteenth century, Ibn Khaldoun hoped for continuing cycles of growth and decay. Today, without enough social "cement" and with the twentieth and twenty-first century technology of destructive weapons, one wonders whether there will be one last cycle of decay, or whether Khaldoun will be on target and man will continue, in little windows of time, to find wisdom and restraint and achieve balance instead of destruction.

One last note. It seems ironic that it is so easy to point out the blundering and plundering of ancient civilizations, yet so hard to look at our own civilization. We deplete the ozone and our forests, and we build weapons for total destruction. Are we aiming to move from order to disorder and decay—or is every civilization much more fragile at any moment than we or people like Ibn Khaldoun want to think?

Hands-on History

Making Japanese Washi Paper

Linda Miller, Trudi Arnold, and Gil Morrison

Using the talents of many people and many disciplines, Linda Miller has developed a multidisciplinary, cooperative class project in papermaking using art, photography, industrial arts, and world history, which might be extended into a cooperative lesson involving the entire school.

Hands-on history encourages students to take part in the traditional Japanese art of making handmade paper. They participate in a "hands-on process" that began in Japan in the 700s and remains the same today. It provides an excellent way for demonstrating and understanding an unusual papermaking process. Students learn that Japanese paper, often called rice paper, is made not from rice but from the inner bark of mulberry fibers. By participating in the step-by-step process of this ancient art, they can become part of a thirteen hundred-year-old tradition and make a paper treasure that will last beyond the class project.

This is an interdisciplinary project. A world studies teacher who has been to Japan designed the program. The art teacher gave the students a short history of the papermaking process, showed them modern uses, and instructed them in the process. An industrial arts teacher designed the frames for papermaking and instructed students in the step-by-step process of making the frames from wood.

Goals and Objectives

The overall goal is that art and world studies students demonstrate the skills of hand-crafted Japanese papermaking in a multidisciplinary cooperative project.

Making Japanese paper will fit into the world studies unit on Japanese culture. Those students will learn the history behind the making of this ancient paper. The industrial arts students will learn how to use materials to make a product. They will practice using various materials and machines that are very similar to the ones that they will be using in industries. They will also learn safety principles when using the machines. The skills that they learn will be carried with them throughout their lives. Photography students will be taking photographs of the other students engaged in the papermaking process and will make a portfolio. They will also produce photo prints using handmade paper by using it as a base for Polaroid transfer images. They will learn to enhance Polaroid transfer images with pastel pencils. Through this the students will gain or reinforce their technical skills in using camera equipment and darkroom techniques. The students will also learn the proper presentation of a photo essay as they complete portfolios of their work. Finally, they will learn archival techniques of matting and mounting their Polaroid transfer images, which they will display in the art department gallery.

Background Information

Like the computer, paper made more information available to more people. The Chinese discovered that writing on paper was easier than printing on palm leaves and cheaper than writing on silk. Paper proved easier to produce than European parchment, easier to transport than Mesopotamian clay tablets. More paper could be produced in more places than Egyptian papyrus. Soon bundles of contracts, laws, tax records, religious teachings, literature, and letters, inscribed on paper, were carted from place to place in back packs or saddle bags. People had access to more ideas from farther away. More people found a reason to learn to read.

The traditional Chinese date for the first production of paper is 105 C.E. By the 700s both the Koreans and the Japanese possessed the technology. In Japan, Buddhist figures, carved on wooden blocks and coated with ink, were pressed on paper. These Japanese block prints were one of the earliest examples of printing. Arabs learned the technology from the Chinese prisoners of war captured at the Battle of Talas in 751. These Chinese artisans were marched to Samarkand to make paper. From there papermaking spread to the Islamic world. Gradually, those with knowledge of the process made their way to Europe, a journey from China that took a thousand years.

Introductory Lecture to Students

Why make paper? To make your own paper gives you a very personal creation; it becomes the art work in itself, you have all sorts of choices that you can determine. You can choose the surface texture. You can choose to place objects in the paper, bits of cloth, ribbon, string, threads, flower petals, grass, etc.

You can choose to tint your paper or dab the paper with a sponge or cloth doused with variegated colors. You will leave a personal mark on your paper by your choices. It is fun to contemplate all the possibilities.

The Japanese people take time to contemplate, to enjoy nature. The Japanese have gardens made especially for quiet meditation. Their Haiku poetry sparsely, but eloquently, expresses their sympathetic outlook toward the beauty of nature. Their papers are to be made with care and respect for the craft itself. Yes, you could buy paper, but never will it have the personal statement of your handmade Washi paper. It is strong and lasting and will convey your creativity.

To provide information on the historical background of Washi paper, there are two good sources. The first is a poster that gives a background history of papermaking plus a step-by-step diagram of the process. "Washi: Paper in Japanese History" can be purchased from the Asia Society in New York. Namji Steinemann was the project director.

The second is a book that gives a detailed account plus illustrations of the ancient Japanese way. *A Guide to Japanese Papermaking* by Donald Farnsworth can be purchased from Magnolia Editions (see right-hand column).

Vocabulary

Mould: Wooden frame with screening to hold and capture paper pulp.

Deckle: Wooden strip frame to place on top of mould to put a curb on the flowing pulp.

Slurry or slop: The tub of pulp mixed with enough water to float the pulp freely.

Stirring the slurry: Using a stirring stick to keep the pulp from clumping.

Kiss-off: Floating the pulp back into the tub when the mould did not pick it up evenly.

Couching: Gently rocking the mould to release the new paper onto the cloth.

Deckled edge: The rough edge of paper left by the deckle.

Tinting: A gentle color addition to the paper added to the pulp or to individual pieces.

Dabbing: Adding color to the finished paper with a small sponge or rag.

Scenting: Adding fragrance to the paper, which may be sprayed on the wet paper, or cologne or perfume can be added to the slurry tub before pulling out the paper.

Sizing: To strengthen the paper, glue may be added to the slurry or may be added to water and brushed on later.

Surface texture: Degree of roughness or smoothness a paper surface will have.

Materials Needed

One mould and deckle per group of students
Paper pulp
One large dishpan per group
Electric blender if grinding pulp from egg cartons
Water
Strainer
Extra-absorbent sponges
Pieces of old sheets of dimensions larger than mould and deckle
Wooden board (Figure 34.1 includes the dimensions of the frame constructed for this project.)
Iron

Note:
- All materials used in papermaking must be rustproof.
- Do not let pulp stand in water too long, or it will rot.
- Do not pour leftover pulp down a drain. Strain out the water and store it.

Mould and deckles and other papermaking materials including ready-made pulp can be obtained from: Magnolia Editions, 2527 Magnolia Street, Oakland, CA 94607, (415) 893–8334, fax (415) 893–8334.

Making the Mould

Figure 34.1 illustrates the frame for papermaking that was constructed in the industrial arts class.

Figure 34.1. **This pattern was used by students in the shop class to construct the wooden moulds for papermaking.**

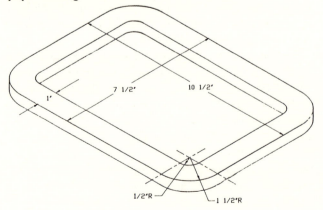

34

The Papermaking Process

1. In a large container or tub, place the pulp and add five or six times as much water to the pulp. The pulp must be free floating in the tub. This mixture is known as the "slurry." It must be stirred, which is called "stirring the slop." A class of thirty students will need five pounds of pulp.
2. Dip the mould, with the deckle over the flat side of the mould, into the slurry. Spread the pulp out away from you. Shake to even the pulp. Make the thickness of the pulp about one-quarter to one-half that of the deckled edge.
3. Pull up the mould and deckle. Let the mould frame rest on the corner of the slurry tub. Let most of the excess water drain off. Press the newly molded paper lightly with a sponge.
4. Carefully remove the deckle.
5. Flip the mould over onto a ready piece of wet rag. Have a thick stack of newspapers underneath the rag.
6. Rock the mould gently from side to side to loosen the paper. This action is called "couching" (sounds like kooching).
7. Remove the mould. Place another wet rag on top. Carefully use a rolling pin to remove more wetness.
8. Have an iron ready on the cotton setting or on medium heat. Leave the paper between the two wet rags and iron it.

Figure 34.2. Paper that has been removed from the mould. *The photography and graphic designs were the work of Trudi Arnold's students, Jaime Carbonara, Bobby Inthavohg, Morena Martinez, and Kathryn Syard.*

9. When most wetness has steamed off, lay the paper on a flat surface to dry.
10. To keep the paper from curling up, place a board or a screen on top to keep it flat. Let it dry overnight.
11. Proceed to decorate the paper in any fashion. The only limit is your imagination. Have fun!

Mongols and Their Importance in World History

A Teaching Module

Helen Grady

One way to structure a world history course is to consider not only the story of civilizations but also the history of nomadic pastoralists, their migrations and impact on sedentary peoples. Using a variety of sources, Helen Grady teaches a unit on the Mongols of the premodern era. As a culminating evaluation for this module on the Mongols, students are asked to assess the role of the Mongols in world history.

To teach world history means the teacher must make conscious decisions of inclusion and exclusion. There is so much material that neither one-year nor two-year sequence courses give us the luxury to include everything. Complicate this with the need to teach skills and the desire to create interactive classrooms, and the demand for choice becomes even more vital. The inclusion of the Mongols in any syllabus I create for world history is a given. In order for students to fully understand the interconnected world of the thirteenth and fourteenth centuries, the Mongols are a must. Obviously, there is a multitude of ways to approach the teaching of the Mongols, and each teacher has his or her focus theme. In this module I will outline one approach focused on the theme of the Mongol migrations and their effects on the environments and cultures of the sedentary peoples they conquered. The module will use a variety of materials: maps, videos, a chronological listing of Mongol invasions, secondary source excerpts, as well as the text.

To begin a lesson on the Mongols, project a transparency of the Mongol Empire in 1290 onto the screen and accompany it with the provocative statement that this is the "largest continuous land empire that has so far existed" (Morgan, p. 5). Note or have students note that it extended from eastern Europe to Korea. Use a current map to show the contemporary countries that were included in this empire to give a fuller idea of its scope. This is an exercise that could be done in groups, with each group having a copy of the Mongol Empire map and one of contemporary

Eurasia or with the whole class using transparencies. Discuss the climate and the land areas that are included, drawing information from students' previous knowledge of geography. Have students guess who created the Mongol Empire. Then elicit from students what they know about the Mongol Empire and what questions they have about it. (This might be a good time to ask about stereotypes of Mongols, not only to show how little of substance is generally known about Mongols, but also to add to a more general discussion on the flaws of stereotyping.) Focus questions should include:

- Who were the Mongols?
- How did they accomplish their empire building?
- What was the Mongols' impact on their conquered peoples?

This introductory mapwork and highlighting of the search questions can take a full period or can be shortened into half of a period depending on your schedule and how much work you want students to do with maps.

Who Were the Mongols?

Depending on how much time can be given to this subject, the identification of the Mongols can be accomplished by any of the following, singly or in combination:

- a homework reading from the text
- an information sheet outlining the essential material created by the teacher
- a handout from one of the sources on the Mongols (pp. 1–11 from Leo De Hartog's *Genghis Khan: Conqueror of the World* offer a brief and accessible account)
- the first twenty minutes of the video "Birth of an Empire" from the series *Mongols: Storm from the East*
- lecture format

As part of a whole-class discussion focused on learning about the Mongols, the following items should be addressed:

- their pastoral lifestyle (compared with other nomadic peoples like the Arabs)
- the hostile environment of the steppes
- their tribal way of life
- their shaman religion
- description of food, clothing, shelter
- duties and roles of men and women
- marriage and burial policies

After essential information is articulated and discussed, remind students of the pattern of relationship of nomadic tribes and settled peoples that has been examined in other situations and recall the values held by those nomadic peoples. Ask: What values do the Mongols hold? This moves the discussion from a recitation of factual information to analysis and inference. Depending again on time and strength of students, you may want to assess the source materials available on the Mongols. Morgan's text on the Mongols (pp. 1–31) provides fine background on this for teachers.

How Did the Mongols Create Their Empire?

Now that students have a more complete sense of who these people were, this question becomes even more vital. Note that it is pretty inconceivable that such a people was able to overthrow Russia, Poland, Hungary, the Balkans, Turkey, Palestine, Iraq, Iran, parts of India, all of Central Asia, China, and Korea. Give some time here for students to speculate in answer to this question. You can record the speculations on the board for greater impact. Distribute some excerpts from sources and a chronology that will help students learn more about how the Mongols built their empire. (See Assignment Sheet #1.)

These readings can be done as a home assignment or in class as part of a group project, again depending on the time frame. Students are to read document excerpts and list anything that could be considered a factor that enabled these nomadic peoples to conquer the most advanced civilizations of their time. Reading and listing of information will take about fifteen or twenty minutes.

When students have completed their work on these source readings (homework or in-class group assignments), have individuals list on the board one factor that each felt was beneficial to the Mongols in their empire-building venture. Students need to explain why and how the factor they selected is important. Factors that should emerge will include:

- Genghis's dream of a world empire;
- Genghis's leadership in uniting the tribes of the steppe and how this worked to eliminate the Chinese model of separation to limit the strength of these peoples;
- advantages of nomads in waging war: surprise, speed, lifestyle, especially hunting skills, which were practiced even though they were no longer essential to economic activity;
- horsemanship, which gave Mongols such mobility;
- willingness to experiment with and adapt new ideas;
- weaknesses and inefficiencies of conquered empires;
- excellent intelligence network;
- tenacity (inferred from chronology).

An excellent source of information on the Mongols' military strategy and how it compares with that of the Europeans is the video "World Conquerors" from the series *Mongols: Storm from the East*. A six-minute segment (22:00–28:00) details weapons, protective clothing, and battle strategies clearly and captures students' imaginations. This can be used to conclude this segment or before students begin sharing their lists of contributing factors.

Review discussion of Mongols to this point. Be sure students understand who the Mongols were and how they managed to create their expansive empire. You can do this by

- giving a short quiz;
- having students write a paragraph, draw a political cartoon, or write a fifty-word newspaper article for homework;
- asking students to check their notes.

How Do Migrating Peoples (Specifically the Mongols) Affect the Environments and Cultures of the Areas They Conquer?

This is the major question of this lesson and will be answered by students as they read the document excerpts on Assignment Sheet #3. This should be begun in class. Divide students into groups (four groups of four, five groups of five, etc.) so that groups may be reconfigured with one member of each group representing his or her group's discussion in a new group. Distribute documents. Explain task. Each student is to read all of the documents given to the group, keeping the focus question uppermost in his or her mind. Depending on the strength of the students, I set up the assignment with more or less structure. If students are particularly strong, I will let them devise their own system for processing the information. If not, I will ask them to categorize their information using columns for political, social, economic, etc., effects. This reading process can be done as a homework assignment or in class depending on time constraints.

When the reading assignment is completed, the members of each group discuss their impressions. A scribe is to be designated by each group to keep track of the group's discussion. The scribe's notes are handed in to the teacher for evaluation of each group's participation and effort. This process should take about twenty minutes. Either a reconfigured group discussion or a whole class discussion should follow this initial group work. Be sure students have noted positive and negative effects, and that they have included issues such as population, trade, cultural exchanges, religious toleration, cities, and artisans. If you touched on the issue of stereotypes at the beginning of this lesson, ask students here if the stereotypes hold and why or why not.

Supplementary Suggestions

Some supplementary activities available to the teacher to pursue additional information on the Mongols with students could be

- an examination of the building of Karakorum using the appropriate video from the series *Mongols: Storm from the East.*
- a reading selection about Genghis Khan's place in history using sources in Michel Hoang's *Genghis Khan,* chapter 15.
- an investigation of Kublai Khan's rule in China and how he borrowed Chinese cultural traditions while maintaining his Mongol identity using the appropriate video in the series *Mongols: Storm from the East.*
- Kublai's rule in China.

Assignment Sheet #1

"The Mongol conquests began with Genghis Khan's unification of the steppe nomads in the first quarter of the thirteenth century. . . ." (Curtin, p. 120)

"All the men in the Mongol Empire over the age of 20 except physicians, priests of any religion or those who washed the bodies of the dead, were liable for military service." (Chambers, p. 67)

"The removal from a town of men of military age was a system in the Mongol method of warfare that was rigorously applied. The method was a double-edged sword: that part of a town's population capable of resistance was removed, to be employed as a terror weapon against the next town. . . . This absolute form of terror sometimes resulted in crushing all will to resist." (De Hartog, p. 131)

"By the sword or by diplomacy, through terror or persuasion, Temujen (Genghis Khan) had subdued or enslaved a hundred peoples. . . .

"Genghis Khan practiced a strategy of systematic intimidation and terror. Too few in number to fight on several fronts, and having little stomach for a long-drawn-out guerrilla war, the Mongols often employed methods that were bloody in the highest degree. . . .

"When they occupied a city or a land they had conquered, they separated families, scattered the inhabitants, taking many into their service . . . as if they were intent on 'breaking' the structures of an entire society." (Hoang, pp. 20, 294, 297)

"The Mongols' tactical supremacy was achieved through frequent exercise that took the form of immense hunting parties in which the army participated as units. Coordination was accomplished in various ways: careful plans were made and distributed among the participants; communications were maintained between units by various means, for example, special messengers or whistling arrows; and finally—perhaps most important—discipline in the Mongol armies was exceedingly strict. No excuse was accepted for failure to carry out one's part of the plan. . . .

"Manpower, economic resources, or technological know-how available in one part of the domain could promptly be mobilized and deployed to meet a need in some other part of the far flung empire. Hulegu's campaign in western Asia . . . can be used to illustrate this point. Troops for his assault on the Assassins and Abbasids came from Mongolia, Turkestan, Iran, the Transcaucasus, and the Golden Horde. Food to sustain these armies came from Armenia, Georgia, and central Asia. Technical specialists to operate the catapults and siege equipment were sent from China. . . ." (Allsen, pp. 6, 219–20)

"Genghis Khan was from a nation of hunters and he shared his people's love of the hunt. 'As soon as the children are two or three years old . . . they begin to ride . . . and then a small bow, suitable in size to their age, is given to them and they are taught to shoot.' " (Ratchnevsky, p. 154)

"The same techniques that were necessary for survival in a herding and hunting environment were, with very little adaptation, those used in warfare. . . .

"All male Mongol adults below the age of sixty were liable for military service. . . .

"It is the character rather than the size of the Mongol army which is crucial. . . .

"According to one story, the invasion of China quickly revealed a serious weakness in Mongol military effectiveness: a cavalry force such as the Mongol army could be supreme in the field, but it was not an adequate instrument for the taking of the walled cities of China. We are told that, faced with a formidable city for the first time, Chingiz Khan offered to raise the siege if he were given 1,000 cats and 10,000 swallows. These were duly handed over. Material was tied to their tails, and this was set on fire. The animals were released and fled home, setting the city ablaze, and in the ensuing confusion the city was stormed. . . .

"The Yam [the Mongol courier/communication system] impressed European observers. It was designed to facilitate the travels of envoys . . . for the transportation of goods . . . the speedy transmission of royal orders from one part of the empire to another; and it provided a framework whereby the Mongols could receive intelligence as quickly as possible." (Morgan, pp. 84, 85, 88, 65, 103–4)

Assignment Sheet #3

"In the early days of the empire, artisans captured in the course of a campaign usually were sent back to the Mongol homeland and made the slaves of princes and military commanders. . . . Realizing their economic and military value, the Mongols always took care to separate the craftsmen before putting the general population to the sword." (Allsen, p. 213)

"No one with a usable skill was overlooked. All of the Mongols' subjects, from the Alan metal workers who produced chain mail for the army to the Chinese physicians who tended Hulegu's health when he came west, were required to place their particular abilities at the disposal of the empire." (Allsen, p. 215)

"The qans of the early Mongol Empire can be divided into two distinct groupings on the basis of their general policy orientation. In one category are those qans—Chinggis Qan, Chaghadai, and Guyug—whom [scholars] describe as steppe traditionalists, the enemies of agriculture and city life, who pursued policies uniformly detrimental to their sedentary subjects; on the other are those rulers—Ogeidei, Mongke, and Qubilai—whom [scholars] regard as champions of centralized imperial authority and advocates of some measure of accommodation with the sedentary population under their control." (Allsen, p. 221)

"East Iran never recovered entirely from the Mongol hurricane. Some towns still show signs of the Mongol destruction; they were unable to regain their former position as centres of Islamic civilization." (De Hartog, p. 131)

"[Ogeidei] had been impressed by the life that he had seen in Samarkand and he began to establish Karakorum as a worthy capital for his empire. The city was extended, public granaries and warehouses were built and a regular system of food supply was organized whereby five hundred wagonloads of food were brought into the city every day. . . . in the hall of his new palace he erected a gold fountain made in the shape of elephants, tigers, and horses. . . ." (Chambers, pp. 57–58)

"The Mongols entered the besieged city and put almost the entire population of Ningxia to the sword." (Hoang, p. 22)

"Mongol warfare followed the steppe tradition. Peoples who resisted were exterminated; others were enslaved, the men were forced to serve in the Mongol forces, the cities were plundered and then abandoned." (Ratchnevsky, p. 169)

"Genghis Khan was not . . . able to divorce himself completely from the traditions of the steppe. He regarded the conquered peoples as belonging to himself and to his family, dividing them among the members of his clan. . . ." (Ratchnevsky, p. 176)

"The effect of the Mongol conquest upon . . . China . . .

has been disputed. Beyond doubt, it knit together the greater empire that endured until the twentieth century. It also increased vastly the contact of this new empire with southern and mid-Asia. The heavy trade of the Yuan (Mongol) period continued into the Ming. . . . the Mongols had thrown open the courts and schools to nearly all languages and religions. . . . Others hold that the shock of the Mongol conquest exhausted the Chinese spirit . . . [and it became] imitative, fearful of new invasion. . . ." (Lamb, pp. 308–9)

"Partial coalescence [in China] between mercantile and official outlooks reached its apogee during the Mongols, who did not share the Confucian disdain for shrewd traders. Marco Polo's reception at Kublai's court illustrates this fact. He was, indeed, only one of many foreign merchants whom Kublai appointed as tax collectors and to other key administrative posts in his empire." (McNeill, *Pursuit,* p. 42)

"The fortresses refused the surrender always demanded by the Mongols at the beginning of a siege. They were therefore vigorously [attacked] and taken by assault with the help of modern devices such as smoke and fireships. . . .

"The Mongol invasion had also brought about certain ethnic changes. . . ." (Spuler, pp. 13, 59)

"Once the Mongols began to live in the country they were subject to manners, modes of dress, and religious beliefs foreign to their tribal mode of life. The force and continuity of Iranian civilization worked to alter their very character. The feudal system of government was retained, Persians were soon named to the highest administrative posts, and the Il Khans became patrons of literature and the arts." (Wilber, p. 51)

"Ghazan converted to Islam, built an Islamic state, [with] himself the autocrat. . . . His purpose was to live in peace and develop the caravan trade. . . ." (Lamb, p. 311)

"The condition of the peasants at this time was appalling, for they were subject to anything from fifteen to thirty different kinds of tax and tribute. . . . It was during the Mongol period that the peasants became in fact slaves of the soil, a position previously unheard of in the Islamic world under Islamic law, which regards workers of the land as freemen. . . . towards the end of the thirteenth century these various systems of taxation had turned whole regions into dust. . . .

"The towns destroyed by the invasion were slow to revive. The attempts of the Mongols to rebuild these towns or create new ones were largely unsuccessful. . . . the markets were no longer being supplied with farm produce from the neighborhood. . . . they dwindled in size. . . . the townspeople were burdened with taxes and other obligations. . . . All this led to a decline in the country's productivity. . . .

"One important aspect of the Mongol conquest is that for

the first time Persia and other large parts of the Muslim world found themselves governed . . . by non-Muslim rulers . . . who ignored differences of religious belief among their subjects. . . . it has been remarked by some scholars that despite the terrible devastation that it brought with it, Mongol rule did provide certain virtues, such as the reunification of large areas, safety of travel, the establishment of new trade routes. . . ." (Bausani, pp. 114–16)

"North China was subjected to a series of destructive campaigns over a period of twenty-five years. . . . the Mongols seriously considered wiping out the whole population . . . to turn the land over to pasture (according to one story). . . . Transoxania and more particularly eastern Persia had to endure something that must have seemed to approximate very nearly to attempted genocide. . . . The figures . . . for the numbers of people massacred are . . . 1,600,000 . . . at the sack of Harat and 1,747,000 at Nishapur." (Morgan, p. 74)

"The Persian plateau is largely lacking in great rivers. Consequently agriculture is . . . dependent on a locally devised form of artificial irrigation, the qanat—an underground water channel that brings the water to where it is needed. Some of these were destroyed during the invasions *and* without effective irrigation . . . much of the land would soon revert to desert. But a more long-term consideration is that qanats, even if not actually destroyed, quickly cease to operate if they are not constantly maintained. . . . land would suffer irreparable damage through neglect of the qanats. With their pasture-oriented minds, the Mongols were not the people to do anything to remedy this." (Morgan, pp. 80–81)

"The Muslims of western Asia . . . were prepared to learn from the Chinese. The most visually striking example of this is to be found in Persian miniature painting of the period. The rocks, the trees and the clouds frequently have a very Chinese look about them. But . . . there are no Persian motifs in the Chinese arts of the Yuan Dynasty. . . . Middle Easterners . . . were valued by the Chinese . . . for . . . technical skills they might possess." (Morgan, p. 195)

"There were a great many European merchants in the Mongol Empire, a considerable number of missionaries, and some ambassadors." (Morgan, p. 198)

"Qubilai . . . did not appoint Chinese to the great offices of state, and the old examination system for entry into the civil service . . . was not revived." (Morgan, p. 110)

"Mongol conquests facilitated trade between the civilizations at each end of Eurasia, making possible the exchange of foods, tools, and ideas on an unprecedented scale. . . . Perhaps the greatest long-term impact of the Mongol drive to the west was . . . that the Mongol conquests played a key role in transmitting the fleas that carried bubonic plague from central Asia to Europe and the Middle East." (Stearns et al., p. 462)

"Kubilai promulgated many laws to preserve the distinction between Mongol and Chinese. . . .

"Kubilai modeled much at his capital and court at Tatu after Chinese precedents. His palace was laid out like those of Chinese emperors. . . . The upper levels of the bureaucracy were organized and run . . . along Tang-Song lines. . . . His generous patronage drew to his splendid court scholars, artists, artisans, and office seekers from many lands. . . . Kubilai displayed a strong interest in all religions and insisted on toleration in his domains." (Stearns et al., pp. 245, 246, 247)

"The same Mongol law and order that made possible a century of intense human interchange between China and the Atlantic coast now quickened the progress of the plague bacillus across Eurasia. The Black Death was the grimly ironic price the world paid for the trans-hemispheric unity of the Pax Mongolica." (Dunn, p. 271)

"Mongol communications had another important effect. Not only did large numbers of persons travel very long distances across cultural and epidemiological frontiers; they also traversed a more northerly route than had ever been intensively traveled before. The ancient Silk Route between China and Syria crossed the deserts of central Asia, passing from oasis to oasis. Now, in addition to this old route, caravans, soldiers and postal riders rode across the open grasslands. They created a territorially vast human web that linked the Mongol headquarters at Karakorum with Kazan and Astrakhan on the Volga, with Caffa in the Crimea, with Khanbaliq in China and with innumerable other caravanserais in between.

"The process of southernization reached its zenith after 1200. . . . The Mongols' control of overland routes between Europe and Asia . . . fostered unprecedented contacts between Europeans and peoples from those areas that had long been southernized. . . .

"In the seventeenth century . . . Francis Bacon . . . singled out three technologies in particular that 'have changed the whole face and state of things throughout the world.' These were all Chinese inventions—the compass, printing, and gunpowder. All three were first acquired by Europeans during this time of hemispheric reorganization [thirteenth century]." (Shaffer, pp. 16, 17, 18)

"From an epidemiological point of view, this northward extension of the caravan trade net had one very significant consequence. Wild rodents of the steppelands came into touch with the carriers of diseases, among them, in all probability, bubonic plague. . . .

". . . the bacillus . . . proceeded to penetrate almost all of Europe and the Near East. . . ." (McNeill, *Plagues*, pp. 133–34, 145)

Bibliography

Allsen, Thomas T. *Mongol Imperialism*. Berkeley: University of California Press, 1987.

Bausani, Alesandro. *The Persians: From the Earliest Days to the Twentieth Century*. Translated by J.B. Donne. London: Elek Books, 1975.

Chambers, James. *The Devil's Horsemen: The Mongol Invasion of Europe*. London: Cassell Publishers, 1988.

Curtin, Philip D. *Cross-Cultural Trade in World History*. Cambridge: Cambridge University Press, 1984.

De Hartog, Leo. *Genghis Khan: Conqueror of the World*. New York: St. Martin's Press, 1989.

Dunn, Ross E. *The Adventures of Ibn Battuta: A Muslim Traveler of the 14th Century*. Berkeley: University of California Press, 1989.

Hoang, Michel. *Genghis Khan*. Translated by Ingrid Cranfield. New York: New Amsterdam Books, 1990.

Lamb, Harold. *The March of the Barbarians*. New York: Doubleday, 1940.

McNeill, William H. *Plagues and Peoples*. New York: Doubleday, 1976.

————. *The Pursuit of Power*. Chicago: University of Chicago Press, 1982.

Morgan, David. *The Mongols*. Cambridge: Blackwell Publishers, 1986.

Ratchnevsky, Paul. *Genghis Khan: His Life and Legacy*. Translated and edited by Thomas N. Haining. Cambridge: Blackwell Publishers, 1991.

Riasanovsky, Nicholas V. *A History of Russia*. New York: Oxford Press, 1969.

Shaffer, Lynda. "Southernization." *Journal of World History* 5 (spring 1994):1–21.

Spuler, Bertold. *The Mongols in History*. Translated by Geoffrey Wheeler. London: Pall Mall Press, 1971.

Stearns, Peter, et al. *World Civilizations: The Global Experience*. New York: HarperCollins Publishers, 1992.

Vernadsky, George. "The Mongol Impact on Russia." *Readings in Russian Civilization: Russia before Peter the Great, 900–1700*. Edited by Thomas Riha. Chicago: University of Chicago Press, 1964.

Wilber, Donald N. *Iran: Past and Present*. Princeton: Princeton University Press, 1958.

36

A Roundtable Discussion

Timothy C. Connell

History comes alive for students in Tim Connell's class when they come dressed to assume the life of the person they've researched. Akbar, Mansa Musa, and Joan of Arc take their places for a roundtable discussion of the period from 1200 to 1600.

Background and Explanation

This is not an original idea. I picked it up at a conference that I attended a numbers of years ago, and older teachers might recognize that it is adapted from the Steve Allen show "Meeting of the Minds."

I use this as the first major project in my sophomore world history course that begins about 1350. Our first unit focuses on the Mongols, followed by a discussion of Europe at the time of the Renaissance, Reformation, and exploration. The assignment has both a written component and a discussion. I would like a solid two-hour block of time for the discussion but must make do with three days of forty-minute class periods. I have classes ranging in size from thirteen to nineteen; teachers with larger classes might need a week to give everyone a chance to respond.

A great frustration with this assignment is the dearth of information about non-Western people. Very little information exists about Cheng Ho and Mansa Musa, whereas volumes have been written about Columbus and Michelangelo. Likewise, the list favors rich, powerful males. On occasion I have had talented students choose someone such as Wat Tyler (leader of a peasant rebellion in England in the late fourteenth century) or Donna Marina (the Native American who advised Cortés). In such a case, the research is indirect in that Cortés is studied, for example, and the student must infer how a native woman would have responded to him. This kind of sophisticated research frustrates many students who do not have the background to make thoughtful inferences.

I tried the costumes as an option this year and quickly realized that I had hit upon a gold mine. It really sets the mood and makes it a special day. Some costumes are better than others. For some reason, students assume that Michelangelo wore a bathrobe, but dressing Mansa Musa in white emphasizes the importance of his hajj. Nothing can compare to the creative students such as one Joan of Arc who came tied to a stake with bright orange flames surging from her body.

I cannot grade the assignment and keep the discussion going, so I find it helpful to videotape the discussion and grade it at home on the weekend. With a separate tape for each class, I can then see the discussion in one showing and write thoughtful comments for each student.

I begin the discussion by asking students to give some background information about themselves, and this helps break the ice, especially for the meek. I more and more rely on general topics in the discussion, so as to involve different kinds of people. Savonarola's fiery Christianity is a wonderful foil to the tolerance of Akbar's Divine Faith. Subjects such as women, power, and wealth stimulate the conversation. Everyone has an opinion about Genghis Khan's terror tactics. On the other hand, getting bogged down with Joan of Arc on the intricacies of the Hundred Years' War bores the others.

What follows below is the assignment as it is given to the students. I have made a few notations in brackets.

Assignment to Students

Introduction and Evaluation

This assignment requires you to investigate the life of a person from world history who lived from about 1200 to 1600. You need to familiarize yourself with this person's life and his or her views.

You will be evaluated in two ways:

1. *Written analysis* (50 points). This essay asks you to argue why your person is so important in history. To write a thoughtful essay you must find out as much as you can about your historical person. Usually this means reading one short biography. See the attached for more details about the essay. [When little information is available, I put more responsibility on the student to know about the time when a person lived. For example, Cheng Ho will focus on Ming China.]

2. *Roundtable discussion* (50 points). In about mid-October we will take three days, and you will present the views of your historical person in a roundtable discussion. You may

bring to this discussion no more than three 3 × 5 index cards containing what information you think is important.

The basis for your grade will be the following:

- thoroughness of research
- historical accuracy
- understanding of key events affecting your person's life
- degree to which you express your ideas in an articulate way
- length of time that you talk

Research

To help you with your research I will give you a list of questions about important matters relating to the life and times of your person. Among other things you will need to consider key events that occurred in this person's life. For example, if you are John Calvin, you must be well versed in the ideas of the Protestant Reformation. Another general topic is that of power. All of these people wielded power in one form or another. What was the basis of their power? To what ends did they use it? Were they successful? [This year was the first that I gave students a list of leading questions, which I have not included here in the interest of brevity. This is mostly for weaker students who focus on minutiae and miss the essentials.]

Selection of Historical Figures

Below are some possibilities to consider. I am open to other choices. Check with me if you have an idea.

Marco Polo, Ibn Batuta, Genghis Khan, Cheng Ho (Zheng He), Vasco da Gama, Suleiman, Mansa Musa, Akbar the Great, Tamerlane, Joan of Arc, Eleanor of Aquitaine, John Calvin, Leonardo da Vinci, Christopher Columbus, Niccolò Machiavelli, Fra Savonarola, Michelangelo, Saladin, King Louis X of France, Hernando Cortés, Mar-

tin Luther. [I follow this with a brief statement identifying each person.]

Costumes

In order to make the situation as real as possible, you will be required to come in costume. Be creative. Although it will not be a major component of your grade, I will take it into account when you are evaluated. Change into costume before class. Do so quickly. Do not go to another class in costume.

Miscellaneous

Bring a small placard with your person's name on it to place in front of you.

You are encouraged to respond directly to the comments of others, especially if your character has a sharply contrasting perspective. For example, Sir Francis Drake, an English

explorer, despised the Spanish. He would think nothing of insulting Queen Isabella of Spain and chastising her for her Catholic beliefs.

Written Analysis

For this exercise you should begin your essay with the following statement:

"I, _____ , was one of the most important figures of the period 1200–1600. Without me and my contributions the history of the world would have been very different."

From this point proceed and explain your basic views on important matters. Discuss what changes you favored, why you felt that they were necessary, and how you went about implementing them.

You may include some biographical information, but keep this to a minimum. You should write in the first person, but use the past tense. Your style may be conversational, but avoid colloquial expressions. [I ask for the essays before the discussion. A deadline that demands something written is more meaningful to my students that one that requires an oral recitation.]

A Note on Sources

As a rule of thumb there is no problem finding adequate sources about Europeans. There is a wealth of information on Joan of Arc, Christopher Columbus, Martin Luther, and others; however, little is available on Ibn Batuta, Mansa Musa, or Cheng Ho. Having said that, there are several sources that my students have found useful. The Chelsea House series entitled *World Leaders Past and Present* is geared to about the junior high level and these books are terrific. They are easy to read, tell a nice story, and have abundant visuals. J. Kelly Sowards, *Makers of World History* (St. Martin's Press), offers several interpretations of a particular person and is especially recommended for brighter students who are not confounded by reading different perspectives about the same person. Michael Hart's *The 100: A Ranking of the Most Influential Persons in History* (A and W Visual Library), can be useful, although it offers only a few paragraphs about each person. An old standby for both European and some non-European people is Will Durant's *The Story of Civilization* (Simon and Schuster). Durant offers wonderful vignettes of people that are seldom bland.

Islam and Slavery in West Africa

Dale M. Owens

Dale Owens's lesson introduces students to the development of the West African slave trade and the role of Muslims in that trade. This historic trend would eventually shape the lives of people on four continents—Africa, Europe, and North and South America.

This particular content focus was chosen to give students additional information about Muslims "outside" of their religious activities. This focus gives students an opportunity to see and understand that Muslims were traders and business people, who, along with indigenous Africans and other Europeans, engaged in the slave trade as a commercial and religious interest.

I have found that this method of presentation of new material gives students an opportunity for participation individually and collectively and enables them to assist each other in arriving at conclusions after a consensus is reached.

Objective

During a two-week period students will read, research, and understand why and how Muslims participated in the slave trade in West Africa. This lesson plan will be an infusion into a unit on Islam that is taught with other major world religions, such as Judaism, Christianity, and Hinduism.

Procedure

Geography plays an important part in global understandings. Students will be asked to locate West African countries where Muslims were involved in the slave trade on an outline map of Africa. Students will also research four to five geographical facts about each country (example: climate, landforms, etc.).The ideas about Muslims' involvement in the West African slave trade will be presented in a brief lecture-discussion introduction, and students will be asked to develop critical thinking questions relative to that topic.

After completion of assigned readings, students will be

divided into groups, where they will exchange the questions they have prepared in order to discuss them and formulate answers after they have reached a consensus. Each group will select a reporter, who will give a summary of the group's discussion.

Overview

Several accounts put Islam in contact with West Africa during the eighth century. Arabs, having overrun North Africa, followed the trade routes across the Sahara Desert to West Africa. The first military expeditions and slave raids were organized between 734 and 740 C.E. by Governor Ubayd Allah B. Al-Habib. This expedition returned to North Africa with not only slaves but also large quantities of gold.[1]

Muslim merchants also developed early contact between West Africa and Islam. Muslims heightening their interest in trade were attracted by the prospect of obtaining large amounts of gold.

Drawn principally by the prospect of obtaining large quantities of gold, a precious metal used as a medium of exchange, North African Muslim merchants came in increasing numbers to settle in the commercial centers along or at the end of the trans-Saharan trade routes.[2]

When the ninth century began, the trans-Saharan trade principally in gold was beginning to make an indispensable contribution to the Islamic market. Like civilizations of old, the Islamic economy functioned not only through its stable currency but also by its slave system and its free labor.[3] Both industrial and domestic slavery were prevalent. All accounts state that slavery under Muslims was never as harsh as eighteenth- and nineteenth-century plantation slavery in North America. Freeing of slaves was frequent, and sometimes slaves became members of the Muslim families.[4]

In exchange for West African slaves and gold, occasional elephant tusks and kola nuts, the North African towns sent across the Sahara camel loads of textiles, metal bars, rods, knives, weapons, ceramics, glassware, and other manufactured goods made in Muslim countries.

What was the attitude of the religion of Islam toward slavery? Islamic notions of the enslavable stemmed from a peculiar worldview. This worldview, as portrayed in Muslim

This lesson was written as part of "Islam and West Africa," a 1994 summer institute at the University of Arkansas, Monticello, funded by the National Endowment for the Humanities.

society, became a simile for the heathen condition—a symbolic representation of the antithesis of Islam.[5] If the slave is to be brought out of his heathenness, it is his submission to Islam that would give him redemption. Thus nonbelief is the signal and underlining principle for the existence of slavery in Islam. Cases have also been made for the so-called Curse of Ham as a reason for enslavement. Although color is not mentioned in the Old Testament, it remained a pretext for enslavement.

For Sundani Muslims of the colonial era, the fate of the men of color remained fettered to the condition of servility. The story of Ham continues to be fated in its endless variations. Although it is refuted by noted Muslim scholars such as Ibn Khaldoun, it continues to cause conflict between lighter-skinned and darker-skinned Muslims.[6]

It is not surprising that Muhammed looked upon slavery as part of the natural order of things. His approach to what was already an age-old institution was reformist and not revolutionary. The Prophet's purpose was to improve the conditions of slaves by correcting abuses and appealing to the conscience of his followers to treat them humanely. He spoke to them at his farewell pilgrimage, "Feed them with what you eat yourself and clothe them with what you wear. If you cannot keep them or they commit any fault, discharge them. They are God's people like unto you and be kind to them."[7]

Muhammed took pains to urge his followers to free their slaves as a way of getting rid of their sins. Some argue that this was an attempt to gradually eliminate slavery; however, others argue that Muhammed gave slavery the moral authority of Islam and assured its legitimacy. Slaves were one of the main props of Arabian pastoral economy and formed an integral part of its social life.[8] Abolishing slavery would have forced Arabs to perform household chores, field tasks, etc. Of course, this bordered on social revolution.

Judaism and Christianity by moral authority justified a two-tiered society where members were part free and part slave. This of course did not go unnoticed by Muhammed. The Old Testament goes into considerable detail in reference to the acquisition of slaves and the manner of their treatment. For those Muslims who still had moral doubts about enslaving people, the Koran contains nothing to cast doubt on the essential rightness of owning a slave. Whatever the Prophet's real beliefs were regarding slavery, they were lost on large numbers of Muslim slaveholders who had a stake in maintaining a system that bestowed huge benefits.[9] Slavery as carried on in Islamic countries bore the characteristics of the age-old practice of enslaving outsiders. Islamic law enforced the rule that no born Muslim could be enslaved. Religious belief and not race, national origin, or territoriality was the determining factor in whether an individual was enslaved.[10]

Under Islamic law there were two prescribed ways of making people into slaves. One was by birth and the other was by jihad, or holy war. Children born to slave parents were themselves slaves. This was a way to ensure that only non-Muslims would be enslaved. Muslims believed that in order for slaves to be brought out of their heathenness, slavery was needed to bring them into submission to Islam, which would give them redemption.[11] Jihad was a unique Islamic way of extending or consolidating Islamic law. Unbelievers who were captured in battle were generally offered the choice of converting to Islam, paying a tax, or fighting to the death. Prisoners were enslaved either in default of payment of tax or to avoid being massacred on the battlefield. Whatever the reason, thousands were brought back to Muslim lands and made into slaves by the conquering armies of Islam.

As late as 1900 Mandingo traders were still entrenched in the slave trade along the coast of Liberia. Mandingo long-distance traders who brought slaves from Guinea into Liberia exchanged them for forest items such as kola nuts. It was reported that Mandingos were the main suppliers of slaves as well as gold along the coast of Liberia in the nineteenth century. As the onslaught of colonials and Europeans increased, the Mandingos resented the disruption of their monopoly of the slave trade. Slaves were exported from Liberia to Spanish plantations in Fernando Po during the 1900s.

The end of the slave trade across the desert dealt a severe blow to the trans-Saharan routes. What accounted for this drop was not so much the enforcement of the anti-slave treaties but the introduction of more attractive modes of transportation and commercial opportunities. Once West African blacks began to send goods to the markets of Hausaland at cheaper prices, the days of the caravan routes were numbered. The camel was no match for the steamship.

The movement to end slavery and its trade was waged over time, and finally in 1807 an act was passed by the English.[12] Pressure was eventually brought on others to follow the example of Great Britain, Denmark, and the United States. France permitted slave trade until 1819, Spain until 1820, and Portugal until 1830.[13]

Despite this progress and the progress made in sheikdoms, slaves continued to be brought into Saudi Arabia. A steady stream of blacks from West Africa was filtered across the porous boundaries by enterprising slave masters from Saudi Arabia, who brought them home and sold them.[14]

Notes

1. Peter B. Clark, *West Africa and Islam.* (Edward Arnold Publishers, 1982), p. 8.
2. Ibid., p. 10.
3. Ibid., p. 89.

4. Phyllis Martin and Patrick O'Meara, *Africa* (Bloomington: Indiana University Press, 1986), p. 89.

5. John Willis, *Slaves and Slavery in Muslim Africa,* Vol. 2: *The Servile Estate* (United Kingdom: Frank Cass, 1985), p. 4.

6. Ibid., p. 10.

7. Murray Gordon, *Slavery in the Arab World* (Franklin, NY: New Amsterdam Books, 1987), p. 19.

8. Ibid.

9. Ibid., p. 21.

10. Ibid., p. 24.

11. Willis, *Slaves and Slavery,* p. 4.

12. Patrick Richards, *Empire and Slavery* (Longmans, Green, 1968), p. 90.

13. Ibid., p. 91.

14. Gordon, *Slavery in the Arab World,* p. 230.

Bibliography

Curtin, Philip D. *Africa Remembered: Narratives by West Africans from the Era of the Slave Trade.* Madison: University of Wisconsin Press, 1967.

Davidson, Basil. *The African Slave Trade.* Boston: Atlantic–Little, Brown, 1980.

Konneh, Augustine. *Indigenous Entrepreneurs and Capitalists.* Bloomington: Indiana University Press, 1992.

Sweeney, Phillip. *The Gambia and Senegal.* Boston: Houghton Mifflin Company, 1993.

Thornton, John. *Africa and Africans in the Making of the Atlantic World 1400–1680.* New York: Cambridge University Press, 1992.

Willis, John. *Slaves and Slavery in Muslim Africa.* Vol. 1: *Islam and the Ideology of Enslavement.* United Kingdom: Frank Cass, 1985.

Did Women Have a Renaissance?

Susan Pojer and Sue Robertson

Using a variety of sources, Susan Pojer and Sue Robertson have constructed a document-based essay question about women in the Renaissance.

Directions for Students

The following question is based on accompanying Documents 1–14. (Some of the documents have been edited for the purpose of this exercise.) Write your answer on the lined pages of the pink essay booklet.

This question is designed to test your ability to work with historical documents. As you analyze each document, *take into account its source and the point of view of the author.* Write an essay on the following topics that integrates your analysis of the documents. You may refer to historical facts and developments not mentioned in the documents.

> *Analyze the educational and social opportunities and/or limitations for upper- and merchant-class women in Renaissance society.*

Historical Background

The Renaissance refers to the period in history between 1350 and 1650 when Italian culture dominated western Europe. Humanistic studies and scholarly analysis of Greek and Latin texts and cultures, the development of vernacular literature, and new artistic techniques and scientific theories emerged. Since the Renaissance influenced only the patrician (upper) and merchant classes, modern historians are examining whether this cultural revival had any effect on the women of Renaissance high society.

Document 1

> I will proceed with the description of the queen's disposition and natural gifts of mind and body, wherein she either matched or exceeded all the princes of her time, as being of a great spirit yet tempered with moderation, in adversity never dejected, in pros-

This material was the product of a July 1994 National Endowment for the Humanities summer institute conducted at Union Theological Seminary, Columbia University, New York, and sponsored by the Renaissance Society of America.

perity rather joyful than proud; affable to her subjects, but always with due regard to the greatness of her estate, by reason whereof she was both loved and feared. . . .

> Latin, French, and Italian she could speak very elegantly, and she was able in all those languages to answer ambassadors on the sudden. . . . Of the Greek tongue she was also not altogether ignorant. She took pleasure in reading of the best and wisest histories, and some part of Tacitus' *Annals* she herself turned into English for her private exercise. She also translated Boethius' *On the Consolation of Philosophy* and a treatise of Plutarch, *On Curiosity,* with divers others. . . .

> —An unknown contemporary describes Queen Elizabeth I, late sixteenth century.

Document 2

> It is more than a monster in nature that a woman shall reign and have empire above man. To promote a woman to bear rule, above any realm, nation, or city, is repugnant to nature, contumely to God, . . . and, finally, it is the subversion of good order, of all equity and justice. When a woman rules, the blind lead the sighted, the sick the robust, the foolish, mad and frenetic the discreet and sober. For their sight in civil regiment is but blindness, their counsel foolishness, and judgment frenzy. Woman's attempt to rule is an act of treason: For that woman reineth above man, she hath obtained it by treason and conspiracy committed against God. . . . [Men] must study to repress her inordinate pride and tyranny to the uttermost of their power.

> —John Knox, *First Blast of the Trumpet Against the Monstrous Regiment of Women,* 1558

Document 3

Percentage of Married Women According to Age, and Average Age at Marriage (Tuscany, 1427–1430)

Age	Total Country	Total City	Total Population
10 and under	0.1	0.5	0.2
11	0.1	0.0	0.1
12	0.5	0.3	0.4
13	1.2	0.5	0.9
14	3.5	4.1	3.7
15	12.0	14.5	12.7
16	26.0	31.1	27.5
17	38.1	43.3	40.0
18	65.0	71.1	66.8
19	68.2	72.4	70.1
20	89.3	87.7	89.2
25	96.1	91.6	94.8
Average age at marriage (in years)	18.1	17.5	17.9

Document 4

In this way they [women] will always seem to be provoked into conversation rather than to provoke it. They should also take pains to be praised for the dignified brevity of their speech rather than for its glittering prolixity. . . .

It is proper, however, that not only arms but indeed also the speech of women never be made public; for the speech of a noble woman can be no less dangerous than the nakedness of her limbs. For this reason women ought to avoid conversations with strangers since manners and feelings often draw notice easily in these situations. . . .

Sophocles, who is certainly no worse than the Venetian I am discussing—and most men consider his better—has termed silence the most outstanding ornament of women. Therefore, women should believe they have achieved glory of eloquence if they will honor themselves with the outstanding ornament of silence.

—Francesco Barbaro, *On Wifely Duties,* early fifteenth century

Document 5

And should we not greatly rejoice that you can be named among those admittedly few but certainly famous women [of the past], when we see that the ancients gloried in the learning of such outstanding women? . . . Rightly, therefore should you also, famous Isotta, receive the highest praises, since you have indeed, if I may so speak, overcome your own nature. For that true virtue which is proper to men you have pursued with remarkable zeal—not the mediocre virtue which many men seek, but that which should befit a man of the most flawless and perfect wisdom. Thus Cicero rightly said: "You young men have a womanly spirit, but that girl has a man's spirit." Therefore, dissatisfied with the lesser studies, you have applied your noble mind also to the higher disciplines, in which there is need for keenness of intelligence and mind.

—Laura Quirini, a Venetian patrician, in a letter to Isotta Nogarola, mid-1440s

Document 6

Here I have in mind someone whose intellect shows the greatest promise, who despises no branch of learning, who holds all the world as her province, who, in a word, burns marvelously with a desire for knowledge and understanding. An ardent and well-motivated person like this needs, I think, to be applauded and spurred on in some directions, while in others she must be discouraged and held back. Disciplines there are, of whose rudiments some knowledge is fitting, yet whereof to obtain the mastery is a thing by no means glorious. In geometry and arithmetic, for example, if she waste a great deal of time worrying their subtle obscurities, I should seize her and tear her away from them. I should do the same in astrology, and even, perhaps, in the art of rhetoric. I say this with some hesitation, since if any living men have labored in this art, I would profess myself to be of their number. But there are many things here to be taken into account, the first of which is the person whom I am addressing. For why should the subtleties of the *status,* the *epicheiremata,* and *krinomena,* and a thousand other rhetorical conundrums consume the powers of a women, who never sees the forum!

—Letter of Leonardo Bruni to Lady Battista Malatesta of Montefeltro, 1424

Document 7

Some say that clerks or priests have written your works for you for they could not come from feminine intelligence. But those who say such things are ignorant, for they are not aware of the writings of other women wiser than you, even prophets who have been mentioned in past times. . . . so I urge you to continue your work which is valid, and not be afraid of me.

—Christine de Pizan, French writer, *Christine's Vision,* 1420s

Document 8

There are already so many women in the world! Why then . . . was I born a woman, to be scorned by men in words and deeds? I ask myself this question in solitude. . . . For they jeer at me throughout the city, the women mock me.

—Isotta Nogarola in a letter to Guarino Veronese, mid-fifteenth century

Document 9

I thought their tongues should have been fine-sliced and their hearts hacked to pieces—those men whose perverted minds and inconceivable hostility [fueled by] vulgar envy so flamed that they deny, stupidly ranting, that women are able to attain eloquence in Latin. [But] I might have forgiven those pathetic men, doomed to rascality, whose patent insanity I lash with unleashed tongue. But I cannot bear the babbling and chattering women, glowing with drunkenness and wine, whose impudent words harm not only our sex but even more themselves . . . ; but any women who excel they seek out and destroy with the venom of their envy.

—Laura Cereta (1469–1499), a Brescian aristocrat, in a letter to Lucilia Vernacula, possibly a fictitious literary character

Document 10

In the case of men, however, public praise was so free in the classical world that sometimes even slaves reached the summit of philosophy. But in our age, in which it is rare even for men to excel in letters, you are the only maiden living who handles a book instead of wool, a reed pen instead of make-up, a metal stylus instead of a needle, and who smears not her skin with white lead, but rather paper with ink. This indeed is as extraordinary, as rare, as new, as if violets took root amid ice, roses in snow or lilies in frost. . . . Indeed, you have so mastered philosophy that you sharply defend and strongly attack set propositions, and you, as a virgin, dare to compete with men in the beautiful race-course of learning in such a way that your sex does not daunt your soul, nor your soul your modesty, nor your modesty your talent. . . .

—Angelo Poliziano, a Florentine humanist, in a letter to Cassandra Fedele, a woman of the Venetian privileged class, 1491

Document 11

I am amazed by the opinion of some men who claim that they do not want their daughters, wives, or kinswomen to be educated because their mores would be ruined as a result. . . . Here you can clearly see that not all opinions of men are based on reason and that these men are wrong.

. . . Similarly, to speak of more recent times, without searching for examples in ancient history, Giovanni Andrea, a solemn law professor in Bologna not quite sixty years old, was not of the opinion that it was bad for women to be educated. He had a fair and good daughter, named Novella, who was educated in the law to such an advanced degree that when he was occupied by some task and not at leisure to present his lectures to his students, he would send Novella, his daughter, in his place to lecture to students from his chair. And to prevent her beauty from distracting the concentration of her audience, she had a little curtain drawn in front of her. In this manner she could on occasion supplement and lighten her father's occupation.

—Christine de Pizan, French writer, *The Book of the City of Ladies,* 1420s

Document 12

My mother wished me to become a nun / To fatten the dowry of my sister / and I obey my Mama / Cut my hair and became one . . . / Mother don't make me a nun / that I don't desire; . . . / I would go quite mad if I was forced to fast / and go to Vespers and Eventide and sing at all hours.

—A fifteenth-century folk song

Document 13

Empresses, queens and duchesses . . . would wish to be considered one of the least of your handmaids, esteeming your condition so much more worthy, so much better than their own.

—Angela Merici, founder of the Ursuline Sisters, speaking to some of her nuns, mid-sixteenth century

Document 14

Zeal for holy chastity and virginity makes a weak young woman or woman of whatever sort stronger than many men, and than the whole world, and than all hell; and when men see such extreme energy and force, they are afraid and jump back dismayed.

—Diego Pérez de Valdivia in his handbook for Spanish nuns

Sources of Documents

1. James Harvey Robinson, ed., *Readings in European History,* Vol. 2 (Boston: Ginn & Co., 1906), found on p. 449 of Donald Kagan, Steven Oziment, Frank M. Turner, *The Western Heritage since 1300,* 4th ed. (New York: Macmillan Publishing Co., 1990).
2. Ibid.
3. Christine Klapisch-Zuber, *Women, Family and Ritual in Renaissance Italy* (Chicago: University of Chicago Press, 1985), p. 110.
4. Benjamin G. Kohl and Ronald G. Witt with Elizabeth B. Welles, *The Earthly Republic: Italian Humanists on Government*

& Society (Philadelphia: University of Pennsylvania Press, 1978), pp. 205–206.
5. Margaret L. King and Albert Rabil, Jr., *Her Immaculate Hand: Selected Works by and about the Women Humanists of Quattrocento Italy* (Binghamton, NY: Medieval and Renaissance Texts and Studies, 1992), p. 113.
6. Gordon Griffiths, James Hankins, and David Thompson, transl., *The Humanism of Leonardo Bruni* (Binghamton, NY: Medieval and Renaissance Texts and Studies in conjunction with the Renaissance Society of America, 1987), p. 244.
7. Margaret L. King, *Women of the Renaissance* (Chicago: University of Chicago Press, 1991).
8. Ibid., p. 196.
9. King and Rabil, *Her Immaculate Hand,* p. 85.
10. Ibid., p. 127.
11. Christine de Pizan, *The Book of the City of Ladies,* trans. Earl Jeffrey Richards (New York: Persea Books, 1982), p. 153.
12. King, *Women of the Renaissance,* p. 86.
13. Ibid., p. 94.
14. Ibid.

Bibliography

Anderson, Bonnie S., and Judith P. Zinsser. *A History of Their Own: Women in Europe from Pre-History to the Present:* Volumes 1 and 2. New York: Harper and Row, 1988.

Chervin, Ronda de Sola. *Prayers of the Women Mystics.* Ann Arbor, Michigan: Servant Publications, 1992.

de Pizan, Christine. *The Book of the City of Ladies.* Trans. Earl Jeffrey Richards. New York: Persea Books, 1982.

Hays, Denys, ed. *The Age of the Renaissance.* New York: McGraw-Hill Publishers, 1967.

Kelly, Joan. "Did Women Have a Renaissance?" In *Women, History and Theory.* Chicago: University of Chicago Press, 1984.

King, Margaret L. *Women of the Renaissance.* Chicago: University of Chicago Press, 1991.

King, Margaret L., and Albert Rabil, Jr. *Her Immaculate Hand: Selected Works by and about the Women Humanists of Quattrocento Italy.* Binghamton, NY: Medieval and Renaissance Texts and Studies, 1992.

Klapisch-Zuber, Christine. *Women, Family and Ritual in Renaissance Italy.* Chicago: University of Chicago Press, 1985.

Labalme, Patricia H., ed. *Beyond Their Sex: Learned Women of the European Past.* New York: New York University Press, 1984.

Lerner, Gerda. *The Creation of Feminist Consciousness: From the Middle Ages to Eighteen-seventy.* New York: Oxford University Press, 1993.

Maclean, Ian. *The Renaissance Notion of Women.* New York: Cambridge University Press, 1985.

Saint Teresa of Avila. *The Life of Saint Teresa of Avila by Herself.* Trans. J.M. Cohen. New York: Penguin Books, 1988.

Stone, Lawrence. *The Family, Sex and Marriage in England, 1500–1800.* Abr. ed. New York: Harper and Row, 1979.

Giuseppe Castiglione

His Life and Works

Michele Hubley

The life and work of the Jesuit artist Giuseppe Castiglione provides Michele Hubley's class with the subject matter for an engaging forum to compare Eastern and Western art, to analyze European and Chinese society, or to consider a life in terms of character and goals.

The story of Giuseppe Castiglione highlights the difficulties the Jesuits faced in China during the Ch'ing dynasty. Castiglione was a Jesuit priest whose sole motivation for exercising his artistic talent was to spread Christianity throughout China. He embodies the heart and soul of the missionary movement in modern China. An examination of the life and works of this talented artist and priest offers a more personal view of court life than most history books can provide, as well as some insights into the basic differences between Chinese and Western art.

Objectives

The American education system should produce young men and women who are highly literate and completely capable of functioning in a rapidly changing world. The system should assure that most students graduate and that those graduates seek to use their knowledge and skills to contribute to American society rather than take from it. This goal appears to be simple enough, but the road to accomplishing it is riddled with potholes, barriers, and detours.

Today's public school teacher not only must teach the curriculum but also must accept the added responsibility of instructing students on the dangers of alcohol, tobacco, drugs, unprotected sex—the list is endless. While researching the life and works of Giuseppe Castiglione, I became particularly impressed by the strong, moral character of this Jesuit priest. Castiglione's one goal, to which he dedicated his life, was to spread Christianity to the people of China. A gifted artist, he used his talent in hopes of accomplishing that one, important aim. Though he probably did not succeed in converting more than a handful of Chinese people to Roman Catholicism, many of his paintings remain and are considered to be splendid examples of both Chinese and Western art. Was Castiglione a failure because he failed to achieve his personal goal, or was he a success in terms of his personal commitment and his contributions to the world?

The objectives of this lesson are:

1. To investigate the life of one particular priest in order to involve the students more personally in the plight of Christian missionaries in Ch'ing China.
2. To point out the basic differences between Chinese and Western art and artists.
3. To examine the character and goals of Castiglione.

Materials Needed

If possible, show reproductions of selected works of Castiglione. Cécile and Michel Beurdeley's book *Castiglione, Peintre jésuite à la cour de Chine* offers the biggest selection of Castiglione's works. Other examples may be found in several of the books listed under "Notes."

Assignment

Divide the class into two or four groups. (If necessary, instruct the class on the rudiments of debate procedure.) Using their class notes and additional research, students should construct arguments to support either the view that Castiglione was a failure because he failed to achieve his personal goal or the view that he was a success in terms of his personal commitment and his contributions to the world. This will provide a forum in which students can discuss issues such as character and commitment without approaching them on a personal or religious level.

Background

There are few people born with a vocation so strong and so enduring that they are willing to give up their homes, their families, and their friends to travel to an unknown land to share their passions with strangers. Most men and women stumble along in mediocre lives denying their talents, preferring to be led rather than to lead. Yet, every once in a while, be it in the pages of history or in our daily lives, we meet a truly inspiring individual. The degree of fame or notoriety is inconsequential. The strength of character and personal integrity of the person are what make the difference and, in the end, are the most important factors in determining the real worth of an individual's contributions to the world.

Giuseppe Castiglione was a painter of some repute and a Jesuit whose name does not crowd the pages of history. Deeply religious, he joined the Society of Jesus and traveled to China to serve as a missionary. Throughout his life, never did he lose sight of his goal to convert the Chinese to Christianity. He was first and foremost a Jesuit. Any artistic talent he may have had, he used in accordance with the philosophy of the Society of Jesus. Therefore, to fully understand the contributions of Giuseppe Castiglione, it will be necessary to explore the forces that drove him to excel both as a human being and as an artist.

> You must realize that man does not only serve God by praying; otherwise all prayer that did not go on for twenty-four hours a day would be too short.
>
> —Ignatius Loyola

The Society of Jesus, whose members are commonly referred to as Jesuits, was founded in the middle of the sixteenth century by Ignatius Loyola. Loyola believed that Jesuit priests should be gifted intellectuals whose main goal should be to advance the Roman Catholic church through the quest for and dissemination of knowledge.[1] Jesuits should be active rather than contemplative and should be expected to do anything necessary to bring the word of God to the pagans. Jesuits should not be cloistered, should wear no habits, and should renounce their individual wills in favor of complete obedience to their superiors.[2] Then, as now, the Society of Jesus was considered radical by the authorities at the Vatican.

During the Ming dynasty, a group of Jesuits under the leadership of Matteo Ricci decided to make a great effort to proselytize the Chinese. For the first time, the Jesuits encountered a culture and a civilization that not only was much older and much more sophisticated than their own, but also was totally opposed and seemingly impervious to outside influence. The Chinese language alone posed a formidable barrier to any idea of a quick understanding of the Chinese and their radically different culture.[3]

Fortunately, Ricci was a rather accomplished diplomat. He understood many of the problems that the missionaries would have to face, and so he proposed a three-part plan to deal with the Chinese. First, it would be necessary to prove to them that there was an advanced civilization on the other side of the world. Second, it would be necessary to assure them that there was much Western knowledge from which they could profit. Third, it would be necessary to convince the Manchus, the scholars, and the elite to embrace Christianity. Without that, there would be no hope of preaching to the general population. In light of the fact that it took Ricci seven years to move from Macao to Peking, he understood that these goals could not be realized in one lifetime.[4]

By the end of the Ming dynasty, the Jesuits had found a kind of niche in Chinese society. Their scientific knowledge and their talents as musicians and painters had earned them respect and had gained them a favorable position at the court.[5] Many of them had learned to speak both Manchu and Chinese and had gained at least a reasonable understanding of the culture and traditions of the land.[6] Clearly, steps one and two of the Ricci plan had been achieved. The final step remained elusive.

The young Jesuits who arrived in China during the Ch'ing dynasty understood considerably more than their predecessors. They knew that they would be considered subjects of the emperor and that they would have to conform to the rules of Chinese etiquette. Willingly, they shared their knowledge and their skills, hoping to build the bridges that would allow them access to the Chinese people. Ultimately, they understood that should the emperor and his court find no value in their presence, they would quickly be dismissed from China.[7] It was against this background that Giuseppe Castiglione, S.J., arrived in Peking in 1715.

Castiglione was born in Milan, Italy, on July 19, 1688. Not much has been recorded about his childhood. At the age of nineteen, he entered the Society of Jesus to begin his novitiate. Unlike other religious orders, which required only one year of study as a novice, the Jesuits demanded two years of rigorous work. Less than half of the young men who began their studies were able to complete the task. Still, the intense studies did not impede Castiglione's painting. During those two years, he completed two paintings for the Chapel of the Novices in Genes.[8]

Once ordained, Castiglione realized that he had become a priest neither to paint nor to spend time examining his own spirituality. He wanted to go to China. For more than a hundred years, the Jesuits had been sending their best and brightest men to China to serve as missionaries. The problem was that in order to go to China, one had to go through Portugal, travel on Portuguese ships, and be introduced to the Chinese by the Portuguese. Consequently, Castiglione applied and was accepted by the Jesuits in Coimbra, Portugal.

During the two-year mandatory stay in Coimbra, Castiglione continued to paint. Thanks to a letter written by Castiglione, which is now in the National Library of Lisbon, it is known that he painted two portraits of the queen of Portugal's children, as well as some paintings for the Chapel of the College of Coimbra. On April 11, 1714, the already well-respected painter of religious subjects and his fellow priest Father Costa boarded a ship called *Our Lady of Hope* and set sail for China.[9]

At that time, the voyage to China was long and arduous. Violent storms and rough seas commonly caused shipwrecks and drownings. Only a man highly motivated to achieve his goal would undertake such a dangerous journey. Fortunately, the ship in which Castiglione sailed arrived safely in Macao in July 1715.[10]

After a brief stay in Macao, Castiglione was permitted to go to Canton. While there, he received instruction in Chinese etiquette: how to stand, how to sit, how to kneel, and where to put his hands. He learned about Confucianism, about the cultural traditions and rules of this new land, and he began his study of the Chinese language.[11] While in Canton, Castiglione took the name Lang Shih-ning, because Western names were difficult for the Chinese to pronounce.[12] Finally, Castiglione was deemed ready to make the long, slow journey to Peking to be presented to the emperor.[13]

The Emperor Kang-hsi was sixty-one years old when he first encountered Castiglione. Though appreciative of the value of the Jesuits, he remained quite reserved regarding the Christian religion. Many restrictions were imposed on the activities of the priests, and the eunuchs displayed impatience with the foreigners and their bizarre ways. Without a doubt, the position of the Church was tenuous, and the missionaries were allowed no forum in which to preach their faith. The presence of Castiglione and the other Jesuits working at the court must be understood against this background.[14]

So Castiglione began his work as an artist for the court. Shortly afterwards, on December 30, 1722, Kang-hsi died.[15] The next emperor, Yung-cheng, ruled from 1723 until 1736. Castiglione spent most of his life in the service of the Emperor Ch'ien Lung, who ruled China from 1736 to 1796.[16]

Life as a court artist was not easy. Every morning, Castiglione and the other artist had to wait at the front gate of the palace until the eunuchs appeared to usher them through the first of many gates. At each gate, they would be kept waiting according to the whims of the jealous eunuchs. Undoubtedly, the eunuchs took a certain degree of pleasure in annoying the artists. Little consideration was given to them in spite of extreme cold and hot temperatures. Nevertheless, Castiglione carried out his duties. He was willing to create in any medium anything that the Emperor Ch'ien Lung commanded. Quietly, unaggressively, and in accordance with the tenets of the Society of Jesus, he was using his talent in the hope of gaining an opportunity to preach and to seek converts for the Roman Catholic church.[17]

Ch'ien Lung perceived himself to be omniscient in all aspects of art. He often corrected or altered the work of court artists. There was no question that his demands had to

be met.[18] Initially, this must have presented a huge problem for Castiglione, whose background and training in art reflected the European style. Castiglione favored the use of highlights and shadows. His paintings took on a mathematical perspective and drew the eye to a central focal point. This was offensive to Chinese standards. The Chinese style of painting was quite opposed to all of that and was much more concerned with the essence of something than with perspective. Fortunately, Castiglione was both skillful enough and sensitive enough to Chinese expectations to adjust his work accordingly.[19]

> Chinese painting emphasizes Yang the light but not the dark Yin. Therefore, it is flat. In the west, a combination of shadows and lights are used. . . . recessed parts of eyes, ears, nose and mouth have dark shadows . . . so they can make their portraits indistinguishable from living persons.[20]

In 1743, there were twenty-two Jesuits living in Peking, seven of whom were in the direct service of the emperor Ch'ien Lung. These seven men, including Castiglione, had to be willing at any moment to do precisely that which the emperor wished.[21] Ch'ien Lung enjoyed spending the summer months at Yuan Ming Yuan, the summer imperial palace, located about sixty miles northwest of Peking. Although the palace was completely destroyed by British and French forces in 1860, some surviving engravings and a few written descriptions give some idea of the once splendid buildings, gardens, and fountains.[22]

In 1747, on the advice of missionaries, Ch'ien Lung determined to make his summer palace a monument to his taste and power by building Italian-style pavilions and extraordinary fountains. In order to accomplish this, he commanded Castiglione to do a great deal of the work. First, Castiglione built the Palace of Delicious Harmony (Hsia'chi). The building was quite reminiscent of Le Petit Trianon de Porcelain erected by King Louis XIV in the garden next to the Palace of Versailles. It was surrounded by fountains spewing water from the mouths of bronze animals. A small bridge and more fountains led to another marble structure and a maze. In the center, the Calm Sea Hall (Hai yen-t'ang) was also designed and built by Castiglione.

Castiglione's talent was also used to construct several other less imposing pavilions such as the House for Feeding Birds (Yang ch'iao). The walls of this structure were adorned with paintings of ships. Most of these buildings were multicolored with white marble pillars, red brick walls, and yellow, blue, or green tiled roofs that sparkled in the sunshine.[23] As always, Castiglione had to follow Ch'ien Lung's wishes for the design of the interior. The emperor wanted no staircases inside because he did not wish to live in the air in the fashion of the Europeans. Most of the furniture and other inside decorations, however, were brought in from Europe.[24]

All in all, the palace and the gardens turned out to be an exotic mixture of Chinese decoration on French-style structures.

Besides the architectural pursuits in the summer palace, Castiglione also accomplished some painting. *The Garden of Extended Spring* is perhaps one of the best-known of his works. Again, in accordance with the taste of Ch'ien Lung, Castiglione captured the emperor, some servants, and the famous concubine from Yarkand, Hsiang Fei, seated on a terrace in front of a belvedere that bears the inscription "Garden of Harmonious Amusement." While the setting is sterile, the technical execution of the work is meticulous.[25]

Another assignment that Castiglione and a few other Jesuits assumed was the design and illustration of the Chinese war campaigns and the conquest of Turkestan. Sixteen memorials were fixed to the walls of a memorial hall on the west shore of Central Lake in Peking. These works were so pleasing to Ch'ien Lung that in 1765 he demanded that they be reproduced by European engravers. Of course, he stipulated that only the best European artists be employed to accomplish this task. Castiglione wrote a letter to the Royal Academy of Painting in France requesting that the work be executed with both precision and delicacy. The principles of the French academy took precedence, so very little of the personal style of the missionaries in the Chinese court remained apparent.[26]

Nevertheless, Castiglione is best known for his painting. While in China, he consistently had to balance his work between Ch'ien Lung's desires and the principles of painting in his native style. This could not have been an easy task. In 1757, he completed a scroll depicting the Kazaks giving horses to Ch'ien Lung. The inscription of the painting, which was written by Ch'ien Lung, reads: "Swift as lightning these horses are veritable dragons, and the emperor has asked Castiglione (Lang Shih-ning) to paint them."[27] Horses were important to the Manchus—almost as important as dragons—and Castiglione painted them well. They look real, although they do not have the superpower that Chinese horse painters such as Jen Jen-fa were capable of depicting.

There is also some evidence that Castiglione used his talent in both enamel and porcelain. Again, artists were not permitted to specialize in any one medium. On one occasion, Castiglione drew some designs for a French painter named Perroni, who had been ordered to paint in the enamel workshop. It is also generally agreed that Castiglione may have been responsible for some of the decorations on porcelain pieces that were part of the imperial collection. The best porcelain of the empire was made in Ching-te-chen. Some of it was sent in white to be decorated by the established artists in the imperial city.[28] Yang describes 107 pieces—84 decorated with birds, flowers, and landscapes and 4 with figures. Both Michel Beurdeley and Lady David believe that these are Chinese scenes executed by a European, most

probably by Castiglione.[29] Lady David owned a silk painting of an unadorned landscape signed by Castiglione, which is found on several pieces of porcelain that are now on exhibit in the museums of Taiwan and Washington, D.C.[30]

Though obviously a talented artist capable of displaying his gift in every medium, Castiglione's raison d'être was to bring Christianity to the Chinese. By the time of his forty-seventh birthday, he had gained considerable knowledge of the court and had the opportunity to see Ch'ien Lung almost every day. Though specifically forbidden to discuss anything of a political nature with the emperor, on several occasions, Castiglione did take the opportunity to intercede on behalf of the Church. One time, the emperor had ordered the death of a young Chinese Christian. Castiglione asked him why he found it necessary to condemn the Christian religion. The emperor replied that he had no wish to damn Christianity. He had simply forbidden the people of the Banners, military organizations, to embrace it. The eunuchs present were so angered that Castiglione had dared to communicate with the emperor that they insisted upon searching him everyday in order to ensure he was carrying no memorials or petitions for Ch'ien Lung.

One year later, Castiglione again approached the emperor regarding the beating of a Chinese novice for having baptized abandoned children. The man had been accused of using "magic water" and was labeled a criminal for having converted to Christianity. Ch'ien Lung offered the same response as last time, but he did stay away from the studios for several days in order to demonstrate his disapproval.[31]

The third incident occurred in 1746. Ch'ien Lung had issued the death sentence on five Dominican missionaries. Castiglione begged the emperor to have compassion on the sorry Catholic religion. The emperor declared that Castiglione was a foreigner and did not understand the customs of China. His decision was irrevocable. Father Sanz was executed in 1747, and the four other Dominicans were killed one year later. Castiglione was asked to concern himself simply with painting.[32]

On one occasion, the emperor arrived at the studio in the morning accompanied by his concubines. The next day, he questioned Castiglione as to which one of the beauties he preferred. At the risk of offending Ch'ien Lung, Castiglione replied that he had not noticed because he had been too busy counting the porcelain squares on the palace wall. In disbelief, the emperor asked for the total. He then asked the eunuchs to recount the squares. Castiglione had been accurate![33]

Giuseppe Castiglione died in Peking on July 17, 1766.[34] Undoubtedly, he was the most talented of all the missionary painters of his time. Although he did offer a few paintings to Christian communities around Peking, most of his work was used to embellish the collections of the imperial palace. In spite of this, Castiglione never stopped believing that he was using his skill and his talent to drive home the spiritual message of Roman Catholicism. He insisted that the only payment he needed was to have the opportunity to witness and to help the missionary effort in China.[35]

In the final analysis, Castiglione's life and work simply reflect his perhaps idealistic desire to be in China and to serve God. Throughout his life, he compromised neither his religious beliefs nor his religious and apostolic responsibilities. He worked within the framework and boundaries permitted by the court, always in the hope of achieving his ultimate goal. He should be remembered first as a man of strong, unwavering character; second, as a Jesuit who, at the very least, represents the futility of the missionary movement in Manchu China; and third, as an artist whose work enlightened Chinese and Europeans alike.

Notes

1. Manfred Barthel, *The Jesuits: History and Legend of the Society of Jesus,* trans. Mark Howson (New York: William Morrow and Company, 1984), p. 41.

2. Ibid., p. 66.

3. Ibid., p. 190.

4. Ibid., pp. 192–93.

5. Jacques Gernet, *A History of Chinese Civilization,* trans. J.R. Foster (Cambridge University Press, 1985), p. 518.

6. Cécile Beurdeley and Michel Beurdeley, *Castiglione, peintre jésuite à la cour de Chine* (Fribourg, Suisse: Office du Livre, 1971), p. 6.

7. Ibid., p. 4.

8. Ibid., p. 11.

9. Ibid., p. 12

10. Ibid., p. 19.

11. Ibid., p. 26.

12. Ibid., p. 22.

13. Ibid., p. 23.

14. Charles E. Ronan, S.J., *East Meets West: The Jesuits in China* (Chicago: Loyola University Press, 1988), p. 117.

15. Beurdeley and Beurdeley, *Castiglione, peintre jésuite,* p. 31.

16. Gernet, *A History of Chinese Civilization,* p. 472.

17. Beurdeley and Beurdeley, *Castiglione, peintre jésuite,* p. 28.

18. Michel Beurdeley, *The Chinese Collector Through Centuries* (Rutland, VT: Charles E. Tuttle Company, 1966), p. 28.

19. Arnold Sitcock, *Chinese Art and History* (New York: Oxford University Press, 1948), p. 214.

20. Ronan, *East Meets West,* p. 107.

21. Beurdeley and Beurdeley, *Castiglione, peintre jésuite,* p. 45.

22. Ronan, *East Meets West,* p. 117.

23. Beurdeley, *The Chinese Collector,* p. 156.

24. Ibid., p. 157.

25. Ronan, *East Meets West,* p. 117.

26. Ibid., p. 119.

27. Ibid.

28. Beurdeley and Beurdeley, *Castiglione, peintre jésuite,* p. 46.

29. Beurdeley, *The Chinese Collector,* p. 177.

30. Ibid., p. 180.

31. Ibid., p. 39.

32. Ibid., pp. 40–42.

33. Ibid., p. 40

34. Ibid., p. 59.

35. Ibid., p. 48.

Reference

Speiser, Werner. *The Art of China: Spirit and Society.* New York: Crown Publishers, 1960.

The Clamor for a Return to Government

Pat Carney

Pat Carney asks students to analyze documents and draw conclusions about the English revolution, 1640–1660, on the basis of the primary sources. With this lesson small student groups have the opportunity to become practicing historians.

Rationale and Unit Overview

The purpose of this unit is to explore popular thought and culture during the English revolution, 1640–1660. The seventeenth century was a period of major religious and political upheaval all over Europe. England itself experienced such turmoil as a civil war between the king and Parliament, the trial and execution of the king, a republican government, and a military dictatorship. Because censorship was lifted during the English revolution, this period offers a unique window in time through which it is possible to study the ideas and attitudes of non-elite groups. All other areas of Europe strictly controlled the press, as did England before and after this period. A study of popular documents of this era provides a deeper insight into English society. The ordinary people were excited by events of the revolution, formulating their own reactions and getting them published. This is, therefore, the only time before the nineteenth century in which one can read what ordinary people in any part of Europe thought about the world in which they lived.

This unit, based on primary sources, introduces the student to the major concerns of the English during the revolutionary upheaval, using excerpts from pamphlets, broadsides, court records, and petitions. It is hoped that by using primary source material, the students will discover that history includes real people like themselves. In addition, by analyzing evidence and drawing conclusions, the students will be engaged in the historian's craft. They will use the materials and the methods that historians use in creating their own interpretations. They will also become more aware that history is an interpretation rather than rote memorization. By analyzing original documents, students will be introduced to issues raised during the English revolution that had significant impact. For example, the ferment of ideas, whether the demand for democracy by the Levellers or the army's experiment in republicanism, contributed to the development of political thought in America. Many issues invite comparison with concerns still relevant today. For example, the women's petition to Parliament can be related to the ongoing struggle to advance women's rights. The cancelation of Christmas festivities can be compared to contemporary issues of censorship and religious freedom.

The unit includes a variety of ideas and activities to engage students in the historical process. Lesson One provides a practice exercise in reading early modern printed texts. Lesson Two deals with three different historical interpretations of witchcraft accusations. Students are asked to consider the social context and belief systems of the seventeenth century. Lesson Three compares the ideas of two radical groups that offered political and social solutions to contemporary problems. Lesson Four presents excerpts from debates in the army held in Putney church in 1647. This discussion considered expansion of the franchise. Lesson Five describes the grim conditions in an English town during a siege in 1648. Lesson Six is based on a petition presented to the House of Commons by women in 1649. This document reflects their concerns and represents their increased involvement in political activity. Lesson Seven focuses on the execution of King Charles I in 1649 and the reactions to this event. Lesson Eight deals with restrictions placed on the traditional popular festivities under a Puritan Parliament. The people reacted to having their "Christmas" taken away. Lesson Nine presents the views of various groups who clamored for a return to government after the death of Cromwell in 1658. Lesson Nine with its documentary evidence is included as a sample lesson from the unit of study.

Unit Objectives

1. Students will examine ideas and reactions of ordinary people published during the English revolution.
2. Students will read primary source material, gather evidence, and make interpretations.

"The Clamor for a Return to Government: Popular Thought and Culture during the English Revolution," *State Papers Domestic, 1625–1665,* Document SP 181219, custody of the Public Record Office, London, England.

3. Students will consider the reliability of evidence and compare conflicting accounts.

4. Students will identify principles of political democracy, such as expansion of the franchise and government by consent, expressed by radical political groups during the English revolution.

5. Students will understand the importance of popular political participation during this period of revolutionary upheaval.

6. Students will examine the arguments expressed by the English in support of representative government.

7. Students will analyze historical interpretations of beliefs, such as witchcraft in the early modern period.

Popular Culture in the Early Modern Period

Conventional histories rely on factual information derived from politics and high culture. In intellectual studies, familiar labels such as "Renaissance" and "Scientific Revolution" reveal the thought of elites during the early period of Western development. But what did ordinary people think and feel in these periods? Culture is not just formal aesthetics, but also includes what ordinary people think and do. In his study of early modern Europe, historian Peter Burke drew a distinction between two cultural traditions. A "great tradition" was transmitted formally in schools and universities and involved the ruling minority. This would include expressions of high culture, such as religious doctrine and political and legal theory. A "little tradition" was transmitted informally and involved the common people. This would include expressions of popular culture, such as annual festivals, ballads, legends, and dances. Historians draw arbitrary boundaries around groups to examine particular cultural elements and to show how these were transmitted. It is the interchange between the "great" and the "little" traditions that increases our understanding of society in the early modern period. Popular culture is a blend of ideas, customs, skills, values, and artifacts that are accessible to all groups within a given society and can be transmitted to the next generation, either orally or in written form. In some cases, popular culture was shared by elite and non-elite types. There were many social interactions in the community that brought people together. In other cases, there was a gap between groups and the focus is on the bottom and middle levels of society.

In early English history, popular culture is an elusive area of study. At least two difficulties impede the search. First, few written sources reveal the attitudes and values of non-elite groups. Many early traditions were passed to the next generation orally. Available records are filtered through the views of elites, who were educated males of the higher classes. When they recorded impressions of attitudes and

beliefs of non-elites, it was not always in the best of circumstances, such as trials for criminal offenses or suppression of rebellions. Second, even when elite sources are available, it is difficult to tell how cultural interchange actually took place. When elites created propaganda to influence commoners, the commoners may have resisted or reacted against the imposition of these views. While the difficulties of investigating popular culture appear enormous, historians of early English history have developed successful approaches to determine what groups had access to cultural elements and how the interchange among groups took place.

The range of common sociability in early modern England is rich and varied. Plays, processions, dancing, and the Maypole celebration brought people together for entertainment and enjoyment. Local parish plays centered on themes of Robin Hood, Maid Marian, and St. George and the Dragon. These performances, held in the church, were intended to raise revenues. Churchwarden records reflect money collected as well as expenditures for props, such as the dragon's tail. Participation in the plays varied by age and gender. The younger, unmarried men acted out versions of Robin Hood, while the older men usually performed St. George and the Dragon. The May Queen was adapted from the May celebration and later incorporated into the Robin Hood plays as Maid Marian. Communal solidarity was also expressed in calendar customs. There were celebrations on New Year's Night and on the first Monday after Twelfth Night, known as Plough Monday, in which a plough was dragged around the parish. Food and drink were demanded in return for performing plays and dances. These occasions allowed merriment for participants and an opportunity to let off steam. Celebrations at Whitsun and Midsummer Day involved the Lord of Misrule, captains of mischief, for whom rules were temporarily suspended. In this carnival atmosphere for only a little while, the lowly reigned and the world was turned upside down.

Popular culture also included recreational activities and social drinking. A football game could involve many neighbors from surrounding parishes or from rival parts of the same village. Other appealing pastimes were cricket, boxing, wrestling, and dueling with simple sticks. Activities that involved a low sensitivity to animal suffering were bear and bull baiting and cock fighting. The most common reaction of the people was meeting in the alehouse. It was a place to drink as well as to meet, gossip, and exchange political news. It also provided a source of activities and games of the people, from dancing and performing plays, to bowls, dice, and cards. Some alehouses had lodging accommodations, but most were small business establishments. The Puritan attack on festivities and disorderly recreations had the effect of making the alehouse more popular, and it became a rival to the parish church.

By 1550, popular literature, such as pamphlets, almanacs,

and chapbooks became available, especially in the towns. Much of the information was religious or utilitarian; only gradually did it begin to reflect political news and propaganda. Being sensationalist in tone, popular literature reinforced some irrational beliefs. The people still lived close to nature, and their level of explanation for misfortune was primitive. They viewed abnormalities as an omen from God or as a foretelling of a future event. A calf born with two heads, for example, could symbolize a division of power. Not until the end of the seventeenth century would attitudes toward causation begin to change. The most systematic attempt to explain natural phenomena was astrology. Handbooks in clear and simple language explained the movements of stars and planets. Almanacs contained phases of the calendar, farming practices, and medical techniques. For the year it was issued, an almanac could also contain prognostications, which were political, religious, and social speculations. Another feature of popular literature was didactic and supported the existing social order. Conduct books asserted the patriarchal authority of the father as head of the household. A wife's first duty was to obey her husband on the basis of the naturalness of subordination. Yet the normal relationship between spouses was presented as loving and based on shared responsibility.

Another function of popular culture in the early modern village was enforcing social norms. Tension sometimes arose over women who were perceived as exhibiting deviant social behavior. Typically, women were viewed as more emotional and subservient to men. Wives were in charge of the household and expected to be obedient and silent. Those who deviated from these norms were called "scolds" who misused their verbal power. They spoke in ways that made trouble in the community by spreading false stories or making fun of an official. This was unsettling to the social order of the community. "Witches" were women whom the community or a member of the community singled out for revenge. There was usually a social and economic gap between the villager who made the accusation and the accused witch. The witch had requested alms or help from a wealthier member of the community who then turned the witch down. Afterwards, the person felt guilty; when a misfortune occurred, he or she would strike out and accuse the witch. Male villagers also enforced community norms of wifely subordination by the charivari (also known as the skimmington or riding the stang). Husbands who neglected their position of authority in allowing their wives to beat them were satirized in a riding. Two villagers would act out the domestic discord accompanied by others beating pots and pans, which created "rough music." Reputation and honor were highly valued by individuals in the early English community.

The attitudes of elites toward popular culture changed in the early modern period. In 1550, popular culture belonged to everyone. The elites alone participated in a learned culture, but they shared the forms and attitudes of popular culture with the masses. But by 1800, the elites withdrew from the culture of the ordinary people and developed a distinctive culture of their own. This was part of a change in the general intellectual climate. The elites objected to popular culture on the grounds that stability was threatened by raucous behavior and on the grounds of morality. The Puritans especially associated popular culture with actions that were not pleasing to God. They attempted to tame popular culture with an attack on parish ales, country dances, and Maypole celebrations. The triumph of the "godly" culture was not limited to Puritan preachers but was shared by local elites who viewed the inversion of norms as something that needed to be suppressed.

The era of the English revolution offers a unique opportunity for the study of popular thought. Before 1640 and after 1660, only the powerful could publish, because of tight control by authorities. While censorship was lifted during this short period, a flood of ideas and reactions was published in response to revolutionary upheaval. The collection of pamphlets made in the 1640s and 1650s by a London bookseller, George Thomason, is a good indicator of the quantity of material published in these two decades. The *Thomason Tracts,* still intact in the British Library, contains over twenty thousand works, which provide insights into the politics and religion of the period as well as revealing the perspective of ordinary men and women. Additionally the *State Papers Domestic* record all correspondence from English people to their government and provide examples of pertinent local issues. All levels of English society took advantage of the press while struggling to make sense of their world. This unit presents a selection of the wealth of ideas expressed in this period. By analyzing these documents, students not only will gain insight into the lives of the early English people but also will see many of the ideas still reflected in contemporary concerns.

The English Revolution: A Chronology

1640–42:   Nonviolent conflict between the Long Parliament and Charles; negotiations over grievances; Charles accepted limitations on royal rights and limits on church.

1642–48:   First civil war and growth of radicalism; Charles went to Scotland and raised his standard, and fighting began; the north was more conservative and fought for Charles.

1642:   Parliament split; some joined the king; fighting continued until 1646; Parliament had victories.

1646–48:   Radical ideas about government and religion grew.

1648–49: Second civil war and the trial and execution of King Charles I; Parliament was successful and created courts separate from the king; the king was accused of treason, found guilty, and executed in 1649; this action (first execution of a ruler) shocked Europe; Parliament decreased in size to the Rump; the monarchy and House of Lords were abolished.

1649–53: Commonwealth was established; the remaining members of the House of Commons ruled; Oliver Cromwell, the head of the New Model Army, grew in power; he subdued the Scots; he was unhappy with the Rump Parliament.

1653–59: Cromwell eliminated the Commonwealth and established the Protectorate, a conservative experiment that was not popular; Cromwell became Lord Protector but functioned as a king; Cromwell was dependent on the army for survival; there was more unrest and use of force to subdue it in this period.

1659–60: After Cromwell's death, his son was unable to lead; the army was disunited and anarchy apparent; General Monck, one of Cromwell's subgenerals in Scotland, came south to London, called the members of the 1640 Parliament to dissolve it; a new legal form of government was set up and elections held; a Convention Parliament invited the son of Charles I to come and rule; the Anglican church and monarchy were restored; return to conservatism because of war weariness and unpopularity of military rule.

Bibliography

Ashley, M. *General Monck.* Totowa, NJ: Rowman and Littlefield, 1977.

Ashton, Robert. *The English Civil War: Conservatism and Revolution, 1603–1649.* New York: W.W. Norton, 1978.

Burke, Peter. *Popular Culture in Early Modern Europe.* New York: Harper and Row, 1978.

Capp, Bernard S. *Astrology and the Popular Press: English Almanacs, 1500–1800.* London and Boston: Faber and Faber, 1979.

Clark, Peter. *The English Alehouse.* London: Longman Group Limited, 1983.

Coward, Barry. *The Stuart Age.* London: Longman Group Limited, 1980.

Cressy, David. *Literacy and the Social Order: Reading and Writing in Tudor and Stuart England.* Cambridge: Cambridge University Press, 1980.

Easton, Susan, et al. " 'A Rude and Disorderly People': Popular Culture and Social Order in England 1550–1700." In *Disorder and Discipline: Popular Culture from 1500 to the Present.* Hands, England: Temple Smith Gower Publishing, 1988.

Harris, Tim. "The Problem of 'Popular Political Culture' in Seventeenth-Century London." *History of European Ideas* 10 (1989): 43–58.

Hill, Christopher. *Religion and Politics in Seventeenth-Century England.* Amherst, MA: University of Massachusetts Press, 1986.

Hutton, Ronald. *The British Republic, 1649–1660.* New York: St. Martin's Press, 1990.

Ingram, Martin. "Ridings, Rough Music and the 'Reform of Popular Culture' in Early Modern England." *Past and Present* 105 (1984):70–113.

Macfarlane, Alan. *The Family Life of Ralph Joselin, A Seventeenth-Century Clergyman.* New York: W.W. Norton, 1970.

Malcolmson, Robert W. *Popular Recreations in English Society, 1700–1850.* Cambridge: Cambridge University Press, 1973.

Reay, Barry, ed. *Popular Culture in Seventeenth-Century England.* London and Sydney: Croom Helm, 1985.

Sharpe, J.A. *Early Modern England: A Social History, 1550–1760.* London: Edward Arnold, 1987.

Spufford, Margaret. *Small Book and Pleasant Histories: Popular Fiction and Its Readership in Seventeenth-Century England.* London: Methuen, 1981.

Stone, Lawrence. *The Causes of the English Revolution, 1529–1642.* London: Routledge and Kegan Paul, 1972.

Wrightson, Keith. "Alehouses, Order and Reformation in Rural England, 1590–1660." In *Popular Culture and Class Conflict, 1590–1914,* edited by Eileen Yeo and Stephen Yeo. Atlantic Highlands, NJ: Humanities Press, Inc., 1981.

Wrightson, Keith. *English Society, 1580–1690.* New Brunswick, NY: Rutgers University Press, 1982.

Lesson:
1659: A Request for Government

Objectives

1. To examine the views of various types of English people, such as gentlemen, apprentices, ministers, freeholders, seamen, and commoners, regarding the government in 1659.

2. To identify the major political issues and grievances that concerned the people.

3. To compose a statement of the type of government that the English wanted for their country in 1659.

Materials and Preparations

For a class of thirty or thirty-two students, assign students to cooperative learning groups of four, with a high achiever, two middle-range students, and a basic student in each group. Make two copies of each document (Documents #1 through #14) for each class. To facilitate collection for reuse, copy documents used within each group on a different color paper. Read the contextual information below.

Lesson Activities (One class period of fifty minutes)

1. Using the lesson in the context of the English civil war, set the stage either through assigned readings in the text or a lecture on the events leading up to the end of the Protectorate under Cromwell after his death in 1658.

2. Explain the assignment and how students will be evaluated. Working in groups, students will read documents and

gather information on the English views of government. Groups will have different documents to analyze. The information gathered will be shared with the class so that they can prepare a composite position statement: "A Proposal for the Government of the English People, 1660." This compilation together with their notes attached to the back will be evaluated.

3. After explaining the assignment, have students form the preassigned groups. Then to groups 1 and 5, give copies of Documents #1, #2, and #3. To groups 2 and 6, give copies of Documents #4, #5, #6 and #7. To groups 3 and 7, give copies of documents #8, #9, #10, and #11. To groups 4 and 8, give copies of Documents #12, #13, and #14.

4. Before they start, indicate to the students how much time they will have to read and gather information (suggested length 15–20 minutes). Within their groups, students should read each document together, look for the following information, and record their findings:

- What types of groups composed the statement?
- To whom was the document directed?
- How did the people describe the war?
- What impositions did the war cause?
- What were their demands?
- What grievances did they have?
- What type of government did the people now want? How would it have been an improvement?

5. After they have finished reading the sources and gathering the information, have each group report what they have found to the class. Students should take notes on information that differs from what they have found.

6. When each group has reported, the students will make a composite position statement: "A Proposal for the Government of the English People, 1660." This should include what types of Englishmen petitioned for a change in government, and it should include supporting evidence from the documents, giving reasons for the type of government desired. Students can compose their own, or the group can make a composite statement. These are turned in for evaluation.

Contextual Information for the Teacher

At the beginning of the Interregnum, the period from 1649 to 1660 between two monarchical reigns, England was a republic under a government known as the Commonwealth. In reality, the Commonwealth was a dictatorship of a radical minority that came to power through the organization of the New Model Army. Since the radicals felt insecure about calling a free election, the Rump Parliament continued to sit. Cromwell dominated the new government. He was a patriotic Englishman and strong-minded Independent, yet he was

not willing to compromise. Nevertheless, he was a prisoner of his own position.

Cromwell faced hostility on all sides. The majority of the English were royalist at heart and weary of the conflicts and changes of the previous decade. Cromwell also faced a hostile Scotland and Ireland, where the disorders in England had encouraged the Catholic Irish to rebel in 1649. In 1650, Charles II, the eldest son of the executed Charles I, landed in Scotland, guaranteed the Presbyterian faith, and led an army against the English. The English army defeated Charles, who fled to the Continent. Cromwell then faced a war with Holland (1652–1654) brought on by the Navigation Act of 1651, which protected English shipping and struck at the Dutch carrying trade.

Cromwell was more successful in his foreign policy than in his domestic policy. He went to Ireland to suppress the rebellion. In the settlement of 1652–1654, he replaced rebel Irish landholders with Protestants. He brought the naval war with the Dutch to a close in 1654. In a war against Spain from 1656 to 1658, the English acquired the sugar island Jamaica in the Caribbean. At home, however, the Rump Parliament resisted an increase in membership and reform of its procedures. In 1653, Cromwell forced its dissolution by appearing in Parliament with his soldiers. He then inaugurated the regime called the Protectorate, taking the title of "lord protector" for himself and placing the country under a written constitution, the Instrument of Government. It provided for a Parliament with a single house whose members were chosen by Puritan sympathizers. Even so, Cromwell had constant conflict with his parliaments, and in 1657 he modified the Instrument to provide a second house to limit the lord protector's power. Meanwhile, to maintain order, Cromwell divided the country into twelve military districts, each commanded by a major general.

The Protectorate disintegrated after Cromwell died in 1658. He was succeeded as lord protector by his son Richard, who proved to be an inept leader. In the country, there was a rising clamor for a new and free Parliament. It was unclear whether there should be new elections or if former members should be included. The army soon seized control but became divided within itself, unable to unite on a single policy. Some of its leaders regarded the restoration of the Stuarts as the best way to end the continuous political turmoil. To ensure the legality of the move, General George Monck (1608–1670), commander of the Protectorate's forces in Scotland, advanced on London, summoned back the Rump, and readmitted the surviving members excluded by Pride's Purge. These promised to dissolve the Long Parliament and order elections for a new one. Everywhere the electors returned royalists under the pressure of eleven years of military rule. The new Parliament restored the House of Lords, and in 1660 Charles Stuart accepted an invitation to return from exile and reign as Charles II.

Document #1

To His Excellency, General Monck. A Letter from the Gentlemen of Devon: in Answer to his Lordships of January 23. to them directed from Leicester.

My Lord,

There is a Letter which hath passed the Press under your Name, dated at Leicester 23. Jan. and directed unto Mr. Rolle, to be communicated to the rest of the Gentry of Devon: &c.,—Whether this be your Excellencies Act or not, is the question. If so it be, we receive it as a noble Respect from General Monk to his Friends and Country-men; if otherwise, we look upon it as the Artifice of an Anti-Parliamentary Faction, under the presence of your Concurrence and Aid, to delude and enslave the Nation.

It is one thing for a person of Honour freely to communicate his Thoughts and Reasonings, (although in favour of a possible mistake) still referring the Issue to the determinations of Divinity, and Reason: and it is another thing, for a Confederate Party to charge such a Person with failings properly their own.

To hasten the dispatch of that little we have to say, the Authours of this, are of that number to whom your Letter directs. We shall proceed according to our Duties, and Instructions, and briefly acquaint your Excellency with the sense of those that have entrusted us.

We shall begin (my Lord) with the Concessions of what we much suspect, and take for granted, that the Letter so inscribed, is really Yours. We are next, to return you the thanks of your Country-men, for the expressions of your Piety and Care, therein contained, and particularly, that in the head of your Army, you have rather chosen arguments of Reason, then of Force.—that you propose the word of God, for your Rule, and the Settlement of the Nation, for your end.—that you take notice of many Factions, and Interests introduced, and yet profess a service to none of them.—That you so earnestly desire to compose old Differences at home, and to prevent new mischiefs from abroad.—And finally; That you submit the Result of all, to a fair, and rational examination.

To profess, and to persue all this, is but like yourself; and to these purposes, we shall not stick to live and dye at your Feet. If upon Discussion of the Reasons to alledge, we assume the Liberty which your Candour allows us, of declaring wherein we differ, we beg to be understood with all tenderness toward your Excellency; to whom, as a stranger to our late Oppressions and Calamities, the State of our Affairs, and Affections, may probably be misrepresented. To observe your own Method; our Letter to the Speaker, importing the recalling of the Secluded Members was the occasion of yours to Us; which sayes, that; Before these wars, our Government was Monarchical, both in church, and State, but (as the case stands now) Monarchy cannot possibly be admitted for the future, in these Nations; because it is incompatible with the several Interests which have ensued upon the Quarrel; viz., the Presbyterian, Independent, Anabaptists, & c. (as to Ecclesiasticks) and the Purchasers of Crown, and Bishops Lands, Forfeited Estates, & c. (as to Civils) by which means, the support itself is taken away; so that the Constitution, qualified to fix all Interests, must be that of a Republique: To which, the Secluded Members of 1648, will never agree, many of them being Assertours of Monarchy, and Disclaimers to all Laws made since their Seclusion: over and

above, that the army also will never endure it. The Conclusion this, that it were better for us to desist from that Paper, and rely upon the Promises of this Parliament, for a due Representative:—a Provision for succeeding Parliaments, and a Peaceable settlement, then by an unseasonable Impatience to embroil the Nation in a fresh Engagement.

From hence it appears, that we might be allowed a Free Parliament, but for four Reasons. First, The Major part Inclines to Monarchy and they that have swallowed the Revenues of the Crown, declare against it. Secondly, The Entangled Interests of this Nation can never be united, but under a Republique. Thirdly, The Army will never endure it. And lastly, it would beget a new war, whereas this Parliament promises to settle us in a lasting Peace.

To all which, in Order, and first, concerning Monarchy, (not as the thing which we contend for) we (onely) wonder, why it is prejudged, and particularly, by those Persons who have sworn to defend it. But, my Lord, you have hit the Reason; they have gained by Dissolving it, and they are afraid to lose by Restoring it. Having put the Father to Death, whom they Covenanted to Preserve; they Abjure the Son, whom they fear to Trust. By Force they would maintain, what by Force they have Gotten. In effect; the Question, is not so much, what Government, as what Governours: A Single Person will down well enough, with the fiercest of them, when it lies fair for any of themselves. Witness the late Protectour, and the later Lambert. Briefly, since the Death of the late King, we have been Govern'd by Tumult; Bandy'd from one Faction to the Other: This Party up to day, That to Morrow; but still the Nation under, and a Prey to the Strongest. It is a feeble Argument against Monarchy, that we never have been happy since we lost it: and yet nothing hath appeared to obstruct our Quiet, but the Divisions of the Booty. What Hath been, Shall be, so long as this Violence continues over us: nor can any other Government Settle the Nation, then that which pleases the Universality of it. And in that, we pretend not to direct our Representatives: but which way soever they encline, we shall with our Lives and Fortunes Justifie, and Obey their Appointments.

Whether we have Reason, or not, in this Particular, let your Excellency Judge.

The second Objection against a Free Parliament, is drawn from the Necessity of a Republique, to reconcile all Interests. To this, we offer, first, that it is not necessary; next, that it is not so much as effectual, to that purpose, and lastly, that a Free Parliament ought to Introduce it, if it were both the one and the other.

The first we prove, thus, It is not the Form of Government, but the consent of the People, that must Settle the Nation. The Publique Debt, must be secured out of the Publique Stock; and that disposed of by an Engagement of the Publique Faith, to such Ends, and Purposes, and the Representatives of the Nation shall deem expedient for the Good of it. In like manner may all other Interests be secured; whether of Opinion, or Property, under what form of Government soever a Free Parliament shall think fit to unite us. That is not Necessary, enough is laid. We are now to deduce from your Lordships Text, that a Free State would be as little effectual also, as to our concernes. You are pleased to intimate the Dangerous Inclination of the People to Monarchy: and to Balance the Satisfaction, the Right, and the Universal Vote of the Nation, with the Interests of some few persons, that would Rule us Themselves, (for that's the English of the Settlement they propose.) By this Argument, a Republique, excludes the Negative, and more considerable Interest, in favour of a

Small, and a Partial one: and if it be granted, that a Free Parliament will never agree upon a Free State, it follows necessarily, that That Form will never do our Business. Lastly, what Government soever is forced upon us, most certainly expire with the Force that imposed it; and the Voice of the People (in this case) is the Declaratory Voice of Providence.

The third Difficulty is. The Army will never endure it. This is to say, You are to be Govern'd by the Sword.

To Conclude; The Fear of a New War, and the promise of a speedy Composure, are the last Suggestions of Disswasion to us. Alas, my Lord, do we not see that Parties are uniting against us, Abroad, and we against ourselves at Home? How certainly shall we be Attempted, and how easily overcome; without such a Medium to Reconcile us All, as may Please us All! but we are promised fair. We beseech your Lordship to consider the Promisers. Are not these the people that vow'd to make our Last, a Glorious King? Just such a Glorious Nation will they make of us. Did they not next abjure a Single Person; and yet after that, set up ANOTHER, with Another Oath? Not to pursue this Subject further: These men we dare not Trust, nor any other of that Leaven, we have no thoughts but of Justice to all Interests; and in order to that Settlement and good we with the Nation, we shall impower our Representatives with the Command of all we are worth, and most remarkably evidence our selves, my Lord,

Your Excellencies Servants.
Jan. 28, 1659
London, Printed for Y.E. 1660.

Document #2

The Declaration of the Gentry, of the County of Norfolk, and of the County and City of Norwich.

We the Gentry of the County of Norfolk, and County and City of Norwich, being deeply affected with the sence of our sad Distractions and Divisions, both in Church and State, and wearied with the miseries of an Unnatural Civil War, the too Frequent Interruptions of Government, the Imposition of several heavy Taxes, and the loud Out-cries of multitudes of undone, and almost Famished People, occasioned by the General decay of Trade, which hath spread it self throughout the whole Nation, and these Counties in particular; and having met together, and consulted what may best remedy, and remove our, and the nations present Grievances and Distractions, Do humbly conceive, that the chief Expedient will be, the recalling of those Members that were secluded in 1648, and sat before the Force put upon the Parliament (We of the County of Norfolk) being by such Seclusion, deprived of any Person to represent us in Parliament, and also by filling up the Vacant Places thereof; and all to be Admitted without any Oath, or Engagement, previous to their Entrance; which being done, We shall be ready to acquiesce, and submit in all things, to the Judgment and Authority of Parliament; without which Authority, the People of England cannot be obliged to pay any Taxes.

This Declaration, subscribed by three hundred Gentlemen, was delivered to the Honourable Will: Lenthall, Speaker of the Parliament, on Saturday the Eight and Twentieth of January, 1659. By the Lord Richardson, Sir John Hobart, and Sir Horatio Tounsend, Baronets.

Document #3

A Letter Agreed unto, and subscribed by, the Gentlemen, Ministers, Freeholders and Seamen of the County of Suffolk Presented to His Excellency, The Lord Generall Monck.

May it please your Excellency,

That our own hearts may not accuse us of a negligence and Supinesse, unbecoming those Distempers we languish under, 'tis our desire, that this Application, humbly and affectionately tendered, may be received, as the Effect of a just and serious resentment. To us, at this distance, the God of Heaven seems to prompt you to do Nobly, by depositing in your hands a full and happy Opportunity, such as conspires to promote those Ends, which are worthy and generous. Your Lordship will need no other Incitements, than the publick Concern, and contriving an abiding Ornament to your Name, It must needs be tedious, to see Government reeling from one Species, from one hand to another. We apprehend it much in your power to fix it. Are our Sacred or civill Liberties dear to us? They sollicite a Restitution to their Legall Boundaries. Let your Lordship cast your eyes upon a Nation, impoverished, disfigured, bleeding under an intestine Sword: Let its agonies, its miseries, its ruines, implore your assistance. To our sense, the onely redresse, under God, lies in a Free and Full PARLIAMENT, whereunto our Ancestors recours'd in resembling Exigencies. And lest your Lordship should suspect these to be our own solitary thoughts, we are not ashamed to acknowledge, that the Presentments of severall Grand-Juries, and the desires of the Sea-men in this County, urged this Addresse; which shall be pursued with all due testimonies of a Cordiall Adhesion to your Lordship in order thereunto.

This letter was delivered at St. Albans, Jan. 18, 1659 by Sir Henry Feron, Baronet, Robert Brook, and William Bloys Esquires.

LONDON, Printed for Thomas Dring. 1659.

Document #4

The humble desires the Knights, Gentlemen, Ministers, Free-holders and Inhabitants of the County and Burrough of Leicester. Delivered to His EXCELLENCY, The Lord Generall Monck, At St Albans the Thirtieth day of January, 1659. by George Fawnt Esquire, High Sheriffe of the said County, William Bootbby, Richard Orton, and Richard Halford Esquires, entrusted for that purpose by the Body of the whole County.

We the Knights, Gentlemen, Ministers, Free-holders, and Inhabitants, of the County of Leicester humbly conceiving, that the first Force put upon the Parliament, hath been an encouragement and occasion to all the rest: And finding that your Excellency (under God) hath been the principall means, for repairing the last interruption, are the more encouraged to desire your assistance, in the promoting of these our just desires, as a visible means of an happy Peace and Settlement of these Nations. And whereas every free-born person of England is supposed to be present in Parliament, by the Knights and Burgesses of the place where he liveth, and thereby is persumed to give his consent in all things that passe in Parliament. There is not (as we are credibly informed) one Knight for all the Counties in Wales, nor for divers Counties in England, and some of them the greatest in England, as that of Yorkshire. We therefore desire, that all vacant places be supplied, whether they became vacant by death, judgment of Parliament: And that those that were secluded by force in the year 1648 may sit again. And that no previous Oath or engagement be put upon any, that is chosen by his Country to sit and vote freely in Parliament.

That the fundamentall Laws of England, the Priviledges of Parliament, the Liberties of the people, and the Property of Goods, may be asserted and defended, according to the first Declaration of Parliament, when they undertook the War; and no Taxes or Free-quarter imposed upon any, without Authority of Parliament.

That the true Protestant Religion may be professed and defended, all Heresies, Sects, and Schisms, discountenanced and suppressed; a lawfull succession of godly and able Ministers continued and encouraged; and the two Universities, and all Colledges in both of them, preserved and countenanced.

That a fitting and speedy course be taken, for paying and discharging the Arrears of such Officers and Souldiers, as submit to Authority of Parliament, and they may be speedily reduced to a lesser number, for easing of the great Taxes and Burthens of these Nations.

LONDON, Printed for Henry Chase, in Chancery-Lane. 1659.

Document #5

A Letter Agreed unto and subscribed by the Gentlemen, Ministers, Freeholders and Seamen of the County of Suffolk. Presented To the Right Honorable, the Lord Mayor, Aldermen, and Common Councell of the City of London. Assembled, January 30th 1659.

RIGHT HONORABLE

Please you to accept this Paper as a testimony, that we are highly and gratefully sensible of those Breathings and Essaies towards Peace, which your Renowned City has lately declared to the World: And we earnestly wish, that our serious and unanimous Concurrence, may ripen them to a perfect Accomplishment. We are willing to consider it as an Omen of Mercy, when we observe the Nation in generall, lifting up its Vowes to Heaven for a Free and Full PARLIAMENT. 'Tis that alone, in its Genuine Sense, which our Laws prescribe and present to us, as the great Patron and Guardian of our Persons, Liberties, and Proprieties, and whatsoever else is justly pretious to us. And if God shall, by your hand, lead us to such an obtainment, after-Ages shall blesse your Memory. 'Tis superfluous to spread before you, your Merchandise decay'd, your Trade declin'd, your Estates wither'd. Are there not many within your Walls, or near them, that in your ears deplore such miseries as these? Your Lordship may believe, that our Prayers and Persons shall gladly promote all lawfull means for our Recovery. And we entreat, that this cheerfull suffrage of ours may be annex'd, as a Labell to your Honourable Intendments.

This Letter was delivered according to its Superscription, by Robert Broke, Philip Parker, and Thomas Bacon, Esquires.

LONDON, Printed for Thomas Dring. 1659

Document #6

Wee the KNIGHTS, GENTLEMEN, MINISTERS, AND FREE-HOLDERS Of the County of Warwick.

Being deeply affected with, and sadly sensible of the present Miseries, which both our selves and the whole Nation groan under, We can no longer forbear to express our Griefs, and Declare our Desires and Thoughts of the most probable means (by Gods assistance) to give some remedy to our present sufferings, and prevent those yet greater Calamities which threaten our speedy and utter Ruine.

The cause of our present Calamities, (we conceive) proceeds from the many revolutions, through Male-Administration of Government, and want of the right Constitution of Parliaments: And that after all our great and intolerable Sufferings, and vast expence of Blood and Treasure, for our Rights and Liberties, and Priviledges of Parliament (which we take to be the good Old Cause) we, with most of the Counties of this Nation, have not our Representatives in a Free Parliament:

We therefore do declare, That we shall not consent to pay any Tax or Imposition, but by our Representatives freely elected, according to the fundamental Laws of this Nation; It being the Indubitate and Indisputable Right of all the free born people of England, that no Tax or Imposition whatsoever, be put upon, or exacted from them, but by their consents had by their Representatives in Parliament.

And we further declare, That we heartily desire the burying of all Animosities and Differences, by a full land General Act of Oblivion and Indempnity: And consideration to be had of Purchasers claiming by Act of Parliament.

And, That no Officer or Souldier who hath ventured his life for the freedome of his Country, and shall continue faithful to those principles, should be hereby discouraged, We also declare, that we shall freely and willingly consent that all such shall receive their Arrears, and be continued so long as the Parliament shall think fit, in order to the safety and preservation of the Nation. And that such Liberty be allowed to Tendere Consciences as is agreeable to the Revealed Will of God in the Holy Scriptures.

We also Declare, That we shall not be wanting to our utmost powers, by all lawful wayes and means, to endevour the effecting of these our Just Desires; And shall think nothing too dear to hazard for the Redemption of our undoubted Rights. And hoping that our most Gracious God hath yet a Mercy for this bleeding Nation, We trust that he will more especially move the hearts of those into whose hands he hath put the most power. And that his Excellency General MONCK, with the honorable City of LONDON, together with all the good people of the Three Nations, will concurre with us in these so just and reasonable things, whose peace, Prosperity and Safety is equally concerned with ours.

(Subscribed by many Thousand hands.)

London, printed for R.L. at the White Lyon in St. Pauls Church-yard. 1660.

Document #7

DECLARATION Of the Nobility, Gentry, Ministry, and Commonalty of the County of Kent. Together with the City and County of Canterbury, the City of Rochester, and the Ports within the said County.

Having with sadness weighed the multiplied calamities wherein we are at present involved, how friendless we are Abroad, and how divided at home; the loud and heart-piercing cries of the poore, and the disability of the better sort to relieve them; the total decay and subversion of Trade, together with the forfeiture and loss of the honor and reputation of the Nation, and (what is more dear to us then all these) the apparent hazard of the Gospel through the prodigious growth of Blasphemies, Heresies and Schism, all which own their birth to the instability of our Governors, and the unsettlement of our Government. Lastly, how in all these, an universal ruine threatneth us, and wil (if not timely prevented) doubtless overwhelm us. We thought it our bounden duties, both as Christians, out of tenderness to our Religion; as English men, to our country; and as Friends, to our selves and our Relations, to represent and publish to the world our just griefs for, and our lively resentments of this our deplorable condition, and to seek all lawful and probable means to remedy and redress the same.

Wherefore having the leading Examples of the renowned Cities of London and Exeter, together with the Counties of the West before our eyes; and the clamours and out-cries of the People alwaies in our ears, (whereof the one encourageth, and the other enforceth us to this our Declaration) we thought that we would not be silent at such a time, when our silence would speak us to be either Assentors to our own ruine, or Abettors of such proceedings as have neither Law nor equity to support them.

We therefore, the Nobility, Gentry, Ministry, and Commonality of the County of Kent, together with the City and County of Canterbury, the City of Rochester, and the Ports within the said County, do by these Presents unanimously Declare, That our desires are for a Full and Free PARLIAMENT, as the onely probable means, under God, to lead us out of this Maze and Labyrinth of confusions, in which we are at present engag'd; that is, that the old secluded Members, so many of them are surviving, may be readmitted into the House, and that there may be a free Election of others to supply the places of those which are dead, without any Oath, or engagement previous to their entrance, these we shall own as the true Representatives of the People; these we shall with our Lives and Fortunes, to the uttermost of our power, assist, and with all cheerfulness submit to, and acquiess in whatsoever they shall Enact or Ordain.

Thus concluding, that all publick spirited men, and good Patriots, wil with all readiness join and concur with us in a matter of so universal concernment, and that we shal find Opposition from none but such as prefer their own private Interests; and temporal respects, to their Religion and laws of the land; we shal as boldly subscribe our Names as we do heartily declare our Desires.

ADVERTISEMENT

The forward zeal of some well-disposed persons, to express their Cordial and unanimous Concurrence with their Countrymen of the several Counties and Cities of England; having caused a Declaration imperfect, in a very weighty and material Clause thereof, to be Printed and published, in the name of the county of KENT, &c. It was thought fit, that the genuine and true copy of the said Declaration should be set forth, as it was intended to be presented to the Speaker, and to the present great Arbitrator of the Nations peace and happiness, General Monck; but through the mis-informations of some unquiet spirits, (who while they may have leave to accuse, will leave no man innocent, nor the State without trouble) the persons of many Gentlemen are secured, and others threatened, by a great force marcht into the Country, the Presentation was necessarily omitted, and the Names and Scriptions not exposed to publick view, for reasons very obvious and evident.

Document #8

His Excellency General Monk, The Congratulation and Address of us the Knights, Divines, Free-Holders, and others of the County of Bucks.

Humbly Sheweth,

That with all possible Gratitude we admire the wise and gracious Dispensation of things by Almighty God, who hath moved your self, and other the worthy Officers with you to such just and honourable Resolutions, as to put your selves into the Breach then, when Tyranny, Irreligion, and all Confusion like a mighty Flood were ready to break in upon us ... Our Credit abroad is impaired, our Trade at home decayed, our Fundamental Laws violated, our primitive Apostolick Religion endangered; the cause of all which we humbly conceive is the force and violence put upon the Parliament in the year 1648. And since to obviate all which evils we request the total removal of that force, and that all surviving Members so secluded, be restored to the discharge of their Trust, Vacancies be supplyed by free Elections according to Law, that no previous Oaths or Engagments be put upon any of them that shall be chosen to fit, and Vote in Parliament. Sir; This is our desire, and as we observe 'tis the voice of the whole people, and that is the voice of God; we doubt not but that you have been reserved for such a time as this; in pursuance of which we are ready to hazard our Lives and Estates.

Document #9

A Declaration and Protest of the Lords, Knights, and Gentlemen In the Counties of Chester, Salop, Stafford, & c. Against all Assembles which impose Taxes upon the People without their consent by their Representatives in a Full, Free and Legall PARLIAMENT.

Having with great trouble, observed the grievances of the People in these late revolutions, and being encouraged by the common consent of this Nation (securing our late endeavours) in their frequent Addresses unto his Excellency the Lord Generall Monck, We have consulted, and thereupon, with them, do declare our Protest against all Powers or Assemblies whatsoever, who impose Taxes upon the People, without their consent by their Representatives, duely elected in Full, Free and Legal Parliament; and that any should seem to countenance that force put upon the Parliament (now called the secluded Members) in the year 1648, by Cromwell and his Conspirators, seemes unreasonable unto us, in that they have publickly disowned the like force since put upon themselves as unlawful: Therefore how the Minor part of National Councils can exclude the Major (which was ever acknowledged the whole) we leave to the consideration of all sober men, and say, That the People ought not to be limitted in their Elections, by unheard of Qualification, contrary to the known Lawes of England: neither that the Members so Elected or forcibly Secluded, should be debarr'd the discharge of their Trust, by any previous Oathes or Engagements whatsoever; for that they were the first Assertors of our Rights and Freedome of Parliaments, unto which they bound themselves (the Nations complying) by Solemne Leagues and Covenants) not to destroy, but to preserve) The breach of which by others we find hath brought these Calamities upon us, all which we hope will be call'd to remembrance, and repented of, as becometh Christians, that at last the Nations may have peace and be setled.

LONDON, Printed for Thomas Poole. 1659.

Document #10

LETTER AND DECLARATION Of the Gentry of the County of NORFOLK, and the County of the City of Norwich,

To his Excellency the Lord Generall MONK.

Right Honorable,

Wee the Gentry of the County of Norfolk, and of the County and City of Norwich, do cordially rejoyce, with many others of these Counties, and of the Nation, for your Excellencies return into your Native Countrey with honour and safety: And that the late Differences in the Armies are now so happily composed without blood-shed; We are desirous to blesse our good God for these mercies, and to acquaint your Lordship, That we have signified the Resentment of our grievances to the Speaker of the Parliament; A true Copie whereof we have here inclosed, sent to your Excellency, least any persons should in our absence misrepresent us or our intentions to your Lordship: We rest.

THE DECLARATION

We the Gentry of the County of Norfolk, and County and City of Norwich, Being deeply affected with the sence of our sad Distractions and Divisions both in Church and State; And wearied with the Miseries of an unnaturall Civil War, The too frequent Interruptions of Government, the Impositions of severall heavy Taxes, And the loud out-cryes of multitudes of undone and almost famished people, occasioned by a generall decay of Trade which hath spread itself throughout the whole Nation, and these Counties in particular; And having met together and consulted what may best remedy and remove Our and the Nations present grievances and Distractions; do humbly conceive, That the chief Expedient, will be, the Recalling of those Members that were secluded in 1648, and sate before the Force put upon the Parliament (We of this County of Norfolk, being by such Seclusion deprived of any person to represent us in Parliament) and also by filling up the vacant places thereof; And all to be admitted without any Oath or Engagement, previous to their Entrance; Which being done, We shall be ready to acquiesce and submit in all things to the Judgment and Authority of Parliament; Without which Authority, the People of England cannot be obliged to pay any Taxes.

The Letter to General Monk, and this Declaration was signed by

Thomas Lord Richardson, Edmond Bacon, Philip Woodhouse, John Hobart, N. Le Strange ...

With many hundreds more of the Knights, Gentry, Citizens, and Free-holders.

LONDON. 1660.

Document #11

The Declaration of the Gentlemen, Free-holders and Inhabitants of the County of Bedford.

Wee the Gentlemen, Free-holders, and Inhabitants of the County of BEDFORD, being truly sensible of the heavy pressures that we lye under, having all our Civill and Religious Rights and Liberties daily Invaded, cannot in this common day of Calamity, be silent, but, with the rest of the Nation, make some enquiry after the way of Peace and settlement: And having met, and considered thereof, do propose, as the most probable means, under God, to compose all our Differences, and cement all our Breaches both in Church and State, the assembling of a Full and Free PARLIAMENT, without any previous Oaths, or Engagements, or Qualifications whatsoever, (saving what was in the year 1648, before the Force put upon the Parliament.) Or, the re-admitting of the Secluded Members to the Execution of their Trusts, with a full and free Supply of their Vacancies by Death. And untill one of these be done, we do declare, We shall not hold ourselves engaged to pay the Taxes imposed upon us, without our Consents so first had in Parliament.

Printed at LONDON, 1659.

Document #12

To His EXCELLENCY The Lord General Monck. The Unanimous Representation of the Apprentices and young men Inhabiting in the City of London.

Humbly Sheweth,

That the glory of our Nation, and the greatest comfort of our Lives in our Civil Interests, consists in the Priviledges and Liberties to which we were born, and which are the undoubted Inheritance of all the free people of England, among which the grand and Essential Priviledge which discriminates free men from slaves, is the interest which every man hath in the Legislative power of the Nation, by their Representatives assembled in Parliament: without which, however we may flatter our selves, or be flatter'd by others, we are truly no better than Vassals govern'd by the will and pleasure of those who have no relation to us or our common Interest.

Now how much this dear Priviledge of the People hath been assaulted by the open violence of some, and secret artifice of others, and to what a deplorable condition we are brought at this present period, when heavy taxes are imposing upon mens Estates, and new Laws upon our Persons without any consent of the people had in a free Parliament, and how generally through the said distractions in Government trading is decayed, and how much we are likely to suffer therby in our times and places, we cannot but Remonstrate to your Excellency, constrain'd through the sense of our present sufferings and apprehensions of greater to implore your assistance most humbly beseeching your Excellency by that ancient love you have born to your Native Countrey, zeal to our Liberties, by that great renowne you have lately gain'd in opposing the cruel Rageing of the Sword by the common cries of the People, and by the hopes and chearful Expectation of all England now fixt upon you; And, lastly, by your own personal concern in the same common cause as a free-born English man, that you would please to use those great advantages Divine Providence hath now put into your hands to the securing your Native Countrey from those dangerous usurpations, and preserving us in those Liberties to which we were borne. That no Tax may be imposed, nor new Law made, nor old abolisht but with the consents of the people had by their Representatives in Parliament, freely to be chosen without terrour or limitations, and freely to sit without any Oath or engagement previous to their entrance, without which special Liberties the Parliament cannot in any construction be esteemed the free Assembly of the People; And by your Excellency's asserting of those our undoubted rights in your present advantages, you will certainly by the blessing of God, and unanimous concurrence of the People accomplish our ends, and will thereby gaine the hearts and hands of the whole Nation, and the City in particular, and purchase to yourself a name that shall make every true English man call you blessed, and Posterity shall hereafter delight to recount the famous Acts of their worthy Patriot.

This was delivered to his Excellency at St. Albans, Thursday, February 2, 1659. by persons Elected for that purpose, and had a very cheerful Reception.

LONDON, Printed by tho. Ratcliffe, Anno Dom. 1659.

Document #13

A Letter and Declaration of the Lords, Knights, Gentlemen and Ministers, of the County of York, and of the Lord Mayor, Aldermen and Common-Councell of the City of York, presented to Generall MONCK, Feb. 17th 1659. at His Quarters at Drapers Hall London, by Sir Thomas Wharton Knight, Brother to the Lord Wharton, John Dawney, Thomas Harrison, and John Legard Esquiers, As also a Letter, with the said Declaration inclosed delivered, by the said Gentlemen to the Lord Mayor directed to him, and to the Common-Councell of the Citty of LONDON. To His EXCELLENCY The Lord Generall Monck.

My Lord,

We find ourselves constrained by writing to supply the Omission of acquainting your Lordship with our thoughts and desires when you passed through our County, which we had then done, if upon so short notice we could have met for a mutuall Understanding; Your Lordship will find in the Inclosed Declaration the sum of our Apprehensions. We thought it not necessary to multiply particulars, but leave all other things to a duly constituted Parliament; neither have we been sollicitous to multiply Subscriptions, trusting more to the weight of the Proposalls than to the number of Subscribers; yet we may safely affirm this to be the sense of the Generallity of the County and City, as your Lordship sees it is of others. We have onely to add our earnest desires to your Lordship, that you would be pleased to further the Accomplishment of what we have represented with such seasonable speed, as that the fear of Friends, and the hopes of Enemies concerning a dangerous Confusion amongst us, may be prevented.

Your Lordships very humble servants,
Thomas Fairfax, Faulconberge
Bar. Bourchier, Vice comes.
Christopher Topham Mayor, & c.

THE DECLARATION

We being deeply sensible of the grevious Pressures under which we lye, and extream dangers we are exposed to at this time, through the violent alteration of our Government, the Mutilation and Interruption of Parliaments: And having no Representatives to expresse or remedy our grievances, have thought it meet (according to the examples of other Counties). . . . And until this, or One of these be done, We cannot hold our selves obliged to pay the Taxes that are or shall be imposed. We not enjoying the Fundamentall Right of this Nation to consent to our own Laws by Equall Representatives.

Subscribed by

Thomas Lord Fairfax, Sir Fran. Boynton, Barr., Thomas Hutton . . .

The said Declaration was also subscribed by the Aldermen and Common-Councell of the City of York.

Document #14

The DECLARATION of the County of Oxon to His Excellency The Lord General Monck. We the Gentlemen, Ministers, Freeholders, and others of the County of Oxon, having a long time groaned under heavy Burthens, do now hereby Declare the Resentments we have of our Grievances, and our just desires as the most visible means of a happy Peace and Settlement of these Nations.

Whereas every Free-born Subject of England is supposed to be present in Parliament, by the Knights of Burgesses of the place of his Residence; and thereby is presumed, to consent to all things that passe in Parliament; it now so hapning, that many Counties are wholly left out, either by Death or Seclusion.

I. We therefore desire, That all places vacant by Death, may be supplyed, and those that were Secluded in 1648, may be re-admitted, that thereby we may be taken into the Share of Government by our Representatives; We having at this time but one of nine, and hint a Burgess, taken up with the Publick Concern of the Chair, from minding our particular Grievances.

II. That no unusual previous Oath may be put upon any that is to sit in Parliament.

III. That no Tax may be put upon us without our Free consent in Parliament.

IV. That the Fundamental Laws of the Land, the Priviledges of Parliament, the Liberty of the Subject, the property of Goods, may be asserted and defended, according to the first Declaration of Parliament when they undertook the War.

V. That the True Protestant Religion may be professed and defended, a lawful Succession of Godly and Able Ministers continued and encouraged, and the two Universities, and all Colledges in or belonging to either of them, Preserved and Countenanced.

These our Just Rights we lay Claime to, as Free-born English-men, and resolve to assert.

This Declaration was signed by above Five thousand considerable Inhabitants of the said County, and delivered to Gen. Monk, on Munday, Febr. 13. at his Quarters at the Glasshouse in Broadstreet London, by the Lord Falkland, Sir Anthony Cope, Mr. James Fiennes, Captain William Cope, Henry Jones, Edward Hungerford Esquires., and other Persons of Quality.

LONDON, Printed for John Starkey, at the Miter, near the middle Temple-gate in Fleetstreet, 1660.

Sources of Documents

1. January 28, 1659–50, Public Record Office, London, *State Papers Domestic, 1625–1665*, SP18/219, 42.

2. January 28, 1659–60, Public Record Office, London, *State Papers Domestic, 1625–1665*, SP18/219, 43.

3. January 28, 1659–60, Public Record Office, London, *State Papers Domestic, 1625–1665*, SP18/219, 44.

4. January 13, 1659, Public Record Office, London, *State Papers Domestic, 1625–1665*, SP18/219, 45.

5. January 30, 1659–60, Public Record Office, London, *State Papers Domestic, 1625–1665*, SP18/219, 46.

6. 1659–60, Public Record Office, London, *State Papers Domestic, 1625–1665*, SP18/219, 54.

7. 1659–1660, Public Record Office, London, *State Papers Domestic, 1625–1665*, SP18/219, 55.

8. 1659–60, Public Record Office, London, *State Papers Domestic, 1625–1665*, SP18/219, 56.

9. 1659–60, Public Record Office, London, *State Papers Domestic, 1625–1665*, SP18/219, 57.

10. 1659–60, Public Record Office, London, *State Papers Domestic, 1625–1665*, 1659–60, SP18/219, 58.

11. 1659–60, Public Record Office, London, *State Papers Domestic, 1625–1665*, PS18/219, 59.

12. February 2, 1659, Public Record Office, London, *State Papers Domestic, 1625–1665*, SP18/219, 60.

13. February 17, 1659, Public Record Office, London, *State Papers Domestic, 1625–1665*, SP18/219, 75.

14. February 13, 1660, Public Record Office, London, *State Papers Domestic, 1625–1665*, SP18/219, 57.

Acknowledgments

Special appreciation is due:

- The National Endowment for the Humanities and the Dewitt Wallace Reader's Digest Fund, which awarded me a Teacher-Scholar grant for the 1992–1993 academic year to do the reading and research to create this unit of study,
- Jefferson County School District R-1, Lakewood, Colorado, which supported the award by granting a year-long sabbatical,
- Marjorie McIntosh, professor of Early Modern England, University of Colorado, Boulder, who guided my efforts, and
- Charles Anderson, my husband and best friend, who provided constant encouragement.

41

Coffee House Discourse

Sammy Crawford

Sammy Crawford places students in a coffee house setting where the conversation is witty and engaging but the issues and ideas discussed are those of the seventeenth- and eighteenth-century philosophers.

This lesson fits into my second semester of world history following the Renaissance. The philosophes are important in the Enlightenment, and having students play roles of the thinkers helps them see the connections between their own lives and interests and those of people who lived and thought and discussed issues (like censorship and who should govern and to what ends) a few hundred years ago. As a global event the ideas discussed had long-range ramifications for revolutions that continue to occur, starting with our own in 1776 and continuing today.

Background

The Enlightenment, or Age of Reason, was marked by attempts to apply laws of nature and reason to all aspects of social and political life—particularly government, education, and censorship. Throughout much of the seventeenth and eighteenth centuries, philosophers and scientists had chances to meet, hear lectures about one another's discoveries, and discuss ideas. Lively discussions took place in coffee houses and salons. Major philosophers of the time include Thomas Hobbes, an English political theorist; John Locke, an English political theorist; Voltaire, a French philosophe, Baron de Montesquieu, a French lawyer and aristocrat; and Jean Jacques Rousseau, a French philosophe who wrote and discussed ideas about education and political theory.

Thomas Hobbes believed that people act out of self-interest. He sought to apply basic laws, similar to those newly discovered in the physical world, to governments. He felt that a strong government must be formed to set rules that control human nature. Without strong rules, people would act selfishly and compete violently. He maintained that a strong rule was necessary to avoid total disorder.

John Locke believed the purpose of government was to protect what he called "natural rights" of its citizens. All people, said Locke, are born free and equal, with a right to life, liberty, and the pursuit of happiness. If a government fails to protect the rights of its citizens, then the people have the right to overthrow that government and establish a better one. Locke's ideas on knowledge and education were closely related to his political ideas. He believed that all children were born without knowledge and would be shaped as adults depending on the kind of experiences they had as children. He compared the mind of a child at birth to a blank slate, filled by experience. Therefore, education was very important.

Voltaire, whose real name was François Marie Arouet, wrote stories and essays in which he attacked and mocked intolerance and superstition. He opposed censorship and vowed to fight for tolerance, especially of different religions. Voltaire believed the best form of government was a monarchy in which the ruler was familiar with the teachings of the philosophes and respected the people's rights.

Baron de Montesquieu admired English freedoms and in a book called *The Spirit of the Laws* put forth the principle of *separation of powers,* the division of authority among three branches of government. He proposed a legislative branch to make the laws, an executive branch to carry out the laws, and a judiciary to interpret the laws, judge lawbreakers, and handle disputes between individuals. He believed individual liberty would be safeguarded by preventing any one group of individuals from gaining control of the government.

Jean Jacques Rousseau proposed new changes in education and social change. He felt that "progress" in the arts and sciences was part of the way of life that corrupted people's natural goodness. He drew a sharp distinction between "civilized people" and what he called the "noble savage." Rousseau argued that people who lived outdoors, in harmony with nature, were happier, less greedy and selfish than people who lived in a civilized society and were unhappy, insecure, and selfish. He believed children should grow up in the country and be allowed to enjoy their youth. He did not, however, believe in democracy. He agreed with many that the common people were incapable of ruling themselves.

Activity for Students

1. Form five groups of students and tell them they are going to have a coffee house discourse, representing the ideas and the philosophes of the Enlightenment. This discourse is meant to provide wise, witty, and intelligent conversation among all citizens represented. Encourage or assign students to do outside reading on the Enlightenment and on the philosophers and how their ideas are different from each other, particularly in the areas of government, education, and censorship. Assign each of the groups to represent one of the five philosophers: Locke, Hobbes, Montesquieu, Voltaire, or Rousseau. Give students time to digest the basic ideas of their philosopher by thinking about his main ideas toward government, education, and censorship. Have each group of students make a sign for their group that can be taped to the front of a student desk so that others can see and remember which philosopher they are representing.

2. Ask students to form a large circle with each philosopher represented by a student group and their sign. Begin the discourse by asking each student in each group to summarize in one or two sentences the basic ideas of his or her philosopher. After all students have spoken, give them five minutes to discuss within their groups attitudes toward government held by their philosopher. Starting around the circle again, ask each student to summarize an idea about government as representative of his or her philosopher. After a short time to discuss in groups, ask students to ask a question of other groups that might be a question a philosopher of the Enlightenment would have asked. After this discussion, follow the same procedure with ideas toward education and censorship.

3. For the final round of the activity, have all the students in turn summarize the ideas of the philosopher they have chosen that they think are most interesting or controversial.

4. The homework assignment could be to have each student write the ideas he or she found most appealing in government, education, and censorship.

For Further Reading

Perry, Marvin. *A History of the World* (Boston: Houghton Mifflin, 1985). Most world history textbooks include majority of information with different details.

Impact of the Europeans upon the City-Systems of the World

Corinne Lathrop Gilb

In terms of political history, the European colonial impact around the world is understood. But Corinne Lathrop Gilb uses the city to evaluate the impact of European imperialism in terms of changes in city-systems.

The purpose of this lesson is to understand how the European networks of trade, missionary activity, and colonial government helped reshape the city-systems of the world and how they contributed to globalization.

Main Changes in City-Systems in World History

There has been a series of stages in world history, each with its own city-system(s). Before Europeans colonized the world, a number of different city-systems had come and gone. Over the four centuries of European colonialism, new city-systems were created. It is important to understand what they were and what created them.

1. Cities had existed in the world a long time before Europeans colonized. True cities began in Mesopotamia around 3500 B.C.E. Cities existed in Egypt, India, and China long before the Christian era. There were cities in Mesoamerica and Peru long before Columbus sailed to America in 1492.

When cities had persistent links with one another, the links helped form a "system of cities." City-systems changed when new kingdoms or empires arose, when trade routes changed, and when religions spread.

In class, discuss how different kinds of systems (political, trading, religious) use different sets of cities that sometimes do not completely overlap. For example, trade routes normally cut across political boundaries.

2. After 1492 Europeans built trading stations in various parts of the world, sometimes in or near existing cities. For example, the British placed stations at Surat, Bombay, Madras, and Calcutta in India near existing Indian settlements. For a while, the Portuguese held Malacca. Later on, the Portuguese used Macao as a base for their Far East trade. In the nineteenth century the British developed Hong Kong, and several European countries established treaty ports in China. The Dutch developed Cape Town in South Africa as a supply base for ships. In West Africa, Europeans often built trading stations along the Atlantic coast or on islands off the coast.

European bases needed some form of government, so administrative centers were created. Calcutta became such a center for the British trading company in India. The French used Pondicherry on India's southeast coast; the Portuguese used Goa on India's southwest coast; and the Spanish took over the Philippines and made Manila their capital there. The Dutch used Batavia in what is now Indonesia. Later on, the British had secondary administrative centers in Penang and then Singapore off the Malaysian coast. In the New World, the Spanish built up ports at Vera Cruz and Acapulco, Cartagena and Panama for trade. The Portuguese developed several ports along Brazil's coast. In Mexico, the Spanish took over the Aztec capital, Tenochtitlán, and renamed it Mexico City. In Peru, they built a new capital, Lima, near the coast to replace the inland Inca capital of Cuzco. The capital of Brazil was first in the northeast and then in Rio de Janeiro.

Religious orders and priests went out to various places in the world, sometimes using their own centers—for example, the French in North America—near forts but separate.

In an examination on a map, locate the mentioned cities and ports.

Discuss differences from what had been before.

3. Cities overseas were closely linked by trade to particular cities in Europe: Lisbon in Portugal; Cadiz and Seville in Spain; Bordeaux, La Rochelle, Nantes, L'Orient, and Rouen in France; Amsterdam in the Netherlands; London, and later also Bristol and Liverpool in England. Governance was directed out of European capitals. Roman Catholic religious orders looked to Rome. These linkages persisted for a long time, often down to the present.

Trace on the map linkages between European and overseas cities. The linkages were reinforced by law and language and personal ties.

4. To have more certain supplies for trade the Europeans developed mines and plantations. Systematic links were developed between these overseas capitals and ports. The spread of plantations in South America, the West Indies, and later in North America created a new market for slaves brought from Africa.

In class, discuss how world city-systems evolved to exploit natural resources and replenish the money supply of Europe.

5. By the late eighteenth century, government in European colonies was becoming more complex. For example, in Spanish America there were representatives of the Spanish government in Cuba, La Plata, and Chile, as well as in Peru and Mexico City. As more areas of India came under British control, the capital of the trading company governing British India was centered in Calcutta. When Britain tried to establish firmer governmental control over thirteen of her American colonies, they declared their independence in 1776. After they agreed on a new constitution, they built a new capital in Washington, D.C.

In class, discuss all the different levels of capitals there might be within a single country and the way they are linked to one another.

6. Since European countries often fought wars with one another, colonies often changed hands. This caused readjustments in trade, government, and religion and in city-systems. For example, the towns in the maritime colonies on Canada's east coast became more important when the British took over Canada from the French in 1763. Halifax became an important naval base and commercial seaport.

Write a brief essay about how changes in the colonial power controlling a city might affect the city's residents.

Note on a map of the world which colonies changed hands.

7. By 1800 many cities in the world were already closely linked to western Europe. Although many former colonies in the Western Hemisphere won independence between 1776 and 1830, they had continuing cultural and economic links to Europe. During the nineteenth century, Europe developed new colonies and built new cities in Australia, New Zealand, Asia, and Africa, and established greater control over the Middle East. New steamship and railroad lines linked the world's networks of cities more closely together so that they were more economically and culturally interdependent. The building of the Suez Canal (completed in 1869) and the Panama Canal (completed in 1914) made the world seem smaller. So did the telegraph, radio, and telephone.

Today, television, satellites, fiber-optic cable, and computers draw the linkages more tightly together.

Locate new nineteenth-century colonies and their major cities on the map.

Discuss in class: Is the world held together by one big network of cities? Or are there subsystems? If the latter, why?

8. When India, Asia, Africa, and the Middle East became independent again in the twentieth century, their cities were linked to global networks of trade and communication. Today, the networks are less dominated by Europe, but they would be different today if the Europeans had not helped to create them.

Write an essay speculating about how they would be different and why.

Further Discussion

How do the global networks operate? (The role of airplanes, radio, satellites, fiber-optic cables under the oceans; the role of multinational corporations)

Why did Amsterdam replace Antwerp, then London replace Amsterdam, then New York City replace London as the most central city for world trade? (Antwerp as the center for Portuguese and Spanish trade when the Spanish rulers held the Low Countries; Amsterdam as a center when the Netherlands won independence from Spain and began aggressive commerce; London, because it could marshal the rest of Britain for resources and as a market and because of the growing size of the British Empire; New York City when the British were distracted by World War I)

Will Shanghai or Hong Kong be the new center of world trade? Why?

How would global networks and city networks be different if the Europeans had not helped create them?

Project to Be Completed by the End of the Term

Prepare two outline maps of the world, one for c. 1492 and the other for some time in the seventeenth century. On the first, using information from the lesson plan, put dots where the major cities were in the Western Hemisphere, Africa, and India. On the other, use different-colored pencils for the Spanish, Portuguese, French, Dutch, and English empires; put dots for the major cities in each empire, including capitals and ports in each of the major European countries. Also locate Rome. Draw lines showing the major trade routes.

On a third map, mark where the Suez (1869) and Panama (1914) canals were built. Draw lines showing the trade routes that used these canals.

In teams of two or four, students should select a city, research its past, and design a pavilion for a 1900 world trade fair. The purpose is to provide the public with basic information about the city and its past and to display its products, its cultural achievements, and its modern conveniences.

Suggested Reading

Collier, Simon, Harold Blakemore, and Thomas E. Skidmore, eds. *The Cambridge Encyclopedia of Latin America.* London: Cambridge University Press, 1985. Has maps, pictures, and bibliography.

Oliver, Roland, and Michael Crowder, eds. *The Cambridge Encyclopedia of Africa.* London: Cambridge University Press, 1981. Has maps, pictures, and bibliography.

Robinson, Francis, ed. *The Cambridge Encyclopedia of India.* Cambridge: Cambridge University Press, 1989.

References

Curtin, Philip D. *Cross-Cultural Trade in World History.* New York: Cambridge University Press, 1984.

Vance, James E., Jr. *This Scene of Man.* New York: Harper's College Press.

Memories of Silk and Straw

Environmental Change in Small-Town Japan

Robert Cummings

Bob Cummings uses Japanese oral histories to examine modernization. Students design projects from the oral histories of villagers who were living in a small Japanese farming community as it became absorbed into a larger urban system.

In the past two years of teaching "Modern East Asian History" to upper-class cadets at the Air Force Academy, I have assigned one project that has excited the interest of every student and helped him or her to discover what Japanese modernization has meant for other than the *genro* and important personalities found in most textbooks. Going beyond a mere review of Dr. Junichi Saga's *Memories of Silk and Straw*,[1] this project makes the stories from a small Japanese town come to life. In fact, the students themselves bring the stories to life with their own creativity. This chapter explains how I've made this project successful in my classroom and will, I hope, inspire others to create similar creative and academically effective projects. Following are the exact instructions to the students contained in the syllabus:

The *Memories of Silk and Straw* Project is to be a creative learning experience based on your reading of this account of early twentieth-century Japan. Using the personal interviews contained in the book (try to integrate as many as possible), develop a segment of a movie script, a scene from an opera, an act of a play, a song cycle, an epic poem, or some other innovative project that captures the spirit of life in a small Japanese community undergoing modernization. Format is flexible, but shoot for something around ten minutes if to be performed. Creative writing projects may be around five to ten pages. All projects will be presented to the class. Approve your proposed format with the instructor beforehand. Your grade will be based on historical content (how accurately you incorporate the book), inventive format, and effective completion. The top two authors will receive a special award.

Memories contains eight segments with fifty-eight stories.[2] I suggest to the students that they should use *at least* seven stories for their particular project, and of course that they should read all the interviews, because (1) they're extremely interesting, and (2) many of the stories are interrelated, and reading them all gives one a better feel for the life of the village. I have allowed collaborative efforts as well, with two to a group. I tell both group members that they will each receive the same grade, and they will each be expected to put in the same effort as one person working alone; whereas an individual, if creating something to be performed, is expected to produce about ten minutes of material, a group project should shoot for twenty minutes.

The students perform, explain, or read aloud all projects on the assigned days. I recruit colleagues to accompany me in the classroom on presentation days to help judge and to give the students an audience for their creative work. Awarding a prize, usually a book on an Asian topic, adds an element of friendly competition to the project. I also videotape the performances, which provides material for me to review when determining grades. Grading "creativity" is naturally a difficult process but not impossible. When determining grades, I weigh the first criterion, historical content (how accurately students incorporate the book), a bit more heavily. Generally, I have found that a student's comprehension of the culture evinces itself in the quality of the product. Some students obviously will integrate stories into a narrative whole much better than others.

Results have ranged from outstanding to mediocre, while every student has enjoyed and benefited from the experience. The approximately twenty students who have completed the project have produced movies, a simulated town meeting, love stories, a song, a poster-art project, and collections of poetry (I'm still waiting for the *No* drama). Many students find themselves relating directly to a particular segment of the Japanese society. One student who loves to do woodworking immersed himself in a study of Japanese techniques of carpentry and integrated the stories involving craftsmen building houses.

At the end of each student's presentation, I direct a short class discussion on the characteristics of Japanese society that particular project has demonstrated, attempting to put the project in historical context. This is history from the "common" person's perspective—social history at its best. One can make it an even more rewarding learning experience by relating it to the material students have previously read in the more standard, statistic-filled textbooks about Meiji political, economic, and military reforms, parliamentary struggles, increases in industrial output, and other less personally captivating, but no less important, aspects of Japanese history. Students find after completing the project that they have not only discovered or resurrected creative talent long dormant, but they appreciate in a deeper way the struggles of the common person, the truly difficult, yet sometimes serene, aspects of premodern life, and the often more difficult aspects of the transition to a modern, industrial state.

Excerpts from *Memories of Silk and Straw: A Self-Portrait of Small-Town Japan*

It must have been in about 1911 or 1912 we had the terrible floods; the whole town was a shambles. The level of the Sakura rose, the river water started rushing along, and Zenikame Bridge was in danger of being washed away. Back then all bridges were made of wood, of course, and the only way to stop the whole thing lifting out of the riverbed was to weigh it down. Everyone in Omachi was asked to fetch out all their two-gallon barrels—maybe a hundred or a hundred and fifty of them in all; the fire brigade then filled the barrels with water as quickly as they could, and piled them on top of the bridge. There was terrible panic and chaos. All the roads in Omachi were underwater. The River Bizen, to the south of the Sakura, was even worse affected: all along it, from Zenikame Bridge to the hill at Shimotakatsu, there was a high wharf, and during the floods you had to walk along the top of this to avoid falling waist-deep in swirling water. The rivers have since been widened and bridges reinforced with steel struts, so there's no longer any real danger of flooding, but in the past, whenever it rained, people were terrified it might result in floods.[3]

—Mr. Ryutaro Terauchi (b. 1905), "In and Around the Rickshaw Station"

You know, in the old days the water in the lake was so much cleaner than it is now. The fishermen's houses stood in a long line along the shore and all the families used the lake water for cooking and washing; there was no need to dig any wells. The water was so clear you could see the bottom out to some distance.

The front was always a lively place then: the sand white in the bright sun, men shouting and heaving on ropes, women carrying huge baskets of fish, and kids playing and getting in the way or sometimes lending a hand. There was life in that scene. But nowadays the lakeside's almost empty; it's a sad, dead sort of place."[4]

—Mrs. Hama Suzuki (b. 1906), "Fishing Nets Three Miles Long"

I didn't usually go up the River Sakura, but on sunny days in the cherry blossom season I used to take parties of villagers on the boat, and we'd go under the railway bridge, past Nioi Bridge, and all the way up the Sakura to Mushikake. That stretch of the river was a tunnel of flowers; I don't think there's anything to match it elsewhere in Japan. The lines of cherry trees continued along both banks up as far as Mushikake Bridge. Fancy barges would float by with rich parties from Tsuchiura in them, dancing and singing and having fun with geisha. On both sides of the river there'd be rows of little stalls selling food and drink to dozens of sightseers. In full bloom, it was spectacular.

But the riverboats all went out of service a few years after the war. With so many cars and trucks around, people began to use the roads for transporting things. Most of the River Kawaguchi was filled in and made into a road, and the cherry trees along the Sakura have all disappeared. Only cars run along the Kawaguchi now. Everything's changed so much, in such a short time.[5]

—Mr. Yukio Komatsuzaki (b. 1902), "By Sail into Town"

So there you have it. The fact is that, since the postwar land reforms, life for us farmers has been far, far better than it was before. A number of schools and colleges have been built near our village, for example. And the whole world, it seems to me, has changed beyond all recognition.[6]

—Mrs. Michi Tsukamoto (b. 1901), "Sakura Village"

Background

Through absorbing personal stories such as these, Dr. Junichi Saga breathes life into the story of environmental change, both positive and negative, occurring in an area of small villages in the Kanto Plain north of Tokyo. This physician's collection of personal interviews was born of his concern that untapped resources of Japan's heritage—the elderly patients he treated daily—were slowly disappearing. Before presenting the interviews, however, Dr. Saga presents a most interesting, though undocumented, background to the area in which he inspired villagers to conjure up their memories of silk and straw.

Tsuchiura, forty miles northeast of Tokyo, was once a castle and post-station town, which gave it a moderate measure of importance during the Tokugawa period (1600–1868), for important parties would stop there on their way to Edo under the alternate attendance system. It nestles the northwest edge of Japan's second largest lake, Lake Kasumigaura. Dr. Saga, however, emphasizes the decline of the area from a historically prominent position and blames the shogunal government for "frequent and severe floods" around the lake over the past two hundred or three hundred years. The River Tone, the second or third largest river in Japan, formerly flowed from the interior highlands southeast into Edo (Tokyo) Bay. Around 1622, Japanese rulers decided to divert the river so that it flowed eastward into the Pacific Ocean to prevent flooding around Edo and to provide irrigation for agriculture in the plains area. This diversion changed the course of everyday life for residents around Tsuchiura.

Dr. Saga implies that shogunal politics may have been involved in this large environmental engineering plot and in the transformation of a formerly politically important province into an "agricultural backwater." The richly endowed province of Hitachi, in which Tsuchiura is now located, was evidently the center of "one of the strongest anti-Tokugawa clans in the vicinity of Edo," the Satake family. The

Tokugawa shoguns, whose capital was in Edo, where the River Tone often flooded, battled with the Satake family, eventually prevailing and forcibly removing the Satake far away to Akita on the very northern tip of the main island of Japan. They then gave the domain to the pro-Tokugawa Tsuchiya clan. According to Saga, though the Tsuchiya lords held important positions in the Tokugawa central government, "the fact that . . . Tsuchiura saw no notable cultural development or artistic achievements testifies to the lack of interest shown by the Tsuchiyas in their lands."[7]

While the rechanneling of the Tone succeeded in saving Edo from further flooding, it began to cause catastrophic floods in the area around Tsuchiura. In addition, sand and mud brought down by the Tone from its upper reaches eventually blocked off the main waterway joining Lake Kasumigaura to the sea. This turned it into a freshwater lake, with only one small channel that linked one part of the lake to the open sea. The lake evidently had an abundance of freshwater and saltwater fish, but the closing of sluice gates in 1973, and perhaps previous environmental changes, explain the nostalgic quality of the fishermen's stories.

The establishment of a naval air training base in the vicinity in the 1920s was another significant development in the history of the region, attested to by stories of swashbuckling aviators, "high-class" geisha, and "low-class" prostitutes.

Today, Tsuchiura is a town of concrete office buildings, apartment blocks, and over 112,000 residents. Many of the rivers have become highways. Nearby is Tsukuba Science City, a "technopolis" with two universities and no fewer than forty-five high-technology research institutes.[8] Dr. Saga has fortunately realized the precious nature of people still living who have experienced the results of these environmental changes, from the flooding, caused by a river diversion three hundred years ago, to the rapid urbanization typical of most of Japan during the twentieth century. The remarkable reminiscences of villagers who have experienced the transformation surrounding this area can personalize students' understanding of the complexities of environmental change.

Yet, while this can make an engrossing narrative of ecological impacts, history instructors must not overlook the opportunity to teach critical analysis and the proper use of sources. As previously noted, Dr. Saga's historical account of the area is undocumented; the critical reader wonders where he gets his information and if local pride might color his account. Dr. Saga, for example, does not mention in his account that the Tokugawa rulers diverted the river at least partly for irrigation purposes. Problems also exist with oral interviews. How reliable are memories sketching sixty to seventy years back? How did the relationship between the interviewer and interviewee affect the story? How accurately did the interviewer understand and record the stories?

These problems need not be a drawback in using *Memories of Silk and Straw* to teach about environmental history or the social history of Japan; in fact, high school and college students can learn much about the uses and limits of oral history. Properly using primary documents is one of the most important aspects of learning about history, and this book can be a great tool to teach students critical thinking skills. Students can use Dr. Saga's narrative and the villagers' stories to discover aspects of Japanese history, including environmental impacts of modernization, often ignored by standard textbooks; yet they must also realize the limitations and the dangers of overinterpreting primary materials. These accounts may not tell us as much about what *actually* happened in history or to the environment, as they tell us what the interviewees, and even Dr. Saga, *perceived* to have happened. Even if the memories are faulty, or Dr. Saga introduces a certain amount of bias into his historical narrative, one can glean useful information from what these people perceive about their own history.

Memories of Silk and Straw is an absorbing book of outstanding narratives. The colloquial, relaxed language will make the student feel as if he or she were personally sitting and chatting with these fascinating personalities. One feels the loss of beauty, such as cherry tree–lined waterways, which often accompanies modernization. One may also physically ache from sharing the bitter, back-breaking difficulties of a peasant's or fisherman's life, and perhaps appreciate the more leisurely lifestyle brought by modernization. Properly used, with an eye toward critical analysis, *Memories of Silk and Straw* can be a rewarding tool in teaching the personal impacts of environmental change.

Notes

1. Junichi Saga, *Memories of Silk and Straw: A Self-Portrait of Small-Town Japan* (New York: Kodansha International, 1990).
2. The segments are entitled "Around the Town," "Boatmen and Fishermen," "Shopkeepers and Tradesmen," "Women of the Town," "Geisha and Officers," "Life at the Countryside," "Crafts and Craftsmen," "At School and at Play."
3. Saga, pp. 59–60.
4. Ibid., p. 77.
5. Ibid., p. 88.
6. Ibid., pp. 179–180.
7. Ibid., pp. 16–17.
8. Ibid., p. 15.

44

Nationalism Poster Project

Daniel Berman, Felicia C. Eppley, Ellen Pike, and Robert Rittner

Daniel Berman, Felicia Eppley, Ellen Pike, and Robert Rittner combine a visual-design activity with critical thinking in this lesson on nationalism. They have developed a practical approach to assessment, which can serve as a model for other evaluations. The poster project was co-authored by Daniel Berman and Timothy Miller of Fox Lane High School, Bedford Central Schools, Bedford, New York, as part of the district's Professional Growth and Development Program.

Directions for Students

Introduction

You will be creating a poster to demonstrate your knowledge and understanding of nationalism. This involves a wide choice of options for you to consider. You will be given a handout of quotations by nationalist leaders organized by continent. Consider the quotations and identify a common theme, illustrated by several quotations, to be the theme of your poster. To make an effective poster you need to consider the following general questions:

1. What is my topic, the one specific concept I must focus on?
2. What is the purpose of the poster? Do I want to inform people, persuade people, elicit a particular emotion (anger, sorrow, pity, etc.)?
3. What do I want people to know? What specific information do I want the viewer to have? What message do I want the viewer to come away with?
4. Who is my audience? Who are the people I want to see and respond to this poster?

The type of poster you make will be a function of your purpose. For example, if you have a story to tell, a cartoon format may be appropriate. If you have information to convey, text may be needed. If you want to spread an idea, symbols may be called for. Keep it *simple*. The overall message must be *clear*.

Procedure

1. Make a *story board*, an outline of the elements of your

poster. It is here that you think through your poster. Your story board should contain all of the elements of your poster (for example, if the poster is to have a red border, label the border on the story board "red"). Make more than one "draft" if necessary. The story board will be handed in along with your finished poster.
2. Check the story board against the check list below to see that all criteria have been met.
3. Make the poster.
4. Perform a self-evaluation. (Be as objective as possible; neither pad nor underestimate your work.)

Check List

1. The Knowledge Base Element

- Is it clear that I know a great deal about my topic?
- Have I developed a good thesis?
- Have I integrated my knowledge and understanding into my poster?

2. The Creative Element

- Design: Does the layout of my poster help get my message across? Is the size and style of the printing effective? Are color choices, or lack thereof, effective?
- Message: Is the wording clear? Are the symbols effective?
- Emphasis: Have the most important elements in the poster been emphasized through placement, color, etc.?
- Shapes: Have I used shapes effectively?
- Symbol, metaphor, analogy: Are they accurate? Are they appropriate?
- Labeling: Are there parts of the poster that would be enhanced by labeling?
- Subtlety: Have I used design and language elements that allow my message to be interpreted at more than one level?

Example of Conceptualizing a Poster Project

Audience: Other students and my teacher.
Topic: Environmental pollution.
Knowledge base: What have I learned about pollution: causes, extent, present effects, probable effects, costs of clean-up, costs of prevention, etc.?

This lesson was written during the Woodrow Wilson National Fellowship Foundation 1993 History Institute for the DeWitt Wallace–Reader's Digest Fund Curriculum Models, Princeton, NJ, 1993.

Implications of knowledge base: How does pollution relate to population trends in my country and the world? How does it relate to industrialization in my country and the world? How do the costs of prevention and clean-up relate to the economic goals of nations in the world? How does the policy-making apparatus in my country relate to my views on what should be done about this problem?

Integration of knowledge base: How do my views about democracy and freedom relate to the mechanisms available to solve this problem? How do my views on healthy economics relate to the solutions for this problem? How do my views on an acceptable living standard relate to this problem? How do my views on the United States' place in the world relate to this problem?

Layout: I may want to consider a circular earth in the center of a large rectangle.

Printing: I will want to use styles and boldness of print to highlight the most important things.

Use of color: I definitely want to use green and blue as environmentally suggestive colors. I may also use green as the color of money and play it off against the destruction of rainforests.

Message: Conservation makes good economic sense (cents).

Emphasis: My theme will center on the economic waste entailed by pollution, so I will emphasize all symbols and wording having to do with costs. I will use a bright green and may outline the green in a bright white to add emphasis. Wording related to cost will either be made bold or have a different style from other wording.

Shapes: Circle as mentioned above. I also will employ dollar or cent signs.

Symbol, metaphor, analogy: I may do something with a play on saving "cents" by polluting, saying that polluting makes no "sense" when pollution costs "dollars."

Labeling: I will have to label any elements that may not be clear to my audience.

Subtlety: I don't want to oversimplify the issue by coming out against pollution. Some pollution is a necessary cost of life: I do not want to raise the issue of who should decide how much pollution is tolerable. So, I will do something with the fact that though in some ways polluting may save money, in others ways it costs more than it saves (high cost of health defects caused by pollution), and therefore there needs to be rational control over the degree of pollution tolerated by any society.

Objectives for Teachers

1. To explore nationalism.
2. To give students guided experience in producing a visual project that involves higher-level thinking skills.

Procedure

1. Arrange students in groups.
2. Give each group a sheet of quotations. (See pp. 220–24.) Students will read quotations and try to reach consensus on main themes.
3. Give students copy of project directions (pp. 219–20). Review them with students. Emphasize importance of story board. (If possible, invite a person with advertising expertise to come in and explain the story-board process to the students.)
4. Ask each group to produce a poster reflecting a theme in its selection of quotations from the handouts.
5. Ask a member of each group to explain the group's poster—reasons for symbols and colors chosen, placement of elements, etc. Teacher can expedite explanation with judicious questioning if necessary. (Teacher might want to invite the art teacher to address the class regarding the basic techniques of composition.)
6. Ask students from other groups to comment on the poster. Is the message clear? Are the symbols effective?
7. Save posters to use as exemplars for subsequent poster activities.

Quotations

Africa

Kwame Nkrumah (1909–1972): Son of a goldsmith, educated at Roman Catholic mission schools in the Gold Coast. Graduated from Lincoln University in Chester, Pennsylvania, 1939, did post-graduate work at the University of Pennsylvania. President of African Students Organization of USA and Canada. In 1945 went to London to study law and there organized a Pan-African Congress. Returned in 1947 to Gold Coast, where he led numerous strikes and boycotts for self-government. Became prime minister in 1952 and became first president of the Republic of Ghana in 1960. Recipient of Lenin Peace Prize, 1962.

> On this journey, I had an opportunity to observe the Prime Minister in action at close range. Among his own people he was a democrat, self-forgetfully identifying himself with the common masses in deed and word each passing hour. He slept, played, and ate with them, sharing his life in a manner that no Englishman or missionary every could. . . . It was his lapsing into sudden silence that drew a line between himself and them. . . . I'd not witnessed any evidence of the fury of which I'd been told he was capable, but there was a hidden core of hardness in him which I was sure that no one could bring to the surface quicker than an Englishman.
>
> —Observations by American author Richard Wright on a visit to the Gold Coast in 1954. From "Freedom Now" by Richard Wright. In *Africa: Selected Readings,* ed. Fred Burke, p. 202. Boston: Houghton Mifflin, 1974.

Patrice Lumumba *(1925–1961): Member of Batatele ethnic group, educated in mission schools, and later worked as a postal clerk. President of Congolese National Movement, an influential political party. Became first prime minister of the independent Republic of the Congo in 1960. Killed by political rivals in 1961.*

> The dawn is here, my brother! Dawn! Look in our faces
> A new morning breaks in our old Africa.
> Ours alone will now be the land, the water, mighty rivers
> Poor African surrendered for a thousand years.
> Hard torches of the sun will shine for us again.
> They'll dry the tears in eyes and spittle on your face.
> The moment when you break the chains, the heavy fetters.
> The evil, cruel times will go never to come again.
> A free and gallant Congo will arise from black soil.
> A free and gallant Congo—black blossom from black seed.
> —From *Dawn in the Heart of Africa* by Patrice Lumumba.
> In *Africa: Selected Readings,* ed. Fred Burke, p. 206.

Tom Mboya *(1930–1969): Son of a Luo farmer, educated in mission schools. Studied in India and at Oxford, led Kenya Federation of Labor. Became president of All-Africa Peoples' Congress in 1958. Popular leader of independence movement in Kenya. Assassinated in Nairobi, 1969.*

> In Africa the belief that we are all sons and daughters of the soil has exercised tremendous influence on our social, economic, and political relationships. Arising from this belief is the logic and practice of equality . . . and the practice of communal ownership of the vital means of life—the land. The hoe became the symbol of work: every able-bodied male and female worked. Laziness was not tolerated. Poverty existed, but it was not due to man exploiting man. . . . there was equality of opportunity—everyone had land and hoe at the start of life.
> —From *African Socialism* by Tom Mboya. In *Africa: Selected Readings,* ed. Fred Burke, p. 212.

Latin America

Simón Bolívar *(1783–1830): Born to a* criollo *family of Venezuela's colonial elite in 1783, Bolívar had joined the independence movement by age twenty-four, later rising as a leader of insurgent forces. He led the liberation of Venezuela, Colombia, Ecuador, Peru, and Bolivia. Though an admirer of George Washington—he carried a lock of the president's hair—Bolívar favored a strong central rule, fearing that U.S.-style federalism would spread anarchy across Latin America. He is considered one of South America's greatest generals and is called* El Libertador *and the George Washington of South America.*

> We are not European; we are not Indians; we are but a mixed species of aborigines and Spaniards. . . . Americans by birth and Europeans by law, we . . . are disputing with the natives for titles of ownership.
> Unity, unity, unity must be our motto in all things. The blood

of our citizens is varied: let it be mixed for the sake of unity.
> —Bolívar quotations taken from Bryan Hodgson, "El Libertador Simón Bolívar," *National Geographic,* March 1994.

José de San Martín *(1778–1850): An Argentine general who fought for independence in the wars with Spain. Born February 25, 1778, a Yapeyu, he was educated in Spain and fought with the Spanish forces against Napoleon. In 1812, he sailed for Buenos Aires, where he joined the Spanish colonies of South America in their rebellion against Spain. He then joined forces with Bernardo O'Higgins, to lead an army over the Andes and drive the Spaniards out of Chile. He later joined forces with Bolívar to liberate Peru. Discouraged by the quarrels that wracked Argentina after liberation, San Martín left with his daughter for Europe, where he died. . . . It wasn't until after his death that he was hailed as the selfless hero he was.*

> The key to San Martín's behavior in South America is to be found in the radical principles which he absorbed in Spain . . . his anti-clericalism; the clauses promising religious toleration in the proclamation issued when he became protector of Peru; his firm belief in the power of education which caused him to . . . found the National Library at Lima; his admiration of British liberalism; and his enlightened attitude to slavery. He was not a political thinker of Bolívar's caliber, but he had deep-seated political convictions.
> —J.C.J. Meteford, *San Martin, the Liberator,* Oxford: Basil Blackwell, 1950

Bernardo O'Higgins *(1778–1842): Born in Chillá, Chile, the illegitimate son of Ambrosio O'Higgins, an Irishman who became the viceroy of Peru. After Spain defeated a Chilean army in 1814, Bernardo joined José de San Martín in Argentina. They crossed the Andes Mountains to Chile in 1817 and defeated the Spanish at Chacabuco. O'Higgins won the final victory over the Spaniards at the Maipo River in 1818. He became the leader of an independent Chile but was ousted from power over his attempts at reform (e.g., land reform, public education, equality for Protestants).*

> His irregular birth, with which his enemies never ceased to taunt him, his education, and his own unassuming tastes, had never predisposed him in favor of the aristocracy. His unsuccessful attempts to secure a certificate of legitimacy and the right to his father's titles had only sharpened the edge of his antagonism. More prudent advisers . . . who shared his egalitarian views but thought it unwise to offend a powerful section of the landed gentry, counseled moderation. But O'Higgins was adamant. "Aristocracy is abhorrent to me," he wrote, "adored equality is my idol."
> —Stephen Glissold, *Bernardo O'Higgins and the Independence of Chile,* New York: Praeger, 1961

Miguel Hidalgo y Costillo *(1753–?): A* criollo, *Hidalgo entered the priesthood and became the rector of the college of*

St. Nicholas. In 1792, he resigned and became the head of the parish of Doloros near Guanajuato. There he plotted with other leading criollos to rebel against Spain (under the guise of resisting Napoleon, who had just toppled Ferdinand VII of Spain). In 1810, the plot was discovered; Hidalgo's cohorts were seized, and he chose to lead the revolt single-handed rather than capitulate. In conjunction with other criollos, he launched the Mexican revolt. On September 16, from the window of his house, he made his famous speech, "El Grito de Doloros" (Cry of Doloros)—his exact words are not known. The next day he told his supporters:

My friends and countrymen: neither the king nor tributes exist for us any longer. We have borne this hateful tax, which only suits slaves, for three centuries as a yoke of tyranny and servitude. . . . The moment of our freedom has arrived; the hour of our liberty has struck . . . you recognize its great value, you will help me defend it from the ambitious grasp of the tyrants. . . . The cause is holy and God will protect it. . . . Long live, then, the Virgin of Guadalupe! Long live Amerce for which we are going to fight.

—Hugh M. Hannil, Jr., *The Hidalgo Revolt: Prelude to Mexican Independence,* Gainesville: University of Florida Press, 1966

Europe

Nicholas Balescu: *Nineteenth-century Romanian patriot, emphasized in 1848 that national rights took precedence over human liberty.*

For my part, the question of nationality is more important than liberty. Until a people can exist as a nation, it cannot make use of liberty. Liberty can easily be recovered when it is lost, but not nationality. Therefore I believe that in the present position of our country we must aim rather at the preservation of our greatly menaced nationality and seek only as much liberty as is necessary for the development of our nationality.

—Hans Kohn, *Hapsburg Empire 1804–1918,* Princeton, NJ, Van Nostrand, 1961, p. 110

Francis Palacky: *Nineteenth-century Czech patriot. On April 11, 1848, he expressed in a letter to the German National Assembly in Frankfurt, which had invited him to participate as a Czech delegate, the principles that prevented him from accepting, which became the principles of the Czech and Slav national policy in the Habsburg Empire.*

I am a Czech of Slav descent and with all the little I own and possess I have devoted myself wholly and forever to the service of my nation. That nation is small, it is true, but from time immemorial it has been an independent nation with its own character; its rulers have participated since old times in the federation of German princes, but the nation never regarded itself nor was it regarded by others throughout all the centuries, as part of the German nation. The whole union of the Czech lands first with the Holy German Empire and then with the German Confederation was always a purely dynastic one of which the Czech nation, the Czech Estates, hardly wished to know and which they hardly noticed. . . .

—Kohn, *Hapsburg Empire,* p. 118

Hungarian Declaration of Independence

The Creator has blessed this land with all the elements of wealth and happiness. Its area of 100,000 square miles presents, in varied profusion, innumerable sources of prosperity. Its population numbering nearly fifteen million feels the glow of youthful strength within its veins, and has shewn temper and docility which guarantee its proving at once the mainspring of civilization in Eastern Europe, and the guardian of that civilization when attacked. Never was a more grateful task appointed to a reigning dynasty by the dispensation of Divine Providence, than that which devolved upon the House of Hapsburg Lorraine. If nothing had been done to impede the development of the country, Hungary would now rank amongst the most prosperous of nations. . . .

But this dynasty which cannot point to a single ruler who has based his power on the freedom of the people, adopted, from generation to generation a course towards this nation which meets the name of perjury. . . .

Confiding in the justice of an eternal God, we, in the face of the civilized world, in reliance upon the natural rights of the Hungarian nation and upon the power it has developed to maintain them, further impelled by that sense of duty which urges every nation to defend its own existence, do hereby declare and proclaim in the name of the nation, lawfully represented by us, as follows:

1st. Hungary with Transylvania, as by law united, with its dependencies, are hereby declared to constitute a free independent Sovereign state. The territorial unity of this State is declared to be inviolable, and its territory to be indivisible.

—Kohn, *Hapsburg Empire,* pp. 132–34

Greek National Assembly: Proclamation of Independence. *On January 27, 1882, "the first year of independence," the Greek National Assembly, which met in the ancient seaport of Epidarus near Argos to work out a provisional constitution, issued the following manifesto to the peoples of Europe.*

We, descendants of the wise and noble peoples of Hellas, we who are the contemporaries of the enlightened and civilized nations of Europe . . . find it no longer possible to suffer without cowardice and self-contempt the cruel yoke of the Ottoman power which has weighed upon us for more than four centuries—a power which does not listen to reason and knows no other law than its own will, which orders and disposes everything despotically and according to its caprice. . . .

The war which we are carrying on against the Turk is not that of a faction or the result of sedition. It is not aimed at the advantage of any single part of the Greek people; it is a national war, a holy war, a war the object of which is to reconquer the rights of individual liberty, of property and honor,—rights which the civilized people of Europe, our neighbors, enjoy today; rights of which the cruel and unheard of tyranny of the Ottomans would deprive us. . . . Nature has deeply graven these rights in the hearts of all men; laws in harmony with nature so completely consecrated them that neither three nor four centuries—nor thousands nor millions of years can destroy them. . . . uniting all our strength, we have formed ourselves into a single armed body, firmly resolved to attain our end, to govern ourselves by wise laws. . . .

—Kohn, *Hapsburg Empire,* pp. 116–18

Karel Havlicek: *Nineteenth-century Czech student and journalist.*

I am very happy that I can proudly say that we Czechs, although insignificant in numbers and power compared to the Russians and Poles, are more highly esteemed by all reasonable and educated men. . . . The Russians are hated everywhere, the Poles are merely pitied everywhere . . . but the world looks on us Czechs with respect seeing . . . how manfully we fight for our preservation, for life, for nationality! Should we perhaps be afraid of the great and many obstacles, should we perhaps become downhearted before the hard and unpleasant road which we must tread? A Czech is not afraid of hard work and obstacles, he is not downhearted, and he does not rely on others. . . . A Czech sets out to do his work and will overcome everything. For the very reason that people work harder among us, there is no doubt that on the better historical foundation we have, and with our better general education, we Czechs will advance in the arts, in literature, and generally in national happiness beyond the Russians and the Poles. . . .

—Harry Carroll Jr., Ainslie T. Embree, Knox Mellon Jr., Arnold Schrier, and Alastair Taylor, *Development of Civilization,* Chicago: Scott Foresman, 1962, pp. 196–99

Douglas Hyde: *Nineteenth-century Irish author, commenting on the revival of Gaelic.*

When we speak of "The Necessity for de-Anglicizing the Irish Nation," we mean it, not as a protest against imitating what is best in the English people, for that would be absurd, but rather to show the folly of neglecting what is Irish, and hastening to adopt, pell-mell, and indiscriminately, everything that is English, simply because it is English. . . . If we take a bird's-eye view of our island to-day, and compare it with what it used to be, we must be struck by the extraordinary fact that the nation which was once, as everyone admits, one of the most classically learned and cultivated nations in Europe, is now one of the least so. . . .

I shall endeavour to show that this failure of the Irish people in recent times has been largely brought about by the race diverging during this century from the right path, and ceasing to be Irish without becoming English. I should also like to call attention to the illogical position of men who drop their own language to speak English, of men who translate their euphonious Irish names into English monosyllables, of men who read English books, and know nothing about Gaelic literature, nevertheless protesting as a matter of sentiment that they hate the country which at every hand's turn they rush to imitate.

I wish to show you that in Anglicizing ourselves wholesale we have thrown away with a light heart the best claim we have upon the world's recognition of us as a separate nationality. What did Mazzini say? That we ought to be content as an integral part of the United Kingdom because we have lost the notes of nationality, our language and customs. It has always been very curious to me how Irish sentiment sticks in this halfway house—

how it continues apparently to hate the English, and at the same time continues to imitate them: how it continues to clamour for recognition as a distinct nationality and at the same time throws away with both hands what would make it so. . . .

—Hans Kohn, *Nationalism: Its Meaning in History,* Princeton, NJ: Van Nostrand, 1955, pp. 146–49

Giuseppe Mazzini: *Nineteenth-century Italian patriot.*

A country is not a mere territory: the particular territory is only its foundation. The Country is the idea which rises upon that foundation; it is the sentiment of love, the sense of fellowship which binds together all the sons of that territory. So long as a single one of your brothers is not represented by his own vote in the development of the nation life—so long as a single one vegetates uneducated among the educated—so long as a single one able and willing to work languishes in poverty for want of work—you have not got a Country such as it ought to be, the Country of all and for all. Votes, education, work are the three main pillars of the nation: do not rest until your hands have solidly erected them. . . .

—*Selected Writing* by N. Gangulee, London: Lindsay Drummond, pp. 113–14

The Declaration Required of New Members by the Action Française

French by birth and by heart, by reason and by will, I will fulfill all the duties of a conscious patriot. I promise to combat any republican regime. The Republic in France is the reign of the foreigner. The republican spirit disorganizes national defense and favors religious actions totally hostile to traditional Catholicism. France must be given a regime which is French.

Our only future lies in the Monarchy such as personified by His Grace, the Duke of Orléans, the heir of forty kings who, in a thousand years, made France. Only the Monarchy assures public well-being, is compatible with order, and prevents public wrongs like anti-Semitism and antipatriotism. The necessary organ of every general interest, the Monarchy revives authority, liberties, prosperity, and honor.

I associate myself with the work of monarchical restoration.

—Leslie Derfler, *Third French Republic: 1870–1940,* Princeton, NJ: Van Nostrand, 1966, p. 150

Asia

Rabindranath Tagore (1861–1941): *Tagore was an Indian poet, philosopher, and supporter of freedom for India. . . . In his many songs and poems, he stirred pride among his Hindu countrymen. He was born in Calcutta and studied law in England. He returned to Bengal, a province of British India and the center of the Hindu cultural and spiritual revival in the 1800s. In 1901, he set up a school at Shantiniketan that tried to blend the best in Hindu and Western culture.*

There is only one history—the history of man. All National histories are merely chapters in the larger one. I am not against one nation in particular, but against the general idea of all nations. What is Nation? It is the aspect of a whole people as an organized power. . . . Nationalism is a great menace.

—D. Mackenzie Brown, *White Umbrella: Indian Political Thought from Manu to Gandhi,* Los Angeles: University of California Press, 1959, pp. 109–10, 114, 115

Sun Yat-sen *(1866–1925): Born of humble parents in Kwangtung province, Sun was educated at mission schools in Hong Kong and Honolulu and became a doctor. From 1895 to 1911, he toured the United States, Japan, and Europe to organize sympathy for republican principles and to seek financial aid for his revolutionary movement against the Manchu dynasty. He is generally called the* Father of the Revolution. *Sun was too idealistic to be an effective political leader; but his* Three People's Principles *(nationalism, democracy, and socialism) became the guiding principles of the Chinese republic, established in 1912. The following excerpt is from a letter written on his deathbed to the Central Committee of the USSR:*

> I charge the Kuomintang to continue the work of the revolutionary nationalist movement, so that China, reduced by the imperialists to the position of semi-colonial country, will become free. With this object I have instructed the Party to be in constant contact with you.
> —Hans Kohn, *Nationalism: Its Meaning in History*, rev. ed., Melbourne, FL: Robert Krieger, 1982, p. 182

Jawaharlal Nehru *(1889–1964): Nehru was born in Allahabad into a distinguished family in the province of Kashmir. (His father, Motilal Nehru, was a follower of Gandhi.) He graduated from Cambridge University in England and returned to India to become active in politics. He supported Gandhi's civil disobedience movements in 1920. He was imprisoned repeatedly by the British for nationalistic activities. When India became independent in 1947, Nehru became prime minister and served in that capacity until his death.*

He worked to establish a democracy and to increase living standards. He favored a state-controlled economy.

> I had long been drawn to socialism and communism, and Russia had appealed to me. Much in Soviet Russia I dislike—the ruthless suppression of all contrary opinion. . . . But there was no lack of violence in the capitalist world. . . . The policy of the British Government in India had resulted in ranging the socially reactionary classes in opposition to political independence . . . under Gandhi's leadership, it [Congress] had produced a wonderful awakening of the masses, and, in spite of its vague bourgeoisie ideology, it had served a revolutionary purpose. It had not exhausted its utility yet and was not likely to do so till the nationalist urge gave place to a social one.
> —From Nehru's autobiography, quoted by Kohn, in *Nationalism: Its Meaning and History*, rev. ed., pp. 175–76, 178

Ho Chi Minh *(1890–1969): Ho was born Nguyen Van Thanh in central Vietnam. He became a Communist in 1920 and helped the French Communist Party. Near the end of World War II, he became head of a Vietnamese government that opposed France's rule. In 1946, fighting broke out between the French and Ho's troops, the Vietminh. In 1954, the Vietminh defeated the French, and an international conference divided Vietnam into two nations. Ho became president of North Vietnam. In the 1950s and 1960s, Ho's Communist government sent supplies and troops to aid rebels in South Vietnam who were trying to overthrow the anti-Communist government there.*

> Today it is a case of the grasshopper pitted against the elephant. But tomorrow the elephant will have its guts ripped out. . . . Patriotic zeal has a triple end: 1) to conquer famine; 2) to conquer ignorance; 3) to conquer the enemy. . . . Every Vietnamese, irrespective of age, sex or status must become a fighter on one of these fronts: military, economic, political or cultural.
> —Jean Lacoutre, trans. Wiles, *Ho Chi Minh: A Political Biography,* New York: Vintage Books, 1968, pp. 277 ff

Sukarno *(1901–1970): Born in Surabaja, Java, Sukarno formed the Partai National Indonesia (P.N.I.) in 1927, seeking independence from The Netherlands. After independence, Sukarno called for a "guided democracy" for Indonesia. By 1960, he held unrestricted power.*

> My philosophy is composed of nationalism, religious belief, and Marxist historical analysis. Our economy was a colonial economy . . . we must change this . . . into a national economy which is clean of imperialism, clean of blood-sucking exploitation by outsiders.
> —Emil Lengyel, *From Prison to Power,* Chicago: Follett, 1964, pp. 204–5

Mohammed Ali Jinnah *(1876–1948): Born in Karachi, India (now part of Pakistan), Jinnah came from a wealthy Moslem family. He studied law in England and became famous as a lawyer in London and Bombay. He was a leader in India's struggle for independence. In 1940, he led Moslem demands for separation from the Hindu majority in India. He is considered the founder of Pakistan. When Pakistan was created in 1947, Jinnah became its first governor general.*

> The majority community have clearly shown their hand that Hindustan is for the Hindu. . . . How can I ask my people to give their blood and money when I have no share in that government and no power to dispose of that money?
> —Percival Spear, *The Oxford History of Modern India 1740–1947*, Oxford: Clarendon Press, 1965, p. 374

Peasant Resistance to Colonial Economic Policy in Nineteenth-Century Tanganyika and India

Connie Wood and Sandra Garcia

Connie Wood and Sandra Garcia designed this lesson to introduce students to the nature of peasant resistance to European colonial power in the late nineteenth century. They introduce this lesson with a discussion of parental authority and child resistance to develop an understanding of colonial rule and local resistance.

The two case studies used in this module may be used in a variety of ways to enlighten units on the industrial revolution, the economics of imperialism, or any global study of resistance movements. Both cases focus on the rural populations of European colonies in the late nineteenth century and how the peasants responded to the pressures created by imperial demands on native land use. When looking at the big picture of world history, we have a tendency to view the common people as passive recipients dominated by the needs and ambitions of the imperial powers. What the case studies offer is the opportunity to study two microcosms with unique historical contexts from which we can draw connections to and make generalizations about what was going on in the world during the nineteenth century. From the studies, we can teach: (1) the European drive to dominate local, colonial economies in the service of their own economy; (2) the varied forms of peasant resistance to European domination; and (3) the tug between traditional subsistence economies and a modern model of commercial economy.

Objectives

1. Students, through journal responses, will explore human reactions to oppression and begin a process of engaging in and understanding this historical phenomenon.
2. Students will use inductive reasoning to speculate on the course of actual historical events.
3. Students will read and interpret primary source material and distinguish points of view.
4. Students will be able to identify a variety of methods of

peasant defiance as well as a variety of colonial administrative responses.
5. Students will be able to demonstrate what they have learned in an analytical piece of writing or in a creative project.

Procedure

Parts to the Module

1. A background history sheet for the teacher on each of the two resistance movements.
2. Two imaginary news articles for each of the movements, one early in the movement and one at the end.
3. Two primary source quotes for each movement, one from the perspective of the peasants and one from the perspective of the colonial power.
4. One chart showing the variety of possible forms of resistance and response.
5. Activity questions and project suggestions.
6. Bibliography.

Order of Activities

1. Assign journal responses based on the questions about personal resistance to authority.
2. Use the chart on peasant defiance (Table 45.1) and do the following activity with the students. Use one sheet of paper and print out the colonial and peasant responses on the right-hand side of the page. Have the students fold the paper lengthwise and respond on the left side to the action/reaction of the student and the parents. Next, have the students find correlations between the responses of the parents and the colonial administration and between the responses of students and the peasants. Be sure the students can verbalize what makes the family dynamic of action/reaction different from the action/reaction between a colonial power and the native population. When

Table 45.1   **Forms of Peasant Defiance**

Action/Reaction	
Your Parent's Action	Colonial Administration's Actions
	Humiliation Taxes Forced labor Land appropriation Slavery
Your Reaction	Peasant Reactions
	Migration Feigned ignorance Work slowdown Theft Smuggling Sabotage Slander Arson Boycotts Strikes Rebellion War

students have responded, they can be led in a discussion comparing different forms of resistance to authority in familiar revolutions such as the American, Latin American, and French revolutions.

3. Students, in groups, read the first news article and discuss the questions.
4. Students read the second article and discuss the questions.
5. Teacher lectures, giving the background information on each resistance movement; students take notes.
6. Students read the firsthand accounts with care and compare them, with special emphasis on point of view. Students can pair off to discuss the similarities and differences between the two native accounts and the two colonial accounts. They should answer the points-of-view questions.
7. Students complete a final assignment to demonstrate their understanding of the unit.

Suggested Assignments

1. Write an essay comparing one of these peasant resistance movements to another rebellion already studied. Students need to elaborate a question or questions that will guide them in writing their essay. Possible areas for comparison: France, China, Russia, Iran, Egypt, Mexico.
2. Complete a project comparing British, French, and German policies toward their colonial populations in the nineteenth century. An interesting question to pursue would be, Which colonial power experienced more resistance in response to its policies and why?
3. Create a "Peoples Handbook to Defiance." Show how to

defy a colonial imperial power. Illustrate your methods.
4. Address the following question: How do the changes brought about by the industrial revolution create a potential for social and political revolution? This question may be answered in a written essay, a series of political cartoons, a play, a visual representation, or any other creative format of the student's choice.

**Background Information for Teachers:
Peasant Resistance in Kumaun, India**

The British Kumaun was located in the Central Himalaya region of India bordering on Tibet and Nepal. It was under colonial domination from 1815 to 1947. During early colonial rule the peasants of this region were characterized as being docile and law abiding. The Bhotiya herdsmen lived in the highland valleys of the Himalayas, herding animals and cultivating grains and vegetables along the steep river valley slopes. The extensive oak and pine forests of the Himalayas played an essential role in peasant subsistence, providing fodder and fertilizer. The chir pine forests, in particular, served as pasture land for the animals. The peasants would burn off the dry grass and pine needles between the trees every year to allow fresh grass to grow for their animals to graze.

Kumaun society was different from the majority of Indian society in the nineteenth century in that it did not have sharp class differences. This agrarian society had long-standing traditions of communal life, which included free use and sharing of the forest land surrounding their villages. While in the rest of India the British found a system where large landowners predominated and there were many small land-owners, tenant farmers, and landless workers, in the Kumaun region by the end of the nineteenth century 90 percent of the land was owned by the peasants who cultivated it.[1]

In the early years of British rule there was little pressure put on Kumaun society to change. Because of its strategic position on the borders of Nepal and Tibet, the Kumaun had status as a good recruiting area for army personnel. Local farmers made a fine fighting force. Because the villagers were important to the army, British land taxes were light and the natives were not pressured to change cultivation to commercial crops. However, with the coming of industrialization and, in particular, the building of the railway network by the British in India, things would change for the Kumaun. The rail industry created demands for commercial forestry to provide the sleepers (railroad ties) for the railway. The rapid destruction of accessible forests in early railroad expansion brought about the creation of a forestry department by the British. In the early days, cedar forests in the Himalayas were drastically exploited until finally the British had to import wood from Europe. Such importation increased the costs so much that the British turned once again to India in search of indigenous sources for the sleepers. In the 1890s, the forestry department focused on the chir pine forests of the Himalayas in the Kumaun region. They found that this tree could be profitable both for sleepers and as a source of resin from which turpentine could be made. The stage was set for commercial or "scientific" forestry; a great change in the level of state interference in the everyday life of the peasants was unavoidable.

As the forestry department's business increased, so also did the demands made on the peasantry of the region. They were called upon to provide coolie labor, and they were expected to abide by the rules set up by the forestry department with respect to the use of the forests, which were now designated as reserves. The rules severely limited peasant use of the chir pine area for grazing their animals and therefore upset the ecological balance the villagers had established to survive. As the villagers were pressed, they responded initially with evasion of the rules and noncompliance with the demands for their labor.

In time the peasants became more actively defiant as a group and received support from local members of the Kumaun Parishad. The Parishad was an organization of local Kumaun journalists, lawyers, and intellectuals initially set up in 1916 to mediate between the state and the peasantry. At its birth, the Parishad swore an oath of loyalty to George V. As things got worse for the peasants, the Parishad, under the leadership of Bandridutt Pande, took a more confrontational position. Bandridutt used his weekly publication, *Shakti,* to criticize both labor policy and forest rules. He spoke to more than ten thousand peasants at a local fair, promising them Gandhi's support in their cause and inciting them to refuse forced labor and to defy forests rules. At the end of his speech he called for a free India, thus connecting the local fight against oppression with the national movement for Indian independence. The Garhwal soldiers who fought under British command were among the most active defiers of British rule when they were on leave in their villages. One of the disenchanted soldiers was quoted as saying that "government was not a Raja, but a Bania [merchant] and Rakshasi [demonic] and the King Emperor was Ravan [demon god]."[2] The rulers had lost their legitimacy in the eyes of the villagers. The king was seen as an abuser rather than the upholder of justice and harmony.

The variety of peasant responses ranged from evasion and noncooperation to organized acts of arson intended to destroy the chir forests being exploited by the British. The British eventually had to give up the practice of forced labor among the villagers of Kumaun and, because of the acts of arson, were forced to amend the laws controlling the villagers' use of the forest land. The battles between the traditional and modern forms of land use in the Himalayas did not end there. Because the Himalayan forests are the only source of softwoods in India, they have been targeted for commercial exploitation since the end of the nineteenth century. As recently as 1973 that area was the center of a peasant-based movement to stop commercial logging called Chipko or tree hugging, which involved peasant men and women defiantly hugging trees in an effort to focus attention on the need to conserve the trees. Forest use is no longer a battle between the native peasantry and the colonial master but an internal, national struggle between Indian peasantry conserving their traditional use of the land and Indian entrepreneurs attempting to make money from commercial exploitation of the Himalayan forests.

Primary Source Material: The India Times

Forestry Department Closes off 3000 acres in Kumaun

Kumaun, India, Special Report, June 3, 1916. Administrative sources in Kumaun reported today the premature felling of at least 28,000 pine trees due to what they have described as "malicious" fires set presumably by local villagers. These chir pine trees are located in the government forest reserves and are exploited both for their resins and as lumber to make sleepers for railroad building. As a result of what the government spokesman has labeled "deliberate and organized incendiarism," the burned trees were no longer useful to the forest department and had to be felled.

Conflict between government officials and highland villagers in Kumaun has been building now for five years since Kumaun forests were designated as reserves. Government use of the forests has increased the demand by officials for coolie labor in the area as well as having restricted the traditional use by villagers of the forest land for grazing their herds.

Officials have been frustrated in their efforts to trace the people responsible for setting the fires. Reacting to what seemed last week to be a chain of general firing, the government has suspended all village rights on several thousand acres of forest for ten years.

Continued Drought and Fires Bring Disaster to Kumaun Forests—Soldiers Involved

Kumaun, India, Special Report, August 8, 1921. In the wake of one of the driest summers on Indian record, the government has reported continuous blazes in the Almora district. When the villagers of the region are called on to help put out the fires, officials report that they are helping to spread the fires instead. In total 2.46 lakh acres of chir pine forest vital for both timber and resin extraction have been burned over and an estimated 819 forest offenses are reported. Among those detained yesterday were four soldiers of the 39th Garhwalis arrested for assaulting forest officials.

This resistance by the region's villagers comes on the heels of their refusal to cooperate with the government demands for labor to transport and provide for the touring forestry officials. Given the total breakdown of the coolie labor system in Kumaun between January and April, the government has been forced to abolish the labor system. It remains to be seen how the government will respond to the ever increasing number of acts defying the forest laws.

Background Information for Teachers: Maji-Maji Rebellion in Tanganyika

In "The Political Economy of Colonial Tanganyika 1890–1930," Walter Rodney asserts that the Maji-Maji Rebellion not only was anti-European and anti-colonial, but also was a movement against economic imperialism. Rodney asserts that the entire trading community, including African and Arab merchants as well as Europeans, was attacked by the rebellious tribesmen, making it a response to changing economic conditions, not just European imperialism. As the industrial revolution created a demand for raw materials and markets, the exploitation factor "trickled down" to the local villagers as is illustrated in this case study.

Germany came late to the colonial acquisition game and did not occupy Tanganyika until 1898. At the time of the rebellion, Germany had a rather tenuous hold on the colony. As was true of most colonial powers, the Germans viewed Tanganyika as an area to be exploited for cash crops under the plantation system. Plantation agriculture required land and labor, which the German colonial administration acquired through legislation and administrative regulations. Of course, the native population was not consulted in the making of the policies.

The Germans sought to convert Tanganyikan agriculture to a cash crop: cotton. The nature of the German policies was both oppressive and exploitative. Generally, a native headman was charged with the responsibility of developing a communal farm for the purpose of raising cash crops. The amount of land required for the plots was increased each year to increase the amount of exportable cotton. Villagers were required to work a specific number of days on those plots. Additionally, the Germans levied taxes on the Africans that forced them to go into the labor market to earn a wage to pay the tax. The plantations then had a ready source of labor for the days the villagers were not required to work. The peasants were under tremendous pressure to produce the export crops, pay German taxes, and try to eke out a living.

Arising at almost the same time as the new German economic policies was a religious movement led by Kinjikitile Ngwale. In a vision, he saw a way to relieve the Africans from German oppression through the use of the *maji*, a protective water (see primary source material, the *Tanganyika Times*, "Germans Hang Native 'Prophet,'" article). The powers of the magic water would render German bullets useless, and, thus, the Africans would be able to drive out the Germans. Devotees of the god Hongo claimed that Kinjikitile's message was from their god, and they actively spread the news about the vision. Across the Tanganyikan lands, people flocked to a sacred site to acquire some of the holy water. The movement became known as the Maji-Maji. The movement of the Hongo priests among the villages also facilitated the spread of rebellious ideas. The Germans viewed the Maji-Maji as a harmless invention of a witch doctor and, therefore, underestimated the power of the spiritual movement to unify the peasants into a cohesive force to defy the colonial administration.

The 1905–1907 Maji-Maji Rebellion was in direct defiance of the German colonial administrative policy. By the time the war was over 75,000 Africans had died. The revolt began in a normally passive area of Tanganyika and spread rapidly. The Germans were ill prepared to respond to the uprising. In fact, early on, they believed the Arab *akidas* (overseers) were at the root of the rebellion, when in fact it was led by Africans. The Africans had the momentum at the beginning of the rebellion but were unable to sustain it as the German officials finally responded with well-armed troops. However, the Africans effectively utilized guerrilla warfare, for which the German forces had no military answer. Eventually, famine and starvation became significant factors in suppressing the rebellion and were responsible for a high number of deaths (see primary source material, the *Tanganyika Times*, "48 Maji-Maji Leaders Executed" article).

Primary Source Material: The Tanganyika Times

Germans Hang Native "Prophet": Unrest Continues in African Colony

Mohoro, Tanganyika, Special Report, August 4, 1905. Kinjikitile Ngwale was executed today by German officials in the African colony of Tanganyika. Kinjikitile was reputed to be the leader of the Maji movement in that colony. The colony has experienced a great deal of unrest in the past several years, since the Germans initiated a system of communal land holding and forced labor that would improve the output of exportable cotton. Villagers have been forced to pool land resources and abandon traditional crops of maize, millet, and rice in favor of export cotton production. Earlier this summer, acts of defiance took place in a region called Nandete when a group of natives pulled ripening cotton plants from the ground. The actions were a sort of war declaration on the Germans. The resistance appears to flow out of a vision by Kinjikitile.

A witness of Kinjikitile's possession in 1904 by the spirit Hongo described it in this way: "He was taken by an evil spirit one day. They saw him go on his belly, his hands stretched out before him. Then, he disappeared in the pool of water. Those who knew how to swim dived down into the pool, but they did not see anything. The following morning he emerged unhurt with his clothes dry and as he had tucked them the previous day. He said, 'All dead ancestors will come back. No lion or leopard will eat men.' "

After the vision, Kinjikitile built a huge spirit hut at a place called Ngaranbe to communicate to the spirit. The location became a pilgrimage site for the natives seeking the holy water called maji. The maji reputedly brings all Africans together in unity and makes them more powerful than the Europeans by protecting the natives from the white man's bullets.

Emboldened by the belief in maji, the Matumbi of Nandete attacked a local official's home on July 30 this year. Governor Gotzen immediately responded with troops, who captured Kinjikitile yesterday.[3]

48 Maji-Maji Leaders Executed: Rebellion in Tanganyika Abates

Songea, Tanganyika, Special Report, February 27, 1906. Forty-eight Ngani leaders of the Maji-Maji Rebellion were hanged today. Among them was Nkoaimputa Gama, a paramount chief of southern Unzioni in the German colony of Tanganyika. The executions are the culmination of the Germans' attempt to regain control of rebellious tribesmen who have been fighting the Germans since July of 1905 over issues related to the growing of cotton and forced labor. The rebellion spread rapidly among the people of the Rufiji Valley into the highlands near Dar es Salaam and to the western reaches of the German colony. In August of 1905, the Germans had been pushed almost to the seacoast. The failure of the native forces to

take Mahenge allowed the Germans time to bring in additional troops to put down the rebellion.

However, the use of guerrilla tactics by the Africans occasioned German use of famine as a means of subduing the natives. Captain Richter, a district officer in Songea commented, "That's right, the fellows can just starve. We shall be sure to get food for ourselves. If I could, I would even prevent them from planting anything. This is the only way that we can make the fellows sick of war." Reports of starvation amongst the people of the highlands have been filtering into the capital city Dar es Salaam. Reports of guerrilla fighting in the south continue to be received.[4]

Points of View

Peasant in India: Government Clerk Who Applied for Exemption from Forced Labor

In days gone by necessities of life were in abundance to villagers ... [and] there were no such Government laws and regulations prohibiting the free use of unsurveyed land and forest by them as they have now. The time itself has now become very hard and it has been made still harder by the imposition of different laws, regulations, and taxes on them and by increasing the land revenue. Now the village life has been shadowed by all the miseries and inconveniences of the present-day laws and regulations. They are now allowed to fell down a tree to get fuels from it for their daily use and they cannot cut leaves beyond a certain portion of them for fodder to their animals. But the touring officials still view the present situation with an eye to the past and press them to supply good grass for their horses, fuels for their kitchens, and milk for themselves and their [retinue] without even thinking of making any payment for these things to them who after spending their time, money, and labor can hardly procure for their own use. In short, all the privileges of village life, as they were twenty years ago, are nowhere to be found now, still the officials hanker after the system of yore when there were everything in abundance and within the reach of villagers.[5]

Peasant in Tanganyika: Eighteen-Year-Old Girl in Chiwata

Our news is this, that the Germans treat us badly and oppress us much, because it is their will. Here at Chiwata there is a court every Wednesday, and many people are beaten and some are imprisoned by order of the German Government. But we, who have for so long been used to govern ourselves, find the laws of the Germans very hard, especially the taxes, because we black people have no money, our wealth consists of millet, maize, oil, and groundnuts, etc. Here at Chiwata two houses have been built, one for the court and one for the prison.[6]

Colonial View in India: Forest Settlement Officer of British Garhwal

The notion obstinately persists in the minds of all, from the highest to the lowest, that government is taking away their forests from them and is robbing them of their property. The notion seems to have grown up from the complete lack of restriction or control over the use by the people of wasteland and forest during the first 80 years after the British occupation. The oldest inhabitant therefore, and he naturally is regarded as the greatest authority, is the most assured of the antiquity of the people's right to uncontrolled use of the forest; and to a rural community there appears no difference between uncontrolled use and proprietary right. Subsequent regulations—and these regulations are all very recent—only appear to them as a gradual encroachment on their rights, culminating now in a final act of confiscation. . . . [My] best efforts have, I hear, failed to get the people generally to grasp the change in conditions or to believe in the historical fact of government ownership.[7]

Colonial View in Tanganyika: German Engineer R.H. Gillman

In the evening I had an interesting talk with old experienced Africans [i.e., settlers] about the natives: "They must feel that the white man is the mbana," the master. The whites must act with the necessary tact and justice, but must always be strict and have all their orders obeyed to at once. If necessary the whip must come in helping.

Kindness is absolutely no good with the niggers, who are used to have someone above, and it is to a great deal due to the fact, that missionaries are too kind and familiar with them, that the present [Maji-Maji] rebellion broke out. . . .

Whether they are the born slaves, as was said by a man, who ought to know them well enough, I can't make out yet, and therefore can't quite agree with the idea, that the putting an end to slavery was a great pity to the country—as the above mentioned gentleman thinks.[8]

Activities

Journal Questions

1. What are the ways you or your peers defy your parents or other authority figures?
2. What are the ways your parents control you?
3. Why do you or your peers defy authority figures?
4. What are the responses to your defiance?

News Article Questions

First Set of Articles

1. What are the facts about the peasant activities? (Who, what, where, when)
2. Why do you think the events are occurring?
3. What questions do you have about the acts of defiance?

Second Set of Articles

1. Repeat the first set of questions.
2. Which of your questions from the first article were answered in the second?
3. What do you still need to know about the conflict to understand the outcome?

Points-of-View Questions

1. Using the information from the reading and the points of view of the peasants, identify the sources of dissatisfaction to the peasants. Compare the two areas.
2. Using the "Forms of Peasant Defiance" chart (Table 45.1), determine which actions the peasants probably utilized before the rebellions took place.
3. How would you describe the tone of the comments made by the Europeans? Which specific words or phrases establish that tone?
4. After studying the European comments, speculate on how the solutions to the rebellions were viewed as "reasonable" options.

Notes

1. Ramachandra Guha, "Saboteurs in the Forest: Colonialism and Peasant Resistance in the Indian Himalaya," in *Everyday Forms of Peasant Resistance,* ed. Forrest D. Colburn (New York: M.E. Sharpe, 1989), p. 68.
2. Ibid., p. 85.
3. Robert O. Collins, "Records of the Maji-Maji," in *Eastern African History,* Vol. 2 of *African History: Text and Readings* (New York: Markus Wiener Publishing, 1990).
4. Ibid.
5. Guha, "Saboteurs in the Forest," p. 72.
6. Collins, "Records of the Maji-Maji," p. 124.
7. Guha, "Saboteurs in the Forest," p. 75.
8. "Gilman Diary 29 October 1905" in John Iliffe, *A Modern History of Tanganyika* (Cambridge: Cambridge University Press, 1979), p. 150.

Selected Bibliography

Adas, Michael. "Market Demand Versus Imperial Control: Colonial Contradictions and the Origins of Agarian Protest in South and Southeast Asia." In *Global Crisis and Social Movements,* ed. Edmund Burke III. Boulder, CO: Westview Press, 1988.

Collins, Robert O. "Records of the Maji-Maji." In *Eastern African History*, Vol. 2 of *African History: Text and Readings.* New York: Markus Wiener Publishing, 1990.

Guha, Ramachandra. "Saboteurs in the Forest: Colonialism and Peasant Resistance in the Indian Himalaya." In *Everyday Forms of Peasant Resistance*, ed. Forrest D. Colburn. New York: M.E. Sharpe, 1989.

Iliffe, John. *A Modern History of Tanganyika.* Cambridge: Cambridge University Press, 1979.

Rodney, Walter. "The Political Economy of Colonial Tanganyika 1890–1930." In *Tanzania Under Colonial Rule,* ed. M.H.Y. Kaniki. London: Longman Group Limited, 1980, pp. 128–63.

Scott, James C. "Everyday Forms of Resistance." In *Everyday Forms of Peasant Resistance,* ed. Forrest D. Colburn. New York: M.E. Sharpe, 1989.

Watts, Michael. "On Peasant Diffidence: Non Revolt, Resistance and Hidden Forms of Political Consciousness in Northern Nigeria." In *Global Crisis and Social Movements,* ed. Edmund Burke III. Boulder, CO: Westview Press, 1988.

Mexican Mural Painting in the United States

The Influence of Mexican Artists During the 1930s

Carrie H. McIver

Mexican wall murals were first brought into the United States during the depression. Carrie McIver introduces students to Mexican nationalism as expressed through the wall murals and provides them with a hands-on experience as well. She offers practical, reassuring advice for teaching art projects in world history.

Introduction

History is most frequently presented as the written word, with occasional illustrations used to enliven the text. Using art as primary source documents allows the visualization of history and promotes student understanding of the human emotions and energy prompting social and political change. Teaching history through art more readily communicates the interaction of people and nations and makes history come alive in the imaginations of our students. At the same time, such lessons allow students to identify with their own cultural roots, because they come, not with empty hands and hearts, but with souls representing a rich cultural heritage that has influenced and enriched them as well as their historical past.

All of the arts represent their time. And, while the arts sometimes reflect those in power, they are also a source of information about those segments of society frequently omitted from our texts. Poetry and music are two of the best art forms to provide information on how "everyone" felt about life and events in the past. (Reflect on the poetry and music produced by slaves, people living during the depression, and people enduring and fighting wars.)

If a teacher feels uneasy about incorporating art (and related art activities) into the lesson, the first planning session will be a challenge. With a little guidance, however, even the first session can be enjoyable. The first stumbling block is usually one of the following two:

• *Teacher uncomfortable using art:* Teachers can first rely on their school history texts; most are now including time lines incorporating events, developments in science, exploration, and the arts. Libraries also provide books with overviews (organized chronologically) in these areas and, of course, books focusing on specific periods. Look through these, keeping in mind you are looking specifically for illustrations of the written word. Check out the books for class use; or, if you're comfortable with a camera, take slides of the illustrations that would be useful for your lessons. (As long as slides are for your use only, and not available to others, most publishers do not deem it necessary to get permission.) Many museums sell slides of works in their collection; thus, when an art work is listed in a book, note its location, and then request from that institution slides, posters, even postcards. Some museums also sell excellent videos on art. Keep in mind that the art should expand the lesson, not "decorate" it. Examples of visual art, music, and literature should be integrated into the day's lesson, involving students in discussion about them. Provide students with opportunities to assess, to imagine, and to make connections.

• *Teacher unsure how to motivate the class to produce art:* Most people in the West claim they can't draw "a straight line with a ruler." Many other cultures of the world have no such anxiety; artistic expression is an expected and enjoyed part of living; thus, everyone "can do it." We all have innate ability to be artistic; it's just been stifled. Art lessons integrated across the curriculum are meant to expand understanding; ability has nothing to do with it. A finished product need not be "beautiful." A primary point to remember: The art lessons should not be abruptly assigned. As an example, in the following lesson on the Mexican muralists students are asked to produce a group mural reflecting their current concerns about today's society. Say nothing about this ultimate goal as you begin study.

As students read the text, show them examples of art reflecting the depression in the United States and the 1910 Mexican Revolution (see lesson for the list of art used as examples, pp. 235–238). With all examples, involve students in discussing interpretations of the art. On some occasions ask students if they discern any parallels in our societies today. As examples of the Bonampak murals are shown, mention that Diego Rivera was especially impressed with the organization of their murals. The Mayan style of organization was related to the real world in that the mural's bottom portion referred to the underground, rising up through daily life to that of the ruler, and finally to the heavens; color was used symbolically. After studying the Renaissance, when an individual artist would be credited with a mural though helpers were employed, Rivera was impressed at the community effort to produce the Mayan murals. As your studies progress, casually suggest that it might be interesting to see what "we" would produce in the mural style of *los tres grandes,* in which society's concerns are represented. As a homework assignment, ask students to make a *quick* sketch reflecting what they feel are today's societal concerns. If some students say they "can't draw . . . with a ruler," respond that it doesn't really matter, it's just a way to visually record their concerns. Ask them to also write a few lines about their societal concerns on the back of the drawing. (Give them inexpensive $8\frac{1}{2} \times 11$ paper for this and ask that they just use their pencils; no need for fancy colors, etc.) The next day, make no mention of the quality of the drawings; focus on the *meaning.* Class discussion should be focused on their individual concerns reflected in their drawings. Use discretion in displaying them; it may be best just to collect the assignment after class discussion. After all, you *told* them their drawing skill was unimportant, so why display it? The drawings are assigned for homework to get the students to focus and commit their ideas to paper with a visual representation. Thus, when a class discussion is held, students have concrete ideas to discuss. (Seeing their drawing at this stage is unnecessary.) If students did not do this individually before the discussion, many would ride the coattails of others, especially the "artists" in the class. This assignment enables all students to contribute ideas, with the class artists unable to dominate at this point. (A few pointers for those teachers who have a student or two who are considered to be artists. These students are good artists for several reasons: usually they have developed a specific style, and as long as they stick to that style they draw well; these students also reinforce their skills by investing a lot of time and effort in their drawings. However, many cannot perform as well in a group setting requiring adaptation to the group. Other students usually defer to these students and let them do the drawing; or, the artist feels too special to acquiesce, she or he refuses to become involved. Have several strategies ready for such occasions. Perhaps this person could do a small focus area and demonstrate brush techniques for others in the group. Acknowledging the personality involved, do not let such an artist dominate or boss others in the group. They need to retain their self-respect and also respect the efforts of others.)

At this time, or a few days later, tell the students you would like the class to divide into groups of about five or six. (Have ready the white butcher paper and tempera paints so they can see the size and colors available. Do not pass out any supplies; students will need time to discuss and plan, using inexpensive small paper for this stage.) Return their sketches, suggesting they look for common themes among their work and ways in which several of their concerns could be represented in one large mural. (I extend this and ask that each group, after developing their themes, ask another group to join them in planning a way to join their murals. This would mean that the borders would meld into one another.)

In order to facilitate cooperative effort I ask that each group divide responsibility; each group member is to grade the quality of his or her own involvement as well as that of the others in the group. If problems arise within the group, the group should discuss and solve its problems. In other words, the focus is on the process: the thought to develop and plan the mural. No one student should come up with the themes or execute the entire mural; it should be a group effort from beginning to end. Let students know your grading will be partly based on their effort and their ability to work well with others. They will also be individually graded on their essays explaining their group's mural. Upon completion of the written assignment, ask the group to produce *one* paper to be displayed at the side of their mural. (As a model, think of the museum labels explaining paintings.)

Exhibiting the murals depends on the teacher and the school. Perhaps it is enough to hang them on the classroom wall, accompanied by the explanatory paper. If the teacher feels the class projects should be shown to other classes, consider an exhibit in the school auditorium, with students explaining their mural's symbolism and content to the audience. Many local banks welcome student work, hanging it in their public areas. Perhaps the history and literature teachers could plan complementary lessons and create a joint exhibit.

In summary, let's refer to the beginning. The best way to encourage student involvement is to place less emphasis on the final product (and, as a result, on their "talent"); instead emphasize the importance of their ideas. As you facilitate the process, ensuring they have the necessary supplies and the groups are working in harmony, get involved yourself through observation. Actively watch them develop their ideas, verbally support their efforts, let them know that their efforts communicate their concerns, that you see what they mean. Ask "active" questions that communicate that you are involved. (For example, if they are doing a landscape, notice if they have all the colors they need and ask if they could use more browns or greens, etc. Conversely, do not comment that they used the "wrong" color, drew something out of proportion, etc.) And, when it comes time to evaluate the final product, get the students involved in the evaluation. If they are critical of their skills, ask them how they would have done it differently. If they become too critical, remind them that the ability to be artistic is an ability we all have. Assure students that there is no right or wrong way; there are techniques. In the West we emphasize the *right* way to do things; papers are graded for exact information; we give little opportunity for imagining or dreaming where there isn't a "right" or a "wrong." Artistic ability can be fostered by releasing anxieties about the correct way of doing things, focusing on the imagination, not what's right. If students genuinely desire to improve their skills, let them know that drawing can be developed through practice and observation, and that the more one draws, the better one gets. Art classes can address techniques, but classes incorporating art across the curriculum need to stress ideas communicated visually. Remember to enjoy the process with your students, and invariably the students will relax and enjoy the process as well.

Applications

This lesson has several possible uses:

Eleventh grade, U.S. history during 1920s–1930s

- industrialization
- the "Red Scare"
- the Great Depression
- the New Deal

Tenth grade, world history

- industrialization and the arts
- revolutions of Mexico and Russia
- Mexico's indigenous heritage and its Hispanic past
- Mexico's influence on the United States (in the 1930s)
- socialism vs. capitalism

Goals

Through an interdisciplinary presentation students will gain insight into the social and political climates of Mexico and the United States during the 1920s and 1930s: the post-revolutionary period of Mexico and the depression and New Deal era of the United States.

Objectives

1. Students will apply the historical data covered in class studies to write a paper on the Mexican muralists, focusing on *los tres grandes* (Jose Clemente Orozco, Diego Rivera,

David Alfaro Siqueiros). Students' papers will reflect the artists' social and political concerns and their influence on the establishment of the Public Works of Art Project in the United States in 1933. Allow about one week.

2. Students will compare and contrast current social and political concerns in the United States with those of the 1930s. Using a mural style of *los tres grandes*, they will work as a team to design and execute a mural for a classroom wall. Allow about two weeks.

Through slides and film or video students will observe the influence of the Mexican intelligentsia on the United States, with the focus on the 1930s. What seems like the influence of one country is, in reality, layers of cultural influence encompassing European and Mayan and Russian or socialist influences. At the conclusion of this study students will:

1. Write a summary paper reflecting and evaluating the following points:

   - North American intelligentsia looked to the Mexicans as cultural and political heroes as a possible way out of the apathy, hopelessness, and confusion of the United States in the early 1930s. Writers and artists were weary of what they perceived to be the self-serving interests of U.S. citizens and governments, and Mexico was perceived as a society working together to produce only what was needed, rather than the "embarrassing excesses" produced by a free-market society.
   - Socialism vs. capitalism: Socialism and Marxism were thought to be more "human" than democracy. Those systems valued social commitment over personal independence and held that the community was more important than the individual.
   - *Los tres grandes* were sophisticated, educated, well-traveled artists initially influenced by European mural tradition, who later became aware of their own cultural heritage, especially the Maya murals at Bonampak. The Maya expressed their complicated concepts of the universe in colors (example: red/East, white/North, black/West, yellow/South, green/center; gods concerned with those areas of the world were represented by those colors). The carefully delineated painted scenes indicated they were executed as a collective project. Murals were typically planned and sectioned to represent progress of an event (example: battle, triumph, sacrifice of prisoners).
   - Mexicans believed strongly in their responsibility to represent all people, to express social concerns with passion; walls belonged to everyone and were not for the glorification of the artist or creator. U.S. New Deal muralists tended to illustrate projects rather than social

issues; they were funded by the government, which preferred to avoid controversy. Mexican artists were provided spaces to paint and were funded by government groups that encouraged the expression of social and political issues.

- Mexican artists also were backed financially by art patrons to produce work in the United States. While some patrons were altruistic, the primary patrons (Dwight Morrow and John D. Rockefeller) were also circuitously trying to protect U.S. companies in Mexico. (Cardenas was in the midst of nationalizing companies. Morrow was the U.S. ambassador to Mexico; Rockefeller represented himself as an art patron rather than an industrialist when he appealed to Cardenas on behalf of the Rockefeller oil holdings in Mexico.)
- Mexican artists were in national favor; "anything" Mexican was popular in the United States, including architecture designed in "Revival Mayan Style."
- Through the success of the Mexican mural projects, artists and writers of the United States approached the federal government suggesting that Mexico provide the model for the WPA Public Works of Art Project.
- Mexican artists met the U.S. depression head on. Having interpreted the Mexican Revolution (one of the first of the world's twentieth-century revolutions), they arrived in the States as experienced political artists.
- Mexican artists were strident and confrontational in their art (this ultimately created conflict; e.g., Rockefeller Center).

2. Produce a mural for the classroom wall.

Assessment

1. Students will be teamed to evaluate their written papers. They will work together to make a joint presentation to the class. A video will be made of each presentation and then be shown to the class as a whole. The class will discuss and evaluate the content and presentation manner, and students will self-evaluate. *Note to teacher:* All too often, students are not part of the evaluation process. When students make presentations, they never have a chance to see themselves perform and thus be in a position to self-evaluate. By making a video, students can self-evaluate.

2. Students will present their murals by discussing the symbolism and themes as they are related to social and political concerns of the current day.

Annotated List of Slides

The object in showing the slides is to visually communicate the dynamic influence of Mexico and *los tres grandes* on the United States, with a focus on the 1930s.

Los tres grandes were three Mexican muralists who greatly influenced both their country and ours. These three, Orozco, Siqueiros, and Rivera, were sophisticated, well-traveled, and professionally trained. It was the standard of the day to send promising Mexican artists to western Europe for advanced study, focusing on the great masters of the Renaissance; many of these students found inspiration in the murals of Michelangelo. Rivera, in particular, realized his own cultural heritage included a great civilization that created murals in bold colors on massive walls. (The elegant cities of the Maya were flourishing at a time when Paris was a small village. The Classic Period of the Maya was 300 C.E.–900 C.E.)

Rivera returned to his own country to continue his studies, going to the southern areas where the Maya civilization had once lived. (It should be noted that descendants of the Maya are living and working today, in the same areas; many of these Maya are well aware of their heritage, continuing to honor and follow some of their ancient beliefs.) Rivera was especially impressed with the murals of Bonampak. These murals had obviously been created as a group project and utilized colors and figure placement to symbolize power and geographical direction. In the 1930s *los tres grandes'* work in Mexico was also inspiring artists to the north, in the United States. This was also the time when the Mexican government was nationalizing companies, many of which had been owned and operated by U.S. companies. One such company was owned by the Rockefeller family; in hopes of avoiding a take-over by the Mexican government, Nelson Rockefeller presented himself as a patron of the arts who would like to expand his support to the artists of Mexico. While, in the end, Rockefeller's oil company was nationalized, he did commission Mexican muralists for large projects in the United States. Their philosophical approach to murals became an inspiration to U.S. artists struggling to survive as WPA workers. In Mexico, muralists felt that the walls belonged to the people, and, therefore, that their art should reflect their heritage and Mexico's political and social transformations. They also believed it was important to produce their murals in contemporary paints (paintings were referred to as "plastic arts") and to execute them with group effort (as the Mayas had done). (It should be noted that George Biddle was among the artists who found inspiration in Mexico, and as a former classmate of Roosevelt's [at Groton], he persuaded FDR to expand his Public Works Projects to include people in the arts.)

The slides that follow will focus first on Mexico, its traditions, its cultural heritage, and its artists. Then, we will see the works of *los tres grandes* produced in the United States. Murals produced for the WPA will be shown next, followed by murals produced by Chicano contemporary artists (influenced by this past confluence of art) in San Diego.

1. **Opening slide: Cover of book *The Mexican Muralists in the United States* by Laurance P. Hurlburt, showing Diego Rivera's *Allegory of California*.** This book is listed in the bibliography and is a valuable resource for historical information and color reproductions (photographs) of art work. See no. 27 for details on Rivera's *Allegory of California*.

2. **Close-up of Mexican candy: Mexico City.** Mexico cities, towns, and villages usually have street vendors selling artificially colored candies, cakes, and jelled desserts. Color enlivens Mexico's clothing, foods, and architecture.

3. **Days of the Dead sand painting: Oaxaca City, Oaxaca.** Trucks of sand and gypsum (a natural mineral used for the white areas) are brought in October 30 and 31 to be used for the large murals made on the central plaza walkways. There is a sense of urgency as night descends on October 31, for that marks the beginning of celebrations for Días de las Muertas (Days of the Dead), which continue November 1 and 2. This is a time to remember deceased family and friends. It is also a time to remind the living that all will die; beauty, wealth, personal power will not stop the inevitable. The skull and skeleton have been used for centuries in Mexican cultures to symbolize death as a part of life, and continue being used today. Look for use of skulls and skeletons in the slides that follow.

4. **Temple door: Palenque, Chiapas.** Palenque was one of the great Mayan civilizations and is located in one of the most southern Mexican states: Chiapas. The Mayas were superb architects, and the door was of special significance as a symbol to the opening of the underworld.

5. **Temple door: Palenque, Chiapas.** As a symbol of the underworld, doors referred to cave openings allowing passage deep within the earth. In such caves, Mayas performed special ceremonies for the gods of the underworld.

6. **Temple complex: Palenque, Chiapas.** The cities of the Mayas were enormous, carefully planned complexes. While we see the remains of this great civilization today, what we don't see is the use of many colors covering the facades of the buildings. Colors were significant and purposefully used as symbols of power and cardinal directions (east was red or yellow or blue-green for Mesoamericans in different regions at different times).

7. **Color panel of mural: Bonampak.** The mural tradition of *los tres grandes* was inspired by the marvelous murals at the Mayan city of Bonampak. This inspiration came as a revelation to Diego Rivera while he was studying painting in Europe. He had been seen as a promising young art student in Mexico and was sent to Europe, as was the custom, for a "proper" education in the arts. When study was focused on the murals of the Renaissance, Rivera awakened to the history of his own country; he realized that the Maya built grand cities utilizing murals not just as decorations but as a record of events and religious communications. He returned to Mexico and began to study the Bonampak murals.

8. ***Sunday Dream in the Alameda Park,* painting by Diego Rivera.** This large painting is set in the famous park of Mexico City, a popular place to gather and stroll. At the center of the painting you will see a *calavera* (skeleton) dressed as an elegant woman. To the right of her is José Guadalupe Posada, whom Rivera considered his artistic father, and who used many *calaveras* in his broadsides. Rivera, portrayed as a young boy, is holding the right hand of the *calavera*. Standing behind him, with a hand on Rivera's shoulder, is Frida Kahlo, Rivera's wife and a great painter in her own right. Kahlo is holding a "yin-yang" (a symbol for opposites: black/white, male/female, right/wrong, etc.). Beside Kahlo is the Cuban patriot José Martí. (Note: This painting is full of symbolism and includes many historical figures.)

9. ***Calavera Zapatista* by José Guadalupe Posada.** This is one of the *corridos* (tabloids or broadsides) produced by Posada (he produced as many as fifteen thousand to twenty thousand). "Zapatista" refers to either Zapata himself (the revolutionary leader representing the peasants in the 1910 Mexican Revolution) or a follower of Zapata.

10. ***Plagues of Mexico* by José Guadalupe Posada.** Many Mexican people died from plagues (yellow fever, etc.).

11. Days of the Dead, Oaxaca City, Oaxaca. Calaveras continue to be used in Mexican celebrations.

12. **Days of the Dead, Oaxaca City, Oaxaca.**

13. **Market stall for Days of the Dead, Oaxaca.** Special sections in the markets are set aside for sellers of celebration items for Días de las Muertas. It is customary to buy these to decorate altars set up to honor deceased family and friends. It is also the custom to buy sugar or plaster-of-paris skulls and paint on them the names of the living, given as special gifts.

14. ***Fiesta of the Dead in the City,* by Diego Rivera.** Look for Rivera's self-portrait looking through the crowd.

15. ***Cuauhtemoc Resurrected: The Torture,* portion of a mural painting by David Alfaro Siqueiros.** The industrial revolution was a time when factories came to dominate and workers were subjugated to the machine, valued less than the inanimate tools of production.

16. ***Prometheus,* mural by José Clemente Orozco, Pomona College, CA.** The murals created for Pomona College represent a pivotal time in Orozco's career. He had been greatly influenced by Michelangelo's work in

the Sistine Chapel, as he had also been by Alma Reed, his patron, who exposed him to Greek mythology. As a teenager Orozco was maimed in an accidental explosion, which destroyed his left hand and impaired his sight and hearing. Octavio Paz, the noted Mexican writer, felt Orozco identified with Prometheus, a Greek mythological character who stole fire from Olympus and gave it to man. (Note the many reds in the mural, communicating the feeling of fire.) It is felt that Orozco used this mural to represent the anguish of society transcending the situation of our "orphanhood."

17. *The Legend of the Races,* **series of murals by José Clemente Orozco, Dartmouth College, Baker Library.** *The Legend of the Races* was painted during 1932–1934. Dartmouth's budget was limited, but a contribution by Mrs. Rockefeller made payment for the murals possible. The murals' theme focuses on heroic self-sacrifice by individuals for the benefit of humanity.

18. **Portion of slide 17 series:** *Ancient Human Migration.* This is Orozco's vision of the murky primeval origins of the indigenous American civilization, representing zeal and competence of the leaders.

19. **Portion of slide 17 series:** *Modern Migration of the Spirit.* A majestic, though horribly mutilated, Christlike figure provides crescendo for Orozco's series. The figure returns to destroy his cross. Orozco felt this represented the "last judgment" and failure of modern American society. Thus, this last panel relates to the first one (slide 18) of the series in that man must once again begin the long and painful journey, struggling for human perfection.

20. *Portrait of Modern-Day Mexico,* **mural by Siqueiros, Santa Monica, CA.** This mural is one of the few executed by Siqueiros still in existence in the United States. As one of the more politically vocal artists, Siqueiros was considered too controversial; in 1933 he was deported from the United States, and many of his murals were eventually destroyed. (In February 1933, Los Angeles police actually stormed into an exhibit and shot and bashed Siqueiros's painting entitled *Blacks.*) Because *Portrait of Modern-Day Mexico* was painted on the walls of a private home (actually, the walls are of the cabana in the garden), it survives today. The wall on the right depicts Mexico's President Calles, whom Siqueiros considered to be the lowest form of corruption; the money bags (white bundles to the left of Calles) represent all the money he took from the people; the gun Calles is holding shows he was "armed to the teeth." Siqueiros also felt Calles was the Mexican equivalent of the United States ambassador to Mexico, Dwight Morrow. The dead men painted on the left represent the martyred workers of Mexico.

21. *Collective Suicide* **by Siqueiros, Museum of Modern Art, New York City.** Siqueiros was always interested in advancing the techniques and mechanics of his paintings; this painting probably represents the best of his "New York style." He considered this a "sculpture-painting" because of the three-dimensionally applied sections of paint. The painting itself is a dynamic confrontation, using machinery and materials of modern industry to produce political art that would radicalize the viewer. The bottom of the painting does not show up well in a slide; in very small scale, people are depicted being consumed by the fires.

22. **California School of Fine Arts mural by Rivera, San Francisco.** The theme is artistic and manual labor and the productive role of the worker in society. This painting by Diego Rivera was completed after *Allegory of California,* but took half the time and is 70 square feet larger. The scaffolding was the compositional device and ultimately became the weakness in the mural, making it overly rigid.

23. *Modern Labor II,* **mural by Rivera, Detroit Institute of the Arts, Detroit.** At a time when the United States was in the deepest throes of the depression, Edsel Ford paid Diego Rivera to produce a series of industrial murals at the Detroit Institute of the Arts. (As an example of the devastating effects of the depression in a one-industry city like Detroit, the 1933 Detroit Institute of the Art's budget plummeted to $40,000 from $400,000 in 1928.) Rivera spent several months sketching in the Ford Motor plants, focusing on twentieth-century industrial technology and its relationship to man. Rivera was exceptional in the use of symbolism for historic detail and political and social commentary. Slide 24 is also a good example of his use of symbolism.

24. *Modern Labor I,* **mural by Rivera, Detroit Institute of the Arts, Detroit.** Both slide 23 and this slide are murals painted at the top of the Garden Court walls in the institute. Under these murals were larger ones focusing on the dualities Rivera saw in nature, man, and technology. Rivera's raw materials reflected advancements in painting technology, and his assistants had a specific task, as was true on the assembly line.

25. *Man at the Crossroads,* **mural by Rivera, originally painted for Rockefeller Center in New York City, and later re-created in a new version in Mexico City.** In 1933, Todd-Robertson-Todd Engineering Corporation (the development manager for Rockefeller Center) commissioned Rivera to paint a mural in the Rockefeller Center building. Mr. and Mrs. John D. Rockefeller supported this commission. In this project, Rivera continued to develop his subject matter incorporating technology and workers. However, this would be Rivera's most

frankly Marxist work in the United States. Rivera predicted the liberation of man from machine by socialist transformation of society. Rivera was a great synthesizer as well as a historian. He used a geographic layout to develop his theme (note the sky-ground placement) and in this painting used the intersecting ellipses to contrast macrocosm and microcosm (i.e., the microscopic and telescopic views of the world). This served to contrast capitalism and socialism as opposing political systems, with capitalism representing the decaying of society (including the use of chemical warfare) and socialism representing the hope for humankind. The Rockefellers knew about, even encouraged, Rivera's use of Lenin as a symbol of true communism in this mural representing "man at the crossroads of life" (Rivera's words). Rivera felt "that the hope of the future lies in the organization of producers into harmony and friendship and the control of the natural forces through high scientific knowledge and the development of the skilled worker. Socialism, if you like." The dull grays and greens of contemporary chemical warfare were juxtaposed with the vibrant reds and joyous activity of a Communist May Day celebration.

What began as an innocent act led the way to the ultimate destruction of the mural. Ben Shahn, an American artist who became famous in his own right, was hired to work on the mural. He called attention to the fact that the contractor's painters were splashing paint on parts of the mural as they sloppily painted the ceiling. As one of the managers investigated the damage, he became aware of the blatant communist viewpoint of the mural. When Rivera was confronted, he said that he would prefer the entire mural be destroyed before he would alter his composition; thus, Rivera had "painted himself into a corner." The controversy became public knowledge as newspapers wrote of the confrontation and provided details of the painting. The poet E.B. White even wrote a satirical poem ("I Paint What I See") about the controversy. Despite a decision to transfer the mural to the Museum of Modern Art, workers destroyed it as removal was begun (even though the mural was painted on a separate surface, which should have facilitated removal).

26. **Detail of slide 25.** This slide shows the most controversial portion of the mural. Lenin is shown joining the hands of black and white workers, and just above his head (in the ellipse) the ascending evolution is represented with a glowing red star (Mars) and a sickle and hammer.

27. *Allegory of California,* **mural by Rivera, City Club, San Francisco.** In September 1930 Rivera had been selected to paint a mural in the San Francisco Stock Exchange Luncheon Club. Since Timothy L. Pflueger "held the purse strings" for payment to Rivera, he was intent on curbing any radical political subject matter in the mural. Rivera stated that his mural would "represent California with the three bases of her richness, gold, petroleum, and fruits. Transportation, rail and marine, will be motifs stressed, and on the ceiling, energy and speed." The overall theme was the idea of liberation; his "geographic plan" began at the bottom with miners and evolved up to the oil rigs, derricks, cranes, and ships. Man's will and spirit transforms gold, wood, and metal into goods that are to liberate the life of man.

28. **Detail of slide 27.** The heroic figure is Mother Earth, the giver (the model was the tennis champion Helen Wills Moody). Her necklace is of wheat. The genius of Mother Earth's son is represented by Luther Burbank (bent over the shovel), John Marshall and another miner panning for gold, and the "American Boy" (shown holding the plane and representing the youthful industry of aviation and the inventive gifts of humankind).

29. **Detail of slide 27.** The lumberman to the left of the young boy represents the redwood timber industry (the model for this figure was Victor Arnautoff, a California painter who would be commissioned to paint murals in San Francisco's Coit Tower). The engineer and the mechanic represent a partnership of imagination and manual labor, and between them is a project. The one political symbol used by Rivera was not discovered by Pflueger, and that is the machine gauge shown by the engineer. Note that the red hand has passed far beyond the safety level indicator. This is Rivera's allusion to the capitalist explosion (revolution) soon to occur.

30. *The Family,* **painting by George Biddle.** As a fellow student at the prestigious private school Groton, Biddle had access to F.D. Roosevelt like no other artist. Biddle was part of the "intelligentsia" looking south to Mexico for inspiration and hope for a better future in the United States. He was impressed with the Mexican muralists and their use of public buildings and walls; thus, he encouraged Roosevelt to include artists, writers, musicians, and actors as part of the WPA workers employed by the government. This Biddle painting does not show particular talent, but his connection with Roosevelt proved invaluable in creating jobs for the artistic community.

31. **WPA Work Notice.** This is a typical work notice issued for specific assignments. While artists were employed only from December 12, 1933, to June 30, 1934 (the end of the funding), sixteen thousand works were produced by thirty-six hundred artists in that time.

32. *California Coast,* **mural by Belle Baranceanu, La Jolla (post office).** Artists receiving the work notices

were not necessarily from the vicinity of their assignment. This mural decorates the wall of the La Jolla, California, post office, but the artist was from another part of the United States. While many excellent murals were produced, this mural represents the bland nature of many. The U.S. government was not as open to murals of political or social ideas as the Mexican government was. With the negative effects of the depression, most murals were to present a more positive view of our potential as a nation.

33. **Coit Tower, San Francisco: Slides 34–36 are in Coit Tower.** The murals around the interior walls of Coit Tower (which overlooks the San Francisco Bay) are excellent examples of WPA commissions. Many of the artists employed for this project had been influenced by and worked with los tres grandes. The murals were renovated in the late 1980s and are in excellent condition. (Postcards of the murals are available at the Coit Tower gift shop.)

34. *Factory Workers*, **WPA mural by Ralph Stackpole.** (Stackpole's son was the model for the youth holding the airplane in mural, slide 27.)

35. *The Orchard Scene*, **WPA mural by Maxine Albro.** Themes for the Coit Tower murals focused on California.

36. *The Pedestrian Scene*, **WPA mural by Victor Arnautoff.** (Arnautoff was the model for the lumberman in mural, slide 27.) This mural contains a few overt references to urban problems. Note the car wreck in the background and the man in the foreground being robbed.

37. *Trouble in Frisco*, **painting by Fletcher Martin.** Impatience with the difficulty of making a living and working in less than perfect environments sparked the kind of conflict depicted in this painting of dock workers.

38. *Employment Office*, **painting by Isaac Soyer.** Reflecting the despair of those seeking employment, this painting is frequently reproduced in U.S. history textbooks.

39–42. **Centro cultural murals by Victor Ochoa, San Diego.** To come full circle, it is important to realize that the Chicano muralists of today also look to their Mexican heritage for inspiration. This old water storage tank has become a cultural center for the Hispanic community around San Diego. Victor Ochoa is an accomplished artist, teaching in San Diego area universities. His sense of personal and cultural history extends to the exterior walls of the center. Note the large painting of a beautiful woman; her head is being overtaken by her skeletal structure—a reference to our vulnerability, to our cycle of living and dying, and to Días de las Muertas.

43. **Chicano Park under the Coronado Bay Bridge, San Diego.** Ochoa was also instrumental in creating the murals painted on the support columns and walls of the bridge to Coronado. And, in true los tres grandes style, these were executed by people working together to express political and social concerns about the lack of any public park available to the San Diego Chicano population. For years, the Chicano community had asked the city government to convert the unused space beneath the bridge (surrounded by their homes) for a park. In frustration, the artists "took the walls" and made it their own. Look at the paintings and you will see references to their Mayan heritage as well as a record of their struggle to obtain this space.

Resources

Books

Berdecio, Roberto, and Stanley Appelbaum. *Posada's Popular Mexican Prints: 273 Cuts by Jose Guadalupe Posada.* New York: Dover, 1972. This softcover book focuses on Posada's illustrations for broadsides or small popular books. These "consumables" were usually discarded after use; as a result, this book provides rarely available reference to Posada's famous illustrations which so influenced Rivera and Orozco.

Beckham, Sue Bridwell. *Depression Post Office Murals & Southern Culture, A Gentle Reconstruction.* Lafayette: Louisiana State University, 1989. The photographs of the murals are in black and white, and most are small, taking up less than a quarter page in most cases.

Bermingham, Peter. *The New Deal in the Southwest: Arizona & New Mexicn.* Tucson: University of Arizona Press, 1980. Small photographs of the murals in black and white, taking up less than a quarter page in most cases.

Bruce, Edward, and Forbes Watson. *Art in Federal Buildings, An Illustrated Record of the Treasury Department's New Program in Paintings and Sculpture.* Volume 1. *Mural Designs, 1934–1936.* Baltimore: John O. Lucas, 1936. E. Bruce was director of the Public Works of Art Project, and his foreword gives an overview of the project, the government's attitude, and the basis of selecting artists.

Drescher, Timothy W. *San Francisco Murals: Community Creates Its Muse, 1914–1994.* St. Paul, MN: Pogo Press, 1994. The softcover book includes colored and black-and-white photographs, ordered geographically, with addresses, artists, and dimensions listed. *Note:* The murals of Coit Tower, which have recently been renovated, are listed in detail.

Federal Arts Project. *Historical Murals in the Los Angeles County Hall of Records.* Washington, DC: Works Progress Administration, 1939. The photographs of murals are all in sepia tones, which is undesirable for accurate portrayal.

Hurlburt, Laurance P. *The Mexican Muralists in the United States.* Albuquerque: University of New Mexico Press, 1989. The focus of this excellent book is on los tres grandes and their influence on mural art in the United States. It has color photographs of their projects in the United States.

Ingle, Marjorie. *Mayan Revival Style, Art Deco Mayan Fantasy.* Salt Lake City, UT: Peregrine Smith Books, 1984. Excellent reference, with color and black-and-white photographs and text on Mayan revival of architecture in the 1920s and 1930s.

Larrea, Irene Herner. *Diego Rivera's Mural at the Rockefeller Center.* Publication by agreement between the Faculty of Social and Political Sciences of the National Autonomous University of Mexico and Epicupes, S.A. de C.V.; 1986 in Spanish, 1987 in English; 2d edition (English), 1990. This oversized book is 228 pages in length and includes color photographs of the mural that Rivera painted with slight variation from the original in El Palacio de Bellas Artes, Mexico City. A chronological account of events leading to the destruction of the controversial mural is augmented with reproductions of newspaper articles appearing at the time (in both English and Spanish). The brief introduction (34 pages, including valuable footnotes) gives an excellent overview of the cultural and political setting contributing to the public uproar over the mural's obvious references to "communist paradise," with Lenin as the unifier and guide. The extensive bibliography is especially helpful.

Leuchtenburg, William E., and editors of *Life. New Deal and Global War,* Vol. 11, *1933–1945.* The Life History of the United States series. New York: Time Incorporated, 1964. The section on art and the New Deal is valuable as a source of information as well as for color reproductions of paintings. It is one of the few sources that has color photographs of New Deal art. It is also one of the few showing paintings that dealt with political and social issues in the United States.

Paz, Octavio. *The Labyrinth of Solitude.* New York: Grove Weidenfeld Press, 1985. This latest edition includes new texts. Two used for this project: "The Present Day" and "From Independence to Revolution." Paz's writings give valuable insight into Mexico and its people.

Reed, Alma M. *The Mexican Muralists.* Santa Clarita, CA: Crown Publishers, 1960. It is important to realize that Reed's account is somewhat flawed in that she tended to distort events and situations to suit her "cause": the reputation of Orozco. However, this book presents brief overviews of many other muralists, not just los tres grandes. She has also written *Orozco* (1956), which

should be read remembering the preceding caveat.

Rodriguez, Antonio. *A History of Mexican Mural Painting.* New York: Putnam, 1969. This book is a valuable reference and is truly a history: it begins with the Mesoamerican murals, going into detail on several important Mayan sites and their influence on the muralists of the 1920s and 1930s. Rodriguez includes a section on two artists who were especially influential in the development of Mexican art. The two, Dr. Arl and José Guadalupe Posada, are generally recognized as a major part of the movement to eschew European artistic style in search of a Mexican style.

Sayler, Oliver. *Revolt in the Arts.* New York: Brentano's, 1930. With contributions by thirty-six representative authorities in the several arts: theater, music, dance, film, literature, and architecture. Fascinating period opinions on the "function of art in the machine age," machine-made vs. handmade.

Magazines

Artnews, April 1982 (pp. 82–87), "New Deal Art Projects: Boondoggle or Bargain?" by Milton W. Brown. Excellent view of New Deal art and good source for colored reproductions of art.

Westways, March 1972 (pp. 24–27), "How a Generation of Artists Worked Their Way Through the Depression."

Film and Videos

America Tropical (23 minutes), 16mm, on Siqueiros's mural in Los Angeles; in color, 1971.

Chicano Park (1 hour), on park in San Diego, produced by KPBS in association with local muralist Victor Ochoa, 1988.

Mexico: The Frozen Revolution (66 minutes), 16mm, 1971. Video originally produced as a 16-millimeter film in 1971. Presents a sociohistorical analysis of Mexico in view of continuing poverty and failed hopes of the 1910 revolution. (Footage from the 1910–1914 uprising is included.) Spanish dialogue with English subtitles. Tricontinental Film, Berkeley, CA.

Orozco's Mural: Quetzalcoatl (23 minutes), 16mm, on Orozco's Journey mural; in color, 1962.

Frida Kahlo (1 hour), produced by PBS. Kahlo was the wife of Diego Rivera and is recognized for her own success as an artist. This video has interesting footage of Rivera working on his U.S. murals and reflects their social and political concerns.

Diego in America (30 minutes), produced by PBS.

Walls of Fire (1 hour), on Siqueiros's March of Humanity mural in Mexico City, the largest mural in the world.

Note to teachers: Availability and sources of films and videos can be obtained by referencing NICEM (National Information Center for Educational Media), published and updated yearly by Plexus Publishing, Medford, NJ. Those produced by Public Broadcasting are listed at either (800) 344–3337 or (703) 739–5276.

Slide Resource

SPARC (Social & Public Art Resource Center), 685 Venice Boulevard, Venice, CA 90291, Attn: Roberto Rubalcava. A slide package is available for $38.92 (includes tax). This package includes 20 slides representing contemporary Chicano murals in California, a book entitled *Signs From the Heart, California Chicano Murals,* and a supplemental teacher guide giving brief descriptions of the slides. Slide sets may be purchased separately for $27.00, and the book may be purchased separately for $21.59.

SPARC has catalogued over 14,000 slides of Chicano murals in California, and these may be purchased separately. It is in the process of cataloguing slides of murals outside California. It does not have catalogued slides of Mexican muralists at the present time.

Carrie McIver, 2527 San Marcos Avenue, San Diego, CA 92104–5031.

Estonia and Namibia

Making Comparisons and Drawing Conclusions

Carol A. Adamson

Carol Adamson's comparative lesson on the newly indepen-dent nations of Estonia and Namibia enhances her students' abilities to identify sources of information beyond the library and to research questions not often found in curricular guides. The lesson is designed to relate to the personal experiences of the students and their families and facilitates the exchange of information between groups.

Introduction

Years ago, at the time when the school I work in changed its name from the Anglo-America School to the International School of Stockholm, I was hired to teach social studies in grades seven through nine. The school followed an old-fash-ioned curriculum that included a whole year of American history in grade eight but nothing at all in grade eight or nine about Sweden, the rest of Scandinavia, or northern Europe, much less the parts of the world from which many of our pupils come. The school assumed I would continue along the path of least resistance—assign work page by page from the very traditional textbooks that lined the classroom shelves; they didn't really care what I did as long as the pupils were well behaved and the parents pleased. This was a wonderful opportunity for me to be creative and experiment with the curriculum.

The curriculum as it stands now incorporates classical history—not just Greece and Rome but the classical histories of the peoples of Eurasia and Africa, ending with the Byz-antine and Muslim empires and medieval Russia, which puts us in touch with prehistoric Scandinavia. At the end of grade eight we visit the archaeological digs at Birka, the most important Viking-age trading center in this part of Sweden.

Grade nine begins with an open classroom at a base camp on Gotland, a Swedish island province in the Baltic Sea. There we visit graveyards dating from the Stone Age, see the monumental barrows and ship graves of Bronze Age chief-tains, walk through leafy meadows and hedgerows that are the result of cultivation begun in the Neolithic, and evaluate more recent hillforts, keeps, country churches, and the mag-nificent remains of Visby, which clearly reveal a wealthy and

violent medieval society. We take up Gotland's prehistoric and medieval patterns of trade, and back in the classroom, our studies extend to the Baltic littoral, the Russian rivers, the Teutonic knights, Muslim merchants, empire building by the Mongols, the Hanseatic League, the Danes, the Poles, the Russians, and the Swedes, and try to follow the political and economic consequences of the activities of these Baltic peoples. Our studies stretch to include this unfortunate cen-tury, the Nazi and Soviet empires and their consequences for this area of the world. We deal with our Baltic neighborhood rather than with the limits of Swedish national history. This year we had the addition of the film *Schindler's List*.

As I see my students from Nigeria and Japan and Colom-bia and Malaysia earnestly bending over their Baltic work and trying to make sense of history, I sense their need for a greater context so that they can more easily evaluate the human condition. I do not want them to go away with the impressions that this part of the world is the only important one, that Hitler and Stalin were the greatest of devils, and that the Holocaust is a narrowly European problem. Each year I choose somewhere else in the world as a focus for comparison. This year, as in some previous years, I chose southern Africa. The class follows the region in current events, and also goes through prehistory, migrations of peoples, Euro-pean colonization and empire building, and political and eco-nomic geography. We also use poetry, excerpts from essays and novels, and a video of the making of *Woza Albert*.

By this time, most of the pupils have a lot to say about human behavior and human conditions. They are able to add to the discussion what they know about Somalia and Burundi, Cambodia and Sri Lanka, the Shining Path in Peru and the Hamas in Lebanon. I then ask them to focus on two newly independent nations they know very little about, and compare them. Because I have two parallel classes, one class is assigned Estonia, the other, Namibia. Their task is to learn all they can about the country they are assigned, formulate and distill their information, and present it to the other class. Meeting together, the classes will then make comparisons, predictions, and perhaps draw general conclusions. The fol-lowing is the study sheet given out as the unit is assigned.

Most of the topics listed require the pupils to apply the methodology they have learned in the previous units about Gotland, the Baltic area, and southern Africa. The pupils are asked to consider the list, and I help them divide up the tasks.

Assignment for Students

You have studied the Baltic area and southern Africa. Now you will study two countries in depth, compare them, and try to draw some conclusions. The two countries are Estonia and Namibia. What could the people of these countries, which are so distant from each other, have in common?

Begin by making a large outline map of the country. Add details as you find them.

The following are points of comparison; can you think of others?

- *Economic geography*
  Major cities
  Natural resources
  Infrastructure
  Industry
  Agriculture
- *Statistics and trends*
  Population
  Population growth rate
  Gross national product
  Gross national product per capita
  Literacy rates
  Primary and secondary school enrollment rates
  Infant mortality
  Average life expectancy
  Physicians and/or hospital beds per unit of population
  National debt
  Imports and exports
- *History*
- *Ethnic groups*
- *Environment*
- *Current events*
- *Law and government*
  Form of government, political parties
  Constitution, laws and courts
  International recognition, memberships and alliances
  Defense

Teacher Information

The large outline map is made by tracing the outline of the country on an overhead projector film and then projecting it on the bulletin board, where it is again traced. The map is then filled in when the pupils find information in a variety of sources and decide on symbols. Pupils realize they need to define, and when looking for information on such things as cities, also gain understanding of other concepts such as urban and rural, towns, villages, and urban settlements. (For the last, they get into a discussion of Soviet collective farms and Bantu homelands and set about finding out what such places were really like.)

When the outline maps of Estonia and Namibia are ready and the pupils begin to add information, I ask them their assumptions about both countries with a view to opening up avenues to learning and finding information and answers. We are fortunate in that, for pupils at this level, we can enlist the help of embassies for information about small countries that is almost never accessible otherwise. Some pupils volunteer to phone the embassies and ask for help and interviews. (Earlier this year, some pupils were very successful at the South African Embassy and came back with interesting impressions, answers to lists of questions posed by the class, and contact with an information officer willing to send over information as it came in.)

The section on statistics and trends allows for learning the value and limitations of statistics, more basic definitions, applied mathematics, and comparisons. Here I have put to use my experience using the World Bank's *Development Data Book,* unfortunately now outdated. Pupils find recent statistics in a variety of sources (World Almanac, embassy material, yearbooks, data bases, etc.), make comparisons, and try to determine trends.

Finding out about the history of countries like Estonia and Namibia is an interesting lesson in itself. We examine the table of contents in all the available texts and come up with absolutely nothing useful. We then find out that there is not much more to be found about older countries such as Finland and Zambia. We then try Sweden in the same tables, with just a little bit more luck, and then Egypt, which isn't mentioned much for the last two millennia. Some pupils become indignant, but most of them begin to see that what they are trying to do in gathering information about Estonia or Namibia and then informing other groups of people about them is important. We then are able to learn something about sources—even primary sources of information.

The almanacs usually list two ethnic groups in Estonia. Embassy data adjust that to about twenty groups, together with the history and problems surrounding this reality. This study is nonthreatening to everybody in the class, and it does provide them with a good definition of ethnic group and the problems that can arise. The pupils then can discuss ethnic conflicts in the Balkans, southern Africa, and elsewhere with greater insight. (There also seems to be a shift away from some traditional European attitudes regarding African ethnic groups when the pupils equate them with Island-Swedes, Ingermanlanders, and Russians.)

Environmental problems are of worldwide concern, and here the pupils have a chance to analyze the problems and try to find out what is being done to solve them. Here is a chance to do more investigative research, and the pupils phone the local offices of the Worldwide Fund, Greenpeace, and the United Nations to supplement the information received from the embassies. We supplement book knowledge with visits to a local water purification plant and fishing fleet, and examination of local pH-values and the damage due to acid rain. This year the class also saw the film *Germinal* and were aghast at the effect of coal mining on people and the natural environment. They immediately asked questions about mining regulations and conditions in Namibia.

Finally, the pupils bring to bear their knowledge of a variety of forms of government and try to diagram the power structure in Estonia and Namibia. They have learned about prehistoric republics and kingdoms, about theocracy, fascism (the corporate state), dictatorship, direct and representative democracy, and anarchy. They have studied Viking law, Gotland's medieval law code, and the fourteenth-century National Swedish Law Code developed by King Magnus Eriksson. They have read about the Nazi-targeted Nuremburg laws and have imagined what it means to live under martial law, or in a place where no one has power enough to enforce the law. They have seen a medieval gallows and eighteenth-century instruments of torture, visited a modern Swedish prison, and discussed crime and punishment in different times and places. They have read and discussed the United Nations Declaration of Human Rights.

Pupil Evaluation

Because there are fifteen pupils in each class, it is possible to encourage, instruct, and evaluate individuals and groups on a daily basis. Each class meets for eighty minutes on Mondays and Tuesdays and forty minutes on Wednesdays. On Mondays and Tuesdays the pupils gather and collate information and discuss issues in small groups. On Wednesdays they share their findings in an informal discussion. During the four-week unit I give two written quizzes on objective information such as basic geography and definitions.

The most difficult part is the final organization and presentation of information to the parallel class. Each group must produce clear and interesting information including audio-visual materials. The following discussions based on the presentations provide one more indication of their efficacy. As a final task, each pupil must write an essay in which he or she compares the two countries and predicts their future development.

Teaching in this style is great fun because it allows so much personal interaction among the pupils as well as between teacher and individual pupils and groups. The seemingly eccentric subject matter is nonthreatening but interesting for the pupils because they can see the possibilities for positive national development as well as potential conflicts (and their solutions) and then relate what they have learned to other more troubled situations in such places as the Horn of Africa, the Caucasus, and the Balkans. Taking on such places directly can lead to more shouting than learning, given the nationalities of the pupils.

Preparing for such a unit of study is well worth the effort. First of all, there is ample opportunity for the teacher to learn a lot, but, most of all, my pupils like to work this way. At the beginning of the year, some of them were insecure without textbooks and workbooks. When they begin to master the skills of research in our library, find that they can extend their skills to the Stockholm Public Library and the Foreign Policy Institute, and even extract bibliographies from the computer system in the cavernous university library and interview diplomats, they begin to take themselves seriously as competent persons. They want to be able to master the vocabulary and the concepts, and they dig deeper on their own. They learn to savor the feeling of "Aha." The other day, when one group of pupils was constructing a time line for Estonia's history, they included the Russo-Japanese War as a step toward Estonian independence in 1918. They were trying to understand that context, and the next day a shy Japanese boy arrived with a Japanese book and in halting English explained how and why the Japanese had prevailed in that war. The idea that the activities of people on the periphery of the Eurasian landmass could have such monumental influence on the lives of people on another periphery left the pupils with an understanding that what you do does make a difference, and that you probably won't always realize the consequences, but that looking back at what people have done and studying the consequences is a useful and fascinating occupation.

48

New Leaders of Nations

Asia and Africa Today

Darlene E. Fisher

Darlene Fisher introduces students to independence movements following World War II using information that is often difficult to acquire. The lesson includes the opportunity for students to discover similarities and differences among leaders, as well as an innovative and useful way to review using the game of "independence bingo."

Rationale

The multiple and varied nations of Asia and Africa and their concerns are often confusing to teach because there are so many developments, and many are not easy to understand, much less connect in logical fashion. Among these developments are the sprouting of many new nations from former colonial empires. One way to make some sense of this development is by following several specific people in specific countries to understand their motivations and actions. The generalizations one can make from these examples can help to make sense of the many varied movements.

Objective

To gain an understanding of the motives and effectiveness of the leaders of today's developing nations and the challenges they face. It is hoped that students will understand these people as fellow humans with goals and problems and not just leaders of abstract movements.

Method

Form students into groups of six. Each member of the group should read and do research about one independence leader described in the following pages as homework or at the beginning of class. Maps would enhance their understanding. Once the reading is complete, students within each group meet to discuss the leaders. Each individual in the group should answer the questions for their leader (see "Questions for Students" below). The answers should be recorded. Everyone should answer the first question before going on to the second, etc. By listening to the answers to each of the five questions, students should begin to see some similarities and differences. They should then answer the two conclusion questions. Answers may then be reported to the class orally or written and given to the teacher for credit. Evaluation should be based on how well the similarities and differences are observed.

Questions for Students

Imagine you are the nationalist leader you read about. How would you answer the following questions? Tell the others in your group the answers. Record your answers on paper.

1. What country did you represent?
2. What education or training did you have?
3. How did you become an important leader?
4. What obstacles did you have to overcome to get power?
5. What problems have you faced as a leader?

After each member of the group has given answers to the above questions, compare the lives and leadership experiences to develop conclusions on the basis of the questions below.

A. What are the common qualities and experiences of a third world leader?
B. What common problems do they face? Anything common in the solutions? Different?

Biographies

Hosni Mubarak—Egypt

On a sunny day of celebration in Cairo in 1981 flags flew and soldiers marched proudly, when suddenly shots rang out. Within minutes Anwar Sadat, president of Egypt, was dead. Who would fill the shoes of the charismatic peacemaker who had been Egypt's leader since the death of Gamal Abdul Nasser in 1970?

Egyptians and world leaders alike held their breath wondering what chaos would result. Quietly Vice President

Hosni Mubarak stepped in to stabilize Egypt and calm the fears. Many were surprised that the hard-working yet largely unknown man had political strengths. He was able to provide some of the steadiness Egyptians needed in the face of the turbulence of Middle Eastern and Arab politics and the desperate problems at home.

In taking the oath of office, Mubarak called upon Egyptians for national unity. "Everyone must ask what he can offer to Egypt and not what he can take from Egypt" (*New York Times,* June 15, 1981). He said of his new post, "This is my fate," and called upon God to guide him and his nation.

Hosni Mubarak was born in 1928 on the Nile Delta, where Sadat also had been born. His education was military. He graduated from the Egyptian air force academy as a fighter pilot and continued his training in the Soviet Union. He joined the Egyptian air force at the age of twenty-two and progressed rapidly through the ranks, becoming director of the Egyptian air force academy seventeen years later. He was air force chief-of-staff in 1969 and commander in chief in 1972.

In 1975 Mubarak became vice president of Egypt. He simultaneously served as a member of the Higher Council for Nuclear Energy and as a leader of the National Democratic Party. He has also served as the chairman of the Organization for African Unity.

Mubarak has a wife, Suzanne, who has a degree in anthropology from the American University in Cairo. She has been making a special effort to improve schools and create public libraries in the interests of improving education and preserving Egyptian culture. Their two sons, Alaa and Gamal, were seventeen and twenty when he became president. They both became bankers. Mubarak likes to keep in shape playing squash and field hockey.

The president of Egypt continues to face many challenges. A primary problem has been religious pressure, for it was Muslim extremists who killed Sadat. They apparently believed that Sadat's efforts to build a more secular state and modern economy were antireligious. Mubarak has supported political efforts of the more moderate members of the Muslim Brotherhood while strongly suppressing extremists. Such efforts have not prevented sporadic extremist attacks on tourists and Egyptians. Police and the military have thus far been supportive of Mubarak's policies and seek to control such outbreaks. That control has its negative side, however, as police can detain those they suspect whenever they choose. There have been reports of torture of those who are suspected of opposition. Conflict between Coptic Christians, approximately 10 percent of the population, and Muslims also erupts from time to time. Yet Mubarak works to strengthen the constitution and the role of the courts in dealing with these problems.

Social problems loom large on the Egyptian scene. Economically, Egypt is heavily dependent on outside aid and is struggling to meet demands from the International Monetary Fund to create more private industry. The necessary economic reforms will make life harder for an already impoverished population that is growing rapidly. Education, health, and related needs must be met.

Egypt under Sadat was isolated from the Arab community when it signed a history-making treaty with Israel. Mubarak has reconciled with his Arab neighbors while maintaining peaceful relations with Israel. Sadat had also dramatically cut ties with the Soviet Union and established connections with the United States. In the post–Cold War era Mubarak seeks to maintain ties with the United States and others but has also established ties with the new nations emerging from the former Soviet Union.

Mubarak has managed to balance international, religious, and social economic pressures thus far. However, problems in all of these areas continue to be his challenges.

P.V. Narasimha Rao—India

Can one apparently frail, elderly man hold together the presently volatile groups of India? Although the tradition of Mahatma Gandhi proves the task can be done under some times and circumstances, today is a new challenge for Prime Minister Pamulaparti Venkata Narasimha Rao, now in his second year of office.

Rao is a small, often unsmiling man, born in 1921. He appears more an intellectual than a politician and yet has played a role in politics most of his life. He speaks at least six languages and has written fiction in three. He is a scholar in the modern Hindi and ancient Sanskrit languages, a poet and linguist. Although steeped in tradition, he is also interested in math and computer technology. He is a widower with eight children.

Born in the southern Indian state of Andhra Pradesh, Rao got his education from Bombay and Nagpur universities. His family were farmers of the Brahmin caste, India's highest social group. As a young man he began to participate in the Congress Party campaigns for Indian independence led by Mohandas Gandhi and Jawaharlal Nehru. He was known primarily as an intellectual, writing materials for the campaigns and finding native roots for important ideas.

At Indian independence in 1947 Rao continued to support the dominant Congress political party led by Nehru and then later, successively, by Nehru's daughter, Indira Gandhi, and his grandson, Rajiv Gandhi (no relation to Mohandas Gandhi). He supported Indira Gandhi in a political party split in 1969, which gained him influence within her branch of the party. The assassinations of first Indira and then Rajiv pushed Rao to a more prominent position as peacemaker and caretaker. He had served loyally in the cabinets of both Indira and Rajiv Gandhi as foreign affairs minister, defense minister, home affairs minister, and human resource development minister. He was chief minister for Andhra Pradesh from 1971 to 1973. Although his loyalty is unquestioned, many wonder whether he has the decisiveness to be a leader of a divided country. He would prefer to focus on reconciliation.

As he became prime minister in June of 1991, Rao was concerned with the stagnating economy. He has chosen a policy encouraging foreign investment to help get the economy going, a policy more open to outsiders than those of the past. Four years of political confusion needed straightening out, and Rao hoped economic progress would help. His general beliefs are based along the lines of Jawaharlal Nehru: Economic progress is important, nations should avoid close entanglement with more powerful powers, and religious extremism should be avoided.

In 1991 the issue of religious extremism was Rao's greatest challenge. Traditional Hindu-Muslim tensions erupted over a temple in northern India. Four hundred years ago a temple to the Hindu god Rama was torn down and a Muslim mosque built. Hindu extremists heated up that issue until a mob tore down the Muslim mosque. Since then, Hindus and Muslims have been beating and killing one another. Each group fears the loss of their rights to worship and wants revenge for mistreatment by others. Hindu groups hope to win a government more anti-Muslim and less secular. Rao's programs for economic progress and investment are challenged by potential chaos.

Note: This biography first appeared in the *CTA Newsletter,* New Trier Township High School, Winnetka, Illinois.

Benazir Bhutto—Pakistan

In an Islamic nation where men are expected to control matters outside the home, a woman, daughter of an executed former prime minister, became prime minister for the second time in October 1993. Benazir Bhutto is a tall, impressive woman who is usually a crowd pleaser. She dresses with the modesty demanded by Islamic social code and is careful to remain properly formal in both political and social relations. Her education has been Western and her political training brutal.

The Bhutto family are wealthy landowners who have been prominent in Pakistani politics but often at odds with other key players such as the president, the army, and the bureaucracy. Her first term as prime minister ended in charges of corruption that put her husband in jail and placed Bhutto under house arrest for the second time in her life.

Benazir Bhutto was born in Karachi, Pakistan, in 1953. An English governess provided her early education. She studied at Roman Catholic schools while retaining her family's and nation's Islamic faith. Her higher education

took place outside Pakistan. She earned degrees from Radcliffe College (Harvard) in 1973 and Oxford in 1976. Her academics focused on politics, government, philosophy, and economics. She considered seeking a job in the foreign service.

Meanwhile, in 1967 her father formed the Pakistan People's Party. Pakistan had been created in 1947 in separate eastern and western sections. In the late 1960s and early 1970s the country faced a civil war in which the eastern portion split off to become independent Bangladesh in 1973. Under a new constitution prescribing a parliamentary form of government, Zulfikar Ali Bhutto became prime minister of the remaining part of Pakistan in 1973. In 1977 he was overthrown by General Zia ul Haq. Zulfikar Bhutto was charged with ordering the murder of an opponent and executed despite international appeals to save his life.

After the death of her father, Benazir Bhutto was kept under house arrest. Her brothers remained abroad. She was released from house arrest in 1986. Her family arranged a marriage for her to a businessman and land developer, Asif Ali Zardari. She became the mother of two daughters and a son. Assuming leadership of the Pakistan People's Party, she was able to win sufficient electoral support to form a coalition government and become prime minister in 1988 after the death of Zia in a plane crash. She soon had problems, however. She was not able to manage all the internal complications of an administration in which forces such as the army and the bureaucracy refused to cooperate, despite her popularity with many of the people. She lost power in 1990.

On her return to power in 1993 Benazir Bhutto faced many problems. Nearly 70 percent of Pakistan's people are illiterate. Many people lack safe water. Corruption in government is deep rooted. Old landed families and newer businessmen prosper, but few others do. Military costs are high. Women have few rights or opportunities. Pakistan has been feuding over territory with its neighbor, India, since the two nations split at independence in 1947. Thus, fear of war justifies large military budgets. Although Pakistan has benefited from U.S. aid, that resource has been cut off in a dispute over the Pakistani development of nuclear weapons. Groups who wish a more traditional Islamic government promise to play a more critical political role, probably further restricting the role of women. Yet the shared Islamic faith is a force holding the nation together. An allegiance to Islam may also help gain financial assistance from oil-rich nations of the Middle East.

Bhutto's Pakistan People's Party has generally maintained an approach to those problems that emphasizes the needs of the people. She favors slum clearance, food for the hungry, health care for the sick, and jobs for the unemployed. She plans to make these reforms while cooperating with private business. However, funding for such programs will be difficult to find, especially if she continues to resist taxing wealthy landowners.

Bhutto's own family presents a challenge to her personal success. At the time of her father's arrest, her two brothers were in England. They remained abroad and engaged in antigovernment conspiracies during Zia's rule. In 1985 her younger brother, Shahnawaz, died mysteriously in France. Meanwhile, her other brother, Murtaza, took refuge in Syria. He returned to Pakistan just after her reelection to take a seat in the assembly and was promptly jailed as an opponent. Her mother, Nusrat Bhutto, has thrown her support to the male line of Murtaza in traditional Islamic custom. Benazir has thus lost an important traditional area of support, her family.

Bhutto faces an uncertain future in Pakistan, but as a female head of an Islamic country, she will be an influence in the international scene, already having drawn attention to her concern for the plight of Bosnian Muslims.

Daniel Arap Moi—Kenya

"Your Excellency, come down to the State House. Kenya has lost its eyes." That message awoke Daniel Arap Moi on August 22, 1978. It meant that President Jomo Kenyatta, founding father of the independent nation of Kenya, was dead. Moi was vice president. Many wondered what would happen now. Would the nation continue? Would its problems continue? Would things get better?

Kenya faced many problems after it became independent from the British. The nation was made up of many ethnic units, both large and small, with much bitterness and rivalry between them. Kenya had a growing middle class, some industry, and a developing, profitable tourist business. Yet its economy was not keeping pace with its population and the hopes of the people. Unemployment grew. Land, which nearly everyone wanted, was a source of conflict, as there was not enough and the elite groups controlled the best land.

As leader of the strongest political party in Kenya, Moi became the new president. He had been active in Kenyan politics for many years. Moi was born to a poor farming family in a village 150 miles north of the capital of Nairobi in 1924. His name was Torotich Arap Moi. *Arap* means "son of" in the Tugen language. When he began attending mission school, he was given the baptismal name of Daniel. After attending the mission school, he attended a government African school while Kenya was still a British colony. In 1945 he became a teacher at a government African school. Later Moi married and had three children, but his family is kept from the public eye.

Although Moi has not claimed to have played a major role in the Kenyan independence struggle, he did hide five rebels and take care of them during the conflict. He was the first national leader to visit Kenyatta in prison and urge his release so that talks for a constitutional independence could occur. The British had established a legislature consisting mostly of white settlers and only a few black Africans. In 1955 the black representative from the Rift Valley resigned, and Moi was appointed to the seat, beginning his political career.

Moi was very involved in politics thereafter. He was a participant in the constitutional discussions before independence as the leader of the Kenya African Democratic Union. Kenyatta led the Kenya African National Union (KANU), a group drawn heavily from the powerful Kikuyu tribe. The two parties formed a coalition to develop a transitional government for independence and later merged. As a member of the tiny Tugen tribe of the Rift Valley Kalenjin ethnic group, Moi provided, in Kenyatta's view, a good political balance between the competing clans of the larger Kikuyu and Luos.

As a supporter of Kenyatta, Moi rose in government positions: minister of education, then local government, and later home affairs. He was also active within the political party as president of KANU for the Rift Valley province. In 1971 he became vice president of Kenya, and that job was his stepping stone to the presidency at Kenyatta's death.

Moi has continued in office since 1978, consolidating his power and discouraging opposition. Kenya has remained relatively stable but has not made the hoped-for improvements. It continues to have relatively good road and telephone networks, small-scale industry, tourism, and a large educated middle class, which are strengths. Many of these strengths are weakened, however, by neglect and reduced through inflation. Moi's response to criticism has been to crack down on the opposition. Some opponents have died in various mysterious circumstances. Magazines have been impounded, and freedom of the press is challenged by libel and sedition charges. Particularly damaging to both the economy and the political situation has been rampant corruption at all levels.

In 1991 major international donors to Kenya withdrew aid. They demanded reforms before aid would be resumed. As a result, Kenya's first multiparty elections in twenty-six years were held in December 1992. International observers considered the elections unfair and manipulated by KANU and the larger Kikuyu and Luo tribes. Moi was reelected with only 35 percent of the vote because the opposition was divided. Little seems to have changed with the election either politically or economically.

Suharto—Indonesia

Indonesia's top leader since 1967, Suharto was born in a bamboo hut in a small village, Kemusuk-Argomalya, on the island of Java. Once it was a collection of bamboo huts. The village is now a showplace of concrete houses and paved roads. The village chieftain is Suharto's half-brother, the only person in town with a satellite dish. Suharto grew up in a poor, divided home. As a young man he hoped for a job as a bank teller but failed to get to work when his one sarong was torn and he could not afford another. Thus, in 1942 when he began hearing Radio Tokyo propaganda, he was unemployed and ready for a change.

The Japanese spread sweet and alluring promises of economic cooperation in a "Greater East Asian Co-Prosperity Sphere." They encouraged the Indonesians to join with Japan against the Dutch colonial masters of Indonesia. Frustrated at Dutch control and exploitation, Suharto and many of his generation joined World War II on the side of the Japanese. Before long they realized that the Japanese were even more brutal taskmasters than the Dutch. By 1945 Suharto had joined a guerrilla movement against the Japanese.

Despite his disillusionment with the Japanese, Suharto had learned from them a vision of a wider world and its relationships and an idea of a united greater Indonesia or "Indonesian raya," beyond his native island of Java. He also came to respect order, discipline, and ruthlessness in the administration of a country. Economic progress seemed to be a Japanese secret of success worth seeking.

As the Japanese surrendered in 1945, the Dutch tried to retake the islands. Suharto joined the opposition to the Dutch and commanded a guerrilla battalion until the Indonesian effort was successful in 1949. After independence Suharto stayed in the army and rose through the ranks as President Sukarno attempted to rule the country. By 1963 Suharto had taken command of the strategic forces based in the capital, Djakarta, thus putting him on the scene of future action. The army itself was full of factions with little agreement.

Sukarno's policy was to try to unite the Islamic, nationalist, Communist, and military forces into a unified nation and government. His theoretical base for this unity was the Pancasila, or five principles. These principles included belief in a god, humanitarianism, nationalism, democracy, and social justice. By 1965 Sukarno's union was falling apart, and he turned to the Communists, many of them Chinese, for support, thus alienating the other groups.

On October 1, 1965, a bloodbath began with a botched Beijing-inspired Communist coup d'état. Someone rounded up six key generals and killed them brutally. Suharto was not on the hit list. Large-scale violence broke out against the Communists and against citizens of Chinese ancestry, who often dominated the local economy. More than 500,000 were killed. At the end of the chaos Sukarno was discredited, and Suharto emerged as a leader of what he called the New Order in Indonesia. By 1967, as Sukarno was eased out of power, Suharto became acting president and in 1968 was formally made president.

The New Order was to be just that: *order.* Communists were not orderly in Suharto's mind and were not a part of it. Fundamentalist Islam was not orderly enough for much favor either, although Suharto seems more friendly to that force in recent years. The army played a critical role in political organizing. The Pancasila remained important as political goals. Opposition was not tolerated. At first opposition was put down brutally, but later discipline was enforced more by courting key people to the government and not allowing the opposition an opportunity. Fewer people were jailed as political prisoners. Favors rather than coercion held more people in line. Nevertheless, human rights organizations are concerned about Indonesia's political prisoners.

The ideal of economic progress was vital to Suharto's concept of the New Order. The oil boom of the 1970s, in which Indonesia enjoyed significant participation, helped Suharto's efforts. Foreign aid gave a boost as well. These efforts brought more rice, roads, schools, markets, and clinics to the villages. He encouraged business and investment and theorized that a prosperous economy would eventually benefit all, although wealthy businessmen were clearly the greatest beneficiaries. Indonesians often use the image of the *wayang,* the classical shadow puppet play, to describe the handling of power in their country. Much is hidden from the eye.

When oil prices fell in the 1980s and Suharto had to scramble for a new economic base, he moved to manufacturing for export and encouraged foreign investment, which appeared to keep Indonesia on its economic feet. The new petrochemical, transportation, and telecommunications industries provide benefits especially to the wealthy elite. The modified free-market economy serves Indonesia effectively for a continued 6 percent economic growth and a growing per capita income.

Suharto begins his work day in the same house he lived in as a military commander, arising at 5:00 A.M. to begin work. By 9:00 A.M. he is at the palace, a former Dutch governor's residence, working through a rigidly scheduled day of visitors and appointments. In the afternoon he often goes to openings and ribbon-cuttings for new projects, all carefully recorded for national television. A monthly TV program features his visits to villages. Evenings are devoted to his prosperous friends and family and private foundations that he has established for charity and influence.

After twenty-seven years Suharto seems firmly in power. He is Suharto Bapak (Suharto Father) and has considerable support at all levels of his nation. Economic success has marked him a winner, but the direction of some of the economic benefits has raised questions. Suharto has six adult children between the ages of twenty-nine and forty-one. Four of them, Tommy, Siti, Sigit, and Bambang, are involved very profitably in Suharto's modern economy, raising questions of whose benefits Suharto is seeking and what his plans for the future might be.

At age seventy-one, Suharto began a new five-year term, his sixth. Many questions are being raised as to whether he can continue. Yet there is little in the way of organized, functional opposition. Any event will be heavily influenced by the role of the military, which is thus far unclear. Parliamentary elections, called "festivals of democracy," have been held every five years, but only the official Golkar Party is legal, and many in Parliament as well as governors and army officials are chosen by Suharto.

Suharto is clearly on top of political developments identifying with the Islamic majority. In 1991 he took a highly publicized pilgrimage to Mecca. King Fahd of Saudia Arabia gave him a new name, Mohammed, to add to his single Indonesian name. Suharto seems to mean stability and progress to Indonesians, who have profited from his rule.

Note: This biography first appeared in the *CTA Newsletter,* New Trier Township High School, Winnetka, Illinois.

Mahathir bin Mohamed—Malaysia

Malaysia's most notable political characteristic is its ethnic mix. The nation is composed of 59 percent Malay, 32 percent Chinese, and 9 percent Indian groups. The Malays are mostly Muslim, and the others are Hindu, Buddhist, Confucianist, and Taoist. Traditionally, the Chinese and Indians have controlled the business of the nation and have prospered. The Malays have been farmers and far less prosperous. Since independence in 1957, the major challenge for the Malaysian government has been to increase opportunities for the Malays and thus avoid potential trouble bred from jealousy. The Malaysian constitution made special provisions for Malays to "catch up," but improvement was not significant. The Malay religion of Islam and the Malay language are official nationally in Malaysia. In the middle of this mixture stands Mahathir bin Mohamed, prime minister. His prescription for avoiding disaster? Provide Malays with an opportunity to participate in a booming economy.

Mahathir was born December 20, 1925, in the Malaysian town of Alur Setar. He received his early education at the Malay school in the town of Sebrang, attended Abdul Hamid College, and received a medical degree from the University of Malaysia in Singapore. After graduation he served as a government medical officer in three locations before going into private practice in 1957.

The 1957 independence of Malaya (which became Malaysia in 1963) led him to reconsider his career plans. In 1965 Mahathir began his political career and was elected to the House of Representatives. He was a member of the UMNO (United Malay National Organization) Party. His political position was so extremely pro-Malay that he was expelled from the party in 1969, the year a race riot broke out in the city of Kuala Lumpur.

Mahathir had advocated using loans and investments to increase Malay participation in the commercial and industrial life of the country. The government began such a program in 1971, calling it the New Economic Policy. In 1972 Dr. Mahathir was readmitted to the party and in 1976 won an election as deputy prime minister. He also served variously as minister of education and minister of trade and industry.

In 1981 Prime Minister Hussein bin Onn was in ill health and stepped down in 1981. Mahathir took the job. He won impressive election victories in 1982 and 1986. Previous prime ministers had come from among the land's traditional princes. Mahathir was the first commoner. He set out to dramatically improve the economy, end corruption, and make the government more efficient. Known as "a man in a hurry," he set about developing heavy industry and looked to Japan and Korea as models for economic development. He has encouraged developing what he says are Japanese qualities such as efficiency, cleanliness, orderliness, thrift, trustworthiness, and especially hard work. His "Look East" policy emphasized Malaysian ties with Asia and Muslim countries first and Western countries second. Foreign involvement has been welcomed as long as Malays are given opportunity. Despite economic setbacks and the falling prices of Malaysia's primary exports of tin, oil, and rubber, the Malaysian economy has made an impressive improvement.

The effort to encourage Malay participation in the economy continues. Yet Mahathir also has to deal with militant fundamentalist Islamic groups, which seek to take the government in the direction of traditional law and reject what are considered Western materialist values. Mahathir has tried to curb the movement without offending those who hold the dominant Islamic faith. Balancing economic development and the Islamic faith is a challenge. It remains to be seen whether Dr. Mahathir has the right prescription.

Mahathir himself is an extremely hard worker who does not drink, smoke, or take much relaxation. He expects others to work hard as well. One day he may dress as a prosperous Western businessman and another day in a traditional Malay tunic, according to the occasion and audience. He insists that government officials always wear a name badge, as he does, so that no one can hide irresponsibly behind anonymity. Politicians should not appear too wealthy, he believes. He and his wife, Dr. Siti Hasmah binti Jahi Mohd Ali, have two daughters and three sons who are educated in England. Mahathir thus is a man of both national and international interests.

Deng Xiaoping—China

Deng Xiaoping, the mastermind of current Chinese political theory, was born August 22, 1904, in Paifangcun, a tiny isolated village in western China. Although they lived in an area of rural poverty, Deng's family had some money and a tradition of scholarship, village leadership, and public service. His father, Deng Wenming, was literate, a captain in the town militia, and a devout Buddhist. Deng Xiaoping was his first son.

Deng's education began with tutoring at home. He was then sent to the nearest town as a boarding student at Guang'an High School number two. Later he went to Chongqing and attended a tutorial run by an old revolutionary who prepared students for work-study programs in France. Deng went to France but was too poor to study. He worked in steel manufacturing, in a Renault auto plant, and as a locomotive fireman. He was so poor that for a time he lived on a glass of milk and a croissant a day. In France he met Zhou Enlai and other Chinese Communists. He joined the Communist Party in 1925, visiting Moscow as he returned to China.

Upon his return to China he began his lifelong activity in the Communist Party of China, assisting the party in a variety of roles. He taught briefly at a military academy. The Shanghai Communists sent him on a dangerous mission to organize the peasants in Guangxi in southeastern China, an extremely dangerous task. He was once attacked by bandits, who threatened his life. He proved very successful in organizing peasants. He would urge them to kill allegedly oppressive landlords. The peasants would then be loyal to the Communist Party, as they could no longer be on the other side. Since he was using very small forces against large ones, he usually lost actual battles, to the dismay of party leaders. Although he had no military training, he was adept at developing his own strategies. He went to the mountains to join Mao Zedong, the key Chinese Communist leader, because he agreed with Mao's emphasis on the necessity of organizing peasants in order to have a successful revolution. Party leadership inspired from Moscow still depended upon urban revolt.

The leadership of the Communist Party based in Shanghai called Deng back to be "struggled with," the first of several serious and painful attacks on him during his career.

The Long March (1934–1935) was the escape of the party members from southern China to Yenan in the north, where they established a new base. Deng began the Long March as an ordinary party member. Mao's forces built up support and fought both the Japanese during World War II and the nationalist Kuomingtang forces led by Chiang Kai-shek until 1949.

After the Communist success in conquering Beijing and much of eastern China, Deng led the forces to wrap up control of the southwest. Mao then appointed him to create his "Third Line," a massive effort to build an industrial and defense complex deep in China, relatively safe from every attack. Mao was impressed with Deng's success in building a railroad between Chongqing and Chengdu and other construction efforts despite tremendous strains on the economy. Mao brought Deng to Beijing and made him his chief assistant. In 1954 Deng became the secretary general of the Communist Party, and by 1956 he was the number four leader.

Deng supported Mao in a number of ways. He never approved of the Hundred Flowers campaign, which allowed freedom of expression and was effective in helping repress the resulting criticisms. He helped defend Mao's theories in arguments with the Russians and verbally attacked Russia's Khruschev for trying to dominate China.

Just as Deng seemed to be very successful, he suffered another setback. Mao and other supporters launched the Cultural Revolution. Many leaders, educated people, and ordinary people were suddenly viewed as enemies of the revolution, tortured mentally and physically, and driven to the countryside or killed. In 1969 Deng and his family were forced to go to Jiangxi in southeast China, where they were confined with no communication, continually harassed, and worked at hard labor. His eldest son was brutally treated and became paralyzed.

Gradually Deng suffered less, and there were signs he would again be accepted in Beijing. In 1973 he returned to Beijing and again became vice premier, a member of the party Presidium and Central Committee. Deng was appalled at the economic chaos that had resulted from the Cultural Revolution. He worked to get administrators out of the menial jobs they were forced into during the Cultural Revolution and returned to government offices. Aware of the failures of the communes, he tried to open the economic system to new ideas and efforts. By 1975 Mao again became concerned with Deng's actions, especially those allowing more individual economic activity. Verbal attack on Deng began again. He was accused of not properly handling demonstrations that occurred after the death of Zhou Enlai, and he was removed from office. Again he had to leave Beijing.

Mao grew increasingly ill and weak. Another old Communist, Marshall Ye, supported and protected Deng in the confusion when Mao died in 1976. Deng again gradually assumed more power. By 1978 he began to take charge, openly ending some communes, providing incentives for greater work, and allowing peasants to earn money. This time he held firmly to power. Any challenge was met with force, despite new economic openness. The result of the open economic activity but closed political actions was the tragedy of the violent repression of the student demonstrations in Tiananmen Square in 1989.

Today Deng is aged and in seclusion. He primarily communicates with the world through his daughters and other assistants. His ideas and his words still determine what is happening in China, however: economic reform but little political change.

Bibliography

Bhutto

"Benazir Bhutto." *The Encyclopedia Americana*. Danbury, CT: Grolier Incorporated, 1993.

"Benazir Bhutto's Long Year Back." *New York Times*. October 9, 1993, p. 22

Current Biography Yearbook 1986. New York: H.W. Wilson Company, 1986, pp. 39–42.

Gargan, Edward A. "Benazir Bhutto Returns as Leader of a Poor and Troubled Pakistan." *New York Times*. October 2, 1993, A:12.

———. "Bhutto Stands by Nuclear Program." *New York Times*. October 21, 1993, A:12.

———. "Ex-Leaders Await Pakistan Vote Tally." *New York Times*. October 7, 1993, A:3.

———. "Following a Tough Act: Bhutto Gets Another Chance to Get It Right." *New York Times*. October 24, 1993, A:3

———. "Pakistan Chief's Dismissal Is Overturned." *New York Times*. May 27, 1993, A:3.

———. "A Talk with Bhutto: Is Her Sure Touch Slipping?" *New York Times*. June 10, 1993, A:3.

MacFarquhar, Emily. "Born to Rule, Bred to Lose." *U.S. News and World Report*. November 5, 1990, pp. 40–42.

"Mommie Dearest." *Time*. January 17, 1994, p. 39.

Deng

"Ailments, Old Age, Do Not Sap Strength of Deng 'Theories.' " *Chicago Tribune*. August 22, 1993, 1:3.

"Congress in China, Re-elects Premier." *New York Times*. March 29, 1993, A:7.

Salisbury, Harrison E. *The New Emperors*. Boston: Little, Brown and Co., 1992.

Mahathir

Current Biography Yearbook 1988. New York: H.W. Wilson Company, 1988.

International Who's Who 1993–94. London: Europa Publications, 1993.

Mauzy, Diane K., and R.S. Milne. "The Mahathir Administration in Malaysia: Discipline through Islam." *Pacific Affairs* 56 (winter 1983–84):617–48.

1992 World Almanac and Book of Facts World Almanac. New York.

Moi

Hempstone, Smith. "Confessions of a Boatrocker." *Los Angeles Times*. June 1, 1993, 5B:2.

International Who's Who 1993–94. London: Europa Publications, 1993.

"Kenya Survives Transfer of Power Smoothly After Kenyatta's Death"; "A President in the Shadow of a Legend"; "Kenya Survives Its Long-Feared Transfer of Power." *New York Times*. November 20, 1978, A:14.

Mubarak

"The Angry Man of the Nile." *U.S. News and World Report*. Vol. 99, October 28, 1985, p. 11.

Curtis, Charlotte. "Books and Suzanne Mubarak" *New York Times*. October 1, 1985.

"Egypt's Acting Leaders." *New York Times*. October 1, 1981, A:8.

Fischer, Dean. "You Can Feel the Damage." *Time*. Vol. 126, October 28, 1985, p. 26.

Gouch, Sara. "Mubarak's 10 Years." *Africa Report*. Vol. 36, November/December, 1991, pp. 38–41.

International Who's Who 1993–94. London: Europa Publications, 1993.

"Mubarak's Address." *New York Times*. October 15, 1981, A:8.

Rao

"Congress Party Loyalist with a Calming Hand." *New York Times*. New York Times Biographical Service, June 1991.

"Economic Austerity Vowed for India." *New York Times*. June 23, 1991, A:3.

"Hindu Opposition Plan to Agitate for India Vote." *Chicago Tribune*. December 31, 1992, 1:10.

Suharto

Bone, Robert C. "Indonesia." *Encyclopedia Americana*. Danbury, CT: 1980, 15:77–96.

Elegant, Robert. "Years of Living Prosperously." *National Review*. June 22, 1992, pp. 22–24.

Scott, Margaret. "Suharto Writes His Last Chapter." *New York Times Magazine*. June 2, 1991, pp. 28–30ff.

Shenan, Philip. "Indonesian President Suharto, 71, Seen Likely to Seek and Get Another Five-Year Term Next Year." *New York Times*. September 3, 1992, A12:1.

Review Exercise: Independence Bingo

To Play Bingo

The teacher reads the information *following* each name, picking at random. Students identify the person or term and put a chip in the square with the corresponding name. The winner is the person with a straight line across, down, or diagonally through the center. The winner must then correctly identify all the names he or she has crossed off to win.

Key

Cairo: The capital and largest city in Egypt.

Gamal Abdul Nasser: The leader of Egypt until 1970.

Anwar Sadat: Tried to establish peace between Egypt and Israel; assassinated by fanatic Muslims.

Hosni Mubarak: Trained as a fighter pilot; as leader of Egypt, he has maintained peaceful relations with Israel and his Arab neighbors.

Muslim Brotherhood: An Islamic religious organization in Egypt with a political agenda.

Fahd: King of Saudi Arabia.

Coptic Christians: A religious minority in Egypt.

Nairobi: The capital of Kenya.

Jomo Kenyatta: Founding father and first leader of Kenya.

Daniel Arap Moi: Selected for the position of vice president of Kenya following independence.

Sanskrit: An ancient Indian language.

Rama: A Hindu god.

Congress Party: The political party that has dominated Indian politics since independence.

Mohandas Gandhi: Led a nonviolent campaign to win independence for India.

Jawaharlal Nehru: First prime minister of India.

Indira Gandhi: Daughter of Jawaharlal Nehru; prime minister; declared state of emergency. Assassinated.

Rajiv Gandhi: Became prime minister of India when his mother was assassinated.

P.V. Narasimha Rao: A highly educated Brahmin who, as leader of India, encouraged foreign investment.

Pakistan: An Islamic country that separated from India at independence.

Bangladesh: Originally the eastern segment of Pakistan.

Zulfikar Ali Bhutto: The first parliamentary leader of Pakistan.

General Zia ul Haq: Established a military dictatorship in Pakistan.

Benazir Bhutto: From a wealthy family of landowners; educated at Radcliffe and Oxford; and twice elected leader of Pakistan.

Indonesia: Occupied by the Dutch and the Japanese before gaining independence.

Golkar: The official political party of Indonesia.

Sukarno: Fought for Indonesian independence from the Dutch.

Suharto: General who overthrew Indonesia's first leader and began a policy of development financed by foreign investment and profits from the sale of oil.

Mahathir bin Mohamed: The first Malay commoner to be elected prime minister.

"Look East": A Malaysian policy that emphasized ties with Asia and Muslim countries before turning to the West.

Khruschev: Communist leader of the Soviet Union.

Beijing: The capital of China.

Mao Zedong: Led the Communist revolution in China.

Long March: The Communist escape from Kuomintang and Japanese forces in 1935–1936.

Chiang Kai-shek: Leader of the unsuccessful Nationalist forces that were defeated by the Communists.

Cultural Revolution: A period when many of the educational and political leaders as well as artists and ordinary people were regarded as enemies of the state and sent to work in the countryside or killed.

Deng Xiaoping: Leader of the Chinese Communist Party who inaugurated an open economic policy and foreign investment and a closed political system.

Tiananmen Square: The site of student demonstrations in 1989.

Independence Bingo Card. Fill in each square with a name or term from the list below. The names and terms may be arranged on the card in any order.

Cairo	Daniel Arap Moi	Pakistan	"Look East"
Gamal Abdul Nasser	Sanskrit	Bangladesh	Khruschev
Anwar Sadat	Rama	Zulfikar Ali Bhutto	Beijing
Hosni Mubarak	Congress Party	General Zia ul Haq	Mao Zedong
Muslim Brotherhood	Mohandas Gandhi	Benazir Bhutto	Long March
Fahd	Jawaharlal Nehru	Indonesia	Chiang Kai-shek
Coptic Christians	Indira Gandhi	Golkar	Cultural Revolution
Nairobi	Rajiv Gandhi	Sukarno	Deng Xiaoping
Jomo Kenyatta	P.V. Narasimha Rao	Suharto	Tiananmen Square

49

United Nations General Assembly Current Problems Project

Mary O. Burton

Mary Burton uses the United Nations General Assembly as the forum for country reports that identify and analyze current problems and propose possible solutions to difficult issues facing current world leaders. In the process, students learn skills useful for a career in business.

Objectives

- Identify, analyze, and report on a current problem in an assigned country.
- Create a solution to the problem.
- Practice skills useful in many jobs and professions today.

Skills

- Researching in current periodicals
- Analyzing information from a variety of sources
- Synthesizing—creating a solution
- Writing a report
- Communicating findings orally
- Debating issues

Student Instructions

United Nations Report

You work for the Foreign Office of (country).

You have been assigned to the staff at the United Nations as a junior assistant for research and analysis. Your job is to prepare a written report for the new ambassador to the United Nations as an overview of the current situation in your country. You will then need to make an oral report to a meeting of the UN General Assembly explaining the problem in your country that needs a solution; you will propose a possible solution.

You will need to have a knowledge of the history of the country in order to make an in-depth analysis of the present status of the country and develop possible options for the future. To obtain this information you will need to research the history of the country, with strong emphasis on twentieth-century events. Next you will have to make a study of a current problem and make an analysis of the situation. Then you will need to analyze the total picture and make projections

for the future to aid your ambassador in making his choices. The ambassador is a busy person, who needs you to select the events in the country's history that have most seriously impacted the current situation. Remember that this is important to the future of your country and that your report will play a vital part in the decisions of the General Assembly. You will give a written report to the ambassador (teacher) and an oral report to a meeting of the General Assembly (the class).

Read about the United Nations on pages ____ in your textbook.

Current Problem: Read at least *eight magazine or newspaper articles* on the problem in current and recent magazines, journals, and newspapers (going back as far as five years or so if you wish).

Turn in note cards on the background and current problem information with the written report. You may photocopy magazine articles and highlight lines instead of making notes if you wish.

Research

Background: Use your text, encyclopedia, or any other source to research the background of your country's problem. Some problems have their roots in the distant past and some in the recent past. Israel's problems could be said to go back as far as Abraham, Vietnam's to the Vietnam War, and Bosnia's to the invasion of the Muslims in the Middle Ages. Many problems have surfaced only in recent years, but most have their roots in the historical development of the country.

Format for Report

Print in blue or black ink or type. Write in paragraph form.

Page 1, Cover Page: Country, Title for problem, Your Name, Period, Date

Page 2, Statement of Current Situation: Describe the (or a major) problem the country is facing today. Identify the problem clearly.

Page 3, Background of the Problem: Describe the cause(s) of and the event leading to the current problem.

Page 4, Analysis of the Current Situation and Proposals for

the Future: Consider the various alternatives. Consider the merits and probable consequences of each of the alternatives. Make a decision on a solution.

Page 5, Bibliography: Follow the sample style shown here.

Book

Crankshaw, Edward. *Bismarck*. New York: Viking Press, 1981.
(author period *title* period place of publication colon publisher comma date of publication period)
Hecht, Jeff, and Dick Teresi. *Bismarck and His Times*. New York: Vintage Books, 1978.

Magazine

Williamson, Donald G. "The Bismarck Debate." *History Today* 24 (1974): 653–661.
(author period "title of article" period [before quote marks] *title of magazine* volume [year] colon page number[s] period)

Encyclopedia

Kent, George O. "Bismarck." *World Book Encyclopedia*. 1988 ed.
(author period "title of article" period name of encyclopedia period edition date period)

Written Report Due: _____

Oral Report

• Present the information from your paper in a two- to three-minute oral presentation. Write on the board for others to see a brief statement of the problem and a brief statement of your proposed solution. You may use a transparency.
• The UN General Assembly will then discuss two or three of these problems and vote on solutions.

Two Other Possible Scenarios

If one of these scenarios is chosen, then there would be no UN General Assembly report, only reports to the board or the embassy staff.

1. Let students be business people working for a company (Coca-Cola, for example) that is planning to set up a new plant in a foreign country and wishes to know whether or not it would be a successful venture. Students would do the same research into a problem and its causes and present a written report to the chairman of the board (the teacher). They would then make recommendations to the board of directors of the company (the class) about the feasibility of a new plant in the country. The board would take action on the basis of the student report.

2. Let the students work for the U.S. Department of State, and be assigned to the staff of the U.S. Embassy in the chosen country as junior assistants for research and analysis. Their jobs would be to prepare a report for the new ambassador

(the teacher). They would also give an oral report to the entire staff (the class).

Notes for Teachers

Students generally enjoy doing the UN project because they are interested in what is going on in the world today and because they like to be able to tell their classmates something that the others do not know.

The project may be assigned in the spring, after the students have some knowledge of events in history and some practice in determining causes and effects. The country could also be assigned at the beginning of the year so that students could begin collecting articles and could follow that country's history when it is covered in class sessions during the year. If this time frame is chosen, introduce the project early; then give the students a few weeks to study the news before selecting a country to study. New problems that arise during the course of the year in countries not already covered could be assigned to new students or to students who are having difficulty finding articles on the country originally assigned.

Provide a list of countries that are highlighted in the news, such as Bosnia, Israel, Egypt, Germany, Russia, South Africa, Rwanda, Japan, China, Ireland. Even though it is not a fully independent country today, Palestine could be included to allow students to see both sides of the problem in the Middle East. Let students choose and rank five of these countries that they would like to study. Sometimes students are aware of problems in some country that is not on the list; allow them to include that name among their five choices. Sometimes in large classes it is necessary to assign two students to one country. If this is done, assign to two students those countries that appear most frequently in the news.

So that students (and teachers) will not feel overwhelmed by this project, emphasize that written reports, with some possible exceptions, should not have more than one page for each section (see "Format for Report" above). Suggest that a *well-written* paragraph or two would suffice. The bibliography may be longer, especially if more than one student is preparing the report. If two students are working on the report, their sections might also have to be longer. Any questions not answered in the written report could be addressed during the oral presentation.

Before the debate in the UN General Assembly, the class should elect a president to preside over the proceedings. This should be preceded by a study of the United Nations. The formality or informality of the debate will depend on how much time is available for the activity. A model UN format would be a good experience but might be more time consuming. After all presentations have been made, the students will choose one problem to discuss. A motion for UN action should be made and voted upon.

A Modest Proposal of the Types of Sources and Materials a Teacher Can Gather to Support the Teaching of World History

Marianna McJimsey

Marianna McJimsey concludes this section with a useful list of possible sources for world historians and their teachers. This list serves as an introduction to be extended and diversified over time.

I have gathered here a sampling of some of the sources and materials I have used or my students at Colorado College have used to supplement a textbook when teaching secondary-school world history. The materials included here:

- simply illustrate the wide range of materials from which one can draw;
- have been used to give flesh and blood to the people who live and have lived in regions of the world unfamiliar to our students;
- reflect the two-year integrated U.S. history/world history curriculum of Colorado Springs School District #11;
- because of the page limits of this listing, do not include examples from all areas of the world, or many videos, films, or multimedia sources.

All of us as history teachers collect materials, texts, and documents to teach history. This particular listing can be added to those that experienced teachers have been using themselves or can be among the first that new teachers use. The important thing is to create your own bibliography of sources that you and your students have enjoyed.

Secondary-school world history is a specialty within the academic discipline of history. Its interdisciplinary nature poses its own challenges, one of which is how to teach the broad themes in history to students whose chronological and geographic sensibilities are being developed. Fortunately, there are many sources upon which we, as historians, can draw, and indeed to which we should also contribute.

Kinesthetic Geography

With homemade salt clay (playdough consistency), students form maps of the areas and countries to be studied. The geography of and relationships among geographic areas are necessary to know in understanding much of history, e.g., Alexander the Great's empire; the Portuguese in Brazil; partition of India and Pakistan; the Balkans in the twentieth century.

When map making has been a consistent part of a history course, at the conclusion of the course students are able to create free-hand maps of the world that reveal important understandings about geographical relationships in history.

Music

Music is one of the most effective avenues through which to introduce high school and middle school students to another country or culture.

Begin the course by asking students to bring their favorite tapes and CDs to play for three minutes at the beginning of class. Gradually intersperse occasions for playing music representative of areas and time periods being studied, e.g., the sitar and tabla music of India, baroque music of Europe, vocal ensembles of Zimbabwe, American jazz.

Find the tapes and CDs at the public library or the music library of a local university or college. Move on to ask the students themselves to conduct the search for the music, e.g., a recording of the koto of Japan, and select what they think is representative to play for the class.

Curriculum Guides and Syllabi

Arab World Notebook. Project of Najda: Women Concerned About the Middle East, 1400 Shattuck Ave., Suite 7, Berkeley, CA 94709, (415) 549–3512.

Brooks, George E., Dik A. Daso, Marilynn Hitchens, and Heidi Roupp. *The Aspen World History Handbook: An Organizational Framework.* Lessons and book reviews for non-centric world history, Aspen World History Institute, 1994.

Coleman, Craig S. *Social Studies Guide on Korea for High*

School Teachers. Los Angeles: Korea Society, 1994.

Friedlander, Jonathan. *The Middle East: The Image and the Reality.* University of California, 1981. Excellent source for teachers; includes lists of resource centers and teaching materials.

Greenberg, Hazel Sara. *A South Asia Curriculum: Teaching About India.* 1994. The American Forum for Global Education, 45 John St., Suite 908, New York, NY 10038.

Korean Studies Council International, PO Box 312, Hartsdale, NY 10530. *Teaching about Korea, Lessons for Students in Grades 4–12.*

Latin America: Land of Diversity, A Comprehensive Multi-Media Social Studies Course on Latin America, Grades 9–12. 1990. Roger Thayer Stone Center for Latin American Studies, Tulane University, New Orleans, LA 70118.

National Center for History in the Schools, 10880 Wilshire Blvd., Suite 761, Los Angeles, CA 90024–4108. E.g., Ancient Ghana: Pre-Colonial Trading Empire; Mansa Musa: African King of Gold (medieval West Africa); Role of Women in Medieval Europe; Wang Mang: Confucian Success or Failure.

Reilly, Kevin. *World History.* New York: Markus Wiener, 1991. Collection of syllabi, rich in suggestions.

Starr, Jerold. *Lessons of the Viet Nam War: Teacher's Manual.* Pittsburgh, PA: Center for Social Studies Education, 1988.

Upper Midwest Women's History Center, Hamline University, 1536 Hewitt Ave., St. Paul, MN 55104–1284. Among the published titles are: *Women in Ancient Greece and Rome, Women in Latin America, Women in Japan.*

Welch, Mike. Dublin City Schools, Dublin, OH 43017. *Blood Ghosts of the Kongo.* My students have found Welch's "Acting Out History" dramas excellent. This one is set in the fifteenth century in what is, today, Zaire.

Journals

Aramco World Magazine. Aramco Services, 9009 W. Loop South, Houston, TX 77096. A beautifully illustrated and written magazine of the Arab world. Articles include bibliographies. Aramco is generous in giving free subscriptions to teachers.

Arts of Asia. 1309 Kowloon Center, 29–39 Ashley Rd., Kowloon, Hong Kong.

Calliope. Cobblestone Publishing, 7 School St., Peterborough, NH 03458–1454, (603) 924–7209 or (800) 821–0115. Although directed at grades 5–10, *Calliope* is useful for older students as well. Themes are related to people and events in world history. There are always bibliographies of books and films. Examples of topics:

Buddhism; the Ming dynasty; Mongols, Shoguns, and Samurai of Japan; Hunnic invasions; Carthage; Judaism. Examples of themes that are developed with a global emphasis: communication, science and technology, transportation, archaeology.

Concord Review. Founded in 1987 to seek and publish exemplary history essays by secondary students in the English-speaking world. Will Fitzhugh, editor, PO Box 661, Concord, MA 01742, (800) 331–5007; email: fitzhugh@world.std.com.

Current History: A World Affairs Journal. 4225 Main St., Philadelphia, PA 19127. An entire issue is devoted to a given topic, e.g., Africa, China. Up-to-date maps and background materials are excellent both for teachers and for secondary-school students.

Journal of World History and the *World History Bulletin.* Richard Rosen, executive director, World History Association, Drexel University, Philadelphia, PA 19104. The *Journal of World History* is the first journal devoted exclusively to world history as a field of research in global, comparative, and cross-cultural history. The *World History Bulletin* includes ideas, materials, and teaching tips for world history courses.

Perspective. National Council for Geographic Education. 16A Leonard Hall, Indiana University of Pennsylvania, Indiana, PA 15705–1087. Excellent column, "Resources in Non-Geographical Publications," e.g., "Climatic Change and the History of the Middle East," *American Scientist* 83 (July–August, 1995):350–355; how major climatic changes altered the course of Middle Eastern history over the past five thousand years.

World Eagle: The Monthly Social Studies Resource: Data, Maps, Graphs. 111 King St., Littleton, MA 01460–1527. October 1995 issue, e.g., included: "Major International Labor Migration Flows," "Lithuania: Profile & Map," "Blank Map of Mexico with State Division," "A Man's Day/A Woman's Day in Africa," "Name Them! Central America."

Literature

Camus, Albert (1913–1960). *The Plague.* New York: Knopf, 1948. Algerian 1957. Written by Nobel Prize for Literature winner. Morality tale of the problem of war.

Chen, Yuan-tsung (1932–). *The Dragon's Village.* New York: Viking Penguin, 1981. Seventeen-year-old Lengling joins a revolutionary theater group carrying out reforms in the Chinese countryside in 1949, and amid tumultuous events she grows toward maturity.

Conrad, Joseph (1857–1924). *Heart of Darkness.* New York: St. Martin's Press, 1996. Confrontation between the "civilized" and the primitive.

Diaz del Castillo, Bernal (1496–1584). *The Bernal Diaz Chronicles: The True Story of the Conquest of New Spain.* ———. *The Discovery and Conquest of Mexico.* New York: De Capo Press, 1996.

Diqs, Isaak. *A Bedouin Boyhood.* New York: Universe Books, 1983. A classic, not only about the Bedouin, but also about boyhood.

Equiano, Olaudah (1789) *The Interesting Narrative of the Life of Olaudah Equiano or Gustavus Vassa, The African.* New York: St. Martin's Press, 1995. Slave narrative.

Franklin, Benjamin (1706–1790). *The Autobiography of Benjamin Franklin.* New York: Viking Penguin, 1986.

Gao, Yuan (1952–). *Born Red: A Chronicle of the Cultural Revolution.* Stanford: Stanford University Press, 1987. Observations on eighteenth-century America and western Europe.

Graves, Robert. *Good-bye to All That.* New York: Double-day, 1957. World War I trench warfare.

James, Cyril L. *The Black Jacobins: Toussaint L'Ouverture and the San Domingo Revolution.* New York: Random House, 1989. Toussaint, 1743–1803.

Kennan, George F. *The Marquis de Custine and His Russia in 1839.* Ann Arbor: Books on Demand. Custine, 1790–1857.

Le Vasseur, Guillaume, and Sieur de Beauplan. *A Description of Ukraine.* Cambridge: Harvard University Press, 1993. Russia in the seventeenth century.

Levi, Primo (1961). *Survival in Auschwitz; The Nazi Assault on Humanity.* New York: Simon and Schuster, 1995.

Llang, Heng, and Judith Shapiro. *Son of the Revolution.* New York: Random House, 1984. Chinese Cultural Revolution, 1966–1969.

Machiavelli, Niccolo (1469–1527). *The Prince.* New York: Oxford University Press, 1984.

Manchester, William (1922-). *Goodbye Darkness: A Memoir of the Pacific War.* New York: Dell, 1987.

More, Thomas (1478–1535). *Utopia.* New York: Cambridge, 1989.

Mullen, Edward J., ed. *The Life and Poems of a Cuban Slave: Juan Francisco Manzano, 1797–1854,* Hamden, CT: Archon Books, 1981.

Narayan, R.K. *The Mahabharata.* New York: Columbia, South Asia Books, 1989.

Oussaid, Brick. *Mountains Forgotten by God.* Colorado Springs, CO: Three Continents Press. Autobiography of childhood in poor Berber family in the Atlas Mountains.

Paine, Thomas (1737–1809). *Common Sense: The Call to Independence.* New York: Viking, 1982.

Remarque, Erich Maria (1898–1970). *All Quiet on the Western Front.* New York: Fawcett, 1987. World War I.

Rolvaag, Ole E. (1876–1931). *Giants in the Earth: A Saga of the Prairie.* New York: HarperCollins, 1965.

Shakespeare, William (1564–1616). *The Tempest.* New York: Bantam, 1988.

Smith, H. Daniel. *Picture Book Ramayana.* Syracuse, NY: Syracuse University, 1981.

Voltaire (1694–1778). *Candide.* New York: Dover, 1991.

Winter, Denis. *Death's Men: Soldiers of the Great War.* New York: Penguin, 1985.

Wollstonecraft, Mary (1759–1797). *Vindication of the Rights of Woman.* New York: Viking, 1993.

Yezierska, Anzia (1880–1970). *Bread Givers: A Novel: A Struggle Between a Father of the Old World and a Daughter of the New.* New York: Persea Books, 1975.

Young, Delbert. *According to Hakluyt: Tales of Adventure and Exploration.* Buffalo: General Distribution Services, 1973. Hakluyt (1552–1616) was a British geographer and promoter of colonization, exploration, and trade who based his writings on interviews with sailors, sea captains, and merchants.

Folk Tales, Short Stories, Poetry, and Fiction

Aesop's Fables. New York: Holt, 1985. Illustrated by Michael Hague. Aesop's fables came to the Western world by Syrian translations into the Greek language with other Oriental tales added.

Agnon, S.Y. *A Simple Story.* New York: Schocken Books, 1935. By the Israeli winner of the 1966 Nobel Prize for Literature.

Attar, Farid ud-Din. *The Conference of the Birds: A Sufi Fable.* Shambhala, 1993. Persian allegorical story of a flock of birds in search of the King of Heaven and Earth.

Bowles, Paul, ed. *Five Eyes.* Santa Barbara, CA: Black Sparrow, 1979. Short stories by North African writers.

Bushnaq, Inea, ed. *Arab Folk Tales.* New York: Pantheon Books, 1986.

Epic of Gilgamesh. Translated by N.K. Sanders. Concord, NH: Paul, 1994. Epic written on clay tablets four thousand or five thousand years ago in Mesopotamia. Mixture of adventure, morality, and tragedy.

Heinrichsdorff, Ava. *Modern Saudi Fiction.* Washington, DC: Three Continents Press, 1987. Short stories of contemporary Saudi culture with portraits of daily life as well as nostalgic pieces on vanishing customs and callings.

Hooke, S.H. *Middle Eastern Mythology.* New York: Viking Penguin, 1963. Much of Greek, Roman, and Celtic mythology has origins in the ancient Middle East. Types of early myths are identified and described by civilization: Sumerian, Babylonian, Egyptian, Ugaritic, Hittite, and Hebrew.

Jaffrey, Madhur, *Seasons of Splendor: Tales, Myths, and Legends of India.* New York: Atheneum, 1985.

Johnson-Davies, Denys, ed. *Egyptian Short Stories.* Washington, DC: Three Continents Press, 1978.

————. *Modern Arabic Short Stories*. Berkeley: University of California, 1994.

Le Carre, John. *The Little Drummer Girl*. New York: Knopf, 1983. Mystery underlining currents at work in the Middle East.

Levy, Ruben. *An Introduction to Persian Literature*. New York: Columbia University Press, 1969. Includes brief history of Persia, Persian verse, early prose and poetry, satirists, and modern writers.

Memmi, Albert. *The Pillar of Salt*. Boston: Beacon Press, 1992. Young boy growing up in a Jewish family in Tunis.

Ramunjan, A.K. *Folktales from India*. Delhi: Penguin, 1993.

Richmond, Diana. *Antar and Abla: A Bedouin Romance*. New York: Quartet Books, 1978.

Salih, Tayeb. *The Wedding of Zein and Other Stories*. Washington, DC: Three Continents Press, 1982.

Schwarz, Leo W., ed. *The Jewish Caravan: Great Stories of 25 Centuries*. New York: Schocken, 1976. Comprehensive anthology spanning twenty-five centuries of Jewish life from the Bible to the present day, including stories from the Apocrypha, the Talmud, the ghetto, Hasidic life, the Holocaust, and also from contemporary Israel.

Zamyatin, Yvgeny Ivanovich (1884–1937). *We*. New York: Viking, 1994. Written in 1920, an inspiration for George Orwell's *1984*. Set in the twenty-sixth century, science fiction of life under regimented totalitarian society of OneState.

Research and Resources for World History

American Historical Association in world history series of short monographs by prominent scholars on broad patterns of human development, recurring themes, and comparative studies such as "The Age of Gunpowder Empires, 1450–1800," by William McNeill; "The World System in the Thirteenth Century: Dead-End or Precursor?" by Janet Lippman Abu-Lughod; "Gender, Sex and Empire" by Margaret Strobel; and "Interpreting the Industrial Revolution" by Peter Stearns.

The Ascent of Man. A thirteen-part video series from the BBC that offers a grounding in world history. Jacob Bronowski traces man's progress from a scientific-philosophic point of view.

Civilization. A thirteen-part video series from the BBC that offers an excellent introduction to world history, with an emphasis on technology. Kenneth Clark places the development of Western culture, from the fall of ancient Greece and Rome to the present day. Illustrated with examples from architecture, art, philosophy, and music.

Davidson, Basil. *The African Genius: An Introduction to African Cultural and Social History*. Boston: Little, Brown, 1969.

Dimmitt, Cornelia. *Classical Hindu Mythology*. Philadelphia: Temple University Press, 1978.

Embree, Ainslie T., ed. *Encyclopedia of Asian History*. New York: Scribner, 1988.

Harvard Ukrainian Research Institute Publications, 1583 Massachusetts Avenue, Cambridge, MA 02138.

Hilton, Anne. *The Kingdom of Kongo*. Oxford: Clarendon Press, 1985.

Jackdaws: Portfolios of Historical Documents. Golden Owl Publishing Company, PO Box 503, Amawalk, NY 10501. E.g., Alfred the Great; China: A Cultural Heritage; Conquest of Mexico; Easter Rising: Dublin 1916; World of Islam; Tutankhamun and the tomb.

Local resources. Develop links with local organizations with international interests. Examples include the United Nations, the Japan–America Society, the Sons of Norway, the English-Speaking Union, the World Affairs Council, and museums.

Maalout, Amin. *The Crusades Through Arab Eyes*. New York: Schocken, 1989.

McNeill, William H. *The Human Condition: An Ecological and Historical View*. Princeton: Princeton University Press, 1980.

————. *Mythistory and Other Essays*. Chicago: University of Chicago Press, 1986.

————. *Plagues and Peoples*, Anchor Press, 1976.

————. *Rise of the West: A History of the Human Community*. Chicago: University of Chicago Press, 1963.

National Archives Publications, Dept. 350, PO Box 100793, Atlanta, GA 30384, 800–234–8861. The National Archives has excellent general guides to using documents in teaching, e.g., *The World in Flames: World War II Documents from the National Archives:* thirty-two posters chronicle World War II. Nearly two hundred images recall, for example, the Battle of Britain, the attack on Pearl Harbor, D-Day, the Battle of the Bulge, and the Holocaust.

Nawab, Ismail, ed. *Aramco and Its World: Arabia and the Middle East*. This 275-page compendium with maps and bibliography as well as a historical narrative is free to libraries by writing: Patrick Flynn, Public Affairs Dept., Aramco, 1800 Augusta, Suite 300, Houston, TX 77057.

Norton, Mary Beth. *American Historical Association Guide to Historical Literature*. New York: Oxford University Press, 1995.

Outreach Services newsletters of the African, East Asian, Latin American, and Russian Studies Centers, University of Illinois, International Studies Building, 910 S. Fifth Street, Champaign, IL 61820. Write to the U.S. Department of Education for complete list of addresses of outreach centers.

Ponting, Clive. *A Green History of the World: The Environment and the Collapse of Great Civilizations*. New York: Penguin Books, 1991.

Roupp, Heidi, and Marilynn Hitchens. *How to Prepare for SAT II: World History.* Hauppauge, NY: Barron's Education Series, 1996.

Sowards, J. Kelley. *Makers of World History.* New York: St. Martin's Press, 1994.

Stavrianos, L.S. *Lifelines from Our Past: A New World History.* Armonk, NY: M.E. Sharpe, 1992.

Stearns, Peter. *World Civilizations: The Global Experience: to 1750.* New York: Talman, 1996.

Teaching Material Index. Center for Middle Eastern Studies, University of Texas, Austin, TX 78712. Free bibliography.

Waddy, Charis. *Women in Muslim History.* White Plains, NY: Longman, 1980. Illustrated book with poems and folktales as well as narrative.

Wolf, Ken. *Personalities and Problems: Interpretive Essays in World Civilizations.* New York: McGraw-Hill, 1994.

World History Standards. National Center for History in the Schools, 18880 Wilshire Blvd., Suite 761, Los Angeles, CA 90024.

Index

Heidi Roupp teaches high school world history, a program she initiated in 1979 in Aspen, Colorado. She recently completed a masters degree in East Asian Studies at Columbia University and has been awarded a Fulbright to India, a Keizai Koho–Japan Foundation grant to Japan, and a Korea Society fellowship to Korea. She is a founding member of the World History Association, as well as current vice president, president-elect. She has also served as a member of the executive board of the Colorado Council for Social Studies. She has had vast experience working with teachers and professors in world history. She participated in a Woodrow Wilson Summer Institute, where she was selected as a member of a national traveling team that presented workshops on world history. She assisted in the development of the World History Standards for grades 5–12. She co-authored *Treasures of the World: Literature and Source Readings for World History* and edited the *Aspen World History Handbook*. She and Marilynn Hitchens recently completed a world history study guide, *How to Prepare for SAT II: World History*.